CHINA UNDER XI JINPING

Studies in Critical Social Sciences Book Series

Haymarket Books is proud to be working with Brill Academic Publishers (www.brill.nl) to republish the *Studies in Critical Social Sciences* book series in paperback editions. This peer-reviewed book series offers insights into our current reality by exploring the content and consequences of power relationships under capitalism, and by considering the spaces of opposition and resistance to these changes that have been defining our new age. Our full catalog of *SCSS* volumes can be viewed at https://www.haymarketbooks.org/series_collections/4-studies-in-critical-social-sciences.

Series Editor
David Fasenfest (York University, Canada)

Editorial Board
Eduardo Bonilla-Silva (Duke University)
Chris Chase-Dunn (University of California–Riverside)
William Carroll (University of Victoria)
Raewyn Connell (University of Sydney)
Kimberlé W. Crenshaw (University of California–LA and Columbia University)
Raju Das (York University, Canada)
Heidi Gottfried (Wayne State University)
Alfredo Saad-Filho (Queen's University Belfast)
Chizuko Ueno (University of Tokyo)
Sylvia Walby (Royal Holloway, University of London)

China under Xi Jinping

An Interdisciplinary Assessment

Edited by
Michał Dahl, Maciej Szatkowski
and Hanna Kupś

Haymarket Books
Chicago, IL

First published in 2024 by Brill Academic Publishers, The Netherlands
© 2024 Koninklijke Brill NV, Leiden, The Netherlands

Published in paperback in 2025 by
Haymarket Books
P.O. Box 180165
Chicago, IL 60618
773-583-7884
www.haymarketbooks.org

ISBN: 979-8-88890-362-9

Distributed to the trade in the US through Consortium Book Sales and Distribution (www.cbsd.com) and internationally through Ingram Publisher Services International (www.ingramcontent.com).

This book was published with the generous support of Lannan Foundation, Wallace Action Fund, and the Marguerite Casey Foundation.

Special discounts are available for bulk purchases by organizations and institutions. Please call 773-583-7884 or email info@haymarketbooks.org for more information.

Cover design by Jamie Kerry and Ragina Johnson.

Printed in the United States.

Library of Congress Cataloging-in-Publication data is available.

Contents

List of Figures and Tables IX
Notes on Contributors XI

Introduction
The Rise of Xi Jinping: Responding to Domestic and External Challenges 1
   Maciej Szatkowski, Michał Dahl and Hanna Kupś

PART 1
Political Dimensions

1   The Characteristics and Evolution of China's Political System under Xi Jinping 15
     Bogdan J. Góralczyk

2   Xi Jinping's Regime Maintenance Paradigm 36
     Yan Chang Bennett

3   The Realpolitik of Xi Jinping Thought 61
     John Garrick

4   Is There a Xi Style of Politics?
   Change and Continuity since 2012 89
     Kerry Brown

5   When Chinese Communist Party (CCP) Meets the Pandemic
   An Authoritarian Resilience? 104
     Yung-Yung Chang

PART 2
Economic Dimensions

6   The Great Chinese Transformation
   From the Third to the First World 151
     Grzegorz W. Kołodko

7   The Belt and Road Initiative, Centralisation of Local Interests and
    Centre-province Relations   167
      Dominik Mierzejewski

8   China's Policy on Climate and Energy towards 2060   192
      Łukasz Gacek

PART 3
Social Dimensions

9   Social Development under Xi Jinping
    Education, Health, and Retirement   217
      Octasiano M. Valerio Mendoza

10 Chinese Nationalism in the Era of Xi Jinping   249
      Joanna Wardęga

11 Competition in the National College Entrance Examination and
    Disparity of Access to Elite Higher Education in China   269
      Tanja Carmel Sargent, Karen Hao and Fei Wang

12 Functionalities of Political Humor in Xi Jinping's Era
    Resistance, Cynicism, Nationalism   301
      Wendy Weile Zhou and Lutgard Lams

PART 4
Cultural Dimensions

13 Opium of the People?
    Religious Politics in the Xi Jinping Era   325
      Martin Lavička

14 Cinema
    Reconsolidation of Party-State Hegemony in a Market Economy   343
      Chris Berry

15 Between Art and Social Responsibility
    The Politics of Music in the Xi Jinping Era   361
      Hanna Kupś

16 Community of Common Language
    The Last Decade in the Advancement of Putonghua 389
    Kamil Burkiewicz

PART 5
Foreign Policy Dimensions

17 China's Belt and Road Initiative as Xi's Personal Legacy Project 413
    Konstantinas Andrijauskas

18 Chinese 'Security' in the Xi Era 432
    David A. Welch

19 China's Space Program and Its Quest for Superpowerhood
    Goals, Strategies, Perception of Challenges 456
    Michał Dahl, Hanna Kupś and Maciej Szatkowski

20 China's Rise to the Global Sports Power 475
    Vic Yu Wai Li and Marcus P. Chu

    Index 499

Figures and Tables

Figures

6.1 The GDP of China and the Big-5 in 2019 index numbers (2009 = 100) 159
6.2 China versus Big-4 GDP of selected countries in percent of China's GDP 160
7.1 Chinese provincial-level government in "Vision and Action" document (2015) 173
9.1 Percentage change in density of higher education institutions from 2011 to 2018 221
9.2 Percentage change in density of undergraduate universities from 2011 to 2018 223
9.3 Percentage change in density of vocational colleges from 2011 to 2018 225
9.4 Percentage change in density of private higher education institutions from 2011 to 2018 227
9.5 Percentage change in tertiary education teachers from 2011 to 2018 230
9.6 Percentage change in higher education enrolment from 2011 to 2018 232
9.7 Percentage change in density of health institutions from 2011 to 2018 234
9.8 Percentage change in density of beds in health institutions from 2011 to 2018 236
9.9 Percentage change in density of medical personnel from 2011 to 2018 239
9.10 Percentage change in density of doctors from 2011 to 2018 241
9.11 Percentage change in pension coverage from 2011 to 2018 244
11.1 Number of students taking *gaokao* and enrolling in college 1977–2017 273
11.2 Distribution of elite (C9, 985 and 211) universities in China 287
11.3 Beijing University enrollment plan by province of origin (2013) 288
11.4 Qinghua University enrollment plan by province of origin (2013) 289
11.5 Zhejiang University enrollment plan by province of origin and rural student special enrollment (2013) 289
11.6a C9 league enrollment by province of origin (2013) 290
11.6b C9 league enrollment per 1,000 *gaokao* takers by province of origin (2013) 291
12.1 Mocking the longevity of Xi Jinping's reign by associating it with marriage pressure 306
12.2 President or Emperor? 309
12.3 Xi Forever 309
12.4 Lying flat and letting it go 311
12.5 No possibility of standing up 311
12.6 New non-cooperative movement – Lying flat 312
12.7 Mocking of US mishandling of the pandemic 314

12.8	Mocking US incapability of handling Afghanistan's politics	315
12.9	Mocking the US for its so-called arrogance and ignorance	316
14.1	Annual box office, People's Republic of China in USD billions	344
18.1	How do people in Taiwan identify?	437
18.2	UN Security Council vetoes	448

Tables

6.1	The value and dynamics of GDP of China, USA and Poland, 1978–2019 (PPP)	153
6.2	Forecasts of recession and growth in 2020–2021 (fall/growth of GDP, %)	159
6.3	Top ten countries of Chinese exports, 2019	161
7.1	The contextualization and the frequency of using the keyword of the Belt and Road in China's provincial-level governments (2013–2019)	178
7.2	Beijing's, Shanghai's, Tianjin's and Chongqing's approaches and contexts of the BRI in the mayor's reports (2013–2022)	183
7.3	Party secretaries in the four municipalities: Chongqing, Shanghai, Tianjin and Beijing	187
8.1	Total energy consumption by source (%)	194
8.2	Electricity generation and generation capacity in China	200
8.3	China and the world: renewable energy installed capacity	203
9.1	Change in the density of higher education institutions	220
9.2	Change in the density of undergraduate universities	222
9.3	Change in vocational colleges	224
9.4	Change in density of private higher education institutions	226
9.5	Change in teachers density in tertiary education	229
9.6	Change in higher education enrolment	231
9.7	Change in the number of health institutions per 10,000 inhabitants	233
9.8	Change in the number of beds in health institutions per 10,000 inhabitants	235
9.9	Change in the number of medical personnel per 10,000 inhabitants	238
9.10	Number of doctors per 10,000 inhabitants	240
9.11	Change in pension coverage	243
11.1	Variations in *gaokao* format in 2012	280
11.2	Implementation schedule of 2014 *gaokao* reforms	283
11.3	2017 percent enrollment into elite higher education institution in Henan, Beijing and Shanghai	291
13.1	Religious freedom provisions in the PRC constitutions	329
14.1	PRC top box office films and their country of production, 2012–2019	344

Notes on Contributors

Konstantinas Andrijauskas
is an Associate Professor of Asian International Relations at the Institute of International Relations and Political Science, Vilnius University (Lithuania), and an Associate Expert at Eastern Europe Studies Centre's China Research Programme (Lithuania). He was formerly a senior visiting scholar at China's Fudan and Zhejiang universities as well as Columbia University under Fulbright scholarship. Dr. Andrijauskas specializes in China-Russia and China-Europe relations in general and Sino-Lithuanian relations in particular.

Yan Chang Bennett
Deputy Course Chair/Coordinator in Multilateral Diplomacy and Climate at the Foreign Service Institute, the training institution of the US Department of State. She holds degrees in political science, international affairs, law, and history. Bennett teaches diplomacy and international affairs as a professorial lecturer at the Elliott School of International Affairs, George Washington University. She has worked previously for Princeton University, at Illinois State University, and the US Department of State. She has publications on the rule of law under the Xi administration, China's emerging political philosophy, and Chinese foreign policy, such as the Belt and Road Initiative. She is working on a number of book projects, including a quantitative comparative examination of China with the United States, the history of American discourse on China, and a history of American policy perspectives on the US-China relationship. Selected publications: "American Strategy in Melanesia: A Discursive examination" (forthcoming); "China's Real Ambitions for the South Pacific" (2022); "Implications of China's Pacific Dream for the United States, Australia, and Allies" (2022); "China's inward and outward facing identities: post-COVID challenges for China and the international rules-based order" (2023). Her views are her own and not representative of the government of the United States.

Chris Berry
is Professor of Film Studies at King's College London. In the 1980s, he worked for China Film Import and Export Corporation in Beijing, and his academic research is grounded in work on audio-visual media of the Sinosphere. Books include: *Cinema and the National: China on Screen* (2006); *Postsocialist Cinema in Post-Mao China: the Cultural Revolution after the Cultural Revolution* (2004); *Film and the Chinese Medical Humanities* (2020); *Chinese Film*

Festivals: Sites of Translation (2017); *Routledge Handbook of East Asian Popular Culture* (2016); *Public Space, Media Space* (2013); *The New Chinese Documentary Film Movement: For the Public Record* (2010); *Electronic Elsewheres: Media, Technology, and Social Space* (2010); *Cultural Studies and Cultural Industries in Northeast Asia: What a Difference a Region Makes* (2009); *TV China; Chinese Films in Focus II* (2008); and *Island on the Edge: Taiwan New Cinema and After* (2005).

Kerry Brown

is Professor of Chinese Studies and Director of the Lau China Institute at King's College, London. From 2012 to 2015 he was Professor of Chinese Politics and Director of the China Studies Centre at the University of Sydney, Australia. Prior to this he worked at Chatham House from 2006 to 2012, as Senior Fellow and then Head of the Asia Programme. From 1998 to 2005 he worked at the British Foreign and Commonwealth Office. He is the author of over 20 books on modern Chinese politics.

Kamil Burkiewicz

is an Assistant Professor at the Institute of Oriental Studies at Adam Mickiewicz University in Poznań. The topic of his PhD dissertation, finished in 2015, as well as some of the further publications concerns languages and cultures of ethnic minorities in PRC, especially the Sui people. The scope of his research interests also covers the language policy in China, earliest written forms of Chinese language and translation studies. His recently published papers include: "Future Written with a Brush Pen: The Role of Classical Chinese in Modern Political Discourse", a chapter in collective monograph *Balancing Changes. Seventy Years of People's Republic of China* (2022); and monograph *Polskie nazwy miejscowe w języku chińskim: Kontekst historyczno-kulturowy, metodologia przekładu i słownik* [Polish Toponyms in Chinese: Historical and Cultural Context, Methodology of Translation and a Dictionary], co-authored with Hanna Kupś (2022).

Yung-Yung Chang

(PhD) is an Assistant Professor in the Asia-Pacific Regional Studies Program (APRS) at the National Dong Hwa University, Taiwan. Her main research interest concerns China's discourse power in digital governance, regional integration in East Asia, China's external relations/foreign policy and politics & security of the Indo-Pacific region. She has conducted research in the UK, Austria, Germany, and Taiwan. She has published in the *Journal of Chinese Political Science, European Journal of East Asian Studies, Politics & Policy* and so on. Her recent publication is "China beyond China, establishing a digital order with Chinese characteristics. China's growing discursive power and the Digital Silk Road" (2023).

Marcus P. Chu
is an Assistant Professor in the Department of Government and International Affairs at Lingnan University, Hong Kong. He has published extensively on the history and politics of sport in the Greater China region. His recent books include: *China's Quest for Sporting Mega-Events: The Politics of International Bids* (2020), *Sporting Events in China as Economic Development, National Image, and Political Ambition* (2021), *China, Taiwan, and International Sporting Events: Face-Off in Cross-Strait Relations* (2022), and *Greater China's Olympic Medal Haul: Beyond Sports Excellence* (2023).

Michał Dahl
Lecturer in the Political Science Division at University of Humanities and Economics in Łódź, Poland. Vice-President of the Center for Eastern and African Studies, member of the Asian Political and International Studies Association, and Association of Asia and the Pacific. His research interests are within contemporary international relations and concentrate on Asia and the Pacific region, international sport organizations, as well as cities in international relations. His recent publications include: monograph *The Role of Cities in International Relations. The Third-generation of Multi-level Governance?*, co-authored with Agnieszka Szpak, Robert Gawłowski, Joanna Modrzyńska and Paweł Modrzyński (2022), *Balancing Changes. Seventy Years of People's Republic of China*, co-edited with Hanna Kupś, Dawid Rogacz and Maciej Szatkowski (2022), and *The Philippines' Strategy Towards the Indo-Pacific Region*, written with Joanna Marszałek-Kawa (2023).

Łukasz Gacek
is a Professor at the Institute of the Middle and Far East at Jagiellonian University, and the Head of the Department of China. He is a political scientist, and an expert in cultural studies. He has completed research fellowships at Fudan University and Xiamen University in China. In 2017–2018, he was employed at KGHM (Shanghai) Copper Trading Co. Ltd. as an Analyst & Business Development Manager. He specializes in modern political systems, security, and international relations in East Asia. The most notable work has revolved around China's energy and environmental policies. He has authored numerous books and research studies on these and other topics, e.g., "Green energy in China: Sustainable development – Environmental

protection – Low-carbon economy" (2015); "Ecological civilization and energy transformation in China" (2020); *China's environmental protection policy in light of European Union standards* (2021); 论中国在欧盟标准方面的环境政策 (2021); *Taiwan under Tsai Ing-wen. Democracy diplomacy* (2022).

John Garrick

LLB (Hon 1, UTS), M.Soc Stud (Sydney), PhD (UTS), is a practicing lawyer in Northern Australia (Northern Territory Law Society) and honorary Charles Darwin University Research Fellow in Law. He has conducted extensive research into Chinese socialist rule of law under President Xi, including directions of China's legal culture and implications for domestic governance and international rule of law. He has written a wide range of publications on China's law reforms including: *Law, Wealth and Power in China: Commercial Law Reforms in Context* (2011); *Law and Policy for China's Market Socialism* (2012); and, with Yan Chang Bennett, *China's Socialist Rule of Law Reforms Under Xi Jinping* (2016).

Bogdan Góralczyk

Political scientist and sinologist, Professor and former Director at the Centre For Europe of the University of Warsaw. Former Ambassador to several Asian states, also with long diplomatic experience in Hungary. He recently published – in Polish – three volumes on China's reform and transformation process (1978–2022). Two of them will soon be available in English as well, including the recent one – *The New Long March. China in the Xi Jinping New Era*. Separately he published – also in Polish – volumes on Myanmar (2021) and Thailand (2023), dealing with the recent volatile domestic situation there.

Karen Hao

is a PhD student at Rutgers University Graduate School of Education. Her research interests lie in early childhood education policy and early interventions for children from disadvantaged backgrounds.

Grzegorz W. Kołodko

Professor of economics, public intellectual and politician, a key architect of Polish economic reforms, Deputy Prime Minister and Minister of Finance, 1994–1997 and 2002–2003. Member of Academia Europaea. Director of Transformation, Integration and Globalization Economic Research (TIGER) at Kozminski University in Warsaw. Author of research papers and books published in 28 languages. Recent books: *China and the Future of Globalization: The Political Economy of China's Rise* (2020); *The Quest for Development*

Success: Bridging Theoretical Reasoning with Economic Practice (2021); *Political Economy of New Pragmatism: Implications of Irreversible Globalization* (2022); *Global Consequences of Russia's Invasion of Ukraine: The Economics and Politics of the Second Cold War* (2023).

Hanna Kupś

is an Assistant Professor at the Centre for Chinese Language and Culture at the Faculty of Humanities of the Nicolaus Copernicus University in Toruń. She received PhD in 2019 and her primary research interests concern traditional Chinese music, including its developments during the New Culture Movement. Going beyond that scope, her recent publications include: *Balancing Changes. Seventy Years of People's Republic of China*, co-edited with Michał Dahl, Dawid Rogacz and Maciej Szatkowski (2022); and monograph *Polskie nazwy miejscowe w języku chińskim: Kontekst historyczno-kulturowy, metodologia przekładu i słownik* [Polish Toponyms in Chinese: Historical and Cultural Context, Methodology of Translation and a Dictionary], co-authored with Kamil Burkiewicz (2022).

Lutgard Lams

is Professor of Media Discourse Analysis and Intercultural Communication at the Faculty of Arts of the KU Leuven – Campus Brussels, heads the Brussels Center for Journalism Studies and is Chair of the Brussels Center for Chinese Discourse Studies workgroup. Her research focuses on ideology and framing in the media, authoritarian discursive practices, identity politics and nationalism in China/Taiwan/Hong Kong, media discourses in and about the Chinese region, strategic narratives in political communication, and electoral campaign discourses. Most recent publications include: "Pseudo-Participation, Authentic Nationalism: Understanding Chinese Fanquan Girls' Personifications of the Nation-State", co-authored with Weile Zhou (2022); "The Red Triangle of the Chinese People, the Chinese Nation and the Communist Party of China: Meaning Generation in Speeches of the Chinese Fifth Generation Leadership" (2023); "Democracy: Quo Vadis? Use and Meaning of 'Democracy' in the Taiwanese English-Language Op-Ed Press at Times of Changing Ruling Parties", co-authored with Charlotte Maekelberghe (2023); "Forging Unity within Diversity: a Discourse-Theoretical Approach to Nation-Building Politics in the Chinese and Taiwanese Contexts" (2021).

Martin Lavička

received his bachelor's degree in Chinese and Japanese philology at Palacký University Olomouc, the Czech Republic, master's degree in International

Relations at National Chengchi University in Taiwan, and PhD in Political Science at Palacký University Olomouc. He is an Assistant Professor at the Department of Asian Studies at Palacký University Olomouc, where he teaches modern Chinese history and Chinese politics. His research focuses on the socio-legal aspects of China's ethnic policies, religious freedoms, and the rule of law. He is currently a visiting research fellow at the Centre for East and South-East Asian Studies at Lund University, Sweden.

Vic Yu Wai Li

is visiting scholar at the School of East Asian Studies, University of Sheffield. He has published on political economy of China's financial opening and Hong Kong's global positioning. His recent works have appeared in *Asian-Pacific Business Review, Global Policy* and *Political Science Quarterly*.

Dominik Mierzejewski

Chair at Center for Asian Affairs (a university-based think-tank), Associate Professor at the Department of Asian Studies at the Faculty of International and Political Studies, studied at the Shanghai International Studies University, Visiting Professor at the Chinese Academy of Social Science granted by the Polish Foundation for Science (2010–2011). His research focuses on China's political development, the rhetoric of Chinese foreign policy and the local government's involvement in China's foreign policy. He published two monographs *China's Selective Identity. State, Ideology and Culture* (co-author, 2019), and *China's Provinces and the Belt and Road Initiative* (2021).

Tanja Carmel Sargent

(PhD) is an Associate Professor of Education, Culture, and Society in the Department of Educational Theory, Policy, and Administration (ETPA) at Rutgers University Graduate School of Education. She is the co-editor of the journal *Chinese Education and Society*. Sargent's work has focused on curriculum and pedagogical reforms in China. Her interest in China grows out of 6 years teaching English in Shanxi Province and Macau from 1993–1999 after she graduated from college and research conducted in provinces across China. Sargent received a PhD in Education and Sociology from the University of Pennsylvania, where she began her research studying the tensions inherent in the implementation of student centered approaches to teaching and learning that focus on the whole child in the context of two important barriers: the ever-present pressure to compete in the National College Entrance Examination (the *gaokao*), and the long-held cultural attitudes supporting teacher and text centered methods. Throughout her career, she has published several articles in leading journals and book chapters. Her publications include an article entitled "Professional learning communities and the diffusion of pedagogical innovation in the Chinese education system" in the journal *Comparative Education Review* (2015).

Maciej Szatkowski

(PhD) sinologist, Assistant Professor at the Institute of Culture Studies of the Nicolaus Copernicus University in Toruń, and director of the Centre for Chinese Language and Culture at NCU. His research focuses on contemporary Chinese culture and literature, particularly Chinese counterculture of the late 1980s and 1990s, as well as drama translation.

Octasiano M. Valerio Mendoza

Associate Professor of Quantitative Methods at the IQS School of Management, Universitat Ramon Llull, Barcelona, Catalunya, Spain. He obtained PhD and MA in International Development at Graduate School of International Development, Nagoya University, Nagoya, Japan. Research interests: international development, economic policies and their effects on inequality and social justice, labor mobility, human capital dynamics, and higher education institutions in China. Recent publications: "Valuing Children: Parents' Perceptions, Spending Priorities and Children's Capabilities", co-authored with Huaxin Wang-Lu and Flavio Comim (2024); "Job prospects and labour mobility in China", co-authored with Huaxin Wang-Lu (2022); "Human capital dynamics in China: Evidence from a club convergence approach", co-authored with Mihály Tamás Borsi and Flavio Comim (2022); "Measuring the provincial supply of higher education institutions in China", co-authored with Mihály Tamás Borsi and Flavio Comim (2018); "Heterogeneous determinants of educational achievement and inequality across urban China" (2018); "Preferential policies and income inequality: Evidence from Special Economic Zones and Open Cities in China" (2016).

Fei Wang

(PhD) is a professor in the Department of Curriculum and Instruction at Shandong Normal University. He received a PhD in Education from Capital Normal University. His work has focused on teacher education, curriculum and pedagogical reforms in China. Throughout his career, he has published over 80 articles in leading journals and three books. In recent years, his main research field has been labor education, and he has participated in the compilation of the "Guidelines for Labor Education in Primary and Secondary Schools" initiated by the Chinese Ministry of Education.

Joanna Wardęga
(PhD) holds the position of Assistant Professor of Political Science at the Institute of the Middle and Far East Studies of the Jagiellonian University in Kraków. She has established and is directing the postgraduate studies program entitled "Contemporary China. Society, Politics, Economy." Her scholarly focus is directed towards the dynamics of Chinese society, encompassing areas such as the interplay of Chinese tourism and nationalism, Chinese cultural heritage, as well as the Chinese diaspora in Poland. Her academic contributions have been published in many publications, which include, but are not limited to: *Chiński nacjonalizm. Rekonstruowanie narodu w Chińskiej Republice Ludowej* [Chinese Nationalism. Nation-Building in the People's Republic of China] (2014), *Współczesne społeczeństwo chińskie. Konsekwencje przemian modernizacyjnych* [Modern Chinese Society. The Consequences of China's Modernization] (2015), *China-Central and Eastern Europe (CEE) Cross-Cultural Dialogue, Education, and Business* (ed., 2016), and *Współczesne Chiny w kontekście stosunków międzynarodowych* [Contemporary China in the Context of International Relations] (ed., 2013). Her scholarly endeavors have also extended to the publication of a multitude of academic papers.

David A. Welch
received his PhD from Harvard University in 1990 and is currently University Research Chair and Professor of Political Science at the University of Waterloo, where he also teaches in the Balsillie School of International Affairs. His most recent book is *Security: A Philosophical Investigation* (2022). His 2005 book *Painful Choices: A Theory of Foreign Policy Change* was the inaugural winner of the International Studies Association ISSS Best Book Award, and his 1993 book *Justice and the Genesis of War* won the Edgar S. Furniss Award for an Outstanding Contribution to National Security Studies. He is co-author of *Understanding Global Conflict and Cooperation*, 10th ed., with Joseph S. Nye, Jr. Of late, he has been working primarily on East Asian security, recently publishing, with Mark Raymond, "What's Really Going On in the South China Sea?" (2022). He is also co-editor of the Cambridge University Press journal, *International Theory*.

Wendy Weile Zhou
is a PhD Candidate in Communication at Georgia State University (GSU). Her research focuses on political discourse, transnational journalism, diaspora media and communication, particularly in the Chinese and American contexts. Her dissertation examines the news practices and career development

of Chinese transnational journalists. Before joining GSU, she served as the Chinese editor for the Global Investigative Journalism Network (GIJN) and as a research assistant at the Journalism and Media Studies Center at the University of Hong Kong, where she earned a master's degree in Journalism.

Introduction

The Rise of Xi Jinping: Responding to Domestic and External Challenges

Maciej Szatkowski, Michał Dahl and Hanna Kupś

Tempora mutantur, nos et mutamur in illis

∴

Against humanity's hopes, the first two decades made it clear that the 21st century is going to be a turbulent time full of challenges. The economic crisis of 2007–2009, terrorist attacks, natural disasters, and progressing climate change as well as constant shifts in the political status quo impacted both countries and their citizens. In the recent years, societies, already tired with subsequent crises, were forced to face new, previously unimaginable, threats. The state that appears at the center of these changes with increasing frequency is China. In 2019, in Wuhan, Hubei province, the first cases of SARS-CoV-2 infection were observed. The People's Republic of China (PRC) was the first to combat the virus, thus becoming a precursor in new branches of internal policy aimed at limiting the spread of the disease, as well as external policy, so-called vaccine diplomacy, which brought about new international disputes and alliances. With the outbreak of the pandemic, China began to gradually isolate itself from the outer world, thus ending the period of relatively favourable attitude towards Western influences which began in the 1980s (see also Gao and Zhang, 2021; Bickenbach and Liu, 2022).

As these words are written, the fight against the pandemic seems to have reached a ceasefire. The zero-Covid policy was discontinued, and the PRC again opened its borders for international tourism. However, the eyes of the world are now focused on a new danger – on 24 February 2022, Russia attacked Ukraine under the false pretext of de-Nazification. China is not an official party to this conflict, yet it seems to be a significant actor. Due to the close political relationship between Beijing and Moscow, the former could play a crucial role in the possible peace process or ceasefire negotiations. The war not only directly caused innumerable deaths and untold damage, but also quickly led to a migration and resource crisis. Nevertheless, the attitude of the international community towards the aggressor turned out to be ambiguous. The war in Ukraine will affect more than just the region itself. Issues regularly raised in the context of the Russian attack include the potential annexation of Taiwan by the PRC (or peaceful reunification of the motherland, as it is depicted by the PRC) as well as its consequences for the international order. At the same time, the war started by Russia causes concern within the Chinese Communist Party (CCP), whose members wonder whether its leader Xi Jinping has backed the right horse in the conflict with Ukraine (see Shin, 2022; Wu, 2023). In the face of numerous internal problems, wrong decisions related to the war in Ukraine may cost the new helmsman dearly, and any significant change in the central government's structure will impact China as well as all territories it controls. Thus, today it is more important than ever to learn about and understand China. The conflict in Ukraine has necessitated immediate interpretations. Researchers and politicians outdo one another, presenting different opinions and analyses. Some directly describe Xi Jinping as an official supporter of Putin, while others perceive the conflict as a proxy war between China and the West, and some anticipate a new Pax Sinica, reaching far beyond East Asia.

1 New Helmsman and a New Course

As a result of a hundred years of humiliations (百年国耻 *bainian guochi*, 1839–1949), still vivid in the Chinese collective memory, in recent years the decision-makers of the PRC have reacted strongly and swiftly to any signs of chauvinism and cultural appropriation appearing in Western media. An issue of great importance at the moment is to develop pride in the achievements of Chinese culture and civilization. Western influence is being limited, the heritage of the Chinese civilization is emphasized, and the greatness and uniqueness of China are promoted by local media and schools. These efforts are part of the cultural rebirth that is supposed to assist in building the Chinese superpower (see also Gries, 2004; Lehman-Ludwig et al., 2023). The presumed goal is to establish China as the center of a Sinosphere, uniting the Chinese living all over the world, including those from Taiwan, Hong Kong, and various diasporas. The Chinese rejuvenation is supposedly a chance to create a Chinese citizen who is free of complex and proud of the achievements of Chinese civilization and Chinese socialism. The new leader brings hope that this project will be implemented.

The political curriculum of Xi Jinping is quite rich. His biography and personal life are a subject of interest to the inhabitants of China. This should not be surprising as he came into power under the banner of fighting corruption, which appeals to the citizens (see also Feldman, 2023). Although he has not managed to curb it entirely, he has limited the phenomenon – even if he showed particular efficiency in tracing corruption among his political rivals (see Feldman, 2023). Leader Xi is without a doubt the strongest general secretary the CPC has had in decades. His trademark is the clear political vision for China's future and the means to achieve it.

Even though Xi Jinping's leadership may still be in its early stage, his impact on China and Beijing's international position has been tremendous. This can be evidenced by, for example, the debate on the conceptual scope of the term "Xi-ism", taking place both inside and outside China, as well as frequent comparisons of Xi's achievements to those of Mao Zedong or Deng Xiaoping (Bougon, 2017: 197). An astute China scholar David Shambaugh also points to the similarities between Chairman Mao and Leader Xi. In the latter's actions, he observes elements of the cult of personality and considers Xi's governance and actions to be guided primarily by politics and ideology (interview with David Shambaugh in: Tiezzi, 2021). The apotheosis of a living leader has not been seen in China since the mid-1970s. Today, however, Chinese propaganda is again turning the person of the leader into a symbol of power and the state, even if the means of expression are much more subtle than those from the times of the Cultural Revolution.

While there is little chance that China will isolate itself in terms of economy and culture as it did in Mao's times, since the beginning of the pandemic it has been keeping its door ajar only to the extent that benefits China. Xi Jinping strives to limit the absorption of Western thoughts and ideas. The mentioned rejuvenation of the Chinese nation includes the promotion of intrinsically Chinese Confucianism as a counterbalance to Western values. For instance, Xi Jinping is considered to be the author of *Xi Jinping: How to Read Confucius and Other Chinese Classical Thinkers* (see Zhang, 2015). The predominant role of this ancient but still relevant philosophy is to cement the power and strengthen the position of a single leader instead of a joint leadership. As a very hierarchical and obedience-enforcing system, Confucianism (as well as Legalism) protects power. Naturally, like socialism, it is used by the authorities partially as a facade, acting as a regulator of the society's relationship with the government, putting the latter in an advantageous position.

2   Setting the Sails

As researched by Guo Baogang, using patterns established by the so-called Western culture in studying China – even though deeply rooted in common thinking – does not allow us to draw valuable conclusions (Guo, 2019). The internal policy of the PRC is a very difficult and delicate area of research.

Analyzing it requires unique competence acquired over years of insightful observation, as well as the ability to make excellent queries, read between the lines, and understand the language of Chinese politics, full of allusions and things left unspoken. Researchers need to seek meanings hidden behind popular metaphors and historical references. The complex and multidimensional Chinese reality, as well as the person of Leader Xi himself, gave us an impulse to attempt grasping these topics. In our book we ask who Xi Jinping is and what China is like under his rule. We are aware that this book tries to present the context for a rapidly changing reality, so perhaps the information and theses included in it will be verified within the next several years. Nevertheless, the readers will find here many interesting analyses by outstanding researchers of China, looking for nuances of the common views on this country. Looking at China from different perspectives – political, economic, social, and cultural – we aim to provide an objective analysis of Xi Jinping's rule *in the years 2012–2022*.

The volume opens with a chapter by Bogdan Góralczyk, one of the most astute Polish researchers of China ("The Characteristics and Evolution of China's Political System under Xi Jinping"). The author analyzes to what degree the political system of the PRC changed under Xi Jinping in the years 2012–2022. The chapter begins with a discussion on the unsuitability of Western labels in the political context of China and on the uniqueness of Chinese political tradition. Góralczyk presents the way the Chinese leaders of the 20th century ruled the country and offers a fascinating, concise presentation of the history of political thought in China. He describes in detail what the CPC is and how it operates. He also lists the changes that have taken place under Xi Jinping, including the abolishment of the two-term rule, and wonders to what extent the autocratic rule of Xi Jinping can impact the shape of the Chinese society, the region, and the world.

In Chapter 2, "Xi Jinping's Regime Maintenance Paradigm," Yan Chang Bennett discusses what "Xi Jinping Thought" (XJPT) is and where this concept will lead China. Bennett describes XJPT as a philosophy of governance, something that has accompanied strong rulers both in China and the West for centuries. Aware of all Western predilections in the assessment of the East, Bennett very carefully selects the methodology used to analyse XJPT and reaches the conclusion that Xi's ideas reflect syncretic thinking about politics that combines the culture of Mao Zedong's rule, Chinese communism, and the (neo)Confucian tradition. The author stresses that Xi's thought is a product of China, a child of its times, formed from the tradition of Chinese thought and concepts long present in China. Analyzing the philosophy of Xi's rule, Bennett does not forget that the leader's message is directed to the Chinese citizens, that he wants to fulfil their (Chinese) dream and this is the context in which his rule should be interpreted.

Some of the motifs described by Yan Chang Bennett are expanded in the following chapter ("The Realpolitik of Xi Jinping Thought") by John Garrick, who attempts to explain the question of how much power Xi Jinping actually holds. Garrick concludes that Xi has more power than Mao Zedong and Deng Xiaoping, although it may not be obvious or noticeable to everyone. The main idea behind this text is to analyse the very fundamentals of XJPT. Garrick wonders to what extent it resembles Mao's thought in its implementation and how deeply it is rooted in the Chinese tradition of Marxist-Leninist ideology with Chinese characteristics. The researcher also highlights the lack of unambiguous assessment of the effects of Chinese reforms in the last three decades, pointing, on the one hand, to the admiration by foreign public opinion and, on the other, to the fears regarding China's new role in the international arena and the criticism of Beijing policy both in its internal and diplomatic aspects.

In turn, Kerry Brown in his chapter "Is There a Xi Style of Politics? Change and Continuity since 2012" contemplates the question of how much of Xi's policy is a continuation of his predecessors' rule, and to what degree it is something new. By resorting to simplifications, journalists often inform the public opinion that Xi Jinping is the new Mao Zedong. By explaining many intricacies of governance processes, Brown provides an exhaustive answer to the question that also underlies this volume: with what kind of rule do we deal here? The author presents the readers with Xi's political biography and captures the *Zeitgeist* in China shortly before Xi Jinping's coming into power. We learn on the example of party discipline how XJPT was shaped and implemented. Above all, we read a fascinating tale of the ideological formation of Xi Jinping and his thought.

The chapter by Yung-Yung Chang ("When Chinese Communist Party (CCP) Meets the Pandemic: an Authoritarian Resilience?") aims to explore the influence of the recent health crisis on the development of the Chinese political regime. The author attempts to explain how COVID-19 tightened and strengthened the control of the authorities over individuals in the name of fighting the pandemic. Accompanied by ubiquitous slogans about peaceful and harmonious coexistence in the society, as well as arguments regarding the importance of national security, the PRC government introduced the Social Credit System, which aroused significant controversies, mainly in the West. Yung-Yung Chang explains the reasons behind the CPC's decisions related to combating COVID-19 and to what extent the pandemic became only a pretext for strengthening and consolidating Xi Jinping's power.

The second part of the monograph is devoted to economic issues, although they're partially mentioned in other sections of the book as well. An introduction to the problem of Chinese economic transformation can be found in the chapter by Grzegorz W. Kołodko, titled "The Great Chinese Transformation: from the Third to the First World". The author presents a synthesis of the Great Chinese Transformation, highlighting the steps China made in the last decades, advancing from the Third to the First World. Kołodko supplements his analysis with detailed economic indicators such as the GDP (PPP and *per capita*), as well as measurements of China's international trade and financial reserves. The author emphasizes that after a successful conclusion of a long fight against poverty, Chinese decision-makers, and above all the Chinese society, must bear the burden of another transformation aiming to build China that is sustainable in economic as well as social and environmental aspects.

The second chapter of the section on economy – "The Belt and Road Initiative, Centralization of Local Interests and Centre-province Relations" by Dominik Mierzejewski focuses on pursuing the local interests in the context of the Belt and Road Initiative (BRI). Adopting the internal perspective allowed Mierzejewski to discuss the relationship between the central government and the province after 1978. Topics related to project implementation within the BRI are often discussed by academic authors and journalists, yet different aspects of internal policy (such as rivalry among provinces, fragmentation, and decentralization in China as well as centralization implemented under Xi Jinping) complement the picture of the largest geopolitical project of the 21st century. The different kinds of center-province relationships presented by the author are illustrated with examples from Beijing, Chongqing, Shanghai and Tianjin.

The chapter by Łukasz Gacek is devoted to Chinese climate and energy policy with the year 2060 in sight ("China's Policy on Climate and Energy towards 2060"). The end date used by the author, and at the same time the main reference point, is the achieving of climate neutrality by the PRC, which was declared by Xi Jinping. Considering that currently China is the world's greatest energy consumer and greenhouse gas emitter, this is a date of great significance for the future of ecosystems, economies and societies – not only in the area of Asia and the Pacific but also on a global scale. The author explains how the policy of decarbonisation is pursued in contemporary China, pointing out the climate- and energy-related premises of the latest Five-Year Plan and the degree to which they have been implemented.

The third part of the monograph concerns the social challenges that have emerged due to the implementation of the "Chinese Dream" and the "great rejuvenation of the Chinese nation" plans. The issues related to the difficulties in achieving sustainable development in different regions of China are introduced in the chapter "Social Development under Xi Jinping: Education, Health, and Retirement" by Octasiano M. Valerio Mendoza. The author presents a series of data on the evolution of the Chinese education system under Xi Jinping, with particular attention paid to the access to higher education institutions, number of teachers and the gross enrolment index. Moving on to the healthcare system, Valerio Mendoza describes the development of medical infrastructure and the changes in the number of medical personnel, ending the chapter with a description of the scope of pension benefits in the aging Chinese society.

An attempt at unifying the nation under a common banner includes, e.g., support for and shaping of nationalist attitudes, which – although already utilized in the past – have been emerging with increased strength since the beginning of the 21st century. Factors leading to this phenomenon and the process of its shaping are the subject of the chapter by Joanna Wardęga, titled "Chinese Nationalism in the Era of Xi Jinping." The author explains the sources of the PRC's ideology and presents the instruments used by the CPC to cultivate patriotic values among the citizens. Wardęga also emphasizes the multiple forms the Chinese nationalism takes – on the one hand it is used by the authorities to legitimize the "only rightful" governance, while on the other it is often a spontaneous initiative of Chinese citizens. Without neglecting the features specific to the ideology in the new helmsman's era, the author depicts new trends that have developed in China together with his doctrine.

The issues related to unequal access to higher education at the provincial and state level are expanded on in the chapter "Competition in the National College Entrance Examination and Disparity of Access to Elite Higher Education in China". Tanja Carmel Sargent, Karen Hao and Fei Wang present here a complex picture of the education system where the future of young people is determined by several factors only partially related to the efforts they have put into learning. The authors provide a comprehensive description of the intricacies of the universities' hierarchy and the impact of the location of these institutions on the student recruitment process. The analysis is complemented by the characterization of reforms that shaped the contemporary form of the famous *gaokao* exam and the centrally-set acceptance limits, to which the candidates must adjust. Problems with levelling social inequalities translate into increased vigilance of the authorities towards any veering off the promoted course.

Considering the mentioned changes, one may wonder what is the attitude of the citizens of China towards the increased nationalist narrative of Xi Jinping's era. This matter is covered in the chapter "Functionalities of Political Humor in Xi Jinping's Era: Resistance, Cynicism, Nationalism", written by Wendy Zhou and Lutgard Lams. Based on the analysis of popular political memes, the authors point to the existence of three main types of attitudes presented by Internet users: creative resistance, playful symbolism, and nationalism. Supported with engrossing and entertaining examples of Internet creativity, the analysis proves the variety of the Chinese cyberspace and the existence of a complex dynamic of dependencies between the CPC and the citizens.

The fourth part of the book focuses on the transformations that occurred in the culture of China in the first decade of Xi Jinping's rule. The modification of earlier practices, which is visible in many aspects, is often an attempt to combine the economic aims with the toughening of the ideological direction. The tendency to control citizens' viewpoints to an ever larger extent is evident in current laws regulating religious practices in China. In the chapter "Opium of the People? Religious Politics in the Xi Jinping's Era", Martin Lavička presents the development of government strategies regarding freedom of belief, in particular Document 19, which since the 1980s has been the basis for the official party line. In this context, the author looks then at the changes that have occurred under the present government. Putting the new regulations and government's narratives under the microscope, Lavička points to the emergence of modified tactics towards religion under Xi Jinping.

The next chapter, written by Chris Berry, is devoted to the issues regarding Chinese cinema ("Cinema: Reconsolidation of Party-State Hegemony in a Market Economy"). The author describes the extensive control system imposed on commercial productions as well as the limitations and ultimate suffocation of all signs of independent cinema. However, Berry also points to the existence of creativity that goes beyond the intentions of the Party leadership, whether it takes the shape of unexpected success of some commercial movies or that of gradual development of artistic cinema. Furthermore, the chapter highlights the importance of cultural configurations created by the authorities in different historical periods.

Focused on the promotion of a specific message and values, the cultural policy of Xi Jinping is reflected in music as well. The chapter "Between Art and Social Responsibility: The Politics of Music in the Xi Jinping Era" written by Hanna Kupś presents the main premises behind the theory of art as formulated by the new helmsman. The guidelines form the ideological basis for the efforts put in promoting socially functional art described later in the chapter. These measures include party-promoted musical works as well as extensive restrictions and means of control that regulate the music industry in China.

Still, the monitoring and cultivation of the attitudes considered appropriate by the Party refer not only to controlling the creators and their works but also to the way they are transmitted, as we are informed by Kamil Burkiewicz in the chapter "Community of Common Speech: The Last Decade in the Advancement of Putonghua". The language policy of Xi and its underlying ideology are described here in the context of the efforts put into spreading *Putonghua* over the last century. From the movement to establish a national language and early legislative activities, through the actions towards language unification in the 1980s and the "crisis of the Chinese language" in the early 2000s, we can follow the evolution of the political and social importance of the standardized Chinese language for the CPC and understand the potential it holds in the eyes of today's authorities.

The fifth and last part of the volume concentrates on the issues of China's foreign policy. These deliberations start with the chapter "China's Belt and Road Initiative as Xi's Personal Legacy Project" by Konstantinas Andrijauskas. The author sketches the concept of the BRI and its evolution, attempting to provide an overview of the project almost a decade after its launch. The analysis takes into consideration the fact that the idea to create the Belt and Road Initiative is ascribed directly to Xi Jinping, thus making it one of the most important – or perhaps the most important – elements of his heritage. Andrijauskas draws attention to the internalization of the BRI and to mechanisms by which Xi can distance himself from the project if the investment fails.

The matter of security, analyzed from the point of view of China, the region, and the world, is expanded upon in the chapter prepared by David A. Welch ("Chinese 'Security' in the Xi Era"). The author highlights different ways in which subsequent generations of Chinese politicians understood security-related issues, pointing also to the evolutionary character of the approach to broadly understood security. Particularly interesting in this context are the views of Xi Jinping. According to Welch, Xi Jinping aligns Chinese security policy with his own assessment of the state, prioritizing activities in the sphere of security to maintain power and exercise control. The chapter discusses China's "core interests" in security policy and points to territorial and maritime disputes, the country's attitude to the international order, and priorities in relationships with other states.

Michał Dahl, Hanna Kupś and Maciej Szatkowski in their chapter titled "China's Space Program and Its Quest for Superpowerhood: Goals, Strategies, Perception of Challenges" analyze the implementation of space program initiatives by the Chinese government. Starting with the fact that the space race is used to strengthen China's position as a superpower, the authors define the goals and strategies formulated by Chinese decision-makers. The chapter also points to Beijing's perception of the threats to the implementation of space programs, including the rivalry with the US in this field. The authors describe the milestones in the Chinese mission to conquer space. The comparison of the ongoing rivalry between China and the US with the Cold War space race proves that the success of the Chinese space program will significantly impact the position of China in the international arena and the dynamics of the processes shaping the world order of today.

The final analysis in this volume is the chapter on Chinese efforts to achieve the status of a superpower in another field – sports, prepared by Vic Yu Wai Li and Marcus Pok Chu ("China's Rise to the Global Sports Power"). The authors put particular emphasis on Xi Jinping's role in developing and implementing the "leading sports nation" strategy with an end date of 2050. The narrative focuses on the Summer and Winter Olympics in Beijing, in 2008 and 2022 respectively. The chapter also points to the importance of campaigns promoting the global competitiveness of China, in particular in sports games, as well as sports exchange initiatives that aim to promote China's image and standing. Li and Chu draw attention to internal aspects of global sports-related ambitions of China, underlining the opportunities and challenges that China will have to face on its way to the status of a global sports superpower.

At the 20th Summit of the CPC in the autumn of 2022, Xi Jinping was elected the general secretary of the Party for the next term. The makeup of the Political Bureau and the number of its members can help predict how much power the leader will be given and how much of it he can hold. The nearest future will reveal how Xi will use the time given to him by the elites, and the next years of his rule will require fresh analyses and overviews. We hope that the readers will find this book both interesting and inspiring and that this publication, prepared in collaboration with Sinologists and experts on China-related issues, will contribute to spreading knowledge about the PRC and facilitate a better understanding of the processes taking place in China during Xi Jinping's era.

References

Bickenbach, Frank and Liu Wan-Hsin (2022) Goodbye China: What Do Fewer Foreigners Mean for Multinationals and the Chinese Economy? *Intereconomics*, 57(5), pp. 306–312.

Bougon, François (2017) *Inside the Mind of Xi Jinping*. London: Hurst & Co.

Feldman, Steven P. (2023) *Xi Jinping's Anticorruption Campaign. The Politics of Revenge*. London: Routledge.

Gao Jinghua and Zhang Pengfei (2021) China's Public Health Policies in Response to COVID-19: From an "Authoritarian" Perspective. *Frontiers in Public Health*, 9 (article 756677), pp. 1–11.

Gries, Peter Hays (2004) *China's new nationalism: pride, politics, and diplomacy*. Berkeley: University of California Press.

Guo Baogang (2019) Sino-Western Cognitive Differences and Western Liberal Biases in Chinese Political Studies. *Journal of Chinese Political Science*, 24, pp. 181–198.

Lehman-Ludwig, Anna, Abigail Burke, David Ambler and Ralph Schroeder (2023) Chinese Anti-Westernism on social media. *Global Media and China*, 8(2), pp. 119–137.

Shin Kawashima (2022) War in Ukraine from China's Perspective: Limited Options for State that Cannot Reject Existing Policies, *Asia-Pacific Review*, 29(2), pp. 35–55.

Tiezzi, Shannon (2021) David Shambaugh on China's Political Personalities, From Mao to Xi. *The Diplomat*, 8 September, https://thediplomat.com/2021/09/david-shambaugh-on-chinas-political-personalities-from-mao-to-xi/, accessed 8 September 2021.

Wu, Guoguang (2023) Interpreting Xi Jinping's Shifting Strategy on the Russia-Ukraine War. *Asia Society Policy Institute*, October, https://asiasociety.org/policy-institute/interpreting-xi-jinpings-shifting-strategy-russia-ukraine-war, accessed 12 November 2023.

Zhang Fengzhi (2015) *Xi Jinping: How to Read Confucius and Other Chinese Classical Thinkers*. Beijng: CN Times Books Inc.

PART 1

Political Dimensions

CHAPTER 1

The Characteristics and Evolution of China's Political System under Xi Jinping

Bogdan J. Góralczyk

1   Tradition

The fundamental problem encountered in Western literature when analysing the developments taking place in China and the People's Republic of China (PRC) stems from our tendency to view Chinese reality through the lens of our own categories and ideas. Often, however, they do not match the nature of this very different, ancient civilization. This attitude is, in some ways, reciprocated: the Chinese have always been, and still are, loath to adopt Western customs and measures. One case in point is the famous reply addressed by emperor Qianlong to British envoy George Macartney when the Chinese ruler, as the Son of Heaven, generously rejected foreign gifts and offers, announcing that:

> Strange and costly objects do not interest me. If I have commanded that the tribute offerings sent by you, O King, are to be accepted, this was solely in consideration for the spirit which prompted you to dispatch them from afar [...]. As your Ambassador can see for himself, we possess all things.
> KISSINGER, 2011: 42

A newer example is, of course, the reception of Marxism–Leninism, which is, after all, the product of Western thinking (even though it spread in Russia and later the USSR) and has been regularly moulded to domestic circumstances (for example, sparking a revolution of the peasantry rather than of the proletariat) by Mao Zedong and other leaders of the Communist Party of China (CPC, alternately called in this article the "Party") following in his tracks. Once they were in charge of the great state spanning half the continent, Marxism was skillfully Sinicized, giving birth to "Maoism". Just to quote an expert on the issue, Stuart Schram: "There can be a little doubt that Mao Zedong (Mao Tse-tung) believed he had defined a new and distinctive Chinese road to socialism, which marked a clear break with many aspects of the Soviet interpretation of Marxism" (Schram, 1989: 201).

The essence of things lies not only in the difficulty of matching words and ideas in languages, or rather civilizations, alien to each other, but is mostly the product of our inability to view China in a holistic way as a compact whole and also the longest-lasting statehood tradition in the world. It is not surprising to see even noted experts on the country confessing that "China's political system is more opaque than most" (Dickson, 2021: 6). The notions, terms, concepts and ideas Chinese use usually do not match our usual formulas and principles, or are given a meaning different from ours.

We have multiple valuable works and studies concerning ancient Chinese history, modern China (understood as the period since the Opium Wars in 1839–1860), or the PRC. It is rare, however, for the West to realise that China means tradition, stability and civilizational continuity or, in the apt words of Lucian W. Pye (1992: 235) a "civilization pretending to be a state", and, moreover, a state proud of its achievement and resources. While Mao Zedong had a heterodox relationship with Chinese tradition, he made it the mainstay of his thinking. His approach has lately and increasingly been copied by the man who has led the PRC since 2012, Xi Jinping. Xi's ideological legitimacy is gradually being underpinned by a "mixture of Chinese philosophy, Maoism, and Nationalism", combined with "fighting against 'deviant behaviour'", as Asia specialist François Bougon describes (Bougon, 2018: 19).

Xi Jinping's rule marks a clear return to China's own domestic traditions, from antiquity to the ideas of Mao in an ideological and conceptual sense, coupled with the Leninist legacy of centralisation, rigour and strict discipline. In each dimension, the point of departure is the Chinese character. Richard McGregor is right in writing that "the Party now markets itself as an inclusive organization with uniquely Chinese roots" (McGregor, 2010: 33). In former times, during the long ages of history, China was ruled by an emperor surrounded by throngs of advisers, for the most part eunuchs, and the ubiquitous bureaucracy. Today, the CPC is the "collective emperor", which sometimes, as in the times of Mao and today under Xi, bears the face of a single leader, while the bureaucrats nowadays are none other than the structures of the ruling and dominating Party.

When analysing China and its political system or governance concepts, we must decide whether or not we will accept that China's entire tradition of emperorship meant the concentration of authority in the hands of one man. It was autocratic and patriarchal by nature, firmly entrenched in the gargantuan bureaucratic apparatus, and supported by a legal system that boiled down to a harsh penal code and an extensive network of penitentiaries.

Lucian W. Pye aptly pays attention to the fact that China has always been "the combination of bureaucratic hierarchy and ideological conformity" (Pye, 1992: 15). Another no less astute researcher of Chinese traditional ruling methods, Étienne Balázs, adds such traits as enlightened despotism, obedience to superiors, constant state control and state intervention, draconian laws, and sometimes even a totalitarian strain (Balázs, 1967: 3–9). All of this together led to a marvel called at times the State Moloch, and at others Chinese particularism.

An attempt to break down this tradition was made by Sun Yat-sen, but his republican and democratic experiment ended tragically in chaotic war waged by private armies of warlords (军阀 *junfa*). On the other hand, once Chiang Kai-Shek (Jiang Jieshi) has consolidated his power, he was eager to return to those old autocratic traditions and near the end of his life, while living in Taiwan, made the birthday of mainland-banned Confucius a state holiday. In the words of his insightful biographer, Jakub Polit, Chiang as a military man already had authoritarian tendencies, so his National Party (国民党 Guomingdang), and the then Chinese Republic, concealed a "Bolshevik skeleton" underneath (Polit, 2008: 593). Later, in Taiwan, when due to circumstances and the constant tensions over the strait martial law was kept up almost all the time, Chiang ruled single-handedly, relying on three people only: his wife, his son Ching-kuo, and Chen Cheng, his prime minister since 1950 (Polit, 2008: 633).

Even less love for democracy was displayed by Chinese communists, who adopted Soviet patterns when they came into power. Their leader, Mao Zedong, was, however, quick to add Chinese tradition to the mix, erecting a system aptly dubbed Confucianist–Leninism. The main trait of that system was its closed and monopolistic nature (Pye, 1992: 13). With the passage of time, it became increasingly clear and palpable that the rule of the CPC, even though assumed to be different and based on entirely distinct ideological foundations, led to the renascence of classical Confucian traits. A new hierarchical state was born, based on traits and values such as "respect, humility, docility, obedience, submission, and subordination to elders and betters" (Balázs, 1967: 18). In the case of the CPC, this was transformed into subordination to the Party, its requirements and those who formed the power elite.

Mao Zedong was indeed at first a revolutionary, guerrilla fighter, rebel and peasant leader, and even a "native philosopher" (Schram, 1989: 191), but near the end of his life he built a system that was all but totalitarian and, paying no heed to individuals, permeated by a revolutionary and ideological fervour ("red better than expert") and once again vindicating the ideal, Confucian in spirit, of rule by an "enlightened individual" whose vision and will was imposed on the Party, state and the entire society. Moreover, attempts were made to export this system (for instance to Cambodia, as exemplary case, or whole Indochina and the global South, under a messianistic mission of "exporting revolution"), an undertaking thoroughly researched in a recent work of Julia Lovell (2019: 139, 257, 261). And so this system, constantly evolving, diverged a long way from anarchic and utopian ideas to the despotism and single-man rule so well-known from Chinese history.

2   Ideology

The official ideology of the ruling Party is Marxism–Leninism, the former in the ideological, the latter in the practical dimension, because, as Bruce J. Dickson rightly says, "Marx provided the ideology of communism; Lenin provided the organization" (Dickson, 2021: 11). Thus, beginning with Mao and Maoism, it was always the case that the ruling ideology was to a greater or lesser extent mixed with practice. The influence of ideology waxed under Mao and waned under Deng, but the ideological and practical framework remained the same. According to these principles, CPC rule can be defined as a dictatorship, and the Party itself as an entity that has monopolized power, and subsequently also propaganda or overarching influence on the life of society in both a material and spiritual sense.

During PRC history, this rule underwent some quite considerable evolution, but the basic ideological tenets remained the same. Even with such an essential change as the transition from the inherently anti-market "Mao era" to the pro-market reforms of Deng Xiaoping and the abandonment of political class struggle in favour of economic growth struggle, the basic formula of the CPC taking the centre stage all over the country was not altered. Moreover, at the very outset of his pro-market reforms on March 30, 1979, Deng laid down the "four cardinal principles" (四项基本原则 *sixiang jinben yuanze*): uphold the socialist road, the dictatorship of the proletariat, the leadership and undivided rule of the communist party, and Marxism–Leninism and "Mao thought" as political paradigms (Deng, 1984: 166–191). These "four cardinal principles" were considered so important that they were enshrined in the constitution and remain in force to this very day.

Yet they have been, as always, dyed with a Chinese tint: since the 13th Congress of the CPC in the autumn of 1987, China's political system has been officially called "socialism with Chinese characteristics", including besides Marxism–Leninism various Chinese theories and ideas listed in the Party's documents as a collection of "Mao Zedong ideas" (毛泽东思想 *Mao Zedong sixiang*), the theories of Deng Xiaoping in addition to the "four principles" named above, the old pragmatic formula of "seeking truth from facts" (实事求是 *shishi qiushi*) [lit. "it is what it is" – trans. note], the idea of reforms and opening to the world (改革开放 *gaige kaifang*), Jiang Zemin's theory of "three representations" (三个代表 *san ge daibiao*) that extended Party membership to the rich, the concept of "scientific development" (科学发展 *kexue fazhan*) championed by Hu Jintao, as well as the "ideas of Xi Jinping" (习近平思想 *Xi Jinping sixiang*) which are analysed in this chapter.

The usual assumption is that the ideological underpinning of CPC rule are "Mao Zedong's ideas", which, in the Western world colloquially, even in specialist literature, are called Maoism. The assumption is not incorrect, but not very accurate either. This is because Mao Zedong's conceptions as party chairman and then state leader evolved along with changing times and developments. It appears that they can be divided into at least four basic stages, or phases:

1. *Revolutionary* (from the formation of the CPC to victory in the civil war with Guomindang, evolving constantly, with no precise end date).
2. *Consolidation and closing of ranks* (from Mao's taking control over the Party during the Long March and the Zunyi conference in autumn 1935 until proclaiming the PRC).
3. *Adaptation* (or the "leaning to one side" and the alliance with the USSR, into which the PRC was forced by circumstances during 1950–1958/60).
4. *"Left deviationism"* (from the Great Leap of 1958–1961 to the Cultural Revolution of 1966–76).

Despite these somewhat essential changes, the basic principles remained unaltered: the system was a greatly centralised state socialism, in which the power was consolidated in the hands of the CPC as the "modern mandarins" and its leader, Mao, as the "modern emperor". It was thus "Confucian Leninism", an authoritarian and, in the final phase of the "Left deviationism", a decidedly totalitarian system, highly anti-market, highly collectivist and anti-individualistic, autarkic and closed to the world, but also greatly "revolutionary" and downright messianic in its rhetoric, wishing to spread these ideals to the whole world. First, "under the gaze of Mao, ideology was replaced by national interest", and then the authorities took a fancy to exporting their ideas, a move that surprisingly temporarily succeeded in one case (Cambodia), producing the well-known and enormously tragic results (Lovell, 2019: 274, 275).

Deng Xiaoping, himself a victim of the "cultural revolution" and single-man rule, made some essential changes to the system; while maintaining the Leninist-minded principle of "democratic centralism" (i.e., Party dictatorship), he allowed market experiments (an anathema for both classical Marxism and Maoism) within the bounds of "socialism with Chinese characteristics", opening to the world and a pragmatic mindset, an approach summed up in the famous saying: "It doesn't matter whether a cat is black or white, as long as it catches mice [it is a good cat]". He also did much to replace single-man rule with limited terms for the highest posts in CPC authorities and, most importantly, introduced the collective leadership formula.

The latter can be compared with the principle of "modern meritocracy" (Góralczyk, 2018: 194), because the construct used in classical Marxist–Leninist parties was skilfully padded with the rudiments of Confucian requirements. These grounds, but also the personal wishes of Deng, were used to select the members of the third and fourth PRC leadership, two sets of names during the term of Jiang Zemin (1989–2002): the post of prime minister was first occupied by hardliner Li Peng, then by agile, skilful and convinced reformer Zhu Rongji and finally the duo of Hu Jintao and Wen Jiabao (2002–2012). The "fifth generation of leaders" (第五代 *di wudai*), headed by the charismatic Xi Jinping, profoundly altered, if not entirely reversed, this system, in the Leninist spirit with its renewed centralization and consolidation of powers in the hands of the Party and its leader. At the same time, great care was taken to ensure that the changes also followed the Marxist spirit in their programmatic and ideological dimension.

Once again, one must stress the important fact that the "fifth generation" of leaders under Xi Jinping decided to supplement the previous ideas of Mao Zedong and pragmatic programmes of Deng Xiaoping with the theory of "three representations" (三个代表 *san ge daibao*) espoused by Jiang Zemin and "scientific development" and other theories of Xi himself, which were again awarded the name of *sixiang*, just like Mao's and unlike the thought of the three previous leaders and their inner circles. The entire package has, with time, following the 19th Congress of the CPC (October 16–17, 2017), become known by the quite baroque appellation of "Xi Jinping Thought on Socialism with Chinese Characteristics in a New Era" (习近平新时代中国特色社会主义思想 *Xi Jinping Xin Shidai Zhongguo Tese Shehuizhuyi Sixang*) (Xinhuanet, n.d.). As such, it was introduced not only in propaganda or to party schools, but also resulted in the establishment of special chairs and institutes at universities.

The exegesis of the entire system would require enormous work, and, moreover, the whole process has not yet been completed. For the time being, we can make only a preliminary guess that, just as in case of Mao Zedong, Xi Jinping's "ideas" will likewise evolve and may still bring some surprises or novelties. On the other hand, analysing the previous output collected in Xi Jinping's "works" (of which three major, not counting many minor volumes have been published already) has so far led to the following preliminary assessments and conclusions. It appears that this leader:

1. following an era of liberalisation (both in economic and market, but much less political, terms), intends to return to the "sources of socialism", which, in the Chinese dress, means Maoism, understood primarily as a system of social justice and more balanced incomes, all under the slogans of "better life" for society (内好生活 *nei hao shenghuo*);
2. has set his sights on eradicating extreme poverty as part of his plan to build a "moderately prosperous society" (小康社会 *xiaokang shehui*), announced already by previous leaders, but not put into effect with much consistency. In this aspect, Xi has peremptorily announced a "victory" and declared that "China has already essentially achieved the goal of building a moderately prosperous society" in early 2019, when "the poverty rate has dropped from 10.2 to 1.7 per cent" (Xi, 2019: 7, 13). In 2021, to mark the one hundredth anniversary of the CPC, the programme was brought to completion, and almost immediately thereafter a new campaign has been introduced, to bring – by 2035 – a "common prosperity" (共同富裕 *gongtong fuyu*) to the country (later, in 2022, suspended indefinitely, due to the lockdown in Shanghai);
3. attempts to make CPC rule more effective, primarily through increased centralisation and control, as well as (self-)discipline of the Party members, resorting for this purpose to more subtle solutions such as the much-bruited "social credit system" (社会信用体系 *shehui xinyong tixi*) that involves artificial intelligence, extensive use of cameras and *big data* processing (Strittmatter, 2018: 80–140);
4. as part of the plan to realize the "Chinese Dream", which he promoted from the outset of his rule, set the overarching goal of "uniting the fatherland" (with Taiwan) on the one hand, and bolstering the power and rank of the Middle Kingdom on the other. This is proved by the slogans of "the great renaissance of the Chinese people" (中华民族伟大复兴 *Zhonghua minzu weida fuxing*) (Xi, 2014: 38, 41) or China as an innovative society (Xi's statements from 2015 and 2017), which he declared his "historic mission" in the upcoming "new era". The best proof is his proposal to divide the history of PRC into the following periods: "getting off the knees" (1949–76), "becoming rich" (1978–2012) and "coming into power" (from 2012) – 从站起来 富起来 到强起来 的历史性飞跃 *cong zhan qilai, fu qilai, dao qiang qilai de lishi xing feiyue;*

5. in all programmes and declarations put in effect so far, irresistibly appears "as someone who places fidelity to ideology above everything else" (Brown, 2017: 227).

Virtually all analysts and observers agree that Xi Jinping inaugurated an era of charismatic and heavy-handed rule. Autocracy is on the rise, while liberal trends are disappearing. As noted by one of the politician's biographers, "Xi is instituting a form of neo-authoritarianism at home, bolstered by a strong state" (Bougon, 2018: 10). On the other hand, noted US expert David Shambaugh defines this new system as "Patriarchal Leninism", and the reality it has established in China as "neo-totalitarian" (Shambaugh, 2021: 336, 337).

It is well known that statesmen are judged not only by their programmes or verbal declarations but also by their entourage. In this respect, one of the more important observations has come from the astute observer of the Chinese internal scene, Cheng Li from the Brookings Institution. He proved that while Xi Jinping's retinue includes pro-market and liberal economists, beginning with the influential deputy minister Liu He, on the other hand his most trusted associates in ideological matters are "noticeably very conservative", such as Huan Kuming, He Yiting and Li Shulei (Li, 2016: 214). The main ideologist in the current line-up of the Standing Committee, Wang Huning, can hardly be counted as liberal either.

All of them together are staunch opponents of liberal democracy, Westernization or even liberalisation in an ideological or political sense. They favour a heavy-handed approach and centralisation, because they are devotees of a slogan long cherished in the inner circles of the CPC that "(democratic) elections do not guarantee competence" (Shambaugh, 2008: 123). As strongly espoused by the recently influential on the Chinese internal scene, as important in this respect Professor Zhang Weiwei from Fudan University, they are convinced that democratic legitimacy is not as important as a method of good and effective governance (Zhang, 2019: 163–174).

An important factor in these calculations is also the trauma caused by the downfall of the USSR, which Western literature fails to fully appreciate, and the conclusions drawn by CPC bodies after that event. This means primarily the need to adapt to new challenges and circumstances, accurately pinpoint the greatest threats, and identify both internal and external dangers. An indispensable addition was "the ideological purity of the Party rank and file" and the need for "self-reflection" of Party members (Shambaugh, 2008: 124, 125).

3 Structure

Considered formally, the CPC is Leninist in spirit, and thus monopolistic in its nature and structure, and totally dominating and strongly hierarchical in its style of governance. In some ways, it resembles classical Marxist–Leninist parties modelled after the Communist Party of the Soviet Union (CPSU). Actually, however, it combines the basic communist party skeleton with Chinese traditions of autocracy, patriarchalism, social discipline and a single entity that dominates the entire power structure. Under its rule, the PRC could well be defined as a single party state, because the formally existing eight democratic parties can hardly be considered serious power centres or forces. Moreover, during the Mao era, the Party could basically be considered identical to the State, so much overlap was there between the two structures, and history seems to be repeating itself under Xi Jinping.

Formally, the highest institution in the power system is the CPC Congress, which meets every five years to choose the supreme leaders for the next term. Since 2012, the CPC has been led by General Secretary Xi Jinping. Subordinate to him is the seven-man Standing Committee of the Central Political Bureau (CBP; Xi Jinping, Li Keqiang, Li Zhanshu, Wang Yang, Wang Huning, Zhao Leji and Han Zheng – in the order of precedence given in official documents). The next level in the hierarchy is the 25-person Central Political Bureau, then the Central Committee made up of more than 370 people, and finally rank-and-file party members whose number has, according to the most recent 2021 data, exceeded 95 million (Weixin, 2021). In addition to the CPC CPB, the Party framework consists of 31 provincial committees, 665 city committees, 2487 county committees, 41,636 town committees and 780,000 village committees (hierarchy of bodies: Li, 2016: 45; figures following the official CPC webpage: http://cpc.people.com.cn/). In some ways, therefore, this is a veritable state within a state and a highly extensive bureaucratic network, just as expected, given Chinese traditions.

I have dealt with the political aspects of CPC functioning on multiple occasions, at times somewhat summarily (Góralczyk, 2018: 194–218), at others more systematically and minutely (Góralczyk, 2021a: 13–30). For the purpose of this study and the clarity of my arguments, I am now going to sketch out only the most important principles governing the functioning and decision-making at the highest CPC levels. Another intent is to demonstrate, in a more visual manner, what essential changes have already been made by Xi Jinping in this system. The system built by Deng Xiaoping and his successors was as follows:

1. The highest authority, as the first among equals, was held by the General Secretary of the CPC CPB, who also acted as the head of

state, the President of the PRC (hence the presidential title commonly assigned to him abroad) and was, moreover, the chairman of the Central Military Commission of the CPC CPB, or essentially the commander-in-chief. Accordingly, the supreme figure in the collective leadership was at one time the head of state, Party and the army.
2. The second person in the state, holding an executive function and acting like another emperor, was the prime minister, whose position was so strong that for years he and the president could be said to govern in tandem, as was the case with Hu Yaobang and Zhao Ziyang, Jiang Zemin and Zhu Rongji, and Hu Jintao and Wen Jiabao.
3. The actual new emperor was, however, not individual but collective, taking the name of the Standing Committee of the CPC CPB (its current composition has already been listed above). This body sits at least once per month and makes all the important decisions, but in a very non-transparent manner, because press releases summarising its meetings are usually laconic and devoid of details.
4. The road to the top echelons is open to those who have already held posts at lower administrative levels; for example, as a provincial manager or a mayor of a large city, for at least one term or more. Xi Jinping himself, before he entered the Standing Committee, was head of the Fuijan (1985–2002) and Zheijang (2002–2007) provinces, and finally, just before joining the central authorities, the first Party secretary in Shanghai.
5. Sitting in the top decision-making circles of the state is restricted to two ten-year terms.
6. The other restriction is the unwritten, but obeyed age constraint: those over 68 are not admitted to the highest bodies. In practice this means that if someone joins such a body at the age or 65 or 66 – a rare occurrence – they are allowed to complete their five year term but could not expect to be elected for another one.

At the 19th CPC Congress, Xi Jinping made two inroads into this system, one of which was of key importance: abolishing the term limit for the Party General Secretary (a privilege that next March was extended to the PRC President by the National People's Congress). In practice, this may mean lifetime rule, although the exact application of this principle is not yet known, because the formula has not been used before. At any rate, despite an established tradition, the Congress did not choose Xi's successor who would replace him at the next, 20th Congress in 2022. We can, therefore, anticipate that Xi's rule will last much longer.

Regardless of the above, the post of "deputy chairman" (deputy president) was established to recognise the merits of Wang Qishan (born 1948) who, during Xi's first term, directly oversaw the unprecedented anti-corruption campaign (not mentioned here, but equally important, at least as another form of closing of ranks and enforcing discipline). Although, due to his age, Wang was no longer eligible to sit in the Standing Committee, whose member he was formerly, practice shows that he is often invited to its meetings.

Moreover, during Xi Jinping's era, control and centralisation have been strongly enhanced, which in practice boils down to the following formula: the CPC keeps the state and government under its thumb (the role of prime minister Li Keqiang, who will leave his post in 2023, in comparison to the three preceding ruling tandems was much reduced, or even, in the words of eminent analyst Cheng Li, "marginalized") (Li, 2016: 12); the Party is kept in check by the almost omnipotent Organization Department, while Xi Jinping himself, as head of the Central Commission for Discipline Inspection, controls the behaviour of members of the Central Committee and other structures.

Another novelty which must be pointed out is that Xi Jinping does not limit himself to a single control function but holds multiple ones, heading many "small leading groups", as a result of which he was awarded the rather accurate moniker of "chairman of everything" (Barmé, 2016).

4   Individuals

In each autocratic system, an important and usually key role is played by the individual who tops the entire hierarchy. Much depends on his character, likes, beliefs and knowledge. In China, a state with paternalistic traditions, where, moreover, the emperor was the Son of Heaven, a sort of connection between the simple folk and the ruling (or even supernatural) powers, where political rule overlapped legislation and extensive bureaucracy, this truth bears out more than anywhere else. Almost every emperor imprinted his mark on the country's life, although the differences were obviously huge and depended on the ruler's charisma, the length of his reign or other personal attributes.

PRC history is no different in this respect, its reality shaped by the traits and personality of those who led the omnipotent and almost omnipresent Party. The astute remarks of Henry Kissinger on Mao Zedong and Deng Xiaoping, both of whom he had the opportunity to meet in person, are uncannily accurate.

> Chinese leaders traditionally have not based their authority on rhetorical skills or physical contact with the masses. In the mandarin tradition, they operate essentially out of sight, legitimized by performance. Deng held no major office; he refused all honorific titles; he almost never appeared on television, and practices politics almost entirely behind the scenes. He ruled not like an emperor but as the principal mandarin.
>
> Mao had governed by counting on the endurance of the Chinese people to sustain the suffering his personal visions would impose on them. Deng governed by liberating the creativeness of the Chinese people to bring about their own vision of the future. Mao strove for economic advancement with mystical faith in the power of Chinese masses to overcome any obstacle by sheer willpower and ideological purity. Deng was forthright about China's poverty and the vast gaps that separated its standard of living from that of developed world.
>
> KISSINGER, 2011: 334

In other words, Mao was an ideologue who believed in the power of ideas, thoughts and concepts. Deng, on the other hand, was pragmatic to the bone, an administrator far removed from any theories or ideologies. They had some traits in common, however: the belief in China's greatness, the faith in and vision of the country's renascence and power to rival the ages of old, although both imagined the future in a slightly different way and used vastly differing methods: Mao wanted to revolutionise China, toppling down everything that was antiquated, while Deng hoisted an economic, even technocratic, not a political revolution upon the nation, drawing upon the hidden strengths inherent in the Chinese people, such as industriousness, resourcefulness and entrepreneurship (which were stifled under Mao).

For this reason alone, PRC history can be divided into the "Mao era" and the "Deng era", the latter lasting slightly longer than the man it was named after. While Mao's rule was continued by the short and today unimportant *interregnum* of Hua Guofeng (1976–78/80), the Deng era technocracy survived during the reign of Jiang Zemin and Zhu Rongji (until 2002) as well as Hu Jintao and Wen Jiabao (until 2012). While Jiang Zemin did make history with his "theory of three representations" (三个代表 *san ge daibiao*), and Hu Jintao proclaimed the building of a "harmonious society" (和谐社会 *hexie shehui*) in Confucian spirit, in the ideological, structural and practical sense they continued the pragmatic and technocratic regime imposed by Deng Xiaoping. It was not until Xi Jinping that a change took place, and only time will tell how deep it is going to be, because his "era" will not yet be completed by the time these words are written.

Nevertheless, we can already attempt to define the most important adjustments and changes made by that leader in CPC and PRC history. They are already numerous and, taken together, lead to the conclusion that the reality of the state and the entire system has once again been thoroughly revised. A deep transition took place, just as when Mao was succeeded by Deng, but now in the opposite direction. The only difference is that those epochs are already closed, although, of course, they still influence the present state of things, and the current one is still open, so what it will ultimately bring remains a mystery. This is all the more so because Xi Jinping's plans and assumptions, even his visions, are far-reaching and of a widely divergent nature. He has already stamped his mark on the country's political life, the functioning of the Party and its programme, as well as the economy and foreign relations.

To summarize as briefly as possible the *list of changes*, of course, of different impact, but all of them of great significance, which already effected or were formally proposed by the current Chinese leader, the following should be noted as foremost:

1. *The vision of "two centenary goals"* (两个一百年 *liange yibainian*), or establishing until mid-2021, the 100th anniversary of the CPC, a "moderately prosperous society" (小康社会 *xiaokang shehui*), which means eliminating extreme poverty and basing national development on a strong, burgeoning internal market and China's own middle class, a goal that was largely achieved (Xi Jinping, 1 July 2021). It is eventually to be followed by "common prosperity" (共同富裕 *gongtong fuyu*) idea raised in late 2021 (and abrogated – temporarily? – in 2021). By 2049, the 100th anniversary of the PRC, China is set to become "a modern socialist country that is prosperous, strong, democratic, culturally advanced, and harmonious" (Xi, 2014: 60).
2. *The vision of an "innovative society"* added to the "two centenary goals" during the 19th Congress of the CPC in October 2017, which assumes that by 2035 China will not only remain the economic and trade superpower it is now but also become a leader in technology and innovation.
3. *The new "dual circulation"* (双循环 *shuang xunhuan*) *development model*, used since 2021, introduced the following scheme: the first circulation is the domestic system with a flourishing middle class and the national market; and the second, auxiliary, means globalisation and external markets. In some ways, this is a reference to Chinese tradition, and especially the renowned late-nineteenth-century principle of Zhang Zhidong (中学为体, 西学为用 *zhongxue*

wei ti, xixue wei yong – "Chinese learning as substance, Western learning for application").

4. *The vision of two new Silk Roads*, or the idea of large communication links and infrastructural investments on land and sea, announced in 2013 and formally known as *Yidai Yilu* (一带一路) – Belt and Road Initiative (BRI), treated in global literature as one of the boldest geopolitical undertakings of all time, not only for China (Shambaugh, 2021: 292).

5. *The idea of "community of common destiny for all mankind"* (人类命运共同体 *renlei mingyun gongtongti*) promoted towards other countries (this issue requires a separate analysis).

6. *The consistently proclaimed idea of unification with Taiwan*, treated as a paramount strategic objective and, at the same time, an attempt to make good for the very badly remembered "century of national humiliation" (百年国耻 *bainian guochi*) from 1839 to 1949 when China, subjected to extreme pressure from the Great Powers, was reduced to misery and poverty, and even lost some of its territory to foreigners (for an excellent study on this, see Wang, 2012).

7. In this context, one can also observe a noticeable *return to nationalism*, ostensibly under the guise of "promoting patriotism" (Dickson, 2021: 192 et seq.), which has become the special penchant not only for the supreme leader and central authorities but also for at least some media who follow in their footsteps (e.g., the vociferous *Huanqiu Shibao – Global Times* daily) or even scientists (an important and meaningful series 这就是中国 *Zhe jiu shi Zhonguo* – "This is China" by Professor Zhang Weiwei; Baidu, n.d.).

8. *The return to autocracy and the preponderance of politics and ideology over economy.* This aspect is noticed by virtually all external observers of China, with an important note added by Kai Strittmatter, who is known for his extremely critical attitude towards the current Chinese government. In his words, "Every autocracy seeks to destroy solidarity and sympathy among its citizens. Today's China is seething with mistrust, and complaints about moral decline have reached a new pitch of intensity" (Strittmatter, 2018: 292). In leader speeches, the main causes are very often portrayed as excessive stratification and "the law of the jungle", with its extreme worship of money and the market, which obviously "must be opposed".

9. *Abolishing the terms of office for the Party leader,* which should be treated as deviating from Deng Xiaoping's legacy and his carefully

cultivated scheme of collective rule, and perhaps even as the wish to introduce lifetime rule for the supreme leader (Dickson, 2021: 27).

10. *The return to Leninist and Marxist traditions*, with increased centralisation and control, the monopoly for power (for the leader himself and the CPC), greater authoritarianism and a noticeably increased presence of the Party propaganda, even in daily life, as well as, equally ubiquitous, signs of a personality cult, which taken together are unmistakably a sign of "harking back to Maoist traditions" (Shambaugh, 2021: 293; Fukuyama, 2020).

11. *The wish to return to traditions, expressed frequently and on many occasions*, in particular to the art and style of ruling, which, as rightly stressed by Francis Fukuyama, who studied these issues, "have been centralized, bureaucratic, and merit-based" (Fukuyama, 2020). Let us add here our own observation that the currently promoted "merits" are bestowed or granted by the Party and are calculated to serve primarily its interests.

12. *Deep reforms in the army and its rapid modernization* (which is, however, not included in this analysis, since it requires a different approach and other study tools).

Considering all this together, it may be concluded that Xi Jinping's term so far and his achievements as the Party, state and army leader demonstrate three conspicuous tendencies: a return to dominating policy and ideology; increased centralisation of authority, and even partocracy and authoritarianism; and setting ambitious goals, including the restoration of a powerful civilization (Góralczyk, 2021b: 289). We may also add the trappings of a personality cult, including the title of Great Helmsman (Shambaugh, 2021: 315). This urges most external observers to propound the thesis that Xi's China is re-enacting the Mao era, although, of course, the world has changed since then, and so has China, which is now a modern and largely urbanised, not a half-feudal, agrarian and poor country. This is the reason why current developments in China are so important for the world.

5 Conclusion

There can be no doubt that Xi Jinping's overarching goal is to retain power for himself and for the CPC which brought him to the top. It also cannot be doubted that all his declared visions, objectives and assumptions listed in this article, from the "centenary goals" through unification with Taiwan to implementing BRI, are treated seriously as tasks to be completed, and by a set deadline, too.

Xi Jinping is a trenchant, charismatic politician who sets highly ambitious goals for himself and the Party. He was the first since the Mao era to bestow on himself the title of "core leader" (核心 *hexin*) in October 2016, just a step away from chairman (主席 *zhuxi*), the sobriquet once applied to Mao and now increasingly to Xi. Above, we said that Xi has even been jestingly but tellingly called the "chairman of everything". In this context, it is worth recalling the warnings that Deng Xiaoping gave at the close of his life to his successors, Jiang Zemin and prime minister Li Peng, in December 1990. He cautioned against returning to arbitrary, one-man rule and urged them to follow the principle that the key to China's stability was the collective leadership of the Central Political Bureau and, in particular, its Standing Committee (Li, 2016: 13).

Xi's epoch ushers in autocracy, centralisation, top-down planning and the return of CPC party apparatus and units to companies and production firms, and even bodies of a private nature (Bogusz and Jakóbowski, 2019: 94). As in the case of silently building national greatness, here also a clear deviation from Deng Xiaoping's legacy is apparent. Politics came to dominate economy and the market again.

On the other hand, Xi's bold visions in the international sphere, from BRI to imposing China's political will on Hong Kong during the pandemic, a move that immediately brought the delicate and very touchy "Taiwan issue" into the spotlight (a topic that lies beyond the scope of this study; for more details, see Góralczyk, 2021b: 183–219), when taken together, made the international public worried about "a new cold war", like John Mearsheimer pointed it out (Mearsheimer, 2021).

In such circumstances, an increasing number of Western academicians are concerned about China's system lurching towards increasing authoritarianism and even totalitarianism, with the help of state-of-the-art technology, including artificial intelligence (already successfully involved in fighting the pandemic). These concerns are also becoming more widespread and noticeable among authors cited in this article (Dickson, Fukuyama, Shambaugh, Strittmatter and others). Meanwhile, Chinese authors join the fray by retorting that liberal democracy, so championed by the US and Western Europe after the fall of the Cold War order, has not proved an effective and universal medicine, as demonstrated by failed attempts to "export" the idea to Iraq and Afghanistan. In other words, the Chinese are convinced that their system is better but by no means "universal" (Li, 2020). Who is right in this dispute, and how it is going to end is for the history books to decide.

The astute Chinese analyst Cheng Li is correct in noting that the establishment of personality cult, acquiring monopolized powerful positions to exert stronger authority and power "would be counter-productive and detrimental, not only for present-day China but also for Xi himself" (Li, 2016: 17). The truth that has come down to us from previous centuries, in both Chinese and universal history, resounds unambiguously: authoritarian or totalitarian regimes can be effective but only in the short term, as sooner or later they have always led to disaster.

Therefore, the final grand question is whether Xi Jinping and his subordinates remember the vision of reforms formulated by Deng Xiaoping in the late 1970s and consisting of three stages or steps (中国改革三步走 *Zhongguo gaige san bu zou*), used by the known intellectual and influential advisor of the current government, Prof. Zheng Yongnian, as a basis for writing and publishing in the PRC (while working in Singapore) a very important volume bearing the same title. He reminded that according to Deng's vision of 1980, the process of transformation and reforms can take as many as one hundred years to achieve and should go through *three basic stages*:

1. Stage one: (re)build state power, or the later *low profile* strategy, 韬光养晦 *taoguang yanghui* (conceal your capabilities, bide your time and avoid the limelight). This process should last for three decades and was basically completed between 1978 and 2008.
2. Stage two: build the citizen's purchasing capacity as part of the idea of establishing a "moderately prosperous society", followed by a new "dual circulation" model of development. This process should likewise take around three decades and thus last from, say, 2012 to 2032/35 (the latter date is notably aligned with plans to introduce an innovative society).
3. Stage three, posited to last another three decades, consists of political reforms, including "liberalisation of the system", without, however, expanding on any details (Zheng, 2012: 3–7).

Xi Jinping, like a true leader, looks at the world, and especially Chinese future (under his hand, naturally) with optimism. Many times and on various occasions, he has stressed that "time is working for China", and in a very important and symbolic CPC 100th anniversary speech made on 1 July 2021 at the Tiananmen gate, he said that, "The great path we have pioneered, the great cause we have undertaken, and the great achievements we have made over the past century will go down in the annals of the development of the Chinese nation and of human civilization" (YouTube, 2021).

Can this entire idea and vision, like the "Chinese Dream" and "centenary goals" of Xi Jinping, be successfully put into effect, and will, once this process is completed in mid-century, China again become an effective, modernised but also liberalised and even democratic (but certainly of a different shade than liberal) civilisation? The mandarins that desire the same as Xi are close to him, but they, too, realise how inert is the matter they have to work with. Xi Jinping himself said at a meeting with the central authorities in early 2021 that "the world is now going through a period of unprecedented shocks, unknown in the last century". They are accompanied with equally unprecedented challenges. The most important ones, according to Xi, were the coronavirus pandemic, supply chain disruptions, deteriorating relations with the West and an economic slowdown. In general, however, he expressed a belief that the current time is a "strategic occasion" for China (Lo and Huang, 2021).

At any rate, as I prove in my recent work, China under Xi Jinping has entered its contemporary "Qin moment" (Góralczyk, 2021b: 287), in analogy with the Qin Shi Huang, the first emperor, who desired to unify all Chinese lands, whatever the costs and resistance encountered. History shows us that the emperor was successful, but his dynasty did not survive for long. What survived, however, were the foundations he laid under the centralised Chinese universe.

One may wonder what this experiment, which has already started in earnest, will lead to. Today's situation is different in that China is not isolated and not a world unto itself. How will others, especially the recently hegemonic United States, and all Western and liberal nations under "value-based order" umbrella, react to these plans? This question has received an additional value after a Xi Jinping – Vladimir Putin Joint Statement of February 4, 2022 (President of Russia, 2022) and went even further after the Russian aggression on Ukraine on February 24th.

As can be seen, since then there is increasing talk about a "new cold war" (with which we will not deal here). However, all those changes and events lead us to the final conclusion: all of them are the best proof that the reforms initiated and put into effect as part of "Xi Jinping's system" bring many challenges, threats and unknowns, both in China itself and, due to the country's potential and importance, abroad and for the whole world. As "the Xi Jinping era" is still an open one, many questions – many of them of great importance – remain unanswered.

References

Baidu (n.d.) Zhang Weiwei, the *Zhe jiu shi Zhongguo* YouTube series, https://www.baidu.com/s?ie=utf-8&medium=0&rtt=1&bsst=1&rsv_dl=news_b_rs&cl=2&wd=%E8%BF%99%E5 %B0%B1%E6%98%AF%E4%B8%AD%E5%9B%BD%E5%85%A8%E9%9B%86%E5%85%8D%E8%B4%B9%E8%A7%

82%E7%9C%8B&tn=news&rsv_bp =1&rsv_sug3=4&rsv_sug1=2&rsv_sug7=100&oq =&rsv_btype=t&f=8&prefixsug =%2520%25E8%25BF%2599%25E5%25B0%25B1 %25E6%2598%25AF%25E4%25B8%25AD%25E5%259B%25BD&rsp=0&inputT =3371&rsv_sug4=5314& x_bfe_rqs=03E80&x_bfe_tjscore=0.100000&tngroupname =organic_news&new Video=12&goods_entry_switch=1, accessed 2 February 2024.

Balázs, Étienne (1967) *Chinese Civilization And Bureaucracy. Variations on a Theme.* New Haven–London: Yale University Press.

Barmé, Geremie (2016) Chairman of Everything. *The Economist,* 2 April, https: //www.economist.com/china/2016/04/02/chairman-of-everything, accessed 2 February 2024.

Bogusz, Michał and Jakub Jakóbowski (2019) Komunistyczna Partia Chin i jej państwo. Konserwatywny zwrot Xi Jinpinga [The Chinese Communist Party and its state. The conservative turnabout of Xi Jinping]. *Raport OSW,* https://www.osw.waw.pl/sites /default/files/Raport_PL_Komunistyczna-partia-chin_net.pdf, accessed 2 February 2024, pp. 1–148.

Bougon, François (2018) *Inside the Mind of Xi Jinping.* London: Hurst & Company.

Brown, Kerry (2017) *CEO, China. The Rise of Xi Jinping.* London–New York: I.B. Tauris.

Deng Xiaoping (1984) *Selected Works of Deng Xiaoping (1975–1982).* Beijing: Foreign Languages Press.

Dickson, Bruce J. (2021) *The Party and the People. Chinese Politics in the 21st Century.* Princeton–Oxford: Princeton University Press.

Fukuyama, Francis (2020) What Kind of Regime Does China Have? *The American Interest,* 20 May, https://www.the-american-interest.com/2020/05/18/what-kind-of -regime-does-china-have/, accessed 2 February 2024.

Góralczyk, Bogdan (2018) *Wielki Renesans. Chińska transformacja i jej konsekwencje* [Great Rejuvenation. Chinese Transformation and Its Aftermath]. Warsaw: Wydawnictwo Akademickie Dialog.

Góralczyk, Bogdan (2021a) Chiński system polityczny. In: Hanna Kupś, Maciej Szatkowski and Michał Dahl (eds.) *70 lat Chińskiej Republiki Ludowej w ujęciu interdyscyplinarnym* [70 Years of People's Republic of China: An InterdisciplinaryApproach]. Warsaw: Wydawnictwo Akademickie Dialog, pp. 13–30.

Góralczyk, Bogdan (2021b) *Nowy Długi Marsz. Chiny ery Xi Jinpinga* [New Long March. China of the Xi Jinping Era]. Warsaw: Wydawnictwo Akademickie Dialog.

Kissinger, Henry (2011) *On China.* New York: The Penguin Press.

Li Cheng (2016) *Chinese Politics in the Xi Jinping Era. Reassessing Collective Leadership.* Washington DC: Brookings Institution Press.

Li Qingqing (2020) Western elite view of China's governance wrong. *Global Times,* 24 May, https://www.globaltimes.cn/content/1189351.shtml, accessed 2 February 2024.

Lo Kinling and Kristin Huang (2021) Xi Jinping says 'time and momentum on China's side' as he sets out Communist Party vision. *South China Morning Post,* 12 January, https://www.scmp.com/news/china/politics/article/3117314/xi-jinping-says-time-and-momentum-chinas-side-he-sets-out, accessed 2 February 2024.

Lovell, Julia (2019) *Maoizm. Historia globalna* [Maoism. A Global History]. Translated by Filip Majkowski. Warsaw: PIW.

McGregor, Richard (2010) *The Party. The Secret World of China's Communist Rulers*. New York: Harper-Allen Lane.

Mearsheimer, John (2021) The Inevitable Rivalry. America, China, and the Tragedy of Great Power Politics. *Foreign Affairs*, November/December, https://www.foreignaffairs.com/articles/china/2021-10-19/inevitable-rivalry-cold-war, accessed 2 February 2024.

Polit, Jakub (2008) *Pod wiatr. Czang Kaj-szek 1887–1975* [Against the Wind. Chiang Kai-shek 1887–1975]. Kraków: Arcana.

President of Russia (2022) Joint Statement of the Russian Federation and the People's Republic of China on the International Relations Entering a New Era and the Global Sustainable Development, 4 February, http://en.kremlin.ru/supplement/5770, accessed 2 February 2024.

Pye, Lucian W. (1992) *The Spirit of China's Politics,* New Edition. Cambridge, MA–London: Harvard University Press.

Schram, Stuart (1989) *The Thought of Mao Tse-tung*. Cambridge: Cambridge University Press.

Shambaugh, David (2008) *China's Communist Party. Atrophy & Adaptation*. Berkeley–Los Angeles–London: University of California Press.

Shambaugh, David (2021) *China's Leaders. From Mao to Now*. New York: Polity.

Strittmatter, Kai (2018) *Chiny 5.0. Jak powstaje cyfrowa dyktatura* [China 5.0. How the Cyber Dictatorship was born].Translated by Agnieszka Gadzała. Warsaw: W.A.B.

Wang Zheng (2012) *Never Forget National Humiliation. Historical Memory in Chinese Politics and Foreign Relations.* New York: Columbia University Press.

Weixin (2021) Zuixin! Zhongguo gongchandang dangyuan zongshu wei 9514.8 wan ming 最新！中国共产党党员总数为9514.8万名 [Up to date! The total number of members of the Communist Party of China is 95.148 million], 30 June, https://mp.weixin.qq.com/s/CVmzqS1to5VuCBGoujclYA, accessed 2 February 2024.

Xi Jinping (2014) *The Governance of China*. Beijing: Foreign Languages Press.

Xi Jinping (2019) Speech at a Symposium on Resolving Prominent Problems in Poverty Alleviation. *Qiushi,* 11(41), pp. n.d.

Xinhuanet (n.d.) Documents. 19th CPC National Congress, http://www.xinhuanet.com/english/special/19cpcnc/documents.htm, accessed 2 February 2024.

YouTube (2021) Xi Jinping delivers speech to mark 100th anniversary of CPC's founding. *YouTube*, July 1, https://www.youtube.com/watch?v=ZYUmztqXEjI, accessed 2 February 2024.

Zhang Weiwei (2019) *Zhonguoren, niyao zixin* 中国人、尼腰子心 [Chinese People, You Need to Be Self-Confident]. Beijing: Zhongxin Chubanshe.

Zheng Yongnian (2012) *Zhongguo gaige san buzou* 中国改革三步走 [Chinese Reform in Three Stages]. Beijing: Dongfang Chubanshe.

CHAPTER 2

Xi Jinping's Regime Maintenance Paradigm

Yan Chang Bennett

1 Introduction

Since Xi Jinping took the helm of the Communist Party of China (CPC) as its paramount leader in 2012, an enormous body of discourse has been generated around Xi himself, on Xi Jinping Thought (XJPT), and on China's global activities and intentions. What is striking in this discourse is the polarization of opinion on what this means for the rest of the world. Some observers, particularly those from an Anglo-American political tradition (that is, from the 'West' or the 'Global North'), see China's rise as a precursor to great power conflict and a threat to the liberal world order. Others see China's rise as appropriate for such a large, historically important country.

When XJPT was officially incorporated it into the Party Constitution in 2017, international incredulity emerged, questioning the validity of what seemed to be state-sponsored dogma rather than 'legitimate' ideological discourse. International observers scoured Xi's speeches attempting to glean a coherent political philosophy. What they found instead were cliches: 'ensuring Chinese Communist Party leadership' and practicing 'socialist core values.' XJPT's lack of apparent novelty has led China observers to question Xi Jinping's place within the pantheon on China's greatest ideologues, Mao Zedong and Deng Xiaoping. Western discourse deriding XJPT as a 'personality cult without the personality,' 'demagoguery,' and 'half-baked' shows the West has found it as subpar as a sect as well (Barmé, 2021; Carrico, 2018). This misses the point of what XJPT does for Xi and China, however – a serious miscalculation on the part of the West.

In the West, when we think of political philosophy or philosophers, we are imbued with mental images and beliefs laden with normative value statements. Those trained in Western philosophical traditions subconsciously revert to a classical political theory model dating back to Aristotle, in which political philosophy is treated as a subset of moral philosophy. Other unconscious/subconscious philosophic influences are evoked by Machiavelli, Montesquieu, Rousseau, Hobbes, and Kant. Here in the United States, if we think of political philosophy at all, it would be to apply ideals, notions, and beliefs surrounding the founding of the United States. In order to understand China – and XJPT in particular – we need to disabuse ourselves of these notions. Instead, the West should first understand what XJPT is, what it is doing for the Chinese state, and how this affects the international community more generally before making normative, comparative statements.

This is difficult. We are often urged to remember that China cannot be understood through a Western lens and that China is not like the West (Brown, 2018; Shambaugh, 2021). Yet we continue to use political theory to interpret China. Theorists from neorealism, neoliberalism and social identity theory, for example, attempt to forecast China's future behavior based on Western models (Gries, 2005; Larson, 2015). These theories provide little predictive power, however. Neoliberal hopes have been dashed, for example, as China's government has become more authoritarian rather than less (Mitter and Johnson, 2021). These methods are imperfect because of distortions based on preconceptions, underlying ideas, and comparative analyses.

This chapter offers a different understanding of China that relies on a teleological examination of XJPT. Rather than evaluating it with political theory and what we think we know about China, this chapter seeks to interpret the relationship through discourse analysis and utilize methodology from historical contextualism and social constructivism. Doing so minimizes distortions created by preconceptions and misunderstanding, leading to a deeper, more nuanced understanding of China's future trajectory. The first section of this chapter seeks to deconstruct Anglo-American perceptions on political philosophy and ideology that inform Western cognitive biases. The second section of this chapter offers a different perspective on how to understand XJPT if it is not an ideology or political philosophy. The third is a description of what Xi and the Party envision as the actual 'Chinese Dream' and what this entails for the international community.

In order to understand both internal and external narratives about China, critical discourse analysis utilizing social constructivism is employed, which places language and linguistic practices at the forefront of interpretation and helps us understand how "discursive, linguistic, and textual boundaries justify certain claims to truth" (Debrix, 2015: xii). Language has a constructivist function in which "by doing what we do with each other and saying what we say to each other," we create the discursive framework of our world (Onuf, 2012: 4). This methodology looks behind language to understand the meanings and ideas attached to it and what this implies to narratives on China. Underlying this interpretation is Foucault's notion of the relationships between statements and how they lead to discursive formations and limitations (Foucault, 1972). This methodology heavily relies on quoted text in order to examine these discursive interrelations; that is, not to prove the truth of what is asserted, but to understand the current dialogue on and about China and how this has affected understanding on China more generally and on XJPT specifically.

Critical discourse analysis also attempts to "locate the meaning of political texts within wider linguistic contexts" (Vucina et al., 2011: 124). This form of inquiry relies upon Foucault's archaeological and genealogical analyses of power and knowledge. These analyses regard "the historically variable ways in which knowledge informs the modes in which we are constituted as subjects" (Vucina et al., 2011: 128). These concepts of knowledge and regimes of truth define how we understand the world and the exercise of power (Foucault, 1972), and therefore must be unpacked in order to understand how they are being applied in a given situation.

2   Political Philosophy and Ideology, Deconstructed

Philosopher Leo Strauss (1957) wrote that the meaning of political philosophy has been debated "since the time when political philosophy first made its appearance in Athens." We do this as a quest for universal knowledge fueled by a desire to understand the elements of a good life and good society in a greater search of the ideal good. This leads to what he calls "invisible value judgments" because, even if we wish not to, we mediate what we see and study through our understanding of political philosophy and its traditions, which acts "like a screen between the philosopher and political things," regardless of whether one cherishes or rejects those traditions (Strauss, 1957: 343–44, 356). Charles Larmore (2020) informs us that Anglo-American political philosophy is seemingly devoted to one concept of social justice after another. Melissa Lane (2018) notes that political philosophy inherently rates the ethics and the nature of politics as well as the relative merits of types of regimes. Western ideas on political philosophy have therefore come to contain qualitative understandings of morality and ethics; regimes can be better or worse than the ideal 'model' we hold in our minds.

For those of us raised and trained in Western political traditions, we are therefore subject to these 'invisible value judgments' and constantly mediate what we see through what we know. This is human. Even those of us who have been educated in other subjects, such as biology or physics, we nevertheless hold preconceptions based on anecdotal knowledge. While we may not have read Hobbes, we 'know' democracy is a far superior alternative to the nasty state of nature in which man lives a short and brutish life. Thus, the very term 'political philosophy' is in itself already laden with embedded meanings on capitalized notions of *truth, justice, and values*. In the West, what we understand to be political philosophy can be viewed as an underlying belief system that guides and directs, not each and every action we take, but animates subconsciously what we do and believe based on these embedded meanings.

The same goes for the notion of an ideology, in which "definitions are rarely neutral with respect to theoretical approaches" (Hamilton, 1987: 18–19). How reality is categorized depends on one's purpose, the questions being asked, and "prior dispositions and commitments to particular explanations of it." Another way to understand ideology is to view it as comprised of 'latent' ideas and beliefs looking at the totality of a group's views, attitudes, and opinions (Lane, 1962) or "underlying cognitive assumptions of belief, or the total structure of the mind including the conceptual apparatus" (Hamilton, 1987: 21).

According to Western traditions on political philosophy or ideology, XJPT is certainly none of these things. The majority of what we understand to be XJPT has been collated into three volumes entitled *The Governance of China*; following its incorporation into the Party Constitution, it also includes all Party documents and policies. XJPT outlines in excruciating detail individual and societal behavior, hierarchies of power, and what goals and objectives the Chinese state plans to achieve. Tsinghua University offers a USD 49 online certificate course for mastering Xi Jinping Thought (Tsinghua University, n.d.). Communist Party members utilize a daily study app to learn XJPT, which they treat as another tedious duty to be borne (Hernández, 2019). As an ideology or political philosophy, XJPT is seemingly not a belief system animating underlying assumptions about the world.

But if it is not a political philosophy in the sense that we understand it, what is it? Inevitably, Confucianism is mentioned (and, equally inevitably, Sun Tzu's *The Art of War*). A Google search on 'Xi Jinping' and 'neo-Confucianism' produces about 22,000 hits, showing a trend to label Xi a neo-Confucianist. This cannot be entirely faulted; the Chinese state references China's long history constantly and Xi also often quotes Confucius. But as a comparison, American presidents often quote the Founders of the United States to underscore so-called 'American values': good citizenship, political virtue, and democratic practices. But no one can name a modern president who is a neo-Washingtonian; no such designation exists because the United States has evolved and changed since 1776. So too has China in 2500 years. When Xi repeats Confucius's dictum 'Do not impose on others what you yourself do not desire,' he is not neo-Confucianist, just as President Ronald Reagan was not neo-Washingtonian by emphasizing the orderly transition of power from one president to another. Despite the attempts to make XJPT a form of Confucianism, which is a highly moralistic and legalistic system for a feudal society, it is certainly not an updated version of this.

There is another aspect to this belief that Xi is neo-Confucianist: it is Orientalist to believe that a modern leader of a nation in the 21st century is placing himself outside of time to become an adherent of a value system from 2500 years ago. Edward Said argued that Orientalists develop "a kind of image of the timeless Orient, [which] unlike the West, doesn't develop, it stays the same. And that's one of the problems with Orientalism is it creates an image outside of history" (Said, 1998: 4). As a contrast, Aristotle's views on democracy help us think about democracy, yet no one seriously asserts neo-Aristotelian thought as ideas on democracy and governance have changed in 2500 years. But in the case of China, it seems acceptable to believe XJPT is 'Confucianism 2.0,' ignoring context and history. This is perhaps because from the Western perspective the Other does things illogically and irrationally as opposed to the logic and rationality of the West (Vukovich, 2012).

At other times, we excavate meaning from the full title: 'Xi Jinping Thought on *Socialism* with Chinese Characteristics for a New Era.' But since Mao's death, "few cadres and members have retained any faith in socialism, let alone Communism, which even Karl Marx deemed a Utopian ideal" (Lam, 2018: 6). Sinologist Steve Tsang (2021) emphasizes it would be highly unlikely Marx would recognize China as a Marxist state (2021). In close readings, XJPT "offers very little in the way of classical Marxist exegesis" and one suspects Xi "would rather not have the readers of *Qiushi* [the leading official theoretical journal of the CPC] thinking too hard about the details of classical Marxist texts' (Greer, 2019). Kerry Brown (2018), author of Chapter 4, notes that Xi Jinping himself would probably not pass Party school exams on Marxist-Leninist thought (2018). Maoism usually creeps into the conversation, but then the discussion revolves around cults of personality and populist tyrannies than XJPT (Shambaugh, 2021; Zhao, 2019). Xi even fails as a sufficiently motivating cult leader. It would be misleading to think that what is currently offered in China is substantially similar to socialism, Marxism, Maoism, or a personality cult.

Others pivot on 'with Chinese characteristics.' This type of interpretation creates the impression XJPT is merely socialism with some Chinese adjectives, however. This interpretation suffers because it is primarily comparative and offers to explain how Chinese socialism is different from our existing notions on socialism, which are based on Marxist preconceptions; more importantly, it creates a rating system based on normative judgments and values. Donald Clarke (2020) observes that comparative law is freighted with similar cognitive biases, which are imbued with normative rhetoric on 'rule of law' from Western intellectuals, who have deemed certain legal features as generally desirable "and movement toward those features as therefore good as well"

(Clarke, 2020: 549–550). Thus, comparison invites normative valuations that can judge China as better – but usually worse – than the West.

That humans love to compare (Suls and Wheeler, 2000) is a barrier to examining XJPT as an original phenomenon. Normative beliefs are deeply embedded in academia's subconscious (Clarke, 2020: 449). We want to compare XJPT as an ideology to other ideologies and find where it fails to meet our standards. Instead, we first need to examine XJPT without comparison to understand its purpose and effects before making value-laden normative statements. It also distracts to make comparisons in general. How Xi is different or similar to Mao, how XJPT is different or similar to Confucianism, Marxism, or Western political traditions; these are unimportant at this stage of analysis. What we can acknowledge is that China once had a very important leader in Mao and that China now has an important leader in Xi. We need to examine what Xi is doing independently from other models because comparison leads to interpretive conclusions by which XJPT suffers.

3 The Regime Maintenance Paradigm

While we are entitled to make normative judgments about the relative value of institutions and systems, "description and value judgment are two different things, and should be addressed separately" (Clarke, 2020: 551). Therefore, XJPT should be first described before it is judged. The best way to describe XJPT, it seems, is teleological, which is to say it is a regime maintenance paradigm. XJPT is a paradigm with the purpose of maintaining the current regime, making Party rule the center of gravity. This purpose undergirds one primary goal: that China regains its status as a great nation, a novel definition not based upon Western normative standards, but as defined by China. Instead of calling XJPT a political philosophy or ideology – because these are normatively-laden terms containing a wealth of preconceptions that invite comparison rather than analysis – let us call it instead a 'paradigm' to avoid such comparison.

Secondly, we must understand XJPT as a syncretic paradigm drawing from very different political philosophies and systems. As Tsang (2021) explains, XJPT is highly syncretic, such that what is going on in China today is something that Karl Marx would not recognize, nor is today's China something that Confucius would recognize. Other scholars describe this process as a "borrow-and-interpret" mechanism (Solé-Farràs, 2016: 283), or one of "ideological compounds" exhibiting synthetic reasoning that utilizes a pragmatic mindset and uses different value systems to fit different situations (Sukhomlinova, 2020). Delia Lin urges an understanding of XJPT as an "attempt by the Xi-led party to project a *novel* ideological universe of discourse that can rival Western political liberalism" (Lin, 2018: 52, emphasis added). Xi's turn to Confucianism, Maoism, socialism, and most recently 'people's democracy' can be explained by describing XJPT as a highly syncretic, novel paradigm drawing upon tenets from many philosophies, which, as we will see, all serve the purpose of keeping the current regime in power. Xi has even stated as such: the "CPC will unite and lead the Chinese people in pressing ahead with the Chinese-style modernization to make *new contributions* to humanity's search for ways to modernize" (Xinhua, 2021, emphasis added). XJPT is thus at once all of these things, but singularly none of these things.

Through educated study of China it is clear that this paradigm serves one purpose. "Xi Jinping's highest priority is to maintain and enhance the legitimacy of the CPC so as to ensure its 'perennial' rule" (Lin, 2018: 54). Tsang (2021) emphatically states that "the Party is everything, no exceptions" with regard to its centrality to China's narrative. In the Chinese legal system, Clarke explains Western observers must come to "grips with the fundamental reality that China is a Leninist one-party state. It does not, either in theory or to the extent of its ability in reality, tolerate independent power centers." In China, "east, west, south, north, and center, in the Party, the state, the military, civil society, and education, the Party leads everything" (Clarke, 2020: 552). Brown underlines the centrality of the Party, especially to Xi, whose first words were to emphasize the Party's responsibility to unite and lead the people toward the purpose of realizing the great revival of the Chinese nation and to provide the 'firm leadership core' for advancing and modernizing China (Brown, 2018: 29–30). He observes that "even someone with no background in Chinese politics would be struck by how" much of Xi's focus is "on the Party, and on its centrality to the narrative of China's national development" (Brown, 2018: 30).

Other scholars have noted outcomes of this paradigm, which are primarily stability and order (Clarke, 2020; Hou et al., 2018; Wang and Tzeng, 2021). This is important because the Party maintains its primacy by ensuring order through top-down control. The CPC promotes the idea that "without the CPC, there would be chaos" and other political parties would only lead to social disorder (Wang and Tzeng, 2021: 18). The CPC leadership preserves stability as a primary function of retaining control of the country (Hou et al., 2018: 240).

Instead of attempting to attribute to XJPT some overarching philosophy, the regime maintenance paradigm describes its actual purpose as one of retaining the CPC as the regime in power. All else flows from this central tenet, such that policies are designed to uphold Party control rather than initiate needed reforms and progress in modernization and economic liberalization is tempered by paradigmatic concerns. This regime maintenance paradigm is not necessarily inconsistent with other theories, but it draws attention to the central purpose of this paradigm rather than its outcomes. The usefulness of the regime maintenance paradigm is borne out by its ability to explain phenomena that otherwise look aberrational and inconsistent. We can take an example of how to conduct such analysis from Clarke, who describes the dilemmas in comparative law. Instead of interpreting Chinese institutions as if their purpose were legal, "we can get further by interpreting them through a different lens, [of] order maintenance," such that "bugs become features, errors become normal behavior." What we see as regression and setbacks is just evolution "or possibly progress *toward a different goal* from the one imagined or wished for by the analyst" (Clarke, 2020: 553, emphasis added). Key questions to ask in this paradigm are how does a particular element keep the Party in power? How does this event or person benefit the Party? What are the Party's interests in this issue?

A third aspect of this paradigm that we need to understand is that this is an organic, evolving system that acts quickly and pragmatically. We can see this through the evolution of discourse coming out of the CPC. A recent change includes tamping down the rhetoric of the hyper-nationalistic 'wolf warrior' diplomacy. Starting in 2017, Chinese diplomats were given the label of 'wolf warriors' for their increasingly aggressive tactics on social media against foreign governments (Westcott and Jiang, 2020). While domestically this was viewed as patriotic, wolf warrior diplomacy did more to damage China's international reputation than to bolster it (Wong, 2021). Wolf warriorism became so problematic that by late 2021, Xi asked Party members, Chinese diplomats, and Chinese media to "set the tone right" by being more modest and humble so as to promote a more "credible, lovable and respectable image of China" (Myers and Bradsher, 2021). Rhetoric along the lines of Deng Xiaoping's 'to get rich is glorious' has evolved in the past three years into adherence to 'core socialist values,' moving away "from the capitalist excesses of the past few decades to a new phase of development based on 'common prosperity'" (Campbell, 2018; Chin, 2022). These are but two examples of the flexibility of the paradigm.

A fourth aspect of this paradigm is that we need to see Xi as a leader selected by the Party. Xi is a product of Party training and has been a loyal foot soldier for the Party in all of his years of service. "The power that Xi is ascribed and which he wields makes no sense outside this context" and Xi's only option is to wield power through and within the Party (Brown, 2018: 5, 38). Throughout Xi's tenure, "all his tasks as leader have been completely focused on the Party and its health, sustainability and centrality" and Xi continually underlines the importance of the Party in all his efforts, which is "an absolutely central and integral part of his leadership" (Brown, 2018: 41–42). Xi is a "very highly disciplined – arguably perhaps the most disciplined – Leninist in the Communist Party's history," and historically Leninists are all about party and party discipline. For Xi, "the Party is right at the core of everything he wants to do; he will not turn on the Party and risk its destruction [because the Party is] the instrument with which he needs to deliver his China Dream" (Tsang, 2021). In the "Resolution of the CPC Central Committee on the Major Achievements and Historical Experience of the Party over the Past Century" (hereafter the "Historical Resolution"), Xi's place in China's history is cemented as the CPC's chief representative, the bearer of XJPT, and the primary figure in achieving the Chinese Dream. Xi is the veritable lynchpin within this paradigm, but he is not the leader of a personality cult by any means.

What we should keep in mind about China, Xi Jinping, and XJPT is that every time we attempt to cram China into Western theoretical models or frameworks, it will defy all expectations. We must remember that China is not following a model with which we are familiar, but one that is novel and evolutionary. The regime maintenance paradigm toggles between the purpose (the centrality of the Party) and the goal (the Chinese Dream), lessening pressure on one to achieve the other as needed in order to maintain forward progress toward the China it envisions. What seems to be inconsistent is merely organic evolution; an example of this is China's recent crackdown that wiped out USD 1.2 trillion in the market value of Chinese private companies, stoking fears about China's economy. But the goal was not to create chaos, rather it was to make clear to China's private companies that "tapping capitalist markets is fine – as long as it is on the ruling Chinese Communist Party's terms" (He, 2021). China also quashed the highly public initial public offering of fintech company Ant Financial, 'disappeared' public figures critical of the government, and fined private companies for breaches of anti-monopoly rules, all to strengthen Party authority over the private sector, despite the effects on the Chinese economy (Peach, 2021). This is all to recalibrate China's economy toward the newly conceived 'common prosperity' narrative (Chin, 2022), the replacement for 'to get rich is glorious'.

4   Xi Jinping Thought, Explained

To reiterate, the argument is that XJPT possesses a main purpose – to perpetuate the Party's political primacy – and that this is the conceptual premise from which to pivot. If we acknowledge the Party's centrality in this paradigm, then actions and statements by the Chinese state become 'sensible' and perhaps we can make better predictions about China's future behavior. In this section, the unifying and totalizing pathways of XJPT will be explained and its seemingly contradictory statements begin to make sense.

4.1 Unifying and Totalizing Roadmap

XJPT is primarily for the domestic consumption of both Party members and the private citizens of China, as indicated in the language that Xi uses. What is being offered in China "is meant for China, it's not for export" (Tsang, 2021). For Party members, it sits at the heart of their identities: "whatever else they are or may be, they all at least believe they should believe in something – and they are told what to believe in. [...] [O]nce these edicts are issued, they don't argue with them" (Brown, 2018: 47). While it may seem odd that Party members require unification of thought, it is inevitable that a party consisting of some 95 million members will require totalization so that they all work toward the same goal: the realization of the Chinese Dream of national rejuvenation through socialism with Chinese characteristics under the helm of Xi Jinping. Former Party scholar and instructor Cai Xia has noted prior difficulties in having that many people work toward the same goal (Ruwitch, 2021), but XJPT has made significant strides in bringing such a large body together in mind and spirit. Since Xi came to power, new CPC membership has decreased because the Party leadership believes it has become "too large and unwieldy." Acceptance into the Party has become as exclusive as getting into an Ivy League school and requires arduous study and inculcation (McMorrow, 2015). Totalizing discourse directed at Party members is necessary and part of the paradigm.

Xi's public statements are other examples of totalizing discourse directed toward Party members. Although most of his speeches are made during Party functions, even when these addresses are made in public forums, Xi never fails to mention the role of the Party or Party members in carrying out the mission of the Chinese Dream: "All Party members must bear in mind," "all Party members must heighten their sense of urgency and responsibility," "all Party members [...] must earnestly study and implement," statements which emphasize the totalization of all Party members to the "system of socialist theories with Chinese characteristics" (Xi, 2018: 37, 16–17). In the "Historical Resolution", Party members are reminded that the "Party is the highest force for political leadership [and] to follow the leadership core," to "uphold Comrade Xi Jinping's core position," and that "all Party members must [...] ensure the whole Party obeys the Central Committee." The Party and "Comrade Xi Jinping at its core has made it clear that the leadership of the Party is the foundation and lifeblood of the Party and the country, and the pillar upon which the interests and wellbeing of all Chinese people depend" (Central Committee of the Communist Party of China, 2021). It is clear Xi is always talking to Party members, who have an important role in the paradigm in maintaining Party primacy and carrying the Party message to the people.

Secondly, the language of XJPT exhorts Party members to direct the Chinese people toward the right path. Since 2012, Xi has been developing a cohesive narrative of China's history and future trajectory to meet the central goal of achieving the Chinese Dream of national rejuvenation. The totalization of the Chinese people, in particular, is very important within the paradigm because Xi and the Party need the Chinese people to adhere to the Chinese Dream as *their* dream. This need is evident in Xi's discourse, which exhibits a great deal of mental imagery putting the Chinese people together on the same path toward a joint destiny, a very specific path the CPC and Xi have deemed necessary in order to achieve the Chinese Dream. In the first articulation of the Chinese Dream in 2012, Xi orated – allegedly extemporaneously – that the road to rejuvenation was about "the past, present and future of the Chinese nation," in which both Party members and the Chinese people must "resolutely keep to the right path that we have found through great difficulties" to determine their joint destiny (Xi, 2018: 37). Xi pronounced that "history shows that the future and destiny of each and every one of us are closely linked to those of our country and nation, for one can only do well when one's country and nation do well" (Xi, 2018: 38). In a more accurate translation, Xi said that "only when the state is well and the nation is well, can everybody be well" (Yang, 2014: 3), emphasizing the wellbeing of the state over that of the individual.

In other speeches, Xi emphasizes the role of the Chinese people in the realization of the Chinese Dream. XJPT exhorts national spirit, which "unites the people and pools their strength, and is the source of rejuvenating and strengthening the country." He emphasizes the need for "great unity among the people" to achieve the Chinese Dream, which "is the dream of our nation and every Chinese." "The Chinese Dream is, in the final analysis, the dream of the people" (Xi, 2018: 42). In another speech, he emphasizes "the people are the creators of history [and] the real heroes and the source of our strength. [A]s long as we *unite as one like a fortress*, there is no difficulty we cannot overcome" (Xi, 2018: 5). Xi also admonishes while "everyone has an ideal, ambition, and dream [...] [w]e are now all talking about the Chinese Dream," emphasizing their joint destiny over their individual desires (Xi, 2018: 37).

Another important aspect to the paradigm is benchmarking achievements to the 'two centenaries,' which are important anniversaries for the CPC, articulated as "the goals of completing the building of a moderately prosperous society in all respects by the centenary of the CPC in 2021 and building China into a modern socialist country that is prosperous, strong, democratic, culturally advanced, and harmonious by the centenary of the PRC in 2049 so as to realize the Chinese Dream of the rejuvenation of the Chinese nation" (Xi, 2018: 47). In the Historical Resolution, particular emphasis was placed on the two Centenary Goals. While the First Centenary Goal was achieved in 2021 by reaching middle income status, the CPC urged the Chinese people and Party that they must "embark on the new journey to accomplish the Second Centenary Goal, and continue striving toward the great goal of national rejuvenation" (Central Committee…, 2021).

While the Chinese Dream has often been compared to the 'American Dream,' it is most emphatically not an American Dream with Chinese adjectives. In the American Dream, the emphasis is on individual freedoms and social and economic mobility achieved through one's own efforts (Pena, 2015; Thoman, 1993). In the Chinese Dream, it is the success of the entire nation as led by the CPC that is the Chinese Dream. Xi in fact tells the Chinese people that they must sacrifice and forsake their individual ambitions for the nation (Xi, 2018).

XJPT often refers back to Marxism, Maoism, and Confucianism to create a long, uninterrupted history from Confucianism to the present. The "Historical Resolution" claims that Mao Zedong Thought was the "first historic step in adapting Marxism to the Chinese context" with Xi Jinping Thought as the "Marxism of contemporary China and of the 21st century," embodying "the best of the Chinese culture and ethos in our times and represent[ing] a *new* breakthrough in adapting Marxism to the Chinese context" (Central Committee…, 2021, emphasis added). Drawing linkages with the past is part of the totalizing discourse as well as a legitimation of the regime. Lin notes the unprecedented revival of Confucianism and the Chinese classics is not so much an actual turn to these philosophies as a "carefully crafted project to establish cultural and ideological legitimacy of the CPC" (Lin, 2018: 54). Creating a long, uninterrupted past helps the Chinese people to 'think' like a nation and to develop national and patriotic sentiment by coupling the past and future to an "instantaneous present" (Anderson, 2006: 24). Benedict Anderson notes that the PRC's successful foundation as a nation was achieved by grounding itself "firmly in territorial and social space inherited from the prerevolutionary past" and showing continuity with such a past (Anderson, 2006: 2). China is therefore not an object from the past nor is it a repetition of the past; XJPT helps link the Party to China's past, which is different than the Orientalist dilemma of being outside of time and history. References to aspects of China's history help the regime further the totalizing discourse that brings together the Chinese people and Party members as one nation.

4.2 Core Socialist Values and 'Inconsistencies'

XJPT also focuses on the promotion of core socialist values (CSV) as totalizing discourse directed at Party members and the Chinese people to help achieve the Chinese Dream. While these were introduced by Hu Jintao, Xi has come to closely embrace CSV (Gow, 2017: 97) because he understands that shared values help bind citizens together toward a common goal (Lin, 2020). These twelve values, represented by twenty-four Chinese characters, include four national values of "prosperity, democracy, civility, and harmony; four social values of freedom, equality, justice, and rule of law; and four individual values of patriotism, dedication, integrity, and friendship" (Lin, 2020). This is part of the Chinese state's efforts to push "consensus-building activities under the umbrella of the 'Chinese Dream' discourse," emphasizing the superstructure of nation in order to create citizens of and for the PRC (Gow, 2017: 92–93).

What must be noted here is that China defines democracy, freedom, and rule of law differently from the West. In China, "freedom is not about a wild horse running wild in the field. Freedom is about knowing who the riders are, where the reins are, and what the constraints are" (Lin, 2020). What we would consider freedom in the West can be defined as an individual's power to act in pursuit of goals without interference by external agencies (Skinner, 2016). Democracy, according to CSV, is about people's democracy, in which the minority submits to the majority, a Marxist-Leninist definition (Lin, 2020). People's democracy, according to the Party, is not fixed and "manifests itself in many forms, and cannot be arbitrarily decided by a few self-appointed judges" from the West (State Council Information Office, 2021a). The Central Committee of the CPC describes this as 'democratic centralism,' which puts in place "sound systems for ensuring [Party] leadership over major work of the state" (Central Committee…, 2021). The Chinese notion of democracy is most likely closest to Hobbesian despotic democracy or demagogic democracy described by Aristotle (Tuck, 2006: 172, 176). From a contemporary liberal democratic perspective, none of this makes sense. But from a regime maintenance perspective, these syncretic definitions make perfect sense with the object of keeping the CPC in power while furthering progress toward the Chinese Dream.

Rule of law in China is perhaps the most contested concept in debates about China, but the fundamental tenet can be simply summarized as 'China does not have rule of law as we, in the West, understand it.' China is far from being a 'rule-based society' and contains what the West views as "numerous inconsistencies, setbacks, and regressions" toward the ideal end-state for a rule of law system (He, 2020: 2). Often recast as "rule by man" or "rule by law" (Jenco, 2010), and even a "turn against law" (Minzner, 2011), Clarke

(2020: 546) comes closest by proposing a stability maintenance paradigm, in which "China has been building a [legal] system for the maintenance of order and the political primacy of the Chinese Communist Party (CPC), not for the delivery of justice." The regime maintenance paradigm is, of course, very similar to this stability paradigm, but the sole focus is on the Party and applied to the entirety of China's institutions, culture, and society. Instead of considering what is going on in China as 'rule of law,' by perceiving them as practices under 'regime maintenance,' the coercive institutions and acts of the state become consistent rather than illegal or illegitimate. This explains the existence of forced labor camps in Xinjiang in which more than a million ethnic and religious minorities have been imprisoned (Maizland, 2021) in direct contravention of the Chinese Constitution. This explains the detentions, arrests, and convictions of civil rights advocates in Hong Kong for sedition and threatening national security (Fan, 2021). And this explains the disappearance of feminists and sexual assault victims from public view because their protest disgraces the state (Bennett and Garrick, 2021). In all these situations, someone or something pose a threat to the Party's centrality and achievement of the Chinese Dream. What seems to be repression of individual civil liberties and violations of rule of law are just aspects of the regime maintenance paradigm. The paradigm goes far to explain the actions of the state, which by Western standards, are extralegal in nature.

5 Will the Real Chinese Dream Stand Up? The China of the 22nd Century

Xi and the Party have marked 2049, the 100th anniversary of the PRC's founding, as the Second Centenary Goal of "building China into a modern socialist country that is prosperous, strong, democratic, culturally advanced and harmonious." It is at that point that "the dream of the rejuvenation of the Chinese nation will then be realized" (Xi, 2018: 38). While 2049 is China's marker for its ascendance to great power status, we have little more than a quarter century until the Second Centenary Goal, which is, in actuality, not a very long time for China to progress from the lowest rung of middle-income status to the type of great power status that China seeks. Synthesizing Xi's and the Party's statements, the China they envision is one in which China will truly be great again and restored to its *rightful* place in the world. Their vision is one in which China is again in the center of the universe, admired by all and bullied by none (Tsang, 2021). Xi is "now simply coming out and demanding the rest of the world pay it due respect." The China Xi envisions is not an American-style superpower with "all the baggage" of heavy international obligations; "Xi has no intention to see China put in that position," but rather desires to "return to a mythical traditional Chinese concept of *tianxia*, 'all under heaven,' when China was that mythical celestial empire, that China by its superiority, both of its political systems and culture, was the center of the universe to which every other country would look up to, respect, and admire." When Xi references China's past greatness, "he is pointing to the height of the empire of the last imperial dynasty in China [...] or indeed the very first Chinese emperor, Qinshi Huangdi" (Tsang, 2021).

Brown has a much more benign vision of China:

> a harmonious nation governed by the hybrid belief systems and philosophies of socialism and traditional Chinese culture [...] [and] a place of tolerance, where people would be free to practise their religion of choice but also responsible for the society around them, meaning that they would never attempt to give their religious ideas pre-eminence over those of others. It would be a society of justice, where people felt they belonged not just to an equal society but to an equitable one, somewhere with strong civic values where the country was not just a vast collection of discrete familial and individual networks. In this society, there would be no ethnic conflicts. [...] There would be satisfaction, contentment and a sense of fulfilment, with people happy in the knowledge they were living in a culture that was deeply rooted, humane and focused on the wellbeing of the individual.
>
> BROWN, 2018: 124

There is another type of future China the liberal world order envisions. Robert Zoellick articulated a future world order in which China, once risen, would become a 'responsible stakeholder' shouldering global security and economic problems and helping to reduce regional and global tensions. This future China, he urged, would recognize the international system that rewarded it with prosperity and so would "work to sustain that system" (Zoellick, 2005: 6, 8).

The apex China within Xi's vision likely leans more toward Tsang's model than Brown's or Zoellick's. Xi has articulated many times that it is following its own path: "We should modestly draw on the achievements of all other cultures, but *never forget our own origin*"; "we *must not blindly copy* the development models of other countries *nor accept their dictation*;" China "will *never follow*" in the footsteps of the big powers" (Xi, 2018: 32, 189, 293, 491, emphases added). Deborah Larson sees that "China wants to restore its former status as a great power, but at the same time to preserve its culture and norms without assimilating Western liberal values" (Larson, 2015: 324). While China seeks out accoutrements of great power status, such as its lunar program, hosting and winning in the Olympic Games, it is averse to taking on obligations to maintain global security, such as using its influence with Russia with regard to the Ukrainian question (Fung, 2016; Goswami, 2020; Lynch III, 2022). The Belt and Road Initiative is another example of China's self-interest and deflection of global responsibilities; lifting nations out of poverty is incidental to its own economic interests in developing infrastructure to support China's trade networks (Bennett, 2022). This apex China does not wield the kind of direct power that the United States holds, but is more a center of gravity around which the world revolves. Nations would be deferential to China, yet at the same time, China "can be the top dog in the world without all the baggage" of international obligations (Tsang, 2021). This China is about maintaining Party rule while deflecting international responsibilities it deems irrelevant to the Chinese Dream.

The kind of international order China would rather have is what it describes as a 'community of common destiny for mankind', which first entered Chinese discourse in 2013 and "prioritizes a state-centered approach to human rights," subordinating individual rights to national interests (China Media Project, 2021). The 'community of common destiny for mankind' embodies the idea that China offers "a Chinese Solution and Chinese wisdom to the reform and innovation of global human rights governance" by relegating all matters to the decision-making of the state and making national sovereignty inviolable to international interference. Member states protested the inclusion of this phrase in the Declaration of Commemoration of the 75th anniversary of the United Nations because they felt it did not reflect the values and beliefs embodied in the UN Charter (China Media Project, 2021; Mitra, 2020). The intent behind this phrase is to persuade the international community to comply with Party mandates and not interfere in China's attainment of the Chinese Dream (Tobin, 2018) while at the same time avoiding international obligations such as maintaining global peace and security, lifting other nations out of poverty, or promoting so-called 'universal values' of gender and racial equality, social justice, and human dignity (Banyan, 2010; Miller, 2022; State Council Information Office, 2021b; The Economist, 2010). Thus, this China continues to be authoritarian, if not more so after having practiced Party-centered policies and rule for more than a century. By extension, foreign countries will likely experience the same kind of treatment Chinese citizens receive, since China has clearly stated it will not adopt Western liberal values, which include concepts of human dignity and social justice.

This 'top dog without the baggage' status does not have a great deal of regard for Western liberal values of individual freedoms or rule of law. We can see this now. The Chinese Constitution is treated as theatre, merely for show rather than for use (He, 2020; Human Rights Watch, 2008). Enforcement of the law depends on the Party's interpretation of order and stability (Clarke, 2020). Enemies of the state – which for China are many – are treated as 'nonhumans' possessing no rights at all (Lin, 2020). Because of its zero-COVID policy, citizens were blockaded in their homes or forcibly dragged out to detention centers while Africans in China were treated with extreme prejudice (Dou, 2021; Human Rights Watch, 2020). The Olympics are another example. In 2008, human rights organizations identified abuses in China that reflected the "Chinese government's wholesale failure to honor its Olympics-related human rights promises," rolling back "some of the most basic rights enshrined in China's constitution," including restriction of free speech and assembly, forcible eviction of migrants, and harassment and restriction of journalists (Human Rights Watch, 2008). Today, in 2022, more than a million Uighurs are imprisoned in mass detentions centers enduring torture, sexual abuse, and sterilization. Chinese citizens are regularly silenced and jailed – sometimes in forced labor camps where conditions are unbearable and treatment is inhuman (Pang, 2021). In fourteen years, China has become more rather than less authoritarian; this is what a "state-centered approach to human rights" looks like.

It is also unlikely that China will become a 'responsible stakeholder' in the sense that the liberal world order would appreciate. China's thoughts on hegemony help inform what a future global order under its helm might look like. China has articulated many times that it will "never seek hegemony, expansion or sphere of influence" (Xinhua, 2021) and

> never force our will upon others nor allow anyone else to impose theirs upon us. We stand for peaceful resolutions to international disputes, oppose all forms of hegemony and power politics, and never seek hegemonism nor engage in expansion. China has stood up. It will never again tolerate being bullied by any nation. Yet it will never follow in the footsteps of the big powers, which seek hegemony once they grow strong. Our country is following its own path of peaceful development. Not every strong country seeks hegemony. China would stick to the path of peaceful development, a mutually beneficial strategy and opening up, and the pledge of never seeking hegemony.
>
> XI, 2018: 32, 189, 293, 491

This, along with the 'community of common destiny for mankind' discourse and China's actions in the Global South along the path of the BRI (Bennett, 2022), tend to reveal that China's idea of hegemony is a self-interested China seeking out 'mutual benefits' from unquestioning global partners.

How long will it take to achieve this dream of ascendance to China's *rightful* place? China will likely enter the lowest rung of high-income status sometime around 2023 by surpassing the World Bank high-income threshold of a per capita income of USD 12,536 (Larsen, 2021). Economists envisage that by 2049 China will be a fully developed nation when compared to some OECD member states (Dollar, 2021). However, the great power status 'without the baggage' is actually a much higher bar. Economists see that China needs to implement serious and painful economic reforms to achieve the same high-income status as the United States (Dollar, 2021; Larsen, 2021; Murach et al., 2020). But these only require time. If the Chinese state takes reform slowly and incrementally, it will be able maintain regime stability while making steady progress to the attainment of the China Dream. But it is likely that this will not be the case by 2049. For China to reach a point where it is on the same economic footing as major powers and where it engages the world on China's terms, the United States – the biggest bully on the block in China's eyes – can no longer be a superpower.

China is certainly not going to confront the United States directly. Although much has been made of its military build-up, China has not had a direct military confrontation since 1979. Recent skirmishes in India and the South China Sea show China is hesitant to start a prolonged military action and does generally align with its 'peaceful development' narrative (Bennett, 2022). Even as a UN Security Council member, it only contributes about 2,500 troops annually toward UN peacekeeping (Gowan, 2020). In contrast, the United States has more than 100,000 forward-deployed military personnel at any one time and spends more on its military than the next ten countries combined. A little under a million troops have cycled through Afghanistan and Iraq, adding up to a formidable amount of combat training (Haddad, 2021). If China does not engage in direct confrontation with the United States, then China simply needs it to go away for the Chinese Dream to be realized. China appears willing to wait it out, whenever that is.

While many think American power has seen its last days with the Trump administration, the United States has the resources and ability to weather great crises. The China Xi envisions is probably closer to coming about by 2100 than it is by 2049 based on these observations, which gives the US and its allies some time to respond to the challenges China's rise and undermining of universal values pose to the rules-based world order. But in 78 years a lot can happen. And while this seems like a very far off date, it is not for China.

6 Conclusion

This chapter proposes that XJPT must be understood without comparison to other ideologies and without insistence on its inconsistencies with other political philosophies; comparison invites subjectivity, we need a theory that examines and describes XJPT in isolation from previous theories. We must understand that using the vocabulary and concepts of political philosophy is not the best way to understand the institutions and practices of XJPT because in a comparative framework analysts treat these inconsistencies as ideological weaknesses. It is also misleading to believe XJPT is just an updated version of ancient ideas and modes of thinking, because this promotes an Orientalist view of China existing outside of time.

This chapter proposes that XJPT represents a novel paradigm in which regime maintenance is its purpose and attainment of the Chinese Dream – as defined by China – is its primary objective. Through educated study of China, it is clear that the Party is the center of gravity for the Chinese state's actions and that its primary goal is to achieve the Chinese Dream of national rejuvenation, an ideal end state as defined by China and not by Western liberal ideas. Xi and the Party have stated numerous times that China will neither blindly copy Western ideology nor accept Western nations' dictation as she reascends to great power status. The novelty of China's great power definition is something that the West needs to appreciate to a greater degree than it does now as China seeks to recontour world order and reorder universal values in ways most beneficial to the Chinese state.

References

Anderson, Benedict R. (2006) *Imagined Communities: Reflections on the Origin and Spread of Nationalism*. New York: Verso.

Banyan (2010) Sources on Universal Values: Background to the Debate. *The Economist*, 29 September, https://www.economist.com/blogs/asiaview/2010/09/sources_unive rsal_values, accessed 1 February 2022.

Barmé, Geremie R. (2021) The Great Reconciler and the End of Chinese History. *The Little Red Podcast,* 21 November, https://podcasts.apple.com/us/podcast/the-lit tle-red-podcast/id1136685378, accessed 24 January 2022.

Bennett, Yan Chang (2022) China's inward and outward facing identities: Post-COVID challenges for China and the international rules-based order. In: Viktor Jakupec, Max Kelly, Michael de Percy (eds.) *COVID-19 and Foreign Aid: Nationalism and Global Development in a New World Order*. London: Routledge.

Bennett, Yan, and John Garrick (2021) What the Peng Shuai Saga Tells Us about Beijing's Grip on Power and Desire to Crush a #MeToo Moment. *The Conversation*, 24 November, http://theconversation.com/what-the-peng-shuai-saga-tells-us-about-beijings-grip-on-power-and-desire-to-crush-a-metoo-moment-172375, accessed 22 January 2022.

Brown, Kerry (2018) *The World According to Xi: Everything You Need to Know about the New China*. London: I.B. Tauris & Co, Ltd.

Campbell, Charlie (2018) Fan Bingbing Going Missing Raises Questions About China's Justice System. *Time*, 19 September, https://time.com/5400559/fan-bingbing-missing-china-justice/, accessed 24 January 2022.

Carrico, Kevin (2018) I Mastered Xi Jinping Thought, and I Have the Certificate to Prove It. *Foreign Policy*, 18 October, https://foreignpolicy.com/2018/10/18/i-mastered-xi-jinping-thought-and-i-have-the-certificate-to-prove-it/, accessed 5 January 2022.

Central Committee of the Communist Party of China (2021) Resolution of the CPC Central Committee on the Major Achievements and Historical Experience of the Party over the Past Century, 16 November, https://english.www.gov.cn/policies/latestreleases/202111/16/content_WS6193a935c6d0df57f98e50b0.html, accessed 26 January 2022.

Chin, Josh (2022) China's Communist Party Quietly Inserts Itself Into Everyday Life. *Wall Street Journal*, 31 January, https://www.wsj.com/articles/chinas-communist-party-quietly-inserts-itself-into-everyday-life-11643644801, accessed 1 February 2022.

China Media Project (2021) Community of Common Destiny for Mankind, 25 August, https://chinamediaproject.org/the_CPC_dictionary/community-of-common-destiny-for-mankind/, accessed 30 January 2022.

Clarke, Donald (2020) Order and Law in China. *University of Illinois Law Review*, 2, pp. 541–596.

Debrix, Francois (2015) *Language, Agency, and Politics in a Constructed World*. London: Routledge.

Dollar, David (2021) Will China Ever Become a Fully Developed Economy? *Brookings Institution*, 10 August, https://www.brookings.edu/on-the-record/will-china-ever-become-a-fully-developed-economy/, accessed 28 January 2022.

Dou, Eva (2021) Locked Down in China's Xi'an amid Coronavirus Outbreak, Residents Subsist on Deliveries of Vegetables. *Washington Post*, 30 December, https://www.washingtonpost.com/world/2021/12/30/china-covid-lockdown-xian/, accessed 1 February 2022.

Fan, Wenxin (2021) China's Campaign to Crush Democracy in Hong Kong Is Working. *Wall Street Journal,* 25 February, https://www.wsj.com/articles/chinas-campaign-to-crush-democracy-in-hong-kong-is-working-11614268174, accessed 1 February 2022.

Foucault, Michel (1972) *The Archaeology of Knowledge: And the Discourse on Language.* New York: Vintage.

Fung, Courtney J. (2016) What explains China's deployment to UN peacekeeping operations? *International Relations of the Asia-Pacific,* 16(3), pp. 409–41.

Goswami, Namrata (2020) Why Is China Going to the Moon? *The Diplomat,* 18 December, https://thediplomat.com/2020/12/why-is-china-going-to-the-moon/.

Gow, Michael (2017) The core socialist values of the Chinese dream: Towards a Chinese integral state. *Critical Asian Studies,* 49(1), pp. 92–116.

Gowan, Richard (2020) China's Pragmatic Approach to UN Peacekeeping. *The Brookings Institution,* 14 September, https://www.brookings.edu/articles/chinas-pragmatic-approach-to-un-peacekeeping/, accessed 28 January 2022.

Greer, Tanner (2019) Xi Jinping in translation: China's guiding ideology. *Palladium,* 31 May, https://www.palladiummag.com/2019/05/31/xi-jinping-in-translation-chinas-guiding-ideology/, accessed 1 January 2022.

Gries, Peter Hays (2005) Social psychology and the identity-conflict debate: Is a "China threat" inevitable? *European Journal of International Relations,* 11(2), pp. 235–65.

Haddad, Mohammed (2021) US Military Presence around the World. *Al-Jazeera,* 10 September, https://www.aljazeera.com/news/2021/9/10/infographic-us-military-presence-around-the-world-interactive, accessed 28 January 2022.

Hamilton, Malcolm B. (1987) The elements of the concept of ideology. *Political Studies,* 35(1), pp. 18–38.

He, Laura (2021) China's Biggest Private Companies Are in Chaos. It's All Part of Beijing's Plan. *CNN,* 4 August, https://www.cnn.com/2021/08/04/tech/china-crackdown-tech-education-mic-intl-hnk/index.html, accessed 17 October 2021.

He, Xin (2020) (Non)Legality as governmentality in China. *University of Hong Kong Faculty of Law Research Paper,* 2020/035. Hong Kong: University of Hong Kong.

Hernández, Javier C. (2019) The Hottest App in China Teaches Citizens About Their Leader – and, Yes, There's a Test. *The New York Times,* 7 April, https://www.nytimes.com/2019/04/07/world/asia/china-xi-jinping-study-the-great-nation-app.html, accessed 13 January 2022.

Hou, Linke, Mingxing Liu, Dali L. Yang, and Ji Xue (2018) Of time, leadership, and governance: Elite incentives and stability maintenance in China. *Governance,* 31(2), pp. 239–57.

Human Rights Watch (2008) *China: Olympics Harm Key Human Rights,* 6 August, https://www.hrw.org/news/2008/08/06/china-olympics-harm-key-human-rights, accessed 1 February 2022.

Human Rights Watch (2020) *China: COVID-19 Discrimination Against Africans*, 5 May, https://www.hrw.org/news/2020/05/05/china-covid-19-discrimination-against-africans, accessed 1 February 2022.

Jenco, Leigh K. (2010) 'Rule by man' and 'rule by law' in early republican China: Contributions to a theoretical debate. *The Journal of Asian Studies*, 69(1), pp. 181–203.

Lam, Willy Wo-Lap (2018) The agenda of Xi Jinping. In: Willy Wo-Lap Lam (ed.) *Routledge Handbook of the Chinese Communist Party*. New York: Routledge.

Lane, Melissa (2018) Ancient political philosophy. In: Edward N. Zalta (ed.) *The Stanford Encyclopedia of Philosophy*. Palo Alto: Stanford University, https://plato.stanford.edu/entries/ancient-political/, accessed 7 February 2024.

Lane, Robert E. (1962) *Political Ideology: Why the American Common Man Believes What He Does*. New York: Free Press of Glencoe.

Larmore, Charles (2020) *What Is Political Philosophy?* Princeton: Princeton University Press.

Larsen, Mathias Lund (2021) China will no longer be a developing country after 2023. Its climate actions should reflect that. *The Diplomat*, 3 July, https://thediplomat.com/2021/07/china-will-no-longer-be-a-developing-country-after-2023-its-climate-actions-should-reflect-that/, accessed 3 July 2021.

Larson, Deborah Welch (2015) Will China be a new type of great power? *The Chinese Journal of International Politics*, 8(4), pp. 323–48.

Lin, Delia (2018) The CPC's exploitation of Confucianism and legalism. In: Willy Wo-Lap Lam (ed.) *Routledge Handbook of the Chinese Communist Party*. New York: Routledge.

Lin, Delia (2020) Freedom Is Restraint: How Core Socialist Values Are Changing Language and Remoulding Humans. *The Little Red Podcast*, 6 January, https://omny.fm/shows/the-little-red-podcast/freedom-is-restraint-how-core-socialist-values-are?in_playlist=the-little-red-podcast!podcast, accessed 4 January 2022.

Lynch III, Thomas F. (2022) Great Power Competition and Beijing's Olympic Moment. *Foreign Policy Research Institute*, 25 January, https://www.fpri.org/article/2022/01/great-power-competition-and-beijings-olympic-moment/, accessed 29 January 2022.

Maizland, Lindsay (2021) China's Repression of Uyghurs in Xinjiang. Backgrounder. *Council on Foreign Relations*, 1 March, https://www.cfr.org/backgrounder/chinas-repression-uyghurs-xinjiang, accessed 1 February 2022.

McMorrow, Ryan W. (2015) Membership in the Communist Party of China: Who Is Being Admitted and How? *JSTOR Daily*, 19 December, https://daily.jstor.org/communist-party-of-china/, accessed 26 January 2022.

Miller, Chris (2022) How Will China Respond to the Russia-Ukraine Crisis? *Foreign Policy Research Institute*, 21 January, https://www.fpri.org/article/2022/01/how-will-china-respond-to-the-russia-ukraine-crisis/, accessed 30 January 2022.

Minzner, Carl F. (2011) China's turn against law. *The American Journal of Comparative Law,* 59(4), pp. 935–84.

Mitra, Devirupa (2020) Explained: Why India joined the West to object to a phrase in the final UN75 Declaration. *The Wire,* 30 June, https://thewire.in/world/explained-un75-declaration-xi-jinping-phrase-india-object, accessed 30 January 2022.

Mitter, Rana, and Elsbeth Johnson (2021) What the West gets wrong about China. *Harvard Business Review,* 1 May, https://hbr.org/2021/05/what-the-west-gets-wrong-about-china, accessed 1 February 2022.

Murach, Michael, Helmut Wagner, Jungsuk Kim, and Donghyun Park (2020) *Trajectories to High Income: Growth Dynamics in Japan, the People's Republic of China, and the Republic of Korea.* Manila: Asian Development Bank.

Myers, Steven Lee, and Keith Bradsher (2021) China's Leader Wants a 'Lovable' Country: That Doesn't Mean He's Making Nice. *The New York Times,* 8 June, https://www.nytimes.com/2021/06/08/world/asia/china-diplomacy.html, accessed 24 January 2022.

Onuf, Nicholas (2012) *Making Sense, Making Worlds: Constructivism in Social Theory and International Relations.* London: Taylor & Francis Group.

Pang, Amelia (2021) *Made in China: A Prisoner, an SOS Letter, and the Hidden Cost of America's Cheap Goods.* Chapel Hill, NC: Algonquin Books.

Peach, Sam (2021) Why did Alibaba's Jack Ma disappear for three months? *BBC News,* 20 March, https://www.bbc.com/news/technology-56448688, accessed 29 January 2022.

Pena, David S. (2015) Comparing the Chinese dream with the American dream. *International Critical Thought,* 5(3), pp. 277–95.

Ruwitch, John (2021) China's 100-Year-Old Communist Party Has More Members Than Most Countries Have People. *NPR Weekend Edition Saturday,* 10 July, https://www.npr.org/2021/07/10/1014914913/chinas-100-year-old-communist-party-has-more-members-than-most-countries-have-pe, accessed 26 January 2022.

Said, Edward (interviewee) (1998) *Edward Said: On Orientalism (Transcript).* Amherst: Media Education Foundation – University of Massachusetts.

Shambaugh, David (2021) *China's Leaders: From Mao to Now.* Cambridge, MA: Polity.

Skinner, Quentin (lecture) (2016) A Genealogy of Liberty [videorecording]. *YouTube,* 1 December, https://www.youtube.com/watch?v=PjQ-W2-fKUs, accessed 27 January 2022.

Solé-Farràs, Jesús (2016) A discourse called China and the PRC's foreign policy and diplomacy. *Journal of Chinese Political Science,* 21(3), pp. 281–300.

State Council Information Office (2021a) China: Democracy That Works. *The State Council of the People's Republic of China,* 4 December, http://www.china-embassy.org/eng/zgyw/202112/t20211204_10462468.htm, accessed 27 January 2022.

State Council Information Office (2021b) Poverty Alleviation: China's Experience and Contribution. *The State Council Information Office of the People's Republic of China*, 1 July, http://www.xinhuanet.com/english/2021-04/06/c_139860414.htm, accessed 27 January 2022.

Strauss, Leo (1957) What is political philosophy? *The Journal of Politics*, 19(3), pp. 343–68.

Sukhomlinova, V. V. (2020) Discovering the synthesis between Marxism and Xi Jinping's thought on socialism with Chinese characteristics for a new era. *Concept: Philosophy, Religion, Culture*, 4(1), pp. 30–38.

Suls, Jerry M., and Ladd Wheeler (eds.) (2000) *Handbook of Social Comparison: Theory and Research*. New York: Kluwer Academic.

The Economist (2010) The debate over universal values, 30 September, http://www.economist.com/asia/2010/09/30/the-debate-over-universal-values, accessed 1 February 2022.

Thoman, Elizabeth (1993) Media, technology and culture: Re-imagining the American dream. *Bulletin of Science, Technology & Society*, 13, pp. 20–27.

Tobin, Liza (2018) Xi's Vision for Transforming Global Governance: A Strategic Challenge for Washington and Its Allies. *Texas National Security Review*, 2(1), pp. 155–66.

Tsang, Steve (2021) 'Xi Jinping Thought': China's Post-Communism Ideology. *YouTube*, 2 December, https://www.youtube.com/watch?v=cMvRxxkXnQ8, accessed 27 January 2022.

Tsinghua University (n.d.) Xi Jinping's Thought on Socialism with Chinese Characteristics for a New Era. *EdX*, https://www.edx.org/course/xi-jinpings-thought-on-socialism-with-chinese-char, accessed 13 January 2022.

Tuck, Richard (2006) Hobbes and Democracy. In: Annabel Brett and James Tully (eds.) *Rethinking the Foundations of Modern Political Thought*. Cambridge: Cambridge University Press, pp. 171–190.

Vucina, Naja, Claus Drejer, and Peter Triantafillou (2011) Histories and freedom of the present: Foucault and Skinner. *History of the Human Sciences*, 24(5), pp. 124–41.

Vukovich, Daniel F. (2012) *China and Orientalism: Western Knowledge Production and the P.R.C.* New York: Routledge.

Wang, Hsin-Hsien, and Wei-Feng Tzeng (2021) Building a hyper-stability structure: The mechanisms of social stability maintenance in Xi's China. *Issues & Studies*, 57(01), pp. 1–22.

Westcott, Ben, and Steven Jiang (2020) China Is Embracing a New Brand of Wolf Warrior Diplomacy. *CNN*, 29 May, https://www.cnn.com/2020/05/28/asia/china-wolf-warrior-diplomacy-intl-hnk/index.html, accessed 25 January 2022.

Wong, Brian Y. S. (2021) China Has an Image Problem – but Knows How to Fix It. *Foreign Policy*, 6 April, https://foreignpolicy.com/2021/04/06/china-image-problem-wolf-warrior-international/, accessed 24 January 2022.

Xi Jinping (2018) *The Governance of China*. Vol. 1. Beijing: Foreign Languages Press.

Xinhua (2021) Xi Urges World Political Parties to Shoulder Responsibility for Pursuit of People's Wellbeing, Progress of Mankind. 7 July, http://www.xinhuanet.com/english/2021-07/07/c_1310046497.htm, accessed 29 January 2022.

Yang, Fan (2014) *The 'Chinese Dream' in Contemporary Media Culture*. Washington, DC: George Washington University.

Zhao, Andrew (2019) The cult of Xi: China's return to a Maoist personality cult. *Synergy: The Journal of Contemporary Asian Studies*, 16 March, https://utsynergyjournal.org/2019/03/16/the-cult-of-xi-chinas-return-to-a-maoist-personality-cult/, accessed 14 January 2022.

Zoellick, Robert (2005) Whither China? From Membership to Responsibility. *National Committee on US-China Relations Gala*, 21 September, https://www.ncuscr.org/fact/robert-zoellicks-responsible-stakeholder-speech/, accessed 29 January 2022.

CHAPTER 3

The Realpolitik of Xi Jinping Thought

John Garrick

1   Introduction: Domestic Narratives/Global Contexts

China's General-Secretary Xi Jinping declared at the April 2021 Boao Forum that the world needed "justice, not hegemony, [that] China would never engage in an arms race or boss others around and meddling in others' internal affairs will not get one any support" (2021a). Xi's words are generally reproduced by China's "mass-media machine" without criticism (Bergin, 2021), as questioning official Chinese Communist Party (CCP) narratives is not permissible domestically (Garrick and Bennett, 2021). Internationally, China has even created a national security law with extraterritorial scope (Hernandes, 2020), and China's public diplomacy has evolved "from listening to telling" (Zhao, 2019). Further, at the 2022 Beijing Winter Olympics, Russian President Vladimir Putin and Xi Jinping made their joint declaration of a "no limits" relationship (The Kremlin, 2022). Against such a backdrop of political power and narrative control, this chapter examines the realpolitik of 'Xi Jinping Thought on Socialism with Chinese Characteristics for a New Era' (hereafter XJT).

XJT was incorporated into the CCP constitution at its 19th Party Congress in October 2017. Xi's (2017a) full report told that Congress: "China must hold high the banner of socialism with Chinese characteristics for the new era [...] and work tirelessly to realize the Chinese Dream of national rejuvenation." XJT has significant implications for China's domestic policy and for the global community, but what exactly is 'Xi Jinping Thought'? What are its guiding principles? What are its implications domestically and for systems of international governance? The following seven chapter-sections draw upon primary Chinese sources and various secondary sources including both Chinese and Western academic and media reports to critically examine the 'realpolitik' underlying the Dream. The theoretical framework for interpretation draws on political economy, international comparative law and legal narrative analysis.

2   What is 'Xi Jinping Thought'?

Xi Jinping's 19th CCP Congress report outlines the key aspects of 'Xi Jinping Thought', identifying China's primary policy objectives going forward: to "ensure and improve living standards through sustainable development" (Xi, 2017a: 23); to condone market "reform and opening" (改革开放 *gaige kaifang*) and encourage Chinese enterprises to "go out" (走出去 *zou chuqu*) – especially along the Silk Road Economic Belt and 21st Century Maritime Silk Road (2017a:2). They are known together as the Belt and Road Initiative, which projects Xi's philosophy globally (Li, 2020: 169).

Notwithstanding setbacks from the COVID-19 pandemic, the Chinese economy has maintained its position as the world's second largest economy with some forecasters predicting China may overtake the US as soon as 2031 (South China Morning Post, 2021).[1] At the same time, power is tightly controlled and deepened within the one-party system with General Secretary Xi holding more power than any Chinese leader before him – Mao Zedong included – although Goodman (2021) points out that although it is reasonable to assume Xi has had close supporters within the leadership of the CCP, and even among former leaders, they are not as visible, for the most part, as was the case for Mao and Deng. This is no bold assertion about Xi's power as he rules a wealthy, modernised country with a powerful military compared to the largely agrarian economy of Mao's time. Xi has taken China to the dark side of the moon (BBC News, 2019),[2] and tested new space capability including nuclear-capable hypersonic missiles that have circled the globe (Financial Times, 2021). In 2018 the CCP amended the country's Constitution, removing the expression that "the President and Vice-President of the People's Republic of China shall serve no more than two consecutive terms" enabling Xi to retain power indefinitely (Xinhua, 2018).

Before this constitutional maneuver, Xi's power between 2013–17 had already been extended, in part, through the execution of his 'Four-Pronged Comprehensive Strategy' (四个全面战略布局 *si ge quanmian zhanlüe buju*; hereafter *Four Comprehensives*). The *Four Comprehensives* is fundamental to understanding 'Xi Jinping Thought', encompassing the interrelated narratives of: 1. building a moderately prosperous society, 2. deepening reform, 3. governing the nation according to law, and 4. tightening party discipline.

---

1   also see Zhu and Orlik (2021), on why this may never happen.
2   Two weeks later the constitutional changes were passed by the annual sitting of the National People's Congress – of the 2,964 votes two delegates voted against the change and three abstained (see BBC News, 2018).

Xi (2017a: 16) stated that the plan for building socialism with Chinese characteristics for the new era is "based on the four-pronged comprehensive strategy", and the 19th Party Congress then incorporated 'Xi Jinping Thought on Socialism with Chinese Characteristics for a New Era' into the CCP's constitution (Xinhua, 2017).

Together the 'prongs' position the CCP at the centre of every aspect of economic development, social cohesion, law and governance, comprising a totalising discourse with precious little room for disagreement or dissent.

3   Building a 'Moderately Prosperous Society'[3]

The political reality of China's socialist market economy follows a Marxist-Leninist ideology with Chinese characteristics (Mitter, 2021a). These 'characteristics' include Chinese experience, over millennia, of a social system that recognizes a central authority free from the checks and balances generally associated with a Western concept of rule of law (see contrasting Chinese and Western 'rule of law' perspectives in: Guo and Garrick, 2020; Garrick and Bennett, 2016; Peerenboom, 2015; Chen, 2010; Berring, 2004; Rose, 2004). Linking the authority structure of the traditional Chinese dynastic rulers with the pragmatic Leninism of today's CCP, the Confucian tradition of relational governance, centred on *the family* and *loyalty to authority*, maps well onto the theoretical frame of 'Xi Jinping Thought'. It can be made useful to the Party; deployed as a tool. Reconciling Marxism-Leninism with the rampant pursuit of wealth and power is, however, another matter. Under Xi's guidance, the CCP constructs a narrative of law-based governance as an instrument that helps legitimise wealth-building and modernization. Despite the growth of an influential private sector, internal CCP practices are still guided by the Leninist concept of 'democratic centralism'.[4] This is meant to allow for debate, discussion, and the development of policy within the CCP, but Lenin's definition of 'democratic centralism' allows for criticism of Party action "*only before* a course of action has been decided upon" (Lenin, 1906).

In 2015, Xi silenced internal dissent with a revised version of the Party's disciplinary regulations, banning groundless criticism of the Party center's (Beijing's) decisions and policies; a year later, Xi was given the title of 'core leader', becoming the personification of the party center (Cai, 2021a; The

---

3   "Moderately prosperous" – as set out in Xi Jinping's full report (2017a: 23).
4   For more on 'democratin centralism' see Ball (2021).

Straits Times, 2016). Garnaut (2019) argues that Marxism-Leninism was interpreted to Mao (and his fellow revolutionaries) by Joseph Stalin, with that version of communism, (as interpreted by Lenin, Stalin and then Mao), being a *total* ideology. The argument holds that Xi has reinvigorated that ideology and CCP congresses now essentially rubber-stamp decisions made by the top party leadership – the vanguard's elite. Indeed, a 'Study Xi, Strong Nation' app was created by the Communist Party's propaganda department in 2019 to promote study of 'XJT', somewhat reminiscent of Mao's 'Little Red Book' (Los Angeles Times, 2020).[5]

'XJT' (Xi, 2017a: 23) – to build a moderately prosperous society – requires China to transition further from a command economy towards a socialist market economy by "innovation-driven development, rural vitalization, coordinated regional and the military-civilian integration strategy." This 'military-civilian' integration element is referred to in more depth in section seven of this chapter and in relation to the theory underlying the Belt and Road Initiative (also see The Soufan Centre (2020) and Konstantinas Andrijauskas's chapter in this volume).

A vital challenge for China's Dream realisation is that the PRC's economic growth remains highly unequal. The wealth of the privileged few princelings and wealthy second-generation elites, (富二代 *fuerdai*), is set against a backdrop of those whose incomes have, proportionately, hardly increased at all.[6] There are two issues here: *income* inequality and *wealth* inequality (with wealth about business, legitimate or otherwise, and income pertaining to employees). Here Knight (2017: 307) made the point that "income inequality is falling whereas wealth inequality continues to rise" [and] "has increased rapidly in recent years" (Knight, 2017:312). The wealth imbalance indicates the 'new normal' narrative has covered up the emergence of a highly diversified capitalist class system within communist China. This has not been lost on China's top leaders. Xi Jinping's 2018 New Year's speech for instance proclaimed:

> As part of our poverty alleviation efforts, 3.4 million people have moved into new and warm homes, and the goal of upgrading 6 million housing

---

5 Also see (Los Angeles Times, 2021) how the app is not always used as the Party intended.
6 The *Hurun Rich List 2021* indicates that "China has pulled away from the USA, leading with 1058 billionaires, up 259, compared with the USA with 696 billionaires, up 70 from last year." (China and the USA make up over half of 'known' billionaires in the world.) See: *Hurun Global Rich List 2021 – Hurun Australia*.

> units in run-down areas has been realized in advance. The improvement of people's well-being has been accelerated, and the ecological environment has gradually improved. The people have gained a stronger sense of fulfillment, happiness, and security. We are now one big step closer to the completion of a moderately prosperous society in all respects [...] It is our solemn commitment to lift all rural residents living below the current poverty line out of poverty by 2020.
>
> XI, 2017b

Whilst not referring specifically to the extreme wealth imbalance, the speech was generally concerned about poverty alleviation in the knowledge that Huron's 2021 'Rich List China' showed the PRC had more billionaires than the US Politically, the need for a transparent system of wealth redistribution remains a fundamental challenge (He, 2021). This was reflected in Xi's August 2021 speech to the 10th meeting of the 'Central Committee on Finance and Economics' when he emphasized the need to "promote common prosperity" (Xinhua, 2021).[7]

The range of challenges in managing China's economic growth and transition to a sustainable development model makes it difficult to fit the process into a particular theoretical framework. At the heart of this interpretive puzzle is a paradox: a so-called 'socialist market economy' developed within a 'state-controlled' property system in which the government owns all the land in perpetuity and is *both* market-player and market-regulator. Striking a balance in this model proves to be elusive (Lun, 2021).

In a discussion of the 'property paradox,' Hu (2016: 132) asserts that China's urban planning has historically been 'land-based' rather than 'population-based': urban expansion has been accompanied by rural migrants moving to cities, often without attaining urban citizenship. At the same time, urbanisation has been associated with depopulation and land loss amongst rural peasants. Hu (2021) further shows that along with glimmering city developments like Shanghai and Shenzhen, China's land use and urbanisation have both been subject to government monopoly and control, with local governments having political and financial incentives to sell land and promote urban growth. Many underlying issues, including corruption, risky financing and

---

7   See speech summary at: Xi Jinping chaired the 10th meeting of the Central Committee on Finance and Economics to emphasize promoting common prosperity in high-quality development and to do a good job in preventing and resolving major financial risks Li Keqiang Wang Huning Han is attending (Xinhua, 2021).

peasant exploitation are attributed to this nexus of political power, monopoly practices and corrupt financial incentivization which is notoriously difficult to stamp out.

Xi's 19th Party Congress report referred more 'delicately' to the central contradiction facing Chinese society, as having "evolved from the ever-growing material and cultural needs of the people and backward social production to unbalanced and inadequate development and the people's ever-growing needs for a better life" (Xinhua, 2017). That 'better life' includes affordable housing, but house price inflation seriously influences China's inequality of total wealth. For some, such as China's Uighur population, the situation could not be more dire despite official claims they are being given new 'vocational education' opportunities (see World Uyghur Congress, 2021; ABC News, 2021; The Guardian, 2021).In China, inequality based on unfairness in treatment or access to opportunities is intensely disliked (see Zang, 2015; Solinger, 2020). But the masses do not always know about such treatment due to intensely censored domestic media and the strict internet 'firewall'. Chinese citizens are nonetheless acutely aware that there remains a deep urban-rural divide with vested interests shaping local level decisions even though it is the central government that sets the rules – Beijing is often reliant on local governments to implement them (see for example: The Economist, 2021; McCuaig-Johnston, 2021). Building a moderately prosperous society and increasing prosperity whilst simultaneously targeting extreme wealth inequality remain conundrums to the CCP's 'deepening reform' agenda and partly explains why Xi's August 2021 speech stressed "efforts to promote *common prosperity* in the pursuit of high-quality development [...] [with] unreasonable incomes to be rectified" (Xi, 2021d).

4   Deepening Reform and Foregrounding 'Common Prosperity'

Xi's (2017a: 30) report highlighted various challenges for deepening reform including the creation of a modern public finance system, a fiscal relationship between central and local governments built upon clearly defined powers and responsibilities, deepened reform of the taxation system, institutional reform in the financial sector and an improved framework of regulation for monetary and macro-prudential policy including "interest rates and exchange rates becoming more market-based." Each of these critical reform areas warrant disaggregation and analysis, but this is outside the scope of this chapter. Xi's report did, however, also emphasise "building the military" (Xi, 2017a: 48). In fact, China's military is now already larger than those of Japan, South Korea,

Taiwan and Southeast Asia combined and challenges US dominance in some areas (see Lowy Institute, 2021). With its economic and military power, China now seeks to forcefully influence international financial, trade and legal systems (Xi, 2021b). Further, Xi's (2021b) CCP 'Centenary Speech' warned that foreign powers will "get their heads bashed" if they attempt to bully or influence the country, and that Beijing would not allow "sanctimonious preaching" – remarks widely seen as directed at the US over criticisms about alleged human rights abuses against the Uighurs and its forceful crackdown in Hong Kong (BBC News, 2021a; for more detail see Human Rights Foundation, 2021).

Until now, China's reform narrative had been more generally associated with a set of macro-economic policies promoting structural reform in the economy and internationalisation of the Renminbi. Indeed, Xi's (2013) "Explanation of the Chinese Communist Party Central Committee Decision on Several Major Questions About Deepening Reform" (*Decision*) made it clear that "ideological unity continues to be forged around Deng Xiaoping's 'two-hands' formula: a market-based economy and uncompromising political control." In the decision, Xi emphasised that rule of law should be advanced under CCP leadership, in line with socialism with Chinese characteristics and with economic structural reform at the centre of deepening reform generally – with core issues identified as dealing well with the relationship between the government and the market, ensuring that the market has a *decisive function* in resource allocation, and giving better rein to the function of government. These views were reinforced in the amendment to the CCP constitution at the 19th Party Congress which enshrined 'XJT' as part of the Party's "guide for action" (Xi, 2017b).[8]

Almost immediately following this elevation of 'XJT', the balancing of state sector/marketization shifted to a greater focus on maintaining the one-party state with "complete coverage under the Party's unified command" (Xi, 2017a: 62). Under Xi, no big privately owned Chinese banks, oil companies, telcos or power providers have been allowed – as legacy state-owned enterprises retain control of those sectors. Now, even China's big-tech companies are being brought under direct party-state control with wealthy bosses like Alibaba's Jack Ma 'disappearing' in November 2020 for several months in a reminder (to all) that the Party is firmly in charge and big data belongs to the State (Yang, 2021). Soros (2021) argues that in fact "Xi regards *all* Chinese companies as instruments of a one-party state". With China's current 'cult of personality'

---

8 At the same time, the Congress approved "Xi's military thinking and the party's 'absolute' leadership over the armed forces" into its constitution (Xinhua, 2017b); also see Xi (2017a: 34) on "advancing law-based governance".

there is only room for one at the top, and the 'decisive role of the market' is, in fact, decided by the Party elite (Birtles, 2021). In this political context assessing if (and how much) agency civil society actors still have is difficult, although Christina Zhou (2020) notes that *any* form of public criticism of the State in China is deeply problematic. Even Party-members who are worried about the hardline, militaristic directions being taken must now speak with very great caution, coded, even amongst friends and family (see Cook, 2022).

With Xi's Belt and Road Initiative incorporated into the CCP Constitution (Xi, 2017a: 2), the PRC seeks to more closely link countries across Eurasia and the Indian Ocean (One Belt One Road Europe, 2021). In 2022 the Chinese Foreign Minister Wang Yi also sought to incorporate 10 islands of the South Pacific under a PRC regional trade and security pact and, although this attempt was unsuccessful, numerous Belt and Road MoUs were agreed (Bennett and Garrick, 2022). Indeed, China's policy banks are providing massive funds to allow Chinese enterprises to operate along the 'Belt' and 'Road' axes, with further funding provided by the Asia Infrastructure Investment Bank (AIIB). The Bank of China has indicated that the aim of the Belt and Road initiative is to make the RMB the main trading and investment currency in the countries involved (Chatzky and McBride, 2020; Belt and Road News, 2019). There are obstacles to the rapid internationalisation of the RMB, however, including China's domestic financial system, in which interest rates are tightly controlled, state-owned banks dominate financial intermediation, and the Chinese stock market faces periodic and deep central government intervention. At the international level, any Chinese leadership in reforming global financial structures faces significant challenges until China's own development strategy is less opaque and more stable. For example, Chinese banks tend to pay interest rates below international standards without regulatory caps, and China still has relatively poorly developed alternatives for domestic consumers looking to invest their savings. This partially explains why most domestic investors cheered when the stock market was rising, but when the bubble burst the Communist Party's distrust of market forces became clear: regulators capped short-selling, pension funds were forced to pledge to buy more stocks, the government suspended initial public offerings and brokers were required to set up a fund to buy shares backed by the Central Bank (see Eslake, 2021). This dilemma remains highly pervasive and is exemplified in the Evergrande property-group crisis (Oi, 2024), with Lam (2021) asserting that "Xi's retrogression to Maoism has sparked rare divergent views from different sectors of the Party."

The 'deepening reform' narrative continues to face immediate and substantial challenges with some of China's leading-edge industries, including information technology, ridesharing, e-commerce and private education provision, being hit with new state-imposed constraints. Chinese equities over 2021 lost over a trillion dollars in value (Callick, 2021). Distinguished Professor at the Henry A. Kissinger Center for Global Affairs at Johns Hopkins University, Hal Brands (2022) even claims that China's large economy is "stagnating". The significant journey from a command economy to allow for *the decisive function of the market* might be far over, but the deepening economic reform narrative will need much more to sustain legitimacy than the centrally driven tropes of intervention, intensified nationalism, the promise of 'common prosperity', fear, surveillance and demand for compliance (see Callick, 2021). Even after prolonged periods of extraordinary economic growth and development, the relentless drive for legitimacy is, in part, where the associated 'legal and governance reform' narrative comes into play – to clarify and strengthen the *socialist nature* of the Party's version of 'rule of law'.

5 Governing the Nation According to Law

Under Xi's leadership, the socialist rule of law with Chinese characteristics is the foundation for all legal reforms. From the CCP's 2014 Plenum five general principles guiding law reform processes were upheld: (1) the leadership of the Party, (2) the dominant position of the people, (3) equality before the law, (4) the combination of the rule of law with the rule of virtue and (5) the need for China to chart its own path. The 19th Party Congress guaranteed that this path will be charted under the *absolute* leadership of the CCP through the official justification of the Party Constitution over the State Constitution (Zhang, 2017). Socialist rule of law with Chinese characteristics can be interpreted as an *instrument* of the CCP leadership with the Party said to reflect *the will* of the people. This is the modern incarnation of an intricate interaction between law and society in China which has been a central feature of Chinese legal tradition. During the Xi era the CCP's enhanced supremacy over the PRC's legal system has noticeably altered the Party–law relationship to the point where there is now little dispute amongst China watchers about the CCP's supremacy. However, opinions *are* divided over the nature of the relationship between the CCP and Chinese law. This will remain a principal issue in Chinese politics and legal studies whilst the Party has monopolised control over the legal system. For instance, CCP propagandists insist that the Party's leadership is compatible with Chinese law, and that there is no conflict between Party supremacy and its version of 'socialist rule of law': Marxist-Leninist legal concepts remain fundamental with the aim to use the law as a political instrument to make the state more efficient (Moritz, 2021).

Xi (2017a: 19) urged "reform of the judicial system and strengthened rule of law awareness among all our people while also enhancing their moral integrity." Xi has spoken on the need for rule of virtue *and* rule of law – with inescapable links to traditional Chinese legal theory (for detail see Teon, 2016). 'Virtue', in the context of 'XJT', includes being "put down in words and borne in people's hearts [...]. If the basic policy, strategy and mode of governance by the rule of law are to be well implemented, rule of law must be combined with rule of morality, so they complement, promote and support each other" (Xu, 2017). In this way the modernization of state governance, and the CCP's governance capability are thought to be advanced.

This is a version of organic-unity theory – of law and state – that contrasts with the 'separation of powers' doctrine characteristic of western legal systems. China does, however, have its own separation of powers issue centred on the modernization of state governance on the one hand, and the CCP's governance capability on the other hand. Zhang (2017: 1) expresses this separation as being "between the Party and the state, within a Party-state." Zhang's argument holds that this domestic issue [notwithstanding recent challenges to rule of law theory in China including arbitrary or non-judicial detentions such as the use of 'Residential Surveillance at a Designated Location' (RSDLs) (see Safeguard Defenders, 2021) and 'black jails'(see Pils, 2017; The Washington Post, 2021)], "doesn't necessarily indicate a failure." Others, such as Professor of Law at King's College, London, Eva Pils, point out that the *Decision* has a "deeply illiberal commitment to power concentration and Party supremacy *over* law" (Pils, 2015: 83; see also Pils, 2016, 2017).

Re-affirming the Party line, China's Chief Justice, Zhou Qiang, as quoted in the state-run (2017), said: "China's courts must firmly resist the western idea of judicial independence and other ideologies which threaten the leadership of the ruling Communist Party."[9] The judiciary in Chief Justice Zhou's model thus essentially becomes part of a taskforce under the Executive Branch. Pils (2016) draws on her work with human rights lawyers to point out that a consequence [of this Executive-led approach] is a deepening repression of legal and political

---

9   Chief Justice Zhou's comments came after the country's anti-graft watchdog said that a mechanism to keep officials in check that is independent of the Communist Party cannot exist in China. The Central Commission for Discipline Inspection (CCDI) pledged to create a national supervisory commission and a corresponding national law as part of a move to reform the oversight system for thousands of Party officials, but the reforms stopped short of placing power outside the Party. See Reuters World News, 2017.

advocacy. Pils's (2017) further view is that the anti-liberal re-conception of legal *process* allows 'rule by fear' techniques to play an increasingly prominent role and be applied more blatantly. By 2021 the repression of civil rights lawyers and 'citizen journalists' for example had confirmed Pils' concerns (see Garrick and Bennett, 2021). Without adequate checks and balances on Party power, political and legal development, civil society is heavily circumscribed by the overarching authority and intense surveillance of the Party-state. The *de facto* application of 'rule of fear' can undermine the *de jure* principle of 'rule of law' as laws are open to *selective* application – to serve non-legal interests such as crushing political opponents, 'protecting' the well-connected, or used as an instrument of coercion.

6 Tightening Party Discipline

Xi's (2017a: 6) report identified "sweeping efforts to strengthen Party leadership and Party building [...] [and a] commitment to examining ourselves in the mirror, tidying our attire, taking a bath, and treating our ailments." This fourth prong of the *Comprehensives* included its own propaganda: the "Three Strict, Three Earnests" (*Three Stricts*) campaign (commonly known on Chinese websites as "Three Stricts and Three Honests").[10] This campaign was required to improve Party discipline and cadre conduct and promotes 'Core Socialist Values' (Gow, 2017: 106; Xinhua, 2016). Core socialist values reflect normative concepts as defined by the CCP, which are "diametrically opposed to the common-sense usage of the same terms used in Western liberal thought, including freedom, democracy, civility and rule of law."[11] By building a normative consensus around socialist values, the CCP aims to strengthen its already dominant position over legal and regulatory systems. Effective courts now require 'virtuous communists' who are tuned into "the actual situation of China and the actual needs of the people" (Zhang, 2019: 175).

Concerned about clear gulfs in theory and practice under Xi, Cai Xia (2021a), a former professor at the Central Party School of the CCP in Beijing, writes

---

10   "The Three Stricts and Three Earnests" are: to be strict with oneself in practising self-cultivation, using power, and exercising self-discipline; and to be earnest in one's thinking, work and behaviour" (Xi 2017a: 6, footnote 1). Also see Wang, 2016.

11   A central element of the Three Stricts campaign focuses on "personal moral character" (Gow, 2017: 106). Gow points out that this "illustrates the CCP's appropriation of the Confucian status of a morally superior person [drawn from *Analects* 15:15]." The CCP's messaging is that a communist must be a virtuous person.

extensively about the course of Xi's tenure, arguing: "the regime has degenerated further into a political oligarchy bent on holding on to power through brutality and ruthlessness [and] has grown even more repressive and dictatorial [...]. A personality cult now surrounds Xi, who has tightened the Party's grip on ideology and eliminated what little space there was for political speech and civil society" (also see Cai, 2021b).

Since Xi's centenary speech the 'actual situation of China' includes authorities naming a new source of corruption – China's "sissy idols" – men deemed by the regime as being 'too effeminate' (South China Morning Post, 2021). Mitter (2021b) points out that "sissy" is a contemptuous expression in Chinese and English, referring to "a trend of young male stars appearing more feminised than *the macho norms* of traditional Chinese masculinity." Mitter (2021b) relates this to a growing trend in PRC domestic politics and society relating to "eliminating difference". His argument on this point is that the [policy of eliminating difference] is related to economics in that although China has reduced poverty, the World Bank still classes a quarter of its population as living on less than USD 5.50 a day. Premier Li Keqiang says China still has 600 million people (around 41 per cent of the population) whose monthly income is barely 1,000 yuan (USD 140) – not even enough to rent a room in a city (Global Times, 2020; BBC News, 2020). Thus, Xi's crackdown on highly visible and super-rich lifestyles sends a message about wealth and income inequality. The Party's hope is that this message will prove popular with the masses. But whether it will bolster Xi's power is more dependent on how senior party cadres regard the revival of a Maoist concept such as "common prosperity", and whether Xi can "purge the PLA and the political-legal apparatus of untrustworthy cadres who might challenge his supremacy" (Lam, 2021). Critically, the Party vanguard's desire to smooth out the vast differences in wealth and income comes hand-in-glove with the drive to impose conformity on political views, language, ethnicity, and gender norms. For Mitter, the price to be paid for the common prosperity policy "seems to be a common culture with little space for serious variation" (2021b).

The policy framework for propagating this homogenisation is grounded in prong four of the *Comprehensives* on tightening Party discipline. The CCP's Sixth Plenum (2017) approved two key documents designed to strengthen Party discipline: (1) "Guidelines on Inner-Party Life in the New Situation" and (2) "Party Regulations on Inner-Party Supervision" (Doyon and Godement, 2017: 4). The 'new situation' included a massive institutionalised anti-corruption campaign, initially launched by Xi in 2013, which proved to be popular. The above guidelines and regulations leveraged increased power to the top Party leadership with key mechanisms to ensure political unity being 'Party study sessions' and 'democratic life meetings'. These focus on Party ideology and improved understandings of the Party's current line and involve "self-criticisms", meant to ensure the unity and purity of the Party, and eradication of the "four [bad] work styles – formalism, bureaucracy, hedonism, and extravagance" (Doyon and Godement, 2017: 5). It is compulsory for core Party officials to attend a democratic life meeting at least once every year.

The above measures are meant to strengthen the Leninist structure of China's 'democratic centralism' and are accompanied by reforms to procedural justice, directly challenging any role for 'judicial independence' (see Cai, 2021a). Indeed, judicial independence is particularly fragile in relation to matters deemed 'politically sensitive' (Guo and Garrick, 2020: 334). Sensitive matters can, for example, include trials involving foreign nationals or internal Party disciplinary matters. For instance, the Party has previously relied heavily on internal political-legal committees and its own extra-legal mechanism, *shuanggui* (双规), to fight internal corruption. Xi (2017a: 61) has called on the Party to deepen reform of the national supervision system with a "National Supervision Law to be formulated [and] supervisory commissions given responsibilities, powers and means of investigation in accordance with law and the practice of *shuanggui* to be replaced by detention." But the notion of procedural justice is a recent introduction to China with Jianfu Chen (2016: 96) noting that it "needs time to be developed and adapted to local conditions." This argument does not necessarily imply a tacit acceptance of extra judicial measures or detention to discipline Party members who are perceived to have strayed from the strict and virtuous requirements of today's CCP. From the Gang of Four trial to Bo Xilai's downfall to Xi Jinping's "tigers and flies" (老虎苍蝇一起打 *laohu cangying yiqi da*) campaign, there are similarities and continuities in the CCP's anti-corruption measures with the CCP both main actor *and* director, eliminating political enemies through publicised campaigns and trials, and non-judicial anti-corruption measures that rely on Maoist rhetoric for legitimization.

For today's CCP-approved discourse, Maoist rhetoric remains a powerful element in operational narratives. It is normative, with core socialist value propaganda disseminated on state media platforms at national, provincial, municipal, district and community administrative levels. Blanket coverage of poster art and digitised forms of propaganda posters are developed and disseminated under the 'Propaganda Department and Central Guiding Committee for Building Spiritual Civilization' (see Gow, 2017: 96). Under CCP direction, anti-corruption campaigns appear to remove not only corrupt officials but others perceived to be politically unreliable, considered "bad elements" bent on destroying the Party (Ho, 2016: 109). Ironically, this has similarities to the way Bo used the organised crime crackdowns in Chongqing to extort businessmen and remove individuals he perceived as threats to his authority.

Under Xi's leadership, the crackdown on dissidents has, in part, been conducted under the cover of tightening discipline and expanded during the conditions of the COVID-19 pandemic (Bernot et al., 2021). The associated broader anti-corruption campaign also stressed the Party's absolute leadership over the People's Liberation Army (PLA) with military corruption, although seldom spoken of in public, targeted by Xi's campaign.¹² Furthermore, the domestic anti-corruption campaign has international implications, as China tenaciously pursues corrupt "fugitives" who have fled overseas to escape charges at home (Lynch, 2021; Feng, 2016; 2017; Wen and Garnaut, 2015). As Fu (2014) argued, corruption is closely correlated with legitimacy, and political leaders in China have found it expedient to use anti-corruption campaigns to remove their political foes and rein in the bureaucracy while enhancing their legitimacy in the eyes of the general public. Fu's "wielding the sword" argument is essentially that the Party's anti-corruption campaign is a tool for the concentration of political power on the one hand, in addition to eliminating corrupt conduct on the other hand.

Against the backdrop of China's anti-corruption campaign and drive to tighten Party discipline, Norman Ho's (2016: 109) view still holds: that the medium-term outlook for consistent procedural fairness and transparent use of the courts is "not so encouraging". For the longer term, there is always a hope that the improvements to judicial capability, procedural fairness and the legal system across China more generally can be built upon (see Reuters, 2017).

At the time of completing this chapter (June 2022) it is clear enough that Beijing is explicitly interested in propagating the PRC's conception of law and legal practice internationally, to establish new legal standards and, together with the Russian Federation, enforce its interests through global systems including global governance of human rights, national sovereignty, security, and territorial integrity. Following Russia's 2022 invasion of Ukraine (and China's failure to condemn it), Washington, London, Brussels, Paris and Berlin are certainly paying special attention to both Russian and the PRC conceptions of 'rule of law'. Moritz (2021) suggests that in-depth knowledge on this topic is imperative to better understand the logic of PRC actions [around its domestic law reforms and applications to global governance] as it seeks to expand and impose its international influence.

7 International Dimensions of 'Xi Jinping Thought'

'XJT' plays a vital role in attempting to unify economic and legal reforms, Party discipline and the 'Chinese Dream' of national rejuvenation. The Dream extends to exerting global leadership, shaping governing international

---

12 *The Economist* (2015: 39) claimed that corruption is worst in departments dealing with logistics, weapons procurement, and political matters (the latter oversees maintaining party loyalty and appointments). Paying bribes for promotion is widespread and 9 of the 16 senior officers (15 being generals) recently disgraced were [at that time] from the PLA's political wing.

institutions to better reflect China's great power status (Kassam and Lim, 2021). The Belt and Road Initiative is, of course, a Xi signature project. In June Xi (2021c) said: "the purpose of proposing the BRI is to inherit the Silk Road spirit, jointly build an open cooperation platform and provide new impetus for the cooperation and development of all countries [...] [and] China has signed cooperation agreements with a total of 140 countries under the BRI in eight years". China routinely promises a 'no strings attached' and 'no ideology' approach for nations signing-up to its pragmatic BRI. Many agreements reached are legally unenforceable Memorandums of Understanding (MoUs) and, as such, are primarily symbolic allowing the parties to celebrate "people-to-people ties" (Xi, 2021c). In fact, there are *always* strings of some sort attached (see BBC News, 2021b; The New York Times, 2021; Global Times, 2021). Along with the BRI, China-led 'Beijing Consensus'-based institutions such as the New Development Bank (NDA) and Asian Infrastructure Investment Bank (AIID) offer developing economies an alternative to the 'Washington Consensus' multilateral development banks (MDBs). So-called neoliberal forms of Western multilateralism are now being seriously challenged (for further detail see Jakupec et al., 2020).

The nexus of growth, law reform and outward-bound Chinese political power does not easily fit into any specific development model. Promoting moderately prosperous and sustainable development, deepening economic reforms so the market can (if allowed) play a more decisive role, governing the country according to the rule of law, tightening party discipline and expanding Beijing's influence globally can all sound reasonable on the surface (see Xi, 2021b). When taken together, different goals can be discerned. The realpolitik of the CCP's totalising grand narrative places the Party at the centre of economic development, social cohesion, law and governance, with Xi in particular, portrayed in state-controlled media as the people's saviour. CCP rule is presented as *the only way* to realise the Chinese Dream (Kembayev, 2015). With this totalising discourse, Palmer's (2020) argument that a climate of fear and control has arisen – like a dangerous phoenix not seen since Mao's cultural revolution era – is highly plausible (also see The Conversation, 2021b). As with any totalising discourse, there is little (or no) room for dissent as revealed in both public and secret silencing of Chinese legal rights lawyers, citizen journalists and other activists (Cook, 2022; Pils, 2017: 2020). This rule by fear approach has affected China's outwards expansion, especially since the PRC's loss-of-face when the United Nations Arbitral Tribunal (2016) (The Hague) ruled unanimously against it.

In the UN Tribunal, constituted under the UN's *Convention on the Law of the Sea*, the 2016 case of *Republic of the Philippines v. the People's Republic of China,* found in favour of the Philippines. The case, initiated in 2013 by the Philippines (as the aggrieved party), ultimately established that the nine-dash line is legally void. The Tribunal concluded that, "to the extent China had historic rights to resources in the waters of the South China Sea, such rights were extinguished [...], incompatible with the exclusive economic zones provided for in the Convention [and] that there was no legal basis for China to claim historic rights to resources within the sea areas falling within the nine-dash line" (see Permanent Court of Arbitration Press Release, 2016). Further, at clause 1181 (p. 464) the Award states that "China violated the Philippines' sovereign rights, caused severe harm to the coral reef environment and aggravated the dispute by involving Chinese naval and law enforcement vessels in support of the construction of a large artificial island within the Philippines' exclusive economic zone." The Tribunal considered it "beyond dispute that both parties are obliged to comply with the Convention" (clause 1201, p. 469 of the Award).

Since that date, China has repeatedly rejected the decision, arguing the Tribunal lacks jurisdiction in the matter even though China is a signatory to the UN Convention on the Law of the Sea. This reflects the realpolitik and tendency of superpowers to ignore international law when it does not suit them. Xi's own reference to the issue in his report simply states (2017a: 2), "construction on islands and reefs in the South China Sea has seen steady progress." It is therefore little wonder that the port acquisitions and other infrastructure along the Maritime Silk Road that have been vigorously pursued have raised concerns across Europe, the US (and elsewhere) – as to whether China intends to use its commercial acquisitions of overseas ports (and other infrastructure) for military purposes, under its stated goals to put civilian technology and resources to military use (Kania and Laskai, 2021: 1; see also The Soufan Centre Intel-Brief, 2020; Bagshaw and Galloway, 2021; Huang, 2018). Furthermore, the COVID-19 pandemic has seen China's overseas diplomatic methods further harden, with so-called 'wolf-warrior' diplomats becoming overtly aggressive, and coercive tactics used to pursue CCP goals (see for example: Feng, 2020; Green, 2019; Andrijauskas, 2019). These examples illustrate why some European nations (and others) are turning away from China's sphere of influence (for further examples see Banka, 2021; Gillespie, 2021). That said, the economic reach and seductive allure of permitted entry to the PRC's huge consumer market persuades many nations to acquiesce to China's advances. After all, money talks.

8   Conclusion

As Carl Minzner (2020) explains, China's reform-era is ending. The core factors that characterized it – political stability, ideological openness, and rapid economic growth – are unraveling. Minzner (2020: 1) shows how, since the 1990s, "a frozen political system has fueled both the rise of entrenched interests within the Communist Party itself, and the systematic underdevelopment of institutions of governance among state and society at large." He adds, "economic cleavages have widened [...] and ideological polarization deepened" (Mizner, 2020: 2). Foreign perceptions of the PRC have wavered between admiration for its developmental advances, perplexity over the unchanging persistence with some hardline efforts – especially when faced with *any* form of criticism – and rising concerns over actual (or imagined) changes in its role and responsibilities as a global power. Global powers do, invariably, face scrutiny and criticism. America is constantly criticized for its role on the world stage; it is also self-critical, allows protest and people can vote. Now China too faces international scrutiny as it exercises great power status. Indeed, China (and the world) has arrived at a dangerous turning point. 'XJT' shows the frail edges in the Marxist-Leninist-CCP guardianship of Chinese society, including incoherent threads in the master-narratives around market reform, socio-economic transformation, and messaging about its peaceful outward expansion under an authoritarian leadership model. Xi (2017b: 8) has, for some time, acknowledged some of these frailties having directly referred to "acute problems caused by unbalanced and inadequate development." Even so, the PRC has greatly enhanced its technological capacities, significantly enlarged its arsenal of weaponry (Blaxland, 2021), and successfully landed spacecraft on the moon (and even Mars) bringing national prestige (see Dahl et al. in this volume on 'China's Space Program and its Quest for Superpowerhood, see also He, 2021)

Despite heavy surveillance and built-in disincentives to protest any perceived injustice, for example, through the 'Social Credit System' (see ABC News, 2020), China's civil society continues to mobilise where possible. 'Citizen journalists', rights lawyers and reporters, for example, continue to cover issues of concern knowing they may be (and often are) arrested by authorities for 'picking quarrels and provoking trouble', with harsh penalties for relatively mundane communication. Some are taken into custody ('administrative detention') for up to 15 days without charge, an increasingly common punishment for simply speaking-up about perceived over-the top authoritarian actions. But as the French philosopher Michel Foucault declared, "as soon as there is a power relationship there is always the possibility of resistance" (see Heller, 1996; O'Farrell, 2008; Cook, 2022). With modern advances in China's surveillance technology including the use of artificial intelligence (AI), the ancient-Chinese proverb 'the mountains are high and the emperor far away' is, however, less applicable. Despite the lengthening shadows of authoritarianism, China's human rights movement proves to be resourceful and resilient (see The Guardian, 2019). But with China's economic and military rise the CCP pursues both domestic and international goals with increasing vigour, and Xi commands the gun.

Following Xi's (2021b) 'centenary speech' no-one should expect China to swallow anything that undermines its interests as it "marches toward the second centenary goal of building China into a great modern socialist country *in all respects*". China's domestic power hierarchy and rising international determination is heavily vested in Xi Jinping. It is unlikely that China's most senior leaders would want to unleash self-destructive ultra-nationalist forces, but there are worrying signs in this new march (Palmer, 2020; The Economist, 2021). 'Little pink' (or 小粉红 *xiao fenhong*) ultra-nationalists *have* been allowed relatively free reign and China's rise sharply impacts global financial, legal and trade regimes. Reliance on international relationships being skilfully managed through negotiation and diplomacy now becomes less likely as the organisations charged with managing multilateral affairs (such as the United Nations, World Health Organisation, World Trade Organisation) have themselves become highly contested spaces (see Mantesso, 2021; Lee, 2020; Feldwisch-Drentrup, 2020). Consensus about what constitutes 'rule of law' is breaking down in some parts of the world, with China's current 'playbook' (Cai, 2021b) enabling the emergence of more illiberal political, security and economic alternatives to those traditional global organisations (also see South China Morning Post, 2021; Lowy Institute, 2021). And where its international level clout has not yet changed things in its favour, China's sway is evident at regional and sub-regional levels where politicians can be more easily influenced and there's even less transparency (Yoshihara and Bianchi, 2020). The unfortunate potential exists in these tensions, at least in the short to medium term, for the US, the EU (and democratic allies) and China (and its allies including Russia – see Schuman, 2020; Gavin, 2021; Kuhrt, 2021) to engage in a dangerous game in which one side can *only* win something by causing the other side to lose it. Russia's illegal invasion of Ukraine illustrates just how vicious this game can become.

With Xi continuing at China's core, this bleak 'grey-zone' (see Garrick, 2021) is now spiralling faster than ever, with democracies facing *strategic competition* with a relentless and emboldened Middle Kingdom. Better ways forward can and must be found. But any compromise that may diminish perceptions of CCP power or legitimacy is definitely not part of Xi Jinping's realpolitik.

References

ABC News (2020) China's Social Credit System is pegged to be fully operational by 2020 — but what will it look like? 1 January, https://www.abc.net.au/news/2020-01-02/china-social-credit-system-operational-by-2020/11764740, accessed 22 November 2022.

ABC News (2021) Journalists allowed inside China's Urumqi Dabancheng detention centre in Xinjiang. 23 July, https://www.abc.net.au/news/2021-07-23/chinas-largest-detention-centre-for-uyghurs/100316712, accessed 10 November 2022.

Andrijauskas, Konstantinas (2019) A Diplomatic Incident in Lithuania Troubles Its Relationship with China. *China Observers in Central and Eastern Europe* (CHOICE), 17 September, https://chinaobservers.eu/a-diplomatic-incident-in-lithuania-troubles-its-relationship-with-china/, accessed 10 November 2022.

Bagshaw, Eryk and Anthony Galloway (2021) Japan warns of crisis over Taiwan, holds grave concerns about China's military build-up. *The Age*, 13 July, https://www.theage.com.au/world/asia/japan-warns-of-crisis-over-taiwan-holds-grave-concerns-about-china-s-military-build-up-20210713-p5898n.html, accessed 10 November 2022.

Ball, Terence (2021) Democratic Centralism: Communist Policy. *Brittanica*, 18 August 2021, https://www.britannica.com/topic/democratic-centralism, accessed 10 November 2022.

Banka, Andris (2021) Baltic states start to turn away from China. *The Strategist*, 7 May 2021, https://www.aspistrategist.org.au/baltic-states-start-to-turn-away-from-china/, accessed 10 November 2022.

BBC News (2018) China's Xi allowed to remain 'president for life' as term limits removed. 11 March, https://www.bbc.com/news/amp/world-asia-china-43361276, accessed 10 November 2022.

BBC News (2019) China Moon mission lands Chang'e-4 spacecraft on far side. 3 January, https://www.bbc.com/news/science-environment-46724727, accessed 10 November 2022.

BBC News (2020) Has China lifted 100 million people out of poverty? 28 February, https://bbc.com/news/56213271, accessed 10 November 2022.

BBC News (2021a) CCP 100: Xi warns China will not be 'oppressed' in anniversary speech. 1 July, https://www.bbc.com/news/world-asia-china-57648236.amp, accessed 10 November 2022.

BBC News (2021b) China: Big spender or loan shark? 29 September, https://www.bbc.com/news/world-asia-china-58679039, accessed 10 November 2022.

Belt and Road News (2019) China is Investing in Europe but there are Strings attached. 20 August, https://www.beltandroad.news/china-is-investing-in-europe-but-there-are-strings-attached/, accessed 10 November 2022.

Bennett, Yan and John Garrick (2022) Implications of China's Pacific Dream for the United States, Australia, and Allies. *Journal of Political Risk*, 10(6), June, https://www.jpolrisk.com/implications-of-chinaa-pacific-dream-for-the-united-states-australia-and-allies/#more-3054, accessed 10 November 2022.

Bergin, Julia (2021) How China used the media to spread its COVID narrative – and win friends around the world. *The Conversation*, 12 May, https://theconversation.com/how-china-used-the-media-to-spread-its-covid-narrative-and-win-friends-around-the-world-160694, accessed 10 November 2022.

Bernot, Ausma, Alexander Trauth-Goil and Sue Trevaskes (2021) China's 'surveillance creep': how big data COVID monitoring could be used to control people post-pandemic. 31 August, https://theconversation.com/chinas-surveillance-creep-how-big-data-covid-monitoring-could-be-used-to-control-people-post-pandemic-164788, accessed 10 November 2022.

Berring, Robert C. (2004) Rule of Law: The Chinese Perspective. *Journal of Social Philosophy*, 35(4), pp. 449–456.

Birtles, Bill (2021) China is cracking down on 'effeminate' men, private tutors and gaming. Here's what that tells us about Xi Jinping's vision. *ABC News*, 3 September, https://www.abc.net.au/news/2021-09-03/xi-jinpings-government-turns-against-capitalism-fame-and-tutors/100421752, accessed 10 November 2022.

Blaxland, John (2021) China does not want war, at least not yet. It's playing the long game. *Asia and the Pacific. ANU*, 5 May, https://asiapacific.anu.edu.au/news-events/all-stories/china-does-not-want-war-least-not-yet-its-playing-long-game, accessed 10 November 2022.

Brands, Hal (2022) The Dangers of China's Decline. *Foreign Policy*, 14 April, https://foreignpolicy.com/2022/04/14/china-decline-dangers/, accessed 10 November 2022.

Cai Xia (2021a) The Party that Failed: An Insider Breaks with Beijing. *Foreign Affairs*, January-February, https://www.foreignaffairs.com/articles/china/2020-12-04/chinese-communist-party-failed, accessed 10 November 2022.

Cai Xia (2021b) A Former Chinese Communist Party Insider on Beijing's Perspective On China's Relationship With The United States. *The Hoover Institution*, https://www.hoover.org/press-releases/hoover-institution-releases-essay-former-chinese-communist-party-insider-about, accessed 10 November 2022.

Callick, Rowan (2021) Helmsman Xi takes China back to the future. *The Strategist*, 3 September, https://www.aspistrategist.org.au/helmsman-xi-takes-china-back-to-the-future/, accessed 10 November 2022.

Chatzky, Andrew and James McBride (2020) China's Massive Belt and Road Initiative. *Council on Foreign Relations*, 28 January, https://www.cfr.org/backgrounder/chinas-massive-belt-and-road-initiative, accessed 10 November 2022.

Chen Jianfu (2016) Efforts toward Procedural Justice in Post-Mao China. In: John Garrick and Yan Chang Bennett (eds.) *China's Socialist Rule of Law Reforms under Xi Jinping*. London: Routledge, pp. 94–108.

Chen, Albert H. Y. (2010) Pathways of Western liberal constitutional development in Asia: A comparative study of five major nations. *Journal of Constitutional Law*, 8(4), pp. 849–884.

Cook, Sarah (2022) Voices From China: What the CCP Doesn't Want You to Hear. *The Diplomat*, 22 February, https://thediplomat.com/2022/02/voices-from-china-what-the-ccp-doesnt-want-you-to-hear/, accessed 10 November 2022.

Doyon, Jérôme and François Godement (2017) Discipline and Punish: Party Power under Xi. *European Council on Foreign Relations. China Analysis*, 14 March, https://ecfr.eu/archive/page/-/ECFR_China_Analysis_Discipline_and_punish._Party_power_under_Xi.pdf, accessed 09 February 2024.

Eslake, Saul (2021) China's economy. *Economist*, 5 June 2021, https://www.saul-eslake.com/topics/topics/asian-economies/, accessed 10 November 2022.

Feldwisch-Drentrup, Hinnerk (2020) How WHO Became China's Coronavirus Accomplice. *Foreign Policy*, 2 April, https://foreignpolicy.com/2020/04/02/china-coronavirus-who-health-soft-power/, accessed 10 November 2022.

Feng Chongyi (2016) China's Socialist Rule of Law: A Critical Appraisal of the Relationship between the Communist Party and Comprehensive Law Reform. In: John Garrick and Yan Chang Bennett (eds.) *China's Socialist Rule of Law Reforms under Xi Jinping*. London: Routledge, pp. 45–58.

Feng Chongyi (2020) What's behind China's bullying of Australia? It sees a soft target – and an essential one. *The Conversation*, 2 December, https://theconversation.com/whats-behind-chinas-bullying-of-australia-it-sees-a-soft-target-and-an-essential-one-151273, accessed 10 November 2022.

Financial Times (2021) China tests new space capability with hypersonic missile. 16 October, https://www.ft.com/content/ba0a3cde-719b-4040-93cb-a486e1f843fb, accessed 10 November 2022.

Fu Hualing (2014) Wielding the Sword: President Xi's New Anti-Corruption Campaign. *University of Hong Kong, Faculty of Law*, http://papers.ssrn.com/sol3/papers.cfm?abstract_id=2492407, pp. 134–157, accessed 09 February 2024.

Garnaut, John (2019) Engineers of the Soul: Ideology in Xi Jinping's China. 17 January, https://sinocism.com/p/engineers-of-the-soul-ideology-in, accessed 10 November 2022.

Garrick, John (2021) The domestic and international consequences of Xi's political philosophy. *The Strategist*, 3 September, https://www.aspistrategist.org.au/the-domestic-and-international-consequences-of-xis-political-philosophy/, accessed 10 November 2022.

Garrick, John and Yan C. Bennett (2021) How China is controlling the COVID origins narrative – silencing critics and locking up dissenters. *The Conversation*, 14 January, https://www.abc.net.au/news/2021-01-14/china-control-covid-origin-message-detention-zhang-zhan/13056420, accessed 10 November 2022.

Garrick, John and Yan C. Bennett (eds.) (2016) *China's Socialist Rule of Law Reforms under Xi Jinping*. London: Routledge.

Gavin, Gabriel (2021) Russia's Romance With China Is All About Keeping Up Appearances. *The Diplomat*, 1 January, https://thediplomat.com/2021/01/russias-romance-with-china-is-all-about-keeping-up-appearances, accessed 10 November 2022.

Gillespie, Alexander (2021) Calling out China for cyberattacks is risky – but a lawless digital world is even riskier. *The Conversation*, 20 June, https://theconversation.com/calling-out-china-for-cyberattacks-is-risky-but-a-lawless-digital-world-is-even-riskier-164771, accessed 10 November 2022.

Global Times (2020) 600m with USD 140 monthly income worries top. 29 May, https://www.globaltimes.cn/content/1189968.shtml, accessed 10 November 2022.

Goodman, David S.G. (2021) Xi Jinping puts his stamp on Communist Party history, but is his support as strong as his predecessors? *The Conversation*, 12 November, https://theconversation.com/xi-jinping-puts-his-stamp-on-communist-party-history-but-is-his-support-as-strong-as-his-predecessors-170874, accessed 10 November 2022.

Gow, Michael (2017) The Core Socialist Values of the Chinese Dream: Towards a Chinese Integral State. *Critical Asian Studies*, 49(1), pp. 92–116.

Green, Mark (2019) China's Debt Diplomacy: How Belt and Road threatens countries' ability to achieve self-reliance. *Foreign Policy*, 25 April, https://foreignpolicy.com/2019/04/25/chinas-debt-diplomacy/, accessed 10 November 2022.

Guo, Yingjie and John Garrick (2020) China's 'Socialist Rule of Law' and the Five Heroes of Mount Langya. *Australian Journal of Asian Law*, 20(2, Article 4), pp. 333–348.

He, Laura (2021) President Xi Jinping turns his fire on China's rich in push to redistribute wealth. *CNN*, 18 August, https://edition.cnn.com/2021/08/18/economy/xi-jinping-china-wealth-redistribution-intl-hnk/index.html, accessed 10 November 2022.

Heller, Kevin Jon (1996) Power, Subjectification and Resistance in Foucault. *SubStance*, 25(1), pp. 78–110. DOI: 10.2307/3685230.

Hernandes, Javier (2020) Harsh Penalties, Vaguely Defined Crimes: Hong Kong's Security Law Explained. *New York Times*, 13 July, https://www.nytimes.com/2020/06/30/world/asia/hong-kong-security-law-explain.html, accessed 10 November 2022.

Ho, Norman P. (2016) Addressing Corruption and the Trial of Bo Xilai: Historical Continuities, Rule of Law Implications. In: John Garrick and Yan C. Bennett (eds.) *China's Socialist Rule of Law Reforms under Xi Jinping*. London: Routledge, pp. 109–21.

Hu, Richard (2016) China's Land Use and Urbanization: Challenges for Comprehensive Reform. In: John Garrick and Yan Chang Bennett (eds.) *China's Socialist Rule of Law Reforms under Xi Jinping*. London: Routledge, pp. 122–133.

Hu, Richard (2021) *The Shenzhen Phenomenon: From Fishing Village to Global Knowledge City*. London (Oxon): Routledge.

Huang, Kristin (2018) Why China buying up ports is worrying Europe. *South China Morning Post*, 23 September, https://www.scmp.com/news/china/diplomacy/article/2165341/why-china-buying-ports-worrying-europe, accessed 10 November 2022.

Human Rights Foundation (2021) *Report on 100 Years of Suppression: The CCP's Strategies in Tibet, The Uyghur Region, and Hong Kong*, August, https://hrf.org/wp-content/uploads/2021/08/CCP-REPORT-FINAL-VERSION.pdf, accessed 10 November 2022.

Huron Report (2021) China Rich List 2021. At: Hurun Global Rich List 2021, *Hurun Australia*, https://hurun.com.au/hurun-global-rich-list-2021/, accessed 10 November 2022.

Jakupec, Viktor, Max Kelly and Jonathan Makuwira (2020) *Rethinking Multilateralism in Foreign Aid: Beyond the Neoliberal Hegemony*. Oxon: Routledge.

Kania, Elsa B. and Lorand Laskai (2021) Myths and Realities of China's Military-Civil Fusion Strategy. Center for a New American Security (en-US), 28 January, https://www.cnas.org/publications/reports/myths-and-realities-of-chinas-military-civil-fusion-strategy, accessed 10 November 2022.

Kassam, Natasha and Darren Lim (2021) How China is remaking the world in its vision. *The Conversation*, 22 February, https://theconversation.com/how-china-is-remaking-the-world-in-its-vision-155377, accessed 10 November 2022.

Kembayev, Zhenis (2015) The Political Theory of 'Four Comprehensives'. *Beijing Review*, 30 April, http://www.bjreview.com.cn/nation/txt/2015-04/28/content_685398.htm, accessed 10 November 2022.

Knight, John (2017) China's evolving inequality. *Journal of Chinese Economic and Business Studies*, 14(4), pp. 307–323.

Kuhrt, Natasha (2021) Russia and China present a united front to the west – but there's plenty of potential for friction. *The Conversation*, 31 March, https://theconversation.com/russia-and-china-present-a-united-front-to-the-west-but-theres-plenty-of-potential-for-friction-157934, accessed 10 November 2022.

Lam, Willy Lo-Lap (2021) Xi Facing Opposition on Different Fronts in Run-Up to Key Party Plenum. *The Jamestown Foundation*, 23 September, https://jamestown.org/program/xi-facing-opposition-on-different-fronts-in-run-up-to-key-party-plenum/, accessed 10 November 2022.

Lee, Karen (2020) The United Nations: An Emerging Battleground for Influence. *Testimony before the US-China Economic and Security Review Commission Hearing on The Chinese View of Strategic Competition with the United States*, June 24.

Lenin, Vladimir (1906) Freedom to Criticize and Unity of Action. In: *Volna 22, Marxists Internet Archive*, https://www.marxists.org/archive/lenin/works/1906/may/20c.htm, accessed 10 November 2022.

Li Mingjiang (2020) The Belt and Road Initiative: geo-economics and Indo-Pacific security competition. *International Affairs*, 96(1), pp. 169–187, DOI:10/1093/ia/iiz240.

Los Angeles Times (2020) Dreams of a Red Emperor: The relentless rise of Xi Jinping. 22 October, https://www.latimes.com/world-nation/story/2020-10-22/china-xi-jinping-mao-zedong-communist-party, accessed 10 November 2022.

Los Angeles Times (2021) How China's Xi Jinping app went from pushing nationalism to scamming women. 23 June, https://www.latimes.com/world-nation/story/2021-06-23/china-study-xi-app-online-scam-romance, accessed 10 November 2022.

Lowy Institute (2021) The Growing Reach of China's Military, 9 August, https://www.lowyinstitute.org/publications/australia-and-growing-reach-china-s-military, accessed 10 November 2022.

Lun Tian Yew (2021) Unleashing reforms, Xi returns to China's socialist roots. *Reuters*, 9 September, https://www.reuters.com/article/china-regulation-xi-analysis-idUSKBN2G50FU, accessed 10 November 2022.

Lynch, Sarah (2021) Chinese prosecutor charged in alleged plot to intimidate citizens to return to China. *Reuters*, 24 July, https://www.reuters.com/world/china/chinese-prosecutor-charged-alleged-plot-intimidate-citizens-return-china-2021-07-22/, accessed 10 November 2022.

Mantesso, Sean (2021) China hits back as it faces growing criticism of its human rights record, treatment of Uyghurs. *ABC News*, 12 May, https://www.abc.net.au/news/2021-07-20/china-responds-to-western-criticism-of-human-rights-record/100295550, accessed 10 November 2022.

McCuaig-Johnston, Margaret (2021) We thought China could become more democratic: Instead, it is becoming totalitarian. *Ottawa Citizen*, 18 January, https://ottawacitizen.com/opinion/mccuaig-johnston-we-thought-china-could-become-more-democratic-instead-it-is-becoming-totalitarian, accessed 10 November 2022.

Mitter, Rana (2021a) China's Crucial Decade. *World Politics Review*, 29 June, https://www.worldpoliticsreview.com/articles/29768/in-china-ccp-leaders-face-a-crucial-decade, accessed 10 November 2022.

Mitter, Rana (2021b) The super-rich, 'sissy boys', celebs – all targets in Xi's bid to end cultural difference. *The Guardian*, 5 September, https://www.theguardian.com/commentisfree/2021/sep/05/super-rich-sissy-boys-celebs-all-targets-in-xis-bid-to-end-cultural-difference?CMP=Share_iOSApp_Other, accessed 10 November 2022.

Mizner, Carl (2020) *End of an Era: How China's Authoritarian Revival is Undermining Its Rise*. Oxford: Oxford University Press.

Moritz, Rudolf (2021) Xi Jinping Thought on the Rule of Law: New Substance in the Conflict of Systems with China. *SWP Comment*, 28 April, https://www.swp-berlin.org/publications/products/comments/2021C28_Jinping_RuleOfLaw.pdf, accessed 10 November 2022.

O'Farrell, Clare (2008) Foucault on Power and Resistance. *Refracted Input*, 3 December, https://clare-ofarrell.com/2008/12/03/foucault-quote-for-december-2008, accessed 10 November 2022.

Oi, Mariko (2024) Evergrande: Crisis-hit Chinese property giant ordered to liquidate. *BBC*, 29 January, https://www.bbc.com/news/business-67562522.amp, accessed 10 February 2024.

One Belt One Road Europe (2019) The 19th CPC National Congress and the 'Belt and Road Initiative', 25 October, http://www.oboreurope.com/en/19th-cpc-national-congress, accessed 10 November 2022.

Palmer, James (2020) How China Shaped the World in 2020, From Wuhan to Xinjiang. *Foreign Policy*, 23 December, https://foreignpolicy.com/2020/12/23/how-china-shaped-the-world-in-2020, accessed 10 November 2022.

Peerenboom, Randall (2015) Fly High the Banner of Socialist Rule of Law with Chinese Characteristics! What Does the 4th Plenum Decision Mean for Legal Reforms in China? *Hague J Rule Law*, 7, pp. 49–74, DOI:10.1007/s40803-015-0003-9.

Permanent Court of Arbitration (2016) The Republic of the Philippines vs The People's Republic of China. The Hague, July 12, https://pcacases.com/web/sendAttach/1801, accessed 10 November 2022.

Pils, Eva (2015) China, the Rule of Law, and the Question of Obedience: A Comment on Professor Peerenboom. *Hague Journal of Rule of Law*, 7, pp. 83–90.

Pils, Eva (2016) Rule of Law Reform and the Rise of Rule by Fear in China. Paper presented at the Law, Authoritarianism and Democracy in Asia Symposium, National University of Singapore, 12–13 December.

Pils, Eva (2017) *Human Rights in China: A Social Practice in the Shadows of Authoritarianism*, NYSE: Wiley.

Pils, Eva (2020) This flies in the face of the civil rights of Hong Kongers. *Mercator Institute for China Studies (MERICS)*, 27 November, https://merics.org/en/interview/eva-pils-flies-face-civil-rights-hong-kongers, accessed 10 November 2022.

Reuters World News (2017) China's Top Judge Warns Courts on Judicial Independence. 15 January, http://www.reuters.com/article/us-china-policy-law-idUSKBN14Z07B, accessed 10 November 2022.

Rose, Jonathan (2004) The Rule of Law in the Western World: An Overview. *Journal of Social Philosophy*, 35(4), pp. 457–470.

Safeguard Defenders (2021) New graphic report takes reader into the heart of China's hidden RSDL prisons. 21 June, https://safeguarddefenders.com/en/blog/new-graphic-report-takes-reader-heart-china-s-hidden-rsdl-prisons, accessed 10 November 2022.

Schuman, Michael (2020) What Happens When China Leads the World. *The Atlantic*, 5 October, https://www.theatlantic.com/international/archive/2020/10/what-kind-superpower-will-china-be/616580/, accessed 10 November 2022.

Solinger, Dorothy J. (2020) The State and Privatisation: The chase for cash and its whitewash. In: Kevin Latham (ed.) *Routledge Handbook of Chinese Culture and Society* (1st edition). London: Routledge.

Soros, George (2021) Investors in Xi's China face a rude awakening. *Financial Review*, 31 August, https://www.ft.com/content/ecf7de34-e595-4814-9cbd-4a5119187330, accessed 10 November 2022.

South China Morning Post (2021a) China calls for boycott of 'overly entertaining' entertainers and 'sissy idols' in continued purge of popular culture industry. 2 September, https://www.scmp.com/news/people-culture/china-personalities/article/3147354/china-calls-boycott-overly-entertaining, accessed 10 November 2022.

South China Morning Post (2021b) When will China overtake the US to become the world's biggest economy? 7 July, https://www.scmp.com/economy/china-economy/article/3140038/when-will-china-overtake-us-become-worlds-biggest-economy, accessed 10 November 2022.

Teon, Aris (2016) China's Legal System and The 'Ten Abominations'. *The Greater China Journal*, 11 May, https://china-journal.org/2016/05/11/china-legal-system-ten-abominations/, accessed 10 November 2022.

The Economist (2015) Military corruption. Rank and vile. 14 Februrary, http://glassyad.ir/magazine/economics_marketing/2015/February/The_Economist_-_14_February_2015.pdf, accessed 10 November 2022.

The Economist (2021) What China Wants: Essay on 'China's Future', https://www.economist.com/news/essays/21609649-china-becomes-again-worlds-largest-economy-it-wants-respect-it-enjoyed-centuries-past-it-does-not, accessed 18 August 2021.

The Conversation (2021) China: don't mistake Xi Jinping's crackdowns for a second Cultural Revolution. 20 September, https://theconversation.com/china-dont-mistake-xi-jinpings-crackdowns-for-a-second-cultural-revolution-167483, accessed 10 November 2022.

The Guardian (2021) 'Show no mercy': leaked documents reveal details of China's Xinjiang detentions. 17 November, https://www.theguardian.com/world/2019/nov/17/show-no-mercy-leaked-documents-reveal-details-of-chinas-mass-xinjiang-detentions, accessed 10 November 2022.

The Guardian (2021) China's Uyghurs living in a 'dystopian hellscape', says Amnesty report. 10 June, https://www.theguardian.com/global-development/2021/jun/10/china-uyghur-xinjiang-dystopian-hellscape-says-amnesty-international-report, accessed 10 November 2022.

The Kremlin (2022) Joint Statement of the Russian Federation and the People's Republic of China on the International Relations Entering a New Era and the Global Sustainable Developmen, 4 February, http://www.en.kremlin.ru/supplement/5770, accessed 10 November 2022.

The New York Times (2021) Lithuania vs. China: A Baltic Minnow Defies a Rising. 8 October, Superpower https://www.nytimes.com/2021/09/30/world/europe/lithuania-china-disputes.html, accessed 8 October 2022.

The Soufan Center (2020) China's Military-Civil Fusion Strategy, 13 August, https://thesoufancenter.org/intelbrief-chinas-military-civil-fusion-strategy/, accessed 10 November 2022.

The Strait Times (2016) As Chinese Communist Party's 'core' leader, Xi Jinping can shape power play. 28 October, https://www.straitstimes.com/asia/east-asia/as-chinese-communist-partys-core-leader-xi-jinping-can-shape-power-play, accessed 10 November 2022.

Washington Post (2021) A detainee says China has a secret jail in Dubai. China's repression may be spreading. 22 August, https://www.washingtonpost.com/opinions/2021/08/22/detainee-says-china-has-secret-jail-dubai-chinas-repression-may-be-spreading/, accessed 10 November 2022.

Wang Hairong (2016) Rule the Party With a Firm Hand. *Beijing Review*, (44), 3 November, http://www.bjreview.com/Current_Issue/Editor_Choice/201610/t20161030_800070457.html, accessed 10 November 2022.

Wen, Philip and John Garnaut (2015) Chinese police chase corruption suspects in Australian suburbs, The Sydney Morning Herald, 15 April, http://www.smh.com.au/world/chinese-police-chase-corruption-suspects-in-australian-suburbs-20150414-1mkwd2.html, accessed 10 November 2022.

World Uyghur Congress (2021) UN Rights Boss Signals She May Move on Xinjiang Without China Nod. *Reuters*, 25 June, https://www.uyghurcongress.org/en/un-rights-boss-signals-she-may-move-on-xinjiang-without-china-nod/, accessed 10 November 2022.

Xi Jinping (2013) An Explanation of the Chinese Communist Party Central Committee Decision on Several Major Questions about Deepening Reform. *Xinhuanet*, 15 November, http://news.xinhuanet.com/politics/2013-11/15/c_118164294.htm, accessed 10 November 2022.

Xi Jinping (2017a) *Secure a decisive Victory in Building a Moderately prosperous Society in All Respects and Strive for the Greatest Success of Socialism with Chinese Characteristics*. Delivered at the 19th National Congress of the Communist Party of China, 18 October, http://news.xinhuanet.com/english/special/2017-11/03/c_136725942.htm, accessed 10 November 2022.

Xi Jinping (2017b) Chinese President Xi Jinping delivers 2018 New Year speech. *China Plus*, 31 December, http://www.china.org.cn/china/2017-12/31/content_50181054.htm, accessed 10 November 2022.

Xi Jinping (2021a) Boao Forum for Asia Annual Conference 2021. *Xinhua*, 18 April, http://www.xinhuanet.com/english/cnleaders/2021Boao/BoaoForum.htm, accessed 10 November 2022.

Xi Jinping (2021b) Xi's speech at CPC centenary ceremony published in multiple languages, *CGTN*, July 20, https://news.cgtn.com/news/2021-07-20/Xi-s-speech-at-CPC-centenary-ceremony-published-in-multiple-languages-123EXzty1Ve/index.html#:~:text=In%20his%20speech%2C%20Xi%20reviewed%20the%20Party%27s%20success,a%20great%20modern%20socialist%20country%20in%20all%20respects, accessed 10 November 2022.

Xi Jinping (2021c) Xi Jinping: China welcomes closer 'Belt and Road' partnerships. *CGTN*, 23 June, https://news.cgtn.com/news/2021-06-23/Xi-Jinping-China-eyes-closer-Belt-and-Road-partnership-11kHYERzNew/index.html, accessed 10 November 2022.

Xi Jinping (August 2021d) Xi stresses promoting common prosperity amid high-quality development, forestalling major financial risks. *Xinhuanet*, 18 August, http://www.xinhuanet.com/english/2021-08/18/c_1310133051.htm, accessed 10 November 2022.

Xinhua (2016) The CPC Central Committee issues 'Regulations on Accountability of the Chinese Communist Party'. *Xinhua*, 17 July, http://news.xinhuanet.com/politics/2016-07/17/c_1119232150.htm, accessed 10 November 2022.

Xinhua (2017a) Inclusion of Xi's Thought Highlight of Amendment to CPC Constitution. *Xinhua*, 29 October, http://news.xinhuanet.com/english/2017-10/29/c_136713559.htm, accessed 10 November 2022.

Xinhua (2017b) Xi's military thinking, Party's "absolute" leadership over army written into CPC Constitution. 24 October, http://www.xinhuanet.com/english/2017-10/24/c_136702143.htm, accessed 10 November 2022.

Xinhua (2018) CPC proposes change on Chinese president's term in Constitution, 25 February, http://www.xinhuanet.com/english/2018-02/25/c_136998770.htm, accessed 10 November 2022.

Xinhua (2021) Xi Jinping zhuchi zhaokai zhongyang caijing weiyuanhui di shi ci huiyi qiangdiao zai gao zhiliang fazhan zhong cujin gongtong fuyu tongchou zuo hao zhongda jinrong fengxian fangfan huajie gongzuo Li Keqiang Wang Yang Wang Huning Han Zheng chuxi. 17 August, http://www.xinhuanet.com/politics/2021-08/17/c_1127770343.htm, accessed 10 November 2022.

Xu Xianming (2017) Rule of Law and Rule by Virtue. *China Human Rights Magazine*, 10 July, http://www.chinahumanrights.org/html/2017/MAGAZINES_0710/8564.html, accessed 10 November 2022.

Yang, Samuel (2021) Alibaba's Jack Ma disappeared for months, but mystery remains over the Chinese billionaire's whereabouts. *ABC News*, 29 January, https://www.abc.net.au/news/2021-01-29/china-jack-ma-reappeared-amid-alibaba-ant-group-investigation/13098016, accessed 10 November 2022.

Yoshihara Toshi and Jack Bianchi (2020) *Uncovering China's Influence in Europe: How Friendship Groups Coopt European Elites*. Washington DC: Center for Strategic and Budgetary Assesments.

Zang Xiaowei (2015) *Understanding Chinese Society* (2nd ed). Routledge: London.

Zhang Xiaodan (2017) Rule of Law within the Chinese Party-State and its Recent Tendencies. *Hague Journal on the Rule of Law*, 9(2), pp. 373–400. DOI: 10.1007/s40803-017-005-3.

Zhang Yupu (2019) Three Aspects of Xi Jinping's Thoughts on Socialism with Chinese Characteristics in the New Era. *Atlantis Press,* Advances in Social Science, Education and Humanities Research, 415, pp. 174–176, 5th International Symposium on Social Science.

Zhao Kejin (2019) The China Model of Public Diplomacy and its Future. *The Hague Journal of Diplomacy*, 22 April, https://brill.com/view/journals/hjd/14/1-2/article-p169_12.xml?rskey=OlMGKv&result=1, accessed 10 November 2022.

Zhou, Christina (2020) China's Communist Party is at a fatal age for one-party regimes. How much longer can it survive? *ABC News*, 5 January, https://www.abc.net.au/news/2020-01-05/chinas-communist-party-is-at-a-fatal-age-for-one-party-regimes/11807138, accessed 10 November 2022.

Zhu, Eric and Tom Orlik (2021) When Will China Rule the World? Maybe Never: The Communist Party wants the world to see China's continued rise as inevitable. In reality, it's anything but. *Bloomberg*, 6 July, https://www.bloomberg.com/news/audio/2021-07-08/china-surpassing-america-s-economy-isn-t-a-sure-thing-podcast, accessed 10 November 2022.

CHAPTER 4

Is There a Xi Style of Politics?

Change and Continuity Since 2012

Kerry Brown

1   Introduction

As the Xi Jinping era in Chinese politics, which began with his appointment as Party Secretary of the Communist Party of China (CPC) has continued, so too has the claim that in some ways his rule represents something different from the past in modern Chinese politics. He is, in the words for instance of former US President Barack Obama, someone who consolidated power as quickly as one of his predecessors, Deng Xiaoping in the late 1970s (Beattie, 2014). According to the *Economist* magazine in October 2017, Xi Jinping was the world's 'most powerful man' (Economist, 2017). This is supplemented by the language that Xi himself uses. In his epic report to the 19th Party Congress on 18 October 2017, he declared that under his leadership China was entering a 'new era'. The confidence of this long oration (almost three and a half hours) was palpable. 'We,' he declared, 'the Chinese people, have greater confidence' (Xi, 2020: 4). He went on 'Our country's underlying values hold greater appeal than ever before, and the wave of positive energy felt throughout society is building.' China, in this context, was well on the way to achieving the 'Chinese Dream' he had talked about a lot in the previous few years.

There are specific areas where the Xi era is different from what has gone before. These will be spelled out later. But in many ways, the lines of continuity between Xi and his predecessors is also striking. This is not a leadership that could be seen as fundamentally breaking the mould of Chinese politics in the way that, for instance, the group around Deng Xiaoping did in the years from 1978. In many ways, Xi is a fundamentally conservative leader. He has espoused a traditional view of the role of the Party, its leadership function, and, more strikingly, the importance of standing fast beside what he himself calls 'traditional Chinese values.' The overarching narratives that his leadership operates in, the fundamental goals it has set himself, while adapted from the immediate past, do not radically break from that. In many ways, Xi's style of power can be seen as a natural development from the situation in which the country finds itself after almost four decades of fast economic growth and material enrichment. His has also been an opportunistic leadership in terms of how it deploys new technologies. But the fundamental strategic objective – to make one party rule sustainable – has not changed from the Mao era.

2   Fundamental Continuities – The Context of Xi's Rise

One of the great mysteries of modern Chinese politics is precisely how Xi rose to be the preeminent leader. A glance back for instance at Cheng Li's assessment of the so called emerging fourth generation of leaders around Hu Jintao in 2001 mentions Xi amongst a range of other leaders as someone who typified the 'taizi' (princeling) faction, then very much out of fashion. Alongside a similar product of the elite political class, Bo Xilai, whose father had also been a high-ranking figure in the Maoist and post-Maoist era, it was noted that Xi had gained the lowest number of votes during an election for membership of the Central Committee of the CPC. This was one of the occasions in which there were more candidates than positions. He had been in good company: Wang Qishan, Deng Pufang (the son of Deng Xiaoping), and Bo were also defeated. This was, as Cheng said, 'the strongest evidence to the opposition to nepotism' (Li, 2001: 165). Five years later, Willy Wo-Lap Lam concurred with this assessment that princelings, as they were called, were still regarded dimly. In his book issued in 2006 in the Hu era, Xi merited only two, brief mentions. One of these remarked that Xi was 'sometimes rated as the most capable and popular of the princelings.' Even so, Lam only saw a Vice Premier position for him in the future (Lam, 2006: 29).

Despite this, Xi's subsequent ascent from 2007 can only be described as meteoric. Whatever the issues with those who were deemed to have an elite background, Xi seems to have surmounted them. With Bo Xilai, he was one of the stars of the 2007 to 2012 period. He was allowed the opportunity to build a case for his eventually being granted that rarest of things in modern Chinese politics – a relatively smooth leadership transition, and, more importantly, the gifting of the main levers of power almost immediately after he came to office in November 2012 – meaning that he was made head of the Party, and, unlike Hu who had had to wait two years for this, directorship of the Central Military Commission, putting him in charge of army affairs.

It is clear at least that an extensive consultation process took place from 2007 to 2012 and Xi's final appointment. I have outlined this in a little detail in *CEO China: The Rise of Xi Jinping* (Brown, 2016). Just who was consulted and how remain largely mysteries. It is one thing to have a list of names and a debate about the merits of each of them, and another to be presented with one name and asked what your feelings might be about this person. What is clear is that amongst the political super-elite, which included former members of the Politburo, and active leaders like Hu and his premier Wen Jiabao in 2012, support for Xi outweighed that for anyone else. Whether this was a full-hearted posture, or simply a case of Xi not being that great, but the rest being even more problematic, it is hard to say. The CPC had become even better at guarding its secrets, and as of 2021 and the time of writing, nothing new has emerged about exactly why Xi came out on top the way he did.

In addition to this, however, Xi was to enjoy two pieces of good fortune. The first was the nature of the leadership he replaced. The Hu style is now best defined as one of egolessness. At the time, critics castigated it as 'wu wei' – the time of 'doing nothing.' Despite the country getting more and more wealthy (a crucial issue which we will come back to a bit later) it seemed that domestically and internationally Hu did little with the new kinds of powers this economic might granted the country. Explosions of unrest in Tibet in 2008, Xinjiang in 2009 and even Inner Mongolia in 2011 were the more dramatic events that showed a shaky grasp on affairs. But almost daily, there were cases of social disturbance, reaching, according to one researcher at the Chinese Academy of Social Science Yu Jianrong, to over 200,000 by 2010. The country seemed beset by ferment. Xi himself in statements he had made while Party Secretary of Zhejiang from 2002 to 2007 had noted in his fast growing and wealthy province that officials more often than not looked like businesspeople. Many of them became associated with high corruption claims. Everyone seemed on the take. The Party was unable to discipline its own, so how could it demand much of others? Hu's largely silent, expressionless persona meant that while vast events were happening, there was no leadership there to craft a narrative that reached out to the public and made them feel they were part of a story. Hu's main ideological phrase, 'Scientific Development', was cold, technocratic sounding, and only highlighted something that Xi himself, in articles in the Party theoretical magazine *Seeking Truth* pointed out – a huge gap between public discourse and that of politicians. Despite this, Hu's evident commitment to process, the utter lack of anything resembling a cult of personality, and the insistence on making sure the transition happened in an orderly way meant that Xi did not have to contend with an immediate predecessor that was inclined to outstay their welcome and continue to interfere. Hu's almost complete invisibility since this November 2012 transition just underlines that this was very much part of the character and the wishes of the person.

On top of this, Xi also had good fortune in his most pressing fellow contenders. Of these, the charismatic Bo Xilai is the most striking case. Bo had used his leadership of Chongqing, the huge city-province in the southwest of the country since 2007 to advertise and lobby for policies he was instigating. These were decidedly populist. They included affordable housing, and a clampdown on local mafia and corruption. On top of this, there were public propaganda campaigns – the 'sing red', where Maoist era songs and phrases were used in public, and the city used new technology to text daily patriotic phrases to citizens. Bo clearly had his sight on higher things, despite only being in the full 25 strong Politburo rather than the 9 strong Standing Committee on which Xi sat. From a clear blue sky, however, calamity struck him in late 2011 when his wife was associated with the death of a British businessman Neil Haywood. The situation spiralled out of control in February the following year when Wang Lijun, the city Head of Police, fled to the American Consulate in neighbouring Chengdu with explosive claims that Bo had been implicated in the murder, and was also associated with widespread corruption and venality. Bo was felled a month later. His wife was given a suspended death sentence later that year, and Bo himself was indited for corruption a year later, expelled from the Party and given a lengthy prison sentence.

Once more, it is impossible to be sure in which ways Bo's case was manipulated and manufactured, and how it was truly a case of his culpability. It may have been a combination of the two. What is sure is that Xi came out the undisputed political winner. His most formidable potential opponent was eliminated. Had this not happened, it is interesting to speculate just how things might have proceeded from 2012, and just how smooth Xi's progress would have been. The overlap between some of Bo's policies and that of the Xi era is striking. All one can say is that in coming to power, Xi enjoyed what the Canadian Michael Ignatieff in his searing account of politics, *Fear and Ashes*, called the most crucial thing of all for success – good fortune (Ignatieff, 2013).

3   Two Pillars – The Story and the Wealth

That Hu Jintao was a poor storyteller did not mean there wasn't a story that needed to be told. That was the fundamental problem with his era in office. There clearly was a huge story. It was one Chinese people along with the rest of the world were watching sometimes in amazement. Much of this Xi's leadership inherited. It put new structures and some new stylistic elements to this, but the fundamental ingredients that Xi inherited in 2012 were already well set in.

The first of these is the easiest to quantify. It can be put very simply. Since entry to the World Trade Organisation in 2001, around the time that Hu himself was preparing to take over as Party leader the next year, the country entered a period of economic growth and productivity such as no society has ever seen on such a scale and at such speed in human history. In the following decade, despite the Global Financial Crisis of 2008–9, China's economy quadrupled in size.

In essence, for all the complexities about the rise of Xi, there is one very prosaic reason why China in 2012 could afford a more confident, ambitious style of leadership – and that was because it was four times wealthier than at the time of the previous leadership transition. Xi inherited this situation. It was the Hu leadership that had built up such huge financial and economic reserves. Since then, the Xi era has been far less successful economically than the Hu one. This is unsurprising. Maintaining such rapid growth was never sustainable. Even so, it meant that Xi's inheritance was a powerful one. He was handed the material basis to do things that no previous leader in modern Chinese history ever had. Deng and to some extent Jiang and Hu, all had to continue to simply produce growth no matter what, because of the extent of poverty their societies still had, and the general levels of backwardness. For Xi, he can be seen as the first leader since the early 1980s who has been able to look beyond simply pumping out GDP growth. His China is therefore not like that of his predecessors. It is not a straightforward developing society, but partially developed. This is best symbolised by the announcement in 2021 that absolute poverty had been eliminated in the country – a remarkable things in view of the situation in 1949 where infant mortality meant the average age people lived to was in their 30s, and where levels of literacy, nutrition, access to clean water and education were amongst the lowest in the world.

That this situation in 2012 can be described economically as radically different to a decade before does not mean therefore that Xi was able to devise a wholly new kind of politics. What is striking is that even though the chief target of the Deng era from 1978 onwards of making economic productivity the key benchmark of success has migrated to more complex, varied outcomes more suitable for a developed rather than a developing country, the overall narrative politically has remained the same. Like his predecessors, Xi is principally a nationalist. He speaks of socialism with Chinese characteristics just as Deng did. He also used the language of creating a great, powerful country, absolutely in line with Mao Zedong's principles. The 'rejuvenation of the Chinese nation', a phrase that has become one of the key slogans of the Xi era and can be seen plastered across notice boards throughout the country, is nothing new – the only difference is that today that rejuvenation and the emotions that it gives rise to are far more tangible and present. China does not hope, as it did in the Mao and Deng eras, to be great again – it is able to show this greatness through the huge size of its economy, the construction of a modern hard infrastructure system across the country (more high speed railways, for instance, than the rest of the world put together, and built in little over a decade), and the fact that in vessel numbers at least it has more ships than the US. Through outward investment and people movement, and the rankings of its universities, China is a major power now. This is manifested in obvious ways, but also in less overt ones – the fact, for instance, that it now consumes the foreign policy attentions of the US is an indirect compliment that China matters. The US does not waste time on non-entities!

The fundamental narrative of the Xi era therefore – of the Party's role in carrying the country forward to fulfil its historic mission to be great and wealthy – are longstanding, and structural. They can be found in the language of Mao, Deng, Jiang, and Hu. These are not innovations. The new element is the economic and geopolitical situation China finds itself in. And while Xi has clearly committed to a more complex view of reform, the general guiding lines of that reformist philosophy – acceptance of a hybrid state-non state model, where the former continues to enjoy a privileged position – have also not changed from the Deng era. Where Deng Xiaoping supported a hugely contested shift from the Maoist preoccupations with class struggle, and the delivery of Utopian social ends through mass campaigns like the Cultural Revolution, towards the acceptance of foreign capital, entrepreneurialism, and a free market to some extent, these sorts of things may be adapted in the Xi era, but they continue. There is no radical disruption or anything in this area that can be seen as a paradigm change. Politically, and economically, Xi has been a conservative leader, not a radical one.

4   Where Is the Ideology? Xi Jinping Thought

When Xi Jinping Thought was written into the State Constitution in March 2018, and time limits for the presidency were removed, many took this as a sign of how Xi was becoming a new kind of autocrat. Not since 1945, in the era before the Party had even come to power, had a person's 'Thought' been put in the Constitution. And this was the guiding ideas of Mao, which had been evolving during twenty years of struggle and fighting to survive for the Party. Xi Jinping Thought had only emerged around 2015. In three years, therefore, it had seemingly risen to the same exalted status as the ideology of the founder, Mao.

Attending to the content of Xi Thought however can prove frustrating. It may well define a practical approach to governance. But it is hard to divine any real ideological content within it. Mao had at least his work on the principle of contradictions, the validity of looking to peasants as a source of revolutionary change rather than city-based proletariat, and the tactics of guerrilla warfare where he had proved a hugely successful innovator. In essence, Mao and his fellow ideologues had achieved the sinification of what was meant to be a universal creed, Marxism-Leninism (Saich, 2021).

For Xi, the only overlap with the former ideology is in the stress on practical actions and resisting over-theorising. In fact, for Xi's three volumes of writings officially published since 2013, they are almost exclusively focussed on practice – the art, as the titles declare 'of governance'. There are no extensive discussions of theoretical issues, even in a Marxist framework. The Xi words, as evinced in this collection, are Confucian in their focus purely on guidance to action, not to trying to address more abstract issues like why humans behave as they do, and what the fundamental principles of political life in China might be.

This can be most easily traced in the genesis of Xi Thought, the Four Comprehensives. These were issued by Xi in December 2014. They were to 'comprehensively build a moderately prosperous society, comprehensively deepen reform, comprehensively implement the rule of law, and comprehensively strengthen Party discipline' (Xinhua, 2015). The emphasis on actionable outcomes has been pursued through the Xi era subsequently. All of these can be seen as simply continuing to construct on what had already been put in place. Building a moderately prosperous society, the first, was a stated aim of the Hu and Wen leadership from the mid-2000s, when they saw that by the end of the following decade, the majority of Chinese would be living in cities, and working more in services than in manufacturing or agriculture. Projections of economic growth showed that the country was heading for middle-income status, with per capita GDP of around USD 13,000 by 2020. This indeed has come to pass. Deepening reform, the second, is so general and wide ranging as to be close to meaningless. In effect, it simply restates a commitment to the Dengist reforms that had started four decades before. This was a highly uncontroversial statement of intent. After all, which contemporary Chinese leader would not want reform? The key thing was to make sure that this was simply the right kind, confined largely to the economic realm, rather than spilling into the more political one – an orthodoxy Xi has abided by. The third, implementing the rule of law, was at least a little more focussed. As shown during the Third Plenum of the 18th Party Congress held in 2013, with its long final statement and explanatory note issued in Xi's name, building a more predictable legal system, and one with more credibility and impact, was a key means of appealing to the emerging middle class. They were the key group in Xi's China, the people who were working in the new cities in emerging industries, graduating from China's many new universities. They were property owners, and often worked in business. Commercial and property law therefore saw attention and support. But the fact that this was not 'rule by law' was politically significant. In criminal areas of law, it was still perfectly possible to be accused of crimes which were regarded as clearly ones of political belief or conscience in North America or Europe. Ensuring that while the law was strengthened and its implementation improved, there was no chance of this then morphing into a tool by which the Party's opponents might attack it was critical. Seeing as the Deng era had seen the wholesale construction of a Chinese legal system from scratch, this Xi-era move was therefore nowhere near as dramatic. Nor did it contradict in any way what had gone before, or radically change things. Its aim was to simply improve.

5 Xi Thought in Practice: Party Building and Party Discipline

If there was a significant shift ushered in by the 'Four Comprehensives' it was in the fourth, and final one: improving party discipline. Here too, there was nothing radical or wholly unexpected. Party discipline has been part of the whole culture of the CPC since its earliest years in existence. Under Mao, in the 1940s during the years of internal exile in Yan'an, there had been campaigns like that of the 'Rescue Movement' around 1943 which sought to purge the Party of what were regarded as unhealthy influences from the Soviet Union or from other factions domestically. These are expertly catalogued by the late Chinese historian Gao Hua, who described in his epic history the ways in which rectification and internal cleansing of cadres became a key means of ensuring that the organisation remained focussed and incorrupt (Hua, 2019).

Rectification campaigns continued after the CPC came to power in 1949. On one level, the Cultural Revolution from 1966 was a series of purges of party elites. Slightly earlier than this, Xi's own father, Xi Zhongxun, had been felled by a smaller such campaign at the start of the 1960s, and removed from power. This was one reason why Xi himself was sent down to the countryside in 1969, because of what was regarded as his bad class background. His years in rural China were to have a dramatic impact on his world view and have been experiences he himself, or party propagandists, have referred to since he came to prominence. As reforms opened up the Chinese economy, and growth accelerated, however, such widescale and systematic clampdowns on cadres became less systemic and more piecemeal. By the Hu era, there was an intensifying sense that in some ways the CPC had lost control of its own foot soldiers. Corruption increased rapidly (Wedeman, 2012). The boundaries between business and politics became blurred, with a widescale and deep collusion between the two, despite regulations in place demanding this did not happen.

Xi was clearly aware of this, and unusually vocal about it, even when only a provincial Party Secretary in Zhejiang from 2002 to 2007. In a series of short essays issued in 2007 in Chinese written by Xi, or on behalf of him, over this period, one of the main topics was the deterioration of cadre ethical standards. High level officials were unwilling to demand good standards of conduct from those under them, or themselves. They just wanted to be 'good mates' with everyone. They were constantly on the take (Brown, forthcoming). The betrayal of their vocation to govern meant that the Party corporately was regarded with little real trust or approval in society generally. The disciplined politicians of the Mao era were now a self-serving, capitalist-looking travesty.

This may well have been a shrewd tactical move by Xi to adopt such a high-minded and often almost moralizing tone during the years of true excess when China's economy was booming. Perhaps he was simply ensuring that he was not regarded as just another member of the princeling elite who was looking after their own family networks and making the Party increasingly into a narrow business concern. When Xi came to power, he referred on the 15th November 2012 in his brief statement issued that day to how the CPC needed to close the gap between it and the public. By 2013, it was already clear how this was going to happen. Under Wang Qishan, a colleague who in 1997 had also failed to get elected to the Central Committee, but who was now regarded as one of the country's most effective politicians, the Central Commission for Discipline Inspection (CCDI), the Party's anti-graft body, launched a struggle that, in terms of intensity, range and depth, was unlike any since the Mao era.

While ostensibly aimed at those accused of misappropriation of state funds, the campaign which continues to this day and has become an almost continuous part of Xi's style of rule, was connected to a concerted effort to train cadres in ideology, to ensure that they understood where their loyalty lay, and to make sure that they were absolutely committed to the CPC's larger mission. That was not to make China rich. It was to have a far larger strategic aim beyond this – to ensure that the country could be rejuvenated, made powerful, and do so under a sustainable, one-party system. Only the Party, Xi stated, could save China. But first, through this process of purging, disciplining and refining its internal culture, it had to save itself. Otherwise, it would simply grow bloated, incompetent, and lose its mandate to rule.

Party building campaigns, heavy doses of party ideological training, the assertion of very strict lines for party messaging and communication, and the taking down even of the highest-level officials if they were connected to corruption, or suspected of being disloyal, are all core features of the Xi era in ways which was not so from the time of Deng onwards. Again, we have to see this in a broader context. The Xi campaigns on the Party are a product of its success over the last few decades in creating a vibrantly marketized, capitalist looking and diverse society – but one that existed under a Communist Party with a monopoly on power. To continue this grand experiment, the Party could not afford to simply sleepwalk into irrelevance, with cadres who were quasi businesspeople and had no political discipline to guide them and save them from temptation. On top of this, Xi's anti-corruption struggle and party ethos all deployed methods that harked back to the Mao era. They just looked different because of the transformed nature of China itself as a country and economy. What they did show clearly to anyone who concentrated on them was the anomaly of how much, within all this change, and Party itself in its structure, the highly hierarchical nature of its leadership, the focus on one key charismatic leader as a strategic resource to convey core Party messages, the CPC had remained unchanged. Xi was proving that he was certainly not in the business of trying to change this situation.

6 Xi-ism and the State's New Capacity

What Xi has had since 2012 however is greatly enhanced state capacity. This is because of technology. If he and his brand of politics is different to any of his predecessors it is not in terms of ideology, or political reform, or even the overarching framework within which policy has been articulated and directed. The great difference is in the rapidly evolving suite of technology that means he is perhaps the first Chinese, and globally largest, techno-autocrat. In the Xi era, the Internet has allowed penetration into the private lives of citizens in ways which would have been unimaginable even in the very invasive Maoist era. Then, the main surveillance work was undertaken by neighbourhood committees. It was extensive but very hit and miss, reliant on imperfect human intelligence (Schoenhals, 2012).

In 21st century China, the vast take up of mobile phones and social media from Weibo to Weixin (WeChat), along with companies like Alibaba and Tencent, specialising in digital services, mean that practically all adults have a digital presence. Through this, the Party knows much about what they like to buy, what websites interest them, what their sentiments are. It can even use this resource, as it did during the anti-corruption struggle, to recruit members of the public to inform on others, or give it information it requires. This has allowed some public service provision to be greatly improved (as it has elsewhere). But unlike with the European Union, as an example, there is almost no proper data protection in the country. On the grounds of security, particularly with the passing of an extensive National Intelligence Law in 2017, state entities can request on the grounds of safeguarding the nation's interest practically anything they feel is important. The parameters of this and other similar laws are immensely broad. Alibaba with its treasure trove of commercial information, therefore, is an open book for the party-state should it chose to demand anything that the company has. The company has no grounds to deny access. The same goes for even foreign enterprises with operations in China. Xi has even reinforced this with the notion of Internet sovereignty – an idea as firm as that applied to physical territory, with notions of non-interference by outsiders and the right to protect one's own space.

Artificial intelligence, and big data mining, have become areas of rapid technological expansion. In the 14th Five-Year Plan passed at the National People's Congress parliament in March 2021, 7 per cent of GDP was committed to research and development. This is to accelerate the process of the country becoming more autonomous in terms of technology, rather than continuing to rely on the US and others. The turbulence of the period after 2017 and the election of Donald Trump as US president speeded up this long-held desire. Once in technology deficit with Europe and others, China is now becoming a world leader in some areas of technology. Many of these have purely commercial use. But some have definite security and political utility. Technology was one of the enablers of the Social Credit Score system, discussed since 2015. A vast and ambitious idea to give everyone in the country a complex range of assessments from their financial to their civic behaviour, as of 2021 its implementation has remained patchy, despite much excited commentary outside of China (Ding and Zhong, 2021). Regardless of this, that such an idea, involving immense data gathering for hundreds of millions of people, is even possible to contemplate shows just how far technology had advanced, and its potential for a political system like that of the PRC under Xi.

The CPC justifies use of anything which can support its grand strategic aims. This means that not exploiting capacity that new technology offers is impossible. The real problems of a unconstrained usage because of political objectives which are all encompassing can be shown in the use of mass surveillance, from face recognition, to a gridlock security system, deployed in the Xinjiang region from 2015. With satellite evidence, and the testament of those who had left the region to move abroad, from 2017 credible reports of the construction of large centres where people were being detained was broadcast outside of China. Increasingly, claims were made about these being concentration camps. The Chinese government when it did release information argued that they were in fact reeducation centres. They stated that in any case by 2021 most of those originally accommodated in the centres had gone back to their homes. Despite this, it was clear that a gigantic experiment in pre-emptive security, at least of the Chinese government, had been undertaken. This had only been possible because of the new and ubiquitous technology the government had at its hands, with telecoms in particular proving important in tracking and controlling people movement.

The Chinese government's argument, vehemently delivered from 2018, was that Xinjiang separatists offered a significant security threat to the country, and the rest of the world, and needed to be dealt with as comprehensively as possible. Xi himself deployed the term 'the Three Evils' to embrace religious extremism, terrorism and separatism. Having observed the American led War on Terror from 2001, the Beijing administration felt it was within its rights to act the way it had. Critics argued that the terrorist incidents in China, from the Kunming railway attack in 2014 to the self-detonated bomb in Tiananmen Square a year later, were not on the scale of the September 11th 2001 terrorist attacks in the US. What is clear is that technology has given state capacity to undertake campaigns that were simply not possible in the past. The Chinese government has none of the ethical or legal restraints that the US and others needed to observe. Nor did it need to deal at least domestically with any significant critics, either in the media or in the public sphere. The long term impact of what it did over 2017 into the 2020s in Xinjiang however is hard to predict. It has clearly created a vast amount of resentment and anger at the many well documented rights abuses and injustices committed during this sweeping campaign. Xinjiang has also been the greatest problem for China's international image, with many labelling the events there as genocide. The Xi leadership in public statements did not recognise any problems or mistakes. Only time will tell if the costs they have had to bear in order to do what they have done were ultimately worthwhile.

7 Xi Politics: Ambitious, and Conservative

Xi politics is conveyed in a highly ambitious and aspirational language. The 'China Dream', a common destiny for mankind, and a 'new era' or 'national rejuvenation' are key buzzwords. The lengthy speech Xi made at the 19th Party Congress in October 2017 was an astonishing manifesto of the many things that the government was promising – better healthcare, better social welfare, better environmental conditions, better quality of life. A Maoist air of Utopianism came through the final third of this speech, even though Xi speaks with the great advantage that many of the things being promised are indeed already in sight.

There are parts of the Xi vision that are fresh. A concerted commitment to environmentalism is one. Xi since his time in Zhejiang at least has recognised that climate change brought about by human activity is not a problem for others, but a specific and important issue for China itself. This area is one where co-operation with the US and others despite all the problems caused by the China-originated COVID-19 pandemic looks positive and hopeful. Because of its size and importance, this is also an area where China is a necessary partner if any solution is to be found. That Xi is so committed to this is good news for China, and the rest of the world.

Xi is talked of often in terms of someone who has accrued power for almost personal reasons. He is, as one commentator labelled him, the Chairman of everything, head of almost all the main power levels in China. His image and his words are ubiquitous. This seems like a cult of personality along the lines that Mao constructed in the latter part of his life. In discussions of Xi's power, the context in terms of what his predecessors gave him to work with, and the ways in which so many of the issues his administration have addressed have been ones where there is a party corporate view which predated his time in power, and which relate to the Party's fortunes and mission rather than to him and any individual interests he might have. There is also the contribution that new and powerful technologies have made to the governance of China. Once these things are taken into account, the real heart of Xi's political programme looks very conservative, and largely focussed on maintaining the status quo. He is certainly not a radical reformist in the way that, for instance, one might argue Deng Xiaoping was. He largely works in the Dengist paradigm. Xi is a nationalist, much like Mao (and all other subsequent leaders). He is a populist too, like Mao. His key group is the rising middle class, to who the language of aspiration, more responsive party administration, legal reform to protect property and commercial rights, and national greatness and security are aimed. In that sense, despite being a communist leader, his vanguard is not the working class or the proletariat, but, ironically, the bourgeoisie.

That bourgeoisie are inherently risk averse and conservative. They have absorbed a memory, through their parents and grandparents, and through what narratives of history they have been taught at school and elsewhere in the country, or a modern history which was one of huge conflict and vulnerability for their country. They also understand that even under the Communists, until very recently, there has been widespread poverty, famine and instability. That Xi presides over a country that looks confident, stable and finally immune to the horrors of the past is therefore a huge selling point to them. It is hard to assess what appetite for political reform there might be in China. But it is safe to say that there is little appetite for attempting anything that might lead to the sort of economic and social costs the Russian's paid after the collapse of their communist system in the 1990s. The idealisation of Western democratic models has eroded since the great financial crisis of 2008, and then the rise of Trump, and the debacle in Afghanistan after American withdrawal in 2021. The Chinese middle class may not be starry eyed about their own system. But as they learned in the COVID-19 pandemic, nor can they look to the governance models of others to give them easy solutions. For Xi, therefore, the insistence remains that China needs to find its own way – and that aping foreign models is not a viable option. Since 2017, with the Trump style of chaotic leadership, and his own refusal to accept the outcome of the 2020 presidential election, encouraging an astonishing attack on Capitol Hill in Washington DC, even American democracy, once regarded as the golden standard, is no longer attractive to many Chinese. It is hard to see young Chinese erect a 'Goddess of Democracy' admiring of foreign models as they did in 1989 during the widescale protests that year.

Despite this, Xi's leadership is different because of its focus on being complete and comprehensive. It is attempting something that may well end up being radical and revolutionary – making one party rule sustainable. The USSR failed to do this, when it collapsed after 74 years in existence in 1991. The CPC will cross the 74 year benchmark in 2023. In some ways, this will be an even more meaningful anniversary that the hundredth one of the CPC's foundation held in July 2021. Historians have observed that the CPC's early years were often ones of deep financial and political dependence on the USSR, where the Communist Party there was already in power from 1917. But under Mao, the sinificaition of Marxism-Leninism meant that it started to define its own brand of communism, shaped by local conditions. Today, this continues through the simple fact that the PRC, amongst the world's major economies, is the only one that practices one party rule under a Marxist-Leninist framework. That it may well do so sometime in the middle of the next decade as the world's largest economy means it is even more of an outlier. In that sense, Xi will have contributed to the shattering of one of the main intellectual and ideological convictions of the modern world – that to be an effective and powerful developed country one has to also be a democracy. The PRC is well on the way to proving that this is not necessarily the case. In this, the odds are that it will succeed, and the world will have to change to accommodate this fact, rather than the other way around.

References

Beattie, Victor (2014) President Obama 'Impressed' by 'Clout' of China's Leader. *Voice of America*, 4 December, https://www.voanews.com/usa/president-obama-impressed-clout-chinas-leader, accessed 5 October 2021.

Brown, Kerry (2016) CEO *China: The Rise of Xi Jinping*. London and New York: I.B. Tauris.

Brown, Kerry (forthcoming) *Xi: A Study in Power*. London: Ikon Books.

Ding Xiaodong and Dale Yuhao Zhong (2021) Rethinking China's Social Credit System: A Long Road to Establishing Trust in Chinese Society. *Journal of Contemporary China*, 30(130), pp. 630–644. DOI: 10.1080/10670564.2020.1852738.

Economist (2017) Xi Jinping has more clout than Donald Trump. The world should be wary. *Economist website*, 14 October, https://www.economist.com/leaders/2017/10/14/xi-jinping-has-more-clout-than-donald-trump-the-world-should-be-wary, accessed 5 October 2021.

Hua, Gao (2019) *How the Red Sun Rose: The Origin and Development of the Yan'an Rectification Movement 1930–1945*. Translated by Stacey Mosher and Guo Jian. Hong Kong: The Chinese University of Hong Kong Press.

Ignatieff, Michael (2013) *Fear and Ashes: Success and Failure in Politics*. Cambridge, Mass.: Harvard University Press.

Lam, Willy Wo-Lap (2006) *Chinese Politics in the Hu Jintao Era: New Leaders, New Challenges*. Armonk and London: M.E. Sharpe.

Li, Cheng (2001) *China's Leaders: The New Generation*. New York and London: Rowman and Littlefield Publishers.

Saich, Anthony (2021) *From Rebel to Ruler: One Hundred Years of the Chinese Communist Party*. Cambridge, Mass.: Harvard University Press.

Schoenhals, Michael (2012) *Spying for the People: Mao's Secret Agents, 1949–1967*. Cambridge: Cambridge University Press.

Wedeman, Andrew (2012) *Double Paradox: Rapid Growth and Rising Corruption in China*. New York: Cornell University Press.

Xi Jinping (2020) *The governance of China, Volume Three*. Beijing: Foreign Languages Press.

Xinhua (2015) President Xi Jinping's "Four Comprehensives" – a strategic blueprint for China. *Website of Foreign Mission of People's Republic of China to the United Nations and Other International Organisations in Vienna*, 26 February, https://www.fmprc.gov.cn/ce/cgvienna/eng/zgbd/t1240817.htm, accessed 5 October 2021.

CHAPTER 5

When Chinese Communist Party (CCP) Meets the Pandemic
An Authoritarian Resilience?

Yung-Yung Chang

1   Introduction

> COVID-19 will turn the democratic recession into a depression, with authoritarianism sweeping across the globe like a pandemic.
> FREY et al., 2020

Many commentaries state that COVID-19 hit the world at a time when democracy was already under threat in many places, and "it risks exacerbating democratic backsliding and authoritarian consolidation" (Ang, 2020; Brown et al., 2020: 1; Pils, 2020; Schmemann, 2020).

The outbreak of the pandemic has often been attributed to the failure of the Chinese political system – namely, authoritarianism (or some may even consider totalitarianism)[1] – mainly due to its lack of transparency and "a culture of secrecy and rigidly centralized (but by no means always functional) command structure" that delayed the determinant actions or measures to stop the outbreak of COVID-19 before it expanded across China and the world (Ang, 2020; Pils, 2020: 1). In this regard, many claim that dictatorships are vulnerable to epidemics and other disasters (Doyle and Zhang, 2011; Gladstein, 2020; Walt, 2020). The main reasons for this are that an authoritarian regime tends to conceal information, that top officials do not realize how serious the situation is until it is too late to introduce effective preventative measures, and that this can only lead to the exacerbation and spread of disease. In brief, people are not allowed to sound the alarm, and would be punished for doing so. The system is relatively fragmented and rigid, not only lacking the participation of civil society but also placing too much emphasis on upward accountability

---

1 For more details concerning the definition and difference between totalitarianism and authoritarianism, please refer to the part 'conceptualization and framework' (3.3.1) later in the chapter.

and performance-based legitimacy (Huang, 2004). Government officials are not accountable to the public but to their higher authorities, and local government performance is mainly measured by tangible assessment of economic development and growth.

However, as the pandemic has spread to other continents, China has created the impression that, as an authoritarian country, it has performed better than many Western democracies in combating the health crisis. From this perspective, China's "handling of the pandemic has been a global model teaching us that China's governance system is better suited to deal with crises" (Pils, 2020: 1). Furthermore, "China and some of its acolytes are pointing to Beijing's success in coming to grips with the coronavirus pandemic as a strong case for authoritarian rule" (Schmemann, 2020: 1). The strong response by the Chinese government has been praised by global health officials. The World Health Organization (WHO) has called China's response to the pandemic "perhaps the most ambitious, agile and aggressive disease containment effort in history" (WHO, 2020a: 16).

> The remarkable speed with which Chinese scientists and public health experts isolated the causative virus, established diagnostic tools, and determined key transmission parameters, such as the route of spread and incubation period, provided the vital evidence base for China's strategy, gaining invaluable time for the response [...]. The implementation of these containment measures has been supported and enabled by the innovative and aggressive use of cutting-edge technologies, from shifting to online medical platforms for routine care and schooling, to the use of 5G platforms to support rural response operations.
> WHO, 2020a: 16–17

Therefore, the relationship between political regimes and crisis management has been the subject of intense debate.

2   Literature Review

Much literature discusses how regime type might influence state responses to the pandemic and affect outcomes (Alon et al., 2020; Bunyavejchewin and Sirichuanjun, 2021; Cepaluni et al., 2020; Frey, Chen, et al., 2020a; Mao, 2021; Piazza and Stronko, 2020). Specifically, which political system, democracy or authoritarianism is better positioned to respond to the pandemic. Yet, studies and literature have not reached a consensus on which political institution is more conducive to crisis management. Nevertheless, there is no denying that both democratic and authoritarian regimes might have their own advantages and disadvantages in alleviating crises (Mao, 2021).

To stress the advantages of the democratic regime in managing crisis such as the COVID-19 pandemic, Frey, Chen et al. (2020a) offer a viewpoint stating that democratic regimes have actually been more effective in controlling the spread of COVID-19 by reducing geographic mobility; namely, the movement of the people. Moreover, to uphold the democratic system, Marston et al. (2020) point out the importance of 'community participation', suggesting that in the long run, citizens are more likely to comply with public health measures if they have a voice or are involved in the process of government policy decision-making (see also Youngs and Panchulidze, 2020). Through "bottom-up inclusion and pluralism" in democracies, trust is more easily built so that public policies can be supported and compiled more effectively (Youngs and Panchulidze, 2020: 6). As Xue's study (2020) shows, political repression of an authoritarian regime has a negative impact on social capital, "defined as the attitudes, beliefs, norms, and perceptions" (p. 5), which further results in resistance to cooperation. Besides, recognizing democratic openness and competitive politics as assets, Kavanagh (2020) stresses the importance of information politics and believes that democracies are better at "building capacity to prevent, detect, and respond to outbreaks" of pandemics (p. 2).

In arguing that authoritarianism is more effective at tackling crises, many focus on the institutional constraints that democratic regimes face, such as the rule of law and pressure from civil society or free media (Boin et al., 2017). Namely, liberal democracies are inclined to have weak governments, since they have to respect popular choice and legal procedures (Fukuyama, 2020). Alon and Li (2020) further point out that an authoritarian regime has a better chance to manipulate the trade-off between security and freedom. That is, government measures through which citizens' freedom will be restrained can guarantee that citizens receive greater security against external threats (Alon and Li, 2020). Additionally, while agreeing that "democracies are more likely to possess strong information capacity which is conducive to crisis management", Mao (2021) admits that the strength demonstrated by authoritarian regimes in tackling crises is a result of the fact that "they are more likely to possess strong coercive capacity, centralized decision-making and implementation capacity, and state-directed mobilization and cooperation capacity" (p. 317). Commentary by Brands (2020) has also suggested that the Chinese model of containing the coronavirus is superior to the democratic one.

While most of the literature centres around the question of whether an authoritarian regime is more effective at curbing the spread of COVID-19 by imposing more stringent measures, and that the COVID-19 pandemic will turn a democratic recession into a depression, this chapter aims to focus on the internal effects of the crisis by asking if and how the pandemic has contributed to the consolidation of the authoritarian regime within China.

Since the outbreak of COVID-19, governments around the world have been facing challenges dealing with the dissatisfaction, agitation, and criticism, as well as distrust of their own citizens. The pandemic has presented a test of each government's capacity to govern during crisis. How to respond to and manage a crisis such as the pandemic in a timely and effective manner has become one of the main criteria when evaluating the performance of governments. While most governments suffered from losing the support of their citizens (e.g., according to Ahrendt et al. (2020), since the outbreak of COVID-19, many EU countries have lost trust in their national governments or institutions), there is one government that stands out: that of China. Trust in the Chinese government has grown during the pandemic. According to the YouGov-Cambridge Globalism Project, "88 percent of Chinese respondents were convinced of their government's leadership in the COVID-19 crisis" (Hilpert and Stanzel, 2021: 3). Similarly, Wang (2021) points out that survey data suggests that there have been "high levels of approval of [the Chinese] government response to [the] pandemic". Accordingly, contrary to the belief that exogenous shock plays a key role in breaking down authoritarian regimes, this chapter argues that the pandemic has served to bolster regime legitimacy and consolidate China's authoritarian governance. The key lies in state capacity, particularly trust in government (Fukuyama, 2020). Namely, the Chinese government has been able to position the pandemic in a regime-state security context that has presented the Chinese Communist Party (CCP) with a chance to fully realize and consolidate its authoritarian model of governance – high-tech surveillance at a nationwide level. To support this argument, this chapter adopts a theoretical framework focusing on conceptualizing key ideas such as state capacity, legibility, discursive power, network/digital authoritarianism (in contrast to liberation technology) and the authoritarian deliberation to explain how technological development has been deployed as a high-tech advanced solution for managing the health crisis in an authoritarian way and legitimizing/securing the regime's governance.

The remaining empirical parts of the chapter will be structured as follows: firstly, the CCP's authoritarian governance under the Xi administration will be examined, addressing the establishment/implementation of the Social Credit System (SCS, 社会信用体系 shehui xinyong tixi), the CCP's increasingly overall-control system. Secondly, COVID-19 will be taken as the catalyst for the Chinese government to legitimize and accelerate such development; and then

China's 'authoritarian responses' to tackle the crisis will be discussed. In addition to analysing the central government's official discourse and documents, the empirical cases of the digital health and tracking system, the Health Code established by Alipay (a subsidiary of Alibaba) and Tencent will be briefly studied. Thirdly, the chapter examines the effectiveness/legitimacy of authoritarian governance from an 'outside-in' perspective by reviewing relevant international narratives led and constructed by China amid the pandemic. The chapter will rely largely on the analysis of documents (official statements/speeches, international reports, news from media outlet, social media posts, etc.). Lastly, the chapter concludes with the far-reaching implication that the pandemic serves the regime's interest not only to legitimize and reinforce its authoritarian governance internally but also to present China as a great, responsible power to export this 'effective model' worldwide.

3   Conceptualization and Framework

Before moving on to consider state capacity, it is essential to clarify and differentiate the terms: authoritarianism and totalitarianism. Both totalitarian and authoritarian regimes are considered as being opposed to democracy, and that they "allow little or no meaningful political competition, participation, and freedom" (Diamond, 1989: 143). Namely, individual freedom of thought and action are discouraged.

The chapter adopts the definition given by Brzezinski to define totalitarianism as:

> a new form of government falling into the general classification of dictatorship, a system in which technologically advanced instruments of political power are wielded without restraint by centralized leadership of an elite movement for the purpose of affecting a total social revolution, including the conditioning of man on the basis of certain arbitrary ideological assumptions, proclaimed by the leadership in an atmosphere of coerced unanimity of the entire population.
>
> BRZEZINSKI, 1962

Thus, as Diamond (1989) displays, totalitarianism is placed at the "most extreme end of the continuum opposite democracy" (p. 143). Comparatively, authoritarianism is defined as:

> political systems with limited, not responsible, political pluralism, without elaborate and guiding ideology, but with distinctive mentalities, without extensive nor intensive political mobilization, except at some points in their development, and in which a leader or occasionally a small group exercises power within formally ill-defined limits but actually quite predictable ones.
>
> LINZ, 1964: 255

The chapter does not disagree the possibility or even the 'fact' (as some analysts or scholars, e.g., Chan (2022), Babones (2021), might have claimed) that China is heading toward becoming a totalitarian state, especially under Xi's administration. Rather than simply firmly stating China's government is totalitarian, this chapter adopts a more 'practical' and cautious approach to ponder and ask whether it is. There is no denying that using the term 'authoritarian' to describe China might not feel accurate enough, considering its increasing scale of surveillance on its population and companies, its suppression of human freedom and ethnic minority, its aggressive actions internationally (such as in the case of South China Sea) to increase influence on the world's stage etc. Yet, the chapter would still follow the mainstream pundits, for instance, the government agencies (such as the US State Department), the non-governmental organization (like Human Rights Watch), and the think thanks (such as Brookings Institution and Freedom house) (Babones, 2021), to characterize China as authoritarian rather than totalitarian country. In sum, this chapter would like to stick with and settle on the term 'authoritarianism' to describe China.

3.1 State Capacity as the Key (Power, Intentionality, Policy Instruments, Resources)

Harari reminds the reader that what will matter most in overcoming this pandemic are the long-term consequences of decisions currently being taken by governments and policy-makers (Harari, 2020). The pandemic has forced the world to stand at a crossroads and choose between "totalitarian surveillance and citizen empowerment" (Harari, 2020). Although many fundamental beliefs, ideologies and concepts between constitutionalism and authoritarianism are not compatible with each other, when it comes to an emerging post-pandemic order, a renewed ideological encounter needs to be anticipated, in which the distinction will not be as simplistic as "democracy good, authoritarianism bad" (Jentleson, 2018: 3). Rather, the importance lies in the strength required for the state to promote and narrate ideas that help to ward off uncertainty and survive a crisis. Just as Jentleson states, within societies, across cultures, and among political systems, "a healthy dose of soft power will go to whichever system shows its own people and the world that it can meet these challenges" (Jentleson, 2018: 3).

By the same token, rather than treating regime type as a decisive determinant of effective crisis response, Fukuyama (2020) stresses state capacity, and above all, trust in government, as a crucial factor. According to him, trust is built on two foundations: citizens' belief in government (in terms of "the expertise, technical knowledge, capacity, and impartiality to make the best available judgments") and trust in the top end of the hierarchy of the political system.

State capacity is therefore taken as a central focus in this chapter when considering the relationship between regime survival and crisis management. In a broader sense, many scholars (Geddes, 1994; Andrews et al., 2017; Skocpol, 1985; Soifer, 2013) refer to state capacity as the ability to implement state-initiated polices and goals. According to Migdal (1988: xiii), state capacity refers to "the ability of state leaders to use the agencies of the state to get people in the society to do what they want them to do". In other words, it is "the degree of control that state agents exercise over persons, activities, and resources within their government's territorial jurisdiction" (McAdam et al., 2001: 78). Furthermore, Levi (1988) and Besley and Persson (2008) consider state capacity to be the ability of states to extract revenue (e.g., taxes) from society to sustain governance and provide public goods. For Krasner and Risse (2014), state capacity is the ability to legitimate monopoly over the means of violence, as well as implement and enforce rules.

Based on all the studies, this chapter adopts the definition proposed by Lindvall and Teorell (2016) that state capacity is "a form of power that is exercised by using specific resources to enhance the effectiveness of specific policy instruments" (p. 16). By doing so, this chapter centres on the ideas of power, intentionality, policy instruments, and resources in the theoretical framework. Generally speaking, state capacity is the ability one state possesses to 'get things done', which inevitably involves the exercise of power (Lindvall and Teorell, 2016). In Dahl's statement (1957), "A has power over B to the extent that he can get B to do something that B would not otherwise do" (p. 202). This power influence further applies at an ideational level: when A influences what B longs for or wants to believe (Lindvall and Teorell, 2016). Besides, the concept of power has further linked state capacity to an analysis of intentionality (Lindvall and Teorell, 2016; Soifer, 2008); namely, that the intended outcomes of state actions matter (Lindvall and Teorell, 2016). State capacity is therefore tailored to explaining specific outcomes. Needless to say, when a state tries to 'get things done' with an intended outcome, it would need to introduce measures or use instruments/tools to do so. Policy instruments, which are the methods that a state adopts to exercise its power, can be categorized as 'coercion', 'incentives' and 'persuasion/propaganda', which correspond to what Bemelmans-Videc et al. (1998) refer to as 'sticks', 'carrots', and 'sermons', respectively (Lindvall and Teorell, 2016). Those three instruments, 'coercion', 'incentives' and 'persuasion' can be further related to what Mann (1984) refers to as 'military power', 'economic power', and 'ideological power' (Lindvall and Teorell, 2016). With these instruments, the state deliberately wants to change the preferences of its citizens to increase their compliance. Lastly, resources are crucial for the state to strengthen its capacity and increase the effect of policy implementation for achieving the specific outcomes. In other words, resources are the assets that the "state can use to improve the way it coerces ('sticks'), bribes ('carrots'), or persuades ('sermons')" effectively (Lindvall and Teorell, 2016: 12).

Under this conceptual framework, the chapter focuses on China's use of 'propaganda' as the policy instrument to persuade its citizens during the pandemic to adjust/change their preferences and obey the rules (mobilizing members to act as neighbourhood behaviour enforcers, implementing full lockdown and mask policies, intensifying the 'grid management' system, establishing mobile cabin hospitals, taking extreme prevention measures and tracking system, etc.) ordered by the central government.[2] Without denying the importance of 'coerces' and 'bribes', 'propaganda' features in the Chinese authoritarian way of strengthening the state capacity to win identification, empathy and support from its citizens. Hence, the expected policy outcome of bringing COVID-19 and social order under control can be ensured, and state capacity can be recognized by the citizens.

In terms of resources, the chapter concentrates on 'information' (especially with regard to information technology and digitalization), one of the three most crucial types of state resources (revenue, human capital, and information) assumed by Lindvall and Teorell (2016), to be the most valuable resources to China for enhancing the effectiveness of its 'persuasion/propaganda' policy instrument for implementation. This implies that the state's accessibility to means of communication and the transfer of knowledge in developing and bolstering state capacity is significant (Lindvall and Teorell, 2016).

---

2   This does not imply that the coerces and bribes are not important policy instruments for China. Rather, this chapter admits that these three instruments are interdependent and are all crucial for governments to have effective policy implementation. It is also through the mechanism of punishment and reward that the CCP has managed to make its population follow the COVID-19 rules and regulations. However, this chapter aims to manifest the importance of 'propaganda/persuasion' as a featured tool for an authoritarian regime to reinforce its state capacity.

3.2 Legibility: Penetrating Society through Collecting Information

While stressing the importance of gathering and processing information/knowledge as one of the fundamental resources for enhancing state capacity, the chapter would like to further apply the concept of legibility to comprehend state capacity, especially in an emergency. Namely, state capacity depends on legibility – "the breadth and depth of the state's knowledge about its citizens and their activities"– to realize effective and centralized governance (Lee and Zhang, 2016: 118). The concept of legibility was originally proposed by Scott (1998; 2009), who argues that a key component of effective governance lies in making society legible to central governmental officials. In other words, states need to penetrate society and identify individual subjects. Accordingly, legibility implies both:

> (a) that the state possesses information about local practices and (b) that this information is rendered in standardized forms (e.g., cadastral maps, birth certificates, property registers) that are understandable to state administrators.
> LEE and ZHANG, 2016: 118

As Scott argues, the modern state has become "devoted to rationalizing and standardizing what was a social hieroglyph into a legible and administratively more convenient format" (Scott, 1998: 2–3). In brief, the theoretical importance of legibility for state capacity lies in facilitating "the establishment of an efficient social order", particularly through "effectively monitor[ing] private behaviour and enforc[ing] rules and regulations" (Lee and Zhang, 2016: 118).

Hence, linking legibility to state capacity is imperative for understanding why China has curbed the expansion of COVID-19 effectively by monitoring its citizens and mobilizing society.

3.3 Anatomizing State Capacity

3.3.1 Make a Strong State Even Stronger: Sustaining the Authoritarian Form of Governance (Intentionality)

There is no denying that in the face of an emergency or crisis, the state is a key actor in guiding society to cope with the challenges and further bring back 'normal' social order. In the case of COVID-19, as Lamond (2020) puts it, "with a crisis of this magnitude, people want a quick, robust, and comprehensive national response that only a strong government can provide". A strong government is often expected in an authoritarian state, since state–society relations are characterized as the state having control over society (Mao, 2021). Nevertheless, while being perceived as strong (strongman politics) from the external perspective, the authoritarian regime is prone to fragility, and stability of the regime has constantly perplexed the leader (Lamond, 2020).

Consequently, the state–regime security nexus is strongly manifested in an authoritarian state. That is, regime security is closely linked to the security of the nation. To secure the state, the security of the regime needs to be ensured. Among other things, it is the stability (both in the sense of political and social order) that matters most for ensuring coexistence of state and regime security.

In accordance with this state–regime security context, in an authoritarian regime, collective stability is prioritized over individual liberty.[3] Most crucially, the underlying principle of realizing stability lies in stable political order to secure public safety. Authoritarianism adheres to the belief that stability of political order is the most important element for individual and collective security, particularly in emergencies (Kreuder-Sonnen and Zangl, 2015). A breakdown in political authority will be considered as a root of anarchic conditions, and a serious threat to peace and security (Hobbes, 2008). Thus, authoritarianism supports the centralization and concentration of power in executive authorities to guard the stability of political order for enhancing security and assuring a stable society (Kreuder-Sonnen and Zangl, 2015).

Needless to say, under authoritarian governance, the authorities "ought to do whatever is necessary, not what is legal" to ensure stability (Kreuder-Sonnen and Zangl, 2015: 6). Authoritarianism is pro-authority and community but against disruption and disorder (Zelikow, 2017). This implies that to achieve stability, the authority is prompted to act in an autocratic and/or arbitrary manner. To be more specific, there are two fundamental features. Firstly, authority relationships are structured vertically with some form of superior authority "whose acts are legally binding also without or even against the constituents"; and secondly, the political authority is not necessarily constituted or constrained by law, which suggests that the power-holders are granted with unlimited discretion to maintain stability, especially in times of emergency (Kreuder-Sonnen and Zangl, 2015: 4). The authorities might, for example, expand executive authority, increase areas of secrecy and state privilege, or expand domestic surveillance (Cooley, 2015; Scheppele, 2004). This is the alternative state, according to Kay, that is "premised on some collective purposes" and is "a rationally regulated cooperative engagement [...] which refers to the repressive character of a totalitarian regime" (Kay, 1998: 20). In

---

3 This does not imply that stability does not matter to liberal democracies. In fact, most orders (including the constitutionalist/democratic ones) count on a certain level of stability. However, the chapter attempts to highlight the extent to which authoritarianism stresses stability and security, as well as the way the authority is exercised to realize stability.

brief, authoritarian authority is very likely constituted by an act of autocratic self-empowerment and not necessarily exercised in accordance with legal constraints when it comes to the preservation of stable and peaceful order (Hobbes, 2008; Kreuder-Sonnen and Zangl, 2015).

In this regard, in times of emergency, for the sake of stability and social order (as well as for the sake of its citizens' health in the case of the COVID-19 pandemic), the authoritarian government is entrusted with implementing measures or taking action that otherwise would be condemned to tackle the crisis. As a matter of fact, those means or actions are taken for the sake of strengthening its state capacity further for authoritarian governance. In other words, it serves the purpose of sustaining the CCP's authoritarian governance and making a strong state an even stronger one.

3.3.2 Propaganda and Persuasion with the Aid of Discursive Power (policy instruments)

While treating propaganda/persuasion as the main policy instrument, this chapter intends to stress how the CCP has narrated the COVID-19 crisis into the national security context to persuade its people to become unified and fight against COVID-19 to win this 'people's war'. Therefore, it is imperative to delve into the concept of discursive power that China exercises to convince its citizens to increase their compliance.

As will be addressed later, technology, data and information are deemed precious resources for the state to enhance its state capacity, but it is important to note that data and information are only meaningful upon narrative interpretation. This notion is in accordance with the constructive epistemology that knowledge is socially constructed (Guzzini, 2000). If knowledge is socially constructed, it is also possible to reconstruct and reinterpret it (Hagstrom, 2012). In this regard, discourse and narrative are the keys to the process of knowledge reconstruction and reinterpretation.

According to Foucault (1926–1984), discourse is understood as "ways of constituting knowledge, together with the social practices, forms of subjectivity and power relations which inhere in such knowledge and relations between them" (Weedon, 1987: 108). The importance of discourse power lies not only in revealing how concepts become comprehensible but also in considering what power relations are manifested. Most crucially, as a social construct, discourse is produced and perpetuated by those who possess the power and mediums of communication (Pitsoe and Letseka, 2013). In addition, as Diamond and Lee point out, discourse functions as "a form of power that circulates in the social field and can attach to strategies of domination as well as those of resistance" (Diamond and Lee, 1988: 185). As Hutcheon underlines, discourse is not only a tool of domination but also an instrument of power (Hutcheon, 1991). In brief, discourse is both "an instrument and an effect of power" (Pitsoe and Letseka, 2013: 24).

Moreover, as mentioned, 'persuasion' as an instrument is closely related to 'ideological power' (Mann, 1984). The inner contents of the discourse and narratives are ideas, and the relations between ideas and narratives are mutually constructed, reinforcing and closely intertwined. According to Schmidt, ideas are the substantive content of narratives (Schmidt, 2008). Without ideas, narratives would be empty, shallow, meaningless and impotent. Without narratives, ideas will not be diffused and cannot survive. Ideas are used for policymakers to create policies, programmes and philosophies (beliefs) (Schmidt, 2008). Ideas have a crucial role to play in constituting political action and exercising power of persuasion in political disputes. Ideational success depends on the communication process, in which narratives act not only as a carrier to deliver and present ideas but also as a 'filter' to embellish, interpret and promote them. Most crucially, the process involves trust-building, and formation of collective action and identity. That is, "individuals accept the obligation to act jointly on behalf of collective beliefs, whether or not they subscribe to them personally" (Wendt, 1999: 219). Once a bright idea of portraying the situation is formed and a narrative is constructed, the "discourse begins about what 'we' should do, [and] a collective can form much more quickly, leading to 'swift trust'" (Wendt, 1999: 347). Therefore, narratives act as idea facilitator to urge people to engage with "'ideological labor' [...] to create a shared representation of the interdependence and the 'we' that it constitutes before anyone has made any behavioural decisions at all" (Wendt, 1999: 346).

By narrating the COVID-19 health crisis into a context of security, the Chinese authority is granted the power to take whatever measures required to enhance stability and guarantee public safety. Although the persuasion-based influence seems to be inconsistent with an authoritarian regime or to clash with the authoritarian governance, the CCP in China has often used 'deliberative venues' to stabilize and extend the CCP's authoritarian rule (He and Warren, 2011). "Combinin[g] authoritarian concentrations of power with deliberative influence" has permeated the authoritarian rule in China (He and Warren, 2011: 269). This kind of 'authoritarian deliberation' is crucial in discourse on public policy (He and Warren, 2011). It aims not to involve more citizen participation or empower citizens to have a say in the policy decision-making process. Instead, it is a nominal means to exercise the discursive power of the CCP and to declare or justify the legitimacy of its governance.

The discursive power exercised by China under Xi's regime has been treated as an indispensable part of displaying China's national comprehensive strength. With its well-organized propaganda apparatus[4] and sophisticated tactics, China employs its discourse/narrative power to influence its domestic population, seeking to perpetuate pro-party-state narratives and deny unfavourable party-state narratives (Atlantic Council, 2020).

3.3.3 Technology and Information as the Resource to Realize 'Persuasion': China's Networked/Digitalized Authoritarianism Model

The logic of the above-mentioned legibility lies in the tendency of the government to simplify complex systems through standardization so that control can be exerted over society and the population (Snow, 2021). In the information age, new information technology (e.g., networked platforms, big data, machine learning, artificial intelligence, cloud computing, new media, and the internet of things, etc.) has penetrated many aspects of daily life. Hence, the so-called digital revolution is well on its way to reshaping society, economy and governance (Drinhausen, 2018). Noteworthy is that digital communication and technologies have meanwhile brought many convenient changes to the legibility of the state capacity. When these changes meet an authoritarian regime, the result is what MacKinnon (2011) calls, 'networked/digital authoritarianism'. By definition, digital authoritarianism, rather than stressing internet freedom,

> is the use of technology by authoritarian governments not only to control but [also] to shape the behaviour of its citizens via surveillance, repression, manipulation, censorship, and the provision of services in order to retain and expand political control.
> KHALIL, 2020: 6

Taking China as an example, MacKinnon (2011) proposes a model of digital authoritarianism to explain how cyberspace can be used by states to stabilize, strengthen and legitimize authoritarian power. In her words,

> Governments and others whose power is threatened by digital insurgencies are learning quickly and pouring unprecedented resources into

---

4 In addition to the Publicity Department, the United Front Work Department, the State Council Press Office, the Ministry of National Defense, the Ministry of Foreign Affairs, and the National Radio and Television Administration, there are government branches such as the CCP's Central Committee, the State Council, and the CCP's Central Military Commission, which are responsible for domestic and international propaganda (Atlantic Council 2020).

> building their capacity to influence and shape digital communications networks in direct and indirect ways.
>
> MACKINNON, 2011: 34

In a similar vein, in the article "Networked Authoritarianism Is on the Rise", Burgers and Robinson (2016) include non-internet networked technology (e.g., facial recognition software) into their discussion and argue that networked platforms have been used as a tool for authoritarian stability. Namely, rather than being 'liberating technologies',[5] networked platforms can contribute to population control and surveillance. With the governance model of digital authoritarianism, the government is not only able to monopolize information and knowledge but also to build itself as a surveillance state. Surveillance enables the authority to send a warning through electronic communications or in person to targeted individuals who are deemed to have broken the rules or certain standards (MacKinnon, 2011).

With a model of networked/digitalized authoritarianism to make society legible, China will gradually evolve into a so-called 'data Leviathan' that operates an "all-encompassing and highly individualized" system of social control and uses "a mix of mechanisms to impose varying levels of supervision and constraint on people depending on their perceived threat to the state" (Roth and Wang, 2019). As a result, a 'surveillance state' with superior legibility consolidating its governing position emerges.

4 Empirical Study: China's Path toward a Surveillance State – Authoritarian Resilience, High Legibility and Strong Discursive Power

4.1 *A Stronger State under Xi's Regime*

China's leadership under President Xi Jinping is working up efforts to make the Chinese Dream come true and, further, to turn China into a great, responsible power again (Chang, 2019). Domestically, marking a sharp break from the previous era, Xi's presidency has concentrated on power expansion and suppressing civil society. In addition to the increased censorship and political control at the society level, China's vast bureaucratic apparatus also faced tightened supervision (Ang, 2020). As Xinhua reports, in enhancing the Party's political building,

---

5 The term was coined by Larry Diamond (2010) to depict "any form of information and communication technology (ICT) that can expand political, economic, and social freedom" (p. 70).

the disciplinary authorities (Central Commission for Discipline Inspection and National Supervisory Commission) should "closely follow the CPC Central Committee with Comrade Xi Jinping at the core in terms of thinking, political orientation and actions" (Xinhua, 2018).

In its 'state-regime security nexus' context, as Scobell et al. (2020: 26) describe, "Chinese leaders are preoccupied with maintaining domestic stability and tend to be ultrasensitive to the prospect of chaos". Ever since Xi came to power, the party has put 'protecting China's national security' on its top agenda (Legarda, 2021). The so-called stability maintenance (维稳 *weiwen*) operations have been stressed as a top priority for Chinese authorities (Wang and Minzner, 2015). In order to increase the government's grip on the country, the CCP established "a centralized and unified national security system built around the concept of 'comprehensive national security'" (Legarda, 2021: 1). Accordingly, in this 'new era' under Xi's administration stressing the coexistence of party and state, state–party integration is the key.[6] The leadership launched a massive structural reform programme to fully integrate state and party organizations. For Xi, the more output-oriented approach, which was adopted by his predecessors, did drive economic growth, prompt societal opening and increase local governments' autonomy; yet, this approach came at the expense of loss of central control and is seen as a threat to sustained CCP leadership (Grünberg and Drinhausen, 2019). To maintain political stability and enhance the CCP's capacity to make China rich and powerful, Xi sees the necessity of "a unified governance system under tighter party leadership and ideological guidance" (Grünberg and Drinhausen, 2019: 4). As Grünberg and Drinhausen put it, "Xi is returning the party to the fore by rebuilding a centralized, hierarchical system around himself as core leader" (Grünberg and Drinhausen, 2019: 3). Under the banner of 'law-based governance', CCP's rule and ideology are codified in laws and regulation, aiming to solidify the Party's hold on power (Jiang, 2013). The expected outcome is an efficient administration steered and supervised by top-level officials to deliver better services and forestall opposition to CCP rule (Grünberg and Drinhausen, 2019). Pils (2020) calls this state–party integration the 'unity of powers'. China's extraordinary degree of unity of powers contributes to the effective governance, and the possibility to save "the greatest possible number of people in an emergency, or prioritizing the collective good" (Pils, 2020). Along with the state–party integration or the high degree of unity of powers, "extending the CCP's social reach is a major policy focus" (Grünberg

---

6 For more information concerning China's state-party system, please refer to Jiang (2013) and Backer (2009).

and Drinhausen, 2019: 2). In order to shore up its societal support and to reinforce its legitimacy, the CCP has intensified the ideological and propaganda work as well as the mobilization of party members to push the CCP's values, messages, and organizational reach beyond the formal administrative apparatus (Grünberg and Drinhausen, 2019). Namely, CCP's power and influences should be omnipresent, consolidated, recognized, accepted, and appreciated in society at large.

It is against this political background that China's responses toward the pandemic crisis should be understood. For Chinese leadership under Xi's administration, the coronavirus is a severe socio-political crisis that could pose a threat to the Communist Party as well as Xi's popularity and legitimacy. Thus, while tackling this health crisis, "the CCP appears to be acting on its concern over regime survival" (Burgers and Romaniuk, 2020).

Notwithstanding, the COVID-19 pandemic crisis has in fact opened a window of opportunity for Chinese authoritarian government to display and strengthen its state capacity as well as to consolidate its power controlling over the country. As Burgers and Romaniuk (2020) describe, "the pandemic exposes a unique opportunity for the CCP to advance the necessary justification for a tightened security policy". The pandemic is treated not only as a threat to the CCP's regime survival but also, most crucially, considered and narrated as a threat to China's national security by amplifying the international critics on China's mishandling of the pandemic. Namely, in coupling the regime security with the national one, the threat of COVID-19 crisis has actually acted as a catalyst for the CCP to call for unification and mobilize its people to corporately fight against the virus. Taking the advantage of the pandemic to launch 'a people's war' at its convenience, the CCP under Xi meant to arouse patriotic sentiment of its people to fight for themselves and make China great again.

As Xinhua (2020b) describes,

> China is waging a people's war to prevent and control the new pneumonia epidemic. The Party Central Committee, with President Xi Jinping at its core, is the 'supreme command' of this people's war.

Winning this war is a matter of national glory. As Xi describes it during his visit to Xi'an Jiaotong University: "Great historical progress always happens after major disasters"; "our nation was steeled and grew up through hardship and suffering" (Myers and Buckley, 2020; YouTube, 2020).

To ensure regime survival, the Chinese government has magnified the danger of the health crisis brought to the national security. By shielding the collective security from being threatened by the epidemic crisis, CCP's governance can be justified, and its power can be consolidated in taking full grip on its citizens. That is to say, in the name of maintaining the stability, as long as the health emergency is placed in a security context, Chinese government is not only able to entrench control under the guise of protecting the people, but also capable of making its people increasingly rely on the capacities of the state to safeguard them, in spite of the fact that the individual agency has been limited to a lager extent (Burgers and Romaniuk, 2020).

In brief, 'with the help' of COVID-19, by asking its people to show compassion in coping with the difficulties of the times, Chinese government has been able to mobilize, penetrate and monitor the society, which are substantial for displaying the effective governance and successful policy implementation of the CCP to combat the pandemic. All of which further serve the purpose to sustain the CCP's authoritarian governance and make a strong state an even stronger one.

4.2 Technology and Information as the Core Resources: Digital Social Control – The Social Credit System

Under Xi's administration, 'digitalization and informatization'[7] are the key items on China's political agenda (Drinhausen and Brussee, 2021). President Xi made a vow to lead the charge 'making China a cyber-power' (The BRICS Post, 2014). In the outline of the 14th Five-Year Plan (2021–2025), it is explicitly stated that China,

> will embrace the digital era, unlock the potential of big data, build China's strength in cyberspace, accelerate the development of a digital economy, a digital society, and a digital government, and transform the pattern of production, lifestyle, and governance models through digital transformation.
>
> THE PEOPLE'S GOVERNMENT OF FUJIAN PROVINCE, 2021

Putting the digitalization and informatization as main CCP's agenda has both domestic and international implications. Externally, China wants to achieve greater technological self-reliance and to improve its position vis-à-vis the world's leading nations (Drinhausen and Lee, 2021). Internally, China aims to realize smart and efficient governance through leveraging information and communication technologies (Drinhausen and Lee, 2021: 41). Although both

---

7 According to Drinhausen and Lee (2021), 'informatization' refers to "the application of digital technology throughout Chinese society" (p. 39).

informatization and digitalization serve more as an umbrella terms to cover various operations involving digital technology, the ambitions of the Chinese party-state are clear: "to expand, integrate and analyse existing data sources to improve and consolidate CCP rule" (Drinhausen and Brussee, 2021: 4).

It is in these circumstances that the SCS was developed, first tested and implemented by the CCP since 2013 and 2015. Since then, it is considered as a crucial tool for Chinese government to govern the society via monitoring people's daily actions to prevent dissent or opposition (Bartsch and Gottake, 2021; Ge, 2019). As Drinhausen and Brussee (2021: 8) point out, the SCS "remains an extension of the existing legal and administrative system under party-state control". As part of the data-driven governance envisioned by the Xi administration, the SCS aims to build a coherent information ecosystem for realizing the CCP's ambition of data-support and efficient governance (Drinhausen and Brussee, 2021). Four key mechanisms are featured to sustain the operation of the SCS: information gathering, information sharing, labelling and joint sanctions (Chen et al., 2018).

It is a comprehensive and aggressive governance scheme that the Chinese government pursues to promote the norms of 'trust' in the Chinese society (Chen et al., 2018). Even though Chinese government has stressed in its official document (Planning Outline for the Construction of a Social Credit System, 2014–2020) that the SCS is founded on laws, regulations, standards and charters, according to Chen et al. (2018), the SCS represents a new mode of governance under the CCP – rule of trust. This rule of trust, in reality, undermines the rule of law because the SCS "imposes arbitrary restrictions – loosely defined and broadly interpreted trust-related rules – to condition, shape and compel the behaviour of the governed subjects" (Chen et al., 2018: 3). The ambiguous and 'constantly expanding' idea of trust is stressed and used as a credible ideology for the CCP to legitimate its rule (Chen et al., 2018).

The SCS is an ambitious project in digital social control. According to Knight (2018: 7), the system is,

> a loose collective of decentralized attempts to ascribe a credit rating to every individual, company, and government body in China. It is unified by a common ideology and a centralized attempt to nudge certain behaviours through a system of reward and punishment.

Based on the designed SCS, a nationwide 18-digit code for all individuals is introduced to rate and rank the citizen according to their integrity, honesty or trustworthiness (Godement, 2018). On the surface, the system can be deemed as an answer to the lack of trust[8] prevailing between individuals in China, in fact, it can collect a huge amount of data concerning every single citizen in the Chinese society. The sources rely on not only the traditional registry system such as financial, criminal, and government records, but also the digital channel via internet such as searching preferences, personalized searching records, interactions on the social media, etc (Bartsch and Gottake, 2021). Importantly, the surveillance systems with help from facial recognition technology are also the major sources for constructing and implementing the SCS (Bartsch and Gottake, 2021). In the pre-pandemic period, security cameras and facial recognition technology have been already on the rise in China. In its official Twitter account, People's Daily (China state-affiliate media) has announced that:

> 'Sky Net', a facial recognition system that can scan China's population of about 1.4 billion people in a second, is being used in 16 Chinese cities and provinces to help police crackdown on criminals and improve security.
> People's Daily, 2018

Even though the SCS is still under construction[9] and at its beginning phase of implementation, with its evolution and adjustment, the SCS has become

---

8   China's 'trustless' society is characterized by "official corruption, business scandals and other fraudulent activities" (Chen et al., 2018: 2). In the official SCS plan released in 2014, grave production safety accidents, food and drug security incidents, commercial swindles, production and sales of counterfeit products, tax evasion, fraudulent financial claims, academic impropriety, etc. are listed as examples of the lack of integrity, trust and sincerity in society (State Council, 2014).

9   To be more specific, in spite of the fact that the SCS is planned to be a country-wide system and that it was supposed to complete the construction by 2020 (State Council, 2014), the SCS is still in the trial stage and in development. According to latest research done by Donnelly (2024), "an estimated 80 percent of provinces, regions and cities have introduced some version of the system" (para. 2). As for the corporation to implement the SCS system, it is relatively advanced with "more than 33 million businesses in China have already been given a score under some version of the corporate social credit system" (Donnelly, 2024, para. 3). Although the SCS is designed as a highly flexible tool, it comes at a cost that the SCS is featured as being fragmented rather than integrated (Drinhausen and Brussee, 2021). As Drinhausen and Brussee (2021) point out, the SCS "is regulated by thousands of documents, [...] and substantial regional differences exist in implementation and evaluation standards" (p. 1). In 2021, Chinese government has released a new five-year plan to "raise public awareness of the law and to improve the law-based social governance" (State Council, 2021). With the new ideological canon of 'Rule of Law', SCS has become a fundamental unit. In the issued 'construction of a rule of law society', the SCS was highlighted as a bolstering pillar of developing China's legal system (Drinhausen and Brussee, 2021). Accordingly, 'Social Credit Law' has been drafted in 2020 to guide the direction of the further development of the SCS (Donnelly, 2024).

a flexible tool for speedy and strict enforcement (Drinhausen and Brussee, 2021). Taking the recent COVID-19 as an example, in order to respond to the health crisis, Chinse government has rapidly deployed the SCS to address new policy priorities: tracking and imposing sanctions on people who violated the pandemic prevention measures (Drinhausen and Brussee, 2021). To be more specific, citizens in various Chinese cities who refused the temperature check, tried to escape from being quarantined, or covered their travel history to COVID-19 high-risk areas on purpose would be put on the blacklist.[10]

With the SCS and the collected data, the CCP hopes to increase its state capacity to provide new access channels to public goods, to construct a trustworthy atmosphere in the society to bring social order in place, and most crucially, to strengthen and reinforce the legitimacy of the CCP (Drinhausen and Lee, 2021).

Altogether, they pave the road for China's enthusiasm and endeavour to develop itself into a surveillance state.

4.3 *COVID-19 Pandemic as a Catalyst: Networked Platform for Health Surveillance – The Establishment of Health Code*

China or the CCP's road toward building a surveillance state has been further catalysed by the outbreak of the COVID-19 pandemic. Based on the observation, a researcher for Human Rights Watch specializing in China comments, "the coronavirus outbreak is proving to be one of those landmarks in the history of the spread of mass surveillance in China" (Mozur et al., 2020).

As mentioned, positing COVID-19 in a regime-state security context helps the Chinese government to "require a build-up of the necessary structures for full-spectrum surveillance of China's citizens" so that public safety can be secured: using drones to enforce quarantine, implementing full lockdowns, limiting movement of the population, requiring mask wearing, and so on (Burgers and Romaniuk, 2020). For instance, the Chinese government has sped up its surveillance capabilities to enforce the pandemic regulations, urged advancements in facial recognition software tied to a network of cameras to trace individuals and catch those who break the rules, as well as applied classic monitoring techniques to control social media for false information concerning the details or outbreak of the pandemic (Lamond, 2020). All in all, this demonstrates the power of personal information as a valuable resource of social control (Roth and Wang, 2019). In brief, China deliberately deploys

---

10   People who are on the blacklist might face punishments, including denial of licenses, permits and access to social services, exclusion from taking public transportation, less access to bank credit, etc.

its development of technology and digitalization (e.g., artificial intelligence and data collection) as tools to manage the health crisis that serves its authoritarian governance to increase social and political control, which further lays the foundations necessary to consolidate its power: high-tech surveillance on a nationwide level.

To respond to COVID-19 and to curb the virus expansion effectively, many countries around the world have already launched or planned to carry out the 'contact-tracing' applications for detecting potential exposure risks in advance. Certainly, China is no exception. The so-called Health Code system is launched in China to take preventive measures against the spread of COVID-19.

According to Liang (2020), the Health Code system has already been applied to 900 million users and implemented in over 300 cities in China. This system is initiated and put into practice by the competition between two leading Chinese tech companies, Alipay (subsidiary of Alibaba) and Tencent in February 2020. The Health Code aims to use date collection to identify citizens' health status, regulate people's lives, and curb the infection as well as expansion of the COVID-19 pandemic. Upon installation, Chinese citizens will have to input personal information (including name, national ID number, medical information, travel history, and COVID-19 contact history, etc.) into the app. Beyond that, the Health Code system also aggregates 'spatial-temporal' data to identify the geographical location of a person and examine the duration of time a person spent in that particular area (Liang, 2020). Furthermore, to ensure whether a person has contacted any potential COVID-19 carrier, Health Code explores users' networks and online transactions (Liang, 2020). Via tracking individuals' travel and contact history as well as the biometric data, a coloured QR cord will then be generated to pin down three levels of health risk: *green* code means that it is normal and the permission is granted for free movement; *yellow* implies potential risks that a 7–14 days home quarantine is required; and *red* assumes suspected or confirmed patients that will need to be sent to the hospital and a 14-day quarantine will be imposed (Tan, 2020).

The colour determination of the Health Code has a wide-range impact on people's lives in China, as the Chinese local authorities demand their people to show the result of the Health Code App whenever they go (supermarkets, public transportation, residential areas, etc.) (Wang, 2020). In a sense, people's daily life and their mobility are dependent on the tri-colour code generated by the Health Code system (Wang, 2020). Additionally, the Health Code system is also linked with the advanced technologies like facial recognition, drones, and thermal cameras, which have also been employed by the Chinese government to combat the COVID-19 pandemic (Liang, 2020; Wang, 2020). According to Wang (2020), in some residential areas where facial recognition technology has been applied to control the access, only people coded green are allowed to enter. This all indicates that in the name of containing the virus, ensuring the safety of the population and the stability of social order, the Chinese government spares no effort to exercise its prerogative to actively leverage new technologies and extensively penetrate society. Concisely, Health Code is "a rating and ranking practice aiming to render citizens to a state of visibility" (Liang, 2020: 3). With all the data collected and restored by the Health Code system, it can contribute to establishing a coherent information ecosystem for China to forge the surveillance state. As Burgers and Romaniuk (2020) put it, the Health Code "has created the latest node in the (further) rise of China's networked authoritarianism model". COVID-19 as well as the Health Code system therefore indicate the far-reaching implication: when placing the health emergency in a security context, it presents the opportunity for the authoritarian regime like the CCP under Xi's administration to secure and propagate its governance model of networked authoritarianism (Burgers and Romaniuk, 2020).

Unquestionably, China is not the only country that uses the application to trace citizens amid the pandemic. However, among all 'contact-tracing' applications, as O'Neill et al. (2020) observe, "some are lightweight and temporary, while others are pervasive and invasive". Based on the database compiled by 'COVID Tracing Tracker', the Health Code system launched by China is the one that belongs to the pervasive and invasive group (O'Neill et al., 2020; O'Neill et al., 2021). First of all, although Health Code was initiated and built by two Chinese tech-companies, it is backed by the central Chinese government and later adopted by the State Council (Tan, 2020). Secondly, the application of the Health Code is not on a voluntary basis. Namely, Chinese citizens are compelled to download the application and use them to keep the record (Huang, 2020; O'Neill et al., 2020; O'Neill et al., 2021). Besides, there seems to be no limitation on how the data will be used. That is to say, the collected data can be further used for purposes other than public health. According to Mozur et al. (2020), "law enforcement authorities were a crucial partner in the system's development" and the Health Code system "appears to share information with the police, setting a template for new forms of automated social control that could persist long after the epidemic subsides".

To sum up, whether it is the elaborately planned SCS or a contingency plan like the Health Code system amid the pandemic, a nationwide tracking system is conducive to standardizing and simplifying the complexity of governance, in which further enables the Chinese government to make its society more legible and controllable. That is, CCP's endeavour to develop the surveillance state would in return reinforce its state capacity and further legitimate its authoritarian governance.

4.4 'Outside-in' Propaganda: Embellishing China's Role as Path-Maker/Finder to Tackle the COVID-19 Crisis

Aside from using information and technology as resources to strengthen the legibility of the governance, the Chinese government has skilfully used its discourse power to divert public opinion and persuade its citizens into believing the authoritarian governance is not only efficient and legitimate but also necessary. The chapter terms it as an 'outside-in' approach to convince its domestic audiences of the government's state capacity and the CCP's legitimacy.

An 'outside-in' perspective[11] is applied to counteract the inward bias against the CCP's governance and divert internal attention, as well as opinions emerging from dissatisfaction or dissent to agreeing and identifying with the CCP's rule. It is a deliberate approach the CCP adopted aiming to drag its own people back into focusing on what is going on in the world amid the pandemic. Namely, it is the attempt to make a distinction between 'what China has achieved' and 'what others have failed'.

This approach relies heavily on the discursive power of China's state capacity. One of the theoretical connotations of discursive power is to be considered as the symbol of one government's soft power to use words to convince and attract followers/audiences. Putting in the Chinese context, Callahan (2015) proposes the 'negative soft power' to explain China's pursuit of soft power by building "the positive Chinese self through the negative exclusion of Otherness" (p. 218). Accordingly, Callahan (2015) points out the importance of the discursive influences by stating that "discourse is a useful heuristic device for understanding how Chinese policymakers and public intellectuals are actively constructing a 'China' and a 'world' to promote their ideological projects" (p. 222). By "drawing symbolic borders between Self and Other", the discourse power can be used to shape, establish, strengthen and preserve the identity (Callahan, 2015: 9). As Breslin (2011:1324) puts it, a sense of "Chinese exceptionalism – an idea that China is fundamentally different from other countries", would then be emerging. To magnify China's contribution and other actors' failure, an empirical example can be found in an animated video entitled "Once Upon a Virus" released by Xinhua news agency (New China TV, 2020). This video uses Lego pieces to mock the United States' coronavirus response and exposes US self-contradiction in facing the COVID-19 outbreak (Yu, 2020).

Intriguingly, to manifest China's exceptionalism, China centres not only around its pandemic management but also puts the narratives in

---

11 The term is inspired by the approach often adopted in the field of business administration to take customers' perspective into account when running a business (Livework, 2021).

connection with its 'unique' Chinese characteristics[12] and governance model led by the authoritarian regime. Xinhua, a representative Chinese news agency, comments:

> For China to have taken determined steps to protect people's lives and ensure normal operations of economic and social activities, it is because the ruling Communist Party of China (CPC) values serving people's interest as its overarching principle, and the right to subsistence and development represents the most fundamental human rights. China's victory of the all-out people's war on the virus speaks volumes about the strong leadership of the CPC and the advantage of China's socialist system in rallying collective forces to counter difficulties and challenges [...]. In stark contrast, certain Western countries, though endowed with advanced medical resources, have been witnessing persistently high levels of infections and huge losses of human lives.
> WANG and WEN, 2021

Nevertheless, for the purpose of persuasion, stressing the constructed Chinese exceptionalism is not enough, it needs to win the affirmation from the outside world (others). That is, to avoid being perceived as arbitrary, the CCP needs to be cautious in selecting the 'speaker', who further confirms and diffuses the narrative. In addition to the official statements, it is through approaching other foreign channels as a bridge to voice and transfer the messages back to its domestic audiences that the CCP would be able to make those narratives more objective (Chang, 2020). Therefore, the external confirmation from abroad has substantial meaning for Chinese people to believe that their government 'is doing the right thing' and they need or can count on the CCP's rule to protect them from this health crisis.

To be more specific, this outside-in approach can be observed from the fact that China has presented and perceived itself as a path-maker/finder and that various control measures and policies adopted or initiated by China are emulated by other countries around the world. While there are many questioning the cost of China's containment policy and casting doubt on those measure to infringe on citizens' civil liberties, many policy makers around the world have indeed eyed the Chinese model to adopt the similar measures (Gunia,

---

12   The term 'Chinese characteristics' was promoted by Deng Xiaoping, emphasizing that "mechanical application of foreign experience and copying of foreign models will get us nowhere", and "in carrying out our modernization programme we must proceed from Chinese realities" in order to "blaze a path of our own" (Deng, 1982).

2020). For instance, keeping social distance, wearing masks, announcing the lockdown, using high-tech techniques to enforce control (drone and the tracking system), etc. can be found in many countries (without respect to political systems) who have been challenged by the COVID-19 health crisis. Referring to a video reported by Russia Today (RT), the CCTV[13] comments that the West (Italy, France, Spain and the US) is using all the preventive measures it criticized China over at the beginning to tackle the COVID-19 crisis:

> To control the spread of the pandemic, Western countries in Europe and the United States have modelled their pandemic prevention measures on those of China. And just a short time ago, when the epidemic was still raging in China, Western countries spared no effort in criticizing China's measures to fight the pandemic.
> CCTV, 2020

> Recently, as the coronavirus spreads around the world, China's experience in fighting the pandemic has prompted European and American countries to follow suit – issuing travel bans, regional blockades, restrictions on entry, drones broadcasting surveillance, and troops participating in anti-pandemic operations.
> CCTV, 2020

> At present, China's experience in fighting the pandemic, including the seven editions of the COVID-19 Treatment Plan and six editions of the Prevention and Control Plan, has been used by more than 100 countries and 10 international and regional organizations worldwide.
> CCTV, 2020

In addition to stressing emulation of the pandemic prevention policy, China also attempts to play up praise, approval or endorsement emerging from the international media.[14]

---

13   The CCTV source is originally in Chinese and is translated into English by the author, as the focus here is to address Chinese discursive power targeting its domestic audiences.
14   Certainly, China has been using its strategy of 'media offensive' – using its sponsored media outlets to manipulate public opinion – creating, projecting, spreading, and even dominating narratives that feature China's positive images and effective governance.

An editorial titled "China's response to COVID-19: a chance for collaboration" makes the comment that, "China's domestic successes in controlling COVID-19 stand in contrast with outcomes elsewhere, and other countries should learn what public health lessons they can" (The Lancet, 2021). This compliment has repeatedly been mentioned and quoted in many Chinese-led media outlets such as Xinhua news and China Daily (Guo and Liang, 2021; Wang and Wen, 2021).

The Lancet further goes, "China's public health measures, as well as the public's compliance, largely owing to high trust in the government, have contributed to the effective response" (The Lancet, 2021). Among other measures, the most dramatic, and controversial one, was the lockdown of tens of millions of people, which is believed to be the largest quasi-quarantine in human history (Gunia, 2020). In praise of China's strong efforts, WHO Director General Tedros Adhanom Ghebreyesus made the following comments:

> The Chinese government is to be congratulated for the extraordinary measures it has taken to contain the outbreak, despite the severe social and economic impact those measures are having on the Chinese people [...]. In many ways, China is actually setting a new standard for outbreak response. It's not an exaggeration.
> WHO, 2020b

This has been widely cited and spread in China's owned state media and official documents, both in Chinese and English. Following suit, the Chinese state-run press agencies also actively play their role as state's mouthpiece to recognize China's 'great successes' in overcoming the health crisis and bringing social order back to the country. To stress the Chinese state's capacity for mobilization and its own route to success, it gives prominence to the governance model led by the authoritarian regime:

> Relying on its overall national strength, China mobilized the people, enhanced R&D, procured supplies, and brought them to those in need rapidly. It mustered the support of the whole country to assist Hubei, and particularly Wuhan, to combat the disease. It pooled all its strength in the shortest period of time, and halted the spread of the epidemic. Hailing the speed and scale of China's response, WHO Director General Tedros Adhanom Ghebreyesus described it as unprecedented, and said it showed the efficiency and the strength of China's system.
> STATE COUNCIL, 2020

Playing up the international praises to impress its audiences, China's officials keep voicing and stressing comments coming from WHO Director General to manifest how remarkable, advantageous, and exceptional the Chinese way, China's system and CCP governance are:

> It is admirable that the Chinese government has shown its solid political resolve and taken timely and effective measures in dealing with the epidemic [...]. President Xi's personal guidance and deployment show his great leadership capability [...]. China's measures are not only protecting its people but also protecting the people in the whole world [...]. Hailing the high speed and massive scale of China's moves are rarely seen in the world [...] it showed China's efficiency and the advantages of China's system. The experience of China is worth learning for other countries.
> MOFA China, 2020; XINHUA, 2020a

To further affirm its domestic audience that 'the Chinese way' to fight against COVID-19 is valuable for others to learn from, the Chinese government feels the necessity to release the 'White Paper' in six various languages (English, French, Spanish, German, Arabic, and Italian) to explain how China's "all-of-government, all-of-society" approach had "achieved notable success in slowing the spread of the virus and blocking human-to-human transmission" (State Council, 2020).

Most crucially, further targeting its domestic audience to persuade them of the CCP's legitimacy and state capacity, China's authorities speak through the mouth of foreign experts and scholars: the Chinese government has not only been able to handle the crisis properly and effectively but also acted as a great, responsible power moving further forward to the international level to share its experiences, provide medical supports and encourage the international cooperation.

According to the report by Xinhua (2020d), foreign experts and scholars were highly positive about China's active international cooperation in epidemic prevention and control, and expressed their willingness to strengthen cooperation with China. The examples that Xinhua (2020d) reported are wide-ranging. The foreign representatives are across different countries (Brazil, Egypt, Italy, Malaysia, Mexico, Korea, Japan, Thailand, Dominicana, Hungary, Nepal, Kyrgyzstan, South Africa etc.), professions (editors, scholars, professors, government officials, business representatives, etc.) and specialized fields (trade and investment, communication & media, sinology, political science, virology, etc.). Yet, they all reached consensus that it is the governance of the CCP and the socialism with Chinese characteristics that create a role model for others to follow. To admire China's approach and the initiatives China has taken against COVID-19:

> Robert Lawrence Kuhn, president of the Kuhn Foundation, USA, said: China's timely containment of the spread of COVID-19 is largely due to the centralized leadership of the CPC.
> XINHUA, 2020d[15]

> Mansour Abul-Azm, executive editor-in-chief of Egypt's newspaper 'The Pyramids' commented, under President Xi Jinping's personal command and deployment, China's attitude towards the epidemic and the measures it has taken are admirable and show the responsibility of a great country. With the correct leadership of the CPC and the superior system of socialism with Chinese characteristics as a guarantee, China will be able to overcome the epidemic and win this battle.
> XINHUA, 2020d

> Federico Masini, director of the Language Centre at the Sapienza University of Rome, and a renowned sinologist said: in this battle, China has taken timely and effective measures and acted swiftly and forcefully. It has shown us the firm determination and outstanding ability of the Chinese government. China has set a model for epidemic prevention in the world.
> XINHUA, 2020d

> Ronnie Lins, director of the Brazilian Association for the Development of Chinese Trade and Culture, explains, the decisive and strong measures taken by the Chinese Party and government provide an example for the world to respond to major public health emergencies. The Chinese government has demonstrated scientific rigour and discipline, and the Chinese people have shown the patriotism and solidarity, reflecting the remarkable strengths of the socialist system with Chinese characteristics.
> XINHUA, 2020d[16]

---

15 The sources from Xinhua (2020a and 2020b) and China Daily are originally in Chinese and translated into English by the author.
16 For more examples, please refer to Xinhua (2020d).

It goes further with the 'speakers' whose ideology are in line with the CCP:

> Thürmer, chairman of the Hungarian Workers' Party, said that China has made great efforts to fight the pandemic and no other country in the world has been able to efficiently mobilize such a large amount of human and medical resources in a short period of time. This fully demonstrates the great power of socialism with Chinese characteristics.
> XINHUA, 2020C

> We highly appreciate that under the leadership of General Secretary Xi Jinping, the Chinese people are united and brave enough to face the challenges, said Bijukchhe, President of the Nepal Workers and Peasant's Party. The response taken by China is a rare success story in the field of public health and sends a positive message to the world. We believe China will prevail as always.
> XINHUA, 2020C

> Chairman of the Central Committee of the Communist Party of Kyrgyzstan Masaliev said that China has experienced many times of hardship in its history, but the Chinese people have always succeeded in overcoming difficulties and hazards. He believes that under the strong leadership of the CPC, the Chinese people will be able to contain the pandemic and eliminate its negative effects.
> XINHUA, 2020C

> First Deputy Secretary of the South African Communist Party Mapaila said that under the leadership of General Secretary Xi Jinping, the Chinese Party and government have shown excellent leadership in the face of the pandemic, which reflects the superiority of a socialist country. The South African Communist Party is proud of China, and our hearts are with you.
> XINHUA, 2020C

Stressing China's contribution to international cooperation, the following foreign experts depict China as a great, responsible power to respond to public health emergencies in a globalized world.

> Chief Economist at the Institute for International Trade and Investment, Noriyoshi Ehara, said: in the course of the epidemic prevention and

control, China has been maintaining good communication with WHO and actively sharing its experience in epidemic prevention with other countries, which is appreciated.

XINHUA, 2020d

Johan Neyts, president of the International Society for Antiviral Research and professor of Virology at KU Leuven in Belgium, said: China is fighting an invisible 'enemy'. China has taken a series of decisive measures to effectively contain the spread of the epidemic, which has given the international community valuable time to respond effectively to this global public health challenge. Medical institutions around the world should assist each other and work with China to overcome the crisis.

XINHUA, 2020d

Malaysian virologist Lin Shijie said that it was because China was the first to share the gene sequence of the new coronavirus that scientists around the world were able to quickly conduct relevant research and develop potent drugs and vaccines in an effort to take the initiative in this epidemic prevention and control blockade.

XINHUA, 2020d

Tharakorn Wusatirakul, deputy director of the Belt and Road Cooperation Research Centre in Thailand, Thai–Chinese Strategic Research Centre (TCSRC) under the National Research Council of Thailand: in the face of the pandemic, the Chinese government has strengthened communication and close cooperation with WHO and other countries, interpreting the concept of the Community with Shared Future for Mankind with its commitment and making outstanding contributions to the maintenance of global public health.

XINHUA, 2020d

Believing in China's further development and that China model has set an example for the world in the post-pandemic era:

Eduardo Klinger, a Dominicanian expert on China, wrote that the resilience of China's economy is incomparable to that of other countries. Faced with the challenges of the epidemic, China has taken initiatives that demonstrate precisely the kind of economic strength, construction capacity and creativity that other countries do not possess.

XINHUA 2020d

> The international community has seen the power of China in this fight against the epidemic and continues to be positive about China's development, according to Enrique Dussel, coordinator of China–Mexico Study Centre at the National Autonomous University of Mexico.
> XINHUA, 2020d

> Professor Patrick Reinmoeller said, now the rest of the world is still busy fighting the pandemic and preventing a second wave, China's innovations to combat the pandemic are setting a good example for other countries to follow. In the process of economic recovery, China may become an important model for many countries to emulate.
> China Daily, 2020

Through the outside-in narrative approach, the CCP clearly aims to affirm and convey China's confidence and capability to win the battle against the virus outbreak. Meanwhile, by doing so, it delivers the message toward the domestic audiences in China that the international community has witnessed the powerful strength of China in the fight against the pandemic. Plus, the China model with Chinese characteristics is widely recognized and will prevail.

5 Conclusion and Implications: From China under Xi to the World under Xi?

In every country, whether in the process of deciding on major policy directions or policy details, there is always a fundamental set of logic that implicitly guides and influences the decision-making. This logic of thoughts may come from ideology, interest needs, collective values, individual intuitive judgment, or a combination of all of these possibilities (Li and Lee, 2009). This is the so-called strategic perspective of the country. For a country like China, with centralized power and the government system under party-state integration, the strategic perspective has both deep and wide impacts on handling its internal and external affairs (Li and Lee, 2009). Under Xi's administration, the grand strategy of rejuvenation to realize the Chinese Dream is emphasized (Goldstein, 2020). No matter how outward-looking or ambitious it might have shown to seem, it should not be overlooked that "the highest priority of Xi and his fellow Politburo members is 'regime survival'" (Scobell et al., 2020: 26). The "pervasive regime insecurity has a subtle but discernible impact on Chinese statecraft" (Scobell et al., 2020: 26). In Xi's eyes, homeland is the centre of the world that "national security begins at home, and regime security is synonymous with national security" (Scobell et al., 2020: 27).

Accordingly, with its party-state integration and through positing the health emergency into a security context, China under Xi's regime has taken the advantage of the virus to make its authoritarian governance as an imperative and indispensable one. For the sake of people's lives/safety and collective public good, CCP has no alternative but to take control over and penetrate the whole of society. With the policy instrument of persuasion and propaganda (drawing support from its discursive strength), Chinese government has managed to present itself as a competent, responsible, and efficient government that bears in mind the interest of its own people. According to Wu's study (2020) of public responses and social relations in times of crisis, "Chinese citizens' satisfaction with government performance during the pandemic is very high". In investigating the relations among government performance, citizen satisfaction, and trust, Van Ryzin (2007) proclaims that the outcome of overall citizen satisfaction is positively related to trust of government. Increasing trust in government further affirms the CCP's state capacity and its governance legitimacy (Fukuyama, 2020).

Besides, in the name of containing the pandemic, the surveillance system with the help of technology has made the society more legible for the centralized, personalized, and powerful government. Since the outbreak of COVID-19, "China has moved past developing and implementing surveillance high-tech model security and control in troubled spots, to a nationwide level" (Burgers and Romaniuk, 2020). In short, rather than posing a threat to the regime's survival, the pandemic has instead contributed to the consolidation of China's authoritarian governance by means of centralizing power and strengthening its state capacity with the aid of the enhanced legibility and tactful storytelling. In consequence, from theory construction, propaganda/discourse framing, and finally to its operational level, the power of the CCP has been further raised, centralized, and consolidated over and over again.

Certainly, at the time of writing the chapter, the pandemic is still ongoing, and it is still open to observe how the pandemic situation can further influence the ruling party, CCP's governance and legitimacy in China, especially given the increasing cases in Shanghai.

China's 'performance' on responding the COVID-19 pandemic has impressed the world with its unprecedented but seem-to-be efficient measures, at least before the Omicron wave hit hard on main cities like Shanghai and led to the subsequent strict lockdowns in the city starting in March 2022. During the

Omicron wave, China's zero-COVID policy,[17] strict measures, and lockdowns have aroused many concerns, doubts, and criticisms within and outside the country, particularly concerning the food supply shortage, economic disruptions and the access to the medical care (Yuan, 2022). Despite the increasing criticism from the citizens, Chinese President Xi has not given any indication that the zero strategy will change but insists that it is "scientific and effective", that officials should "keep a clear head and unswervingly adhere to the general policy of dynamic zero-COVID"[18] (Xinhua, 2022). Besides, Xi also demonstrated China's firm stand on zero-COVID policy, stating that China "will resolutely struggle against all words and deeds that distort, doubt and deny our epidemic prevention policies" (Xinhua, 2022). To ensure the policy will be implemented without facing obstacles or protests, censorship with assistance from its developed technology has been imposed by the Chinese government. Many reports or videos, which reveal information tending to question or challenge the necessity or sustainability of the zero-COVID policy, have been forced to remove or delete from the social media. Through collecting the data, censoring its population, blocking the unfavourable information, encouraging the set-up of the rewarding mechanism to whistle-blowers for disclosing potential COVID-infected cases, and framing the tactful 'put-people-and-their-life-first' as well as 'China-has-its-special-circumstance-but-is-one-of-the-most-successful-countries-in-the-world-in-combating-COVID' narratives, Chinese government has nonetheless enhanced the legibility, centralized its power, and strengthened its state capacity.

Yet, making a strong state an even stronger one is not the enduring solution to a sustainable governance in an interdependent and globalized world. Showing the concern that China's zero-COVID strategy is not sustainable, Dr Tedros Adhanom Ghebreyesus of the WHO, who once praised China's COVID-policy, comments: "The virus is evolving, changing its behavior [...]. With that (…) changing your measures will be very important" (Song, 2022). However, in response to WHO's concern, Foreign Ministry Spokesperson Zhao Lijian made a clear statement in the press conference that:

---

17 The zero-COVID strategy has been the major pillar of China's COVID policy for over 2 years and has been considered a key success in keeping the virus at bay at the start of the pandemic, in contrast to other countries in the world (Yuan, 2022).

18 For promoting, supporting and justifying the zero-COVID strategy, as usual, Chinese government has expressed its position through foreign experts and officials, to back its policy priority up. For more specific examples on how foreign experts and official spoke in favor of China, please refer to State Council (2022).

> I would like to stress one last point that the Chinese government has formulated and implemented the dynamic zero-COVID policy based on China's national realities and has been adjusting prevention and control protocols based on the changing conditions. The purpose is solely to protect people's life and health to the greatest extent possible and underpin sustained, sound and steady economic and social development. In China, we have the foundation, the conditions and the capability to achieve dynamic zero-COVID. We have every confidence in winning this hard battle and making greater contributions to the united global response.
>
> MOFA China, 2022

With the experiences of handling COVID-19, China has exhibited its ability to "control the population, deter unrest and enhance stability-maintenance" (Burgers and Romaniuk, 2020). In contrast with 'other countries' who failed to offer effective public health response and economic restart, China's example further suggests a plausible pathway that the almighty Chinese government is therefore more confident and encouraged to promote the model of authoritarian governance at the international level. As Pils (2020) puts it, "most concerningly, China's 'emergency responses' have brought to the fore the features of a system that China's current leadership is touting as superior to the liberal-democratic order" (p. 7). This might point to the future trajectory of China's influences in the international sphere:[19] authoritarian resilience by defining the essence of 'good governance' and transforming the norms of the world order. Consequently, an extreme scenario could be imagined: an overstated and prettified 'community with a shared future' favoured by China could ultimately turn out to be an Orwellian world of surveillance, propaganda, and censorship. That is, Big Brother operates the governance machine, supervises the cameras with facial recognition software and drones, calculates the social credit points, defines individuals with scores, creates a society with the atmosphere of trust and stability, and eventually establishes the *peaceful* and *harmonious* order. That being said, what happens in China might not stay only within China.

---

19 For more details concerning China's international influences exercised by its growing discursive power amid the pandemic period, please refer to Chang (2020).

References

Ahrendt Daphne, Jorge Cabrita, Eleonora Clerici, John Hurley, Tadas Leončikas, Massimiliano Mascherini, Sara Riso and Eszter Sándor (2020) Living, working and COVID-19. http://eurofound.link/ef20059, accessed 16 July 2021.

Alon, Ilan, and Shaomin Li (2020) COVID-19 Response: Democracies vs. Authoritarians. *The Spectator*, 27 March, https://spectator.org/covid-19-response-democracies-v-authoritarians/, accessed August 18, 2021.

Alon, Ilan, Matthew Farrell, and Shaomin Li (2020) Regime type and COVID-19 response. *Business Review.*, 9(3), pp. 152–160.

Andrews, Matt, Lant Pritchett, and Michael Woolcock (2017) *Building State Capability: Evidence, Analysis, Action*. Oxford: Oxford University Press.

Ang, Yuen Yuen (2020) When COVID-19 meets centralized, personalized power. *Nature Human Behaviour*, 4, pp. 445–447.

Atlantic Council (2020) China's Shift Toward Discourse Power. https://www.jstor.org/stable/pdf/resrep27615.5.pdf, accessed 18 August 2021.

Babones, Salvatore (2021) Yes, You Can Use the T-Word to Describe China. *Foreign Policy*, 10 April, https://foreignpolicy.com/2021/04/10/china-xi-jinping-totalitarian-authoritarian-debate/, accessed 16 July 2021.

Backer, Larry Catá (2009) The party as polity, the Communist Party, and the Chinese constitutional state: a theory of state-party constitutionalism. *Journal of Chinese and Comparative Law*, 16(1), pp. 101–168.

Bartsch, Bernhard and Martin Gottake (2021) *China's social credit system*. https://www.bertelsmann-stiftung.de/fileadmin/files/aam/Asia-Book_A_03_China_Social_Credit_System.pdf, accessed 8 October 2021.

Bemelmans-Videc, Marie-Louise, Ray C. Rist and Evert Oskar Vedung (1998) *Carrots, Sticks & Sermons: Policy Instruments & Their Evaluation*. New Brunswick: Transaction Publishers.

Besley, Timothy and Torsten Persson (2008) Wars and State Capacity. *Journal of the European Economic Association*, 6(2–3), pp. 522–530.

Boin, Arjen, Paul 't Hart, Eric Stern and Bengt Sundelius (2017) *The Politics of Crisis Management: Public Leadership Under Pressure*. Cambridge: Cambridge University Press.

Brands, Hal (2020) Coronavirus Is China's Chance to Weaken the Liberal Order. *Bloomberg*, 17 March, https://www.bloomberg.com/opinion/articles/2020-03-17/coronavirus-is-making-china-s-model-look-better-and-better, accessed 19 September 2021.

Breslin, Shaun (2011) The 'China model' and the global crisis: from Friedrich List to a Chinese mode of governance? *International Affairs*, 87(6), pp. 1323–1343.

Brown, Frances Z., Saskia Brechenmacher and Thomas Carothers (2020) How Will the Coronavirus Reshape Democracy and Governance Globally? *Carniegie*, 6

April, https://carnegieendowment.org/2020/04/06/how-will-coronavirus-reshape-democracy-and-governance-globally-pub-81470, accessed 8 June 2021.

Brzezinski, Zbigniew K. (1962) *Ideology and Power in Soviet Politics*. New York: Praeger.

Bunyavejchewin, Poowin and Ketsarin Sirichuanjun (2021) How regime type and governance quality affect policy responses to COVID-19: A preliminary analysis. *Heliyon* (7).

Burgers, Tobias and David R. S. Robinson (2016) Networked Authoritarianism Is on the Rise. *Security and Peace*, 34(4), pp. 248–252.

Burgers, Tobias and Scott N. Romaniuk (2020) Can the Coronavirus Strengthen China's Authoritarian Regime? *The Diplomat*, 10 March, https://thediplomat.com/2020/03/can-the-coronavirus-strengthen-chinas-authoritarian-regime/, accessed 20 May 2021.

Callahan, William A. (2015) Identity and security in China: the negative soft power of the China dream. *Politics,* 35(3–4), pp. 216–229.

CCTV (2020) RT shuole dashihua dangchu piping zhongguo de fangyi cuoshi xifang dou yongshang le. *CCTV*, 23 March, http://m.news.cctv.com/2020/03/22/ARTIF4Zs2T0F6EASPkmM2Leu200322.shtml, accessed 18 June 2021.

Cepaluni, Gabriel, Michael Dorsch, and Reka Branyiczki (2020) Political Regimes and Deaths in the Early Stages of the COVID-19 Pandemic, 29 March. https://ssrn.com/abstract=3586767, accessed 8 May 2021.

Chan, Melissa (2022) China isn't just 'authoritarian' any more. It's scarier.*The Washington Post,* 31 January https://www.washingtonpost.com/opinions/2022/01/31/china-authoritarian-fascism-totalitarian-uyghurs-surveillance/, accessed 25 February 2022.

Chang Yung-Yung (2019) Understanding the Belt and Road Initiative (BRI). An Initiative to Make China Great Again? *European Journal of East Asian Studies,* 18, pp. 7–35.

Chang Yung-Yung (2020) The Post-Pandemic World: between constitutionalized and authoritarian orders – China's narrative power play in the pandemic Era. *Journal of Chinese Political Science,* 26(1), pp. 27–65.

Chen Yu-Jie, Ching-Fu Linand Han-Wei Liu (2018) 'Rule of Trust': The Power and Perils of China's Social Credit Megaproject. *Columbia Journal of Asian Law,* 32(1), pp. 1–36.

China Daily (2020) 【Zhongguo naxie shi'er】Waiguo zhuanjia: hou yiqing shidai "Zhongguo moshi" wei shijie shuli bangyang. *China Daily*, 26 May, https://cn.chinadaily.com.cn/a/202005/26/WS5ecce262a310eec9c72bb74b.html, accessed 20 May 2021.

Cooley, Alexander (2015) Authoritarianism Goes Global. *Journal of Democracy,* 26(3), pp. 49–63.

Dahl, Robert A. (1957) The Concept of Power. *Behavioral Science,* 2(3), pp. 201–215.

Deng, Xiaoping (1982) Opening speech at the 12th National Congress of the Communist Party of China. *China Daily*, 20 Ocotber, https://www.chinadaily.com.cn/china/19thcpcnationalcongress/2010-10/20/content_29714514.htm accessed 20 May 2021.

Diamond, Irene and Lee Quinby (ed.) (1988) *Feminism and Foucault: Reflections on Resistance*. Boston: Northeastern University Press.

Diamond, Larry (1989) Beyond Authoritarianism and Totalitarianism: Strategies for Democratization. *The Washington Quarterly*, 12(1), pp. 141–163.

Diamond, Larry (2010) Liberation Technology. *Journal of Democracy*, 21(3), pp. 69–83.

Donnelly, Drew (2024) China Social Credit System Explained---What is it and How does it work? https://joinhorizons.com/china-social-credit-system-explained/, accessed 26 May 2024.

Doyle, Randall and Boshu Zhang (2011) *Modern China and the New World: The Reemergence of the Middle Kingdom in the Twenty-first Century*. Maryland: Lexington Books.

Drinhausen, Katja (2018) China's digital revolution. In: A. S. Francois Godement, Marcin Przychodniak, Katja Drinhausen, Adam Knight, Elsa B. Kania (ed.) *The China dream goes digital: Technology in the age of Xi*. London: European Council on Foreign Relations, pp. 2–4.

Drinhausen, Katja and Vincent Brussee (2021) China's social credit system in 2021: from fragmentation to integration. *Merics*, 9 May, https://merics.org/en/report/chinas-social-credit-system-2021-fragmentation-towards-integration, accessed 18 August 2021.

Drinhausen, Katja, and John Lee (2021) The CCP in 2021: smart governance, cyber sovereignty and tech supremacy. *Merics*, 9 May, https://merics.org/en/ccp-2021-smart-governance-cyber-sovereignty-and-tech-supremacy, accessed 8 August 2021.

Frey, Carl Benedikt, Chinchih Chen, and Giorgio Presidente (2020a) Democracy, Culture and Contagion: Political Regimes and Countries Responsiveness to COVID-19. 13 May, https://www.oxfordmartin.ox.ac.uk/publications/democracy-culture-and-contagion-political-regimes-and-countries-responsiveness-to-covid-19/, accessed 25 July 2021.

Frey, Carl Benedikt, Giorgio Presidente, and Chinchih Chen (2020b) COVID-19 and the future of democracy *Cerp.org*, 20 May, https://voxeu.org/article/covid-19-and-future-democracy, accessed 28 July 2021.

Fukuyama, Francis (2020) The Thing That Determines a Country's Resistance to the Coronavirus. *The Atlantic*, 30 March, https://www.theatlantic.com/ideas/archive/2020/03/thing-determines-how-well-countries-respond-coronavirus/609025/, accessed 7 August 2021.

Ge, Christina (2019) The Historical Roots of the Social Credit System. *Brown Political Review*, 30 March, https://brownpoliticalreview.org/2019/03/historical-roots-social-credit-system/, accessed: 25 May 2021.

Geddes, Barbara (1994) *Politician's Dilemma: Building State Capacity in Latin America*. Berkeley: University of California Press.

Gladstein, Alex (2020) Dictatorships Are Making the Coronavirus Outbreak Worse. *WIRED*, 2 March, https://www.wired.com/story/opinion-dictatorships-are-making-the-coronavirus-outbreak-worse/, accessed 26 June 2021.

Godement, Francois (2018) Introduction. In: François Godement, Katja Drinhausen, Marcin Przychodniak, Adam Knight, Elsa B. Kania and Angela Stanzel (ed.). *THE CHINA DREAM GOES DIGITAL: TECHNOLOGY IN THE AGE OF XI*. London: European Council on Foreign Relations.

Goldstein, Avery (2020) China's Grand Strategy under Xi Jinping: Reassurance, Reform, and Resistance. *International Security*, 45(1), pp. 164–201.

Grünberg, Nis and Katja Drinhausen (2019) The Party leads on everything. China's changing governance in Xi Jinping's new era. *Merics*, 30 September, https://merics.org/en/report/party-leads-everything, accessed 8 August 2021.

Gunia, Amy (2020) China's Draconian Lockdown Is Getting Credit for Slowing Coronavirus. Would It Work Anywhere Else? *TIME*, 13 March, https://time.com/5796425/china-coronavirus-lockdown/, accessed 25 July 2021.

Guo, Wenrui, and Jun Liang (2021) Global health challenges require global responses, cooperation: The Lancet. *Xinhua*, 14 April, http://en.people.cn/n3/2021/0414/c90000-9838931.html, accessed 10 June 2021.

Guzzini, Stefano (2000) A Reconstruction of Constructivism in International Relations. *European Journal of International Relations*, 6(2), pp. 156–162.

Hagstrom, Linus (2012) 'Power Shift' in East Asia? A Critical Reappraisal of Narratives on the Diaoyu/Senkaku Islands Incident in 2010. *The Chinese Journal of International Politics*, 5, pp. 267–297.

Harari, Yuval Noah (2020) The world after coronavirus. *Financial Times*, 20 March, https://www.ft.com/content/19d90308-6858-11ea-a3c9-1fe6fedcca75, accessed 10 September 2021.

He, Baogang and Mark E. Warren (2011) Authoritarian Deliberation: The Deliberative Turn in Chinese Political Development. *Perspectives on Politics*, 9(2), pp. 269–289.

Hilpert, Hanns Günther and Angela Stanzel (2021) China-Winning the Pandemic... for Now. *SWP*, 7 January, https://www.swp-berlin.org/10.18449/2021C01/, accessed 16 July 2021.

Hobbes, Thomas (2008) *Leviathan*. Oxford: Oxford University Press.

Huang, Lanlan (2020) Broad use of health codes raises privacy and legality concerns. *Global Times*, 17 June, https://www.globaltimes.cn/content/1191847.shtml, accessed 25 May 2021.

Huang, Yanzhong (2004) The SARS Epidemic and its Aftermath in China: a political perspective. In: Adel Mahmoud, Stacey Knobler, Stanley Lemon, Alison Mack, Laura Sivitz and Katherine Oberholtzer (ed.) *Learning from SARS*. Washington DC: National Academy of Sciences, pp. 116–136.

Hutcheon, Linda (1991) *Discourse, power, ideology: Humanism and post-modernism.* New York: Routledge.

Jentleson, Bruce (2018) The Post-Liberal International Order World: Some Core Characteristics. *Lawfare* 9 September, https://www.lawfareblog.com/post-liberal-international-order-world-some-core-characteristics, accessed 28 April 2021.

Jiang Shigong (2013) Chinese-Style Constitutionalism: On Backer's Chinese Party-State Constitutionalism. *Modern China,* 40(2), pp. 133–167.

Kavanagh, Matthew M. (2020) Authoritarianism, Outbreaks, and Information Politics. *The Lancet Public Health,* 5(3), pp. E135–E136.

Kay, Richard S. (1998) American Constitutionalism. In: Alexander Larry (ed.) *Constitutionalism: Philosophical Foundations.* Cambridge: Cambridge University Press, pp. 16–63.

Khalil, Lydia (2020) Digital Authoritarianism, China and COVID. *Lowy Institute for International Policy,* November, http://www.jstor.org/stable/resrep27665, accessed 7 February 2024.

Knight, Adam (2018) Credit: The god of China's big data era. In: M. P. François Godement, Katja Drinhausen, Adam Knight, Elsa B Kania and Angela Stanzel (ed.). *The China Dream goes Digital: Technology in the Age of XI.* London: European Council on Foreign Relations, pp. 7–9.

Krasner, Stephen D., and Thomas Risse (2014) External Actors, State-Building, and Service Provision in Areas of Limited Statehood: Introduction. *Governance,* 27(4), pp. 545–567.

Kreuder-Sonnen, Christian, and Bernhard Zangl (2015) Which Post-Westphalia? International organizations between constitutionalism and authoritarianism. *European Journal of International Relations,* 21(3), pp. 568–594.

Lamond, James (2020) Authoritarian Regimes Seek To Take Advantage of the Coronavirus Pandemic, *Center for American Progress,* 6 April, https://www.americanprogress.org/issues/security/news/2020/04/06/482715/authoritarian-regimes-seek-take-advantage-coronavirus-pandemic/, accessed 5 October 2021.

Lee, Melissa M. and Nan Zhang (2016) Legibility and the Informational Foundations of State Capacity. *The Journal of Politics,* 79(1), pp. 118–132.

Legarda, Helena (2021) China's new international paradigm: security first, *Merics,* 15 June, https://merics.org/en/chinas-new-international-paradigm-security-first, accessed 8 July 2021.

Levi, Margaret (1988) *Of Rule and Revenue.* Berkeley: University of California Press.

Li Jiun-Rong and Lee Ching-Yi (2009) Lun 'heping yu fazhanzhanlue guanxia de hexie shijieyu hexie shehui' [The "Harmonious World" and "Harmonious Society" Policies under China's Strategic Perspective of "Peace and Development"]. *Prospect and Exploration,* 7(6), pp. 27–50.

Liang Fan (2020) COVID-19 and Health Code: How Digital Platforms Tackle the Pandemic in China. *Social Media + Society* 6(3), pp. 1–4.

Lindvall, Johannes and Jan Teorell (2016) State Capacity as Power: A Conceptual Framework. STANCE *Working Paper Series* (1),https://lucris.lub.lu.se/ws/portalfiles/portal/102775891/WP_1_Lindvall_and_Teorell_State_Capacity_as_Power_A_Conceptual_Framework.pdf, accessed 10 February 2024.

Linz, Juan J. (1964) An authoritarian regime: the case of Spain. In: Erik Allardt & Yrio Littunen (ed.), *Cleavages, Ideologies and Party Systems*. Helsinki: Westermarck Society.

Livework (2021) What is an outside-in perspective? *Live and work studio*. https://www.liveworkstudio.com/monthly-magazines/what-is-an-outside-in-perspective/, accessed 25 September 2021.

MacKinnon, Rebecca (2011) Liberation Technology: China's "Networked Authoritarianism". *Journal of Democracy*, 22(2), pp. 32–46.

Mann, Michael (1984) The Autonomous Power of the State: Its Origins, Mechanisms and Results. *Archives européenne de sociologie*, 25, pp. 185–213.

Mao Yexin (2021) Political institutions, state capacity, and crisis management: A comparison of China and South Korea. *International Political Science Review*, 42(3), pp. 316–332.

Marston, Cicely, Alicia Renedo and Sam Miles (2020) Community participation is crucial in a pandemic. *The Lancet*, 395(10238), pp. 1676–1678.

McAdam, Doug, Sidney Tarrow and Charles Tilly (2001) *Dynamics of Contention*. Cambridge: Cambridge University Press.

Migdal, Joel (1988) *Strong Societies and Weak States*. Princeton: Princeton University Press.

MOFA China (2020) Xi Jinping meets with World Health Organization Director-General Tedros Adhanom Ghebreyesus. https://www.mfa.gov.cn/ce/cede//chn/zt/coronavirus/t1736817.htm, accessed 18 August 2021.

MOFA China (2022) Foreign Ministry Spokesperson Zhao Lijian's Regular Press Conference on May 11, 2022. https://www.fmprc.gov.cn/mfa_eng/xwfw_665399/s2510_665401/2511_665403/202205/t20220511_10684604.html, accessed 25 May 2022.

Mozur, Paul, Raymond Zhong, and Aaron Krolik (2020) In Coronavirus fight, China gives citizens a color code, with red flags. *The New York Times*, 1 March, https://www.nytimes.com/2020/03/01/business/china-coronavirus-surveillance.html, accessed 25 July 2021.

Myers, Steven Lee and Chris Buckley (2020) In China's Crisis, Xi Sees a Crucible to Strengthen His Rule. *The New York Times*, 20 March, https://www.nytimes.com/2020/05/20/world/asia/coronavirus-china-xi-jinping.html, accessed 28 June 2021.

New China TV (2020) *Once upon a virus*. YouTube, https://www.youtube.com/watch?v=XVTbNQUg7sY, accessed 12 November 2021.

O'Neill, Patrick Howell, Tate Ryan-Mosley and Bobbie Johnson (2020) A flood of coronavirus apps are tracking us. Now it's time to keep track of them. *MIT Technology Review*, 20 May, https://www.technologyreview.com/2020/05/07/1000961/launching-mittr-covid-tracing-tracker/, accessed 19 October 2021.

O'Neill, Patrick Howell, Tate Ryan-Mosley and Bobbie Johnson (2021) MIT Technology Review's COVID Tracing Tracker, https://docs.google.com/spreadsheets/d/1ATalASO8KtZMx__zJREoOvFhonmB-sAqJ1-CjVRSCOw/edit#gid=0, accessed 25 October 2021.

People's Daily (2018) https://twitter.com/PDChina/status/978444380066390016, March 27, accessed 23 August 2021.

Piazza, Kelly Senters and Kylie Stronko (2020) Democrats, authoritarians, and the coronavirus: Who is winning at policy efficacy? *Global Policy*, 12 June, https://www.globalpolicyjournal.com/articles/health-and-social-policy/democrats-authoritarians-and-coronavirus-who-winning-policy, accessed 18 June 2021.

Pils, Eva (2020) China's Response to the Coronavirus Pandemic: Fighting Two Enemies. *Varfassungblog.de*, 20 May, https://verfassungsblog.de/chinas-response-to-the-coronavirus-pandemic-fighting-two-enemies/, accessed 25 August 2021.

Pitsoe, Victor and Moeketsi Letseka (2013) Foucault's Discourse and Power: Implications for Instructionist Classroom Management. *Open Journal of Philosophy*, 3(1), pp. 23–28.

Roth, Kenneth, and Maya Wang (2019) Data Leviathan: China's Burgeoning Surveillance State. *The New York Review*, 16 August, https://www.nybooks.com/daily/2019/08/16/data-leviathan-chinas-burgeoning-surveillance-state/, accessed 20 July 2021.

Scheppele, Kim Lane (2004) Law in a Time of Emergency: States of Exception and the Temptations of 9/11. *Journal of Constitutional Law*, 6(5), pp. 1001–1008.

Schmemann, Serge (2020) The Virus Comes for Democracy. *The New York Times*, 2 April, https://www.nytimes.com/2020/04/02/opinion/coronavirus-democracy.html, accessed 17 July 2021.

Schmidt, Vivien A. (2008) Discursive Institutionalism: The Explanatory Power of Ideas and Discourse. *The Annual Review of Political Science*, 11, pp. 303–326.

Scobell, Andrew, Edmund J. Burke, Cortez A. Cooper, III, Sale Lilly, Chad J. R. Ohlandt, Eric Warner, and J.D. Williams (2020) *China's Grand Strategy: Trends, Trajectories, and Long-Term Competition*. Santa Monica: RAND Corporation.

Scott, James C. (1998) *Seeing Like a State: How Certain Schemes to Improve the Human Condition Have Failed*. New Haven: Yale University Press.

Scott, James C. (2009) *The Art of Not Being Governed: An Anarchist History of Upland Southeast Asia*. New Haven: Yale University Press.

Skocpol, Theda (1985) Strategies of Analysis in Current Research. In: Peter B Evans, Dietrich Rueschemeyer and Theda Skocpol (ed.) *Bringing the State Back In.* Cambridge: Cambridge University Press, pp. 3–38.

Snow, Thea (2021) The (il)logic of legibility: why governments should stop simplifying complex systems. *Medium.com*, 10 February, https://medium.com/centre-for-public-impact/the-il-logic-of-legibility-why-governments-should-stop-simplifying-complex-systems-f8822752d753, accessed 27 June 2021.

Soifer, Hillel (2008) State Infrastructural Power: Approaches to Conceptualization and Measurement. *Studies in Comparative International Development*, 43, pp. 231–251.

Soifer, Hillel David (2013) State Power and the Economic Origins of Democracy. *Studies in Comparative International Development*, 48(1), pp. 1–22.

Song Wanyuan (2022) China: Why is the WHO concerned about its zero-COVID strategy? *BBC News.* 10 January, https://www.bbc.com/news/59882774, accessed: 18 May 2022.

State Council (2014) Shehui xinyong tixi jianshe guihua gangyao (2014–2020 nian) de tongzhi [Planning Outline for the Construction of a Social Credit System (2014–2020)]. *China Copyright and Media*, 25 April, https://chinacopyrightandmedia.wordpress.com/2014/06/14/planning-outline-for-the-construction-of-a-social-credit-system-2014-2020/, accessed 8 August 2021.

State Council (2020) Fighting COVID-19: China in Action. 16 June, https://english.www.gov.cn/news/topnews/202006/07/content_WS5edc559ac6d066592a449030.html, accessed 5 August 2021.

State Council (2021) China releases new five-year plan on legal awareness. http://english.www.gov.cn/policies/latestreleases/202106/16/content_WS60c93527c6d0df57f98db3f6.html, accessed 8 August 2021.

State Council (2022) "Chongfen zhanxian dui renmin shengming jiankang de gaodu fuzhe"—guoji shehui jiji pingjia Zhongguo yiqing fangkong jianchi "dongtai qingling" zongfangzhen bu dongyao (The international community positively evaluates China's adherence to the general policy of 'dynamic zero' in the prevention and control of the epidemic). 19 April, https://www.gov.cn/xinwen/2022-04/19/content_5685932.htm, accessed 8 August 2021.

Tan Shining (2020) China's Novel Health Tracker: Green on Public Health, Red on Data Surveillance. *Cisc.org*, 4 May, https://www.csis.org/blogs/trustee-china-hand/chinas-novel-health-tracker-green-public-health-red-data-surveillance, accessed 25 June, 2021.

The BRICS Post (2014) Xi vows to make China a cyber power. https://www.thebricspost.com/xi-vows-to-make-china-a-cyber-power/, accessed 18 May 2021.

The Lancet (2021) China's response to COVID-19: a chance for collaboration. *The Lancet*, 397. https://www.thelancet.com/pdfs/journals/lancet/PIIS0140-6736(21)00823-0.pdf, accessed 25 June 2021.

The People's Government of Fujian Province (2021) Outline of the 14th Five-Year Plan (2021–2025) for National Economic and Social Development and Vision 2035 of the People's Republic of China. 8 September, https://www.fujian.gov.cn/english/news/202108/t20210809_5665713.htm, accessed 6 September 2021.

Van Ryzin, Gregg G. (2007) Pieces of a Puzzle: Linking Government Performance, Citizen Satisfaction, and Trust. *Public Performance & Management Review*, 30(4), pp. 521–535.

Walt, Stephen M. (2020) The Realist's Guide to the Coronavirus Outbreak. *Foreign policy*. 9 March, https://foreignpolicy.com/2020/03/09/coronavirus-economy-globalization-virus-icu-realism/, accessed 25 May, 2021.

Wang Bin and Xin Wen (2021) Xinhua Commentary: China's stringent COVID-19 control measures people-centered, coordinated approach. *Xinhuanet*, 17 August, http://www.news.cn/english/2021-08/17/c_1310132944.htm, accessed 28 September 2021.

Wang Yuhua and Carl Minzner (2015) The Rise of the Chinese Security State. *THE CHINA QUARTERLY*, 222, pp. 339–359.

Wang, Maya (2020) China: Fighting COVID-19 With Automated Tyranny. *The Diplomat*, 1 April, https://thediplomat.com/2020/03/china-fighting-covid-19-with-automated-tyranny/, accessed 28 June 2021.

Wang, Peter (2021) What Do the Chinese Think about Their Government's Response to COVID-19? *The Chicago Concuil on Global Affairs*, 26 March, https://www.thechicagocouncil.org/commentary-and-analysis/blogs/what-do-chinese-think-about-their-governments-response-covid-19, accessed 25 June 2021.

Weedon, Chris (1987) *Feminist practice and poststructuralist theory*. Oxford: Blackwell.

Wendt, Alexander (1999) *Social Theory of International Politics*. New York: Cambridge University Press.

WHO (2020a) Report of the WHO-China Joint Mission on Coronavirus Disease 2019 (COVID-19). 28 February, https://www.who.int/publications/i/item/report-of-the-who-china-joint-mission-on-coronavirus-disease-2019-(covid-19), accessed 8 June 2021.

WHO (2020b) WHO Director-General's statement on IHR Emergency Committee on Novel Coronavirus (2019-nCoV). 30 January, https://www.who.int/director-general/speeches/detail/who-director-general-s-statement-on-ihr-emergency-committee-on-novel-coronavirus-(2019-ncov), accessed 8 June 2021.

Wu, Cary (2020) How Chinese citizens view their government's coronavirus response. *The Coversation*, 4 June, https://theconversation.com/how-chinese-citizens-view-their-governments-coronavirus-response-139176, accessed 18 July 2021.

Xinhua (2018) CPC meeting reviews work rules of rural organizations, disciplinary inspection agencies, 26 November, http://www.xinhuanet.com/english/2018-11/26/c_137632863.htm, accessed 25 May 2021.

Xinhua (2020a) China Focus: Xi voices full confidence in winning battle against novel coronavirus, 28 January, http://www.xinhuanet.com/english/2020-01/28/c_138739962.htm, accessed 28 May 2021.

Xinhua (2020b) Fighting the "epidemic", Xi Jinping conveys confidence to the world that China will win. 21 February, http://www.xinhuanet.com/politics/xxjxs/2020-02/21/c_1125604458.htm, accessed 28 May 2021.

Xinhua (2020c) Waiguo zhengdang lingdaoren he zhiming renshi dui zhongguo zhansheng xinxing guanzhuang bingdu yiqing chongman xinxin. 2 November, http://www.xinhuanet.com/world/2020-02/11/c_1125560346.htm, accessed 28 May 2021.

Xinhua (2020d) Zhongguo shuli le shijie fangyi de dianfan – Xi jinping zhuxi tongchou tuijin xinguan feiyan yiqing fangkong he jingji shehui fazhan gongzuo bushu huiyi zhongyao jianghua zai guoji shehui yinqi relie fanxiang. http://www.xinhuanet.com/2020-02/25/c_1125623376.htm, accessed 28 May 2021.

Xinhua (2022) The Standing Committee of the Political Bureau of the CPC Central Committee held a meeting with Xi Jinping hosting the meeting. 5 May, http://www.gov.cn/xinwen/2022-05/05/content_5688712.htm, accessed 4 June 2022.

Xue, Melanie Meng (2020) Autocratic rule and social capital: evidence from imperial China. https://economics.yale.edu/sites/default/files/autocracy_ada-ns.pdf, accessed 18 June 2021.

Youngs, Richard and Elene Panchulidze (2020) Global Democracy & COVID-19: Upgrading international support. https://www.idea.int/sites/default/files/publications/global-democracy-and-covid-19.pdf, accessed 28 June 2021.

YouTube (2020) Xi Jinping's speech at Xi'an Jiaotong University on April 24, 2020: epidemic prevention and control is also a historical opportunity to turn crisis into opportunity. https://www.youtube.com/watch?v=O_cVuHBnk6s, accessed 16 July 2021.

Yuan, Shawn (2022) Zero COVID in China: what next? *thelancet.com* (399), 14 May, https://www.thelancet.com/journals/lancet/article/PIIS0140-6736(22)00873-X/fulltext, accessed, 28 May 2022.

Yu Wimmas (2020) 【Xinguan bingdu】Xinhuashe「Lego」donghua pengji meiguo xieze. SBS, 4 May, https://www.sbs.com.au/chinese/cantonese/zh-hans/chinese-state-media-releases-animated-propaganda-video-mocking-us-coronavirus-response, accessed 28 May 2021.

Zelikow, Philip (2017) Is the World Slouching Toward a Grave Systemic Crisis? *The Atlantic*, 11 August, https://www.theatlantic.com/international/archive/2017/08/zelikow-system-crisis/536205/, accessed 18 May 2021.

PART 2
Economic Dimensions

CHAPTER 6

The Great Chinese Transformation

From the Third to the First World

Grzegorz W. Kołodko

1   Three Worlds in One

The idea of the so called Third World was never clear. In the decades preceding the great post-socialist transition boosted by Poland's political breakthrough of 1989, it was most often assumed, without going into the intricacies of terminology and definition, that the first world is the highly developed capitalism headed by the United States, the second world is the state socialism with the Soviet Union (USSR) at the helm, and the Third World is all the rest – most often poor and backward countries, in many cases, especially in Africa – ones still shaking off the legacy of colonialism. One would also often refer to this group of countries as developing countries, though in many cases development was not one of their characteristics. In such a triple division, the Third World was characterised by low output and living standards, by a large population and a quick growth thereof. Even back then one already had to wonder to which world China belonged. Certainly not to the first one, from which it was separated by an unbridgeable gap, but to the second or third one?

China did not wish to be classified as the "second world" as it did not accept the "with the Soviet Union at the helm" formula, while being unable to put itself at its helm. Maybe in the very beginning of the People's Republic of China's (PRC) existence, in early 1950s, it had accepted Soviet political predominance but later this changed. Curiously, Mao Zedong in the final years of his rule put the USSR in the same group as the USA. In 1974, he said: "In my view, the United States and the Soviet Union belong to the first world. The in-between Japan, Europe and Canada belong to the second world. The third world is very populous. Except Japan, Asia belongs to the third world. So does the whole of Africa and Latin America" (Mao, 1974).[1] Of course, the "Third World"

---

1   It would be interesting to know where Chairman Mao saw the place of Central and Eastern European countries in his classification. Probably not in "Europe" but rather by the Soviet Union's side, so in the "first world".

defined this way should have had China at its helm to be able to stand up to the other two worlds and follow its own, only legitimate way towards a better future.

At that time China was already the world's most populated country, inhabited by 22.5 percent of global population, but it was also one of the poorest countries with a very backward agriculture producing as little as 2.8% of global output. To realise how extreme the poverty was there, it is enough to be aware that, according to today's poverty measure (USD 3.20 per person a day at purchasing power parity (PPP)), in the initial years of the PRC more than 99% of the society suffered from it! This was truly a country of paupers. *Now the poor people represent less than 1%.*[2] The ambitious Chinese plan to eliminate poverty altogether in 2020 would mean a position where the economy and social policy provide everyone with a net annual income above RMB 2300, an equivalent of USD 324 at the market exchange rate, and of USD 684 at PPP. Unfortunately, the perturbation brought by the COVID-19 outbreak will doubtlessly delay this historic achievement.

There is a saying I once heard in Africa: "If you want to go fast, go alone, if you want to go far, go together". China is showing to all humankind – both the rich and, more importantly, the poor – that one can both go fast and far. In just a lifetime of two generations – between 1979 and 2020, when the population figure has risen by 45%, from 970 million to 1.4 billion. In other words, China increased its output measured with GDP the unprecedented 40 times! It is hard to believe but these are the facts.[3] Considering the purchasing power and its changes, GDP grew from USD 690 billion to nearly 27 trillion. According to the same PPP measure, GDP per capita rose nearly 27 times in this period, exceeding the world average by 6–7%.

---

[2] During the four decades of China's market reforms and opening to the world, over 850 million people got out of poverty. However, as many as 373 million people are still living on less than USD 5.50 a day over there, that is below the poverty line set for upper-middle income economies, a category to which China belongs (World Bank, 2020).

[3] At constant prices of 2010, China's real GDP rose from nearly 290 billion dollars in 1978 to 11.5 trillion in 2019. "World Bank national account data, and OECD National Accounts data files" (https://data.worldbank.org/indicator/NY.GDP.MKTP.KD?locations=CN, accessed 11 May 2020).

As is always the case with such comparisons, we are dealing with a whole lot of methodological issues as there is more than one way to calculate and more than one comparative measure. According to other estimates, China's GDP per capita has risen from just USD 1,600 in 1978 to almost 16,000 in 2019, or exactly 10 times. In both cases these are values calculated at constant prices of 2018 but subject to different assumptions and appraisals of changes to the purchasing power, hence the significant differences (Table 6.1). The author of those alternative estimates, The Conference Board, in particular, believes that the official Chinese data seriously underestimate the historical base or point of reference – income in 1978 (CB, 2020).

It is hard to miss the almost identical GDP level per capita in the USA in 1978 and in Poland in 2019. If the differences in the level of development and living standards only boiled down to that, the countries would not be so far apart. After all, what are four decades on the long path of history?

According to the World Bank's classification, developed high-income countries are economies with a GNI per capita of USD 12,375. This time it's not GDP but Gross National Income (GNI), though the two categories are not far apart. For China, GNI is lower than GDP by around 6% and in 2019–2020 it could

TABLE 6.1   The value and dynamics of GDP of China, USA and Poland, 1978–2019 (PPP)

	Official data			Alternative estimation		
	1978	2019	Quotient 2019/1978	1978	2019	Quotient 2019/1987
Total GDP Billion 2018 US$						
China	691	26,952	39.0×	1,516	21,956	14.5×
USA	7,252	20,993	2.9×	–	–	–
Poland	476	1,257	2.6×	–	–	–
Per capita GDP 2018 US$						
China	723	19,387	26.8×	1,586	15,973	10.1×
USA	32,574	63,126	1.9×	–	–	–
Poland	13,631	32,775	2.4×	–	–	–

SOURCES: THE CONFERENCE BOARD TOTAL ECONOMY DATABASE (CB, 2020) AND OWN CALCULATIONS

be estimated at USD 10,200. Hence, the high-income country status is not far away; all it takes to reach it is a 20% growth. Once the shock related to the COVID-19 pandemic has been successfully dealt with, this should take three, maybe four years.[4] And that is how, in merely half a century, between 1974–2024, when Mao rightly saw China in the Third World, the country will have moved its economy to the first world. The whole story is far more complicated, because quantity is not all that counts. Sometimes it even counts less than quality.

2   Long, Long Time Ago …

The Chinese path to the "first world" has a rich and complex history. On a short timeline, it is usually traced back to its opening to globalisation and the attendant liberal economic reforms of Mao's *de facto* successor, Deng Xiaoping (1904–1997). His famous quip: "It doesn't matter if a cat is black or white, as long as it catches mice" is truly the quintessence of pragmatism that have informed Chinese market reforms of the past four decades.

A yet shorter timeline starts with the change of narrative during the rule of Xi Jinping, the party's current leader since the end of 2012, and the President of the PRC since the spring of 2013. Deng advised humility and mostly inward orientation, saying in 1990 "hide your strength and bide your time", whereas Xi believes that this time has already come, and he is promoting the "Chinese Dream" (Xi, 2014) as well as economic and political external expansion. China is moving from the "peaceful growth" to an "assertive growth", as declared in the documents from the 19th National Congress of the CPC. Xi said: "The path, the theory, the system, and the culture of socialism with Chinese characteristics have kept developing, blazing a new trial for other developing countries and nations to achieve modernization. It offers a new option for other countries and nations who want to speed up their development while preserving independence; and it offers Chinese wisdom and a Chinese approach to solving the problems facing mankind" (China Daily, 2017: 8). He quite unequivocally stated:

---

4   This may happen but does not have to. Some think that the post-pandemic world will prove much worse for China, which will slow down its growth and greatly lengthen its path to catching up with richer economies. According to those opinions, the West may isolate itself more, blocking the influx of Chinese capital, slow down the knowledge-and technology-sharing and introduce further trade restrictions. The decline in mutual trust will also affect the West-East relations.

"It is time for us to take centre stage in the world and to make a greater contribution to humankind" (Financial Times, 2017).

On a very long timeline of the past, the situation varied. At times China was closer to more developed countries and economies, occasionally even leading the world, some other times the distance was growing and sometimes it was even lagging far behind. Leaving aside ancient times – the highly developed civilisation of Confucius era (551–479 B.C.) – these days there are frequent mentions of great sea voyages of admiral Zheng He (1371–1433), who reached Arabia and eastern coasts of Africa 600 years ago. Rather than by an expansion akin to the one brought by Columbus's voyages to America, these escapades were followed by an utter retreat, which has been never fully explained. Most probably it was necessitated by the need to focus on the heavy load of internal problems, not by a weird phobia of the then emperor of the Middle Kingdom. Today China has a presence in these regions again and there is no indication of its intention to withdraw, quite the contrary. There are those in global politics that would be happy should China's mounting internal problems cause it to take in the sails also this time. That will not happen as this time China is unfurling them to better overcome the difficulties experienced back home by penetrating other parts of the world.

In the late 16th and early 17th century some of the illustrious European minds had high regard for Chinese achievements, treating them as a sign of higher level of development. Gottfried Leibniz (1646–1716), German philosopher and mathematician believed that in the field of exact science the West was at the leading edge, while the Chinese surpassed Europeans in "practical philosophy", in the way it organised the society where "laws are beautifully directed towards the greatest tranquillity and order" (Obbema, 2015: 18). Leibniz, learning about China from Catholic missionaries returning from there, and living in a Germany ravaged by the Thirty Years' War (1618–1648), wished Chinese missionaries would arrive in Europe and dreamt of a new global culture combining the best of China and Europe. Some 300 years have passed; missionaries –now civilian rather than Jesuit ones – imbued with all kind of ideas travel both ways with unprecedented frequency, and yet this longed-for global culture is still far ahead...

Half a century later, Voltaire (1694–1778), a great philosopher and writer of the Enlightenment, wrote of China with esteem. He was certainly inclined to do so by the background of crisis and chaos prevailing in the pre-revolutionary France. When in 1764 he observed: "Their empire is the best that the world has ever seen" (Obbema, 2015: 18), he presumably met with similarly critical reactions to those experienced by today's apologists of the complex Chinese reality. Voltaire even created poems about the Qianlong Emperor (1711–1799), whom he perceived as a Platonic philosopher-king.⁵ By contrast, his contemporary, Montesquieu (1689–1755), treated China as a "despotic state, whose principle is fear" (Obbema, 2015: 19). Some Sinosceptics would concur with him also today.

Hard as it is to believe, 200 hundred years ago China produced 32 percent of global output. It will be easier to understand, however, when we realise that back then the country was inhabited by more people than now in relative terms – 38 percent of the world's entire population. There were more than three times as much of Chinese people as Europeans; 381 and 122 million respectively. Then there came a period of slowdown and regression. While first Europe, and then North America were gathering momentum as a result of subsequent industrial revolutions, China – not without help from some empires of Western Europe – descended into stagnation. In the late 19th and early 20th century it was a semi-colonised economy. That "century of national humiliation" is often recalled today. It is known to all primary school pupils, making them even prouder of their homeland's contemporary achievements and avid for something worthy of being the Chinese Dream of 21st century.

History never repeats itself to the letter, but sometimes the contemporaries cannot help but be reminded of the past. The Chinese were once already the object of fear, or to be more exact, that of scaremongering, amid a surge of xenophobia. The end of 19th century in both North America and Europe went down in history as the inglorious time of 'Yellow Peril'. It was essentially an anti-Asian racism where fear of migrants from the region was deliberately instilled in the local population, and disgraceful racist practices were resorted to, at times, on the grounds of the obvious superiority of the American and European civilisation. In the USA the *Chinese Exclusion Act* was enacted in 1882 (repealed only in 1943 and the Senate was kind enough to apologise for it only in 2011). Had it not done it back then, this certainly would not have happened now, with a Republican majority.

Whereas in Europe in the late 19th century the German Kaiser Wilhelm II would fuel the hatred towards the Chinese with the threatening vision of their invading hordes. It was to that end that he sent to his distant cousin, the tsar of Russia Alexander III, a drawing depicting a Chinese dragon trampling over the Christian Europe. The multiple copies of the image had a vast success as contemporarily do some chauvinistic and racist memes.

---

5   In our day and age, the lack of such poems can be hardly made up for to the President of the PRC by paeans in his honour written in prose in a dozen or so of Chinese institutes established "to study and interpret Xi Jinping Thought on Socialism with Chinese Characteristics for a New Era". This smacks of cult of personality, which the Chinese leader does not need.

The inability to go with the creative and pro-development flow of 19th century industrial revolutions, as well as the social and military shocks of the first half of the 20th century caused China to be incapable, for a couple of generations, of overcoming a systemic – economic and political – collapse. China's GDP in mid-20th century, when the People's Republic of China was founded, with the Communist Party of China at its helm, represented no more than a meagre 2% of the global output. This fall – as a fall it was – in the form of a drastic downward slide in just 130 years from a situation where the country produced one third of the global output to producing merely its one-fiftieth, coupled with the immense population it affected, was an unprecedented process.

3   From Ever More to Ever Better

Now, at PPP, China's GDP is back to ca. 20% of the world's output. Over time, the figure will keep growing; one day reaching again over 30%, like two centuries ago. This has its obvious determinants and less obvious implications. It is the Chinese political and economic system that has enabled such progress, especially in the period of opening and reforms after 1978 (Halper, 2010; Lin, 2012; Economy, 2018). However, it comes at a huge cost and yields negative consequences the GDP figures fail to mirror. Particularly acute are the *ecological costs* in the form of environmental devastation and the immense scale of *income inequalities*. These two areas – in addition to the need for economic equilibrium especially with respect to finance and trade – represent the greatest challenges in the coming decades. Improving the environmental situation and reducing income and wealth differences are issues of more importance than constantly maximising the rate of the traditionally defined economic growth.

Naturally, the latter cannot be disregarded. After all, it is the value of goods produced and services supplied that provides the material foundations of life and determines the wellbeing. Moreover, maintaining a relative balance on the labour market requires, as can be estimated, at least a 5% GDP growth rate. The economy needs to absorb each year over a dozen million employees migrating to industry and services located in urban areas. This is one of the conditions for keeping social peace, much more important than catching up with and outpacing others. After all, the reason why China has the policy of fast economic growth in place is not to be able to outdo Japan and the USA in terms of output, but to better satisfy the needs of its numerous population.

China has picked up speed. Its economic dynamic greatly exceeds that of highly developed countries, constantly reducing the gap.[6] What also matters in the context of geopolitics (Malinowski, 2019) is that in the second decade of the 21st century India's economy is growing almost just as fast. In the previous 30 years it was not the case, which is of significance for discussions comparing different political and economic models. Between 1980–2009, India's GDP rose 7.2-fold, in China, as much as 26.7-fold. In that time, India, which until 1992 had a higher income per capita, was left far behind by China. In turn, while total GDP in China in the decade of 2010–2019 slightly more than doubled, in India it almost doubled. Consequently, now a Chinese person's average income is nearly two and a half times as high as that of an Indian person (see Figure 6.1).

Though we are already living in a beyond-GDP reality (Kolodko, 2014; Stiglitz et al., 2018; Koźmiński et al., 2020), let us dwell a while longer on the GDP analysis. It is important because also in this field a lot will change due to the turmoil caused by the COVID-19 pandemic. As a matter of fact, according to the estimates of the IMF, economic growth is to still continue in 2020 in those former Third World's largest two economies, though on a much lesser scale as a result of the lockdown of part of the economy, intended to prevent the spreading of the contagion, and the disruption of the transnational supply and production chains (Kolodko, 2020b). In the World Economic Outlook (WEO) for spring IMF forecasted for China and India a GDP growth of 1.2 and 1.9%, respectively, in 2020 and an exponential growth of 9.2 and 7.4% in 2021 (WEO, 2020).[7] For highly developed countries a major downturn in output was expected (see Table 6.2).

Should such scenarios materialise, China's GDP at PPP will increase from ca. 128% of the US level in 2019 to 144% in 2021 or – reversing the perspective – the US income will decrease from 78 to 70% of that of China. This is indisputably not the effect desired by the President Donald Trump, whose policy is intentionally designed to weaken relatively the Chinese economy and *Make America Great Again*! in this context. Therefore, the scale of shifts taking place

---

6 It is worth comparing, subject to all relevant methodological reservations, the economic dynamic of China with the country of the most successful post-socialist transition, Poland (Piatkowski, 2018; Kolodko, 2020a). Well, Poland's GDP approximately tripled in the three decades between 1990 and 2019, whereas that of China increased as much as 15 times. Per capita, for Poland this is still more or less three times as much, because the population has slightly decreased, while for China, as we know, the real income per capita has grown approximately 12 times. (For more on the complicated situation in the initial period of Polish transformation, see Kolodko and Rutkowski, 1991 and Nuti, 2018).

7 At the same time, the European Commission forecasted China's GDP growth in 2020–2021 at 1.0 and 7.8% (EU, 2020).

THE GREAT CHINESE TRANSFORMATION

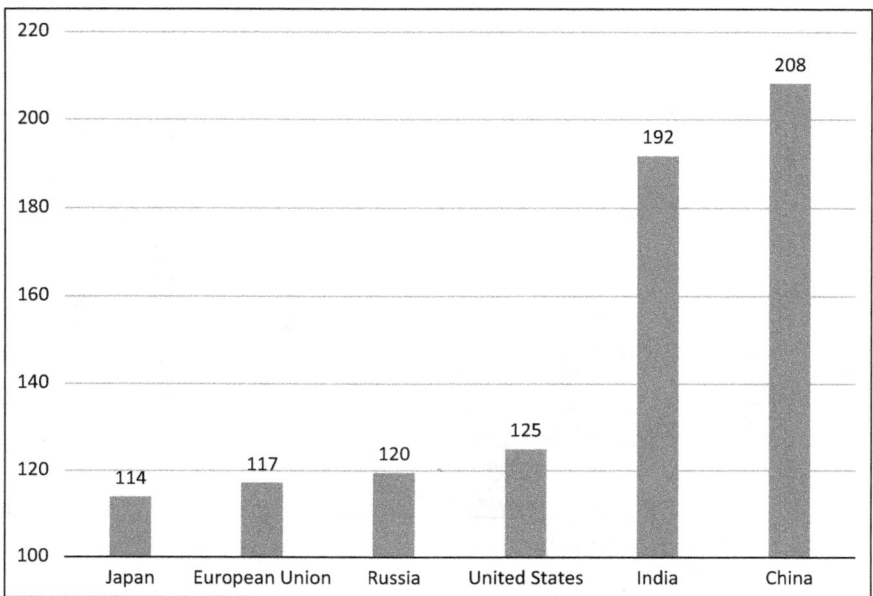

FIGURE 6.1 The GDP of China and the Big-5 in 2019 index numbers (2009 = 100)
SOURCE: OWN CALCULATIONS BASED ON THE DATA OF WEO (2019)

TABLE 6.2 Forecasts of recession and growth in 2020–2021 (fall/growth of GDP, %)

Country	2020	2021	2021 (2019 = 100)
China	1.2	9.2	110.5
India	1.9	7.4	109.4
Japan	−5.2	3.0	97.6
Russia	−5.5	3.5	97.8
USA	−5.9	4.7	98.5
World	−3.0	5.8	102.6

SOURCE: WEO (2020)

on the global scene is gigantic. Let me just point out that the China's national income estimated this way is only counterbalanced by the sum total of income of the US, Japan and Russia (see Figure 6.2).

China's total national income (PPP-weighted GDP) is more than one-fourth higher than that of the US, whereas at the current exchange rate it is still much,

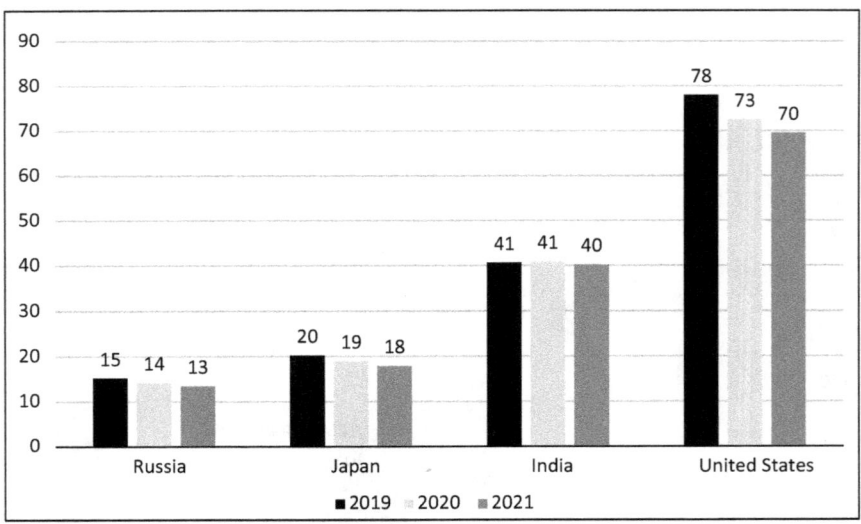

FIGURE 6.2 China versus Big-4 GDP of selected countries in percent of China's GDP
Note: In PPP
SOURCE: WEO (2020)

nearly one-third, lower. In 2019 these figures stood at ca. USD 21 trillion and 14.4 trillion. A better and more informative category is income at purchasing power parity as this figure tells us how much it is actually worth, or, more precisely, what comparable value of goods and services it can be converted into, considering the international price differences. If we were to stick in our analyses to income calculated at the market exchange rate, adopting the simplifying assumption that these countries will maintain post-2020 the average GDP growth rate at the level achieved in the year preceding the COVID-19 pandemic, meaning 2.3 and 6.1%, respectively, then China's GDP, reaching USD 26 trillion (at constant prices for 2019), will exceed the USA's level in 2030.

What also, and sometimes especially, matters in the global economic cooperation and rivalry for political supremacy is how China's output impacts other countries. It was not until 1995 that China made it to the very end of the list of top 15 global exporters and, just after 18 years, in 2013, it took the lead which it will continue to hold in the foreseeable future.[8] China's total international

---

8 With the incredible frictions caused by the COVID-19 pandemic and the often chaotic economic policy reactions, it is rather a question of unforeseeable future.

TABLE 6.3 Top ten countries of Chinese exports, 2019

	USD bln	%
United States	418.6	16.8
Hong Kong	279.6	11.2
Japan	143.2	5.7
South Korea	111.0	4.4
Vietnam	98.0	3.9
Germany	79.7	3.2
India	74.9	3.0
Netherlands	73.9	3.0
United Kingdom	62.3	2.5
Taiwan	55.1	2.2

SOURCES: INTERNATIONAL TRADE CENTRE BASED ON GENERAL CUSTOMS ADMINISTRATION OF CHINA STATISTICS (TRADE MAP, 2020) AND OWN CALCULATIONS

trade amounted to USD 4.6 trillion in 2019, with exports up by 0.5% and imports down by 2.8% compared to the preceding year (see Table 6.3).

Let us also note that the relatively very high exports to Hong Kong are nearly entirely re-exported to other countries, all over the world. So, the actual exportation of goods to respective foreign markets is higher than revealed by the data quoted here.

In the last year before the pandemic that shook the world economy, including the international trade, China had a positive balance of USD 421.5 billion, higher than in the preceding year, despite the sanctions resulting from the trade war waged by the USA. China remains the USA's largest trade partner as, regardless of the protectionist restrictions imposed by President Trump's administration, it is the recipient of goods worth over half a trillion dollars, that is one fifth of total US exports.

Another thing that matters in the global rivalry is the state's financial reserves, in which respect China, again, with foreign currency reserves worth the equivalent of USD 3.1 trillion, ranks first worldwide.[9] These reserves were

---

[9] It is also worth noting that both Hong Kong and Taiwan have reserves that in both cases greatly exceed USD 400 billion. Hence, looking at the so-called Greater China, its currency reserves go up to USD 4 trillion.

ca. USD 750 billion higher in 2014, but in the following five years they were sensibly used by financial policy to stabilise the economy and stimulate the output growth. It is worth pointing out here that Beijing holds a third of reserves in US securities, binding these two economies even further. Two thirds are distributed among other reserve currencies, Euro having the greatest share, tailed by Yen, Hong Kong Dollar,[10] British Pound Sterling, Korean Won, Australian and Canadian Dollars, and Swiss Franc. Approximately USD 100 billion is held in gold. It is the China central bank's large-scale purchases of the latter in recent years that have led to a major increase in the prices of this precious metal.

On the other hand, only ca. 2% of the global currency reserves are held in the Chinese currency. It can be estimated that other countries' central banks have accumulated in RMB no more than the equivalent of a quarter of a trillion of dollars. That is the current status but it will change and RMB's share of global currency reserves will systematically, though slowly, rise. Undoubtedly, at first at the expense of US dollar, which will also have its political implications. Furthermore, China, provoked by the US hostility and aggressive trade policy that hinders economic development, is consistently setting up a parallel financial system, which will help go around USD-based payment mechanisms (Economist, 2020a). Currently, the way the international financial clearing system works means that a vast number of international trade transactions cannot be concluded bypassing USD. This enables the USA to impose severe sanctions on others or blackmail them with a threat of sanctions, which is being experienced by Iran these days and which also threatens to befall its trade partners.

Sometimes hostile emotions virtually lead to loss of reason. This is what can be said of prominent representatives of the US political establishment formulating accusations against China and demanding financial compensation for the losses sustained by the US economy as a result of the COVID-19 pandemic. The media have reported on the fantastic idea popularised by sources within the administration that the White House is thinking of cancelling part of USD 1.1 trillion debt to China to 'punish' the country for the pandemic (Economist, 2020b). "Congressional Republicans such as Sen. Lindsey O. Graham (S.C.) have increasingly demanded the United States 'make China pay big time' over the damage" (Washington Post, 2020). Senator Marsha Blackburn went even further, reaching the absurd, as she "floated waiving interest payments to China for any holdings of US debt, 'because they have cost our economy

---

10   Hong Kong dollar, HKD, is *de facto* pegged to the USD under the currency board regime, so from the macroeconomic perspective both currencies can be treated similarly.

already USD 6 trillion and we could end up being an additional USD 5 trillion hit'" (Washington Post, 2020). Such public declarations by major-league politicians are the grist to the mill of xenophobia as if there was not enough of it already. During the electoral campaign, striving for re-election of President Trump, his henchmen are paying for media ads insinuating that "China is killing our jobs and now, killing our people" (Washington Post, 2020). Chinese state-owned media were quick to respond, fanning the nationalist emotions with invectives against Mike Pompeo, the US Secretary of State, calling him "evil", "insane" and a "common enemy of mankind" (Washington Post, 2020).

A fascinating though often nasty clash between geo-economics and geo-politics is underway (Kolodko, 2020c). Both these mega-processes are interconnected, but – assuming that we manage to avoid the ruinous hot war, which assumption I consistently make – in the world of tomorrow, economic processes will be undoubtedly of crucial importance. Power relations will be determined by how these unfold rather than by subjective desires and ambitions of politicians for whom power and influence are everything, and solving social and economic problems only serves as an instrument of their dominance. From this standpoint, China's relative position in the global arena will continue to grow stronger for many years to come as its economy will grow in both absolute and relative terms, though no longer at the rate it did until recently.

4 Conclusions

China not only does not fall under the rule of "communism" (Sun and Zhang, 2020), but thanks to its unique features continues to grow at an above-average pace. Following the victorious, several decade-long war on poverty, it is in for another war, this time one to protect natural environment. Also, this one can be won over time, and this will prove the *conditio sine qua non* of the Chinese specific political and economic system – so-called Chinism (Kolodko, 2018) – a being accepted by next generations. Earlier on, China, and especially its leaders, were unwilling to sacrifice maximising the traditionally defined (in the narrow quantitative terms) economic growth rate. Now, on the eve of being promoted to the group of high-income countries, it must sacrifice the same at the altar of development that is triply sustainable: economically, socially and environmentally. If it manages to do that, it will peacefully win another era on the never-ending path of development.

Acknowledgements

This chapter is a reprint of G.W. Kołodko's article under the same title, originally published in "Acta Oeconomica" in 2020 (Vol. 70, Issue S, pp. 71-83).

References

CB (2020) The Conference Board Total Economy Database. *The Conference Board*, April, https://www.conference-board.org/data/economydatabase/index.cfm?id=27762, accessed 11 May 2020.

China Daily (2017) Xi Jinping and His Era. 18–19 November.

Economist (2020a) The Pandemic is Driving America and China Further Apart. 9 May https://www.economist.com/leaders/2020/05/09/the-pandemic-is-driving-america-and-china-further-apart, accessed 10 May 2020.

Economist (2020b) There is less Trust between Washington and Beijing than at any Point since 1979. 9 May, https://www.economist.com/united-states/2020/05/09/there-is-less-trust-between-washington-and-beijing-than-at-any-point-since-1979, accessed 10 May 2020.

Economy, Elizabeth C. (2018) *The Third World Revolution: Xi Jinping and the New Chinese State.* New York: Oxford University Press.

EU (2020) *European Economic Forecast, Institutional Paper 125.* Brussels: European Commission, https://ec.europa.eu/info/sites/info/files/economy-finance/ip125_en.pdf, accessed 8 May 2020.

Financial Times (2017) Xi Jinping Signals Departure from Low-Profile Policy. 20 October, https://www.ft.com/content/05cd86a6-b552-11e7-a398-73d59db9e399, accessed 8 May 2020.

Halper, Stefan (2010) *The Beijing Consensus: How China's Authoritarian Model Will Dominate the Twenty-First Century.* New York: Basic Books.

Kołodko, Grzegorz W. (2014) The New Pragmatism, or Economics and Policy for the Future. *Acta Oeconomica,* 64(2), pp. 139–160, http://tiger.edu.pl/aktualnosci/2014/acta-ocevonomica-64-2014.pdf, accessed 10 May 2020.

Kołodko, Grzegorz W. (2018) Socialism, Capitalism, or Chinism? *Communist and Post-Communist Studies,* 51(4), pp. 285–298, http://tiger.edu.pl/CPCS_2018.pdf, accessed 10 May 2020.

Kołodko, Grzegorz W. (2020a) Economics and Politics of Post-Communist Transition to Market and Democracy. The Lessons from Polish Experience. *Post-Communist Economies,* 32(3), pp. 285–305, DOI:10.1080/14631377.2019.1694604.

Kołodko, Grzegorz W. (2020b) After the Calamity: Economics and Politics in the Post-Pandemic World. *Polish Sociological Review,* 2(210), pp. 137–155.

Kołodko, Grzegorz W. (2020c) Chinism and the Future of the World. *Communist and Post-Communist Studies*, 53(4), pp. 260–279.

Kołodko, Grzegorz (2020d) The great Chinese transformation: From the third to the first world. *Acta Oeconomica*, 70(s), pp. 71–83.

Kołodko, Grzegorz W. and Michał Rutkowski (1991) The Problem of Transition from a Socialist to a Free Market Economy: The Case of Poland. *The Journal of Social, Political and Economic Studies*, 16(2), pp. 159–179.

Koźmiński, Andrzej K. and Adam Noga, Katarzyna Piotrowska, Krzysztof Zagórski (2020) *The Balanced Development Index for Europe's OECD Countries, 1999–2017*. Cham, Switzerland: Springer Briefs in Economics.

Lin, Justin Yifu (2012): *Demystifying the Chinese Economy*. Cambridge: Cambridge University Press.

Mao Zedong (1974) Chairman Mao Zedong's Theory on the Division of the Three World and the Strategy of Forming an Alliance Against an Opponent. *The Ministry of Foreign Affairs of the Republic of China*, https://www.fmprc.gov.cn/mfa_eng/ziliao_665539/3602_665543/3604_665547/t18008.shtml, accessed 07 May 2020.

Malinowski, Grzegorz (2019) China, Geopolitics and Geoeconomics. How Not to Fall into the Trap of Narration? *Acta Oeconomica*, 69(4), pp. 495–522.

Nuti, Domenico M. (2018) *The Rise and Fall of Socialism*. DOC Research Institute, Berlin, https://doc-research.org/2018/05/rise_and_fall_of_socialism/, accessed 09 May 2020.

Obbema, Fokke (2015) *China and the West: Hope and Fear in the Age of Asia*. London – New York: I.B. Tauris.

Piatkowski, Marcin (2018) *Europe's Growth Champion: Insights from the Economic Rise of Poland*. Oxford – New York: Oxford University Press.

Stiglitz, Joseph E., and Jean-Paul Fitoussi, Martine Durand (2018) *Beyond GDP: Measuring What Counts for Economic and Social Performance*. Paris: OECD.

Sun Feng and Zhang Wanfa (2020) *Why Communist China isn't Collapsing: The CCP's Battle for Survival and State-Society Dynamics in the Post-Reform Era*. Lanham – Boulder – New York – London: Lexington Books.

Trade Map (2020) Trade Map. Trade Statistics for International Business Development, www.trademap.org/Country_SelProductCountry.aspx?nvpm=1%7c156%7c%7c%7c%7cTOTAL%7c%7c%7c2%7c1%7c1%7c1%7c1%7c%7c2%7c1%7c, accessed 10 May 2020.

Washington Post (2020) US Officials Crafting Retaliatory Actions Against China Over Coronavirus as President Trump Fumes. 30 April, https://www.washingtonpost.com/business/2020/04/30/trump-china-coronavirus-retaliation/, accessed 10 May 2020.

WEO (2019) *World Economic Outlook, October 2019*. Washington D.C.: IMF, https://knoema.com/IMFWEO2019Oct/imf-world-economic-outlook-weo-october-2019, accessed 08 May 2020.

WEO (2020) *World Economic Outlook, April 2020: The Great Lockdown*, Washington, D.C.: IMF, https://www.imf.org/en/Publications/WEO/Issues/2020/04/14/weo-april-2020, accessed 8 May 2020.

World Bank (2020) The World Bank in China. Washington D.C., https://www.worldbank.org/en/country/china/overview, accessed 7 May 2020.

Xi Jinping (2014) *The Governance of China*. Beijing: ICP Intercultural Press.

CHAPTER 7

The Belt and Road Initiative, Centralisation of Local Interests and Centre-province Relations

Dominik Mierzejewski

1   Introduction

After Xi Jinping announced the Belt and Road Initiative in Astana (September 2013), China became the global power with superpower ambitions and an overall strategy to dominate or at least revive its previous historical position in international relations. On the one hand, these views dominate the international discourse, on the other they should be enriched by the vital dimension of the Belt and Road – the complexity of domestic relations between central government and provinces. The complexity of centre-province relations has been discussed mainly since Deng Xiaoping took the initiative in the late 1970s and provided an opening-up period. The economic reforms were mainly based on the decentralization approaches and after 1989 the government in Beijing realised that further fragmentation inside the country might lead to the future collapse of the People's Republic of China. From the above-discussed perspective, the Belt and Road Initiative signals the collective action with centralized interests by the government in Beijing. The collective actions, navigated and monitored by the political centre in Beijing, should be simultaneously undertaken at the domestic and international scenes. Moreover, to limit domestic fragmentation, Beijing discussed with provinces regional integration projects, for example, the Yangtze River Economic Belt as part of the Belt and Road Initiative. This, at least in theory, should result in more coordinated development between the eastern part of China and the inland part of China (Liu and Liu, 2017). The international dimension of China's local governments' activities is seen through the concept of internationalization and city diplomacy.

In order to present the domestic picture of the Belt and Road Initiative, the chapter looks inside China's domestic discussions and adoptions of the central government initiative of the Belt and Road. It adresses the following questions: what are the realities in centre-province relations in China? How does the central government understand the Belt and Road Initiative within the domestic context? Moreover, finally, how do the local authorities see the central government initiative, and how do the four municipal governments of Beijing, Shanghai, Tianjin and Chongqing approach the Belt and Road Initiative and their roles in China's public diplomacy? The chapter opens the discussion about the domestic drivers behind China's Belt and Road Initiative and argues that critical for understanding the initiative are dyadic relations between central and provincial-level government and the design of the central government to coordinate and integrate China's fragmented development.

2   The Complexity of China's Centre-Local Relations

Since the late 1970s, Deng Xiaoping advocated for more decentralised reforms in China. On the one hand, four cordial principles announced in March 1979 secure China's one-party system. However, on the other, the economic development was highly decentralised, with the province as the key player in the national economy. But, this problem was not new. As argued by Arthur Doak Barnett (1967): "The conflict of regional power versus central power, a theme in Chinese political history, has by no means been solved by the Communists". Even under Deng Xiaoping's reign, the problem remained unanswered and each province used protectionist practices to keep its economic growth. China's local protection is generally industry-specific, mainly including particular industries that are the basis of local fiscal sources or local economic development and stable social industries that have a deterrent effect on unemployment and inflation (Goodman, 1994). From this perspective the central government hoped to play the role of coordinator and sponsor of the division of labour approach. The critical issue appeared in the 1980s, when Beijing needed to manage interprovincial commodity. Then, the lesson was learned and as said by Hendrischke (1999), the central government regulated the competition over foreign investments and markets, however, the lower level of competition over the domestic market resulted in informal tax preferences, incentives and other protectionism mechanisms (Hendrischke, 1999: 8–9). In the eyes of Carl Riskin (1987), the needed reforms stressing specialisation and division of labour would significantly increase the need for coordination, which might either be strengthened through bureaucratic command planning or a more outstanding market role. These two opposite directions shape China's domestic realities. In the time of reform in China, both ideas were included. In this regard, Zheng Yongnian (2007) presents the model of centre-local relations that is mainly governed by three institutions: coercion, bargaining, and reciprocity. The coercion institution is mainly embodied in the institution of planned economy and nomenclature system. Bargaining serves as the vehicle for resolving conflicts between the centre and the provinces; in the end, it leads to reciprocal control and promotes the joint agenda between both. Due to the cultural code of behaviour within the guanxi network, reciprocity is seen as an obligatory institution. The concept of reciprocity implies actions contingent on rewarding reactions from others that cease when these expected reactions are not forthcoming (Zheng, 2007: 55–71). More analytical approach was introduced by Jae Ho Chung who argues that three main perspectives should be taken into consideration: cultural, structural and procedural. The cultural perspective discusses the significance of historical continuity of centrifugal tendencies and popular belief of provincialism over the national integration. The structural finds the conflict in the distribution of power between local and central governments while the procedural originates the conflict from the lack of appropriate channels for communication (Chung, 1995: 489). The bargaining institution was also introduced by Linda Chenlan Li (2003). She argued that the significant relations between central and local should be perceived as bargaining with the centre for more favourable policies and locals would manoeuvre to gain more from the political centre. The most important relations are between Beijing and provincial-level governments as argued by Dreyer (2010). However, while having limited autonomy the provincial-level governments have faced challenges from the lower-level officials and need to manoeuvre within their local interests and goals (Dreyer, 2010: 137). Moreover, as China's reforms and opening-up policies illustrate the local government competition has been reflected in eight areas: project competition, the competition of industrial chain development, competition for talents, science and technology, fiscal and financial competition, infrastructure competition, competition for environmental systems, policy systems and management efficiency (Chen and Gu, 2019: XVI). The horizontal competition is strengthened by the policy of "first-in-trial" rights mainly based on the comprehensive reform pilot zone that allows the local governments to compete over the central government resources and own position in the political system of China (Mierzejewski, 2021: 13).

The above-discussed phenomenon, as observed and criticised by the New Left school in the early 1990s, led to the fragmentation of China and the possible collapse of the country (Mierzejewski, 2009). After June 1989, the conservative faction inside the Communist Party of China took the lead. Wang Shaoguang and Hu Angang (1993), in their "Report on China National Power", perceived that the decentralisation led to the weakening of the central government's capacity and has the potential to lead to political disintegration. The New Left believed that radical decentralisation was the main obstacle to forming a unified national market economy, as China experienced throughout the reform. This view was shared by Wang Huning (1993), then a professor at

Fudan University, a current member of the Standing Committee of the Central Committee, and a key advisor in the ideological sphere of the Middle Kingdom. In 1993 in the paper entitled "The need for politics in the socialist market economy," he urged the government for a more centralised social management system. In the light of the growing economic disintegration, Wang Huning called for a more significant role of politics in the socialist market economy while putting aside the market forces. The Chinese academia and policymakers were afraid of intra-country division that might lead to the domestic partition of China. This was reflected in China's past when the country was fragmented, not unified and weak in the international arena. The phenomenon of fragmented China led to the Qing dynasty's collapse. In the view of the New Left intellectuals, strong vertical management could help the systems eliminate the interference of the interests of the local government and formulate public policies based on the needs of the entire country and society. Secondly, the direct management of public affairs by the central government is intended to reduce the system's dependence on the "people, finances and materials" of the local government and strengthen the supervision of power within the system to prevent and restrain corruption. For the centralisation promoters, the positive significance of vertical management in promoting administrative efficiency is unquestionable. From the existing practice, one of the core contents of the pre-reform is to decentralise local governments and stimulate market vitality. The next point discussed in the literature touches on the issue of effectiveness. For instance, Alwyn Young (2000) argues that the liberalisation and transformation of the PRC between 1980 and 1990 can best be illustrated as a process of devolution. The market-driven Chinese economy is less efficient than the old planned economy because the former had carved up the country into local economic disintegration. Moreover, the above-mentioned horizontal competition and lack of clear division of tasks between central and local governments lead to colossal competition, massive production duplication, inefficient allocation of production outputs, trade wars and even local authorities' conflicts (Pei, 2009: 117). As the final product, it leads China to overcapacity and pushes the government to organise the global infrastructure investment to rescue the local economies and, per se China's economic growth (Li, Jiang and Cao, 2019).

The second important feature that plays a decisive role is the nomenclature system. During the reform period, the nomenclature system was decentralised, and the centre lost its control over the nomenclature to prefectural, city and county party committees (Chen, 2003: 29–30). In this sense, the anti-corruption campaign in China is connected with the nomenclature system. It allows the central government to make bureaucratic changes and promises to regain control over the party structures across the country. Only by implementing a more centralised government can the accomplishment of ongoing processes such as urbanisation, changes in the *hukou* system and the regional integration process be possible. At the same time, the Belt and Road Initiative has assisted the anti-corruption campaign that generated enthusiasm across the country and serves as a massive political campaign. Even though the general public might applaud China's centralisation and anti-corruption campaign, the nomenclature system in centralised and decentralised China makes horizontal competition more intense. Under Xi Jinping the anti-corruption campaign and the Belt and Road Initiative serve as the tool for replacing people, not changing the whole mechanism of the horizontal competition. As in the past to win their position in Beijing, the local policymakers look to develop their provinces and, by introducing the pilot projects system, receive more incentives from the central government and be praised as the positive forces in the country. Regardless of the domestic or foreign policies, the ultimate goal for them is to be labelled as the national example for others to follow.

3 The Central Government's Domestic Ostensible Integration Plans

From the central government's perspective, by introducing the Belt and Road Initiative and interprovincial projects like the Yangtze River Economic Belt, the central government has tried to narrow the gap and the competition among the local authorities. The ultimate goal here is to unify China more and conduct more coherent economic policies. The Belt and Road Initiative has attempted to build a vehicle for common interests or a "community of shared interests" (利益共同体 *liyi gongtong ti*) inside China by pushing the local governments to one collective goal. This understanding went together with Yu Jie and Jon Wallace (2021) when they said that apart from the global outreach, "the Belt and Road is seen as a crucial element in the Chinese government's efforts to stimulate economies of the country's central provinces, which historically lag behind richer coastal areas". These promises, however, are mainly challenged by the fact that China is not a unified market far from protectionist practices. As argued in the Report published by the World Bank and the National Development and Reform Commission, "Inefficiencies in how labour, land, and capital are being distributed across China's territory are holding down China's urbanisation and spatial development" (World Bank, NDRC Report, 2019: 114). The Chinese government's most significant dilemma is not to build new roads, railways, or any infrastructure projects but rather intelligent way to plan, utilise and manage its infrastructure investments. Those needs, however, are challenged by the horizontal competition that enables the government to conduct effective economic policies.

Moreover, the horizontal competition and cooperation by implementing the BRI transfer the interprovincial competition from the domestic arena worldwide. Nevertheless, to make this competition effective, the central government attempted to introduce the division of labour concept, discussed further in the last subchapter. After four-five years of the campaign of the Belt and Road, the central government recognised the comparative advantages of each province. It allowed each to be effective in one or two areas. This should narrow the domestic horizontal competition and bring a more united market inside the country (Mierzejewski, 2021: 231–232).

Essential aspects that define the division of labour as specialisation are understood as dividing tasks into discrete activities among individuals within the organisation or between more substantial units (Smith and Snow, 1976: 520–522). By imposing the division of labour delivered in March 2015 by the Ministry of Foreign Affairs, Ministry of Trade and National Development and Reform Commission as "Vision and Actions," the central government tried to bring together diverse interests and limit provincial-level lobbying in Beijing as well as provincial competition inside the country. By naming the provinces "the pace-setter and main force in the Belt and Road Initiative," the central government presents different roles for different local actors. The document names the pivotal provinces and cities in China's infrastructure projects. In other words, by publishing "Vision and Action," the Beijing government selected the most active actors. It also allowed them to contribute to the Beijing-sponsored initiative with its financial resources. Going through the document it is particularly important to find the provinces excluded from the project like Jiangsu, Shanxi or Guizhou and Hebei (see Figure 7.1).

The majority of provincial actors, even landlocked ones, were given tasks to open up the country and utilise the opportunities given by the Belt and Road. The central government, by using a variety of labels as 'windows', 'core area', 'strategic channels', 'key bases', and 'international transport corridor', encourages the provinces to develop the concepts further and answer with more specific policies while competing internationally unified the market domestically (Vision and Action, 2015).

In order to secure its prominent position, the Beijing government promotes the concept of coordinated development and promises to deliver regional integration by commonalities: mutual coordination, support, promotion and adjustment. Most scholars in China postulated the strengthening of the urbanisation process, advocating further integration between urban and rural areas and creating effective and coordinated development. The very first pilot zone

THE BELT AND ROAD INITIATIVE   173

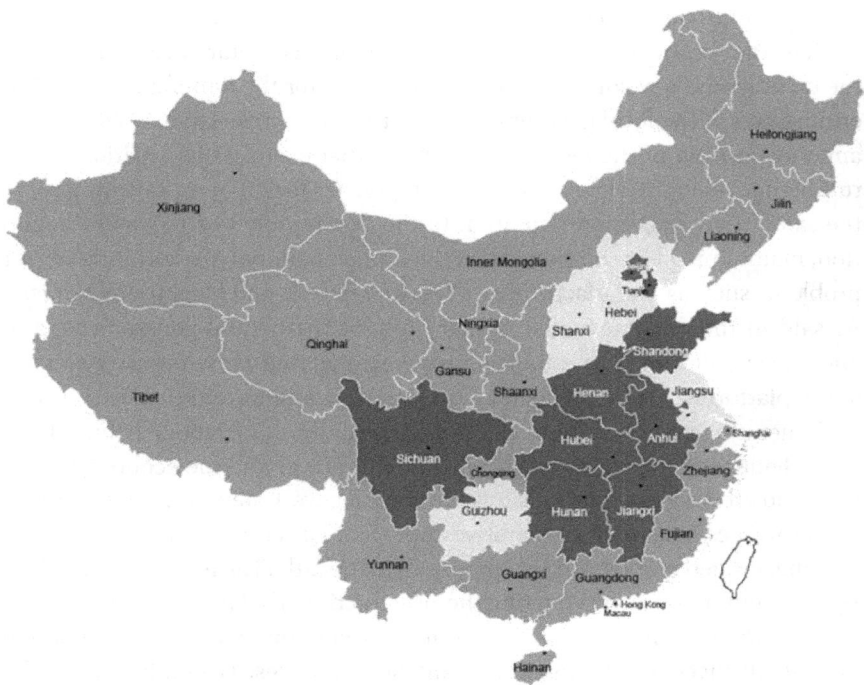

FIGURE 7.1   Chinese provincial-level government in "Vision and Action" document (2015)
LEGEND: GREY: PROVINCIAL-LEVEL GOVERNMENTS MENTIONED BY "VISION AND ACTION" (V&A), DARK GREY: CITIES OR PROJECTS MENTIONED BY V&A, LIGHT GREY PROVINCIAL-LEVEL GOVERNMENT OMITTED BY V&A. MAP DESIGNED AND PREPARED BY JOANNA BECZKOWSKA

of integrating both areas was proposed by the Jiangsu Party Committee when they discussed the city as the centre and the countryside areas as a belt where the city would provide development opportunities. In the 1980s, during the Five-Year Plan (FYP), the central government discussed organising the regional institutions responsible for shaping common economic space and bringing more integration into China's fragmented economy (Hu, 2014: 3–4).

After years of discussions and even implementation, the major principles for the regional coordinated development were assigned by the State Council and the Central Committee in 2018. The first principle, "combination of market leadership and government guidance" (市场主导与政府引导 *shichang zhudao yu zhengfu yindao*) reflects the mixed nature of China's approaches to coordinated development. However, the market forces are given priority, but the government's role is one step behind and can create the reason for interfering. The second, even more important, is the dominant role of the central government in designing the new mechanism (顶层设计 *ding ceng sheji*) that clarifies the responsibilities of the lower level in the hierarchical structure of the coordinated development and is responsible for the flaming mobilisation enthusiasm of the local governments. The third principle established the paramount position of the central government that exercises its position as the rule settler that formulates differentiated policies for different regions and, at the same time, pays more attention to the development of regional integration, maintaining fair competition in the unified national market, and prevent problems such as manufacturing policy depressions and local protectionism. As said in the document, the primary role of the central government is to encourage enterprises to establish cross-regional and cross-industry cooperation platforms, strengthen close cooperation among cities within urban agglomerations, and promote the industrial division of labour (China Gov., 2018). Following the ongoing centralization of power and the economic problems and growing external tensions the central government has tried to stimulate provinces for a more cooperative approach. The concept of constructing a national unified market was first proposed in the 14th Five-Year Plan (FYP). The 14th FYP emphasizes 'accelerating the construction of a large unified domestic market' and calls for 'optimizing the market environment by benchmarking against advanced international rules and best practices.' The unification of the domestic market was to be delivered by common, rules, and policies across different regions and industries, and effectively eliminating local protectionism, industry monopoly, and market segmentation. In other word the central government tried to reverse the last 30 years of reforms that were driven by horizontal competition (14th Five Year Plan 2021).[1] Morever in December 2023 the State Council issued special regulation about linking foreign and domestic markets "Notice on Issuing 'Several Measures for Accelerating the Integrated Development of Domestic and Foreign Trade'" (State Council, 2023). In order to push the "dual circulation economy" into more effective outcome the State Council encouraged local authorities to deepen Pilot Programs for Integration of Domestic and Foreign Trade: cultivate enterprises that integrate domestic and foreign trade, cultivate industry clusters for integrated development of domestic and foreign trade and accelerate the construction of domestic and foreign trade brands (State Council, 2023).

However, despite the centralization of local development in China, the central government often proposes regulations that are quite vague, typically

---

1 See the full translation of the 14th Five-Year Plan for National Informatization: https://digichina.stanford.edu/work/translation-14th-five-year-plan-for-national-informatization-dec-2021/, accessed 12 February 2024.

based on the concept of coordination (协调 *xietiao*). Apart from coordinating the future development of the concept of *xietiao*, it reflects in a no-fixed principle mechanism backed by the promises of the division of labour, leading toward more effective coordinated cooperation and securing the central position of Beijing. However, it fails to translate into full integration. The Yangtze River Economic Belt project serves here as an illustrative example. The significant points in the document issued in September 2014 were dedicated to introducing the division of labour between the participants, promoting modernizing and upgrading industrial capacity. The State Council passed regulations regarding the "golden corridor," which covered an area of 2.1 million square kilometres and accounted for more than 40% of China's population and 45% of the economic output (Asian Development Bank, 2017). According to the guidelines, the Chinese government hoped to secure openness for western China and provide practical inter-province cooperation. This approach goes together with the external opening-up of the western regions. Going further, the major points in the document were dedicated to developing new technologies in inland navigation, modernizing river ports, and testing new solutions with "economic demonstration areas". Interestingly the central government assigned the role to each particular province: to strengthen Yunnan as a "bridgehead" (桥头堡 *qiaotoubao*) in China's foreign policy, connect the Silk Road Economic Belt and 21st Century Maritime Silk Economic Road, build a YREB hub (枢纽 *shuniu*) in Chongqing, and an international link (纽带 *niudai*) in Sichuan province. As environmental issues have grown increasingly important, major concerns have arisen regarding environmental cooperation between provinces (YREB Guidelines, 2014 and 2016).

Nevertheless, facing the realities of horizontal competition, the division of labour failed to work and the central government was left with the position of ultimate arbiter. The majority of the provinces were assigned to the same industries: the information technology industry was seen as a key industry for six of the eight actors, with the Internet of Things (IoT) being essential in three provinces; all provinces and municipalities were designated to work in the biology and biomedicine industry (Mierzejewski, 2021: 124). In the case of the Yangtze River Economic Belt, as discussed above, there is a low degree of economic integration within the belt. The provinces mainly trade within the province rather than between provinces. It creates the situation where the central government needs to manage the relations between quasi-self-reliant entities rather than one unified market. In this regard, the central government wins its paramount position and strengthens vertical control over the provinces.

4 The Belt and Road Initiative: Local Adoptions and Perspectives

After the Belt and Road Initiative was announced, the provincial-level government presented its positions within the Belt and Road Initiative. By using different types of labels such as 'central era', 'bridgehead', 'radiation centre', 'pawn' or 'linking/bonding point' in the yearly reports delivered in the Local People's Congresses, the provincial and municipal governments have discussed the self-given roles within the BRI and present their willingness for cooperation with the central government under a "new umbrella". Moreover, they discuss special "local" BRI projects. Levels of adoption and willingness for further integration with pan-regional projects, mainly the Yangtze River Economic Belt, Beijing-Tianjin-Hebei Metropolitan Area or limiting to its backyard, as in Guangdong, presents rather a lukewarm approach to the BRI. But still, as in the past of the Great Leap Forward and Reform and Opening-up, the guidelines of the Belt and Road at the local level were understood as the signal for horizontal competition. The central government shapes the new BRI appraisal system and opens the space for the local race. The cargo trains to Europe are a very illustrative example. Started by multinational Dell, HP and Foxconn in Chongqing and Chengdu, the trains became the calling card of the Belt and Road Initiative. In 2019, for example, Xi'an took the lead with 2133 trains per year, followed by Yiwu, Chongqing, Suzhou, Chengdu, Zhengzhou, Wuhan, Harbin, and Hebei, Quanzhou, Changsha, Xiamen, Nanchang, Shenyang (Mierzejewski, 2021).

Furthermore, making the political confession to the role of Chairman Xi Jinping also expressed their readiness to take part in the central government project. As acknowledged from the quantitative approach, Sichuan province was the most "optimistic" about the project, while Heilongjiang policymakers from the governor's office discussed the BRI less (see Table 7.1). As declared by the local authorities, Sichuan province under the BRI had accelerated the pace of Reform and Opening-up. It optimistically stated that the *vitality of innovation in the whole society has continued to increase* and strengthen economic cooperation with Western European countries as well as with Hong Kong and Macau. On the other hand, the Governor of Heilongjiang Lu Hao was the only governor in China to express a very passive approach by declaring "active docking" (积极对接 *jiji duijie*) with the BRI, and "docking" (对接 *duijie*) with the BRI (Mierzejewski, 2021: 68). Apart from these two extremes, the provinces present somewhat balanced views and skillfully present their communications strategies to gain extra resources from Beijing. The majority declared active integration and participation, and only Hainan, Yunnan, Liaoning, Hunan provinces, Guangxi Autonomous Region and two municipalities, Shanghai and Beijing, declared to serve the Belt and Road Initiative. The approach of *fuwu* (服务) "to serve" positioned the above-mentioned government as the most subordinated to the central government policies (see Table 7.1).

Taking the municipalities directly governed by the State Council as the example of different approaches to the Belt and Road Initiative, the peculiarities and commonalities of approaches should be distinguished. The municipalities of Beijing, Tianjin, Shanghai, and Chongqing present their geographical locations as the most important in navigating regional development plans and the BRI initiative that leads to limiting the fragmentation of China's domestic market. The second common feature of the four municipal governments was the declaration to utilise the BRI in strengthening relations with Hong Kong, Macau, Taiwan and the Chinese overseas. The last common feature between all four governments is the declared support for local companies to "go global" and set up their business worldwide by close cooperation with the countries along the Belt and Road.

Chongqing is an active player in building a logistic hub, a 'bonding point' between the BRI and Yangtze River Economic Belt, part of the Western development with its "outstanding" geographical position and unique role between domestic development and international cooperation. Moreover, the Chongqing municipal government claims to provide the impetus for further development in international productivity cooperation and takes a leading role in exporting China's overcapacity. Chongqing's approach, however, differs from other municipalities with provincial-level status. Interestingly, the government and officials referred more to Xi Jinping's position and his visit to Chongqing in January 2016 than to the Belt and Road itself (China Daily, 2016). The local authorities mentioned the pivotal role of bringing the development to the local level but were also stimulated by Xi's message of being an important part of China's economic diplomacy. This resulted in Chongqing's project with Singapore, namely the China-Singapore (Chongqing) Connectivity Initiative (CCI) introduced through central government channels. Both governments have helped to catalyse USD 3 billion in multi-currency financing deals. This deal allows Chongqing to play the role of a relatively independent financial center in western China and positions itself as the player superior to the neighboring Sichuan province. The most crucial feature of Chongqing's role under the BRI was the train connection between Chongqing and Duisburg. As the local policymakers advocate, this project has allowed the city to be the actual bonding point between inland and coastal China. Interestingly, over the years of power centralization by Xi Jinping the narratives about the BRI have changed from competition-oriented to the more conciliatory tone of the joint project and mutual support in delivering benefits under the Belt and Road Initiative (Chongqing Local Gov. Reports, 2013–2022).

TABLE 7.1 The contextualization and the frequency of using the keyword of the Belt and Road in China's provincial-level governments (2013–2019)

Province	Frequency	State initiative	Central gov. initiative	Active integration	Active participation	Serve BRI	Make good usage of BRI	Opportunity
Sichuan	26	YES		YES	YES		YES	YES
Hainan	17	YES	YES	YES	YES	YES	YES	YES
Guangxi	17	YES			YES	YES		
Gansu	16	YES		YES			YES	
Shaanxi	14	YES	YES	YES				
Zhejiang	14	YES		YES	YES			
Jiangxi	12	YES		YES				
Xinjiang	12	YES	YES			YES	YES	
Yunnan	12	YES				YES	YES	
Liaoning	12	YES		YES	YES	YES	YES	
Tianjin	11				YES			YES
Shandong	11				YES			
Jiangsu	11	YES		YES	YES			YES
Ningxia	11	YES	YES	YES				YES
Guizhou	10				YES			
Shanghai	10	YES			YES	YES		
Guangdong	10	YES			YES			
Jilin	9	YES		YES	YES			YES
Henan	9	YES						

TABLE 7.1 The contextualization and the frequency of using the keyword of the Belt and Road in China's provincial-level governments (2013–2019) (cont.)

Province	Frequency	State initiative	Central gov. initiative	Active integration	Active participation	Serve BRI	Make good usage of BRI	Opportunity
Hunan	9					YES		
Hubei	9	YES	YES	YES				
Hebei	9	YES						
Inner Mongolia	9	YES						YES
Anhui	8	YES						YES
Chongqing	8	YES	YES	YES				
Tibet	7	YES		YES				
Beijing	7		YES	YES		YES		
Qinghai	7	YES		YES				
Shanxi	6	YES		YES				YES
Fujian	5			YES				
Heilongjiang	4	YES						

SOURCE: THE AUTHOR'S OWN COMPILATION IS BASED ON QUANTITATIVE DATA ANALYSES FROM THE LOCAL GOVERNMENTS' REPORTS (2013–2019) AND CONTEXTUALISES THE BRI FROM THE PERSPECTIVE OF KEYWORDS: 国家 "一带一路" GUOJIA "YI DAI, YI LU" – STATE-SPONSORED BRI, 中央政府 ZHONGYANG ZHENGFU ZHENGCE – CENTRAL GOVERNMENT POLICY, 主动融入 ZHUDONG RONGRU– ACTIVE INTEGRATION, 服务 "一带一路"/服务国家总体外交 FUWU "YI DAI, YILU"/FUWU GUOJIA ZONGTI WAIJIAO – SERVE BRI/SERVE NATIONAL FOREIGN POLICY (ONLY IN THE CASE OF HAINAN), 对接 "一带一路" DUIJIE "YI DAI, YI LU" BE PART OF BRI, DOCK TO THE BRI, 用好 "一带一路" YONGHAO "YI DAI, YI LU" – USE THE OPPORTUNITY, 积极参与 JIJI CANYU – ACTIVE PARTICIPATION. ALL DOCUMENTS ARE DOWNLOADED FROM HTTP://DISTRICT.CE.CN/, ACCESSED 13 JUNE 2022

The second city, Shanghai, declares that it would participate, serve, and implement decisions from the national level and see itself as an example for the other local governments. As the financial hub for China, Shanghai discusses trade and financial cooperation under the BRI and new modes of cooperation with transnational companies based on the most advanced technologies. The city recognises itself as the "bridgehead" in international trade and a part of the local, regional development of the Yangtze River Economic Belt and Yangtze River Delta. The Shanghai government declares to adapt to the new trend of economic globalisation and to be part of China's economic development. Furthermore, the Shanghainese promise to accelerate the construction of a new open economy system and play the role of the bridgehead that serves the country's BRI construction. Interestingly the BRI allows the local government to present itself as the vanguard of the city reform, namely to coordinate reforms at the district and the city level. As a place known for its internationalisation of trade and finances, Shanghai offers the venue for China International Import Expo. However, over the years of COVID-19 Shanghai government has presented a less optimistic view of the Belt and Road: in 2021 the city promised to expand the trade with regions along the BRI and in 2022 declared "active participation and joint efforts to deliver BRI high-quality development" (Shanghai Local Government Reports, 2015–2022).

The third city, Tianjin, sees the BRI as part of the national strategy for opening up the country that is related to the "go global strategy". For Tianjin, the government is the "window of opportunity" that should be used to the fullest to benefit the local economy. The free trade zone is the most important example of delivering economic growth. The city government also declares active international cooperation with Europe, Arab countries and Africa. Apart from the investment, Tianjin announced the opening of ten new "Luban Workshop" in Africa and cooperated with the Ministry of Foreign Affairs to promote the "global Tianjin" project. The city's globalisation has also been possible by providing the venue for international events such as the Belt and Road International Port Cities Symposium, Tianjin Summit, and National Private Enterprise Trade and Investment Fair. From looking into foreign trade partners, the exchanges and cooperation with international sister cities have been named an essential part of Tianjin's international activities. Apart from the international activities under the BRI, domestic integration has been perceived as part of the activities under the BRI umbrella. The construction of the BRI has gone with the coordinated development of Beijing, Tianjin and Hebei Metropolitan Area. Interestingly during the COVID-19 pandemic, the municipal government did not refer to common efforts, as in the case of Chongqing and Shanghai, but precisely named foreign projects realized in the foreign countries e.g., Luban workshop in Africa (Tianjin Local Government Reports, 2015–2022).

As early as 2015 Beijing capital government declared the BRI as part of the opening-up policy and promised to serve the national strategy of the BRI. The city government also saw its actions as part of keeping the international market open for Chinese products. As the political centre, Beijing is the inspection centre for imported products and a partner for typical projects with Asian Development Bank and Silk Road Fund. Moreover, the BRI is seen as part of the "go global" policy and Beijing as an essential part of the China-Mongolia-Russia Economic Corridor. However, most important for the Beijing city government was the fact that it was the host city of the BRI Forum and, by all these means, contributed to the national policies. Providing the venues for the central government's initiative is one of the most critical parts of Beijing's international activities. Moreover, the capital city declares itself to be the international hub for "young talents" (by opening International Talents District Pilot Zone) as well as the hub for "unicorns-start-ups". As declared in the governmental reports, implementing a three-year action plan for jointly building the BRI was considered the central direction that guides the city in its international activities. What makes Beijing government different from the local government is that the international productivity cooperation is directed toward Germany and Japan as part of the BRI international activities. The last feature of municipal government international outreach, namely being part of China's public diplomacy and promoting the Chinese narrative, was less critical. Only Beijing's mayor mentioned "the power of discourse" in his Report in 2019. He promised the city of Beijing would participate in the global technological competition and strengthen the power of discourse in the international arena. During the COVID-19 pandemic, the local government declared to be active in navigating external actions of the local businesspeople and non-governmental organizations, while in 2022 the governor introduced the language of "common efforts to bring benefits under the Belt and Road policies" (Beijing Local Government's Reports, 2015–2022). Making the comparison between four municipal governments it is worth noticing that only Beijing's local government fails to declare domestic coordination, but was also the only one that describes its position as part of China's public diplomacy and the servant of the Belt and Road Initiative. Utilizing the sister cities platform Tianjin was the only single government to declare participation in this global forum, while Chongqing sees the central government as the crucial force behind the economic development of western China under the Belt and Road Initiative. The above-presented approach calls Beijing for bigger engagement with the

Chongqing government and Chen Min'er the party secretary in the city (see Table 7.2).

Bringing back the initial understanding of horizontal competition among the local municipalities, in this case, Beijing, Shanghai, Tianjin and Chongqing, the biggest winner is Chongqing – the most subordinated city as seen from the local governments' reports. Compared to all three cities, the government in the western city was given a unique incentive: the international project with Singapore. The growing role of Singapore was driven by the fact that both sides had cooperated in the Chongqing China-Singapore (Chongqing) Demonstration Initiative on Strategic Connectivity (the Chongqing Connectivity Project). According to the Implementation Agreement on China-Singapore (Chongqing) Demonstration Initiative on Strategic Connectivity, both sides established a management committee with four sub-committees dedicated to financial services, aviation, transport logistics, and information-communication technology. The logic behind Chongqing's cooperation with Singapore was mainly based on the aspiration of the local government to be the centre and pivot to the surrounding nine provinces and attract more private capital from wealthier regions in China. The project allowed the city of Chongqing to position itself as a financial hub: in November 2018, during the Financial Summit, Chongqing's government approved fintech cooperation between Chongqing and Singapore (Mierzejewski, 2021). As said in November 2021, the New International Land-Sea Trade Corridor is a trade and logistics passage jointly built by Singapore and provincial-level regions of western China with Chongqing as the leader (Global Times, 2021).

On the one hand, the international projects in Chongqing are part of the municipal government's effective policies, but on the other they should be viewed as the part of central authorities managing horizontal competition among the most trusted people. Analyzing the international activities of the particular municipal governments we need to understand the importance of the nomenclature system mainly managed by the Department of Organization under the Central Committee. Moreover, from the provincial level together with Guangdong and Xinjiang Autonomous Region the four cities' party secretaries have been placed in the Central Committee. In the case of the three cities of Chongqing, Beijing and Shanghai the former party secretaries: Chen Min'er, Cai Qi and Li Qiang have a political past tied with the presence of Xi Jinping in Fujian and Zhejiang. Only the party secretary in Tianjin is not politically experienced in Xi Jinping's places. Interestingly, this political structure has enabled Shanghai and Chongqing to foster closer mutual cooperation. Operating under the concept of the dual circulation economy, both cities have carved out a space for joint collaboration. In January 2020, Shanghai

TABLE 7.2 Beijing's, Shanghai's, Tianjin's and Chongqing's approaches and contexts of the BRI in the mayor's reports (2013–2022)

	Approach to the BRI	Domestic coordination	Economic development	Sister cities cooperation	International activities	Part of China's public diplomacy/ power of discourse
Beijing	Serve the national strategy, Opening up the country, Provide the venue for the central government BRI events e.g. BRI Forum	N/A	build the investments platform and jointly build a science and technology innovation park	N/A	Promoting "go global" strategy, close relations with Hong Kong, Macau, Taiwan and the Chinese overseas, promoting international young talent program, deepen cooperation, with key cities along the China-Mongolia-Russia Economic Corridor,	Power of discourse together with international technological competition
Shanghai	active implementation and participation in the BRI strategy be the bridgehead for the BRI	Coordination with YREB and Yangtze River Delta	the construction of an international financial centre and a scientific and technological innovation centre, shaping the open economy	N/A	Promoting "go global" strategy, close relations with Hong Kong, Macau, Taiwan and the Chinese overseas, promoting international financial centre	N/A

TABLE 7.2 Beijing's, Shanghai's, Tianjin's and Chongqing's approaches and contexts of the BRI in the mayor's reports (2013–2022) *(cont.)*

	Approach to the BRI	Domestic coordination	Economic development	Sister cities cooperation	International activities	Part of China's public diplomacy/ power of discourse
Tianjin	Deep integration into the BRI national strategy, active participation in building the BRI, the BRI is seen as the window of the historical opportunity for the city.	Coordination with Beijing-Tianjin-Hebei metropolitan area	accelerate the construction of overseas industrial parks and key projects	Important in the BRI international activities	Promoting "go global" strategy, close relations with Hong Kong, Macau, Taiwan and the Chinese overseas, Promote Euro-Asian Land-Bridge as the transport corridor, promoting Luban Workshop in Africa	N/A
Chongqing	Active participation and integration in the national strategy of the BRI	Coordination with YREB, be the hub for the development of Western China	Development is only possible by the support of the central government and Xi Jinping in particular, development of the financial centre in western China	N/A	Promoting "go global" strategy, close relations with Hong Kong, Macau, Taiwan and the Chinese overseas, promote Chongqing-Duisburg cargo train connection	N/A

SOURCE: THE AUTHOR'S COMPILATION IS BASED ON THE QUALITATIVE RESEARCH OF BEIJING, SHANGHAI, TIANJIN AND CHONGQING (2015–2022), ALL DOCUMENTS ARE DOWNLOADED FROM HTTP://DISTRICT.CE.CN/, 16 JUNE 2022

and Chongqing signed a memorandum of cooperation for the Shanghai-Chongqing direct express line in Shanghai, marking a new era of cooperation between the two cities (Shanghai Gov., 2020). Furthermore, the political position of Chen Min'er has allowed Chongqing to shape its financial hub with the support of the Shanghai Stock Exchange, Guotai Junan Securities, and other Beijing-based financial institutions (IChongqing, 2023). Capitalizing on this collaboration, the Chongqing Municipal Commerce Commission stated that the China International Import Exhibition was heralded as 'a window for China's opening-up and cooperation,' providing a platform for both domestic and international collaboration (Chongqing Gov., 2023) and implement the aggrement on fast water transport channel with Yangtze River (Xinhua, 2023). As said, before the political position of the local party secretary matters. Li Qiang, current prime minister, former party secretary in Shanghai served as the party secretary in Wenzhou (Zhejiang province) and then in 2004 became the head of the Secretariat under Xi Jinping, then the provincial party secretary. Chen Min'er, the second of Xi Jinping's protégé served as the head of the Department of Propaganda of Zhejiang province and next as vice-governor. For almost 20 years he served as a party bureaucrat at various levels in the city of Shaoxing. Prior to his post in Chongqing, he governed Guizhou as the governor and the party secretary. Cai Qi, serving as the party secretary in Beijing started his professional career in Fujian province as the party secretary of Sanming city, and then was elevated to Zhejiang's Quzhou, Taizhou and Hangzhou as the mayor of the cities. His political career accelerated in 2010 when he became the head of the Department of Organization as well as a member of the Standing Committee of the Party. In 2013, he became the Executive vice governor of Zhejiang province. The fourth person at the municipal level Li Hongzhong started his political activities in north-east of China Liaoning province and then was based in southern Guangdong province e.g., as the mayor of Shenzhen city. Between 2007 and 2016 Li Hongzhong served as governor and then as party secretary in Hubei. In November 2022, before the National People's Congress, several significant political appointments were made. Li Qiang was elevated to the then future position of prime minister. Concurrently, Cai Qi, previously holding a post in Beijing, was appointed as the first-ranked secretary of the Secretariat of the Chinese Communist Party, with his former position being taken over by Yin Li, the ex-governor of Sichuan province and party secretary in Fujian. Additionally, Chen Min'er replaced Li Hongzhong as the party secretary in Beijing, while Li Hongzhong assumed the role of the first-ranking vice chairperson of the Standing Committee of the National People's Congress (see Table 7.3). among the four local leaders, Chen Min'er, one the leader of the four municipalities directly governed by the State

Council, enjoyed the strongest position. His position as the party secretary in Chongqing was reflected by privileges given by the central government, especially to those who supported the cooperation with Singapore and local interagtion between Chongqing and Shanghai.

The Belt and Road Initiative, together with the ongoing ongoing various unification projects, is conceived as a comprehensive external and internal project that intends to limit the fragmentation inside China. As illustrated in the chapter, the Belt and Road Initiative shows the duality of engagements: central-local and local-local have not been changed, and any centralised government cannot change this substantial vertical and horizontal competition, not only interprovincial but also intraprovincial. By presenting the different levels of adoption of the Belt and Road initiative, e.g., Sichuan and Heilongjiang, the local authorities show their expectations and different level of political confession in the central policies. Moreover, most provincial-level governments declared active integration and participation in the central government project showing their cautiously optimistic approach. In other words, by signalling only integration, the localities use the central government concept to position themselves in horizontal competition and vertical relations with Beijing. At the same time, the central government needs to carefully manage the different interests of provinces with special money transfers and press them to integrate inside the country. However, this also raises the question of the level of unification inside China. Being politically integrated, China is fragmented when it comes to its economic structure. From the perspective of the central government, the fragmentation allows Beijing to execute its paramount position and serves as the ultimate arbiter inside the political system of China. As illustrated by the Yangtze River Economic Belt project, where after years of negotiations, provinces across the domestic belt took the same industries for development. The central government's plan to develop an integrated "Golden Corridor" of the Yangtze River failed to exemplify interprovincial integration.

Moreover, even the international tasks scheduled by the central government might be easily bypassed but also shape the platform for horizontal competition. Not all local governments are interested in taking part in the race, however as illustrated by the development of train connections to Europe: Sichuan and Chongqing were comfortable in taking part in the competition. Public diplomacy, serves here as the second-best example. The central government guides the localities to be part of China's public diplomacy, as illustrated by the four municipalities approach. But officially the only local government in Beijing declares to promote the power of discourse but at the same time not being part of the central public diplomacy agenda.

TABLE 7.3   Party secretaries in the four municipalities: Chongqing, Shanghai, Tianjin and Beijing

Municipality	Party secretary	Political past
Chongqing	Bo Xilai (2007–2012)	Minister of Commerce, Governor of Liaoning, Mayor of Dalian
	Zhang Dejiang (2012)	Party Secretary of Guangdong
	Sun Zhengcai (2012–2017)	Party Secretary of Jilin, Minister of Agriculture
	Chen Min'er (2017–2022)	Party Secretary of Guizhou, Governor of Guizhou, Head of Department of Propaganda of Zhejiang
	Yuan Jiajun (2022-)	Party Secretary of Zhejiang, Governor of Zhejiang
Shanghai	Xi Jinping (2007)	Party Secretary of Zhejiang
	Yu Zhengsheng (2007–2012)	Party Secretary of Hubei, Minister of Construction
	Han Zheng (2012–2017)	Mayor of Shanghai
	Li Qiang (2012–2022)	Party Secretary of Jiangsu, Governor of Zhejiang, since 2023 Prime Minister
	Chen Jining (2022 -)	Mayor of Beijing, Minister of Environmental Protection, President of Qinghua University
Tianjin	Zhang Gaoli (2007–2012)	Party Secretary of Shandong
	Sun Chunlan (f) (2012–2014)	Party Secretary of Fujian
	Huang Xingguo (2014–2016)	Major of Tianjin
	Li Hongzhong (2016–2022)	Party Secretary of Hubei, Governor of Hubei, Party Secretary in Shenzhen
	Chen Min'er	Party Secretary in Chongqing
Beijing	Liu Qi (2002–2012)	Mayor of Beijing, Minister of Metallurgical Industry
	Guo Jinlong (2012–2017)	Mayor of Beijing

TABLE 7.3 Party secretaries in the four municipalities: Chongqing, Shanghai, Tianjin and Beijing (cont.)

Municipality	Party secretary	Political past
	Cai Qi (2017–2022)	Mayor of Beijing, Mayor of Hangzhou, Head of Organizational Department of Zhejiang, since 2022
	Yin Li (2022–)	Deputy party secretary of Sichuan province, governonr of Sichuan, Party Secretary of Fujian

SOURCE: AUTHOR'S OWN COMPILATION BASED ON WEBPAGE HTTP://DISTRICT.CE.CN/ZT/RWK/, 12 FEBRUARY, 2023

To sum up, the Belt and Road Initiative should be seen from the domestic arena as the vehicle for the centralization of local interests. However, by far it does not translate to more integrated China as an economic body. By positioning itself within the Belt and Road Initiative as a domestic and international player the local government has used horizontal competition. The behaviours shown by the second administrative division resulted in maintaining the status quo as before the centralised model of governance introduced by Xi Jinping.

Acknowledgements

The paper is written as part of the research project "The Role of Local Governments in China's Foreign Policy", supported by the National Science Center based on UMO-2017/25/B/HS5/02117.

References

Asian Development Bank (2017) People's Republic of China: Preparing Yangtze River Economic Belt Projects, https://www.adb.org/sites/default/files/project-documents/50343/50343-001-tar-en.pdf, accessed 11 February 2024.

Beijing Local Government's Reports (2015–2022) district.ce.cn, accessed 16 June 2022.

Chen Futao (2003) Tanxi Zhongguo defang zhengfu de duiwai shiwu (On local governments' foreign affairs activities in China). *Xingzhengyu fa* (Administration and Law), 12, pp. 28–38.

Chen Yuxian and Gu Wenjing (2019) *Regional Government Competition*. New York, London: Routledge.

China Daily (2016) President Xi visits and encourages Chongqing, https://www.chinadaily.com.cn/china/2016-01/06/content_22961676.htm, accessed 11 July 2022.

China Gov. (2018) Zhonggong zhongyang guowuyuan guanyu jianli gengjia youxiao de quyu xietiao fazhan xin jizhi de yijian (The Central Committee of the Communist Party of China and the State Council Opinion on Establishing More Effective New Mechanism for Regional Coordinated Development), http://www.gov.cn/zhengce/2018-11/29/content_5344537.htm, accessed 12 January 2022.

Chongqing Government (2023) Chongqing zai Shanghai juhang touzi maoyi hezuo kentan hui tuijie fazhan youshi – zengjia shuangxiang touzi, gongxiang 'Chongqing jihui'. (Chongqing holds an investment and trade cooperation meeting in Shanghai to promote development advantages – increasing bilateral investment, sharing the 'Chongqing Opportunity'), http://www.cq.gov.cn/ywdt/jrcq/202311/t20231106_12519214.html, accessed 10 February 2024.

Chongqing Local Government's Reports (2013–2022), http://district.ce.cn/, accessed 16 June 2022.

Chung Jae Ho (1995) Studies of Central-Provincial Relations in the Peopole's Republic of China: A Mid-term Appraisal. *The China Quarterly*, 142, pp. 487–508.

Doak, Barnett A. (1967) *Cadres, Bureaucracy, and the Political Power in Communist China*. New York, London: Columbia University Press.

Dreyer, June Teufel (2010) *China's Political System. Modernization and Tradition*. New York: Longman.

Global Times (2021) Singapore-Chongqing connectivity strengthens, facilitating trade, 25 November, https://www.globaltimes.cn/page/202111/1239911.shtml, accessed 11 July 2022.

Goodman, David (1994) The politics of regionalism, Economic Development, conflict and negotiation. In: D. Goodman, G. Segal (eds.) *China Deconstruct, Politics, Trade and Regionalism*. London, New York: Routledge.

Hendrischke, Hans (1999) Provinces in competition: region, identity, and cultural contraction. In: Hans Hendrischke and Feng Chongyi (eds.) *The Political Economy of China's Provinces. Comparative and competitive advantage*. London, New York: Routledge, pp. 1–31.

Hu Jun (2014) *Zhongguo quyu xietiao fazhan jizhi tixi yanjiu* (The research on organizational structures of China's regional coordinated development). Beijing: Zhongguo shehui chubanshe.

IChongqing (2023) Chongqing Forms Strategic Cooperation with China's Leading Financial Institutions, 1 September, https://www.ichongqing.info/2023/09/01/chongqing-forms-strategic-cooperation-with-chinas-leading-financial-institutions/, accessed 10 February 2024.

Li Chenlan Linda (2003) *Center and Provinces, China 1978–1993, Power as Non-zero sum.* Oxford: Clarendon Press.

Li Ping, Jiang Feitao and Cao Jianhai (2019) *Industrial Overcapacity and Duplicate Construction in China. Reasons and Solutions.* Singapore: World Scientific.

Liu Hui and Liu Weidong (2017) 'Yidai yilu' jianshe yu woguo quyu fazhan zhanlüe de guo guanxi yanjiu (Study on Relationship between the Belt and Road Initiative and Regional Development Strategies of China). *Bulletin of Chinese Academy of Sciences,* 32(4), pp. 340–347, http://www.bulletin.cas.cn/publish_article/2017/4/20170402.htm, accessed 15 February 2022.

Mierzejewski Dominik (2009) Not to Oppose but to Rethink.The New Left Discourse on the Chinese Reforms. *Journal of Contemporary Eastern Asia,* 8 (1), pp. 15–29.

Mierzejewski Dominik (2020) The Role of Guangdong and Guangzhou's Subnational Diplomacy in China's Belt and Road Initiative. *China: An International Journal,* 18 (2), pp. 99–119.

Pei Minxin (2009) *China's trapped transformation.* Boston: Harvard University Press.

Riskin, Carl (1987) *China's Political Economy. The Quest for Development Since 1949.* Oxford: Oxford University Press.

Shanghai Government (2020) Innovation forum highlights Chongqing's emerging prominence. 6 March, https://www.shanghai.gov.cn/nw48081/20210603/b64ca8e754694a319758d28b49904aa6.html, accessed 10 February 2024.

Shanghai Local Government's Reports (2015–2022) http://district.ce.cn/, accessed 16 June 2022.

Smith, David and Robert Snow (1976) The Division of Labor: Conceptual and Methodological Issues. *Social Forces,* 55, pp. 520–528.

State Council (2023) Guanyu jiakuai nei wai mao yitihua fazhan de ruogan cuoshi (Several Measures for Accelerating the Integrated Development of Domestic and Foreign Trade). 11 December, https://www.gov.cn/zhengce/content/202312/content_6919596.htm, accessed 12 February 2024.

Tianjin Local Government's Reports (2015–2022) http://district.ce.cn/, accessed 16 June 2022.

Vision and Action (2015) Full text of the Vision for Maritime Cooperation under the Belt and Road Initiative. 20 June, http://english.www.gov.cn/archive/publications/2017/06/20/content_281475691873460.htm, accessed 12 September 2021.

Wang Huning (1993) Shehuizhuyi shichang jingji de zhengzhi yaqiu; xin quanli jiegou (The Political Needs for Socialism Market Economy: New Power Structure). *Shehui Kexue* (Social Science), 2, pp. 3–7.

Wang Shaoguang and Hu Angang (1993) *Zhongguo guojia nengli baogao* (*A Study of China's State Capacity*). Changchun: Liaoning Renmin Chunbanshe.
World Bank, NDRC Report (2019) Innovative China. New Drivers of Growth. https://openknowledge.worldbank.org/bitstream/handle/10986/32351/9781464813351.pdf?sequence=7&isAllowed=y, accessed 15 February 2022.
Xinhua (2023) Hu Yu zhidazhikuai xian zhuli Changjiang 'huangjin shuidao' dongneng jiakuai shifang ("The Shanghai-Chongqing Direct Express Line aids in accelerating the release of energy along the Yangtze River's 'Golden Waterway'"). 21 August, http://www.news.cn/fortune/2023-08/21/c_1129815327.htm, accessed 10 February 2024.
Young, Alwyn (2000) The Razor's Edge: Distortions and Incremental Reform in the People's Republic of China. *Quarterly Journal of Economics,* 115(1091135).
YREB Guidelines (2014) Guowuyuan guanyu yituo huangjin shuidao tuidong Changjiang jingji dai fazhan de zhidao yijian guo fa (2014) 39 hao (The State Council Guidelines on promoting the development of the Golden Corridor of the Yangtze River Economic Belt), 25 September, http://www.gov.cn/zhengce/content/2014-09/25/content_9092.htm, accessed 23 January 2022.
YREB Guidelines (2016) Changjiang jingji dai fazhan guihua gangyao (Development Plan Outline for the Yangtze River Economic Belt), 12 September, https://www.planning.org.cn/law/news_view?id=5141, accessed 12 February 2024.
Yu Jie and Jon Wallace (2021) What is China's Belt and Road Initiative (BRI)? *Chatham House,* 13 September, https://www.chathamhouse.org/2021/09/what-chinas-belt-and-road-initiative-bri, accessed 16 February 2022.
Zheng Yongnian (2007) *De facto Federalism in China. Reforms and Dynamics of Central-Local Relations.* Singapore: World Scientific.

CHAPTER 8

China's Policy on Climate and Energy towards 2060

Łukasz Gacek

1   Introduction

Climate change, resulting in the rise in sea-level, extreme weather conditions, including hurricanes, tornadoes, floods, droughts, wildfires, the increasing spread of infectious diseases, is compounding threats to the availability of food, drinking water and healthcare to humanity. Mitigating climate disaster requires to take rapid actions at the national and international level. When it comes to this issue, no nation is more important than China, that emits today more greenhouse gases than the entire developed world combined. China's attitude towards climate change and energy has changed in recent years. At the 2015 United Nations Climate Change Conference in Paris, where a historic compromise was reached to keep the increase in global average temperature to well below 2°C above pre-industrial levels, China played a constructive role in climate negotiations. This contrasted with the situation during the Copenhagen Climate Change Conference in late 2009, when China was accused of sabotaging the talks. In particular, it failed to agree on limiting greenhouse gas emissions. At the time, Chinese negotiators opposed to combine domestic and international commitments on climate change. The Paris deal suggests that Beijing's authorities are willing to play a more constructive role in the global climate regime. The argument in favour of change in the China's position is a result of adopting more sustainable development model, which will help contribute to environmental, social and economic improvements. Changes observed in China's environmental and climate policy do not result from a philanthropic imperative. Indeed, they indicate the need to create a solid foundation for further economic development. Fostering innovation for green growth is perceived as a key to upgrade China's future competitiveness. Climate change has been already recognized by China as the main non-traditional security threat to the country's sustainable development. China's steps towards green transition can be considered both practical and also beneficial for boosting the economy through innovative green technologies, create sustainable industry and transport, reduce pollution and tackle climate change. China's commitments to achieve carbon neutrality before 2060 and peak CO_2 emissions before 2030, incorporated into the overall layout of building an 'ecological civilization', indicate the direction of long-term ambition and priorities.

This chapter aims to describe China's policies and actions responding to climate change. It also discusses four major reasons that justify why China's stance on climate change has shifted, which include public concern about pollution and climate change, promotion of the new development pattern for high-quality and sustainable economic growth, priority on investing in renewable energy, and boosting mechanisms for green development under the Belt and Road Initiative. The structure of this chapter reflects these dimensions and it is preceded by the analysis of energy and climate policy developments in recent years.

2   The Evolution of Energy and Climate Policy in China

Over the last two decades, China has significantly changed its attitude to the problem of climate change and has already taken some steps to transform its economy and make it more sustainable. Since the country introduced reform and opening-up in 1978, the economy has seen a spectacular growth at an average annual rate of nearly 10%. China's gross domestic product has surged from 149 billion US dollars in 1978 to almost 15 trillion US dollars in 2020 (The World Bank, 2022a). After more than 40 years of reforms, China became the world's second-largest economy in nominal terms, behind the United States, and the largest in terms of purchasing power parity (PPP). Such rapid economic development had a lot of negative consequences. It has brought about a rising demand for energy. Meanwhile, primary energy consumption increased rapidly from 0.57 to 4.9 billion tons of coal equivalent (tce) (China Statistical Yearbook, 2021). As a result, China has overtaken the US as the world's biggest consumer of energy. Its share of the global total primary energy consumption was 26.1% in 2020. This is far more than was consumed by the North America (19.4%) and whole Europe (13.9%) (BP, 2021). Over the course of the last four decades China has heavily relied on conventional fossil fuels to drive its economic growth. Its energy structure was dominated by coal (Table 8.1) and was characterized by a low energy and carbon efficiency.

For a long time, China prioritized economic growth, based on the rapid pace of industrialization and the improvement in the living standards over greenhouse gas emissions reduction. China has generated growth at the expense of the environment, creating problems with air pollution, water scarcity, and soil contamination.

TABLE 8.1   Total energy consumption by source (%)

	1978	1990	2000	2005	2010	2015	2020
Coal	70.7	76.2	68.5	72.4	69.2	63.8	56.8
Crude oil	22.7	16.6	22.0	17.8	17.4	18.4	18.9
Natural gas	3.2	2.1	2.2	2.4	4.0	5.8	8.4
Primary electricity and other energy	3.4	5.1	7.3	7.4	9.4	12.0	15.9

SOURCE: CHINA STATISTICAL YEARBOOK (2021)

This approach corresponded to the Chinese stance during the 1972 UN Stockholm Conference on the Human Environment. Conference was hold under the iconic slogan 'Only One Earth' and it was the first international conference on environmental protection with Chinese involvement. At the time 26 principles were adopted. Among them, Principle no. 13 provided a groundbreaking solution, by emphasizing the need for careful planning and rational management of natural resources. It imposed an obligation on states to adopt an approach to development planning which would integrate into such planning relevant environmental factors (Sohn, 1973: 473). During the conference, China firstly emphasized the right to development over environmental protection (Dierci quanguo huanjing baohu huiyi, 1983–1984). China stressed the importance of industrialization and economic growth, while at the same time did not link environmental pollution with social and economic development (Jin and Liu, 1987). However, it has shaped the country's understanding of environmental and climate issues. In 1973, China held its first national Conference on Environmental Protection in Beijing. The leading Group of Environmental Protection of the State Council was formed a year later, and then reorganized into the State Administration of Environment Protection. The conference formulated the nation's first guiding principles concerning environmental issues, known as the '32-character policy', which included 'overall and rational planning; comprehensive utilization; turning harms into benefits; relying on the people; public participation; protecting the environment; and bringing benefits to the people' (全面规划，合理布局，综合利用，化害为利，依靠群众，大家动手，保护环境，造福人民 *quanmian guihua, heli buju, zonghe liyong, hua hai wei li, yikao qunzhong, dajia dongshou, baohu huanjing, zaofu renmin*) (Shengtai huanjing bu, 2013). In 1975 environmental protection was first written into China's five-year plan. In 1979 China promulgated its first Environmental Protection Law. It was revised ten years later. By the end of 1983 Premier Li Peng announced that environmental protection is one of China's basic and long term national policies (Shengtai huanjing bu, 2013).

The United Nations Framework Convention on Climate Change (UNFCCC) that was adopted at the Rio Earth Summit in 1992 can be perceived as an environmental turning-point for China. The 'Earth Summit' concluded that the concept of international partnership is essential to achieve sustainable development and ensure a better future for all (United Nations, 1992). A milestone was reached in Japan's Kyoto on 11 December 1997 when a Protocol was adopted to fight climate change. It entered into force on 16 February 2005 (United Nations, 1998). According to this, developed countries were obligated to achieve a target of a 5.2 per cent reduction in greenhouse gas emissions below 1990 levels by 2012. China and India were exempted from that agreement. China has approved the Kyoto Protocol on 30 August 2002. Despite the lack of a reduction target for greenhouse gas emissions the decision was generally considered as an important boost to the fight against global warming. At the time, China reaffirmed the key principle of 'common but differentiated responsibility' (共同但有区别的责任 *gongtong dan you qubie de zeren*) and well-known formula of 'the right to development'. It argued that rich, developed countries had contributed about 60–80% to the global temperature rise, while developing countries only about 20–40% (Wei et al., 2012: 12911–12915). That's why they must assume greater responsibility for tackling climate change. During the 2009 United Nations Climate Change Conference (Copenhagen Summit), Chinese Premier Wen Jiabao said the principle of 'common but differentiated responsibilities' is the long-term goal of the international community in addressing climate change and is not negotiable (Wen, 2009). It would be very difficult to defend this argument, due to the fact that currently China is not only the world's largest energy consumer, but also is the largest emitter of greenhouse gases worldwide. China's CO_2 emissions share increased steadily over the last three decades. China became the world's top energy consumer and CO_2 emitter, accounting for 29% of global emissions, compared to 10% in 1990. It is also the largest PM, NOx and SO_2 emitter in the world. At present China also becomes the highest sulfur dioxide (SO_2), nitrogen oxide (NOx), and particulate matter (PM) emitter in the world. However, the external perceptions of China's role in international climate talks has changed considerably since 2009. At the Copenhagen conference, China was described as a 'dead weight' or a 'wrecker' in its negotiating strategy (Gao, 2018: 213–239).

In contrast, six years later the Chinese delegation took a constructive part in the climate negotiation, when the Paris Agreement set out a roadmap to limit global warming to below 2°C (United Nations, 2015). Since then China has been more often portrayed as the leader of the global fight against climate change. Surveys conducted among delegates and observers of the Conference of the Parties (COP) of the United Nations Framework Convention on Climate Change show that China, next to the United States and the European Union is now most often identified as the leading voice in this struggle. In this 'fragmented leadership landscape' there's no single unquestionable leader in climate change (Parker, Karlsson and Hjerpe, 2017: 244).

Currently, China points out, climate change and energy issues are prominent global challenges that concern the common interests of the international community and bear on the future of the Earth. The willingness and motivation of the international community to jointly cope with challenges continue to rise, and the key is to take concrete actions. In that context Xi Jinping, Chinese President and General Secretary of the Communist Party of Central Committee of the Chinese Communist Party, expounded China's goal of building 'a community of shared future for mankind' (Xi, 2017a). This crucial question refers to China's changing perception of global governance manifested by instrumental promotion of its own idea of 'community of shared future for mankind' (人类命运共同体 *renlei mingyun gongtongti*). It is explained by exporting 'Chinese wisdom' (中国智慧 *Zhongguo zhihui*) or 'Chinese solution' (中国方案 *Zhongguo fang'an*) abroad. From Beijing's perspective such approach reflects its constructive attitude of participating actively in international cooperation on climate change. This strategic narrative was also designed to win the support of the global community.

China tries to build its image as a responsible actor in international relations, presenting constructive ideas to address global issues such as climate change and environmental challenges. And that explains why China eventually accepted the Glasgow Climate Pact (United Nations, 2021). However, at the final session of COP26 in Glasgow on 13 November 2021, China, together with India, Iran, Venezuela and Cuba insisted to modify the coal text, from 'phase out' to 'phase down' at the last minute. China and Russia, also refused to sign the Global Coal to Clean Power Transition Statement, which emphasized 'the transition away from unabated coal power generation in the 2030s (or as soon as possible thereafter) for major economies and in the 2040s (or as soon as possible thereafter) globally' (UN Climate Change Conference UK, 2021). Despite this, China, once again, demonstrated its international power in order to became an active player in climate negotiations. China's active participation in the climate change negotiations shows that the authorities in Beijing are trying to influence international affairs to a greater extent than before. However, in the global quest to ensure the sustainable development of conventional and clean energy, China is aware that top-down climate management under the aegis of the UN has little impact on individual countries. The proposed green targets and programs for sustainable development in the medium and long term in countries along the Belt and Road demonstrate China's aspiration to become a leader in the dissemination of green technologies. This crucial issue should also be considered in the context of China's approach to global governance manifested by its own idea of "community of shared future for mankind".

3 Public Concern over the Climate Change and Environmental Degradation

Recent shift in China's climate policy is an answer to public concern about climate change as well as the determination of Chinese authorities to adopt number of policies, measures and actions which help to reduce emissions (Gacek and Tkaczyński, 2021). Such policies are linked to its domestic environmental problems including air pollution, water scarcity, soil contamination, desertification, and deforestation (Gacek, 2020: 36–71). Recent surveys reveal that the majority of Chinese are concerned about global climate change. In the public's eye the government is supposed to lead on climate change (Li, 2018). In response to these concerns government initiated a series of campaigns to promote energy efficiency and conservation and low-carbon development, encouraging a sustainable lifestyle. Over the course of the last years China has also enacted a law targeting air pollution (amendment to the Law on Prevention and Control of Air Pollution, 2018), water (amendment to the Law on the Prevention and Control of Water Pollution, 2017) and soil (Soil Pollution Prevention and Control Law, 2018). The Chinese authorities have introduced a new paradigm with the planned construction of an 'ecological civilization' (生态文明 *shengtai wenming*), with the aim of reducing pollution and transforming China's existing development model. Beijing authorities underline the unity between nature and mankind (天人合一 *tianren heyi*), by taking appropriate actions to face the problems of ecology and biodiversity as well as solutions to tackle climate change by cutting atmospheric pollution, especially carbon dioxide emissions (Gacek, 2020; Pan, 2015; Vltchek and Cobb Jr., 2019; Cao, 2014). Innovative scientific and technological solutions are expected to address existing environmental threats and combat climate change while allowing the country to maintain a high rate of economic development. This centrally adopted approach allows China to strengthen its environmental and climate change policies. It has a positive impact on local environmental governance and raises public awareness of today's environmental challenges. It also helps to shape China's image as a responsible player in the international community. There's no doubt that by promoting vision of 'ecological civilization' Beijing tries to set up a new framework for the discussion on climate.

Since taking office in 2013 President Xi Jinping tried to link the ecological civilization with realizing 'the dream of a great rejuvenation of the Chinese nation'. It underlines the need to concentrate on protection of resources and the environment to promote the promotion of the green and low-carbon development (Xinhua, 2013). The 19th Congress of the CCP in October 2017 gave new impetus to the construction of an ecological civilization. As Secretary General of the Party, Xi Jinping spoke about accelerating the reforms associated with the ecological civilization and the formation of a 'beautiful China,' signaling the need for a holistic approach to environmental protection and promoting environmentally friendly growth models. The concept of the ecological civilization has been encapsulated in the Party's statute (Xinhua, 2017a). The importance of this issue is also illustrated by the fact that the concept of the ecological civilization was included in the content of the Basic Law of December 4, 1982, as amended in 2018 (Zhongyang zhengfu menhu wangzhan, 2018).[1] References to the ecological civilization have also appeared in the amendment to the Environmental Protection Law of December 26, 1989 – i.e., the Law of April 24, 2014, which entered into force on January 1, 2015 (Zhongyang zhengfu menhu wangzhan, 2014). It corresponded with setting up of the Ministry of Ecology and Environment and the Ministry of Natural Resources in March 2018. Since then MEE is responsible for managing greenhouse gas emissions and combating the negative effects of climate change.

Confronted by the challenges of climate change, China President Xi Jinping announced that China will aim to hit peak emissions before 2030 and for carbon neutrality by 2060, when speaking to the UN General Assembly in September 2020 (Xinhua, 2020a). For the first time, China has set a clear long-term mitigation goal of carbon neutrality. The announcement is being seen as an important step in the global fight against climate change. It's worth to add that 'dual carbon' goals were included in China's overall plan for ecological conservation, and in the promotion of the development of a green and low-carbon circular economy (Xinhua, 2021a). The plan to achieve net-zero

---

1 Article 46 (6), 'The building of an ecological civilization' (生态文明建设 *shengtai wenming jianshe*). Amended by the Law of 11 March 2018 amending the Constitution of the PRC.

greenhouse gas emissions by the year 2060 corresponds with Xi Jinping's declaration of taking additional steps to deliver 2030 ambitions. At Climate Ambition Summit in December 2020 he stated that in the perspective of 2030, China would aim to cut carbon intensity per unit of GDP by more than 65% from 2005 levels (compared to its initial commitment of 60–65%), increase non-fossil fuels in primary energy consumption to around 25% (compared to 20% in the existing target), increase the forest stock volume by 6 billion cubic meters (compared to 4.5 billion in the current target) and bring its total installed capacity of wind and solar power to over 1,200 gigawatts (no previous target) (Xinhua, 2020b). These commitments undoubtedly show some progression from original climate targets. The overall trajectory to achieve carbon neutrality before 2060 was established in the National 14th Five-Year Plan (2021–2025). First of all, the plan did not set a specific economic growth target which should steer local governments away from the pursuit of economic growth at all costs, emphasizing instead the importance of such issues as climate change and environmental degradation. However, China has not indicated an increase in ambition with its new intensity targets. The carbon intensity target is on the same level as in the 13th Five-Year Plan (2016–2020). Similarly, the energy intensity reduction target by 13,5% is less ambitious than in the prior five-year period when it was 15%. It also set a goal of 20% non-fossil energy in total energy consumption (Xinhua, 2021c). It signals rather a modest acceleration to reach carbon-neutrality target. Apart from rising investments in renewables, China still perceive fossil fuels as the bedrock of its energy security. In the last decade China undertook efforts to diversify its power mix by increasing the share of hydro, wind, solar and nuclear power capacity and gradually switching from coal to natural gas in the residential heating and industrial sectors. Yet it does not change the fact that the country's energy system and economy are still reliant on coal which accounts for nearly 60% of electricity generation (Table 8.2).

China uses more coal than the rest of the world combined (54.3% in 2020). China is also the world's largest producer (50.7%) and importer of coal (20.8%) (BP, 2021). Fossil fuels produce large quantities of CO_2 when burned. So it is not a surprise that China is the world's largest emitter of carbon dioxide and other warming gases. And furthermore, it continues to build new coal power plants domestically. China has pledged to reduce its coal-fired power generation as part of a plan to become carbon-neutral. However, reduction plans will not begin until after 2025. According to International Energy Agency power generation is expected to increase by 9% year-on-year in 2021 (International Energy Agency, 2021). A report published in December 2021 by researchers from

TABLE 8.2   Electricity generation and generation capacity in China

Indicator	Power production (GWh)	Installed generation capacity (MW)	Newly installed generation capacity (MW)
Total	7,623,600	2,200,580	190,870
Hydro power	1,355,200	370,160	13,230
Thermal power	5,174,300	1,245,170	56,370
Nuclear power	366,200	49,890	1,120
Wind power	466,500	281,530	71,670
Solar power	261,100	253,430	48,200

SOURCE: ZHONGGUO DIANLI QIYE LIANHE HUI (2021)

China's State Grid Corporation said that the need to satisfy increased demand for require to build up to 150 gigawatts of new coal-fired power capacity by the end of 2025, bringing the total to 1,230 gigawatts (Stanway, 2021). Faced with an economic slowdown and downturn caused by the COVID-19 pandemic in recent times, Chinese provinces used coal to boosting growth in the short term begin. Current stimulus plans look a bit like a strategy to recover from the 2008 financial crisis, mainly based on investments in high-carbon infrastructure. Luckily, the scale of these plans is beyond comparison. Therefore, we are unlikely to see a rapid increase of emissions.

4   China's New Development Pattern

China's approach to climate is determined by promotion of the new development pattern of high-quality and sustainable economic growth, which also integrates a wider range of targets of environmental quality. Knowledge and innovation started to play a crucial role in fostering competitiveness and economic growth in the long-term period (Gacek, 2018: 5–32). Good example of that shift is Chinese strategic initiative Made In China 2025 (MIC 2025) (Guowuyuan, 2015), inspired by Germany's 'Industry 4.0.' Initiated in 2015, the plan calls for breakthroughs in key technologies, as well as improve quality and efficiency.

It also aims to reduce China's resilience on foreign technology imports. The implementation of innovation-driven development strategy aims to upgrade manufacturing base and laid out strategic emerging industries to ensure competitiveness of Chinese manufacturing sector both domestically and globally. The comprehensive strategy highlighted 10 priority sectors, which include new information technology, numerical control tools and robotics, aerospace equipment, ocean engineering equipment and high-tech ships, railway equipment, energy saving and new energy vehicles, power equipment, new materials, biological medicine and medical devices, and agricultural machinery (Guowuyuan, 2015). MIC2025 focuses on green development, especially on enforcing green manufacturing methods. It became a flagship program for energy saving and new energy vehicles. Green development strongly corresponds with the government's strategies to combat climate change. Initiative also creates the opportunity for China to be the leader in the clean energy manufacturing industries. Environmental concerns and climate change stimulate the development of the breakthrough innovations. In this context research and investment in clean energy is trending up in the global growth of patent application for climate change mitigation technologies. Companies in China filed 81% (6,992) of the renewable energy patents in 2018/2019 (Geary, 2020).

According to the World Bank data China was categorized as an upper-middle-income country with GNI per capita of 10,550 US dollars in 2020, compared to only 200 US dollars in 1978 (The World Bank, 2022b). The World Bank classifies economies into four income groups: low, lower-middle (1,046 – 4,095 US dollars), upper-middle (4,096 – 12,695), and high income (> 12,695 US dollars) (Hamadeh, Van Rompaey and Metreau, 2021). The Chinese government defines incomes ranging between 60,000 and 500,000 RMB (9,600–80,000 US dollars) per year as middle class (Zhongguo "Zhongchan" shou huo shuzi jieding: jiating nian shouru 6 wan – 50 wan, 2005). The Center for Strategic and International Studies informed that, by 2018 more than half of China's population (707 million) was considered to be middle class, compared with only 3% in 2000 (China Power Team, 2017).

After 1978 China's development policy was determinated by large-scale capital investment and rapid productivity growth. The state gave priority to the objective of achieving rapid economic growth. A semi-marketized economy for a long time relied on state intervention (Knight, 2016:–159). A GDP target was crucial for local officials. However eventually it turned out to be a major source of distortions in the economy. For this reason China officially abandoned its pursuit of growth at any costs towards emphasizing the importance of environmental protection. China attached importance to deepen ecological environment management reform, greater efficiency of natural resources and improvement of innovation in clean energy technologies. The environmental measures have been incorporated into the overall local government evaluations. The Decision of the Central Committee of the Communist Party of China on Some Major Issues Concerning Comprehensively Deepening the Reform stated that "We will improve the development progress evaluation system, correct the bias of evaluating political achievements merely by the economic growth rate. We will increase the weight of other evaluation indicators such as resources consumption, environmental damage, ecological benefits, excess production capacity, sci-tech innovation, production safety and new debts, while more emphasis will be put on employment, residents' income, social security and public health" (Zhonggong zhongyang guanyu quanmian shenhua gaige ruogan zhongda wenti de jueding, 2013).

It confirms that China has identified the environment as one of the largest potential sources of instability. During the opening of the 19th National Congress of the Communist Party of China on 18 October 2017, Xi Jinping revived the slogan of 'common prosperity' (共同繁荣 gongtong fanrong) by calling for reduction of the income and regional inequality, and improvement of the living standards. He underlined that "The wellbeing of the people is the fundamental goal of development. We must do more to improve the lives and address the concerns of the people, and use development to strengthen areas of weakness and promote social fairness and justice." He also said: "The needs to be met for the people to live better lives are increasingly broad. Not only have their material and cultural needs grown; their demands for democracy, rule of law, fairness and justice, security, and a better environment are increasing" (Xi, 2017b).

5   Action for Clean Energy

China's decision to increase its climate ambition correlates with enhancing their renewable energy capacity. China is already a global leader in renewable energy. Currently it is the largest global producer of wind and solar energy and the largest both domestic and outbound investor in renewable energy. BloombergNEF (BNEF) stated that global investment in the low-carbon energy transition reached the record 501.3 billion US dollars in 2020. Investment in new renewable energy capacity alone came at 303.5 billion US dollars. China's energy transition investment was the largest of any country in the world, with 134.8 billion US dollars in total. Renewable energy capacity investment reached 83.6 billion US dollars, while electric transport 45.3 billion US dollars (BloombergNEF, 2021). China is responsible for nearly one-third of world's total installed renewable energy capacity. In 2020 China accounted for nearly

32% of the world's installed renewable energy capacity with 895 gigawatts. At the time the world's total installed renewable energy reached 2,799 gigawatts (Table 8.3). China alone was responsible for 28% of the world's total installed capacity in hydro power, 38% in wind power, and 35% in solar power (International Renewable Energy Agency, 2021).

Development of the renewable energy sector is one of the priorities for the Chinese government. Development strategy reaffirmed an existing targets of boosting its total installed capacity of wind and solar power and increasing the share of non-fossil fuels in primary energy consumption, that was previously announced by President Xi Jinping during the Climate Ambition Summit in 2020. According to data from the National Energy Administration, by the end of 2020, 15.9% of China's primary energy consumption came from non-fossil energy, surpassing a target of 15% set for 2020. As a result more than 40% of installed power generation capacity came from renewable resources (Guojia nengyuan bu, 2021).

For a long time the incentive policy was an important force to promote the rapid development of the renewables in China. Chinese central and local governments offered a lot of forms of support for the production of energy from renewable sources, i.e., by tax incentives, credits, preferential tarrifs policies, technical support, renewable obligations and green certificates, guaranteed access to the electricity grid for renewable energy generators, requirements for purchase of renewable power.

The main drivers for rapid transition to renewable energy are the increasing cost-competitiveness of renewable energy technologies, improved energy security and improvement of air quality and human health. The costs of renewable energy has consistently rapidly declined as the world started implementing low-emission development strategies in response to climate change.

TABLE 8.3   China and the world: renewable energy installed capacity

	Total renewable energy (MW)	Hydropower (MW)	Wind energy (MW)	Solar energy (MW)
China	2 799 094	1 331 889	733 276	713 970
World	894 879	370 160	281 993	254 355

SOURCE: INTERNATIONAL RENEWABLE ENERGY AGENCY (IRENA) (2021)

Analyses prove that levelized costs of renewable and nuclear energy generation are falling below that of fossil fuels (International Energy Agency, Nuclear Energy Agency, Organisation for Economic Cooperation and Development, 2020; International Renewable Energy Agency, 2021). Concerns about growing energy import dependency impact China's energy security. China imported 72.5% of its crude oil supply in 2019. At the same time natural gas and coal import dependency reached respectively 40.6% and 7.7% (International Energy Agency, 2020). For some time shale gas was considered as an alternative. Chinese government even set ambitious goals for shale gas production, but some factors related to exploration, production and hydraulic fracturing proved too challenging. Therefore, renewable energy systems can improve energy security by adding diversity to an overall electricity generation. Renewable sources like wind and solar may introduce some concerns about variability into the power grid. On the other hand they are widely available and, in many cases, cost competitive. Above all, however, renewables allow cutting carbon emissions and help to mitigate climate change.

China is expanding its domestic market for clean energy technologies. Currently, China holds a dominant position in wind and solar power generation. Among top 10 global wind turbine manufacturers in 2020 there were 6 from China. Goldwin maintained its third position (Global Wind Turbine Industry Factsheet 2020, 2021). In addition 8 Chinese enterprises were among top 10 PV module suppliers by volume in 2021, with LONGi being the number one. Positions from 1 to 6 were occupied by Chinese enterprises (Colville, 2022). This strategy undoubtedly brings substantial economic returns. China has already become a major exporter of clean energy technologies. In addition, a rapid switch to to renewables create more and more jobs. Clean power employment worldwide reached 12 million in 2020. China created 4.7 million jobs in this area, which represents 39% of total (International Renewable Energy Agency, International Labour Organization, 2021).

In electric vehicles, China's command is even greater (Gacek, 2020: 167–214). According to data released by the China Association of Automobile Manufacturers, China's ownership of new energy vehicles (NEVs), including battery electric, plug-in hybrid, and fuel cell vehicles, reached 7.84 million by the end of 2021, representing 59% increase compared to 2020. These were 2,6% of the country's total vehicle stock. Among them, the ownership of battery electric vehicles reached 6.4 million (Gong'an bu, 2021). Only a decade ago, China established a mid-term strategy for NEV development (Energy-Saving and New Energy Vehicle Industry Plan for 2012 to 2020), that aimed to increase production and sales of pure electric cars and plug-in hybrid vehicles to 500,000 and more than 5 million by 2020 (Zhongyang zhengfu menhu wangzhan, 2012).

The next China's New Energy Vehicle Industrial Development Plan for 2021 to 2035 ("Plan 2021–2035") aims to build a green, and internationally competitive automobile industry (Xin nengyuan qiche chanye fazhan guihua (2021–2035 nian) (zhengqiu yijian gao), 2019). These plans set detailed development targets for the NEV industry, including policies, market strategies, and technology advancement. In addition, China also dominates global battery supply chains (Pattisson and Firdaus, 2021) and it holds over three-fourths of the world's manufacturing capacity for lithium ion battery cells (Statlista, 2022). Benchmark Mineral Intelligence stated that Chinese companies accounted for 80% of the world's total production of raw materials for advanced batteries in 2019. Among 136 lithium-ion battery plants in the pipeline to 2029, 101 are based in China (Moores, 2020). As a result, China is not only recognized as the world's largest automotive market, but also it has taken the lead in the manufacturing of key parts.

6 Path toward Green Development along the Belt and Road

China's new climate commitment may have a positive impact on countries along the Belt and Road. It could also help shape China's image as a responsible player in the international community. If China encouraged countries along the BRI to adopt more strict climate policies by supporting the rapid scale-up of green investment and financing, it would chart a new course in the global climate effort.

China promotes the green development of the BRI. At the First Belt and Road Forum in 2017, Xi proposed the idea of an international coalition for green development on the BRI (Xinhua, 2017b). Two years later, during the Second BRI Forum, the Chinese leader called for the promotion of green infrastructure projects and green financing (Xinhua, 2019). It illustrates radical change compared to the previous policy. China has so far given primacy to 'dirty energy' investments making considerable use of state support. China Global Investment Tracker statistics prove that so far around 45% of investments with Chinese capital along the BRI were conducted in energy and metals. Brownfield investments were the most popular (China Global Investment Tracker, 2022).

Chinese developers have so far given primacy to 'dirty energy' investments, making considerable use of state support. Continued implementation of projects under the BRI carries the risk that more energy in the world will be derived from traditional sources than from renewable ones (Shearer, Brown and Buckley, 2019; Tsinghua University Center for Finance and Development,

Vivid Economics, ClimateWorks Foundation, 2019), which cast a shadow of uncertainty over the Paris Climate Agreement's objective of limiting global warming to well below 2°C. To date, China has pursued its own self-interest by eliminating some overcapacity among companies responsible for the largest volume of emissions. At the same time, it has 'exported' excess capacity to other countries. Chinese investment in energy, transport, and other sustainable infrastructure has blocked the development of new technologies for decades to come and is affecting the development paths of many countries that are part of the BRI, particularly China's neighboring countries in Central Asia.

Over the time this attitude may change for two reasons. In the middle of 2021 the world's seven largest advanced economies (G7) agreed to stop international financing of coal projects. China's response followed a few months later. In September 2021 Chinese President Xi Jinping announced that China will not build new coal-fired power plants abroad anymore, while at the same time will increase its support for developing countries to pursue green and low-carbon development (Xinhua, 2021b). In fact, the Chinese supported development of coal-fired power overseas has already slowed down in the past few years, due to the decreasing costs of renewables and declining needs for coal from host countries. A report prepared by the Centre for Research on Energy and Clean Air shows that over the last five years 4.5 times as much coal power capacity with Chinese involvement has been shelved or cancelled than commissioned (Centre for Research on Energy and Clean Air, 2021).

In July 2021, the Chinese government issued 'Green development guidelines for overseas investment and cooperation'. According to these regulations, where local standards are insufficient, they require Chinese enterprises to 'follow international green rules and standards.' The guidelines enhance 'enterprises to speed up integration with the global green supply chain, carry out green procurement, and purchase environmentally friendly products and services'. The document also named investments in solar, wind and other forms of clean energy as key areas for investment (Shangwu bu, 2021). It is a significant upgrade compared to the 'Guidelines for Environmental Protection in Foreign Investment and Cooperation' from 2013 which obligated Chinese enterprises to 'understand and observe provisions of laws and regulations of the host country concerning environmental protection' (Shangwu bu, 2013). These decisions correspond with green bond catalogue issued by China's top regulators including People's Bank of China (PBoC), China's Central Bank, the China Securities & Regulatory Commission (CSRC) and the National Development and Reform Commission (NDRC), which exclude fossil fuels from their green bonds taxonomy (Fatin, 2020). It stands in conflict with the green finance taxonomies proposed by the European Union, Republic of Korea and Russia that have identified natural gas as green. However, such situation can pave the way for China to become a global leader in promoting high requirements and optimized standards in terms of financing green energy. In comparison, Chinese green taxonomy catalog did not include gas, LNG as well as coal-fired energy activities. Hence, it can be presumed that Chinese enterprises will be more active in greening its overseas investments. Rather than investing in less cost effective coal-fired power plants overseas China can export its renewable energy technologies combined with some business models along the BRI countries. By emphasizing a new model of building relations with other countries based on the principle of mutual benefit, China may obtain control over the main supply chains, but also to consolidate its presence in the world.

7   Conclusions

Climate change and biodiversity loss lead to ocean acidification, sea level rise and global warming as well as an increase in the frequency and severity of fires, storms or periods of drought. Climate change also affects human health and wellbeing. There is no doubt that a fight against climate change and global warming requires more decisive action from all countries in the world. In this particular area much depends on China, which alone is responsible for over one fourth of total global emissions. However, its engagement in global climate governance over the past decade has been changing dramatically. Currently, China plays an active role in the climate change negotiations under the terms of the Paris Agreement. In addition it has also set a roadmap to peak its carbon dioxide emissions before 2030 and achieve carbon neutrality by 2060. Systemic shift observed in China's climate policy is determined by four principles.

Firstly, it is an answer to public concern about climate change which stimulates Chinese authorities to adopt more strict policy instruments to reduce greenhouse gas emissions. China faces great challenges to accomplish coal phase-out in the coming decades. These 'dual carbon' goals were included in the overall plan of building an 'ecological civilization', and promotion the development of a green and low-carbon circular economy.

Secondly, China has adopted a new development model, the priority of which is to promote scientific and technological innovation. Such solutions are expected to address existing environmental threats and combat climate change while allowing the country to maintain a high rate of economic development. This paradigm also underlines the need to concentrate on protection of resources and the environment as well as the promotion of the green and low-carbon development.

Thirdly, China has introduced ambitious plan to expand renewable energy capacity in the coming decade in an effort to meet its core climate goals. According to estimates, the share of non-fossil fuel sources in energy mix will reach around 20% and 25% by the years 2025 and 2030 respectively. Advanced green energy technologies enhance new economic growth areas, expand markets and allow to build country's competitiveness. China has emerged as the world leader in renewable energy, in particular wind and solar, as well as in related technologies such as electric vehicles. An accelerated the green transition and the rapid phase-out of coal place China in a leading position when it comes to taking the initiative in international cooperation on climate change.

Finally, China gradually clarifies its vision for a Green Belt and Road Initiative which encourages investing in and scaling up green infrastructure, energy, transportation, and finance. It would be a crucial issue for BRI countries facing serious energy shortages and requiring significant investment in this sector in the coming years. Eventually China's environmental overseas investment commitments would also demonstrate the effort to integrate its response to curb the global warming threat with its long-term sustainable development vision.

References

BloombergNEF (2021) Energy Transition Investment Trends. Tracking global investment in the low-carbon energy transition. https://assets.bbhub.io/professional/sites/24/Energy-Transition-Investment-Trends_Free-Summary_Jan2021.pdf, accessed 19 January 2022.

BP (2021) Statistical Review of World Energy 2021. https://www.bp.com/content/dam/bp/business-sites/en/global/corporate/pdfs/energy-economics/statistical-review/bp-stats-review-2021-full-report.pdf, accessed 19 January 2022.

Cao Baoyin (2014) *Ecological Civilization of Contemporary China*. Beijing: China Intercontinental Press.

Centre for Research on Energy and Clean Air (2021) 4.5 times as much overseas coal capacity linked to China cancelled or shelved than progressed to construction, June, https://energyandcleanair.org/wp/wp-content/uploads/2021/06/CH-Overseas-Coal-Briefing.pdf, accessed 19 January 2022.

China Global Investment Tracker (2022) Worldwide Chinese Investments & Construction (2005–2021). https://www.aei.org/china-global-investment-tracker/, accessed 19 January 2022.

China Power Team (2017) How Well-off is China's Middle Class? *China Power*, 26 April, https://chinapower.csis.org/china-middle-class/, accessed 19 January 2022.

China Statistical Yearbook (2021) *Total Energy Consumption and Its Composition*. http://www.stats.gov.cn/tjsj/ndsj/2021/indexeh.htm, accessed 19 January 2022.

Colville, Finlay (2022) The top 10 PV module suppliers in 2021 – part one. *PV-Tech*, 13 January, https://www.pv-tech.org/revealed-the-top-10-pv-module-suppliers-in-2021-part-one/, accessed 19 January 2022.

Dierci quanguo huanjing baohu huiyi (1983–1984) (第二次全国环境保护会议 (1983 年12月31日-1984年1月7日)) (2018) *Zhongguo huanjing bao* (中国环境报), 13 July, http://www.mee.gov.cn/zjhb/lsj/lsj_zyhy/201807/t20180713_446638_wap.shtml, accessed 19 January 2022.

Fatin, Leena (2020) China's top regulators announce they will exclude fossil fuels from their green bonds taxonomy. It's a major development! *Climate Bonds Initiative*, 10 June, https://www.climatebonds.net/2020/06/chinas-top-regulators-announce-they-will-exclude-fossil-fuels-their-green-bonds-taxonomy-it, accessed 19 January 2022.

Gacek Łukasz and Jan W. Tkaczyński (2021) *China's environmental protection policy in light of European Union standards*. Göttingen: Vandenhoeck & Ruprecht Verlage Unipress.

Gacek, Łukasz (2018) Nowe źródła wzrostu gospodarczego Chin: wiedza i innowacje. *Sinologia. Roczniki Humanistyczne*, LXVI (9), pp. 5–32.

Gacek, Łukasz (2020) *Cywilizacja ekologiczna i transformacja energetyczna w Chinach*. Poznań: Wydawnictwo Naukowe FNCE.

Gao Xiaosheng (2018) China's Evolving Image in International Climate Negotiation: From Copenhagen to Paris. *China Quarterly of International Strategic Studies*, (4) 2.

Geary, James (2020) 'Green' energy patents filed globally jump 28% in a year as pace of innovation accelerates. *EMW*, 31 January, https://www.emwllp.com/latest/a-rise-in-green-energy-patents-filed/, accessed 19 January 2022.

Global Wind Turbine Industry Factsheet 2020: Top 10 Largest Wind Turbine Manufacturers (2021) *BizVibe*, 26 May, https://blog.bizvibe.com/blog/energy-and-fuels/top-10-wind-turbine-manufacturers-world, accessed 19 January 2022.

Gong'an bu: 2021 Nian quanguo ji dongche baoyou liang da 3.95 yi xin nengyuan qiche tongbi zeng 59.25% (公安部：2021年全国机动车保有量达 3.95 亿新能源汽车同比增 59.25%) (2022). *Pengpai xinwen* (澎湃新闻), 12 January, https://m.thepaper.cn/baijiahao_16264518, accessed 19 January 2022.

Guojia nengyuan bu (国家能源局) (2021) Guo xin ban juxing Zhongguo kezaisheng nengyuan fazhan youguan qingkuan fabuhui (国新办举行中国可再生能源发展有关情况发布会), 30 March, http://www.nea.gov.cn/2021-03/30/c_139846095.htm, accessed 19 January 2022.

Guowuyuan (国务院) (2015) Guowuyuan guanyu yinfa "Zhongguo zhizao 2025" de tongzhi (国务院关于印发《中国制造2025》的通知), 19 May, http://www.gov.cn/zhengce/content/2015-05/19/content_9784.htm, accessed 19 January 2022.

Hamadeh, Nada, Catherine Van Rompaey and Eric Metreau (2021) New World Bank country classifications by income level: 2021–2022, *The World Bank*, 1 July, https://blogs.worldbank.org/opendata/new-world-bank-country-classifications-income-level-2021-2022, accessed 19 January 2022.

International Energy Agency (IEA) (2020) Oil, gas and coal import dependency in China, 2007–2019, 18 December, https://www.iea.org/data-and-statistics/charts/oil-gas-and-coal-import-dependency-in-china-2007-2019, accessed 19 January 2022.

International Energy Agency (IEA) (2021) Coal 2021. Analysis and forecast to 2024, December, https://iea.blob.core.windows.net/assets/f1d724d4-a753-4336-9f6e-64679fa23bbf/Coal2021.pdf, accessed 19 January 2022.

International Energy Agency (IEA) and Nuclear Energy Agency (NEA) Organisation for Economic Cooperation and Development (OECD) (2020) Projected Costs of Generating Electricity, https://iea.blob.core.windows.net/assets/ae17da3d-e8a5-4163-a3ec-2e6fb0b5677d/Projected-Costs-of-Generating-Electricity-2020.pdf, accessed 19 January 2022.

International Renewable Energy Agency (IRENA) (2021) Renewable capacity statistics 2021, Abu Dhabi.

International Renewable Energy Agency (IRENA) (2021) Renewable Power Generation Costs in 2020, Abu Dhabi.

International Renewable Energy Agency (IRENA) and International Labour Organization (ILO) (2021) Renewable Energy and Jobs – Annual Review 2021, Abu Dhabi, Geneva.

Jin Rui Lin and Liu Wen (1987) Environmental Policy and Legislation in China. *Proceedings of the Sino-American Conference on Environmental Law*, 16 August, https://scholar.law.colorado.edu/proceedings-of-sino-american-conference-on-environmental-law/11, accessed 19 January 2022.

Knight, John (2016) The Societal Cost of China's Rapid Economic Growth. *Asian Economic Papers*, (15)2, pp. 138–159.

Li Jing (2018) Does the Chinese public care about climate change? *Chinadialogue*, 21 September, https://chinadialogue.net/en/climate/10831-does-the-chinese-public-care-about-climate-change/, accessed 19 January 2022.

Moores, Simon (2020) China controls sway of electric vehicle power through battery chemicals, cathode and anode production. *Benchmark Mineral Intelligence*, 6 May, https://www.benchmarkminerals.com/membership/china-controls-sway-of-electric-vehicle-power-through-battery-chemicals-cathode-and-anode-production/, accessed 19 January 2022.

Pan Jiahua (2015) *China's Environmental Governing and Ecological Civilization*, Heidelberg: Springer.

Parker, Charles F., Christer Karlsson, Mattias Hjerpe (2017) Assessing the European Union's global climate change leadership: from Copenhagen to the Paris Agreement. *Journal of European Integration*, (39)2, pp. 239–252.

Pattisson, Pete and Febriana Firdaus (2021) 'Battery arms race': how China has monopolised the electric vehicle industry. *The Guardian*, 25 November, https://www.theguardian.com/global-development/2021/nov/25/battery-arms-race-how-china-has-monopolised-the-electric-vehicle-industry, accessed 19 January 2022.

Shangwu bu (商务部) (2013) Shangwu bu huanjing baohu bu guanyu yinfa "duiwai touzi hezuo huanjing baohu zhinan" de tongzhi, shangwu bu duiwai touzi he jingji hezuo si (商务部环境保护部关于印发《对外投资合作环境保护指南》的通知, 商务部对外投资和经济合作司), 28 February, http://www.mofcom.gov.cn/article/b/bf/201302/20130200039930.shtml, accessed 19 January 2022.

Shangwu bu (商务部) (2021) Shangwu bu shengtai huanjing bu guanyu yinfa "duiwai touzi hezuo luse fazhan gongzuo zhiyin" de tongzhi (商务部生态环境部关于印发《对外投资合作绿色发展工作指引》的通知), 15 July, http://images.mofcom.gov.cn/hzs/202107/20210716144040753.pdf, accessed 19 January 2022.

Shearer, Christine, Melissa Brown and Tim Buckley (2019) *China at a Crossroads: Continued Support for Coal Power Erodes Country's Clean Energy Leadership*. Institute for Energy Economics and Financial Analysis.

Shengtai huanjing bu (生态环境部) (2018) Law on Prevention and Control of Air Pollution (中华人民共和国大气污染防治法), https://www.mee.gov.cn/ywgz/fgbz/fl/201811/t20181113_673567.shtml, accessed 8 February 2024.

Shengtai huanjing bu (生态环境部) (2017) Law on the Prevention and Control of Water Pollution (中华人民共和国水污染防治法), https://www.mee.gov.cn/ywgz/fgbz/fl/200802/t20080229_118802.shtml, accessed 8 February 2024.

Shengtai huanjing bu (生态环境部) (2013) Dierci quanguo huanjing baohu huiyi (第一次全国环境保护会议), 13 July, http://www.mee.gov.cn/zjhb/lsj/lsj_zyhy/201807/t20180713_446637.shtml, accessed 19 January 2022.

Sohn, Louis B. (1973) The Stockholm Declaration on the Human Environment. *The Harvard International Law Journal*, (14)3, pp. 423–515.

Soil Pollution Prevention and Control Law (中华人民共和国土壤污染防治法) (2018), Shengtai huanjing bu (生态环境部), https://www.mee.gov.cn/ywgz/fgbz/fl/201809/t20180907_549845.shtml, accessed 8 February 2024.

Stanway, David (2021) China fires up giant coal power plant in face of calls for cuts. *Reuters*, 29 December. https://www.reuters.com/markets/commodities/china-fires-up-giant-coal-power-plant-face-calls-cuts-2021-12-28/, accessed 19 January 2021.

Statlista (2022) Share of the global lithium-ion battery manufacturing capacity in 2020 with a forecast for 2025, by country. https://www.statista.com/statistics/1249871/share-of-the-global-lithium-ion-battery-manufacturing-capacity-by-country/, accessed 19 January 2022.

The World Bank (2022a) GDP (current USD) – China. https://data.worldbank.org/indicator/NY.GDP.MKTP.CD?locations=CN, accessed 19 January 2022.

The World Bank (2022b) GNI per capita, Atlas method (current USD) – China, World Bank national accounts data, and OECD National Accounts data. https://data.worldbank.org/indicator/NY.GNP.PCAP.CD?locations=CN, accessed 19 January 2022.

Tsinghua University Center for Finance and Development, Vivid Economics, ClimateWorks Foundation (2019) Decarbonizing the Belt and Road: A Green Finance Roadmap, September, https://www.climateworks.org/wp-content/uploads/2019/08/BRI_Exec_Summary_v10-screen_pages_lo-1.pdf, accessed 19 January 2022.

UN Climate Change Conference UK (2021) Global Coal to Clean Power Transition Statement, 4 November, https://ukcop26.org/global-coal-to-clean-power-transition-statement/, accessed 19 January 2022.

United Nations (1992) Rio Declaration on Environment and Development, 14 June, https://www.un.org/en/development/desa/population/migration/generalassembly/docs/globalcompact/A_CONF.151_26_Vol.I_Declaration.pdf, accessed 19 January 2022.

United Nations (1998) Kyoto Protocol to the United Nations Framework Convention on Climate Change. https://unfccc.int/resource/docs/convkp/kpeng.pdf, accessed 19 January 2022.

United Nations (2015) Paris Agreement. https://unfccc.int/files/essential_background/convention/application/pdf/english_paris_agreement.pdf, accessed 19 January 2022.

United Nations (2021) Glasgow Climate Pact, 13 November. https://unfccc.int/sites/default/files/resource/cma2021_L16_adv.pdf, accessed 19 January 2022.

Vltchek Andre and John B. Cobb Jr. (2019) *China and Ecological Civilization*. PT. Badak Merah Semesta.

Wei Ting et al. (2012) Developed and developing world responsibilities for historical climate change and CO_2 mitigation. *PNAS*, (109)32, pp. 12911–12915.

Wen Jiabao (2009) Ningju gongshi jiaqiang hezuo tuijin yingdui qihou bianhua lishi jincheng (温家宝：凝聚共识加强合作推进应对气候变化历史进程), 19 December, *Renmin Ribao* (人民日报).

Xi Jinping (2017) Secure a Decisive Victory in Building a Moderately Prosperous Society in All Respects and Strive for the Great Success of Socialism with Chinese Characteristics for a New Era Delivered at the 19th National Congress of the Communist Party of China, Ministry of Foreign Affairs of the People's Republic of China, 18 October, https://www.mfa.gov.cn/ce/ceil/eng/zt/19thCPCNationalCongress/W020171120127269060039.pdf, accessed 19 January 2022.

Xi Jinping (习近平) (2017) Juesheng quanmian jiancheng xiaokang shehui duoqu xin shidai Zhongguo tese shehuizhuyi weida shengli (决胜全面建成小康社会夺取新时

代中国特色社会主义伟大胜利). *Renmin wang* (人民网), 28 October, http://cpc.people.com.cn/n1/2017/1028/c64094-29613660.html, accessed 19 January 2022.

Xin nengyuan qiche chanye fazhan guihua (2021–2035 nian) (zhengqiu yijian gao) (新能源汽车产业发展规划 (2021-2035年)) (2019) *Gongye he xinxihua bu zhuangbei gongye si* (工业和信息化部装备工业司), 3 December, http://www.miit.gov.cn/n1278117/ n1648113/c7553623/part/7553637.pdf, accessed 19 January 2022.

Xinhua (新华) (2013) Shengtai wenming guiyang guoji luntan 2013 nian nianhui kaimu. Xi Jinping zhi hexin (生态文明贵阳国际论坛 2013 年年会开幕。习近平致贺信), 20 July, http://www.xinhuanet.com//politics/2013-07/20/c_116619686.htm, accessed 19 January 2022.

Xinhua (新华) (2017a) Juesheng quanmian jiancheng xiaokang shehui duoqu xin shidai Zhongguo tese shehui zhuyi weida shengli (决胜全面建成小康社会夺取新时代中国特色社会主义伟大胜利), 18 October, http://www.xinhuanet.com//politics/19cpcnc/2017-10/27/c_1121867529.htm, accessed 19 January 2022.

Xinhua (新华) (2017b) Xi Jinping zai "yadai yilu" guoji hezuo gaofeng luntan kaimu shi shang de yanjing (习近平在"一带一路"国际合作高峰论坛开幕式上的演讲), 14 May, http://www.xinhuanet.com//2017-05/14/c_1120969677.htm, accessed 19 January 2022.

Xinhua (新华) (2019) Xi Jinping zai di er jie "Yidai-yilu" guoji hezuo gaofeng luntan kaimushi shang de zhuzhi yanjiang (习近平在第二届"一带一路"国际合作高峰论坛开幕式上的主旨演讲), 26 April, http://www.xinhuanet.com/silkroad/2019-04/26/c_1124420187.htm, accessed 19 January 2022.

Xinhua (新华) (2020a) Xi Jinping zai di qishiwu jie lianheguo dahui yiban xing bianlun shang de jianghua (习近平在第七十五届联合国大会一般性辩论上的讲话), 22 September, http://www.xinhuanet.com/politics/leaders/2020-09/22/c_1126527652.htm, accessed 19 January 2022.

Xinhua (新华) (2020b) Xi Jinping zai qihou xiongxin fenghui shang de jianghua. Jiwang-kailai, kaiqi quanqiu yingdui qihou bianhua xin zhengcheng (习近平在气候雄心峰会上的讲话。继往开来，开启全球应对气候变化新征程), 12 December, https://baijiahao.baidu.com/s?id=1685886202481384721&wfr=spider&for=pc, accessed 19 January 2022.

Xinhua (新华) (2021a) Xi Focus: Xi attends video summit with French, German leaders, 17 April, http://www.xinhuanet.com/english/2021-04/17/c_139885734.htm, accessed 19 January 2022.

Xinhua (新华) (2021b) Xi Jinping zai di qishiliu jie lianheguo dahui yiban xing bianlun shang de jianghua (习近平在第七十六届联合国大会一般性辩论上的讲话), 22 September, http://www.gov.cn/xinwen/2021-09/22/content_5638597.htm, accessed 19 January 2022.

Xinhua (新华) (2021c) Zhonghua renmin gongheguo guomin jingji he shehui fazhan di shisi ge wu nian guihua he 2035 nian yuanjing mubiao gangyao (中华人民共和

国国民经济和社会发展第十四个五年规划和2035年远景目标纲要), 13 March, http://www.gov.cn/xinwen/2021-03/13/content_5592681.htm, accessed 19 January 2022.

Zhonggong zhongyang guanyu quanmian shenhua gaige ruogan zhongda wenti de jueding (中共中央关于全面深化改革若干重大问题的决定) (2013) *China.org.cn*, 12 November, http://www.china.org.cn/china/third_plenary_session/2014-01/16/content_31212602.htm, accessed 19 January 2022.

Zhongguo "Zhongchan" shou huo shuzi jieding: jiating nian shouru 6 wan – 50 wan (中国"中产"首获数字界定：家庭年收入6万-50万) (2005) *Zhongxin wang* (中新网), 19 January, https://www.chinanews.com.cn/news/2005/2005-01-19/26/530046.shtml, accessed 19 January 2022.

Zhongguo dianli qiye lianhe hui (中国电力企业联合会) (2021) 2020 nian dianli tongji jiben shuju yilanbiao (2020 年电力统计基本数据一览表), https://www.cec.org.cn/upload/1/editor/1611623903447.pdf, accessed 19 January 2022.

Zhongyang zhengfu menhu wangzhan (中央政府门户网站) (2012) Guowuyuan guanyu yinfa jieneng yu xin nengyuan qiche chanye fazhan guihua (2012—2020 nian) de tongzhi (国务院关于印发节能与新能源汽车产业发展规划（2012—2020年）的通知), 28 June, http://www.gov.cn/zwgk/2012-07/09/content_2179032.htm, accessed 19 January 2022.

Zhongyang zhengfu menhu wangzhan (中央政府门户网站) (2014) Zhonghua renmin gongheguo huanjing baohu fa (zhuxi ling di jiu hao) (中华人民共和国环境保护法（主席令第九号）), 24 April 24, http://www.gov.cn/zhengce/2014-04/25/content_2666434.htm, accessed 19 January 2022.

Zhongyang zhengfu menhu wangzhan (中央政府门户网站) (2018) Zhonghua renmin gongheguo xianfa (中华人民共和国宪法), 11 March, http://www.gov.cn/guoqing/2018-03/22/content_5276318.htm, accessed 19 January 2022.

PART 3

Social Dimensions

∴

CHAPTER 9

Social Development under Xi Jinping
Education, Health, and Retirement

Octasiano M. Valerio Mendoza

1   Introduction

The Xi Jinping Era accentuates several vital turning points amidst China's meteoric rise from a low-income and undeveloped nation in the 1980s to a middle-income country in 2015. Furthermore, as the country continues its journey towards becoming a developed nation, slower economic growth rates, an aging population, and low levels of human capital present important challenges for China's future prosperity. The share of its labor force with tertiary education still falls considerably short compared to developed economies (Borsi et al., 2022). Similarly, the health conditions of its young rural population may hamper its future development prospects (Emmers et al., 2021; Wang et al., 2019; Zhou et al., 2020). Furthermore, as the Chinese population ages, human capital accumulation will decelerate, labor force participation will decrease, and consumption power will decline (Cai, 2020; Ye et al., 2021). Evaluating the dynamics of education, health, and retirement across Chinese provinces is essential to identify regions at risk of entering development traps (Valerio Mendoza et al., 2022).

To this end, this chapter investigates the evolution of education, health, and pension policies during the Xi Jinping Era (2012–2018) to identify heterogeneities in the provision of higher education, health facilities, and pension coverage between provinces. The findings provide insights into the challenges facing the harmonious revival of the Chinese nation.

The rest of the chapter is structured as follows: Section 2 provides an overview of the education policies implemented during the last decade and their effects on educational disparities across Chinese provinces. A similar analysis for health facilities and pension coverage is given in Sections 3 and 4, followed by a discussion and concluding remarks in Section 5.

2   Education

In the two decades that preceded the Xi Jinping Era (XJE), the PRC had taken enormous strides in terms of education kickstarted by the Nine-Year Compulsory Education Law of 1986. As compulsory education enrollment and completion rates surged dramatically, so did the demand for upper-secondary and tertiary education (Borsi et al., 2022). However, the country did not have a sufficient supply of high schools and colleges, producing severe bottlenecks for continued educational attainment. These demands were met by creating more upper-secondary schools, including vocational high schools and higher education institutions (HEIS), specifically at the turn of the century (Hu and Hibel, 2014; Knight et al., 2017; Valerio Mendoza, 2018). As a result, educational attainment levels in China have achieved tremendous growth.

However, these human capital development efforts were not homogenously fruitful across all regions in China. Consequently, by 2010, there were regional inequalities in educational resources, attainment, and opportunities (Li et al., 2014; Luo et al., 2018; Valerio Mendoza et al., 2022; Wu et al., 2020; Xiang et al., 2020; Zhang et al., 2020). In particular, coastal provinces benefited most compared to non-coastal ones. Not coincidentally, coastal regions also had the highest expansion of primary, secondary, and tertiary institutions (Borsi et al., 2022).

Nevertheless, recent policies prioritizing equality in education and promoting access to education in disadvantaged areas have been implemented (Xiang et al., 2020). These include the "National Medium and Long-Term Educational Reform and Development Plan Outline," "Further Improvements of the Funding Guarantee System for Urban and Rural Compulsory Education," the "High School Education Popularization Plan (2017–2020)," and the "Central and Western Higher Education Revitalization Plan" (Ministry of Education, 2016; 2017). The Central Government provided subsidies to central and western provinces to promote secondary and tertiary educational attainment through these plans. For instance, 10 billion yuan (approximately 1.5 billion USD) was designated to build 100 universities in these inland regions.

The remainder of this section analyzes to what extent different aspects of China's education system have improved across Chinese provinces since the start of the Xi Jinping Era in 2012. Specifically, it examines the supply of higher education in terms of institutions and teachers, and access to higher education in terms of enrollment.

2.1 The Supply of Higher Education Institutions

A large-scale expansion of higher education institutions in China began in 1999. Although the number of HEIs grew considerably across all provinces, comparing absolute numbers can be misleading, as the populations of each region vary (Borsi et al., 2022). Therefore, population-weighted measures for the supply of HEIs are most appropriate, as they indicate how many institutions (supply) a province has in relation to its inhabitants (demand). The Chinese Higher Education Density Index (CHEDI) provides a population-weighted measure of HEIs for each region in China (Valerio Mendoza et al., 2021). The CHEDI is the ratio of the share of HEIs (out of the total HEIs in China) and its population share. A value of 1 indicates that a province has an equal share of HEIs relative to its population share. For example, if a province has 30% of the country's HEIs and 30% of the country's population, its CHEDI would equal 1.

Accordingly, values greater than 1 indicate a disproportionately high share of HEIs relative to the population, while values lower than 1 indicate similarly low share. Table 9.1 reports the CHEDI for all HEIs for the 31 Chinese provinces in 2000, 2011, and 2018. Additionally, it compares the changes in HEI density during the periods before (2000–2011) and the Xi Jinping Era (2011–2018). The last row of the table indicates the mean CHEDI, for which a value of 1 would indicate equality among all the provinces. The mean value decreased from 1.28 to 1.13 in the pre-Xi Jinping era and declined to 1.12 during this period. While there were 12 provinces with a disproportionately low supply of HEIs in 2011, this number decreased to 9 in 2018 (Sichuan, Guangdong, Henan, Shandong, Guangxi, Yunnan, Hebei, Hunan, and Gansu). Furthermore, the changes in CHEDI from 2011 to 2018 reveal that those provinces that benefitted most during the previous 10 years did not continue to reap the disproportionate rewards of the expansion. For instance, Beijing, Tianjin, Anhui, and Shanghai had a reduction in CHEDI during the XJE, while the most prominent winners were Guizhou, Qinghai, Jiangxi, and Xinjiang.

Furthermore, Figure 9.1 shows the geographical distribution of changes in the provincial CHEDI during the XJE. It reveals that all the westernmost provinces except Tibet have improved their higher education densities since 2011, contrary to most coastal and central areas. Notably, while Guizhou was not prioritized during the pre-XJE period (CHEDI decreased by 5% to 0.74), it had the highest gains after 2011, achieving a proportionate share of HEIs.

However, looking at the total number of HEIs can be misleading, as not all HEIs offer the same types of degrees. For example, four-year universities offer undergraduate degrees and above, while two-year HEIs, or vocational colleges, offer a shorter variety of higher education. Therefore, Table 9.2 examines the changes in the density of undergraduate universities before and after the start

TABLE 9.1   Change in the density of higher education institutions

Province	2000	2011	2018	% change 2000–2011	% change 2011–2018
Anhui	0.76	1.11	1.00	46%	−10%
Beijing	5.00	2.59	2.24	−48%	−14%
Chongqing	0.80	1.14	1.12	43%	−2%
Fujian	1.09	1.30	1.20	19%	−8%
Gansu	0.77	0.92	0.98	19%	7%
Guangdong	0.78	0.71	0.71	−9%	0%
Guangxi	0.73	0.84	0.80	14%	−5%
Guizhou	0.77	0.74	1.03	−5%	40%
Hainan	1.18	1.16	1.08	−1%	−7%
Hebei	0.89	0.83	0.85	−7%	3%
Heilongjiang	1.26	1.21	1.13	−4%	−7%
Henan	0.64	0.73	0.74	15%	1%
Hubei	1.06	1.06	1.15	0%	8%
Hunan	0.92	1.02	0.95	10%	−6%
Inner Mongolia	0.89	1.16	1.11	30%	−4%
Jiangsu	1.12	1.02	1.10	−9%	8%
Jiangxi	0.87	1.04	1.14	19%	10%
Jilin	1.53	1.11	1.20	−27%	8%
Liaoning	1.79	1.37	1.39	−24%	2%
Ningxia	1.46	1.40	1.47	−4%	5%
Qinghai	1.57	0.90	1.06	−43%	18%
Shaanxi	1.38	1.33	1.28	−4%	−4%
Shandong	0.73	0.83	0.76	15%	−8%
Shanghai	2.69	1.69	1.40	−37%	−17%
Shanxi	0.93	1.17	1.14	26%	−3%
Sichuan	0.57	0.63	0.69	11%	9%
Tianjin	3.39	2.12	1.93	−37%	−9%
Tibet	1.34	1.26	1.10	−6%	−13%
Xinjiang	1.19	0.92	1.01	−22%	10%
Yunnan	0.66	0.79	0.85	20%	8%
Zhejiang	0.89	0.93	1.00	5%	7%
Mean	1.28	1.13	1.12	0%	1%

Note: Density refers to the ratio of a province's share of the total HEIs to its population share. A value of 1 indicates a proportionate share of HEIs in relation to a province's population share.
SOURCE: AUTHOR'S CALCULATION USING THE CHINESE HIGHER EDUCATION INDICATORS (VALERIO MENDOZA, BORSI, AND COMIM, 2021)

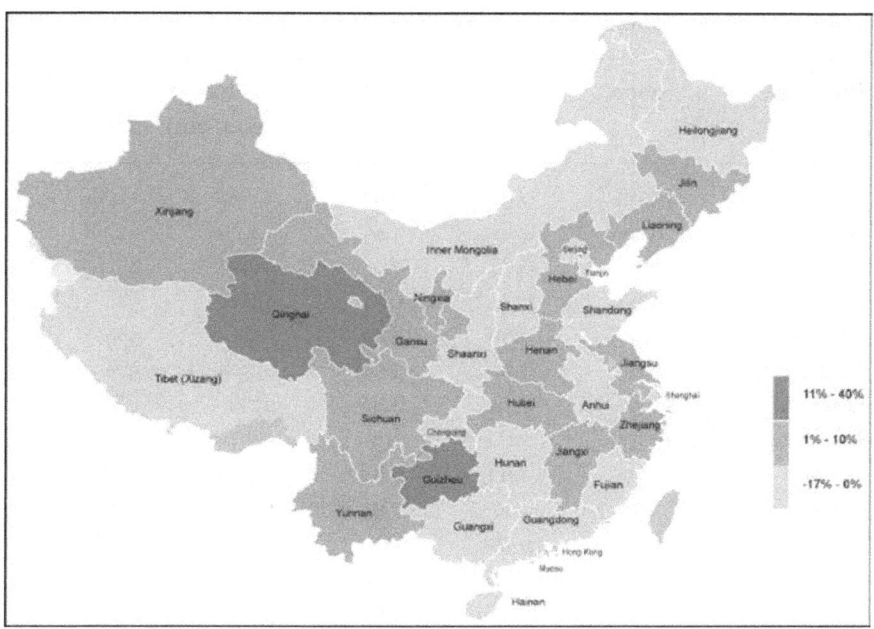

FIGURE 9.1   Percentage change in density of higher education institutions from 2011 to 2018
SOURCE: AUTHOR'S ELABORATION USING THE CHINESE HIGHER EDUCATION INDICATORS (VALERIO MENDOZA, BORSI, AND COMIM, 2021)

of the XJE. The mean CHEDI for four-year universities decreased from 1.19 to 1.14 during the XJE, suggesting an lessening of the disparities between provinces. In particular, the table shows that in 2011, 19 regions had a disproportionately low share of universities. By 2018, this number had decreased to 16 provinces. Those that gained the most during the XJE were Guangxi, Hebei, Jiangsu, Guizhou, Shanxi, Hubei, Zhejiang, and Jiangxi.

Additionally, Figure 9.2 illustrates that the density of universities improved mainly in central and a few coastal areas. However, Qinghai and many borderland provinces such as Tibet, Inner Mongolia, Heilongjiang, Jilin, and Liaoning had decreased university CHEDIs. This decline suggests that higher-quality institutions may not have been promoted in these areas.

Table 9.3 reports the changes in CHEDI for two-year vocational colleges across Chinese provinces before and during the XJE. The mean values suggest that disparities regarding the distribution of vocational colleges have not decreased during the XJE. This rise indicates that vocational HEIs continue to be concentrated in some areas more than others. The number of regions with a disproportionately low supply of vocational colleges has decreased from

TABLE 9.2   Change in the density of undergraduate universities

Province	2000	2011	2018	% change 2000–2011	% change 2011–2018
Anhui	0.68	0.90	0.80	34%	−11%
Beijing	8.19	4.61	3.45	−44%	−25%
Chongqing	0.97	0.84	0.91	−13%	8%
Fujian	0.68	1.01	1.06	48%	5%
Gansu	0.91	0.89	0.94	−2%	5%
Guangdong	0.85	0.61	0.64	−29%	5%
Guangxi	0.58	0.74	0.82	27%	11%
Guizhou	0.51	0.80	0.90	58%	13%
Hainan	1.07	0.93	0.84	−13%	−9%
Hebei	0.70	0.81	0.91	16%	11%
Heilongjiang	1.18	1.32	1.15	12%	−13%
Henan	0.47	0.66	0.64	41%	−3%
Hubei	1.07	1.11	1.29	3%	16%
Hunan	0.62	0.77	0.83	25%	8%
Inner Mongolia	0.90	0.79	0.75	−12%	−5%
Jiangsu	1.22	0.95	1.07	−22%	13%
Jiangxi	0.82	0.87	1.04	7%	19%
Jilin	1.59	1.66	1.52	5%	−9%
Liaoning	1.84	1.68	1.64	−9%	−3%
Ningxia	1.52	1.28	1.31	−16%	2%
Qinghai	1.64	0.86	0.75	−47%	−13%
Shaanxi	1.64	1.75	1.60	7%	−8%
Shandong	0.76	0.85	0.75	12%	−12%
Shanghai	3.05	2.16	1.76	−29%	−19%
Shanxi	0.85	0.86	1.00	2%	15%
Sichuan	0.54	0.65	0.69	19%	6%
Tianjin	3.83	2.29	2.15	−40%	−6%
Tibet	2.44	1.62	1.33	−34%	−18%
Xinjiang	1.14	0.81	0.82	−29%	1%
Yunnan	0.65	0.71	0.74	9%	5%
Zhejiang	0.93	0.99	1.16	7%	18%
Mean	1.41	1.19	1.14	0%	0%

Note: Density refers to the ratio of a province's share of the total HEIs and its population share. A value of 1 indicates a proportionate share of HEIs with respect to a province's population share.
SOURCE: AUTHOR'S CALCULATION USING THE CHINESE HIGHER EDUCATION INDICATORS (VALERIO MENDOZA, BORSI, AND COMIM, 2021)

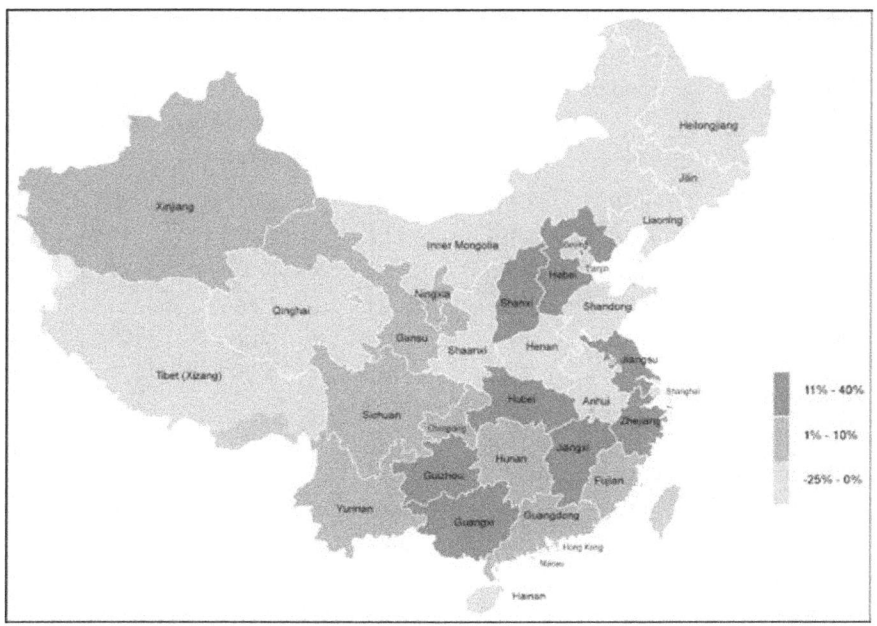

FIGURE 9.2   Percentage change in density of undergraduate universities from 2011 to 2018
SOURCE: AUTHOR'S ELABORATION USING THE CHINESE HIGHER EDUCATION INDICATORS (VALERIO MENDOZA, BORSI, AND COMIM, 2021)

11 in 2011 to 10 in 2018. The biggest improvements in the density of two-year HEIs were in Ningxia, Gansu, Sichuan, Yunnan, Xinjiang, Jilin, Qinghai, and Guizhou. Figure 9.3 illustrates that these regions are westernmost and borderland areas. Some of the regions exhibit contrasting patterns. Some coastal and central provinces increased their university densities but not their vocational ones. Similarly, some western and border provinces increased their vocational CHEDIs but not their university CHEDIs. These results suggest that the central government may be implementing different strategies for the various regions in the XJE. They prioritized better quality HEIs in the coastal and central locations while promoting vocational higher education in the innermost and frontier provinces. Nonetheless, it is also evident that aside from the four municipalities, Tibet is the only one that has experienced decreases in both its four-and two-year CHEDIs.

Finally, since most universities in China are public, the chapter also examines the evolution of private enterprises during the XJE. Private universities in China have a reputation for low quality (Liu, 2020). "Such public–private HEIs increased access to tertiary education at overpriced tuition fees but raised

TABLE 9.3 Change in vocational colleges

Province	2000	2011	2018	% change 2000–2011	% change 2011–2018
Anhui	0.86	1.24	1.18	43%	−4%
Beijing	1.13	1.29	1.15	14%	−10%
Chongqing	0.59	1.32	1.30	124%	−1%
Fujian	1.59	1.48	1.33	−7%	−10%
Gansu	0.61	0.93	1.03	54%	10%
Guangdong	0.70	0.77	0.78	10%	1%
Guangxi	0.92	0.89	0.78	−3%	−13%
Guizhou	1.09	0.69	1.15	−37%	66%
Hainan	1.31	1.30	1.30	0%	0%
Hebei	1.12	0.83	0.80	−26%	−4%
Heilongjiang	1.36	1.14	1.11	−17%	−3%
Henan	0.84	0.77	0.83	−8%	7%
Hubei	1.04	1.03	1.03	−2%	1%
Hunan	1.30	1.16	1.06	−10%	−9%
Inner Mongolia	0.87	1.38	1.42	58%	3%
Jiangsu	0.99	1.05	1.12	6%	7%
Jiangxi	0.93	1.13	1.23	22%	9%
Jilin	1.45	0.76	0.92	−48%	22%
Liaoning	1.73	1.16	1.17	−33%	1%
Ningxia	1.38	1.46	1.61	6%	10%
Qinghai	1.49	0.91	1.34	−39%	46%
Shaanxi	1.07	1.05	0.99	−1%	−6%
Shandong	0.69	0.82	0.78	19%	−5%
Shanghai	2.25	1.37	1.08	−39%	−22%
Shanxi	1.03	1.36	1.27	32%	−6%
Sichuan	0.60	0.62	0.70	3%	13%
Tianjin	2.85	1.99	1.73	−30%	−13%
Tibet	0.00	1.03	0.89	76%[a]	−13%
Xinjiang	1.25	0.99	1.19	−21%	20%
Yunnan	0.67	0.83	0.94	24%	13%
Zhejiang	0.84	1.08	0.85	28%	−22%
Mean	1.11	1.09	1.10	6%	3%

a Percentage change for Tibet is calculated using its 2003 value of 0.59.
Note: Density refers to the ratio of a province's share of the total HEIs and its population share. A value of 1 indicates a proportionate share of HEIs with respect to a province's population share.
SOURCE: AUTHOR'S CALCULATION USING THE CHINESE HIGHER EDUCATION INDICATORS (VALERIO MENDOZA, BORSI, AND COMIM, 2021)

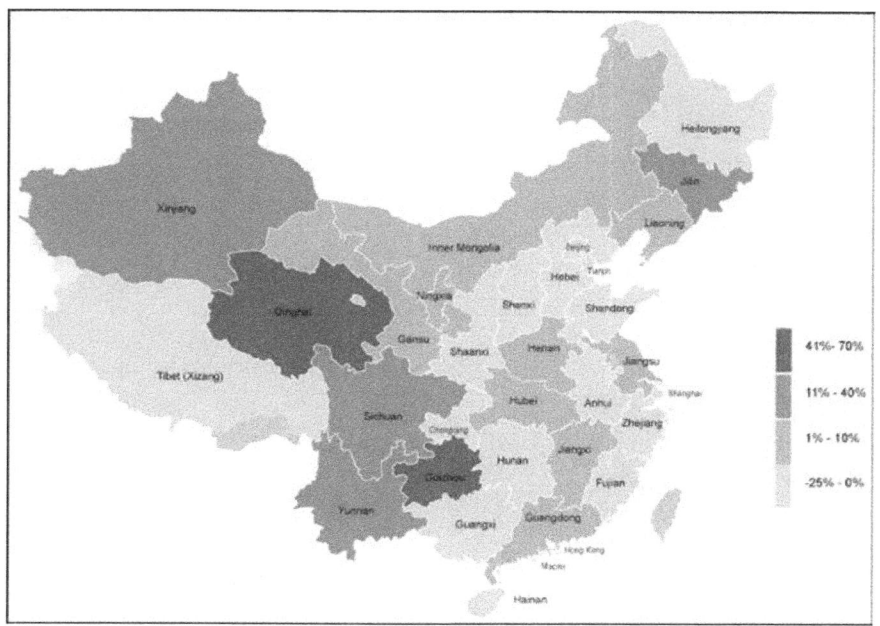

FIGURE 9.3   Percentage change in density of vocational colleges from 2011 to 2018
SOURCE: AUTHOR'S ELABORATION USING THE CHINESE HIGHER EDUCATION INDICATORS (VALERIO MENDOZA, BORSI, AND COMIM, 2021)

criticisms over their adherence to regulations regarding recruitment practices and financial management" (Borsi et al., 2022). Table 9.4 indicates the changes in CHEDI for private HEIs. The mean values suggest that disparities have slightly increased from 2011 to 2018. However, the number of provinces with private CHEDI values lower than 1 have decreased from 18 to 17 in the XJE. In terms of gains during the XJE, Tianjin, Guizhou, and Jilin have more than tripled their private HEI densities. At the same time, Shanxi, Jiangxi, Hebei, Zhejiang, Hubei, Xinjiang, and Sichuan have experienced substantial increases. The map in Figure 9.4 indicates that many private HEIs have yet to be promoted in several regions. Once more, Tibet did not have a single private HEI in 2018, suggesting there is ample room for the growth of all types of institutions in this province.

2.2   *The Supply of Higher Education Teachers*

The previous subsection evaluated the growth of higher education in China in terms of physical supply; however, an indication of the quality of higher education can be appreciated in the number of employed teachers, not just

TABLE 9.4 Change in density of private higher education institutions

Province	2000	2011	2018	% change 2000–2011	% change 2011–2018
Anhui	1.13	1.11	0.94	−2%	−15%
Beijing	3.09	1.72	1.39	−44%	−19%
Chongqing	1.84	1.78	1.60	−3%	−10%
Fujian	2.48	2.43	1.74	−2%	−28%
Gansu	0.55	0.14	0.50	−76%	272%
Guangdong	1.46	1.06	0.85	−28%	−20%
Guangxi	0.30	0.90	0.93	202%	4%
Guizhou	0.37	0.20	0.79	−47%	296%
Hainan	3.58	2.38	1.63	−34%	−31%
Hebei	0.85	0.77	0.91	−10%	18%
Heilongjiang	0.75	1.00	0.85	33%	−15%
Henan	0.60	0.89	0.73	49%	−18%
Hubei	0.95	0.96	1.35	1%	39%
Hunan	0.43	0.79	0.85	83%	8%
Inner Mongolia	0.60	0.98	0.75	63%	−24%
Jiangsu	0.39	1.10	1.15	184%	5%
Jiangxi	1.02	1.08	1.27	6%	17%
Jilin	1.59	0.76	1.25	−52%	65%
Liaoning	1.36	1.43	1.43	5%	0%
Ningxia	2.53	1.09	1.11	−57%	2%
Qinghai[a]	0.00	0.00	0.32	0%	−2%
Shaanxi	1.95	1.67	1.48	−14%	−11%
Shandong	1.10	0.97	0.76	−12%	−22%
Shanghai	6.18	2.37	1.49	−62%	−37%
Shanxi	0.44	0.68	0.77	55%	13%
Sichuan	0.33	0.52	0.77	57%	50%
Tianjin	2.84	0.26	1.46	−91%	469%
Tibet	0.00	0.00	0.00	0%	0%
Xinjiang[b]	0.00	0.47	0.70	−12%	48%
Yunnan	0.66	0.90	0.79	35%	−12%
Zhejiang	0.62	0.83	1.10	34%	34%
Mean	1.29	1.01	1.02	8%	35%

a Percentage change for Qinghai is calculated using its 2015 value of 0.32.
b Percentage change for Xinjiang is calculated using its 2005 value of 0.53.
Note: Density refers to the ratio of a province's share of the total HEIs and its population share. A value of 1 indicates a proportionate share of HEIs with respect to a province's population share.
SOURCE: AUTHOR'S CALCULATION USING THE CHINESE HIGHER EDUCATION INDICATORS (VALERIO MENDOZA, BORSI, AND COMIM, 2021)

SOCIAL DEVELOPMENT UNDER XI JINPING 227

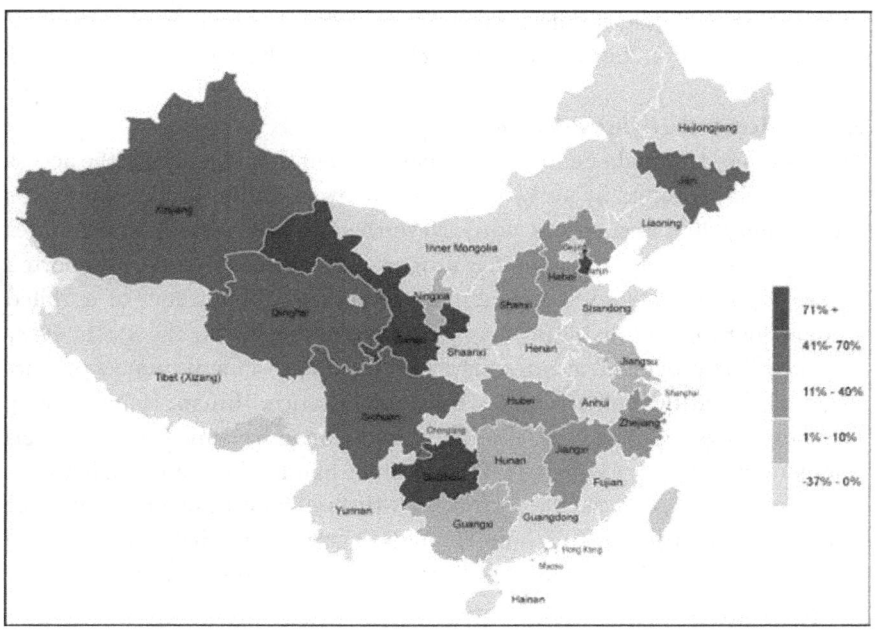

FIGURE 9.4 Percentage change in density of private higher education institutions from 2011 to 2018
SOURCE: AUTHOR'S ELABORATION USING THE CHINESE HIGHER EDUCATION INDICATORS (VALERIO MENDOZA, BORSI, AND COMIM, 2021)

the number of HEIs. Therefore, this subsection analyzes the evolution of the number of teachers per 10,000 inhabitants during the XJE. Table 9.5 reveals that at the beginning of the twenty-first century, the average number of higher education teachers among the 31 Chinese provinces was 1.49 for every 10,000 people. By 2011, this figure had more than tripled to 4.49 and increased during the XJE by a further 21%. It is important to note that the density of teachers has increased in every province during the XJE. However, the distribution of teachers is somewhat unequal. For example, Guangdong, Shandong, Henan, and Jiangsu each have more than 10 higher education teachers per 10,000 inhabitants, more than double the number of 17 other provinces, and more than ten times the ratio for Tibet, Qinghai, and Ningxia. The regions that have improved their tertiary teacher ratios during the XJE are Guizhou, Henan, Yunnan, Guangxi, Ningxia, Gansu, Guangdong, Chongqing, and Sichuan, all of which exhibited an increase between 30% and 60% from 2011 to 2018. The geographic distribution of the changes in teacher ratios during the XJE is depicted in Figure 9.5. Guizhou stands out as a province that has benefitted considerably from increases in both HEIs and teachers during this period.

2.3 Access to Higher Education

As the demand for higher education remains higher than the supply, the access to HEIs is determined by a rigorous entrance examination process known as the *gaokao* (Qian and Smyth, 2011). Nevertheless, this subsection examines how access to tertiary education has progressed in the last decade, as reported in Table 9.6. Once more, it is essential to note that the number of enrolled students per 10,000 inhabitants has continued to rise during the XJE in every province. The provincial average increased from 74.47 in 2011 to 91.32 in 2018. Regional disparities remain quite large. For instance, Hunan, Hebei, Hubei, Sichuan, Jiangsu, Guangdong, Shandong, and Henan have more than 100 tertiary students per 10,000 people. On the other hand, Tibet and Qinghai have less than 10. Nonetheless, the provinces with the highest percentage change during the XJE include Guizhou, Guangxi, Yunnan, Qinghai, Xinjiang, and Henan. These provinces are located mainly in the westernmost regions, as shown in Figure 9.6.

3 Health

The market-oriented health reforms initiated in the 1980s decentralized healthcare financing, transferring responsibilities from central to local governments. Healthcare services were then financed through local taxation, leading to inequalities between the rich coastal provinces and the less-economically advantaged ones, particularly in rural areas (Hougaard et al., 2011). The reforms considerably diminished doctors' income and caused inadequate accessibility, affordability, and patient healthcare utilization (Eggleston et al., 2008). Moreover, while public hospitals dominate the market for health services delivery, there was no regulation to integrate them with private hospitals or the primary care system (Liu et al., 2021).

In 2009, however, the nation introduced a countrywide reform to repair its massive healthcare system (Burns and Huang, 2017; Liang and Burns, 2017; Milcent, 2018; Süssmuth-Dyckerhoff and Then, 2017; Zhou et al., 2021). In the following years, government healthcare expenditures increased significantly. Furthermore, the number of public hospitals, beds, doctors, and equipment increased considerably. Consequently, China has achieved near-universal health coverage, covering more than 95% of the population (Liu et al., 2020;

TABLE 9.5 Change in teachers density in tertiary education

Province	2000	2011	2018	% change 2000–2011	% change 2011–2018
Anhui	1.51	5.12	6.11	239%	19%
Beijing	3.49	5.96	7.11	71%	19%
Chongqing	1.04	3.31	4.29	218%	30%
Fujian	0.98	3.97	4.66	305%	17%
Gansu	0.72	2.21	2.89	207%	31%
Guangdong	2.04	8.29	10.82	306%	31%
Guangxi	0.93	3.35	4.52	260%	35%
Guizhou	0.72	2.19	3.62	204%	65%
Hainan	0.16	0.80	1.01	400%	26%
Hebei	1.94	6.28	7.55	224%	20%
Heilongjiang	1.62	4.48	4.60	177%	3%
Henan	2.02	8.20	11.54	306%	41%
Hubei	3.04	7.90	8.34	160%	6%
Hunan	2.03	6.12	7.27	201%	19%
Inner Mongolia	0.89	2.42	2.69	172%	11%
Jiangsu	3.31	10.39	11.64	214%	12%
Jiangxi	1.04	5.00	5.74	381%	15%
Jilin	1.75	3.56	4.03	103%	13%
Liaoning	2.75	5.87	6.25	113%	6%
Ningxia	0.19	0.62	0.82	226%	32%
Qinghai	0.21	0.37	0.47	76%	27%
Shaanxi	2.07	5.92	6.85	186%	16%
Shandong	2.48	9.46	11.27	281%	19%
Shanghai	2.05	3.96	4.46	93%	13%
Shanxi	1.05	3.75	4.19	257%	12%
Sichuan	1.84	6.74	8.70	266%	29%
Tianjin	1.01	2.89	3.14	186%	9%
Tibet	0.08	0.23	0.26	188%	13%
Xinjiang	0.79	1.73	2.08	119%	20%
Yunnan	0.92	2.95	4.01	221%	36%
Zhejiang	1.61	5.23	6.34	225%	21%
Mean	1.49	4.49	5.40	212%	21%

Note: Density refers to the number of teachers per 10,000 inhabitants.
SOURCE: AUTHOR'S CALCULATION USING THE CHINA STATISTICAL YEARBOOKS (NATIONAL BUREAU OF STATISTICS OF CHINA, 2000–2018)

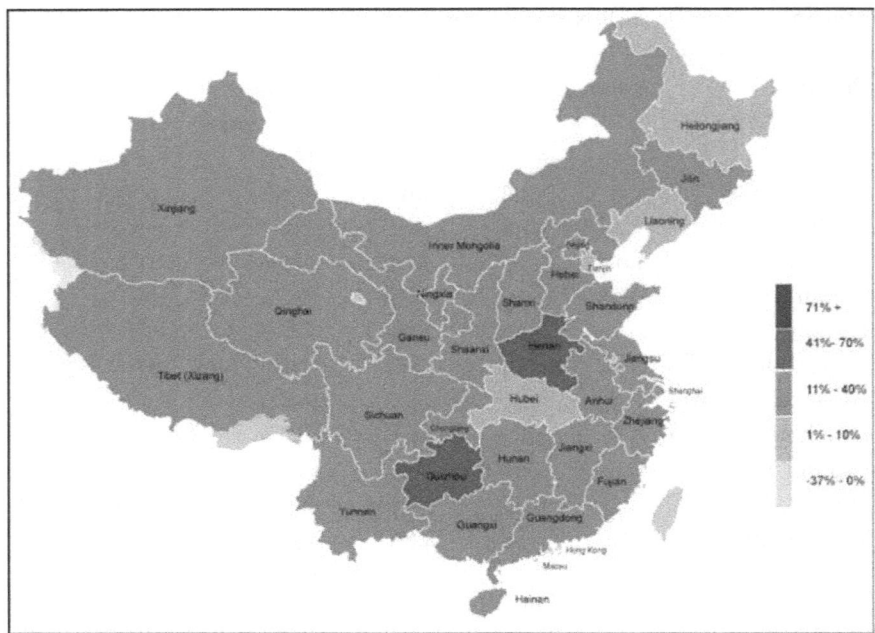

FIGURE 9.5   Percentage change in tertiary education teachers from 2011 to 2018
SOURCE: AUTHOR'S ELABORATION USING THE CHINA STATISTICAL YEARBOOKS (NATIONAL BUREAU OF STATISTICS OF CHINA, 2000–2018)

Yue et al., 2021). Moreover, China is the global leader in the digitalization of healthcare (Milcent, 2018).

This section proceeds to analyze how different elements of China's healthcare system have developed during the Xi Jinping Era. It investigates the physical health infrastructure and the population-weighted medical staff for 31 provinces. Specifically, it evaluates not just the number of hospitals and doctors, but the number of beds and medical personnel per 10,000 inhabitants, which are considered primary medical care resources reflecting a region's capability of dealing with mild diseases and providing healthcare services (Liu et al., 2020).

3.1   Health Infrastructure

While it is evident that the healthcare infrastructure has experienced an expansion since the turn of the century, this subsection explores how these changes were distributed across the 31 Chinese provinces and how much occurred during the XJE. Table 9.7 reports the number of health institutions per 10,000 inhabitants in each region for 2000, 2011, and 2018. The mean values indicate

TABLE 9.6 Change in higher education enrolment

Province	2000	2011	2018	% change 2000–2011	% change 2011–2018
Anhui	19.18	99.13	113.91	417%	15%
Beijing	28.03	58.79	59.49	110%	1%
Chongqing	12.63	56.78	76.28	350%	34%
Fujian	13.79	67.48	77.24	389%	14%
Gansu	8.26	40.53	48.36	391%	19%
Guangdong	30.60	152.73	196.32	399%	29%
Guangxi	12.37	60.01	94.22	385%	57%
Guizhou	7.98	34.41	68.75	331%	100%
Hainan	1.92	15.67	18.92	716%	21%
Hebei	25.26	114.93	134.26	355%	17%
Heilongjiang	21.01	71.00	73.21	238%	3%
Henan	27.34	150.01	214.08	449%	43%
Hubei	35.77	134.03	143.82	275%	7%
Hunan	26.58	106.79	132.68	302%	24%
Inner Mongolia	7.19	38.44	45.53	435%	18%
Jiangsu	45.18	165.94	180.63	267%	9%
Jiangxi	14.86	82.86	105.44	458%	27%
Jilin	18.10	56.28	65.83	211%	17%
Liaoning	30.79	90.22	96.32	193%	7%
Ningxia	1.75	8.79	12.53	402%	43%
Qinghai	1.35	4.57	7.03	239%	54%
Shaanxi	24.47	96.48	105.48	294%	9%
Shandong	32.53	164.56	204.08	406%	24%
Shanghai	22.68	51.13	51.78	125%	1%
Shanxi	12.50	59.45	76.56	376%	29%
Sichuan	24.56	113.93	156.47	364%	37%
Tianjin	11.91	44.97	52.33	278%	16%
Tibet	0.55	3.24	3.57	489%	10%
Xinjiang	8.10	25.87	37.49	219%	45%
Yunnan	9.59	48.76	76.47	408%	57%
Zhejiang	19.24	90.75	101.94	372%	12%
Mean	17.94	74.47	91.32	343%	26%

Note: Enrollment rates refer to the number of students per 10,000 inhabitants.
SOURCE: AUTHOR'S CALCULATION USING THE CHINA STATISTICAL YEARBOOKS (NATIONAL BUREAU OF STATISTICS OF CHINA, 2000–2018)

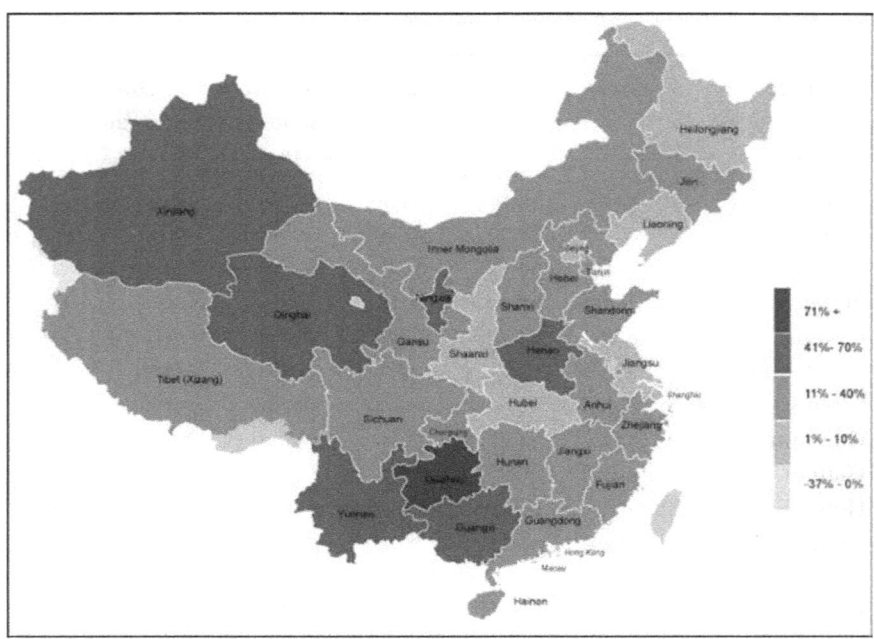

FIGURE 9.6   Percentage change in higher education enrolment from 2011 to 2018
SOURCE: AUTHOR'S ELABORATION USING THE CHINA STATISTICAL
YEARBOOKS (NATIONAL BUREAU OF STATISTICS OF CHINA, 2000–2018)

that although the average health institutions per 10,000 inhabitants more than doubled from 2.89 in 2000 to 7.55 in 2011, this figure decreased to 7.54 during the XJE. Furthermore, there is a large disparity among the provinces. Tibet has the highest health institution concentration (19.90), approximately double that of the remaining top five highest provinces: Gansu, Qinghai, Hebei, and Shanxi. At the lower end, Shanghai, Tianjin, and Anhui have 2.18, 3.64, and 3.94, respectively. Moreover, 11 provinces suffered reductions in their population-weighted health institutions: Jiangxi, Hunan, Tibet, Henan, Guangxi, Shaanxi, Xinjiang, Heilongjiang, Fujian, Beijing, and Hubei. On the other hand, Chongqing, Tianjin, Shandong, and Jilin experienced growth of approximately 10% or higher. Figure 9.7 depicts the geographical distribution of the gains in health institutions per 10,000 inhabitants during the XJE. It reveals that the highest increases of at least 11% occurred in three coastal regions, while many central areas, the two westernmost provinces, and the north-easternmost province suffered declines. The remaining regions' values grew by an average of 3%.

While the number of health institutions is an important indicator of a region's health infrastructure, these may vary in size and quality. Therefore,

TABLE 9.7 Change in the number of health institutions per 10,000 inhabitants

Province	2000	2011	2018	% change 2000–2011	% change 2011–2018
Anhui	1.10	3.83	3.94	248%	3%
Beijing	4.53	4.70	4.67	4%	−1%
Chongqing	3.29	6.05	6.62	84%	9%
Fujian	2.88	7.30	7.00	154%	−4%
Gansu	2.86	10.39	10.58	263%	2%
Guangdong	1.56	4.37	4.53	180%	4%
Guangxi	2.89	7.33	6.85	154%	−6%
Guizhou	2.39	7.48	7.80	212%	4%
Hainan	3.41	5.49	5.70	61%	4%
Hebei	3.10	11.07	11.26	258%	2%
Heilongjiang	2.11	5.67	5.39	169%	−5%
Henan	1.13	8.11	7.43	615%	−8%
Hubei	1.96	6.19	6.17	216%	0%
Hunan	3.76	9.04	8.15	140%	−10%
Inner Mongolia	3.31	9.23	9.71	179%	5%
Jiangsu	1.75	4.01	4.13	129%	3%
Jiangxi	1.94	8.72	7.86	350%	−10%
Jilin	2.07	7.20	8.39	248%	17%
Liaoning	3.00	8.04	8.27	168%	3%
Ningxia	2.46	6.46	6.47	163%	0%
Qinghai	3.57	10.36	10.61	190%	2%
Shaanxi	2.95	9.72	9.14	230%	−6%
Shandong	1.90	7.08	8.11	272%	14%
Shanghai	3.19	2.02	2.18	−37%	8%
Shanxi	4.23	11.23	11.32	165%	1%
Sichuan	4.00	9.42	9.78	135%	4%
Tianjin	2.98	3.27	3.64	10%	12%
Tibet	4.79	21.77	19.90	354%	−9%
Xinjiang	3.63	7.88	7.42	117%	−6%
Yunnan	3.15	5.02	5.17	59%	3%
Zhejiang	3.64	5.59	5.71	53%	2%
Mean	2.89	7.55	7.54	179%	1%

SOURCE: AUTHOR'S CALCULATION USING THE CHINA STATISTICAL YEARBOOKS (NATIONAL BUREAU OF STATISTICS OF CHINA, 2000–2018)

FIGURE 9.7 Percentage change in density of health institutions from 2011 to 2018
SOURCE: AUTHOR'S ELABORATION USING THE CHINA STATISTICAL
YEARBOOKS (NATIONAL BUREAU OF STATISTICS OF CHINA, 2000–2018)

the number of beds in public health institutions per 10,000 inhabitants is a complementary indicator that reflects the caring capacity of healthcare institutions in each province. These values are reported in Table 9.8 for 2000, 2011, and 2018. The averages indicate that although there was a significant increase from 27.86 to 39.10 in the pre-XJE, the number of beds grew by an even larger amount to 59.88 during the XJE. The inequality between provinces is much lower, whereby the region with the highest ratio, Liaoning, has 72.13, compared to the lowest value of 43.72 in Tianjin. These figures suggest that despite the disparities in actual institutions evidenced above, the capacities of the provinces are less dispersed. Furthermore, it is worth highlighting that every single area increased its capacity during the XJE by an average of 54%. The province to benefit most was Guizhou, which raised its number of beds per 10,000 people by 101%. On the other hand, Tianjin, Beijing, and Shanghai increased their values by 20%, 22%, and 26%, respectively. Furthermore, Figure 9.8 suggests that most provinces improved their healthcare capacities at similar rates. A cluster in the central and central-west regions experienced the highest gains, while the remaining areas improved at different rates.

TABLE 9.8 Change in the number of beds in health institutions per 10,000 inhabitants

Province	2000	2011	2018	% change 2000–2011	% change 2011–2018
Anhui	20.33	34.22	51.88	68%	52%
Beijing	52.20	46.91	57.38	−10%	22%
Chongqing	23.06	39.60	70.95	72%	79%
Fujian	26.42	33.39	48.85	26%	46%
Gansu	23.62	37.01	61.70	57%	67%
Guangdong	19.43	30.94	45.56	59%	47%
Guangxi	17.98	32.72	51.95	82%	59%
Guizhou	15.60	33.87	68.22	117%	101%
Hainan	26.11	32.48	47.97	24%	48%
Hebei	25.31	36.81	55.84	45%	52%
Heilongjiang	31.65	43.11	66.29	36%	54%
Henan	20.93	37.24	63.35	78%	70%
Hubei	25.36	38.90	66.50	53%	71%
Hunan	21.85	39.07	69.92	79%	79%
Inner Mongolia	28.20	40.54	62.75	44%	55%
Jiangsu	23.62	37.52	61.05	59%	63%
Jiangxi	21.91	30.21	53.68	38%	78%
Jilin	33.30	44.08	61.76	32%	40%
Liaoning	45.58	49.24	72.13	8%	46%
Ningxia	24.91	40.35	59.59	62%	48%
Qinghai	31.91	40.66	64.84	27%	59%
Shaanxi	26.59	41.09	65.66	55%	60%
Shandong	23.87	43.18	60.57	81%	40%
Shanghai	46.80	45.62	57.34	−3%	26%
Shanxi	34.46	43.72	56.02	27%	28%
Sichuan	22.93	41.58	71.80	81%	73%
Tianjin	39.96	36.47	43.72	−9%	20%
Tibet	24.42	31.65	48.84	30%	54%
Xinjiang	38.13	56.78	71.93	49%	27%
Yunnan	22.99	37.44	60.29	63%	61%
Zhejiang	24.29	35.66	57.89	47%	62%
Mean	27.86	39.10	59.88	48%	54%

SOURCE: AUTHOR'S CALCULATION USING THE CHINA STATISTICAL YEARBOOKS (NATIONAL BUREAU OF STATISTICS OF CHINA, 2000–2018)

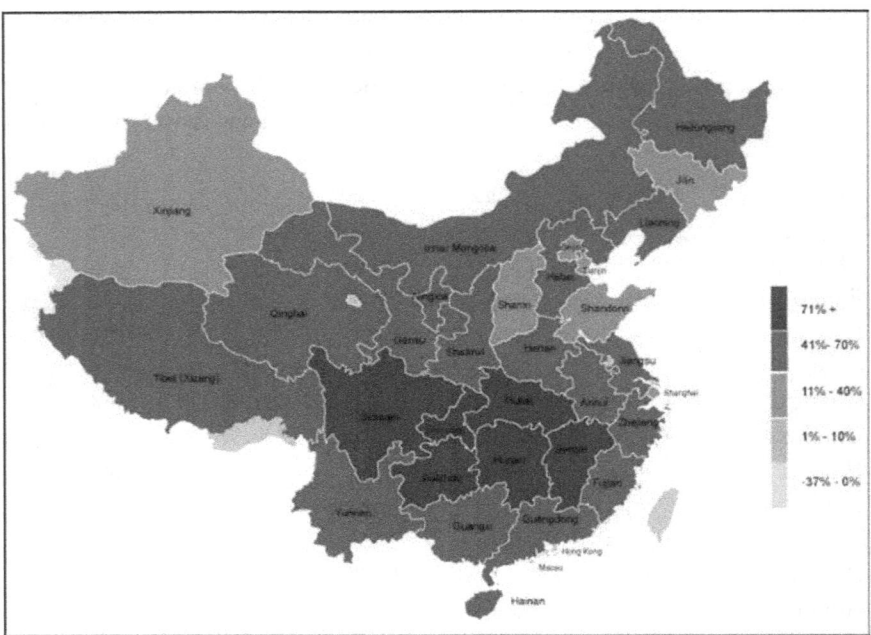

FIGURE 9.8 Percentage change in density of beds in health institutions from 2011 to 2018
SOURCE: AUTHOR'S ELABORATION USING THE CHINA STATISTICAL
YEARBOOKS (NATIONAL BUREAU OF STATISTICS OF CHINA, 2000–2018)

3.2 Health Staff

While the gains in health infrastructure discussed in the previous subsection are important, the quality of a region's healthcare provision can also be measured as a population-weighted number of medical personnel. Since the skills of medical staff vary, the analyses consider the total medical personnel and medical doctors separately. Table 9.9 reveals the change in medical personnel before and after the start of the XJE. The mean values indicate considerable gains during both the pre-XJE and XJE periods. However, disparities in medical personnel are evident, with the capital Beijing leading with 151.39 personnel per 10,000 inhabitants, followed by Tibet, Shaanxi, and Zhejiang with 106.98, 106.34, and 102.74, respectively. At the other extreme, Anhui has 67.52 medical staff per 10,000 people. Nevertheless, each province improved their medical staff ratios during the XJE by an average of 38%. The highest gains were in Guizhou at 84%, followed by Yunnan and Jiangsu at 74% and 51%, respectively. On the other hand, the lowest improvements were in Heilongjiang, Tianjin, and Shanxi with 14%, 15%, and 18%, respectively. The map in Figure 9.9 further illustrates that a group of western regions and a couple of coastal ones benefited the most in terms of medical personnel during the XJE. At the same time, the remainder of the provinces all improved at similar rates.

Moreover, changes in the number of doctors per 10,000 inhabitants are reported in Table 9.10. The results indicate an enormous overall improvement during the XJE compared to the period from 2000 to 2011. While the mean values increased only slightly, from 19.26 in 2000 to 20.10 in 2011, they jumped to 26.32 during the XJE. Despite the gains, regional disparities remain. Beijing has the highest ratio of doctors at 46 per 10,000 people, followed by Zhejiang and Shanghai with values of 33 and 30, respectively. At the lower end, Jiangxi, Anhui, Yunnan, and Guangxi have fewer than half the population-weighted doctors as the capital, ranging from 19 to 22. Nonetheless, all provinces increased their ratios of doctors during the XJE, except for Beijing, Tianjin, and Shanghai. Since the three municipalities already had high numbers of doctors given their populations, it appears they were not prioritized during the XJE. Once more, Guizhou was the province that benefitted most during the XJE, improving its number of doctors per 10,000 inhabitants by 109%. The second- and third-highest were Henan (79%) and Tibet (71%). The map in Figure 9.10 reveals that most central and western provinces experienced gains in their shares of doctors. However, some northern areas experienced below-average increases, such as Xinjiang, Heilongjiang, Liaoning, and Inner Mongolia.

4 Retirement

Many populations are aging rapidly worldwide, increasing pressure on pension systems. China is no exception, as it has surpassed its demographic dividend. The Chinese Pension system consists of a combination of public pension schemes, employer-sponsored programs, and private annuity insurance policies. By 2018, 942,930,000 people were insured by the three types of pension programs indicating that China is on track to achieve universal pension coverage (MOHRSS, 2022). Before 2015, there were four Chinese public pension schemes: i) the basic old-age insurance (BOAI) system; ii) Public Employee Pension (PEP); iii) the Urban Resident Pension (URP); and iv) New Rural Social Pension (NRP) (Fang and Feng, 2018). While the BOAI and PEP are for employed workers in private and state-owned sectors, the URP and NRP are for non-employed individuals. Its urban pension system relies on the BOAI, which was established in 1951, and reformed in 1997 to include a contribution by employers of 20% of the wages paid and stipulated that employees with at least 15 years of contribution history were entitled to pension benefits. On the other hand, employees must contribute 8% of their wages. Therefore, under

TABLE 9.9 Change in the number of medical personnel per 10,000 inhabitants

Province	2000	2011	2018	% change 2000–2011	% change 2011–2018
Anhui	30.90	52.85	67.52	71%	28%
Beijing	117.52	116.76	151.39	–1%	30%
Chongqing	37.87	58.51	87.94	54%	50%
Fujian	34.49	58.49	80.82	70%	38%
Gansu	37.81	56.82	78.50	50%	38%
Guangdong	37.82	59.65	80.94	58%	36%
Guangxi	33.40	61.03	85.34	83%	40%
Guizhou	27.05	48.75	89.83	80%	84%
Hainan	48.80	64.85	87.15	33%	34%
Hebei	41.56	62.03	82.58	49%	33%
Heilongjiang	58.37	69.41	79.41	19%	14%
Henan	35.31	66.41	89.87	88%	35%
Hubei	53.15	63.42	88.20	19%	39%
Hunan	41.53	58.83	80.85	42%	37%
Inner Mongolia	55.19	70.60	95.26	28%	35%
Jiangsu	43.92	61.00	91.83	39%	51%
Jiangxi	36.64	54.50	70.09	49%	29%
Jilin	62.83	70.16	89.50	12%	28%
Liaoning	70.77	72.80	89.91	3%	23%
Ningxia	48.92	65.37	95.64	34%	46%
Qinghai	50.10	68.29	98.51	36%	44%
Shaanxi	44.98	73.60	106.34	64%	44%
Shandong	42.61	71.56	95.69	68%	34%
Shanghai	90.80	75.23	98.27	–17%	31%
Shanxi	59.90	75.59	89.00	26%	18%
Sichuan	37.22	62.82	89.47	69%	42%
Tianjin	84.42	73.97	84.94	–12%	15%
Tibet	42.64	73.19	106.98	72%	46%
Xinjiang	65.60	75.97	91.31	16%	20%
Yunnan	35.75	46.49	80.70	30%	74%
Zhejiang	42.82	68.50	102.74	60%	50%
Mean	50.02	66.37	90.53	42%	38%

SOURCE: AUTHOR'S CALCULATION USING THE CHINA STATISTICAL YEARBOOKS (NATIONAL BUREAU OF STATISTICS OF CHINA, 2000–2018)

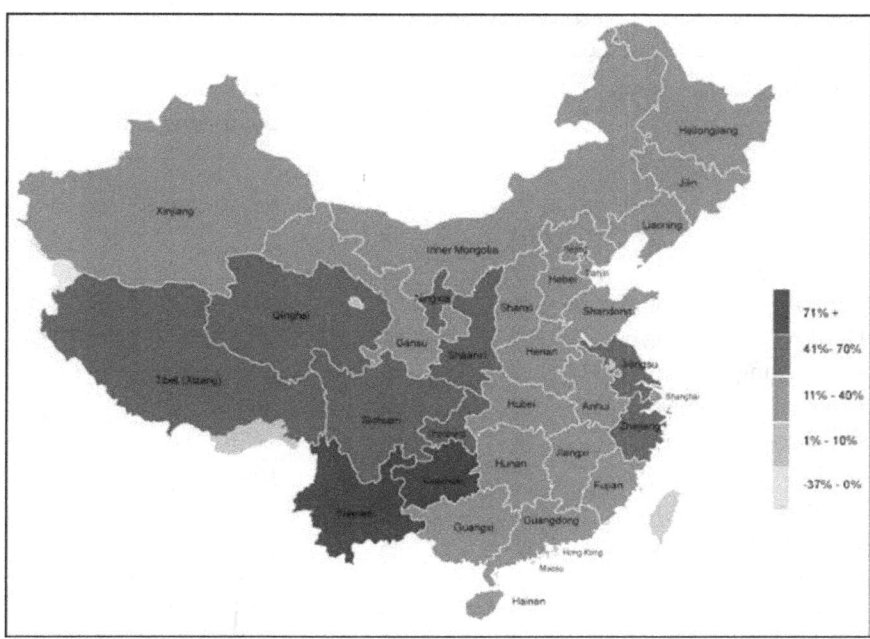

FIGURE 9.9 Percentage change in density of medical personnel from 2011 to 2018
SOURCE: AUTHOR'S ELABORATION USING THE CHINA STATISTICAL
YEARBOOKS (NATIONAL BUREAU OF STATISTICS OF CHINA, 2000–2018)

the BOAI, employers and employees must jointly make contributions (Zhao et al., 2022).[1] For those working in the non-profit public sector and for government employees, PEP was formed in 1953. A notable difference was that the scheme was more generous in benefits and did not require employee contributions. However, in 2015, PEP was merged into the BOAI scheme and the contribution and benefits for public employees were switched to those of BOAI.

Similarly, in 2009, the Chinese government introduced the New Rural Social Pension (NRSP) for rural citizens to provide income for senior rural residents (Pan et al., 2021). The URP was created in 2011 to cover people of urban areas who are unemployed. Both NRSP and URP are voluntary programs supported by government grants where individual accounts are funded through individual donations. However, there are obvious differences between areas and between urban and rural inhabitants since the quantity of contributions is dependent

---

1 The BOAI retirement eligibility age is 50 for female blue-collar workers, 55 for female white-collar workers, and 60 for males.

TABLE 9.10 Number of doctors per 10,000 inhabitants

Province	2000	2011	2018	% change 2000–2011	% change 2011–2018
Anhui	11	12	20	9%	67%
Beijing	47	54	46	15%	−15%
Chongqing	15	15	25	0%	67%
Fujian	13	18	23	38%	28%
Gansu	15	15	23	0%	53%
Guangdong	15	22	24	47%	9%
Guangxi	10	14	22	40%	57%
Guizhou	12	11	23	−8%	109%
Hainan	16	17	24	6%	41%
Hebei	14	19	28	36%	47%
Heilongjiang	21	20	24	−5%	20%
Henan	12	14	25	17%	79%
Hubei	17	17	26	0%	53%
Hunan	14	16	26	14%	63%
Inner Mongolia	22	23	29	5%	26%
Jiangsu	16	18	29	13%	61%
Jiangxi	13	13	19	0%	46%
Jilin	23	22	29	−4%	32%
Liaoning	24	23	28	−4%	22%
Ningxia	16	19	28	19%	47%
Qinghai	19	20	27	5%	35%
Shaanxi	18	17	26	−6%	53%
Shandong	16	19	29	19%	53%
Shanghai	38	38	30	0%	−21%
Shanxi	20	24	27	20%	13%
Sichuan	16	17	25	6%	47%
Tianjin	33	30	28	−9%	−7%
Tibet	34	14	24	−59%	71%
Xinjiang	25	22	25	−12%	14%
Yunnan	15	14	21	−7%	50%
Zhejiang	17	26	33	53%	27%
Mean	19.26	20.10	26.32	8%	40%

SOURCE: AUTHOR'S CALCULATION USING THE CHINA STATISTICAL YEARBOOKS (NATIONAL BUREAU OF STATISTICS OF CHINA, 2000–2018)

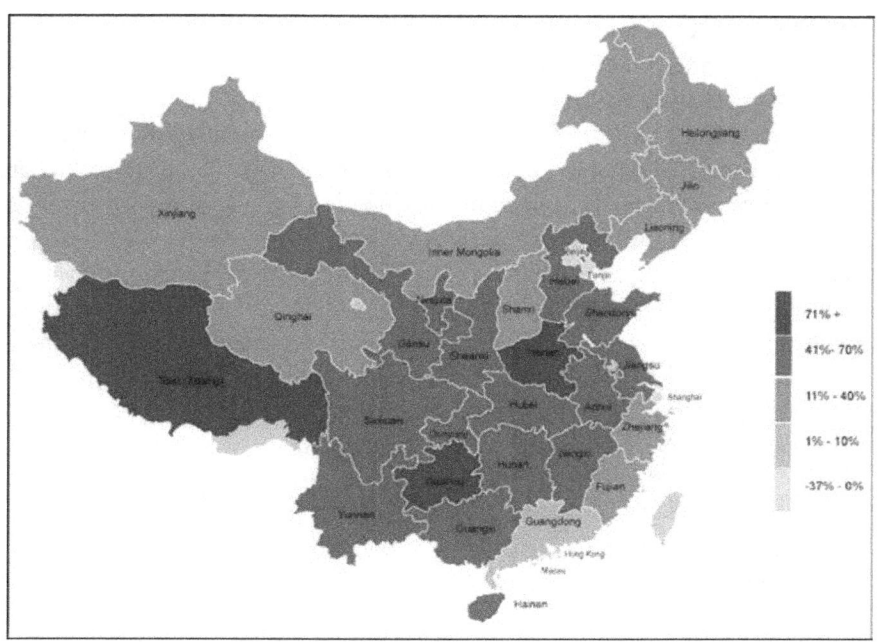

FIGURE 9.10 Percentage change in density of doctors from 2011 to 2018
SOURCE: AUTHOR'S ELABORATION USING THE CHINA STATISTICAL YEARBOOKS (NATIONAL BUREAU OF STATISTICS OF CHINA, 2000–2018)

on regional economic situations. The NRSP was extended to all rural counties by the end of 2012 and incorporated with the urban pension program in 2014, renamed Urban-Rural Resident Social Pension (URRSP) (Fang and Feng, 2018).

Additionally, in 1991, the employer-sponsored pension system was established. However, most firms cannot afford to offer pension programs and have little motivation to do so. As a result, the coverage is quite little as compared to BOAI (Zhao et al., 2022). Furthermore, employer and employee contributions and investment returns are tax-exempt as of 2014. Lastly, the household savings-based private annuity insurance, on the other hand, is comparatively new, is provided as a wealth management product, and has had annual growth rates of 17% since 2001 (Jiang and Ni, 2020). Despite being in its early stages, a pilot program was released at the start of 2018 to offer individual income tax-deferred annuity insurance products in Shanghai, Fujian Province, and Suzhou Industrial Park.

This section uses the China Health and Retirement Longitudinal Study (CHARLS) to evaluate the evolution of pension coverage in China during the XJE. The CHARLS is a large-scale national survey managed by the National

Development Academy of Peking University and designed to study adults older than 45 and their families. The section uses the initial (2011) and fourth (2018) waves of CHARLS to examine how pension coverage has changed across the 28 provinces it includes.[2] Table 9.11 reports the change in pension coverage from 2011 to 2018. Pension coverage is defined as participating in any public or private pension program specified by the CHARLS questionnaires.

The results indicate a dramatic increase, whereby less than a third of the sample in 2011 had pension coverage, while almost 90% had access to a form of pension program in the 2018 sample. However, the coverages across provinces are not homogenous. While Tianjin, Guangxi, Jilin, and Heilongjiang have coverage rates below 78%, more than 98% of the respondents in Beijing had access to a pension plan. Furthermore, while Shanghai is the only region with a decrease in pension coverage, the respondents in Fujian raised their coverage by 840%. Similarly, respondents in Anhui, Yunnan, Shanxi, Gansu, and Guizhou increased their coverage by over 500%. Moreover, Figure 9.11 illustrates that the dramatic increase in pension coverage evident in the CHARLS surveys considerably affected most regions.

5 Conclusion

This chapter has analyzed the evolution of education, healthcare, and pension coverage across Chinese provinces during the Xi Jinping Era. As China transitions toward an advanced economy and high-income nation, it faces many challenges to its development path. It can no longer rely on high growth rates fueled by investment and production. Therefore, it must generate a higher quality growth from R&D, innovation, and human capital. The latter is important since research has shown that countries with an insufficient supply of human capital can enter development traps. Two components of human capital, education and health, are analyzed in this chapter. The results reveal that despite significant overall gains, regional disparities remain. Furthermore, the analysis of the XJE also highlights the prioritization of certain areas and differing strategies for distinct regions.

The expansion of higher education has focused on developing undergraduate universities in coastal and central regions while promoting vocational colleges in westernmost and borderland provinces. Tibet is the only province

---

2 Hainan, Ningxia, and Tibet are excluded from the CHARLS. For details concerning the CHARLS surveys, refer to http://charls.pku.edu.cn/ or see Zhao et al., 2014. For the baseline data or sampling information see Zhao et al., 2013.

TABLE 9.11 Change in pension coverage

Province	2011	2018	% change 2011–2018
Anhui	10.74	93.04	766%
Beijing	79.57	98.08	23%
Chongqing	55.02	85.2	55%
Fujian	10.02	94.21	840%
Gansu	14.78	95.78	548%
Guangdong	21.04	85.91	308%
Guangxi	24.46	72.81	198%
Guizhou	14.87	90.41	508%
Hebei	21.7	94.16	334%
Heilongjiang	66.16	77.99	18%
Henan	28.16	94.66	236%
Hubei	27.67	94.65	242%
Hunan	22.19	93.67	322%
Jiangsu	49.83	91.02	83%
Jiangxi	31.21	86.19	176%
Jilin	33.33	76.55	130%
Liaoning	40.11	92.15	130%
Inner Mongolia	33.53	83.09	148%
Qinghai	18.3	95.54	422%
Shaanxi	36.11	95.33	164%
Shandong	25.91	91.67	254%
Shanghai	93.1	87.5	−6%
Shanxi	14.23	94.72	566%
Sichuan	22.76	82.45	262%
Tianjin	51.28	70.63	38%
Xinjiang	33.98	90.38	166%
Yunnan	13.69	95.32	596%
Zhejiang	62.14	81	30%
Total	28.57	89.19	212%

Note: Pension coverage refers to access and participation in public or private pension programs.
SOURCE: AUTHOR'S CALCULATION USING THE 2011 AND 2018 CHARLS

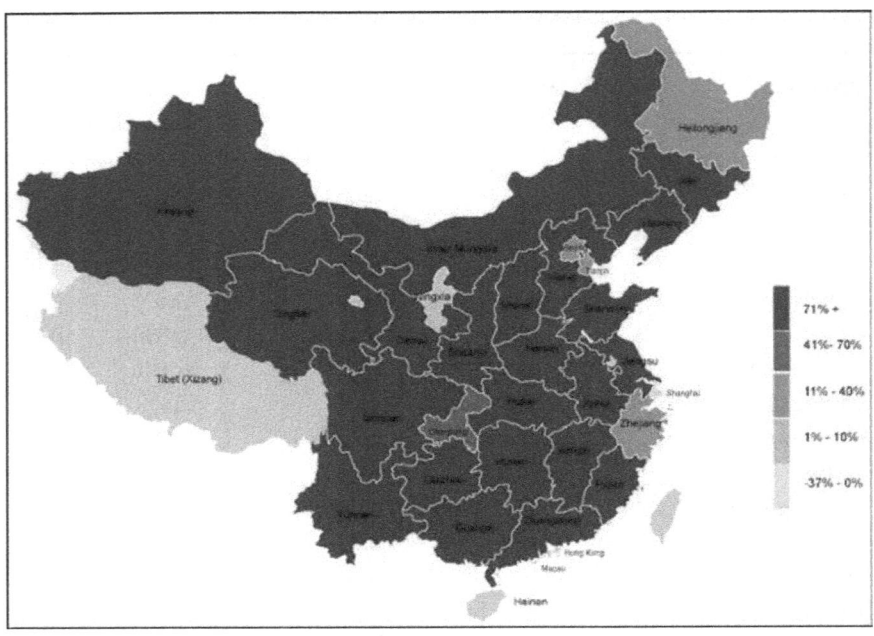

FIGURE 9.11 Percentage change in pension coverage from 2011 to 2018
SOURCE: AUTHOR'S CALCULATION USING THE 2011 AND 2018 CHARLS

that has not benefited from the expansion of HEIs regarding its population. Nevertheless, the increase in teacher and enrollment ratios are more evenly distributed across areas. An advanced economy will require a better trained and highly skilled labor force. Currently, the share of China's labor force with a college education is far below that of high-income countries which is why it is important to continue the higher education expansion, particularly in those regions still suffering from an undersupply as identified here.

Similarly, some research has highlighted the poor health of children in rural areas as an obstacle to China's modernization objectives. Enhancing the provision and quality of health is important. The results show that although improvements in the number of health institutions are not equal across regions, the improvements made to the capacity of institutions measured by the number of beds, medical personnel and doctors seem to have prioritized central and western areas, reducing regional disparities.

Lastly, improvements in pension coverage are evident across all regions, hinting at improving retirement conditions nationwide. As the nation's demographic dividend comes to an end, China's aging society becomes a higher burden that can only be ameliorated through pension reforms. Public and private pension programs will struggle to provide for the increasingly aging population because of a decreasing labor force. The PRC has tried to address the declining birth rates via loosening the One-child Policy, to Two-child in 2016, which soon became a Three-child Policy in 2021. High education costs and property prices remain big deterrents for couples to consider having more children.

Guizhou Province is a clear winner in the XJE and has benefited the most from improvements in HEIs, teachers, enrollment, health institutions, beds, medical staff, doctors, and pension coverage. On the other hand, some westernmost regions, or those bordering other countries, appear to have made modest gains, suggesting a low prioritization.

The results discussed in this chapter present useful policy insights for China's 14th Five-Year Plan for National Economic and Social Development and Long-Range Objectives for 2035. It identifies the extent to which the XJE has prioritized the joint prosperity of developed and less-developed areas. Similarly, it identifies regions that may have been neglected and thus should be included when implementing regional coordinated development strategies. Reducing the regional disparities presented here is vital as the XJE advances in creating a harmonious and prosperous nation by promoting a more balanced development and unified society. While China has enjoyed four decades of unprecedented gains in terms of education, health and pension coverage, the needed reforms and improvements to continue developing are much more difficult to implement and remain an important challenge that Xi Jinping must overcome to achieve his development targets of 2030–47.

References

Borsi, Mihály Tamás, Octasiano Miguel Valerio Mendoza, and Flavio Comim (2022) Measuring the provincial supply of higher education institutions in China. *China Economic Review*, 71, 101724. DOI:10.1016/j.chieco.2021.101724.

Burns, Lawton Robert and Yanzhong Huang (2017) History of China's Healthcare System. In: Gordon G. Liu and Lawton Robert Burns (eds.) *China's Healthcare System and Reform*. Cambridge: Cambridge University Press, pp. 31–74. DOI: 10.1017/9781316691113.004.

Cai, Fang (2020) The Second Demographic Dividend as a Driver of China's Growth. *China & World Economy*, 28(5), pp. 26–44. DOI:10.1111/cwe.12350.

Eggleston, Karen, Li Ling, Meng Qingyue, Magnus Lindelow, and Adam Wagstaff (2008) Health service delivery in China: a literature review. *Health Economics*, 17(2), pp. 149–165. DOI:10.1002/hec.1306.

Emmers, Dorien, Qi Jiang, Hao Xue, Yue Zhang, Yunting Zhang, Yingxue Zhao, Bin Liu, Sarah-Eve Dill, Yiwei Qian, Nele Warrinnier, Hannah Johnstone, Jianhua Cai, Xiaoli Wang, Lei Wang, Renfu Luo, Guirong Li, Jiajia Xu, Ming Liu, Yaqing Huang, Wenjie Shan, Zhihui Li, Yu Zhang, Sean Sylvia, Yue Ma, Alexis Medina, and Scott Rozelle (2021) Early childhood development and parental training interventions in rural China: a systematic review and meta-analysis. *BMJ Global Health*, 6(8), e005578. DOI: 10.1136/bmjgh-2021-005578.

Fang, Hanming and Jin Feng (2018) The Chinese Pension System. NBER Working Paper No. 25088, National Bureau of Economic Research, Cambridge, MA.

Hougaard, Jens Leth, Lars Peter Østerdal, and Yi Yu (2011) The Chinese healthcare system. *Applied Health Economics and Health Policy*, 9(1), pp. 1–13. DOI:10.2165/11531800-000000000-00000.

Hu, Anning and Jacob Hibel (2014) Changes in college attainment and the economic returns to a college degree in urban China, 2003–2010: Implications for social equality. *Social Science Research*, 44, pp. 173–186. DOI:10.1016/j.ssresearch.2013.12.001.

Jiang, Yawen and Weiyi Ni (2020) Impact of supplementary private health insurance on hospitalization and physical examination in China. *China Economic Review*, 63, 101514. DOI:10.1016/j.chieco.2020.101514.

Knight, John, Quheng Deng, and Shi Li (2017) China's expansion of higher education: The labour market consequences of a supply shock. *China Economic Review*, 43, pp. 127–141. DOI:10.1016/j.chieco.2017.01.008.

Li, Shi, John Whalley, and Chunbing Xing (2014) China's higher education expansion and unemployment of college graduates. *China Economic Review*, 30, pp. 567–582. DOI:10.1016/j.chieco.2013.08.002.

Liang, Xiaofeng, and Lawton R. Burns (2017) China's Public Health System and Infrastructure. In: Gordon G. Liu & Lawton Robert Burns (eds.) *China's Healthcare System and Reform*. Cambridge: Cambridge University Press, pp. 75–116. DOI:10.1017/9781316691113.005.

Liu, Haimeng, Chuanglin Fang, and Yupeng Fan (2020) Mapping the inequalities of medical resource provision in China. *Regional Studies, Regional Science*, 7(1), pp. 568–570. DOI:10.1080/21681376.2020.1848615.

Liu, Ning, Zhuo Chen, and Guoxian Bao (2021) Unpacking the red packets: institution and informal payments in healthcare in China. *The European Journal of Health Economics*, 22(8), pp. 1183–1194. DOI:10.1007/s10198-021-01330-z.

Liu, Xu (2020) The Development of Private Universities in Socialist China. *Higher Education Policy*, 33(1), pp. 1–19. DOI:10.1057/s41307-018-0114-8.

Luo, Yan, Fei Guo, and Jinghuan Shi (2018) Expansion and inequality of higher education in China: how likely would Chinese poor students get to success? *Higher Education Research & Development*, 37(5), pp. 1015–1034. DOI:10.1080/07294360.2018.1474856.

Milcent, Carine (2018) *Healthcare Reform in China*. Cham: Springer International Publishing. DOI:10.1007/978-3-319-69736-9.

Ministry of Education (2016). Gāoděng Jiàoyù Bù "2016 nián gāoděng Jiàoyù Bù gōngzuò yàodiǎn" yìnfā de tōngzhī [Notice on printing and distributing the "2016 work points of the higher education department of the ministry of education"]. 26 February, http://www.moe.gov.cn/s78/A08/tongzhi/201604/t20160407_237073.html, accessed 20 September 2022.

Ministry of Education (2017). Jiàoyù Bù děng sì bùmén guānyú yìnfā "Zhōngxiǎoxué jiēduàn jiàoyù pǔjí jìhuà (2017–2020 nián)" de tōngzhī [Notice of the ministry of education and other four departments on the issuance of the "high school stage education popularization plan (2017–2020)"]. 30 March 2017, http://www.moe.gov.cn/srcsite/A06/s7053/201704/t20170406_301981.html, accessed 20 September 2022.

Ministry of Human Resources and Social Security (MOHRSS) (2022) Rénlì Zīyuán hé Shèhuì Bǎozhàng Bù "2021 nián rénlì zīyuán hé shèhuì bǎozhàng shìyè fāzhǎn tǒngjì gōngbào" [Statistical Bulletin on the Development of Human Resources and Social Security Undertakings in 2021]. 7 June, http://www.mohrss.gov.cn/SYrlzyhsh bzb/zwgk/szrs/tjgb/202206/t20220607_452104.html, accessed 20 September 2022.

National Bureau of Statistics of China (2000-2018) *China Statistical Yearbook*. Beijing: China Statistics Press.

Pan, Guochen, Shaobin Li, Zhixiang Geng, and Kai Zhan (2021) Do Social Pension Schemes Promote the Mental Health of Rural Middle-Aged and Old Residents? Evidence From China. *Frontiers in Public Health*, 9. DOI:10.3389/fpubh.2021.710128.

Qian, Joanne Xiaolei and Russell Smyth (2011) Educational expenditure in urban China: income effects, family characteristics and the demand for domestic and overseas education. *Applied Economics*, 43(24), pp. 3379–3394. DOI: 10.1080/000368 41003636292.

Süssmuth-Dyckerhoff, Claudia and Florian Then (2017) China's Healthcare Reform: Status and Outlook. In: Gordon G. Liu and Lawton Robert Burns (eds.) *China's Healthcare System and Reform*. Cambridge: Cambridge University Press, pp. 137–149. DOI: 10.1017/9781316691113.007.

Valerio Mendoza, Octasiano Miguel (2018) Heterogeneous determinants of educational achievement and inequality across urban China. *China Economic Review*, 51, pp. 129–148. DOI:10.1016/j.chieco.2017.11.006.

Valerio Mendoza, Octasiano Miguel, Mihály Tamás Borsi, and Flavio Comim (2021) Indices of the supply of Chinese Higher Education [Data set]. *Zenodo*. DOI:10.5281/zenodo.5753098.

Valerio Mendoza, Octasiano Miguel, Mihály Tamás Borsi, and Flavio Comim (2022) Human capital dynamics in China: Evidence from a club convergence approach. *Journal of Asian Economics*, 79. DOI:10.1016/j.asieco.2022.101441.

Wang, Lei, Mengjie Li, Sarah-Eve Dill, Yiwei Hu, and Scott Rozelle (2019) Dynamic Anemia Status from Infancy to Preschool-Age: Evidence from Rural China. *International Journal of Environmental Research and Public Health*, 16(15), 2761. DOI:10.3390/ijerph16152761.

Wu, Lingli, Kun Yan, and Yuqi Zhang (2020) Higher education expansion and inequality in educational opportunities in China. *Higher Education*, 80(3), pp. 549–570. DOI:10.1007/s10734-020-00498-2.

Xiang, Lili, John Stillwell, Luke Burns, and Alison Heppenstall (2020) Measuring and Assessing Regional Education Inequalities in China under Changing Policy Regimes. *Applied Spatial Analysis and Policy*, 13(1), pp. 91–112. DOI:10.1007/s12061-019-09293-8.

Ye, Jinqi, Ziyan Chen, and Bin Peng (2021) Is the demographic dividend diminishing in China? Evidence from population aging and economic growth during 1990–2015. *Review of Development Economics*, 25(4), pp. 2255–2274. DOI:10.1111/rode.12794.

Yue, Xiaomeng, Yuxiang Li, Jiuhong Wu, and Jeff J. Guo (2021) Current Development and Practice of Pharmacoeconomic Evaluation Guidelines for Universal Health Coverage in China. *Value in Health Regional Issues*, 24, pp. 1–5. DOI:10.1016/j.vhri.2020.07.580.

Zhang, Ganggang, Jie Wu, and Qingyuan Zhu (2020) Performance evaluation and enrollment quota allocation for higher education institutions in China. *Evaluation and Program Planning*, 81, 101821. DOI:10.1016/j.evalprogplan.2020.101821.

Zhao, Fang, Jiayi Xu, and Guanfu Fang (2022) The heterogeneous effects of employment-based pension policies on employment: Evidence from urban China. *Journal of Asian Economics*, 78, 101420. DOI:10.1016/j.asieco.2021.101420.

Zhao, Yaohui, John Strauss, Gonghuan Yang, John Giles, Peifeng (Perry) Hu, Yisong Hu, Xiaoyan Lei, Man Liu, Albert Park, James P. Smith, Yafeng Wang (2013) *China Health and Retirement Longitudinal Study: 2011–2012 National Baseline User's Guide*. Beijing: National School of Development, Peking University.

Zhao, Yaohui, Yisong Hu, James P. Smith, John Strauss, Gonghuan Yang (2014) Cohort Profile: The China Health and Retirement Longitudinal Study (CHARLS), *International Journal of Epidemiology*, 43(1), pp. 61–68.

Zhou, Huan, Ruixue Ye, Sean Sylvia, Nathan Rose, and Scott Rozelle (2020) "At three years of age, we can see the future": Cognitive skills and the life cycle of rural Chinese children. *Demographic Research*, 43, pp. 169–182. DOI:10.4054/DemRes.2020.43.7.

Zhou, Mei, Shaoyang Zhao, and Mingwei Fu (2021) Supply-induced demand for medical services under price regulation: Evidence from hospital expansion in China. *China Economic Review*, 68, 101642. DOI:10.1016/j.chieco.2021.101642.

CHAPTER 10

Chinese Nationalism in the Era of Xi Jinping

Joanna Wardęga

Contemporary patriotic sentiments used by leaders of the Communist Party of China (CPC) to strengthen their power are creating anxiety around the world. However, the use of nationalism as a political tool in China is not a phenomenon that appeared with the start of Xi Jinping's rule. It did not even begin with China's economic growth, although it undoubtedly became more prominent in the early twentieth century. The resurgence of young Chinese nationalist sentiment captured major worldwide attention in 2008. That was an eventful year. In the early spring, the Chinese experienced the anti-Chinese reaction of the West to the Beijing Summer Olympic Games that they were so proud of. They began to be discouraged from using foreign media services perceived as hostile to their homeland, and even launched an anti-CNN campaign. In May, the nation united in the face of the tragedy of the Sichuan earthquake. In the summer, the Chinese celebrated the multilateral success of the 2008 Summer Olympics. It was certainly a favorable period for the rise of Chinese nationalism, but it was not its beginning. To fully understand this phenomenon, it is worth describing the historical background at least in outline, especially since many themes appear over and over again in Chinese nationalist discourse.

During the Imperial China period, nationalism did not yet exist; it was rather a kind of cultural chauvinism, defined by the term "culturalism" (Townsend, 1996: 11–14) or "Sinocentrism" (Kajdański, 2005: 241–242). It was based on the belief that the Chinese share a common, unique cultural heritage, while the peoples around them were considered culturally inferior. However, in the nineteenth century, the weakening of the state, violations of its sovereignty, unequal treaties, and territorial losses proved that it was impossible to maintain a belief in China's uniqueness and superiority. The decline of cultural chauvinism coincided with the birth of Western nationalism, while Sinocentrism was not in line with the modern understanding of the state and had to give way to the emerging Chinese nationalism. This early nationalism had two faces: it was directed against the Manchus ruling China, who were blamed for the weakness of the state, and against foreigners who made China a semi-colony, or, as Sun Yat-sen called it, a "hypo-colony" (Sun, 1927: 38–39), which was even more humiliating. Neither during the revolutionary movements nor after the overthrow of the empire was there a uniform vision of the emerging nation, and even after the establishment of the Republic of China, nationalism was not homogeneous in Chinese political discourse. For instance, liberal republicans favored civic nationalism, revolutionary Zhang Binglin referred to the "Chinese race" (de Barry and Lufrano, 1999: 309–310), and the communists viewed the nation from the perspective of social classes (Mao, 1999: 86–93). Some non-Han groups developed their own national consciousness and started striving for independence: so-called "small nationalisms" emerged (Duara, 1993: 9–32). Therefore, threat to territorial unity made it necessary to evolve the concept of the Chinese nation, which came to be seen as a political community rather than an ethnic one.

In the 1930s in the face of the Japanese invasion, the reference to nationalism brought the Communist Party of China popularity and an increased membership. After the victory in the civil war, the Maoists gained the right to define what the Chinese nation was and who could be included in it, as well as who should be considered an internal enemy and excluded from the community (Fitzgerald, 1999: 78–80). An external enemy, against whom the nation can define itself, can be useful to strengthen national spirit. Among these external enemies in the history of the People's Republic of China were, first of all, Japan and the United States, as well as the Soviet Union after the Sino-Soviet split in 1960. The concept of an enemy who oppressed the nation is essential for the nation to celebrate its liberation and appreciate the heroes, as the Communist Party presents its role in Chinese history.

The Chinese nation's definition was finally clarified as *Zhonghua minzu* (中华民族), a concept used by Liang Qichao for the first time in 1901 (Zheng, 2019). This term denotes the unity of the Chinese nation, consisting not only of Han Chinese but also of all other ethnic groups co-existing in the Chinese land. Nowadays in China, there is an understanding of the nation in both the political and cultural sense. It justifies the need for the unity of the Chinese state within borders that include not only the Han but also minorities, and not only the inhabitants of the People's Republic of China but also other territories and people of Chinese origin. The Greater China concept would include, in addition to the PRC, Hong Kong, Macau, Taiwan and, to some extent, the Chinese diaspora. Within the PRC, the Chinese nation includes not only Han Chinese but also 55 ethnic minorities. The right of non-Han peoples to self-determination is limited to a certain amount of autonomy that some of them may have obtained within the Chinese state. Han ethnocentrism, combined with unrealized independence or larger autonomy ambitions of some of the non-Han peoples, causes tensions between the Han majority and ethnic minorities. This seems to be all the more evident due to an assimilation policy based on the new policy of "deep mingling" (深度交融 *shendu jiaorong*) proposed by Xi Jinping (Wang, 2020).

As mentioned, the concept of Greater China is also directed outside the state. The unification of China (i.e., the inclusion of Hong Kong, Macau, and Taiwan) in the People's Republic of China has been the goal of all the Chinese communists from Mao Zedong to Xi Jinping. This pursuit was already partially successful when Hong Kong was returned to China in 1997, and Macao in 1999. According to mainland China's expectations, Taiwan should also "return" to the homeland, which was written in the preamble to the constitution (Constitution of the PRC, 1982). Greater China includes members of the Chinese diaspora as part of an imagined community united by common roots, a common culture and blood (Lu, 2014). However, emigrants were not always perceived in such a positive way. During the Ming and Qing dynasties, emigrants were considered contemptible for abandoning their homeland for the inferior – from a cultural chauvinism perspective – barbarian countries, and neglecting the spirits of their ancestors. In the PRC, until the end of the 1970s, Chinese from abroad were treated with some suspicion. It has changed since the inauguration of Deng Xiaoping's program of reforms and opening-up. The diaspora's involvement in Chinese affairs has been welcomed, in a sense that goes beyond economics, especially in the realization of Xi Jinping's great rejuvenation of the Chinese nation (Xi, 2017).

In 1978, Deng Xiaoping started the modernization processes and the opening-up policy. That was the beginning of profound transformations of the economic and social system and limited political changes. The passing of the first generation of communist leaders, the tragic legacy of the Cultural Revolution, the initiated reforms and opening policies, and the parallel influx of Western ideas led to the erosion of Maoist ideology. Even today, Mao's ideas remain among the flagship slogans in the ideology of the Communist Party of China and the Chinese constitution, but their real impact on social life is negligible. As a result, the existing ideological foundations of the ruling party began to shake. To maintain the legitimacy of its power, the CCP had to seek an alternative source of power. During the first decades of the modernization and opening policy, economic growth was used to build a positive image of the party, but it could not remain the source of its legitimacy forever. Nationalism seems to have become an important source of unity for Chinese society of all classes and ethnic backgrounds under the leadership of the CPC. This is, however, a different type of nationalism to that of the early days of the People's Republic of China. The patriotic attitude acquired a different meaning: it began to be associated primarily with supporting economic and technological development of China, opposing Western hegemonism, and striving to unify the country.

1 Patriotic Education in Different Dimensions

The events in Tiananmen Square in 1989 were considered a failure of indoctrination, and the authorities recognized the need to increase pressure on nationalism. The protesting youth was described as insufficiently patriotic and therefore vulnerable to foreign influences hostile to China. Patriotic education of young people was given additional importance as a preventive measure against possible further unrest. In April 1990, Deng Xiaoping supported the patriotic education campaign in a speech "Reviving the Chinese People" (振兴中华民族 *Zhenxing Zhonghua minzu*). He explained China's need for stability to continue its development, and the fact that only the CCP could guarantee such conditions (Deng, 1990). That implied that people who opposed the government would actually be standing up against the country. The peak of the patriotic education campaign coincided with the Hong Kong handover (Guo, 1998: 167). In the twenty-first century, students are exposed to patriotic education that goes beyond school lessons, including entertainment, multimedia, TV programs, movies, cartoons, and music.

Focus on the future and reclaiming China's past glory to its rightful place in the world is an important element of Chinese nationalism, but it also includes references to history, both glorified past and traumatic events. The memory of the past is not only passed on as part of the school curriculum of patriotic education but also presented in national museums and memorial sites across the country. The official historical narrative comprises carefully selected elements of history, both moments of national glory and martyrdom, which, as Ernest Renan (1994: 17–18) noted, is of particular importance for the national community. In the Chinese case, so-called the "century of humiliation" (百年国耻 *bainian guochi*) plays a major role. In official historiography, this is the period when the Chinese people were defeated by foreign forces. This period began with the Opium Wars, when China was downgraded from a powerful civilization to the position of "the sick man of Asia." According to the Maoist interpretation, the "century of humiliation" ended in 1949 with the victory of the communist revolution and Mao's declaration of China's reawakening. However, the Western world did not accept the shift in the balance of power, and, therefore, the struggle to remove the remains of the national humiliation was not yet over. This has become an important goal of Chinese foreign policy, along with full unification, and also remains the key historical narrative for Xi Jinping, who often refers to national humiliation and has proposed the China Dream (中国梦 *Zhongguo meng*) and "the great rejuvenation of the Chinese people" (中华民族伟大复兴 *Zhonghua minzu weida fuxing*). It is noteworthy that the concept of *bainian guochi* was not entirely negative, as it included a hope that the Chinese people would recover from humiliation. As the Chinese saying states, remembering past misfortunes helps you appreciate present happiness (忆苦思甜 *yi ku si tian*).

The Chinese authorities use numerous tools to implicate national values: the above-mentioned educational system, state media, public ceremonies, and political anniversaries, such as the recent 100th anniversary of the CPC, symbols, myths, national holidays, monuments and public buildings, as well as art, including cinematography. These works by the "engineers of the nation" can be perceived as instruments of social control, serving the ruling class to maintain and strengthen the legitimacy of its rule.

Cinema was used politically almost from the beginning of its existence. The Chinese communists efficiently developed film production and distribution channels to promote the achievements of the new regime. Today, the production of films promoting the CCP, socialism, and unity in multi-ethnic diversity, films about the history of the PRC, the heroism of the People's Liberation Army, the tragedies of the Sino-Japanese war, and the successes of modernization policy, is continued with the support of public funds. There are also movies about ancient China, showing the greatness of Chinese civilization and also praising authoritarian power. Celebrated historical anniversaries serve as a pretext to strengthen this message. Due to the 70th anniversary of the founding of the PRC, 2019 was a year for patriotic blockbusters such as the epic, seven-part anthology *My People, My Country* (我和我的祖国 *Wo he wo de zuguo*), which was followed by *My People, My Homeland* (我和我的家乡 *Wo he wo de jiaxiang*) and *My Country, my Parents* (我和我的父辈 *Wo he wo de fubei*). In 2021, a film celebrating the 100th anniversary of the founding of the Communist Party of China appeared: *1921*. One of the patriotic movies, the Korean War drama *The Battle at Lake Changjin* (长津湖 *Zhangjin Hu*) turned out to be the highest-grossing film in China that year. On the one hand, patriotic films carry a specific message addressed to the Chinese themselves, and on the other, they are considered as elements of Chinese soft power. Nevertheless, the effectiveness of Chinese soft power in this area is undoubtedly lower than that of the United States of America.

2 Good Government or "Without the Communist Party There Will Be Chaos"

According to traditional Chinese cosmology, the morality of the emperor, the Son of Heaven, and the proper observance of rituals were necessary to ensure balance in the natural world and society. The emperor should have special virtues, the most important of which were truth, benevolence, and glory. He should possess a true knowledge, revealed both through study, and through divination and astrology. The good ruler is characterized as presenting a proper attitude towards the people, compassionate and generous, as he should take care of the material needs of his subjects. The ruler should also secure the glory of Chinese civilization in the economic, political, and cultural dimensions; for example, by maintaining military power or domination over feudal states. As emphasized by the political scientist and sinologist Vivienne Shue (2004: 30–34), even after the fall of the empire, these three virtues – having true knowledge, being generous towards the people, and ensuring the glory of the nation – remained the determinants of the ideal moral government.

Since the time of Deng Xiaoping, real power has been "seeking truth in facts"; that is, rationalism and pragmatism. Being generous with the people has meant maintaining economic development and fighting corruption. The Chinese Dream concept announced by Xi Jinping has two dimensions: collective, consisting of building the country's strong position in the interest of all Chinese; and individual (i.e., building the prosperity of individual Chinese). These actions are to lead to "great rejuvenation of the Chinese nation." The current government is trying to show that it cares about society by fighting corruption, which has become a particularly important element of Xi's policy, and taking care of environmental protection. When it comes to securing the glory of Chinese civilization, the CPC sees itself as the only force that can defend Chinese honor internationally and further increase China's importance. Many actions are aimed at showing the Chinese that the party cares about the country's image in the international arena and is erasing past humiliations. The party also refers to Chinese heritage, emphasizing that it dates back 5000 years, which is also supposed to justify China's special place in the world. The government shows care for cultural heritage, unlike during the Cultural Revolution, protecting historical monuments, applying for entries on the UNESCO World Heritage List, and trying to recover lost historical artefacts from abroad (Kraus, 2010: 201–221). All these ideas can be found in the rhetoric of President Xi when he talks about the Chinese Dream.

At the heart of contemporary nationalism is the regime's claim that loving country and loving Communist Party are the same. Even during the reign of Mao, criticized old teachers who considered themselves patriots, were asked, "What country do you love? Communist or Guomindang?" (Fitzgerald, 1999: 84–85). At that time, patriotism did not mean love for the place of origin, rivers, land, and cities but love for the state ruled by specific authorities. Deng Xiaoping also asked:

> Is loving the motherland something abstract? If you don't love the new China led by the Communist Party, what motherland do you love? We do not ask all our patriotic compatriots in Xianggang (Hong Kong) and Aomen (Macao) and in Taiwan and abroad to support socialism, but at the least, they should not oppose socialist New China. Otherwise, how can they be called patriotic?
> HUGHES, 2006: 18–19

The narrative about the unique role of the party is also repeated by Xi Jinping, stating that "without the Communist Party of China, there would be no new China and no national rejuvenation" (CGTN, 2021). As Xi emphasizes, "Party, government, military, society, education, east, west, south, north, center, the party leads all" (党政军民学, 东西南北中, 党是领导一切的 *Dang zheng jun min xue, dong xi nan bei zhong, dang shi lingdao yiqie de*) (Xue, 2018).

Over the past decades, nationalism has been used by the Communist Party of China in its domestic and foreign policy. In the internal dimension, we can see the phenomena of the reconstruction of the Chinese nation. This policy can be understood through the theories of constructivism, which recognizes the nation as an ideological entity created by nationalism. The party, emphasizing its merits in creating the modern power of the state, refers to its history, party leaders of all generations, and the figure of Mao Zedong as the creator of the new China. Due to the popular sentiment towards the old, idealized times, this leader is not only portrayed as a national hero but sometimes treated as a "deity" in nationalist religion (Wardęga, 2012).

3   Popular Nationalism Meets Top-Down Nationalism

It cannot be denied that in China there is a strong, top-down nationalism of the Communist Party of China, developed through the entire state apparatus, and especially through the education system and media control. This type of nationalism can be considered a continuation of state-building nationalism prior to the founding of the People's Republic of China, although the form of the CPC's nationalism has changed since the 1940s.

The phenomenon of Chinese nationalism, however, is much too complex to be fully explained only as a phenomenon created from above and imposed on society. The activities of the CPC are accompanied by grassroots initiatives, movements, and social activities. A people's response to party nationalism is popular nationalism with slightly different characteristics. The spontaneity of this phenomenon should not be underestimated, although these movements are sometimes related to fostering nationalism by the Communist Party.

Bottom-up nationalism is a kind of safety valve, one of the few ways of expressing public opinion in China. This is particularly evident on the internet, where state censorship and manipulation exists, but the authorities leave a relatively large amount of freedom to nationalists. Web commentators were called "a new pattern of public opinion guidance" by President Hu Jintao (Bandurski, 2008). The internet seems to be a home for online activists, whose actions reflect the state-nationalist discourse. Some of the pro-Chinese and pro-party commentators, such as the so-called 50 Cent Party (五毛党 *wu mao dang*) are indeed being paid for their comments, but many of them operate on their own. There are netizens called "little pink" (小粉红 *xiao fenhong*) or young women active online, who use the term "big brother China" (阿中哥哥 *A Zhong gege*) and see the relationship between the motherland and the people as one of idol and fan, with a strong emotional connection.

Many Chinese people are truly passionate patriots, and thanks to China's impressive economic development and growing importance in international relations, they gain a genuine sense of pride in the achievements of their own nation. It is worth noting that Chinese online patriots come not only from mainland China but also from the diaspora and, therefore, are not solely dependent on the influence of official, party-controlled information channels and distortion of information. Among Chinese nationalists there are also young people returning from their studies in Western countries, and they often bring disappointment with the West. They see an economic miracle in China, its modern cities, advanced infrastructure, and high-speed railways, in which China is leading the way over other countries, so naturally they feel national pride. It gives them a sense of community.

This pride in being Chinese has gained a clear economic dimension in recent years, as it manifests itself in support for Chinese brands, Chinese design, and pride in innovation and product quality. Domestic sales and consumption are growing, which has been very important during the global economic crises of the early twenty-first century. There is also a clear revival in the fashion for Chinese traditional clothes, such as qipao, worn by the younger generation, who proudly present them on social media. Chinese live-streaming e-commerce leaders, such as Viya Huang or Li Jiaqi, are involved in the promotion and sale of local Chinese products.

The pride of the young generation feeds off a rising, assertive China, but at the same time, young Chinese nationalism is based on a strong sense of national degradation and humiliation, which is also experienced today from the West. It is not so much about the continuation of the "century of humiliation," which has long since passed thanks to the Communist Party, as the omnipresent propaganda teachings. It is mainly about the contemporary frustration that the West has not acknowledged that China has changed and cannot be underestimated and disregarded as it used to be. In this vision, China's enemies seek to break up the nation and weaken its economic power, using pretexts such as human rights. The voices of condemnation of Chinese politics around the world, such as those concerning Tibet, Xinjiang, economic domination, increasing armament, or environmental problems, are leading to an increase in anti-foreign sentiment. This perspective is a development and continuation of the "century of humiliation" that is sometimes more radical than the official narrative.

4 Chinese Nationalism with Xi's Thought Characteristics

In general, Chinese nationalism appears to be following a similar course under Xi Jinping's rule as in previous periods. However, two of its features have stood out in particular in recent years. Chinese nationalism is becoming more and more aimed at the domestic audience, not the foreign one, which may be driven by domestic insecurity (Weiss, 2020). Secondly, nationalist sentiment is becoming more and more apparent in Chinese society.

This does not mean that the Chinese authorities are not interested in how the world perceives China or that they have stopped trying to build a proper and true, according to them, image of China. Since the 2008 anti-CNN campaign, official criticisms of the international media for its coverage of China and accusations of anti-China bias seem to have become increasingly commonplace (Hewitt, 2011: 14–25). At least some ordinary citizens share the concern about foreign media objectivity towards China (Hewitt, 2011: 95–108). Chinese politician Zhu Muzhi, once a director of the State Council Information Office, said that some foreign countries "have prejudices or have wrongly believed rumors, therefore what they think about China is not the true image of China," and that is why Chinese journalists should "present a comprehensive and real picture of China to the outside world so that you can see the true image of China" (Parker, 1991). The role of the Chinese media is to influence the opinion of

Chinese society, but it also goes beyond the country's borders (Shan, 2014: 199). There are various media platforms whose task is to build China's international image: multilingual TV channels and China Radio International, printed publications, and online resources. China's efforts to influence how it is perceived on the international stage have been more visible in recent decades through its efforts to shape a positive image of a peace-loving country with rich culture and economic strength (Wang, 2003: 48–49). Attempts to use the soft power of Chinese culture and language are visible in the activities of the global network of more than 500 Confucius Institutes. However, the debate about these institutions in many Western countries has been mostly negative about the ties of the CIs to the Chinese authorities. Therefore it remains doubtful whether these efforts are working as expected (Jura and Kałużyńska, 2013; Wang, 2003). But maybe this message is simply meant for the diaspora and the internal audience, not for foreign ones?

The national dimension of nationalism seems to be more important. When the rulers use nationalism in their politics, the dangers of it being taken over by another political force appear. As a result, if such other actors proved to be more effective in empowering the Chinese people, they could assume legitimacy. Of course, in China there is no threat that a rival party will remove the Communist Party from power in elections. The threads criticizing the too-lenient attitude of the authorities were visible in popular publications as early as the 1990s. "Saying no" (说不 *shuo bu*) nationalism was based on national pride, and was radical, chauvinistic and critical of the Party's international politics, considered too conciliatory. Song Qiang (1996a, 1996b, 2009), the co-author of three manifesto books of this trend, spoke not of nationalism (民族主义 *minzu zhuyi*) but of a new patriotism (新爱国主义 *xin aiguo zhuyi*).

Nowadays, the image of assertive, even aggressive, diplomacy appears in the discussion of Chinese activities in the international arena. Harsh diplomacy, unofficially called "wolf warrior diplomacy," is a term borrowed from a nationalistic action movie (战狼, *Zhan Lang*, 2015). It includes assertive nationalism, attacking foreign critics, highlighting foreign shortcomings and has been clearly visible during the COVID-19 pandemic (Weiss, 2020). The reason for conducting wolf warrior diplomacy by Beijing might be an attempt to meet the expectations of the Chinese people (Wu, 2020), who demand "major country diplomacy" (大国外交 *daguo waijiao*), in the words of Xi Jinping (Chen, 2018).

Popular anger visible online and in nationalistic demonstrations can be seen as a factor that enables the tenacity of unelected leaders in diplomacy. Despite the risk of the nationalist social movement breaking free from any control, the Chinese authorities are often tempted to use this "people's voice" as a justification for various actions in their foreign policy. The reference in diplomacy to anti-foreign protests may be a double-edged sword. Repressing anti-foreign demonstrations could help create an image of a moderate authority in relations with foreign countries. On the other hand, the CPC may be accused by its own citizens of being unpatriotic. Party leaders seem aware that people cannot be completely silenced. However, their tactics towards self-organizing grassroots nationalists and their antiforeign protests vary over time, as well as in relation to the specific countries against which the demonstrators are protesting (Weiss, 2014: 219–220).

Japan has been a particularly frequent target of protests in China. As early as the 1990s, there were protests demanding recovery of the uninhabited islets and rocks in the East China Sea administered by Japan and called the Senkaku Islands in Japan, and of the Diaoyu Islands in the PRC. Large-scale demonstrations against Japan's bid for a permanent seat at the UN Security Council broke out across China in 2005; at the same time, a number of online petitions against such a decision circulated on the internet. At the time, the PRC's diplomats to the United Nations launched a sort of moral offensive. They spoke out very frequently, criticizing Japan's revisionist policy, Tokyo's approval of a new history textbook that ignored Japan's wartime atrocities, visits by the Japanese prime minister and high officials to Yasukuni shrine, which commemorates fourteen A-class war criminals among other Japanese war causalities, lack of compensation for war-time sex slaves, unlawful seizure of the Diaoyu Islands, etc. In the same year, a wave of more or less spontaneous protests swept through many Chinese cities, demanding that the islands of Diaoyu/Senkaku be joined to China and opposing attempts to whitewash history in Japanese school textbooks, as well as official visits to Yasukuni. There were also social campaigns encouraging the boycott of Japanese goods. These actions took place with the quiet consent of the authorities. In the next few years, Chinese and Japanese governments sought to repair bilateral ties, and the Chinese authorities prevented large-scale anti-Japanese protests and censored nationalist content on the internet. During the trawler collision incident near the disputed Diaoyu/Senkaku islands in 2010, there were efforts to restrain anti-Japanese demonstrations. Tokyo's purchase of three of the Diaoyu/Senkaku Islands led to violent anti-Japanese demonstrations and riots in 2012 and 2013. Chinese patriotic citizens called for a boycott of Japanese products again. At that time, a combination of central diplomatic actions with grassroots activities was observed, and the Chinese foreign minister refused to condemn the protesters. The problem of disputed islands and historical Sino-Japanese problems returns every few years, and the tendency of the authorities to repress nationalist sentiments or – on the contrary – to tolerate or even strengthen them, along with the assertive diplomacy, seems to depend on current foreign policy goals.

The anti-American protests, which also sometimes take harsh forms of street protests, can be viewed in a similar way. In 1999, after the mistaken bombing of the Chinese embassy in Belgrade by NATO planes, the authorities did not interfere in grassroots protests in front of the US Embassy and consulates for two days. The then Chinese vice president, Hu Jintao, supported the legal demonstrations which "fully reflected the Chinese people's great fury at the atrocity of the embassy attacks by NATO and the Chinese people's strong patriotism" (CNN, 1999). It was not until the unrest began to threaten international trade and tourism that President Hu Jintao appeared on television to calm the atmosphere. Non-governmental nationalists criticized the authorities for agreeing to pay the American side compensation for the damage to American consulates that took place during the protests (Zhao, 2005). Similarly, in 2001, after a collision between American and Chinese aircraft over the South China Sea, the authorities initially acted to intensify the protests and did not present the US president's apology in state-owned media. When the patriotic demonstrations grew stronger, the Chinese authorities began to criticize them. However, some topics, such as the condemnation of American imperialism and mourning the martyred Chinese pilot, were kept up. During both these events, Chinese cyber-nationalists became active simultaneously with the protests in the streets. Patriotically motivated hackers called "red hackers" (红客 *hong ke*) attacked, among others, the websites of the White House and the US embassy in Beijing, and blocked several hundred other sites.

Later, anti-American themes appeared in various protests. In 2016, large demonstrations were organized following the ruling by the Permanent Court of Arbitration in The Hague rejecting China's territorial claims to nearly the entire South China Sea. The state media defined the verdict as the result of a conspiracy by the US, but when the protests took a sharp course – for instance, against the KFC fast-food chain – the state-owned media tried to calm the mood, emphasizing that destroying the property of other Chinese in the name of patriotism is not patriotic (Jun, 2017). During the tensions between China and Korea over US deployment over Terminal High Altitude Area Defense (THAAD) in 2017 and 2018, a combination of the state's reaction and various state-dependent institutions with grass-roots actions was visible. It soon influenced cultural and economic exchange between China and Korea: cultural exchange, including concerts by popular K-pop artists, was suppressed by the authorities; Korean dramas were removed from television; and group travel to Korea was banned. The grassroots nationalists organized anti-South Korea protests, including protest action in front of supermarkets of the Lotte

Corporation, and encouraged boycotts of Korean brands (Glaser, Sofio and Parker, 2017).

Chinese tourists also become pawns in the nationalist game. The growth of the middle class in China is influencing the number of wealthy Chinese tourists traveling abroad, so the possibilities for the Chinese authorities to use their economic strength to "punish" an unfriendly country are also increasing. When political tensions arise, some individual tourists give up traveling to countries that are considered hostile towards their homeland, not for security reasons but because they do not want to be condemned as unpatriotic (Cheng, Wong and Prideaux, 2016). Due to the intensification of the Sino-Japanese conflict over the Diaoyu/Senkaku islands in 2012 and 2013, the number of departures to Japan dropped significantly (Fu, 2012). Individual decisions were supported by state-owned tourism institutions that stopped promoting tours to Japan and offered full reimbursement for cancelled trips to Japan. In 2014 and 2015, due to the conflict over the islands in the South China Sea, the number of Chinese visiting the Philippines dropped significantly (Department of Tourism, 2021). The crisis in Sino-Korean relations related to the THAAD shield also had an impact. Interest in Korea among the Chinese was related to, inter alia, the popularity of the South Korean popular culture (한류 *Hallyu*) and, as a result, Chinese tourists outnumbered the previously dominant Japanese there. However, from the second half of 2016, the number of departures to South Korea began to decline. The largest outflow was recorded in March 2017, immediately after the Korean government's official decision to install the shield, and the crisis continued for a year. In the most difficult months, the number of tourists dropped by 70 percent compared to the previous year (Wardęga, 2021: 148–151).

Patriotism can be expressed through economic issues and consumer behavior not only in the field of tourism. Economic pressure manifests itself in the boycotts of some companies, initiated on the internet. It seems that most Chinese cyber-nationalists are not passive executors of the CPC's notions but rather members of a community gathering online that responds spontaneously to real or imagined hostility towards China. Young Chinese often support boycotts against foreign brands, companies, and celebrities who are believed to have offended the Chinese people. Many of the cases of such insults relate to the recognition of Taiwan as independent from China. In 2018 Marriott apologized for the mistake, as the company listed as independent countries not only Taiwan but also Tibet, Hong Kong, and Macau, as did Qantas and Delta airlines, which described Tibet and Taiwan as countries on their websites (Chan, 2018). In 2021, John Cena apologized, and did so in quite fluent Chinese, for calling Taiwan a country, which could have jeopardized the popularity of the movie *Fast and Furious 9* in China. The delicacy of the Tibet issue forced Daimler to apologize in 2018 for posting a quote from the Dalai Lama on its social media, as outrage by Chinese internet users threatened its luxury cars sales in China. During the protests following the Hong Kong government's announcement of the "Fugitive Offenders and Mutual Legal Assistance in Criminal Matters Legislation (Amendment) Bill" in 2019, support for these protests was also considered hostile to China. The NBA decided to cut off from the views of Daryl Morey, manager of the Houston Rockets, who tweeted support for Hong Kong's pro-democracy protesters. The Western media's coverage of human rights in Xinjiang is also a sensitive issue not only for the authorities but also for Chinese nationalists. In 2021, the US announced a ban on the import of Xinjiang cotton due to Uyghurs' forced-labor, and several clothing companies announced that for ethical reasons they would not use cotton from the region. Chinese consumer boycotts have hit H&M, Burberry, Tommy Hilfiger, Hugo Boss, Adidas, and Nike. Dozens of Chinese celebrities withdrew from their advertisements, and campaigns to support Xinjiang cotton were organized all over China.

Economic blackmail can be also used at the highest, state level to achieve a country's goals internationally. The most famous such cases are the Chinese ban on Norwegian whole-salmon imports in retaliation for the 2010 Nobel Peace Prize for Liu Xiaobo, restrictions on coal imports from Australia in 2020 after it demanded an international investigation into the origins of the COVID-19 virus, and trade sanctions taken against Lithuania in 2021, when the country agreed to open a Taiwanese Representative Office in Vilnius.

In the context of economy, the role of the Chinese diaspora should be mentioned. In Southeast Asia, the Chinese have constituted significant minorities. In 2011 Chinese in Asian countries made up as much as 75% of the entire foreign population. Indonesia is home to the largest number of Chinese: 8 million (almost a fifth of the total diaspora), followed by Thailand with 7.5 million, and Malaysia with 6.5 million (Poston and Wong, 2016: 356). Many ethnic Chinese in Southeast Asia achieved high economic status. Formerly, Chinese leaders, such as Zhou Enlai, advised them to assimilate in a new country. However, from the early years of reform and opening-up, Chinese expatriates were encouraged to invest in their homeland and bring know-how to China.

In the past, in Indonesia and Malaysia, isolation from the environment and cultivated cultural and religious separation in combination with control over a disproportionately large part of the economy contributed to the development of anti-Chinese sentiments, laws discriminating against Chinese and even persecution of them. At present, concern about China's growing international influence has increased the suspicions that the Chinese authorities will mobilize people of Chinese origin to take pro-China activities in other countries.

Even though the Chinese diaspora is diverse in terms of the level of their assimilation, national identity, and views on the authorities in Beijing, their loyalty to the host country is sometimes questioned by the fellow citizens.

Xi Jinping sees the importance of overseas Chinese as a support in the rejuvenation of the Chinese nation. At the seventh Conference for Friendship of Overseas Chinese Associations (世界华侨华人社团联谊大会 *Shijie Huaqiao Huaren Shetuan Lianyi Dahui*) in 2014 Xi mentioned "tens of millions of overseas Chinese (海外侨胞 *haiwai qiaobao*) all over the world, members of the big Chinese family", and that they "were aware of the Chinese blood in their veins" and "have been faithful to the traditions of their ancestors". Xi described the "enthusiastic support of the compatriots for the cause of Chinese revolution, construction and reform, and contribution to the development and growth of the Chinese nation, and the promotion of the motherland" (Lu, 2014). The Chinese diaspora abroad has been mobilized to become part of the Chinese Dream both by investing and acting as advocates for Chinese interests abroad (Nawrotkiewicz, 2021).

Nowadays, many of the *haiwai qiaobao* visit the homeland of their ancestors, renew contacts with distant families, learn Mandarin Chinese, and send their children to study in the PRC. The involvement of the diaspora is also symbolic. Their solidarity is revealed through demonstrations of support for China – for example, during the 2008 Olympic Games – when they stood in opposition to the protests of human rights defenders and supporters of an independent Tibet. This solidarity is also visible (at least in declaration) the other way around, and was particularly well seen during the COVID-19 outbreak, when attacks against ethnically Chinese individuals residing in Western countries caused outrage and a harsh reaction from the Chinese public.

Among the measures of patriotism there is also the defense of Chinese culture. In 2018, Dolce & Gabbana (D&G) put out a series of advertisements for its fashion show. In the ads, a Chinese woman was eating Italian food with chopsticks, which was considered racist and ridiculing Chinese culture. In response to online criticism, the withdrawal of Chinese celebrities from the fashion show, and a boycott of D&G products by Chinese consumers, the fashion house was forced to react. The company issued an immediate apology and explanations about the hacking attack on Stefano Gabbana's account, which included a comment that was particularly offensive to China and the Chinese. Nothing helped the brand to regain its image. As a result, Dolce & Gabbana lost its position among the dominant luxury brands (Parker, 2019).

The internet also becomes a public shaming arena when a member of a national community is caught being disloyal to the nation. In 2008, Chinese student Wang Qianyuan was targeted for an online "human flesh search engine"

(人肉搜索 renrou sousuo). For her attempts to mediate between Chinese and Tibetan students during an anti-China demonstration on the Duke University campus in Durham, she was denounced as a traitor. Details of her identity have been disclosed on the internet. Even her parents living in China were forced to go into hiding for some time (Dewan, 2008). During the pandemic, even mild criticism of the officials' early handling of the coronavirus problem by writer Fang Fang from Wuhan was depicted as an unpatriotic act, and Fang was called a traitor. Such events may seem trivial compared to big politics, but they stimulate the actions of Chinese nationalists no less than the problems of Taiwan or Hong Kong (Deng and Lin, 2020).

•••

Another Chinese proverb says that "the water that bears the boat is the same that swallows it up" (水能载舟亦能覆舟 shui neng zai zhou, yi neng fu zhou). Even within China, there appear voices warning against indulging domestic populism and leniency towards extreme nationalism. He Yiting, former executive vice-president of the Central Party School, said that China should "continue to expand opening-up, actively and prudently handle relations with major countries, and prevent the rise of domestic populism" (Wang, 2021). Political scientist Zhang Ming said, "[The authorities] will keep using the weapon of nationalism, but it seems they want to control it so it won't backfire. And that is very difficult to do" (Jun, 2017). It seems the party is trying to control the dragon it has awakened.

Finally, it is worth emphasizing the role of the West in strengthening nationalism in China. The sources of the first explosion of national sentiment in republican China, the May Fourth Movement in 1919, were the decisions of the Paris Peace Conference, which were unfavorable to China: former German territories in Shandong were granted to Japan, and the Chinese voice was ignored. However, the sense of injustice being done to China by the West is not just about history. It reappears with every exhortation and instruction directed towards Beijing by Western leaders, defenders of Uighur rights in Xinjiang, supporters of Tibetan independence, etc. Demonstrations in defense of human rights in China organized in the West are perceived as an interference in China's internal affairs by both the Western authorities and by ordinary citizens, and they intensify the xenophobic mood. This was the perception of the intentions to boycott the 2008 Olympic Games, and it should be expected that the diplomatic boycotts of the 2022 Winter Games will be perceived in a similar way. Treating Chinese nationalists as manipulated, deprived of free will CPC marionettes and not as conscious citizens and patriots is self-deception.

Meanwhile, more and more Chinese are simply aware of the power and importance of their own state, as well as of injustice in mutual relations with Western countries. Even without being supporters of the Communist Party, they may appreciate that the Chinese leaders are trying to force the world to return to the "proper" system of international relations.

References

Bandurski, David (2008) China's Guerrilla War for the Web. *Far Eastern Economic Review,* 6(171), p. 41.

CGTN (2021) Without the CPC, there would be no New China and no national rejuvenation: Xi, 9 October, https://news.cgtn.com/news/2021-10-09/Without-the-CPC-no-New-China-and-no-national-rejuvenation-Xi-14dsV3qEpP2/index.html, accessed 10 December 2021.

Chan, Tara Francis (2018) 'Economic blackmail': Zara, Qantas, Marriott and Delta Air Lines reverse position on Taiwan for fear of angering China. *Insider,* 17 January, https://www.businessinsider.com/zara-marriott-qantas-apologized-to-china-listing-taiwan-as-country-2018-1?IR=T, accessed 10 December 2021.

Chen Xiangyang (2018) Xi Jinping waijiao sixiang zhiyin xin shidai Zhongguo tese daguo waijiao. *Zhongguo Wang,* 9 August, http://www.china.com.cn/opinion/2018-08/09/content_58290909.htm, accessed 10 December 2021.

Cheng Mingming, Anthony IpKin Wong and Bruce Prideaux (2016) Political Travel Constraint: The Role of Chinese Popular Nationalism. *Journal of Travel & Tourism Marketing,* 34(3), pp. 383–397, DOI:10.1080/10548408.2016.1182456, accessed 10 December 2021.

CNN (1999) China gives green light to embassy protests, but warns against violence. 9 May, http://edition.cnn.com/WORLD/asiapcf/9905/09/china.protests.02/, accessed 10 December 2021.

Constitution of the People's Republic of China, adopted on 4 December 1982, http://www.npc.gov.cn/zgrdw/englishnpc/Constitution/node_2825.htm, accessed 10 December 2021.

de Bary, William Theodore and Richard Lufrano (eds.) (1999) *Sources of Chinese Tradition.* New York: Columbia University Press.

Deng Chao and Liza Lin (2020) In Xi Jinping's China, Nationalism Takes a Dark Turn. *The Wall Street Journal,* 22 October, https://www.wsj.com/articles/in-xi-jinpings-china-nationalism-takes-a-dark-turn-11603382993, accessed 10 December 2021.

Deng Xiaoping (1990) *Zhenxing Zhonghua minzu (1990 nian 4 yue 7 ri),* http://www.reformdata.org/1990/0407/1795.shtml, accessed 10 December 2021.

Department of Tourism, Republic of the Philippines (2021) Tourism Demand Statistics, http://www.tourism.gov.ph/tourism_dem_sup_pub.aspx, accessed 10 December 2021.

Dewan, Shaila (2008) Chinese Student in US Is Caught in Confrontation. *New York Times*, 17 April, https://www.nytimes.com/2008/04/17/us/17student.html?pagewanted=all, accessed 10 December 2021.

Duara, Prasenjit (1993) Provincial Narratives of the Nation: Centralism and Federalism in Republican China. In: Harumi Befu (ed.) *Cultural Nationalism in East Asia: Representation and Identity*. Berkeley: Institute of East Asian Studies, pp. 9–32.

Fitzgerald, John (1999) The Nationless State: The Search for a Nation in Modern Chinese Nationalism. In: Jonathan Unger (ed.) *Chinese nationalism*. New York, London: M.E. Sharpe, pp. 56–85.

Fu Guangyun (2012) Jingji shuaitui neng fou ci xing Riben. *Guoji Jinrong*, 10 October, http://paper.people.com.cn/gjjrb/html/2012-10/10/content_1123586.htm, accessed 10 December 2021.

Glaser, Bonnie S., Daniel G. Sofio and David A. Parker (2017) The Good, the THAAD, and the Ugly China's Campaign Against Deployment, and What to Do About It. *Foreign Affairs*, 15 February, https://www.foreignaffairs.com/articles/united-states/2017-02-15/good-thaad-and-ugly, accessed 10 December 2021.

Guo Yingjie (1998) Patriotic Villains and Patriotic Heroes: Chinese Literary Nationalism in the1990s. In: William Safran (ed.) *Nationalism and Ethnoregional Identities in China*. London–New York: Routledge, pp. 163–188.

Hewitt, Duncan (2011) *International media coverage of China: Chinese perceptions and the challenges for foreign journalists*. Reuters Institute for the Study of Journalism, https://reutersinstitute.politics.ox.ac.uk/sites/default/files/2018-11/International_media_coverage_of_China.pdf, accessed 10 December 2021.

Hughes, Christopher R. (2006) *Chinese Nationalism in the Global Era*. London–New York: Routledge.

Jun Mai (2017) China vows to nip patriotic protests in the bud to maintain stability. *South China Morning Post*, 13 January, https://www.scmp.com/news/china/policies-politics/article/2061884/china-fears-sovereignty-rows-neighbours-may-spark, accessed 10 December 2021.

Jura, Jarosław and Kaja Kałużyńska (2013) Not Confucius, nor Kung Fu: Economy and Business as Chinese Soft Power in Africa. *African East-Asian Studies. The China Monitor*, 201(1), pp. 42–69.

Kajdański, Edward (2005) *Chiny. Leksykon. Historia, gospodarka, kultura*. Warsaw: Książka i Wiedza.

Kraus, Richard (2010) The politics of art repatriation: nationalism, state legitimation, and Beijing's looted zodiac animal heads. In: Peter Gries and Stanley Rosen (eds.) *Chinese Politics. State, society and the market*. Abingdon: Routledge, pp. 199–221.

Lu Jia (2014) Xi Jinping huijian di qi jie Shijie Huaqiao Huaren Shetuan Lianyi Dahui daibiao, The State Council of the People's Republic of China website, 6 June, http://www.gov.cn/xinwen/2014-06/06/content_2695778.htm, accessed 10 June 2022.

Mao Tse-Tung (1999) On Tactics Against Japanese Imperialism (December 27, 1935). In: Mao Tse-Tung and Stuart R. Schram (eds.) *Mao's Road to Power: Revolutionary Writings 1912–1949. Tom 5.* New York: M.E. Sharpe, pp. 86–93.

Nawrotkiewicz, Joanna (2021) Beyond Patriotic Education: Mobilizing Chinese Diaspora in Thailand. *Centre for Asian Affairs Papers*, https://www.osa.uni.lodz.pl/fileadmin/user_upload/Jednostki/Osrodek_Spraw_Azjatyckich/CAA_Papers/2021/CAA_Paper_JN_March_2021.pdf, accessed 10 June 2022.

Parker, Jeffrey K. (1991) New propaganda office pledges 'true image' of China', *UPI News Agency*, 13 June, https://www.upi.com/Archives/1991/06/13/New-propaganda-office-pledges-true-image-of-China/2314676785600/, accessed 10 December 2021.

Parker, Olivia (2019) Dolce & Gabbana Falls 140 Places in Asia's Top 1000 Brand Ranking. *Jing Daily*, 18 June, https://jingdaily.com/dolce-gabbana-brand-ranking/, accessed 10 December 2021.

Poston, Dudley L Jr, Juyin Helen Wong (2016) The Chinese diaspora: The current distribution of the overseas Chinese population. *Chinese Journal of Sociology*, 2(3), pp. 348–373. DOI:10.1177/2057150x16655077.

Renan, Ernest (1994) Qu'est-ce qu'une nation? In: John Hutchinson and Anthony Smith (eds.) *Nationalism*. Oxford–New York: Oxford University Press, pp. 17–18.

Shan Shi-lian (2014) Chinese cultural policy and the cultural industries. *City, Culture and Society* 5(3), pp. 115–121. DOI: 10.1016/j.ccs.2014.07.004, accessed 10 December 2021.

Shue, Vivienne (2004) Legitimacy Crisis in China? In: Peter Hays Gries and Stanley Rosen (eds.) *State and Society in 21st Century China: Crisis, Contention, and Legitimation*. New York-London: Routledge, pp. 24–49.

Song Qiang, Huang Jisu, Song Xiaojun, Wang Xiaodong, Liu Yang (2009) *Zhongguo bu gaoxing: da shidai, da mubiao ji women de neiyouwaihuan*. Beijing: Jiangsu Renmin Chubanshe.

Song Qiang, Zhang Zangzang, Qiao Bian, Gu Qingsheng (1996a) *Zhongguo keyi shuo: bu. Lengzhanhou shidai de zhengzhi yu qinggan jueze*. Beijing: Zhonghua Gongshanglian Lianhe Chubanshe.

Song Qiang, Zhang Zangzang, Qiao Bian, Gu Qingsheng (1996b) *Zhongguo haishi neng shuo bu*. Beijing: Zhongguo Wenlian Chubanshe.

Sun Yat-sen (1927) *San Min Chu I: The Three Principles of the People*. Shanghai: China Committee, Institute of Pacific Relations.

Townsend, James (1996) Chinese nationalism. In: Jonathan Unger (ed.) *Chinese nationalism*. New York, London: M.E. Sharpe, pp. 1–30.

Wang Hongying (2003) National Image Building and Chinese Foreign Policy. *China: An International Journal* 1(1), pp. 46–72. DOI:10.1353/chn.2005.0019.

Wang Zhewu (2020) Chunfeng huaru run bianjiang – lici zhongyang Xinjiang gongzuo zuotan hui huigu. *Kunlun Wang Xinjiang Dangjian Wang*, 1 December, http://www.xjkunlun.cn/dswx/dszl/90810.htm, accessed 10 December 2021.

Wang, Amber (2021) China must watch for signs of rising nationalism spurred by tensions with the West, warns former top official. *South China Morning Post*, 10 March, https://www.scmp.com/news/china/politics/article/3124899/china-must-watch-signs-rising-nationalism-spurred-tensions-west?module=inline&pgtype=article, accessed 10 December 2021.

Wardęga, Joanna (2012) Mao Zedong in present-day China – forms of deification. *Politics and Religion*, 2 (VI), pp. 181–197.

Wardęga, Joanna (2021) Znaczenie turystyki dla międzynarodowej pozycji Chin. In: Hanna Kupś, Maciej Szatkowski, Michał Dahl (eds.) *70 lat Chińskiej Republiki Ludowej w ujęciu interdyscyplinarnym*. Warszawa: Wydawnictwo Akademickie Dialog, pp. 135–158.

Weiss, Jessica Chen (2014) *Powerful Patriots: Nationalist Protest in China's Foreign Relations*. Oxford: Oxford University Press.

Weiss, Jessica Chen (2020) China's Self-Defeating Nationalism. *Foreign Affairs*, 16 July, https://www.foreignaffairs.com/articles/china/2020-07-16/chinas-self-defeating-nationalism, accessed 10 December 2021.

Wu Jing (director) (2015) *Zhan lang* [Motion picture]. China: Spring Era Films.

Wu Wendy (2020) Is it time for China to leash its Wolf Warrior diplomats? *South China Morning Post*, 12 August, https://www.scmp.com/news/china/diplomacy/article/3097134/it-time-china-leash-its-wolf-warrior-diplomats?module=inline&pgtype=article, accessed 10 December 2021.

Xi Jinping (2017) Full text of Xi Jinping's report at 19th CPC National Congress. Secure a Decisive Victory in Building a Moderately Prosperous Society in All Respects and Strive for the Great Success of Socialism with Chinese Characteristics for a New Era. Delivered at the 19th National Congress of the Communist Party of China. *China Daily*, 4 November, https://www.chinadaily.com.cn/china/19thcpcnationalcongress/2017-11/04/content_34115212.htm, accessed 10 June 2022.

Xue Wangbo (2018) Zenyang renshi "dang shi lingdao yiqie de" xie ru dangzhang? *Zhongguo Gongchandang Xinwen Wang*, http://cpc.people.com.cn/n1/2018/0125/c123889-29787340.html, accessed 10 December 2021.

Zhao Suisheng (2005) Nationalism's Double Edge. *The Wilson Quarterly*, 29(4), pp. 76–82, https://www.jstor.org/stable/40261493, accessed 10 December 2021.

Zheng Dahua (2019) Modern Chinese nationalism and the awakening of self-consciousness of the Chinese Nation. *International Journal of Anthropology and Ethnology*, 11(3). DOI:10.1186/s41257-019-0026-6.

CHAPTER 11

Competition in the National College Entrance Examination and Disparity of Access to Elite Higher Education in China

Tanja Carmel Sargent, Karen Hao and Fei Wang

1   Introduction

From June 7th to June 8th, 2022 the Chinese nation was once again preoccupied with the annual National College Entrance Examination (高考 *gaokao*). This year, President Xi Jinping offered guidance and advice to exam takers. Xi wished to downplay the hierarchy of the higher education institutions in China saying: "We should support qualified colleges and universities in their efforts to grow into leading institutions. But we should not place them in a hierarchy, rather we should encourage each college or university to highlight its own strengths and strive to build first-class disciplines and facilities" (China Daily, 2022). This is at the heart of Xi's Double First-Class (双一流 *shuang yiliu*) Project that aims to raise the quality of higher education in China by increasing the number of world class institutions and disciplines across the nation. With respect to the *gaokao* takers, Xi also expressed his hopes that students would "not only concentrate on book knowledge but also care about the people, the country and the world, and assume [their] responsibility for society" (China Daily, 2022). This latter sentiment captures the concern of China's leaders that the competitiveness of the *gaokao* has led to an overemphasis on teaching and learning for the test that has had a negative impact on the quality of education and the development of the whole person.

A key element of Xi Jinping Thought has been the pursuit of 'common prosperity' (共同繁荣 *gongtong fanrong*) which aims to counteract the widening social inequality brought about by the decades of market reform that have made China the economic powerhouse that it is today (Dunford, 2022). The dilemmas surrounding reform of the examination system in China are intimately tied to the tensions between excellence and equity that are inherent in the Chinese education system. The national college entrance examination has served as a key mechanism for social selection and mobility in Chinese society. It has been the prime instrument used in the centralized allotment of spaces in the stratified system of Chinese higher education. The competitiveness of the *gaokao* in China has also been an important reason for increased numbers of Chinese international students in universities around the globe (Fong, 2011). Chinese students make up the majority of the international students studying around the world (IIE Open Doors, 2021) and, while there are a number of motivations for Chinese students and their families to make this choice, the number one reason cited by the International Institute for Education has been "limited places available to study at (highly prestigious) universities in the home country" (Chao, 2018).

In recent decades, China has seen an enormous expansion in the massification of higher education and, as a result, college graduates have been having an even more difficult time securing stable employment especially in their desired fields (Bai, 2006; Ma, 2019; MyCOS Research, 2017; Ren, 2022). As a result of the difficulties of employment, the expansion of higher education opportunity has, paradoxically, increased the competition to enter into an elite university due to the fact that graduation from an elite university in China has come to be perceived as the only means of conferring employment opportunities post-graduation (Bai, 2006). Indeed, empirical studies have confirmed that top-tier university graduates in China earn more, and find greater job satisfaction, than graduates from lower tier universities (Hartog, Sun and Ding, 2010). The stakes are highest for working class and rural Chinese families who see success in the exams as a way out of a life of toil and manual labor but who are also underrepresented in institutions of higher education, most especially in elite institutions (Jia and Ericson, 2017; Li et al., 2015). In addition to the inevitable inequality in access to higher education by social background, there are systemic interprovincial differences in *gaokao* competitiveness that result from the hierarchical system of higher education; the uneven distribution of institutions of higher education across China; preferential university admissions policies for local residents; the centralized allotment of provincial quotas for spots in elite institutions of higher education, as well as trends in the centralization and decentralization of the administration of *gaokao* format and content.

Haifeng Liu and Qiong Wu (2006) review the history of the development and evolution of the *gaokao* and describe its positive role in Chinese society for the promotion of meritocracy and social mobility; as a motivational tool for the promotion of learning and literacy throughout society; and as a powerful mechanism for translating educational policy into educational practice. They also describe the negative consequences of the national college entrance examination system, including the degree to which severe *gaokao* competition affects the quality of education due to heavy over-emphasis on teaching to the test, and heavy workloads and pressures on students and teachers with resulting negative effects on mental and physical health (Liu and Wu, 2006).

In recognition of the trickle-down effect of the *gaokao* on educational quality – including test-oriented teaching methods, the narrowing of curriculum content, and a negative impact on student well-being – in the year 2000, the government instituted a series of ambitious educational reforms, known as the New Curriculum Reforms (新课程改革 *Xin Kecheng Gaige*) (Dello-Iacovo, 2009). The aims of the reforms were to facilitate a shift from examination-oriented education to quality (素质 *suzhi*)-oriented education that focused on the development of the whole child, reduced the study burden, and fostered such capacities as creativity, innovation, collaboration, self-expression, engagement, enjoyment of learning, inquiry skills, problem-solving abilities, and ability to apply knowledge in practice (Guan and Meng, 2007). The plan also included reforms to the administration and content of the *gaokao* including decentralization, to the provincial level, of textbook selection and examination format and content. As a result, the structure of the *gaokao* varied considerably across the provinces and this stimulated public debate about the ways in which the New Curriculum Reforms and the implementation of the "new *gaokao*" were affecting inter-provincial competition for university spaces.

In spite of over two decades of New Curriculum Reform implementation, the importance of the *gaokao* as a means of selection into higher education has not diminished. The *gaokao* remains a highly trusted social institution and is viewed as a rare fair and equitable pathway in Chinese society for individuals to control their own fate rather than rely on social connections (Liu and Wu, 2006; Zheng, 2010). As the saying goes "everyone is equal in front of the test scores" (分数面前人人平等 *fenshu mianqian ren ren pingdeng*) (Liu and Wu, 2006: 12). These attitudes, notwithstanding, interprovincial disparity in *gaokao* competitiveness, which translates into inequality of access to elite higher education, is common knowledge in China (Zheng, 2010; Fu, 2018), but is not well-documented in the international literature.

At the heart of questions about promoting greater equality in *gaokao* competition and access to higher education in China is the system of provincial quotas for university spaces. In May 2019, just before the *gaokao*, an incident captured public attention in China. Thirty two top students from Hebei Province, who were determined to get spots at one of the two top universities in China, Beijing University and Qinghua, managed to change their household registration (户口 *hukou*) and student residency (学籍 *xueji*) in order to be eligible to sit for the *gaokao* in Guangdong Province under the name of a private school, Fu Yuan High School in Shenzhen. The school hoped to benefit by increasing the rate of entry of its students into elite universities, and the students hoped to benefit from the lower scores required for entry into elite universities for students from Guangdong Province relative to the scores needed for students from Hebei Province. This incident stimulated heated debate across the nation. On the one hand, parents in Guangdong were enraged that these Hebei students illegally tried to use spaces from the Guangdong provincial quota for entry into elite higher education; on the other hand, the incident raised emotions around the issue of inequality in *gaokao* competition according to province of origin (Huxiu, 2019).

Up until now, a clear description of the *gaokao* process and its role in the distribution of access to elite higher education in China is lacking in the international literature. This paper provides a background overview of the nature of *gaokao* competition and university enrollment policy in China.

We investigate the following research questions:
1. To what extent is there a difference in the intensity of *gaokao* competition across provinces in China?
2. What has been the impact of recent *gaokao* reforms on inter-provincial differences in *gaokao* competition?

In this paper, we draw on both international and Chinese academic literature; policy documents; official websites, including the Ministry of Education of China website, Provincial Education Department websites, and the websites of individual higher education institutions; other online media sources; and publicly available census data and university enrollment data from 2013 to investigate the degree of equality in *gaokao* competition by province of origin of the examinee. We organize our investigation of the changing social landscape of the *gaokao* around four main dimensions: 1) the clearly delineated hierarchy of higher education institutions in China, 2) the decentralization/recentralization of *gaokao* content and administration; 3) the centralized system for assigning quotas of higher education spaces; and 4) the uneven distribution of elite universities around the nation combined with preferential enrollment for local residents.

2 Hierarchy of Higher Education

In recent decades, there has been a dramatic expansion in access to higher education. The expansion has been facilitated by an increasing role of the market which has given sudden rise to a large proportion of private institutions of higher education (Zha, 2009; Yang, 2004). Qiang Zha (2009: 42) describes these changes as "perhaps, the most profound changes of institutional patterns and the largest expansion ever seen in the world higher education community".

COMPETITION IN THE NATIONAL COLLEGE ENTRANCE EXAMINATION 273

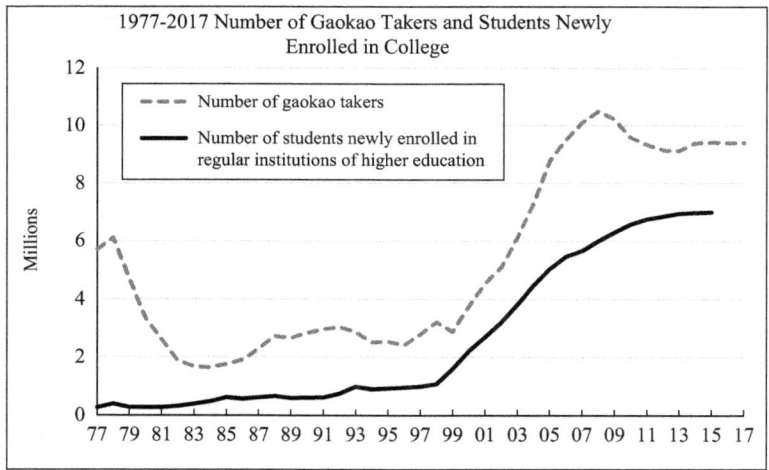

FIGURE 11.1 Number of students taking *gaokao* and enrolling in college 1977–2017
SOURCES: COMMUNIST PARTY OF CHINA NEWS, 2013; SINA EDUCATION NEWS, 2010, 2011, 2012; PEOPLE'S DAILY ONLINE, 2014a, 2016; CHINA EDUCATION ONLINE, 2017b

From 2000 to 2016, the total number of regular[1] higher education institutions increased from 1041 to 2631 (Ministry of Education of China, 2017a). The expanding demand for higher education has been powered by the increasing number of students completing basic education and entering into secondary schools, especially in urban areas. This has in turn led to an increase in the number of *gaokao* takers.

Figure 11.1 shows the trends in the number of *gaokao* takers between 2000–2017 which is accompanied by a corresponding dramatic increase in the number of students enrolled in all-types of "regular" four-year institutions of higher education and three year 专科 *zhuanke* (associate's) degree programs that are approved by the Ministry of Education. Figure 11.1 also shows the downward trend in demand since 2008 as a result of population decline, rising tuition costs and also the increasing popularity of studying abroad.

---

1   Institutions of higher education are officially divided into two categories: "regular institutions of higher education" (普通高等学校 *putong gaodeng xuexiao*) and "adult institutions of higher education" (成人高等学校 *chengren gaodeng xuexiao*). Regular institutions of higher education include all four years colleges that are accredited by the Ministry of Education whether public or private, and three year colleges (专科学校 *zhuanke xuexiao*) that offer more technical-vocational training (Ministry of Education of China, 2017a).

While, overall, access to higher education has witnessed a dramatic expansion, there is still a large gap between those who take the *gaokao* and those who eventually enroll in a program of higher education. Furthermore, due to the hierarchy of the higher education system, competition to get into elite programs of higher education remains fierce. At the top of the higher education system are the publicly funded universities that have received heavy central government investment as part of a series of government investment projects aimed at enhancing the quality of China's higher education. These include the 211 and 985 projects and the more recent Double First-Class (双一流 *shuang yiliu*) Project (Ministry of Education of China, 2017b).

211 Project. In 1995 the central government implemented the 211 Project, which entailed a heavy investment in raising the quality of higher education with a particular focus on raising research capacity (National Development and Reform Commission, Ministry of Education, and Ministry of Finance of China, 1995; Ministry of Education of China, 1998). The 211 Project constituted the largest government investment in higher education since the founding of New China (Ministry of Education of China, 2008). The People's Daily (2008) reported the following:

> China had more than 1,700 standard institutions of higher education (in 2008), and only 6 percent of them [were] "211 Project" schools. However, Project 211 schools take on the responsibility of training 4/5 of doctoral students, 2/3 of graduate students, 1/2 of students abroad and 1/3 of undergraduates. They offer 85 percent of the State's key subjects; hold 96 percent of the State's key laboratories; and utilize 70 percent of scientific research funding.

985 Project. Beginning with Beijing University and Qinghua University in 1998, and expanding to 39 universities in total, the 985 Project targeted the top universities from the original 211 Project universities for further investment of over 30 billion RMB with the aim of bringing this select group of universities up to the level of world-class universities (Cheng, 2011). At the pinnacle of the 985 universities were the 9 members of the "Chinese Ivy League" known as the C9 universities that were recognized as having already achieved world-class status. These are Beijing University, Qinghua University, Fudan University, Harbin Institute of Technology, Nanjing University, Shanghai Jiaotong University, University of Science and Technology of China, Xi'an Jiaotong University and Zhejiang University (Han, 2009).

Double First-Class (双一流 shuang yiliu) Project. In the Xi Jinping era, the 211/985 Projects were replaced with the Double First-Class Project which was instituted in January 2017 with the release of the document "Implementation measures to coordinate the development of world-class universities and the construction of First-Class Disciplines." The project aims to bring 42 universities to the level of world class institutions and about 100 disciplines in 95 universities up to the level of world class disciplines. The list of disciplines and universities was released in September 2017. All the 39 previous 985 Project schools and only 3 of the previous 211 Project schools are among the First–Class universities. However, all of the previous 211 universities are included on the list of universities to develop First–Class disciplines as well as an additional 25 universities that were previously not 211/985 Project universities (Charlesworth Group, 2017). First–Class disciplines fall into 12 categories. Four categories are in Natural Science (these categories include civil engineering, systems science, agricultural resources and environment, mining, traditional Chinese medicine and so on), and eight in Humanities and Social Science (these categories include Marxist theory, Chinese history, drama and film, ethnology, music and dance and so on) (Charlesworth Group, 2017).

The former 211 and 985 universities and current Double First-Class universities are at the top of those universities in China that belong to the "first tier" (一本 *yiben*) universities which have all received funding and investment from the Ministry of Education (Yao et al., 2010). These universities receive the most public support for research. As a result these universities are shooting up in the world rankings. In 2014, only two of the C9 universities made it into the Times Higher Education Rankings top 100 in the world, with Beijing University and Qinghua ranked at number 48 and 49 in the world respectively (Times Higher Education, 2014). By 2019, Qinghua was at 22, Beijing University was at 31 and the University of Science and Technology of China located in Hefei, Anhui entered the top 100 at place number 93 (Times Higher Education, 2019). In 2022, there are now a total of six Chinese universities listed in the top 100. Beijing and Qinghua University were both tied at number 16, and four more universities entered the top 100: Fudan university (60), Zhejiang University (75), Shanghai Jiaotong (84), and University of Science and Technology (88) (Times Higher Education, 2022). Clearly, according to the Times Higher Education ranking, China is fast achieving its goal of raising up world class higher education institutions.

The second tier (二本 *erben*) universities are mostly funded by the provincial and local governments and can be considered teaching universities (Yao et al., 2010). The universities in the third tier (三本 *sanben*), are composed of independent colleges and private universities. Many *sanben* universities are run by private corporations or jointly run by public and private institutions, so the tuition fees are much higher than *yiben* and *erben* universities. In recent years, many prestigious first and second tier public universities have operated their own colleges on the side that are independent of the "mother university". These independent colleges borrow the name and reputation from their "mother university", but they are money-making institutions and are considered third tier universities. Examples of top ranking third tier universities include the Zhuhai College of Jilin University; Wanfang College of Science & Technology, Henan Polytechnic University; and Wuhan University of Science and Technology (China Education Online, 2016). The tuition at these private institutions can be ten times or more than that of public universities. While students from disadvantaged backgrounds will tend to be overrepresented among the lowest scorers on the *gaokao* and thus overrepresented among the students wanting to attend a third tier private college, the exorbitant costs can be an insurmountable barrier for most lower-class urban families and most rural families. In a study of private colleges, Wang (2011) found only 10 percent of students in her sample of private colleges came from rural backgrounds. The *sanben* cutoff score is recognized as the bottom line score for examinees to enroll in a university. If an examinee's score does not reach the *sanben* cutoff score, they can still enter higher education at a vocational or technical college where they can earn the lesser *zhuanke* (associate) diploma.

The college admission process happens in a strict time sequence by matching specific groups of universities by descending order of priority with specific groups of *gaokao* scorers (Yangguang gaokao: kaosheng yu jiazhang dianzi duben, 2009). *Gaokao* takers are ranked at the provincial level by their *gaokao* scores in relation to "lines" that correspond to the minimum score, or cutoff score, to enter the first tier, second tier, and third tier universities and colleges. For example, in 2017 the *yiben* line in Shandong province was 433 for the natural science track and 483 for the liberal arts track (China Education Online, 2017a). Anyone scoring above this *yiben* line would be eligible for selection into top universities around the nation. The provincial Higher Education Admission Office announces the major cutoff scores for the year around June 20 in most provinces. The time sequence for enrollment is outlined in the Yangguang Gaokao Manual (Yangguang gaokao: kaosheng yu jiazhang dianzi duben, 2009) as follows:

1) Four year university pre-enrollment (本科提前批次 *benke tiqian pici*): military universities, armed police colleges, public security colleges (or public security departments in a comprehensive university), sport universities (or sport departments in a comprehensive university), art

colleges and some international politics colleges. These schools are the first to enroll students who apply for them. Applicants to these kinds of schools are either outstanding in all respects or have special ambitions or strengths in these fields.

2) Four year university group one (本科第一批次/一本 *benke diyi pici/ yiben*): In this round of selection, top colleges, including those administered by the Ministry of Education, colleges administered by other ministries in the central government, former 985 and C9 universities, most of the previous 211 universities, are matched with top scorers in the *gaokao* and release their decisions.

3) Four year university group two (本科第二批次/二本 *benke di'er pici/ erben*): In this round the non-key colleges, mostly those administered by provincial governments will select from the remaining students and release their decisions.

4) Four year university group three (本科第三批次/三本 *benke disan pici/ sanben*): In this round the third tier universities which are predominantly the independent or private colleges (独立/民办学院 *duli/minban xueyuan*) select from the remaining students.

5) Three year college group one (专科第一批次 *zhuanke diyi pici*): selection for public *zhuanke* colleges or *zhuanke* majors in four year colleges.

6) Three year college group two (专科第二批次 *zhuanke di'er pici*): selection to private higher vocational schools approved by the Ministry of Education.

In summary, the system of higher education is organized according to a clear and purposeful hierarchy. Sitting at the top of the pyramid of higher education are the prestigious, yet affordable, research-oriented first-class public universities that receive heavy investment from the central government; and at the bottom of the pyramid are private colleges and higher vocational schools that are inferior but expensive and receive little central government support. Given the inevitable sociocultural factors contributing to disadvantage for students from poor, rural and ethnic minority backgrounds who have a lesser likelihood of entry into a first tier university, the system of public elite education ends up being a subsidy for students from families with higher social status (Yao et al., 2010). Furthermore, as we will explain later in the chapter, the unequal distribution of elite universities around China, combined with preferential local enrollment policies, results in inequality of access to elite higher education by province of origin.

3 The Impact of Recent *Gaokao* Reform on Inter-Provincial Differences in *Gaokao* Competition

Over the past two decades there has been a pendulum swing from centralization to decentralization and back to limited re-centralization of *gaokao* format, content and administration. This has mirrored the shifting governance relationship between the government and higher education from a trend towards decentralization towards the more recent trend towards greater recentralization (Han and Xu, 2019). Wenkuo Zhou (2014) argued that the rationale for the decentralization of the college entrance exams was that it could better take into account regional differences in economics and education and the regional heterogeneity of student development; increase the validity and reliability of such high-stake tests; and promote the implementation of the New Curriculum reform movement. Furthermore, there were fears about test question leak such as in the 2003 incident when a high school senior in Nanfang County, Sichuan Province broke into the county department of education and stole the *gaokao* test papers (China Court Network, 2022). Yong Zhao and Wei Qiu (2012: 318) argued that a major incentive for the decentralization of curriculum and the college entrance exams in the first two decades of the 21st century was the "concern that the central government's excessively tight control was a barrier to improving the quality of education, and the belief that more local autonomy would bring innovative ideas and strategies".

However, decentralization policies have led to increasing inequality and a weakening of ideological control. Critics argued that under the *gaokao* decentralization policies the quality of the *gaokao* tests could no longer be guaranteed, that the policies made it difficult to compare educational outcomes across the provinces; and that they raised doubts about the equality of the *gaokao* process. Furthermore, it was argued that decentralization could not really decrease the risk of leaking questions (Sun, 2004). Many parents, teachers and students were not happy with the decentralized approach to the *gaokao* either (Wang and Wang, 2011). The Xi Jinping era brought about a new recentralization of a broad range of policies for the purposes of fostering greater equity, cracking down on corruption, increasing control and accountability, and strengthening ideological control (Kojima, 2020; Teets, 2018). This policy climate along with the perceived disadvantages of *gaokao* decentralization caused a gradual return to greater centralization of the examination system.

Since the reinstatement of the *gaokao* in 1977 after the Cultural Revolution, three distinct periods of *gaokao* reform can be identified delineated by important policy reform documents, Phase I (1977–2002) – Unified *gaokao;* Phase II

(2002–2014) – Provincial autonomous test design (分省自主命题 *fensheng zizhu mingti*); Phase III (2014–) Limited recentralization of the *gaokao*.

Phase I: Unified national gaokao 1977–2002. During this period, all provinces around the nation used the same textbooks and participated in the same examination. The format of the *gaokao* was uniform across the country (Shanghai always being an exception) consisting of the 3+3 format – the three core subjects Chinese, Mathematics and English and the final three depending on whether a student was social science track (文科 *wenke*) or science track (理科 *like*). *Wenke* track students took History, Geography and Politics and *like* students took Physics, Biology and Chemistry.

Phase II: Provincial autonomous test design 2002–2014. Concomitant with the implementation of the New Curriculum Reforms, in accordance with the guidelines in the 1999 "Opinions on further deepening the reform of the examination and enrollment system" (关于进一步深化普通高等学校招生考试制度改革的意见 *Guanyu jin yi bu shenhua putong gaodeng xuexiao zhaosheng kaoshi zhidu gaige de yijian*), (Ministry of Education of China, 1999) the content and administration of the *gaokao* was gradually decentralized from the national unified *gaokao* to the provincial level (分省自主命题 *fensheng zizhu mingti*). The reforms to the format of the exams were commonly characterized as a move from 3+3 to 3+X, where X was a comprehensive integrated, interdisciplinary test that consisted of history, geography and politics (文综 *wenzong*) for *wenke* students, and physics, chemistry and biology (理综 *lizong*) for *like* students or a selected single subject. Formats varied considerably across provinces. The various formats used around the nation in 2012 are shown in Table 11.1. The detailed notes that follow Table 11.1 reveal the complexities of the *gaokao* format and the significant differences across provinces.

The decentralization reforms began in Beijing (although Shanghai has been doing its own thing since 1985), and gradually expanded to Shandong and 16 other provinces. In 2013, only 15 provinces were still using the centralized old version of the *gaokao*. They were Heilongjiang, Jilin, Hebei, Henan, Inner Mongolia, Shanxi, Ningxia, Gansu, Qinghai, Xinjiang, Tibet, Guizhou, Yunnan, Guangxi, Hainan. These latter provinces did not meet the conditions necessary to administer a provincial level version of the *gaokao*. In order to administer a provincial level version of the *gaokao* the provincial department of education needed to submit a proposal to the provincial government and the proposal then had to be approved by the Ministry of Education. The deputy director of the National Education Examinations Authority, Ying Shuzeng, said in a 2007 interview: "The examination institutions in these provinces must have the ability to make proposals, the ability to organize and manage, and have enough accomplished experts in a complete range of disciplines. In some provinces,

TABLE 11.1 Variations in *gaokao* format in 2012

2012 *gaokao* formats	Provinces/Municipalities	Total Score
3+X[a]	26 provinces (including Beijing, Guangdong, Tianjin, Ningxia, Shanxi, Henan, Gansu, Tibet and Xinjiang)	750=150×3+300×1
3+1(Subject Test)[b]	Shanghai	600=150×(3+1)
3+(1+1+4) (Academic Proficiency Tests)[c]	Jiangsu	480=200+160+120; 6A/B/C/D
3+3+4(Basic General Exams)[d]	Hainan	790=150×3+100×3+400×10%
3+X+1(Optional Module)[e]	Zhejiang	750 (810)=150×3+300×1+(60)
3+1(Technology)		550=150×3+100
3+X+1(Test of Basic Abilities)[f]	Shandong	750=150×3+240×1+100×60%

Notes: Gaokao models and total points by region in 2012, selected regions. Source: Provincial Education Bureau websites.

a The X refers to an integrated exam in humanities (文综 *wenzong*) or sciences (理综 *lizong*).

b One subject among Physics, Chemistry, Biology, History, Geography and Politics.

c For liberal arts students, the total score of the Chinese test and Math test was 200 (200=160+40) and 160 respectively. For natural science students, the total score of Chinese test and Math test were 160 and 200 (200=160+40) respectively. The 40 meant they had to take an extra set of questions in either Chinese or Math test and that part had a value of 40 points. The total score of the English test was 120 for both. The Academic Proficiency Tests (学业水平测试 *Xueye Shuiping Ceshi*) referred to seven tests: Physics, Chemistry, Biology, History, Geography, Politics and Technology. Students only got Pass or Fail for Technology. If the student passed the test, he or she will be permitted to get the bonus scores from other tests. In the other six tests, four were compulsory subjects and two were elective subjects. Students could get bonuses for each A they gained in compulsory subjects but not elective subjects. 1A= add 1 point to your score; 2As= add 2 points to your score; 3As = add 3 points to your score; 4As= add 5 points to your score. An A in an elective subject did not count. Students could only get 5 extra points at maximum.

d The Basic General Exams (基础会考 *Jichu Huikao*) included seven options of subjects such as Politics, History, Geography, Chemistry, Biology, Physics as well as Information Technology. In order to help students build up a comprehensive background of knowledge, liberal arts students were required to take three tests of science-related disciplines, while natural science students had to take three tests of liberal arts disciplines. Information Technology was obligatory for all students. The raw score of Academic Proficiency Test was to be multiplied by 10% before adding to the overall score on the *gaokao*.

e The Optional Module (自选模块 *Zixuan Mokuai*) contained 18 questions covering 16 elective parts across all 9 subjects. Students chose any 6 questions to answer. Students who applied for *yiben* universities were required to answer the Elective Section in the subject related to the major they wanted to apply to.

TABLE 11.1   Variations in *gaokao* format in 2012 *(cont.)*

f   The Test of Basic Abilities (基本能力测试 *Jiben Nengli Ceshi*) widely covered basic knowledge of 10 (or more) subjects and general knowledge aiming to test comprehension and creative application and problem solving (Li, 2007). Shandong applied 3+X+1 in 2014.

due to the lack of key colleges and universities, and incomplete expertise across the disciplines, proposals for an independent *gaokao* will be difficult" (Yuan, 2007).

During provincial autonomous test design phase, not only did the format of the *gaokao* vary among provinces and regions, the content of the individual *gaokao* test papers also differed across provinces. The content of the *gaokao* in each province was independent of the format used. Two provinces using a 3+X structure may have had entirely different content in each of the exam papers. The most important reforms affecting the content of the *gaokao* were the New Curriculum Reforms. The questions in the new *gaokao* were designed in line with the overarching goal of all-round development and according to the goals of the New Curriculum standards: Knowledge and Skill, Process and Method, Attitudes and Values. The new *gaokao* was supposed to emphasize lifelong learning, inquiry and application, and the capacities for innovation and problem solving (Li, 2007).

During this phase, textbook publishing was also decentralized. Tanja Sargent and Xiao Yang (2010) outline the extent of the decentralization of the textbooks. Prior to the New Curriculum Reforms, only one publishing house was authorized to produce textbook materials, the People's Education Press. After the implementation of the New Curriculum Reforms, publishing houses from around the nation were able to produce textbooks that were designed in accordance with the New Curriculum standards. In 2006, over 10 publishing houses were approved to produce curriculum materials for Chinese language arts in primary and middle schools. These included People's Education Press, Jiangsu Education Press, Beijing Normal University Press, Language and Literature Press, Educational Sciences Press and others (Sargent and Yang, 2010). Textbooks that were produced needed to be approved by a committee under the Ministry of Education in charge of textbook review, the National School Textbook Examination Commission (Wang, 2008). The decision about the choice of which textbooks to use in the schools was made at the provincial and county levels. Given the fact that there were many different publishing houses producing textbook materials, there was an inevitable decoupling of examinations from the textbook content. The first students to take the new *gaokao* were those in the first provinces to begin New Curriculum implementation in high schools in 2004. These provinces were Guangdong, Ningxia,

Shandong and Hainan (Wang, 2008). All 31 provinces began implementation of New Curriculum Reforms in high schools in 2012. Tests designed by the China National Education Examinations Authority (NEEA) and tests designed at the provincial level in China were used concurrently and there was a great deal of mixing and matching. Some provinces designed only the Chinese, English and Math tests and used the Science and Social Science tests that were designed by the NEEA. Although the policy of provincial autonomous *gaokao* administration intended to include more local economic, cultural and geographic characteristics and better reflect regional differences, it was criticized for leading to inconsistency between exams and textbooks (Zhang, 2011).

Phase III: Limited recentralization of the examinations (2014-). The 2014 "Suggestions of the State Council regarding deepening of reform and implementation of the testing and enrollment system" (国务院关于深化考试招生制度改革的实施意见 *Guowuyuan guanyu shenhua kaoshi zhaosheng zhidu gaige de shishi yijian*) (State Council, 2014) introduced four major reforms to the *gaokao*. These reforms began gradual implementation starting in 2014 in Shanghai and Zhejiang and only then beginning gradual roll out in provinces around the nation. The implementation start dates for each of the provinces are shown in Table 11.2. When reform implementation began in a province, only the first year high school students were affected. This first group were then the first to sit for the examinations under the new policies three years later.

The key features of this round of *gaokao* reforms included the following:

1) First, the gradual reunification once again of the format and content for the three main subjects, Chinese, Math and English. However, the English exam can be taken twice and students can choose their highest score.
2) In addition to the three main subjects of Chinese, Math and English, test-takers can choose three out of six subjects that they take in a series of provincial level tests (高中学业水平考试 *Gaozhong Xueye Shuiping Kaoshi*). They can choose the three scores from the provincial level tests that they would like to report and have a chance to take these tests two times.
3) The new reforms also eliminate the science and humanities tracks since these tracks were originally created to prepare students for the now eliminated science and humanities exams.
4) There is also the beginning of a new approach to making measures of all-round development (综合素质 *zonghe suzhi*) available for use as reference material (参照材料 *canzhao cailiao*).

In June 2022, there were three types of *gaokao* implementation occurring simultaneously: 1) provincial autonomous test design in four places: Beijing,

TABLE 11.2 Implementation schedule of 2014 *gaokao* reforms

Province/City	Start date for students in first year of high school	First year test takers will take reformed *gaokao*
Zhejiang, Shanghai	2014	2017
Beijing, Tianjin, Shandong, Hainan	2017	2020
Jiangxi, Hubei, Guangdong, Jiangsu, Hebei, Chongqing, Hunan, Anhui, Heilongjiang, Liaoning, Jilin, Guizhou, Shanxi, Inner Mongolia, Henan, Sichuan, Fujian, Tibet,	2018	2021
Liaoning, Guangxi, Shaanxi, Yunnan, Gansu, Qinghai, Xinjiang	2019	2022

SOURCE: SOHU EDUCATION (2017)

Shanghai, Zhejiang and Tianjin; 2) NEEA designed test (Yunnan, Sichuan, Guangxi, Guizhou, Tibet, Shaanxi, Xinjiang, Ningxia, Jilin, Heilongjiang, Inner Mongolia, Qinghai, Gansu, Anhui, Jiangxi, Shanxi, Henan; 3) Hybrid design: NEEA designed the three core subjects of Chinese, Math and English and the province designed the tests for the remaining subjects (Shandong, Hebei, Hubei, Hunan, Jiangsu, Fujian, Guangdong, Hainan, Chongqing, Liaoning) (Zhihu, 2022).

What have been the implications for equity of access to higher education of the centralization, decentralization and recentralization of the *gaokao* design, content and administration?

The most recent reforms to the *gaokao* are both centralized and decentralized. The English, Math and Chinese scores are still not comparable nationwide because the top 4 provinces/municipalities are still able to design their own tests. The extent to which the *gaokao* is decentralized, makes it more difficult to compare across provinces the minimum scores that are needed to access elite institutions, thus reducing the transparency related to disparity in access to elite higher education for students from provinces outside of Beijing and Shanghai. As long as the centralized quota system for number of spots in higher education available for each province is the real determinant for entry into elite universities, the decentralization and recentralization of *gaokao* format, design and content is not likely to impact the relative competitiveness to gain access to elite higher education in China.

4 Centralized System for Assigning Provincial Quotas of Higher Education Spaces

The centralized system of assigning provincial quotas for higher education spaces has long been a subject of controversy (Wang, 2010; Fu, 2013a). Haiwen Zhou (2018) argues that there is a long history behind the provincial quota system that dates back to the imperial civil service examination system. He traces debates about whether it is better to have test equality or regional equity from the Song Dynasty (960–1279 AD) to the Qing Dynasty (1644–1912 AD). Test equality is a selection process based entirely on scores, whereas regional equity ensures that success is equitably distributed across all regions of the country. According to Zhou (2018), in the Song Dynasty, success was based entirely on the scores and this resulted in 95 percent of the successful candidates (进士 *jinshi*) coming from the South. On the contrary, in the Ming and Qing Dynasty, regional quotas spread the success more evenly across the country. Liu (2012) covers the more recent history of the development of the provincial quota system. At the start of the founding of New China in 1949 all the student selection was centralized and scores were the only criterion. Beginning in 1951 there was a move away from a sole focus on scores towards quotas for special individuals, especially workers and peasants. In 1958, the preliminary establishment of a provincial quota system was complete and after the period of the Cultural Revolution (during which time examinations were completely abolished) the provincial quota system was revitalized in 1987 according to the policy outlined in the "Temporary regulations for the creation of a regular higher education institution recruitment system based on student origin" (普通高等学校招生来源计划编制工作暂行规定 *Putong gaodeng xuexiao zhaosheng laiyuan jihua bianzhi gongzuo zanxing guiding*). Although the stated intent has been to promote regional equality of access to higher education, the provincial quota system, in concert with the policies of local protectionism, has resulted in disparity of access to higher education and, in particular, access to elite higher education (Fu, 2013a).

Much mystery still surrounds the exact criteria and considerations that are used to determine the contemporary provincial college enrollment allotment or quota (Fu, 2013a). Specific policies regarding the proportion of students that must be enrolled at the *yiben* universities in China cannot be found, however, an attempt to outline the effects of the provincial quotas in practice reveals the complexity of navigating decisions about choice of institution and choice of major. The process assigns provincial quotas, not only to a class of universities but to each university and then to each major. For many majors in a particular university there are no spaces at all for students from a particular province. In order to navigate the process, a student must become aware of the minimum cutoff scores for their province for entry into a particular level of higher education (*yiben* for example) and then whether or not there is a major at a particular university that has spaces for students from their province, and then what the minimum score is for that major at that particular university. Thus university aspirants need to consider three main factors in their choice of program: 1) provincial cutoff scores for *yiben, erben* and *sanben* lines, 2) cutoff scores for each particular individual university, 3) and the cutoff scores for each major. The provincial cutoff scores for each level of university are determined by the provincial Higher Education Admission Office (省招办 *Sheng Zhao Ban*) which ranks the scores of all examinees in the province. The provincial cutoff scores are then determined based on the lowest score for the student who was admitted into each level.

To help students and parents access information about the *gaokao*, the Ministry of Education administers a professional website "Yangguang Gaokao: Student and Parent Electronic Manual." Each province also has its own official *gaokao* website. Examples of such websites include the website of the Beijing Education Examinations Authority (*Beijing Jiaoyu Kaoshi Yuan*, http://www.bjeea.cn) and the website of the Shandong Provincial Academy of Education Recruitment and Examination (*Shandong Jiaoyu Zhaosheng Kaoshi Yuan*, http://www.sdzk.cn/). Here parents and students can access *gaokao* enrollment information including *yiben, erben and sanben* cutoff scores for each province, provincial *gaokao* policies, provincial quota plans and provincial cutoff scores for each major at every university. The cutoff score is the sole standard for evaluating whether a student has met the minimum requirements of a particular major in a desired university. All of the various cutoff scores produced in the college admission process are generated as a result of the centralized college admission quota system. These websites offer recruitment quotas, minimum score cutoffs, and enrollment numbers by major for all universities and colleges.

In many provinces, the policy of "first apply for your preferred university and major, then receive your scores" (先报志愿, 后处分 *xian bao zhiyuan, hou chu fen*) is still in place. How this works is that, shortly after the exam is taken, the test paper is published online with correct responses marked. Students must estimate their total *gaokao* score and use this to determine their chances for entry into a particular major at a particular university based on the cut-off scores from the previous year. Students submit their university applications for several universities at each level, rank ordered according to their preferences, online to the provincial admission office. If a student's score meets the cutoff criteria, the provincial admission office sends the application files to the respective departments of each university according to the students' application (Yangguang gaokao: kaosheng yu jiazhang dianzi duben, 2012).

The complexity of the university selection process creates demand for professional guidance. A burgeoning for-profit educational consultant industry has emerged to offer guidance for families about how to choose the right university and profession. This industry has been criticized for price gouging and lack of regulation (Tian, 2018). Xi's 2021 crackdown on 'disorderly expansion' in the education industry focused mainly on the 120 billion USD after-school tutoring market but was part of a broader movement to increase regulation that will likely have implications for the education consulting industry as well (Liu, 2022).

5 Uneven Distribution of Elite Universities Across China and Local Preferential Enrolment

Elite universities are unevenly distributed across China, with the largest number concentrated in Beijing (See Figure 11.2). In 2013, there were thirty six 985/211 Project schools in Beijing, fifteen in Shanghai, fourteen in Jiangsu, and eleven in Shaanxi. Eleven provinces had only one 211 school in the province including provinces such as Gansu, Shanxi, Inner Mongolia, Henan, Tibet, and Qinghai. Since almost all the schools receiving money as part of the Double First-Class Project were former 985/211 schools the pattern remains the same today.

Through the 985, 211 and Double First-Class projects, however, the central government has been endeavoring to distribute resources into the development of world class higher education across the nation. This notwithstanding, the persistence of the uneven distribution of elite universities across the nation, combined with a policy which allows preferential enrollment for students in the locality of the university is the crux of the issue of inter-provincial inequality in *gaokao* competition (Fu, 2013b). While higher education institutions receive a large proportion of funding from the central government they are also heavily funded by the local and provincial governments and so they are allowed to give preference to local residents (Fu, 2013b). Requirements ensuring that outside students are also enrolled are enforced too. Central government policy requires universities under the jurisdiction of provincial or local governments to allot at least 30 percent of their spaces to students

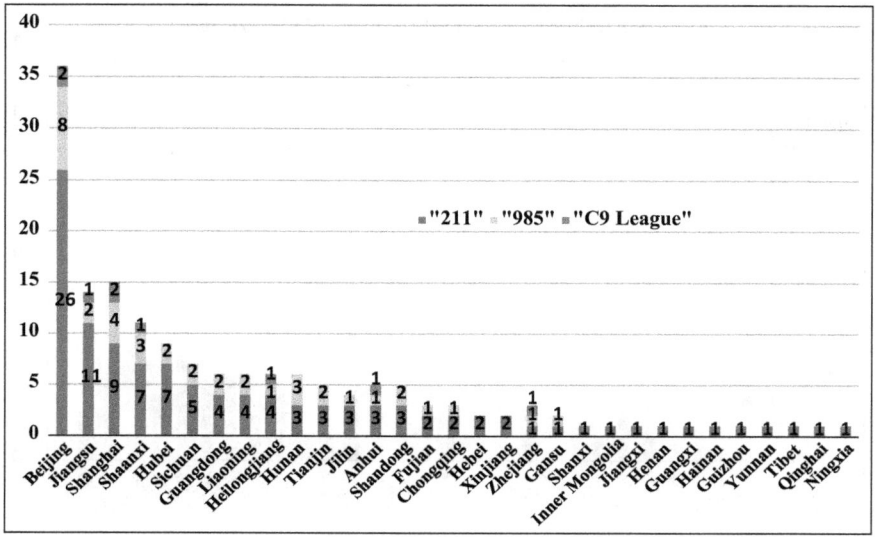

FIGURE 11.2 Distribution of elite (C9, 985 and 211) universities in China
SOURCE: MINISTRY OF EDUCATION OF CHINA, 2008

of other provinces. This is especially true in the case of the elite universities which are disproportionately located in Beijing, with Jiangsu and Shanghai far behind Beijing in the number of elite universities but still with a disproportionate number compared to the rest of the country (Fu, 2013b). Students who are residents in these locations have a much greater chance of gaining access to spots at elite institutions.

What does this mean for examination competition for students across different provinces in China? Henan province has been known for having the most severe competition for university access. In 2011, the undergraduate college admission rates in Henan were less than 34 percent, with an admission rate of only 5 percent into top tier universities (Liu, 2012). In contrast, in 2011, Beijing and Shanghai's undergraduate admission rates were 56 percent and 66 percent respectively, and their top tier admission rates were 24 percent and 20 percent respectively (Liu, 2012). Zhang Qiang (2011) found that for every 10,000 students taking the *gaokao* in Beijing in 2009 there were 66.8 spots allotted at Beijing University; for students taking the test in Tianjin, a neighboring city to Beijing, the number was 10.2; for every 10,000 *gaokao* takers in Shanghai the number was 4.8; and the average for the rest of the country was only 2.2. The proportion from Henan was only 1 for every 10,000 test takers and, even lower than this, was Anhui with the lowest proportion of .66. This meant

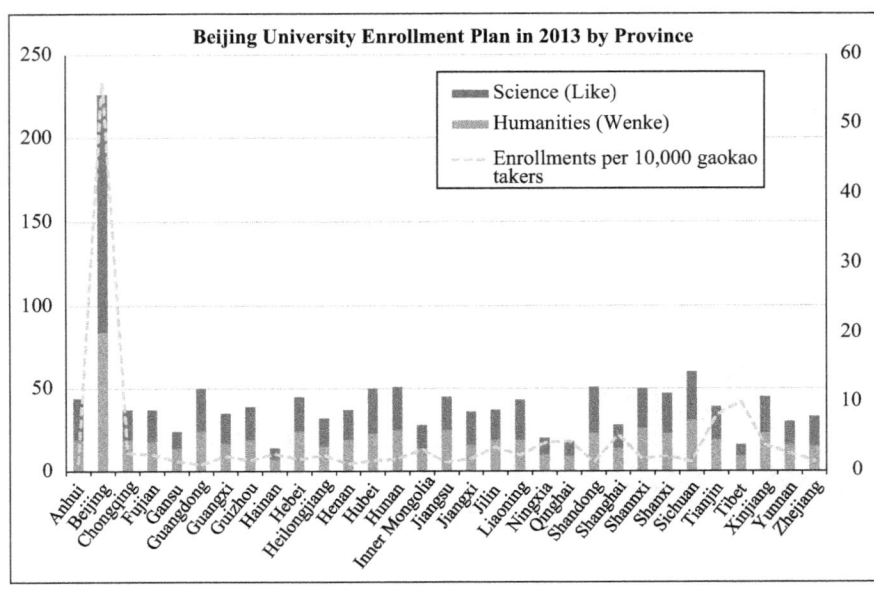

FIGURE 11.3 Beijing University enrollment plan by province of origin (2013)
SOURCE: ADMISSION WEBSITE OF BEIJING UNIVERSITY, 2013

that, in 2009, the chance for a Beijing student to enter into Beijing University was 100 times that of the chance for a student in Anhui. Likewise, the relative probability for non-Shanghai *gaokao* test takers to enter in Fudan University was even more disproportionate than these figures for Beijing University. For example, a Shanghai test taker's probability of entering in Fudan was 288 times that of a student from Inner Mongolia (Zhang, 2011).

Analysis of 2013 enrollment plans of Beijing University and Qinghua University (the last year enrollment plans were publicly available on the university websites) revealed the high percentage of students from Beijing as compared with students from other provinces (see Figures 11.3 and 11.4).

Likewise, Zhejiang University, a former member of the C9 league had an even more striking preference for students from Zhejiang (See Figure 11.5).

Zhejiang University is the only former C9/985/211 university in the province and so providing local preference for Zhejiang students the opportunity for elite education is a high priority. As a result, of all provinces and municipalities, Zhejiang has the highest actual number of students, and the third highest proportion of *gaokao* takers attending a C9 university (see Figures 11.6a and 11.6b).

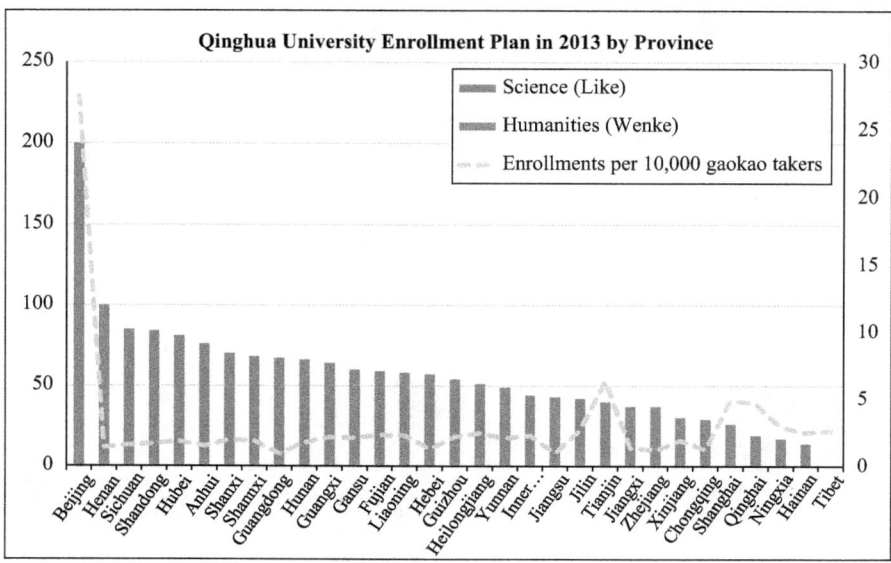

FIGURE 11.4 Qinghua University enrollment plan by province of origin (2013)
SOURCE: ADMISSION WEBSITE OF QINGHUA UNIVERSITY, 2013

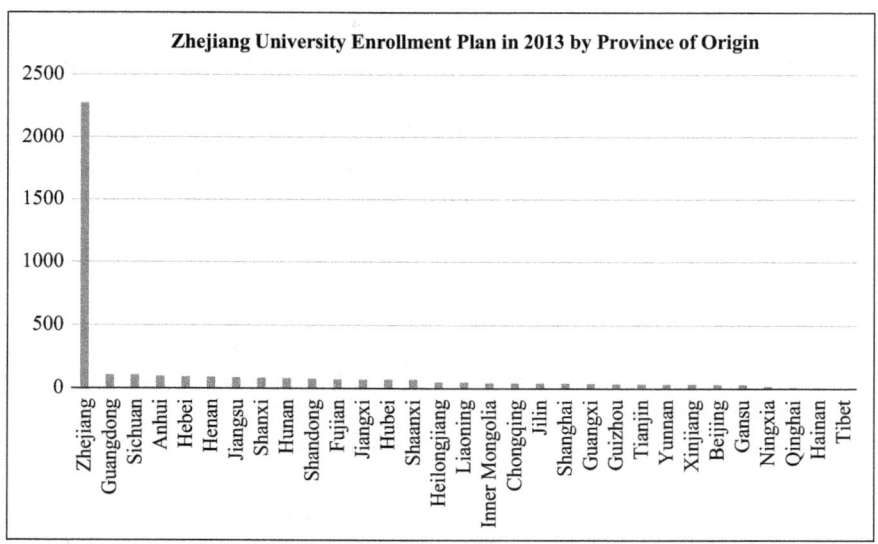

FIGURE 11.5 Zhejiang University enrollment plan by province of origin and rural student special enrollment (2013)
SOURCE: ADMISSION WEBSITE OF ZHEJIANG UNIVERSITY, 2013

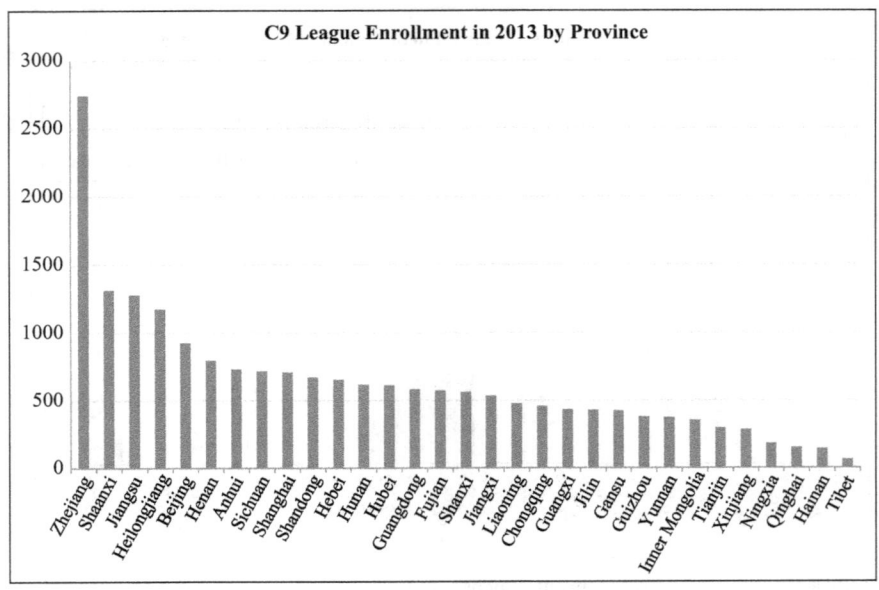

FIGURE 11.6A   C9 league enrollment by province of origin (2013)
SOURCES: ADMISSIONS WEBSITES OF C9 UNIVERSITIES

Analysis of enrollment data from all the C9 universities also reveals interesting trends. Guangdong, Shandong and Henan are the three most populous provinces in China and so they also have high numbers of *gaokao* takers. Henan has relatively high actual numbers of students in C9 institutions, coming in 6th according to actual numbers of students in a C9 university (see Figure 11.6a). When taking number of *gaokao* takers or population into account, however, the disproportionate access for students in locations with the highest number of most elite universities becomes apparent. Proportion of C9 enrollments per 1,000 *gaokao* takers in 2013 was far higher in Beijing, Shanghai and Zhejiang (see Figure 11.6b). However, it is also interesting that when taking the number of *gaokao* takers and population into account, enrollment into the elite C9 universities in places such as Qinghai and Tibet is just above average (see Figure 11.6b). This is partly due to the fact that they have sparser populations and lower numbers of *gaokao* takers. When taking number of *gaokao* takers into account we also see that Shandong, Henan and Guangdong are at the bottom in terms of C9 enrollment and conclude that the competition for the most elite education in China is indeed the highest in these provinces (see Figure 11.6b).

Enrollment data from 2017 and later are no longer publicly available on many university websites but data available on the influential Chinese web

COMPETITION IN THE NATIONAL COLLEGE ENTRANCE EXAMINATION 291

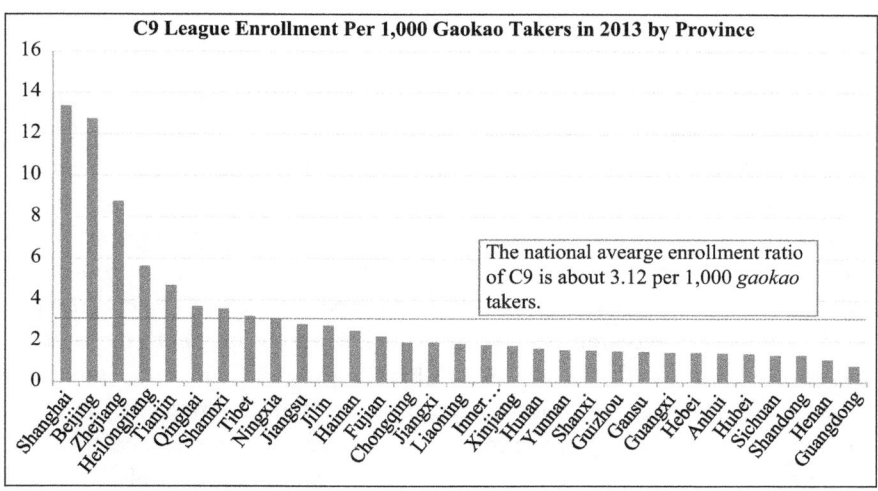

FIGURE 11.6B C9 league enrollment per 1,000 *gaokao* takers by province of origin (2013)
SOURCES: ENROLLMENT: ADMISSIONS WEBSITES OF C9 UNIVERSITIES. NUMBER OF *GAOKAO* TAKERS: CHINA EDUCATION ONLINE, 2013; SINA EDUCATION NEWS, 2013

portal Sohu.com suggests that disparities in lack of access to elite education have persisted. Table 11.3 shows Sohu's figures from 2017 to compare access to elite university education in Beijing, Shanghai and Henan.

In summary, the uneven distribution of higher education institutions, combined with preferential policies for local residents, has resulted in a disparity of competition in the *gaokao* across provinces.

TABLE 11.3 2017 percent enrollment into elite higher education institution in Henan, Beijing and Shanghai

	Henan	Beijing	Shanghai
Top tier (*yiben*)	5.28	18.28	18.91
985	1.14	4.29	5.33
211	4.14	13.99	13.58
Provincial level key universities (*erben*)	13.08	48.78	40.71

SOURCE: SOHU EDUCATION (2017)

6   Discussion

This chapter has investigated the extent to which there is a difference in the intensity of *gaokao* competition across provinces in contemporary China. We also wanted to understand the impact of recent *gaokao* reforms on interprovincial differences in *gaokao* competition during the Xi Jinping era. We found evidence to suggest a persistent difference in intensity of *gaokao* competition across provinces. We argue that several factors combine to contribute to these inter-provincial disparities in the competitiveness of the *gaokao*. The first factor is the hierarchical system of higher education, that continues to be cultivated under the Double First-Class Project, with Qinghua University and Beijing University at the very top of the system, followed by the other members of the C9 league, the former 985 Project universities and then the former 211 Project universities. These make up most of the so-called first tier (一本 *yiben*) universities. Whether or not the *gaokao* is centralized or decentralized, the minimum *gaokao* score, or cut-off, for entry into these elite first tier universities varies by province. Decisions about provincial quotas are made in collaboration between the central and provincial governments. The central government has provincial quotas to guarantee *gaokao* takers across the country some degree of access to the most elite universities, but also provides for some degree of local preferential treatment for local *gaokao* takers. However, due to the fact that elite universities are unevenly distributed across the nation, competition for entry into an elite university varies by the province of origin of the examinee. Beijing has an especially disproportionate number of elite universities and so, given local preferential admissions policies, Beijing students have lower *gaokao* competition than do students in other provinces.

Preferential enrollment is partly to do with the financing of higher education. The 211 Project and 985 Project universities were generally co-funded by the central and the local government and received local preferential enrollment policies in exchange for local funding support, preferential tax measures, and land use policies (Zhang, 2011). Xi Jinping's Double First-Class Project has somewhat succeeded in reducing this inequality as it has expanded the central government funding to provide access to elite higher education to broader number of universities and departments across China (Charlesworth Group, 2017) but the disparities still persist. Martin Carnoy, Isak Froumin, Prashant Loyalka, and Jandhyala Tilak (2014) provide an overview of theories of the main state purposes for investment in higher education including social efficiency and social equity. The social efficiency theory argues that investment in higher education benefits the society at large, including through advancing social development, capital accumulation, economic growth and state revenue. The social equity theory of state investment in higher education argues that, since the disadvantaged in society tend to also be educationally disadvantaged in access to higher education, "if a society values fairness and places social and political value on ensuring equity, the public aspect of education would include financing it in ways that mitigate such disadvantage" (Carnoy et al., 2014: 360). In China, the state has endeavored to simultaneously pursue both the goals of social efficiency and social equity. Heavy state investment in developing "world class" universities through the Double First-Class Project (Ministry of Education of China, 2017b) in Xi Jinping's China is focused on both social efficiency goals, aimed at training elite talent that will drive China's continued growth and development as it emerges as a global superpower, and also on expanding access to elite education to a larger population of the educational disadvantaged across a greater geographic area. Other policies, implemented concurrent to the Double First-Class Project, pursue the social equity goals of state investment in higher education including affirmative action policies for minority students (Clothey, 2005; Sautman, 1998) and recent policies that specifically target raising the enrollment opportunities for rural students by requiring quotas of rural students in specific universities (Ministry of Education of China, 2019; Ministry of Finance of China, 2012).

Other social trends affecting the complex social, cultural and political context of contemporary *gaokao* competition include allowing specific universities greater autonomy to make their own admissions decisions based on multiple criteria which tends to favor urban city dwellers with richer stores of social, cultural and financial capital (Xiong, 2018). There has also been a dramatic increase in families with financial means who are opting out of the *gaokao* all together and preparing their children to attend college abroad by enrolling them in private 'international' high schools or international tracks in prestigious public schools (Xiang and Shen, 2009). In these schools, students can opt to take the Scholastic Aptitude Test (SATs) or the International Baccalaureate (IB) exams, thus providing these advantaged students with alternative options and pathways (Tu, 2016; Wright and Lee, 2014).

Another social phenomenon in China that affects the large numbers of migrant students in Chinese cities is the persistence of the household registration system (*hukou*) which grants social services benefits based on the residency status of the individual. In many localities, individuals are only entitled to social services based on where they hold official residency (Wu and Treiman, 2004). Students can apply for any university across China but migrant students have been required to sit for the *gaokao* in the province where they hold a residence permit (*hukou*) and have therefore been subject to the provincial quotas where they sit their exam (Zhang and Sargent, 2019). This has been one of the factors affecting migrant students' access to higher education as, even if they were born and raised in Beijing or Shanghai and attended school there, they have been excluded from the local preferential enrollment policies available to their classmates holding city residency. Cities have been required to provide basic education for migrant students and, increasingly, there is pressure to allow migrant students to take the *gaokao* in their new cities but acquiring permission to do so has been challenging (People's Daily Online, 2014b) and many high school students have had to continue to sit for the *gaokao* in the province and city where they are residents.

Does the central control of provincial quotas promote equity or exacerbate differences in access to higher education? It is likely that if the government did not have centralized provincial enrollment quotas, the distribution of students at elite universities would be even more skewed geographically. On the other hand, the decentralized policy of allowing local jurisdictions the right to a certain degree of local protectionism is the key source of inequality in access to elite higher education in China.

Whatever the case, ultimately, the attainment of greater equality of access to elite higher education in China will have to be through central government intervention using policy levers to find ways to balance the quest for both quality and equality. For now, even in the face of rapid changes in global and internal mobility, and in China's changing role in the world, the central role of the *gaokao* in determining the fate of the majority of China's citizens remains unchallenged.

References

Admission Website of Beijing University (2013). http://www.gotopku.cn/data/detail.php?id=5220, accessed 2 July 2013.

Admission Website of Qinghua University (2013). http://join-tsinghua.edu.cn/publish/bzw/7540/2013/20130609145724862478439/20130609145724862478439_.html, accessed 2 July 2013.

Admission Website of Zhejiang University (2013). http://zdzsc.zju.edu.cn/index.php?c=Index&a=detail&catid=16&id=628, accessed 2 July, 2013.

Bai Limin (2006) Graduate unemployment: Dilemmas and challenges in China's move to mass higher education. *The China Quarterly*, 185, pp. 128–144.

Carnoy, Martin, Isak Froumin, Prashant K. Loyalka, and Jandhyala B. G. Tilak (2014) The concept of public goods, the state, and higher education finance: a view from the BRICS. *Higher Education*, 68(3), pp. 359–378.

Chao, Chiang-Nan (2018) Why so Many Chinese Students Come to the US for their Higher Education. *Asian Journal of Education and e-Learning*, 6(3), pp. 61–68.

Charlesworth Group (2017) The Chinese Double First-Class University Plan. 3 October, https://cwauthors.com/article/double-first-class-list, accessed 22 June 2019.

Cheng Ying (2011) A Reflection on the Effects of the 985 Project. *Chinese Education & Society*, 44(5), pp. 19–30.

China Court Network (2022) Quanguo shouli gaokao shijuan bei tou an xuanpan. 27 August, https://www.chinacourt.org/article/detail/2003/08/id/77885.shtml, accessed 13 June 2022.

China Daily (2022) Xi Focus-Quotable Quotes: Xi Jinping on higher education. 7 June, https://www.chinadaily.com.cn/a/202206/07/WS629f0539a310fd2b29e61344.html, accessed 10 June 2022.

China Education Online (2013) 2013 Numbers of students taking the *gaokao* in provinces across the nation. http://www.eol.cn/html/jijiao/gao/gkrs/gkrs.shtml, accessed 6 February, 2024.

China Education Online (2016) 2016 nian Zhongguo sanben daxue paiming (qian 100 qiang) quanwei gongbu. 25 June, https://gaokao.eol.cn/news/201607/t20160725_1433562.shtml, accessed 20 June 2019.

China Education Online (2017a) 2017 nian Shandong gaokao fenshu xian gongbu. 24 June, https://gaokao.eol.cn/shan_dong/dongtai/201706/t20170624_1533690.shtml, accessed 19 June 2019.

China Education Online (2017b) 9.4 million students took the *gaokao* in 2017. 6 June, https://gaokao.eol.cn/gkbm/bmxx/201706/t20170606_1522469.shtml, accessed 6 February 2024.

Clothey, Rebecca (2005) China's policies for minority nationalities in higher education: Negotiating national values and ethnic identities. *Comparative Education Review*, 49(3), pp. 389–409.

Communist Party of China News (2013) The number of college entrance examinations has declined for five consecutive years, with only 9.12 million people taking the exam in 2013. 6 June, http://cpc.people.com.cn/n/2013/0606/c87228-21761786.html, accessed 6 February, 2024.

Dello-Iacovo, Belinda (2009) Curriculum reform and 'quality education' in China: An overview. *International Journal of Educational Development*, 29(3), pp. 241–249.

Dunford, Michael (2022) The Chinese Path to Common Prosperity. *International Critical Thought*, 12(1), pp. 35–54.

Fong, Vanessa (2011) *Paradise Redefined: Transnational Chinese Students and the Quest for Flexible Citizenship in the Developed World*. Stanford, CA: Stanford University Press.

Fu Yiqin (2013a) China's Unfair College Admissions System. *The Atlantic*, 19 June, https://www.theatlantic.com/china/archive/2013/06/chinas-unfair-college-admissions-system/276995/, accessed 8 June 2022.

Fu Yiqin (2013b) Problems of Place: Do Quotas in China's College Admissions System Reinforce Existing Inequalities? *Tea Leaf Nation*, http://www.tealeafnation.com/2013/06/problems-of-place-do-quotas-in-chinas-college-admissions-system-reinforce-existing-inequalities/, accessed 8 June, 2022.

Fu Yiqin (2018) Data Analysis: Regional Inequalities in Chinese College Admissions. 7 June, https://yiqinfu.github.io/posts/china-college-admissions-regional-inequalities-tsinghua/, accessed 20 June 2019.

Guan Qun, and Meng Wanjin (2007) China's new national curriculum reform: Innovation, challenges and strategies. *Frontiers of Education in China*, 2(4), pp. 579–604.

Han Shuangmiao and Xu Xin (2019) How far has the state 'stepped back': An exploratory study of the changing governance of higher education in China (1978–2018). *Higher Education*, 78(5), pp. 931–946.

Han Yafei (2009) China establishes "Ivy league", academic credits mutually recognized. *PKU News*, 15 October. https://english.pku.edu.cn/news_events/news/campus/1268.html, accessed 21 June 2024.

Hartog, Joop, Sun Yuze, and Ding Xiaohao (2010) University rank and bachelor's labour market positions in China. *Economics of Education Review*, 29(6), pp. 971–979.

Huxiu (2019) Shenzhen gaokao yimin fenbo beihou. 18 May, https://www.huxiu.com/article/299877.html, accessed 20 June 2019.

IIE Open Doors (2021) Leading Places of Origin. https://opendoorsdata.org/data/international-scholars/leading-places-of-origin/, accessed 21 April 2021.

Jia, Qiong, and David P. Ericson (2017) Equity and access to higher education in China: Lessons from Hunan province for university admissions policy. *International Journal of Educational Development*, 52, pp. 97–110.

Kojima, Kazuko (2020) Politics under Xi Jinping: Centralization and its Implications. *Public Policy Review*, 16(3), pp. 1–21.

Li Wensheng (2007) An renkou bili anpai zhaosheng jihua de gongpingxing – Luan Zhongguo zhengfa daxue de zhaosheng gaige. *Hubei Zhaosheng Kaoshi*, 176, pp. 41–44.

Li Hongbin, Loyalka Prashant, Rozelle Scott, Wu Binzhen, and Xie Jieyu (2015) Unequal access to college in China: How far have poor, rural students been left behind? *The China Quarterly*, 221, pp. 185–207.

Liu Jinsong (2012) Mingxiao zhaosheng diyu chabie diaocha. *Gongchandangyuan*, 2012(7), p. 26.

Liu Haifeng and Wu Qiong (2006) Consequences of college entrance exams in China and the reform challenges. KEDI. *Journal of Education Policy*, 3(1), pp. 7–21.

Liu Yi-Ling (2022) The Larger Meaning of China's Crackdown on School Tutoring. *The New Yorker*, 16 May, https://www.newyorker.com/culture/culture-desk/the-larger-meaning-of-chinas-crackdown-on-school-tutoring, accessed 9 June 2022.

Ma Ying (2019) *Chinese University Graduates' Reflexivity on Social Networking during First-job Search*. Unpublished Dissertation. Hong Kong: University of Hong Kong.

Ministry of Education of China (1998) Jiang Zeming zai qingzhu Beijing daxue jianxiao 100 zhounian dahui shang de jianghua. 4 May, http://www.moe.edu.cn/publicfiles/business/htmlfiles/moe/moe_177/200407/2475.html, accessed 9 June 2019.

Ministry of Education of China (1999) Guanyu jin yi bu shenhua putong gaodeng xuexiao zhaosheng kaoshi zhidu gaige de yijian. http://www.law-lib.com/law/law_view.asp?id=14335, accessed 14 June 2019.

Ministry of Education of China (2008) "211" gongcheng jianjie. http://www.moe.gov.cn/publicfiles/business/htmlfiles/moe/moe_846/200804/33122.html, accessed 14 June 2019.

Ministry of Education of China (2017a) Quanguo gaodeng xuexiao mingdan. http://www.moe.edu.cn/srcsite/A03/moe_634/201706/t20170614_306900.html, accessed 19 June 2019.

Ministry of Education of China (2017b) Jiaoyubu caizhengbu guojia fazhan gaige wei guanyu gongbu shijie yiliu daxue he yiliu xueke jianshe gaoxiao ji jianshe xueke mingdan de tongzhi. http://www.moe.gov.cn/srcsite/A22/moe_843/201709/t20170921_314942.html, accessed 20 June 2019.

Ministry of Education of China (2019) Jiaoyubu guanyu zuohao 2018 nian zhongdian gaoxiao zhaoshou nongcun he pinkun diqu xuesheng gongzuo de tongzhi. http://www.moe.gov.cn/srcsite/A15/moe_776/s3258/201803/t20180320_330724.html, accessed 20 June 2019.

Ministry of Finance of China (2012) Guanyu shishi mianxiang pinkun diqu dingxiang zhaosheng zhuanxiang jihua de tongzhi. http://yss.mof.gov.cn/mofhome/mof/zhengwuxinxi/zhengcefabu/201204/t20120423_644817.htm, accessed 20 June 2019.

MyCOS Research (2017) *2017 nian Zhongguo benkesheng jiuye baogao*. Beijing: Social Science Academic Press.

National Development and Reform Commission, Ministry of Education, and Ministry of Finance of China (1995) "211" gongcheng zongti jianshe guihua. 18 November, http://law.people.com.cn/showdetail.action?id=2593495, accessed 9 June 2019.

People's Daily Online (2008) Over 10 billion yuan to be invested in "211 Project". 26 March, http://english.people.com.cn/90001/6381319.html, accessed 9 June 2019.

People's Daily Online (2014a) The number of applicants for this year's college entrance examination has dropped again in many places, with Beijing declining for the 10th consecutive year. 12 May, http://politics.people.com.cn/n1/2016/0512/c1001-28344014.html, accessed 6 February 2024.

People's Daily Online (2014b) Gaokao for migrant students, education equality for China. 7 June, http://en.people.cn/n/2014/0607/c90882-8738239.html, accessed 12 June 2019.

People's Daily Online (2016) Today, 9.4 million candidates entered the college entrance examination room. 7 June, http://edu.people.com.cn/n1/2016/0607/c1053-28416061.html, accessed 6 February 2024.

Ren Shuli (2022) China's Big Problem That Xi Jinping Can't Solve. *Washington Post,* 9 June, https://www.washingtonpost.com/business/chinas-big-problem-that-xi-jinping-cant-solve/2022/06/09/e3b27a6c-e84c-11ec-a422-11bbb91db30b_story.html, accessed 10 June 2022.

Sargent, Tanja and Yang Xiao (2010) State-sponsored knowledge for the global age: global and traditional values in the Chinese language arts curriculum. In: Emily Hannum, Hyunjoon Park, Yuko Goto Butler. *Globalization, Changing Demographics, and Educational Challenges in East Asia,* Bingley, UK: Emerald Group Publishing Limited, pp. 99–121.

Sautman, Barry (1998) Affirmative action, ethnic minorities and China's universities. *Pacific Rim Law & Policy Journal,* 7, p. 77.

Sina Education News (2010) The number of people taking the *gaokao* in 2010 was 650,000 less than last year. 7 June, http://edu.sina.com.cn/gaokao/2010-06-07/0751250358.shtml, accessed 6 February 2024.

Sina Education News (2011) In 2011, the number of college entrance examination candidates nationwide was 9.33 million, which dropped by another 240,000. 3 June. http://edu.sina.com.cn/gaokao/2011-06-03/1114298442.shtml, accessed 6 February 2024.

Sina Education News (2012) The number of college entrance examination applicants in 2012 was 9.15 million, a decrease of 1.4 million in 4 years. 7 June, http://edu.sina.com.cn/gaokao/2012-06-07/0627341310.shtml, accessed 6 February 2024.

Sina Education News (2013) 2013 Ranking by number of students taking the gaokao in provinces across the nation. 5 September. http://edu.sina.com.cn/gaokao/2013-05-09/1441379477.shtml, accessed 6 February 2024.

State Council (2014) Guowuyuan guanyu shenhua kaoshi zhaosheng zhidu gaige de shishi yijian. 4 September, http://www.gov.cn/zhengce/content/2014-09/04/content_9065.htm, accessed 14 June 2019.

Sohu Education (2017) 2017 percent enrollment into higher education institutions across the nation. http://www.sohu.com/a/161789769_567589, accessed 9 June 2019.

Sun Jinming (2004) Gaokao fensheng zizhu minti de lixing sikao. *Dangdai Jiaoyu Kexue,* 2004(24), pp. 21–24.

Teets, Jessica (2018) Assessing Xi Jinping's Recentralisation of Power. *Asia Dialogue,* 1 September. https://theasiadialogue.com/2018/01/09/assessing-xi-jinpings-recentralisation-of-power/, accessed 6 June 2022.

Tian, Bula (2018) Shei lai guan guan gaokao zhiyuan tianbao tianjia zixun. *People.cn*, 21 June, http://opinion.people.com.cn/n1/2018/0621/c1003-30071573.html, accessed 21 June 2019.

Times Higher Education (THE) (2014) World University Rankings. https://www.timeshighereducation.com/world-university-rankings/2014/world-ranking#!/page/0/length/25/sort_by/rank/sort_order/asc/cols/stats, accessed 12 June 2019.

Times Higher Education (THE) (2019) World University Rankings. https://www.timeshighereducation.com/world-university-rankings/2019/world-ranking#!/page/0/length/25/sort_by/rank/sort_order/asc/cols/stats, accessed 12 June 2019.

Times Higher Education (THE) (2022) World University Rankings. https://www.timeshighereducation.com/world-university-rankings/2022#!/page/0/length/25/locations/CHN/sort_by/rank/sort_order/asc/cols/stats, accessed 15 June 2022.

Tu Mengwei (2016) Chinese one-child families in the age of migration: middle-class transnational mobility, ageing parents, and the changing role of filial piety. *The Journal of Chinese Sociology*, 3(1), p. 15.

Wang Houxiong (2010) Research on the influence of college entrance examination policies on the fairness of higher education admissions opportunities in China. *Chinese Education and Society*, 43(6), pp. 15–35.

Wang Houxiong and Wang Shicun (2011) Butong liyi qunti dui gaokaozhidu gongpingxing rentongdu de diaocha yu fenxi. *Jiaoyu celiang yu pingjia*, 09, pp. 4–18.

Wang X. (2011) Research on higher education enrollment opportunities of rural students in China. *University Academic*, 5, pp. 66–73.

Wang Z. (2008) Xinkebiao xia gaokao fangan de zhiding he shishi. *Dangdai Jiaoyu Kexue*, 11, p. 8.

Wright, Ewan, and Moosung Lee (2014) Developing skills for youth in the 21st century: The role of elite International Baccalaureate Diploma Programme schools in China. *International Review of Education*, 60(2), pp. 199–216.

Wu Xiaogang, and Donald J. Treiman (2004) The household registration system and social stratification in China: 1955–1996. *Demography*, 41(2), pp. 363–384.

Xiang Biao, and Shen Wei (2009) International student migration and social stratification in China. *International Journal of Educational Development*, 29(5), pp. 513–522.

Xiong B. (2018) Gaoxiao zizhu zhaosheng zhengce shishi: Gongpingquan yu jiandu. *Shanghai Jiaoyu Pingu Yanjiu*, 5 (October 2018), pp. 4–26.

Yang Rui (2004) Toward massification: Higher education development in the People's Republic of China since 1949. In: John C. Smart, *Higher education: Handbook of theory and research*. Dordrecht: Springer, pp. 311–374.

Yangguang gaokao: kaosheng yu jiazhang dianzi duben (2009). http://gaokao.chsi.com.cn/z/db2009/, accessed 9 June, 2019.

Yangguang gaokao: kaosheng yu jiazhang dianzi duben(2012). http://gaokao.chsi.com.cn/z/2012gkbmfslq/fsx.jsp/, accessed 9 June 2019.

Yao Shujie, Wu Bin, Su Fang, and Wang Jiangling (2010) The impact of higher education expansion on social justice in China: A spatial and inter-temporal analysis. *Journal of Contemporary China*, 19(67), pp. 837–854.

Yuan X. (2007) Jiaoyubu kaoshi zhongxin fu zhuren Ying Shuzeng tan gaokao gaige. *The People's Daily*, http://edu.people.com.cn/GB/5636042.html, accessed 2 July, 2013.

Zha Qiang (2009) Diversification or homogenization: How governments and markets have combined to (re)shape Chinese higher education in its recent massification process. *Higher Education*, 58(1), pp. 41–58.

Zhang Qiang (2011) Diversity or Discrimination? A Constitutional Analysis of the Admission Quota Scheme in Chinese Universities. *Peking University Law Journal*, 2011(2), p. 248.

Zhang Donghui and Tanja Sargent (2019) Education for Migrant Children in China. In: Mark D. Weist, Aradhana Bela Sood and Caroline S. Clauss-Ehlers (eds.) *Social Justice for Children and Young People: International Perspectives*. Cambridge: Cambridge University Press.

Zheng Ruoling (2010) On the rationality of the college entrance examination: Analysis of its social foundations, functions, and influences. *Chinese Education and Society*, 43(4), pp. 11–21.

Zhao Yong and Qiu Wei (2012) Policy changes and educational reforms in China: Decentralization and marketization. *On the Horizon*, 20(4), pp. 313–323.

Zhihu (2022) 2022 nian quanguo gaokao shijuan fenlei. 7 June, https://zhuanlan.zhihu.com/p/525390973, accessed 17 June 2022.

Zhou Haiwen (2018) A model of institutional complementarities in ancient China. *Eastern Economic Journal*, 44(2), pp. 286–304.

Zhou Wenkuo (2014) Fensheng mingti hengxiang bijiao jiazhi jiangdi de yuanyin fenxi he duice yanjiu. *Dangdai Jiaoyu Kexue*, 2014(14), pp. 48–50.

CHAPTER 12

Functionalities of Political Humor in Xi Jinping's Era

Resistance, Cynicism, Nationalism

Wendy Weile Zhou and Lutgard Lams

1   Introduction

In the socio-political realm, political humor has long been a critical mirror that reflects the fabric of state-society relations. Particularly in China, historically, the political, cultural, and social functions of political humor have been entrenched in Chinese people's everyday life and use of language (Davis and Chey, 2013; Yang and Jiang, 2015). Its online presence exemplifies the interwovenness of cultural norms, power dynamics, and technological influence. In the past 20 years, given that flourishing internet platforms have offered alternative spaces for incorporating and disseminating grassroots viewpoints, political humor has been considered the key force of empowerment and liberation in Chinese civic society (Yang, 2009). Meanwhile, memes, as an eye-catching identity-branding instrument, have long been co-opted by political and commercial forces to either claim discursive control or generate tangible profits (Gong and Yang, 2010).

Noticeably, China's porous cyberspace, which managed to absorb a certain amount of resistance previously, has been more strictly regulated and surveilled under Xi's reign. Meanwhile, the state has become more skillful at channeling and appropriating public opinion and popular culture, especially waging nationalist campaigns to enhance legitimacy (Lams and Zhou, 2023).

These twin factors of entanglement and transformation beg the following questions: What is the role of humor in Chinese contemporary political culture? How is political humor created, represented, and articulated in Xi Jinping's era? To provide some answers, this chapter critically analyzes Chinese digital memes to disentangle the three major types of humor functions: 1) creative resistance, i.e., pushing the state-dictated limits of speech and upsetting the dominant power relations; 2) playful symbolism, i.e., maintaining entertainment as a priority and political participation on a symbolic level; 3) participatory nationalism, i.e., adopting and revamping the state-sanctioned nationalistic narratives. Therefore, the current study sets out to better understand the new trends of political culture in Xi's era, and more broadly, the hyper-interactive social media environment and the image of the Chinese nation-state, as projected in the popular samples investigated later in the study. Through the study, we find that the Chinese digital space accommodates different stances towards the current socio-political climate, exemplified through the three distinct functions of humor. The state-society relationship is symbiotic and fluid rather than antagonistic and fixed: the state and the society rely on each other to create viral memes, channel opinion, and recontextualize or re-articulate social reality.

2 Literature Review

In line with the triple functionalities of resistance, cynicism, and nationalism, as indicated in the title, this section presents a bird's eye view of some relevant literature about the functions of political humor. The focus lies on the roles of resistance and cynicism or playful symbolism since these have been discussed extensively in earlier studies. The third function (nationalism) is not as prevalent in the literature, except for studies by Guo and Yang (2019), who explored memetic communication and consensus mobilization in the cyber nationalist movement, and Liang (2020), who presented a content analysis of a meme war between Taiwanese and Chinese nationalists on Facebook.

In contemporary popular culture, memes have been defined as "collective folk texts that spread because people remix and remake them" (Mcculloch, 2020: 253). They can be satirical or parodic expressions depending on their imitative origin and moral function. Like parodies, they are "cultural replications" (Mcculloch, 2020: 260) and creative distortions that "draw on a shared understanding of some linguistic expressions" (Mcculloch, 2020: 253).

In the digital era, humorous Internet memes are considered as groups of digital cultural items that enjoy large-scale circulation and imitation. They are text and image combinations that share similarities of form/content/attitudes (Shifman, 2014; Dancygier and Vandelanotte, 2017) and have become a ubiquitous source of political participation. The virality of memes lies in the fact that the online environment not only revolutionizes the speed and scale of text circulation but also diversifies the interpretation, increases hyper-textuality and intertextuality, and blurs the lines between producers and consumers (Jenkins, 2014; Jenkins et al., 2013).

2.1 Political Humor as Creative Resistance

Forms of humor, including satire, irony, and parody, have long been studied as subversive non-violent resistance against the hegemonic power and its discourses in both democratic (Freedman, 2009; Punathambekar, 2015) and non-democratic contexts (Moreno-Almeida, 2021; Wedeen, 2013). In practice, political humor can function as a censorship-bypassing tool. In the digital communication environment, the emergence of online humor, like *E-gao* (or parodies), e.g., Steamed Bun and Grass Mud Horse, has created opportunities to articulate critiques of and grievances about state-sanctioned policies and use of power (Meng, 2011; Gong and Yang, 2010). Through innovative sentence-making and multimedia-remixing, online users have exposed important social problems including corruption, social disparity, and class differences, and thus highlighted the importance of public intervention in the top-down power hierarchies (Yang and Jiang, 2015).

Humor has been a particularly useful discursive channel in digital social activism campaigns (Lee, 2016; Yang, 2009). It forms a connective action network and discourse prototype with loose organizational coordination that allows different personal agendas and engagement strategies (Bennett and Segerberg, 2012). Since digital humor is incorporated within the emancipating effects of the internet, it can contribute to transforming state-society relations and even triggering a certain level of democratization (Tang and Bhattacharya, 2011; Esarey and Xiao, 2011).

2.2 Political Humor as Playful Symbolism

Different from the previous note on powerful resistance, some literature suggests the humorous expressions are "light-hearted frivolity" purely for fun (Holm, 2017), or depoliticized forms of public venting and are not aimed at or capable of disrupting the authoritarian rule (Nordin and Richaud, 2014; Lagerkvist, 2010). Instead, these satirical memes can help social media users accumulate cultural capital, form online subcultural communities, and foster collective identities.

Specifically, in the Chinese context, *E-gao* is an "individualized comic parody" and "technology-enabled cultural intervention" (Gong and Yang, 2010: 16) that reflects the society's shift to self-development, individualistic lifestyles, and materialistic pursuits in the post-Mao era (Sun and Lei, 2017; Rosen, 2004). Online satire has become a young generations' window to relieve stress and regain personal autonomy when encountering entrenched social problems (e.g., income gap, lack of social mobility, cultural split from the past), rather than to initiate actual resistance against the regime (Zou, 2020; Gong and Yang, 2010; Tan and Cheng, 2020). The interlocking of popular culture, play, and politics has long been witnessed in the discussions among Chinese online users. The expressions are neither "benign online entertainment" nor "overt political activism" but rather exist in between (Yang et al., 2015; Yang, 2003). For example, Chinese online users use 'diaosi' (or "losers"), 'jiucai' (or "garlic chives"), to either represent their underprivileged social status (Yang et al., 2015) or ridicule state-capitalist neoliberalism (Pang, 2021). But, apart from criticizing societal affairs, they are self-mocking through underlining their sense of inferiority when encountering socially privileged elites, rather than a direct confrontation with the top leadership. The toad worship memes, referring to the former president Jiang Zemin, are employed to seek entertainment, which prioritizes their playful characteristics over their subversive meanings (Fang, 2020).

Political memes can disseminate positive emotions, such as empowerment, solidarity, hope, and gratitude, especially among marginalized groups categorized by gender, ethnicity, and social status (Leung, 2009; Phillips and Milner, 2017; Jackson and Welles, 2016), and through public crises like COVID-19 (Flecha Ortiz et al., 2021). Meanwhile, they can also underline negativity and discrimination through attacks and harassments in nationalistic, racist, misogynistic, and sexist discourses (Polak and Trottier, 2020; Wu and Wall, 2021). Specifically, through Chinese nationalistic memes, the attitude of contempt and superiority was projected in direct and straightforward verbal attacks during disputes over sovereignty claims and other national interests (Min, 2009; Li, 2011).

3 Method

3.1 *Analytical Method*

This research adopted the method 'guerrilla ethnography' to track the evolution and changes of the forms, content, and emotions revealed through the memes across the sites. This method, focusing on the "openness, fluidity, and connections" of internet spaces (Yang, 2003: 471), has been widely employed to study the online discussions among Chinese nationalistic and patriotic groups (Fang and Repnikova, 2018; Han, 2015) as well as social activists (Yang, 2003). Specifically, this approach involves close reading of the textual/visual messages, the comparisons of the ideational meanings of memes over time and across different sites, and the mapping of group relations through interactions, including sharing, commenting, and liking.

As such, multi-modal discourse analysis (MDA), including a critical discourse analysis and semiotic analysis, was employed to examine the meanings and connotations of the specific kind of political humor shown through various semiotic modes integrated into one artifact. Multimodality refers to

FUNCTIONALITIES OF POLITICAL HUMOR IN XI JINPING'S ERA 305

how multiple modes are used for communicative purposes (Kress and van Leeuwen, 2006). This analysis mainly focuses on the combination of pictures and texts adopted by the internet memetic artifacts.

3.2 Data Collection

This study aims to shed light on the forms and functions of political humor in Chinese politics. Therefore, the analysis focuses on the extensively circulated humorous political memes that are either widely shared and discussed on Chinese social media, including the messaging app WeChat and the microblog service Weibo, the Q&A site Zhihu, as well as the video site Bilibili or have been covered by foreign news sites or discussed on Twitter (an important site of dissident voices in Chinese politics) or China Digital Times (a site that collects censored political messages in China). We zoomed in on the internet culture between 2013 and 2020 under Xi's leadership, and selected memes that met the following criteria: 1) They had to be humorous memes discussing or alluding to political issues/events/ideologies/figures; 2) The topics were associated to major Chinese socio-political events; 3) They were mainly created by Chinese users, targeting a Chinese audience, were widely discussed and shared either on the Chinese or international social media; 4) The memes were using both textual and visual elements to convey satirical or parodical messages.

To select the memes, we conducted a thorough keyword search on both Chinese social media and foreign websites as mentioned above, by focusing on words and phrases that specify important political figures (e.g., 'Xi Jinping'), genre (e.g., 'satire'/'irony'/'mocking'), and context (e.g., 'Chinese politics', 'Chinese leadership'). Altogether, we gathered 1,512 memes, and kept 597 after removing 1) the duplicate artifacts (i.e., possess similar image compositions and textual meanings), 2) those that did not convey humor straightforwardly, and 3) whose visual messages and written texts were not connected to each other either on the semiotic level or in the socio-political context.

We conducted three rounds of coding for detailed interpretation. First, we grouped the remaining memes into three categories based on the functions, i.e., 1) creative resistance; 2) playful symbolism; and 3) participatory nationalism. Second, under these categories, three sub-themes were identified: 1) criticism of Xi's leadership (258 memes); 2) cynical self-mockery from the grassroots public, combined with societal criticism (136 memes); 3) ironical comments about anti-China forces or rival countries (203 memes). Third, per sub-theme, we selected for in-depth analysis three prominent groups of memes (253 in total) that attracted relatively more news coverage and online discussions: 1) memes of 2018 Constitution Revision (related to Xi's leadership's term); 2) memes of 'Lying Flat' (related to cynical self-mockery and societal criticism); 3) memes of the US government (related to the foreign rival). For the convenience of interpretation, the empirical analysis below offers one or two representative samples for each function and group of memes to demonstrate the semiotic meanings and discusses some socio-political implications. The artifacts shown below are screenshots taken by the web browser's application.

4 Empirical Analysis of Humorous Memes

4.1 *Creative Resistance: Mocking Xi's Long Presidency*

No pressure on marriage. On February 25, 2018, China's top legislature, the National People's Congress officially abolished the two-term presidential limits as set out by the 1982 Constitution to curb the power of an incumbent leader and avoid political turmoil (Buckley and Wu, 2018). This bold move triggered predictions over China's political future and gave rise to a wealth of digital satire that poked fun at Xi's personal ambitions which are believed to complicate China's political future.

Figure 12.1 offers an entertaining comparison between Xi's time in office and the expected time for marriage. This screenshot, originally posted on WeChat and later circulated on Twitter, shows an anonymous internet user quipping, "My mom urged me to get married within the term limit of President Xi. Now

FIGURE 12.1 Mocking the longevity of Xi Jinping's reign by associating it with marriage pressure
RETRIEVED OCTOBER 31, 2021, FROM TWITTER (2018). THE POST SAYS, "MY MOM URGED ME TO GET MARRIED WITHIN THE TERM LIMIT OF PRESIDENT XI. NOW I AM RELIEVED" (AUTHORS' TRANSLATION)

i am relieved".[1] In addition, this internet user attached an image with the flag of the Party, the emblem of the Chinese Communist Party, and a telling slogan "Always follow the Party's footsteps". Underlying the multimodal message is a demonstration of full political loyalty. To generate laughter, the reader has to be both reminded of Xi's term extension and be familiar with the commonplace conversation between young people and parents about marriage pressure.

Subversion against the official decision is discursively achieved through the transgression of the Confucian ideal that has been observed within Chinese society for centuries. In the conventional Confucian family tradition, the descendants of the family have the responsibility to secure social stability through marriage and have children to carry through the ancestral legacy. Till today, generational gaps of marital views are still permeating everyday life, as a representation of the conflict between traditional culture and contemporary norms of personal freedom. In the meme, the user's mom states that the marriage urgency hinges on the limits to Xi's presidency. Now, since the constitution revision theoretically has removed the time restrictions to holding presidential office, the burdens of partner-searching can be minimized. This irony exposes two layers of societal tensions: 1) the gap between traditional family dynamics and the modern romantic relationships advocated by younger generations; 2) the tension between the decision-making on the individual level (i.e., personal marriage) and the political level (i.e., presidential term).

The act of extending Xi's power thwarts the older generation's expectation of their children's early marriage, and at the same time, gives young people some breathing room for personal development. This reflects the commotion triggered by the unexpectedness of the constitutional change and foregrounds the immense impact of this historical decision, since it can even settle generational disputes over marriage timing. On the semiotic level, the incongruence of the message generates the satirical laughter about the irrationality and unpredictability of Xi Jinping's prolonged reign. Specifically, given the urgency of marriage timing, the mother set the deadline to coincide with the end of Xi's term, expected to be five years later (the normative-surface meaning), but now that Xi's term has theoretically become unlimited, the daughter's marriage is no longer a priority (the deviant-implicit meaning). The authorial intent "to reach not only full comprehension of the ideational content, but also a sense of mutual enjoyment and solidarity" (Lams and Zhou, 2020: 349), at understanding the gap between "both scripts – the normative one (surface meaning)

---

1   All translations of the memetic texts are provided by the authors.

and the deviant one (implicit meaning)" – needs to be captured by all participants to the communicative event (Lams and Zhou, 2020: 349).

Also, the successful posting on Chinese internet accentuates the role of satire in circumventing the Chinese censorship while retaining its potential of resistance. From a multi-modal perspective, both the text and the image employ the strategy of irony to reduce the likelihood of being silenced. The text embeds the incisive critique of Xi's position as a perpetual leader in a safe and colloquial style of referring to President Xi as 'Xi dada [dad]'. This strategy of using an intimate kinship term softens Xi's leadership to a caring parental figure. The image demonstrates the adherence to the party-state decision-making.

Xi as an emperor and Xi as an ageing man. The following memes expose the absurdity of Xi's long term through comic visualization, created by political cartoonist Badiucao. Figure 12.2 portrays Xi as an emperor, and Figure 12.3 displays Xi's face as an ageing man. In Figure 12.2, the signifier consists of the emperor's symbols, including the traditional red crown and necklace, often seen on rulers in Qing Dynasty, the last ancient dynasty before China stepped into modernity. The signified is the idea of the one-man rule, as written in the text, which subjects China to strict official hierarchies and power abuse without the safety net of the checks and balance system. Similarly, Figure 12.3 re-appropriates Xi's official photo by restyling it into an ageing man with a wrinkled face and grey hair (signifier), but he still wears a suit and appears as a leader (signifier), holding on to power (signified). This ridicules Xi's aspiration for perennial rule through highlighting his lost physical capability and mocks the rigidity of the party-rule that even keeps an unqualified man in office.

Altogether, the three images confront the official decisions and Xi's authority as a leader. The memetic articulations reveal what is perceived as an unjust decision-making process by showing its unprecedented consequence in everyday life (Figure 12.1). They reflect Xi's expansion of his own orbit of power (Figure 12.2) and expose the leader's inability of ruling long (Figure 12.3). The adjacent and explicit referential terms directly challenge the political order by questioning the regime legitimacy: Is China moving towards a one-man rule? This question leads to the next inferential query: How does this impact both society's and the individuals' wellbeing? Also, this alternative way of decoding official rule and encoding resistance offers spaces for constructing an alternative imagined community, a common function in Chinese political satire, as noticed by Meng (2011).

FIGURE 12.2 President or Emperor?
RETRIEVED OCTOBER 31, 2021, FROM INDEX ON CENSORSHIP (2018)

FIGURE 12.3 Xi Forever
RETRIEVED OCTOBER 31, 2021, FROM INDEX ON CENSORSHIP (2018)

4.2 Playful Symbolism: Mocking the Self and Criticizing Society Through 'Lying Flat'

As one of China's top 10 viral memes in 2021 (Li, 2021), 'Lying flat' (躺平 *tangping*) epitomizes the young generations' struggles with the hyper-competition and resistance against extra labor throughout work and life. It originates from the post titled "Lying Flat is justice" in April 2021 on the Chinese popular online forum Baidu Tieba. The author narrates his two-year experience meeting minimum materialistic desires without a job (Ji and He, 2021). Naturally, this resonated with young people's dismay at the rat race and soon became popular across the internet.

This series of memes features a central figure—an animal, person, or a comic figure-physically lying on a surface of an object, a sofa, or the ground, accompanied by a text message about the need to 'lie flat'. For example, Figure 12.4 shows a typical lazy person who stays at home, sliding from the sofa to the ground while clinging to the mobile phone. Figure 12.5, the 'Paralyzed Geyou' (葛优躺 *geyou tang*), a popular figure originally from the 1993 comedy *I Love My Family*, was recontextualized to signify the desire for taking distance from the over-competitiveness and high social expectations. Figure 12.6 portrays a group of cute kittens tortured by exhaustion and lying flat together.

As the text shows, this alludes to the 'non-cooperative movement', a non-violent protest led by Indian political activist Mahatma Gandhi to resist British rule over India. The target of the meme is social stagnation and structural limits that create numerous hurdles, and overly high standards for personal achievements. Without direct challenge to the regime, young people are voicing their grievances of the family and workplace pressure through cynical measures, including not getting married, not studying diligently, not working hard, not buying houses (Kuo, 2021).

The playfulness of the 'lying flat' meme is reflected through 1) the self-mockery made possible by the visualized frustration and depression, and 2) the creative memetic replication and reinterpretation of meanings. The act of 'lying flat', embodied through the corpse-like body and the look of disenchantment and tiredness conveys the feeling of powerlessness or even worthlessness. It generates a bitter laughter from realizing the limits of self-development, which turns disappointment into humor that can "mitigate or obfuscate their own negative or nihilistic feelings" (Tan and Cheng, 2020: 95). Noticeably, diverse meanings of 'lying flat' emerge: 1) re-focusing on self-fulfillment rather than adhering to the mainstream ideals for perfect life (Figure 12.4); 2) escaping the stress by distancing oneself from the endless competitive routine (Figure 12.5); 3) strengthening the sense of collectiveness among young people against the culture of progress (Figure 12.6). The overarching attitude of cynicism distinguishes the

FIGURE 12.4 Lying flat and letting it go
RETRIEVED DECEMBER 12, 2021, FROM ZHIHU (2021).
THE TEXT READS, "I AM LYING FLAT NOW. FEEL FREE
TO JOIN ME OR NOT."

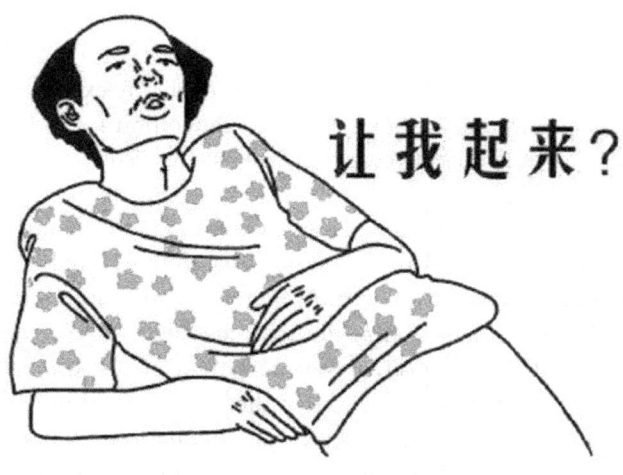

FIGURE 12.5 No possibility of standing up
RETRIEVED DECEMBER 1, 2021, FROM BANDURSKI
(2021). THE TEXT READS, "WANT ME TO GET UP?
THIS IS NOT POSSIBLE IN MY LIFETIME."

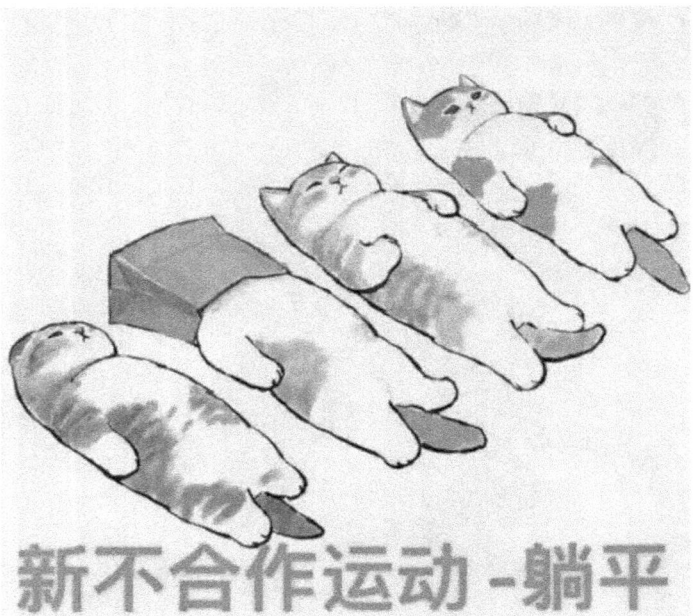

FIGURE 12.6 New non-cooperative movement – Lying flat
RETRIEVED DECEMBER 12, 2021, FROM BANDURSKI (2021).
THE TEXT SAYS, "NEW NON-COOPERATIVE MOVEMENT – LYING FLAT."

'lying flat' approach from the alternative activist mode of explicitly exposing the suffocating social climate in that it shows a passive separation from the normative standards instead of launching collective protests or disobedience campaigns.

Meanwhile, the original emphasis by the memetic community on the disillusionment of the future of personal development was co-opted and reinterpreted by the state propaganda machinery as ordinary people's temporary rest to reduce stress and to eventually realize the state-ideology of 'positive energy', i.e., the optimistic attitude and positive behaviors in social life (Xinhua News, 2021). Subsequently, the room for playful parodies has been trimmed down after state media and Xi dismissed the 'lying flat' phenomenon as 'shameful' and to be avoided. The terms and chat groups related to 'lying-flatism' have been heavily censored or removed (Bandurski, 2021).

4.3 Nationalism: Mocking the US

Mocking the US administration that blames China as a virus carrier. Nationalistic memes, as in Figure 12.7, boosting national pride and a sense of superiority, have gained popularity after China's effective control over the COVID-19 pandemic. The underlying narrative is the defiance against Western society's criticism of China's political system and its top leadership. As a counter-reaction, it underscores the socio-economic attainments that legitimize party-state governance. Particularly, memes of Sino-US rivalry reflect and hype up this narrative.

In Figure 12.7, a satirical cartoon mocks the US government's strong focus on China as the origin of the COVID-19 pandemic while itself being plagued by the virus. The US, symbolized through the uncle Sam image, is holding a huge club to knock down China, represented by the image of a doctor wearing a hermetically closed-off medical suit dedicated to the fight of the pandemic. Meanwhile, the virus, portrayed as an invading warrior, is pointing its gun at the back of the US, which exposes that the US society has been suffering from the rampant contagion due to the Trump and Biden administrations' mishandling of the pandemic. The post on the Chinese social media platform Weibo accuses the US of excelling at blaming others but failing to curb the virus circulation.

This meme signifies China's patriotic branding as the savior of humankind and responsible big power while the US only cares about its short-term political agenda without having a long-term strategic plan. Also, the memetic visualization maintains the long-held notion of US' interference into China's internal affairs, ranging from human rights issues over sovereignty disputes regarding the South China Sea, Hong Kong, Taiwan, China's global aspirations (e.g., the impact of Belt and Road), and its attempt to present an alternative to the international global order by showing the vitality of its political system. The satirical humor derives from two contrastive elements: 1) The US administration is dedicated to launching political attacks against China, while China focuses on the combat with the pandemic; 2) The US prioritizes chasing China over addressing its domestic problems. Therefore, from the Chinese party-state's perspective, the US is incurring a double-layered moral indebtedness to China (i.e., its 'unwarranted' criticism and stigmatization of the Chinese government) and its own domestic society (i.e., insufficient attention and measures to manage the pandemic outbreaks in the US). Overall, mocking the strategic and moral failures of the US leadership heightens the comparative effectiveness of the Chinese governance approach.

FIGURE 12.7 Mocking of US mishandling of the pandemic
RETRIEVED OCTOBER 31, 2021, FROM WEIBO (CHINESE YOUTH LEAGUE, 2021). THE POST SAYS, "YOU FAIL IN CONTROLLING THE PANDEMIC, BUT EXCEL AT SHIFTING THE BLAME."

Irony of US incapability of controlling Afghanistan's political scenarios. In Figure 12.8, the video clip compares the two speech clips from former US President Bush and incumbent President Biden about the US role in Afghanistan's politics. In 2004, when deploying military forces in Afghanistan, Bush made the statement that "Peace will be achieved by helping Afghanistan develop its own stable government." In 2021, Biden delivered the following remarks about the US strategic plan when he decided to withdraw troops from Afghanistan: "It [US mission in Afghanistan] was never supposed to be creating a unified, centralized democracy."

The circularity of handing the Afghanistan regime, i.e., taken from the hands of the Taliban back to the Taliban, contrasts with the democratization rhetoric

FIGURE 12.8 Mocking US incapability of handling Afghanistan's politics
RETRIEVED DECEMBER 12, 2021, FROM WEIBO (QINGCHUN HUBEI, 2021).
THE WEIBO POST SAYS, "AFTER FOUR US PRESIDENTS, A 20-YEAR WAR,
AND MORE THAN 174 THOUSAND CASUALTIES, THE US (GOVERNMENT)
'SUCCESSFULLY' TRANSFERRED THE AFGHANISTAN REGIME FROM THE
HANDS OF THE TALIBAN TO THE HANDS OF THE TALIBAN."

from the two US administrations and exposes the political hyperboles of the US government's diplomatic stances. In addition, the emoji of a smiling dog face adds a tone of defiance and mockery and situates China in the position of a distant onlooker and commentator.

The two above-mentioned posts about the US, originating from the youth wing of the ruling Communist party, the China Youth League, were widely circulated on the microblog Weibo. The frequent use of playful, satirical memes stemming from official sources evidences the deep involvement by the state propaganda, now also digitalized to channel public opinion. Based on the state-provided prototype, a wide array of bottom-up anti-US memes emerged. For example, the Chinese video site Bilibili published a series of cartoons called 'Poland Balls', which ridicules the short US history and its so-called insufficient understanding of other countries. The video creators portray each country as a ball-shape comic figure wrapped by its national flag. Figure 12.9 is a screenshot of a video mocking the US for mistaking other countries' names. The ball on the right, Latvia, was mistakenly recognized as Austria by the US on the left. Also, the site produces memes that symbolize the cordial relationships between China and other countries, highlighting a long-held resentment against what is perceived as US attempts at worldwide policing.

In contrast with the more explicit attacks against Hong Kong and Taiwan, the discursive rivalry with the US is, in this example, rather implicit. As Li (2011) and Min (2009) point out, online users ridicule pro-independence Taiwanese and Hong Kongers for being ignorant of China's economic status and people's livelihood, and these attacks are more direct and explicit in sovereignty conflicts. Differently, as mentioned earlier, criticism of the US is made effective through illustrating the political absurdity and flaws of US government decision-making, e.g., over-emphasis on other countries' mistakes while neglecting its own problems, with implicit references to China's achievements. In other words, the pro-active exposure of failures and guilt of the outgroup offers the nationalistic tones more socio-political capital for justifying claims by the ingroup.

FIGURE 12.9 Mocking the US for its so-called arrogance and ignorance
RETRIEVED DECEMBER 20, 2021, FROM BILIBILI (2017). THE TWO COMMENTS REGARDING THE US SAY (FROM TOP TO BOTTOM): "WHERE ARE THE US SUNGLASSES? I DISLIKE YOU DID NOT PUT THEM ON"; "IT MUST BE THE US BALL THAT RECOGNIZES THE WRONG NATIONAL FLAG AGAIN, AGAIN, AGAIN, AND AGAIN."

5 Concluding Remarks

In Xi Jinping's era, contemporary Chinese society has been undergoing drastic socio-political changes. As a mirror of state-society relations, political humor represents and articulates the tensions and dynamics through three perspectives: 1) creative resistance that directly disrupts the political order; 2) playful symbolism that consolidates the collective identity with diversified, personalized expressions; and 3) nationalistic propaganda that unifies top-down and bottom-up support for the regime. Specifically, the act of subversion is realized through heavy use of irony that questions the top leader's capability and regime legitimacy. Creative resistance functions through the mocking of the party-state decision-making and discourses (e.g., 'Xi as emperor' and 'Xi as an ageing man' memes), and the reflection on the influence of official decisions on individuals' daily lives (e.g., 'no pressure on marriage' memes). Exemplified by the 'lying flat' memes, playful symbolism underscores the isolation from or rebellion against the mainstream culture in a cynical, passive manner through its entertaining memetic creations. Differently, the playful memes do not generate direct confrontation with the official order but instead maximize the reachability across the political spectrum and enhance the sense of communal belonging through reduced political sensitivity and enlarged room for humorous interpretations. Last but not least, nationalistic memes aim to boost Chinese national pride and debunk the negative portrayals of China through foregrounding the defects and failures of governance in foreign countries (especially the US) in comparison with Chinese leadership's wise policies.

Beyond the control-resistance binary, this study identifies the Chinese internet, including its ironical content, as a highly interactive and complicated public sphere, which has evolved under political and technological conditions. Particularly, the state's monitoring and participation is a double-edged sword: on the one hand, they reinforce the information control; on the other, they also enrich the narratives, providing more materials that can be re-appropriated for subversion against the state. Furthermore, facilitated by the participatory culture in social media, the memes create a symbiosis between state and society: both the state and society can be the producer, marketeer, consumer, commentator of the memetic expressions. Rather than simply eschewing or espousing each other, the two sides maintain nuanced and unstable relationships that vary according to the context.

Broadly, this study demonstrates that supported by the hyper-interactivity in the present social media era, political humor in China under Xi entails a wide range of public functions, including acts belonging to the three categories of resistance, symbolism, and nationalism. The Chinese party-state has intensified the scale and depth of propaganda and censorship efforts, but shifting spaces still exist for non-state participation in the digital world through subcultural approaches. Future research might contextualize the gratifications of Chinese internet users, and especially how the networking purpose of this humor is associated with the netizens' identities and the technological affordances of the platforms used.

References

Bandurski, David (2021) The 'lying flat' movement standing in the way of China's innovation drive. *Brookings*, 8 July, https://www.brookings.edu/techstream/the-lying-flat-movement-standing-in-the-way-of-chinas-innovation-drive/, accessed 30 December 2021.

Bennett, W. Lance and Alexandra Segerberg (2012) The Logic of Connective Action. *Information, Communication & Society*, 15(5), pp. 739–68.

Bilibili (2017) [Bolan Qiu] Meiguo Qiu You Rencuo Guoqi Le_Bilibili. *Bilibili*, https://www.bilibili.com/video/BV1Dx411t7DP/, accessed 20 December 2021.

Buckley, Chris and Adam Wu (2018) Ending Term Limits for China's Xi Is a Big Deal. Here's Why. *The New York Times*, 10 March, https://www.nytimes.com/2018/03/10/world/asia/china-xi-jinping-term-limit-explainer.html, accessed 12 December 2021.

Chinese Youth League (2021) Kangyi Ni Buxing, Shuaiguo Diyiming. *Weibo*, 8 August, https://m.weibo.cn/3937348351/4668254784326603, accessed 31 October 2021.

Dancygier, Barbara and Lieven Vandelanotte (2017) Internet Memes as Multimodal Constructions. *Cognitive Linguistics*, 28(3), pp. 565–98.

Davis, Jessica Milner and Jocelyn Chey (eds.) (2013) *Humour in Chinese Life and Culture: Resistance and Control in Modern Times*. Hong Kong: Hong Kong University Press.

Esarey, Ashley and Qiang Xiao (2011) Digital Communication and Political Change in China. *International Journal of Communication*, 5, pp. 298–319.

Fang, Kecheng (2020) Turning a Communist Party Leader into an Internet Meme: The Political and Apolitical Aspects of China's Toad Worship Culture. *Information, Communication & Society*, 23(1), pp. 38–58.

Fang, Kecheng and Maria Repnikova (2018) Demystifying 'Little Pink': The Creation and Evolution of a Gendered Label for Nationalistic Activists in China. *New Media & Society*, 20(6), pp. 2162–85.

Flecha Ortiz, José A, Maria A Santos Corrada, Evelyn Lopez, and Virgin Dones (2021) Analysis of the Use of Memes as an Exponent of Collective Coping during COVID-19 in Puerto Rico. *Media International Australia*, 178(1), pp. 168–81.

Freedman, Leonard (2009) *The Offensive Art: Political Satire and Its Censorship Around the World from Beerbohm to Borat*. Westport: Praeger.

Gong, Haomin and Xin Yang (2010) Digitized Parody: The Politics of Egao in Contemporary China. *China Information*, 24(1), pp. 3–26.

Guo, Xiaoan and Shaoting Yang (2019) Memetic Communication and Consensus Mobilization in the Cyber Nationalist Movement. In: Hailong Liu (ed.) *From Cyber-Nationalism to Fandom Nationalism*. Abingdon–New York: Routledge, pp. 72–92.

Han, Rongbin (2015) Defending the Authoritarian Regime Online: China's 'Voluntary Fifty-Cent Army'. *The China Quarterly*, 224, pp. 1006–25.

Holm, Nicholas (2017) *Humour as Politics*. Cham: Springer International Publishing.

Index on Censorship (2018) The amazing banned memes from China, 1 March, https://www.indexoncensorship.org/2018/03/amazing-banned-memes-china/, accessed 31 October 2021.

Jackson, Sarah J. and Brooke Foucault Welles (2016) #Ferguson Is Everywhere: Initiators in Emerging Counterpublic Networks. *Information, Communication & Society*, 19(3), pp. 397–418.

Jenkins, Eric S. (2014) The Modes of Visual Rhetoric: Circulating Memes as Expressions. *Quarterly Journal of Speech*, 100(4), pp. 442–66.

Jenkins, Henry, Sam Ford, and Joshua Green (2013) *Spreadable Media: Creating Value and Meaning in a Networked Culture*. New York: New York University Press.

Ji, Siqi and Huifeng He (2021) What is 'lying flat', and why are Chinese officials standing up to it? *South China Morning Post*, 24 October, https://www.scmp.com/economy/china-economy/article/3153362/what-lying-flat-and-why-are-chinese-officials-standing-it, accessed 12 December 2021.

Kress, Gunther and Theo van Leeuwen (2006) *Reading Images: The Grammar of Visual Design*, 2nd Edition. London: Routledge.

Kuo, Lily (2021) Young Chinese Take a Stand against Pressures of Modern Life – by Lying Down. *Washington Post*, 5 June, https://www.washingtonpost.com/world/asia_pacific/china-lying-flat-stress/2021/06/04/cef36902-c42f-11eb-89a4-b7ae22aa193e_story.html, accessed 12 December, 2021.

Lagerkvist, Johan (2010) *After the Internet, Before Democracy: Competing Norms in Chinese Media and Society*. Bern: Peter Lang.

Lams, Lutgard and Wendy Weile Zhou (2020) Humorous Ambiguity and Dissimulation as Discursive Vehicles for Political and Social Critique in Chinese Society. *Versus*, 131(2), pp. 347–360.

Lams, Lutgard and Wendy Weile Zhou (2023) Pseudo-Participation, Authentic Nationalism: Understanding Chinese Fanquan Girls' Personifications of the Nation-State. *Asian Journal of Communication*, 33(1), pp. 38–59.

Lee, Siu-yau (2016) Surviving Online Censorship in China: Three Satirical Tactics and Their Impact. *The China Quarterly*, 228, pp. 1061–80.

Leung, Louis (2009) User-Generated Content on the Internet: An Examination of Gratifications, Civic Engagement and Psychological Empowerment. *New Media & Society*, 11(8), pp. 1327–47.

Li, Hongmei (2011) Parody and Resistance on the Chinese Internet. In: David Kurt Herold and Peter Marolt (eds.) *Online Society in China: Creating, Celebrating, and Instrumentalising the Online Carnival*. London: Routledge, pp. 71–88.

Li, Jane (2021) 'Lying Flat' Is Officially One of China's Top Memes of 2021. *Quartz*, 7 December, https://qz.com/2099309/lying-flat-is-officially-one-of-chinas-top-memes-of-2021/, accessed 12 December 2021.

Liang, Fan (2020) Talking Politics via Images: Exploring Chinese Internet Meme War on Facebook. In: Thomas Herdin, Maria Faust, and Guo-Ming Chen (eds.) *De-Westernizing Visual Communication and Cultures*. Baden-Baden: NOMOS, pp. 163–82.

McCulloch, Gretchen (2020) *Because Internet: Understanding How Language Is Changing*. New York: Riverhead Books.

Meng, Bingchun (2011) From Steamed Bun to Grass Mud Horse: E Gao as Alternative Political Discourse on the Chinese Internet. *Global Media and Communication*, 7(1), pp. 33–51.

Min, Dahong (2009) Dui Zhongguo Wangluo Minzu Zhuyi de Guancha Fenxi – Yi Zhongri Zhonghan Guanxi Wei Duixiang. *China Computer-Mediated Communication Studies*, 3, pp. 131–43.

Moreno-Almeida, Cristina (2021) Memes as Snapshots of Participation: The Role of Digital Amateur Activists in Authoritarian Regimes. *New Media & Society*, 23(6), pp. 1545–66.

Nordin, Astrid and Lisa Richaud (2014) Subverting Official Language and Discourse in China? Type River Crab for Harmony. *China Information*, 28(1), pp. 47–67.

Pang, Laikwan (2021) China's Post-Socialist Governmentality and the Garlic Chives Meme: Economic Sovereignty and Biopolitical Subjects. *Theory, Culture & Society*, 39(1), pp. 81–100, accessed 12 December 2021.

Phillips, Whitney and Ryan M. Milner (2017) Decoding Memes: Barthes' Punctum, Feminist Standpoint Theory, and the Political Significance of #YesAllWomen. In: Stephen Harrington (ed.) *Entertainment Values: How Do We Assess Entertainment and Why Does It Matter? (Palgrave Entertainment Industries)*. London: Palgrave Macmillan UK, pp. 195–211.

Polak, Sara and Daniel Trottier (eds.) (2020) *Violence and Trolling on Social Media: History, Affect, and Effects of Online Vitriol*. Amsterdam: Amsterdam University Press.

Punathambekar, Aswin (2015) Satire, Elections, and Democratic Politics in Digital India. *Television & New Media*, 16(4), pp. 394–400.

Qingchun Hubei (2021) Meiguo Jiangyu Taliban Juxing Gaoji Huiwu. *Weibo*, 8 October, https://m.weibo.cn/2321615032/4690311987855797, accessed 12 December 2021.

Rosen, Stanley (2004) The State of Youth/Youth and the State in Early 21st-Century China: The Triumph of the Urban Rich? In: Peter Gries and Stanley Rosen (eds.) *State and Society in 21st Century China: Crisis, Contention and Legitimation.* New York: Routledge, pp. 159–79.

Shifman, Limor (2014) *Memes in Digital Culture.* Cambridge: The MIT Press.

Sun, Wanning and Wei Lei (2017) In Search of Intimacy in China: The Emergence of Advice Media for the Privatized Self. *Communication, Culture and Critique,* 10(1), pp. 20–38.

Tan, K Cohen and Shuxin Cheng (2020) Sang Subculture in Post-Reform China. *Global Media and China,* 5(1), pp. 86–99.

Tang, Lijun and Syamantak Bhattacharya (2011) Power and Resistance: A Case Study of Satire on the Internet. *Sociological Research Online,* 16(2), pp. 10–18.

Twitter (2018) My favorite meme so far, 25 February, pic.twitter.com/tlaKJ4oJyG, accessed 31 October 2021.

Wedeen, Lisa (2013) Ideology and Humor in Dark Times: Notes from Syria. *Critical Inquiry,* 39(4), pp. 841–73.

Wu, Yan and Matthew Wall (2021) COVID-19 and Viral Anti-Asian Racism: A Multimodal Critical Discourse Analysis of Memes and the Racialization of the COVID-19 Pandemic. *Journal of Contemporary Chinese Art,* 8(2–3), pp. 107–27.

Xinhua News (2021). Juexing Niandai, YYDS, Shuangjian, 2021 Niandu Shida Wangluo Yongyu Fabu. 7 December, http://www.news.cn/politics/2021-12/07/c_1128137 881.htm, accessed 12 December 2021.

Yang, Guobin (2003) The Internet and the Rise of a Transnational Chinese Cultural Sphere. *Media, Culture & Society,* 25(4), pp. 469–90.

Yang, Guobin (2009) *The Power of the Internet in China: Citizen Activism Online.* New York: Columbia University Press.

Yang, Guobin and Min Jiang (2015) The Networked Practice of Online Political Satire in China: Between Ritual and Resistance. *International Communication Gazette,* 77(3), pp. 215–31.

Yang, Peidong, Lijun Tang, and Xuan Wang (2015) Diaosi as Infrapolitics: Scatological Tropes, Identity-Making and Cultural Intimacy on China's Internet. *Media, Culture & Society,* 37(2), pp. 197–214.

Zhihu (2021) SCI Lunwen He Jiucaimen De Ai Yu Chou, 7 September, https://zhuan lan.zhihu.com/p/408028779, accessed 12 December 2021.

Zou, Sheng (2020) Beneath the Bitter Laughter: Online Parodies, Structures of Feeling and Cultural Citizenship in China. *Global Media and Communication,* 16(2), pp. 131–47.

PART 4

Cultural Dimensions

CHAPTER 13

Opium of the People?
Religious Politics in the Xi Jinping Era

Martin Lavička

1 Introduction

Following the Third Plenary Session of the 11th Central Committee of the Chinese Communist Party (18–22 December 1978), during which Deng Xiaoping's policy of Reform and Opening Up (改革开放 *gaige kaifang*) received the green light, China began an economic and social transformation with which it would be difficult to find a parallel in the modern history of any other country. The post-Mao period enabled increased liberalisation and decriminalisation of religious practices across China. The considerably more relaxed atmosphere in Chinese society during the reform period revived and rehabilitated numerous aspects of Chinese culture, which had disappeared during the almost thirty years of various adventurist campaigns led by Mao and his followers. Therefore, the 1980s and 1990s witnessed a significant increase in the number of believers, newly built or rebuilt religious sites, and printed religious books (Flocruz and Cooper, 1999: 68–72). The intensity of religious revival that followed surprised the government, which thought that after decades of anti-religious policies and atheistic education, there would be not that many believers left in the country, and that those few would be mainly among the elderly (Chan, 2005: 87). Despite the growing number of governmental constraints on religious matters, the number of believers has been steadily rising[1] in China, according to Chinese sources (CGPRC, 2009; Yang, 2012: 93–95). Growing numbers of religious followers and the increasing role of religions in Chinese society alarmed the Party, as the "spiritual realm" was getting beyond its control (McCleary and Barro, 2019: 25). However, it is control of every aspect of Chinese society that is crucial for the Party to survive. Especially after Xi Jinping assumed his state and Party leadership, pressures for even greater consolidation of control of society further increased.

---

1 Wenzel-Teuber's (2017: 27–28) statistical research shows an increasing percentage of religious believers in China for all religions except Islam.

After the founding of the PRC, the institution responsible for overseeing religious affairs was the Religious Affairs Bureau, established in 1951 and later becoming the State Administration for Religious Affairs (SARA). It managed the official religious associations of five recognised religions in China: the Buddhist Association of China, the Chinese Taoist Association, the Islamic Association of China, the Three-Self Patriotic Movement, and the Chinese Patriotic Catholic Association. In 2018, all functions of the SARA were incorporated into the United Front Work Department, suggesting tightened control over religious affairs by the Party (Joske, 2019). According to the Central Committee of the Chinese Communist Party, this reorganisation would strengthen and centralise the leadership over religious work and continue its Sinicisation (中国化 *Zhongguohua*)[2] and adaptation to socialist society (Xinhua, 2018).

The recently published Freedom in the World Report on China's freedom of religious expression states that "the CCP regime has established a multifaceted apparatus to control all aspects of religious activity, including vetting religious leaders for political reliability, placing limits on the number of new monastics or priests, and manipulating religious doctrine according to party priorities" (Freedom House, 2021). The report mentions that Protestant Christians, Tibetan Buddhists, Uyghur Muslims, and Falun Gong practitioners face severe constraints, while Chinese Buddhists or Taoists face less persecution (Freedom House, 2021). However, numerous reports confirm that under Xi Jinping, even Buddhists and Taoists face increasing restrictions. Places of worship of all religious beliefs are being Sinicised, repurposed, or demolished across the country for being allegedly unauthorised or not in line with local urban planning. In reality, even state-approved places are not spared from desecration. Citing a preacher from Hebei, "for local governments, reducing the number of believers and religious venues is a political achievement. [...] The government can demolish churches as illegal at any time, and believers can do nothing about it" (Yang, 2020).

After the 9/11 attacks in the USA, the general attitude towards Muslim minorities significantly worsened. The ensuing Global War on Terrorism linked the East Turkestan Islamic Movement (ETIM) with global terrorist networks. It enabled Beijing to intensify its crackdown on perceived separatists, terrorists and religious extremists (the so-called three evil forces – 三股勢力 *sangu shili*) living in the eastern part of the country, the Xinjiang Uyghur Autonomous

---

2 In the sense of "Sinicisation from above" (Madsen, 2021: 1) or "Chinafication" (Yang, 2021: 16–17).

Region, in the name of counter-terrorism measures (Roberts, 2018: 8). In mid 2010s, the situation in Xinjiang significantly worsened. Researchers and international media began reporting about the incarceration camps, enforced labour and various repressive social re-engineering policies, some calling it a "cultural genocide" (Roberts, 2020: xiii, 236). Moreover, the initial restrictions on Uyghurs in Xinjiang extended to other parts of the country and other Muslim groups in China, including Kazakh and even the Hui.

Han Chinese culture has been determinedly dominated by the secular ideology of Confucianism, which does not pay much attention to spiritual matters. But at the same time, religion has been crucial for minorities "dedicated to religion," such as Tibetans and Uyghurs (Mackerras, 1999: 25). Therefore, attempts to control religious affairs create tensions between autonomy and loyalty to the government. In this sense, religion epitomises shortcomings in the Party's effort to legitimise its leading role through social policy (Potter, 2003: 318). In his book, David Shambaugh (2008) stated that the Communist Party is dealing with its own atrophy while adapting to new circumstances. However, what we see now is the increasing *controlocracy* in China (Ringen, 2016: 138), fuelled by the use of state-of-the-art technologies. The growing control of every aspect of people's lives is necessary for the Party to mitigate its ideological emptiness and "atrophy" and control the masses.

The following part of this chapter helps gain an understanding of the basic framework of China's religious policies and the highly problematic status of religious freedoms in an increasingly authoritarian regime, deriving its legacy from the essentially atheist thought of Marxism and Leninism.

2   Basic Framework

The 2018 government whitepaper on freedom of religious belief states that "China adopts policies on freedom of religious belief based on national and religious conditions to protect citizens' right to freedom of religious belief [...] under the staunch leadership of CPC Central Committee with Xi Jinping as the core" (SCIO, 2018: Preamble).

According to Article 36 of the still-valid 1982 Constitution, "[c]itizens of the People's Republic of China enjoy the freedom of religious belief," and they cannot be discriminated against based on religion. The same paragraph also states that "[n]o state organ, public organization, or individual may compel citizens to believe in, or not believe in, any religion." The third paragraph adds that the Chinese state "protects normal religious activities," and that "[n]o one may make use of religion to engage in activities that disrupt public order, impair the health of citizens or interfere with the educational system of the state." The last paragraph states that "religious bodies and religious affairs are not subject to any foreign domination." What is meant by "foreign domination" is explained in the 2018 whitepaper, highlighting the history of Catholicism and Protestantism as foreign religions "controlled and utilised by colonialists and imperialists" (SCIO, 2018: Ch. 1).

The following Table 13.1 shows the evolution of the constitutional protection of religious freedom. Compared with the one-sentence mention in the 1954 and 1978 Constitutions and incorporation of religious freedoms into a set of many other rights in the 1975 Constitution, the 1982 version is the most elaborate, yet still highly vague in its wording. But compared with the 1975 and 1978 Constitutions, it lacks any call for promoting atheism, suggesting the liberalisation of religious freedoms in China in the early 1980s (MacInnis, 1989: 7).

The official attitude during the period that followed the Third Plenary Session of the 11th Central Committee of the CCP (henceforth Third Plenum) can be understood from the so-called Document 19.[3] An English translation appeared in Donald E. MacInnis's study *Religion in China Today: Policy and Practice* (1989). Document 19 was issued by the Central Committee of the Chinese Communist Party on 31 March 1982 and consisted of twelve chapters.[4] They provided a party-state view on religious issues in post-Mao China and a blueprint for religious work in the following years (Chinese Communist Party Central Committee, 1987).

According to the first chapter, religion should be understood as a "historical phenomenon" and "product of the history of society." It exists because of the "helplessness of the people in the face of the blind forces alienating and controlling them [...], the fear and despair of the workers in the face of great misery generated by the oppressive social system" and the "oppressor classes [using] religion as an opiate" to control the masses (McInnis, 1989: 10). These oppressors included the feudal landowners; reactionary warlords; the capitalists who controlled Buddhist, Taoist and Islam leadership; and the colonialists and imperialists who manipulated the Roman Catholic and Protestant church (McInnis, 1989: 11). We can see the materialisation of this narrative in the last paragraph of the 1982 Constitution's Article 36 (see Table 13.1).

---

3 The official title of the document is "The Basic Viewpoint and Policy on the Religious Question during Our Country's Socialist Period."
4 The Chinese version from 1987, used as a reference for this chapter, is missing the eleventh chapter titled "International Relations of China's Religions"; therefore, it consists only of eleven chapters in total.

TABLE 13.1 Religious freedom provisions in the PRC constitutions

Constitution – article	Provision
1954 – Article 88	Citizens of the People's Republic of China enjoy freedom of religious belief.
1975 – Article 28	Citizens enjoy freedom of speech, correspondence, the press, assembly, association, procession, demonstration and the freedom to strike, and enjoy freedom to believe in religion and freedom not to believe in religion and to propagate atheism. The citizen's freedom of person and their homes shall be inviolable. No citizen may be arrested except by decision of people's court or with the sanction of a public security organ.
1978 – Article 46	Citizens enjoy freedom to believe in religion and freedom not to believe in religion and to propagate atheism.
1982 – Article 36	Citizens of the People's Republic of China shall enjoy freedom of religious belief. No state organ, social organization or individual shall coerce citizens to believe in or not to believe in any religion, nor shall they discriminate against citizens who believe in or do not believe in any religion. The state shall protect normal religious activities. No one shall use religion to engage in activities that disrupt public order, impair the health of citizens or interfere with the state's education system. Religious groups and religious affairs shall not be subject to control by foreign forces.

SOURCES: NPC, 1954; NPC, 1975; NPC 1978; NPC, 1982

The document further states that religion will keep its influence even within the socialist society, and that its eradication therefore has to be considered a long-term task for the government. Moreover, the text offers a clear warning to Chinese policymakers: "those who expect to rely on administrative decrees or other coercive measures to wipe out religious thinking and practices with one blow are even further from the basic viewpoint Marxism takes toward the religious question. They are entirely wrong and will do no small harm" (MacInnis, 1989: 10–11). Instead, the document advises radically improving material wealth, education, and culture so that the need for religion among Chinese eventually disappears.

The third part of Document 19 discusses how the CCP has handled religious matters since 1949. It admits that there were many "twists and turns" and "some major errors" during the Cultural Revolution. These errors are attributed to the Lin Biao–Jiang Qing clique, who "wantonly trampled upon the scientific theory of Marxism–Leninism and Mao Zedong Thought concerning the religious question" (McInnis, 1989: 12). Nevertheless, the text affirms that after the Third Plenum, the wrongdoings were rectified step by step. The main task now is to "consolidate and advance the patriotic political alliance in each ethnic religious group [and] strengthen education in patriotism and socialism" (McInnis, 1989: 13). As will be shown later, the question of religious personnel education to serve the Party interests became one of the critical points of Chinese religious policy in the following decades.

The following part of Document 19 explains the Party's understanding of the freedom of religious belief: "every citizen has the freedom to believe in religion and also the freedom not believe in religion" (McInnis, 1989: 14). A few lines later, quite interestingly, the document contradicts this statement by saying that "we Communists are atheists and must unremittingly propagate atheism" (McInnis, 1989: 14). It further reiterates that people cannot be coerced or discriminated against regarding their spiritual preferences, because the "Party's basic task is to unite all people" (McInnis, 1989: 14). At the same time, religion should be a private matter. Therefore, it must not "meddle in the administrative or juridical affairs of state, [or] intervene in the schools or public education" (McInnis, 1989: 15). It further states that minors (under the age of eighteen) cannot be forced to be religious, or attend religious activities or places. Furthermore, religion must not be used to oppose the Party leadership and the socialist system (McInnis, 1989: 15). Disconnecting youth from their religious traditions and practices is an apparent attempt to erode the influence of religion on people in China (Lavička, 2021a: 71).

The next part of the document focuses on so-called "religious professionals". The majority of them are "patriotic, law-abiding, and support[ing] the socialist system" (MacInnis, 1989: 15–16). But it is necessary to "unrelentingly yet patiently forward their education in patriotism, upholding the law, supporting socialism, and upholding national and ethnic unity" (MacInnis, 1989: 16). It is also crucial to foster a new generation of patriotic and loyal religious personnel who will effectively link the Party with the people (MacInnis, 1989: 20). The part dealing with the restoration and administration of religious buildings also explains the meaning of "normal religious activities", which could be held in designated places and believers' homes if it is a custom. However, it suggests that Protestant gatherings in homes should not be allowed, although this prohibition "should not be too rigidly enforced" (MacInnis, 1989: 18).

Chapter nine reiterates that freedom of religious belief does not apply to Party members who cannot freely believe in any religion. This policy does not apply to them, because "[u]nlike the average citizen, the Party member belongs to [a] Marxist political party, and there can be no doubt at all that s/he must be an atheist and not a theist" (MacInnis, 1989: 20). However, certain flexibility should be applied when dealing with the Party members from ethnic minorities, who should be gradually educated to "shake off the fetters of a religious ideology" (MacInnis, 1989: 21). At the same time, the Communist Party must be "vigilant and oppose any use of religious fanaticism to divide our people, [or] [...] the unity among our ethnic groups" (MacInnis, 1989: 22). Furthermore, all anti-revolutionary or criminal forces hiding behind the façade of religions must be punished according to the law (MacInnis, 1989: 22).

The opening-up period also led to increased contacts with religious organisations abroad. Document 19 states that although friendly international connections are supported on the one hand, on the other hand, the country must protect its people from foreign infiltration, in particular from imperialistic countries such as the Vatican or Protestant foreign-mission societies (MacInnis, 1989: 23). Therefore, it is also necessary to oversee donations and other funding sources coming from abroad (MacInnis, 1989: 23).

The last part of Document 19 sums up the overall strategy of the CCP: "Party's religious policy is not just a temporary expedient but a decisive strategy based on the scientific theoretical foundation of Marxism/Leninism and Mao Zedong Thought, which takes as its goal the national unification of the people for the common task of building a powerful, modernized socialist state" (MacInnis, 1989: 25).

Further clarification of governmental policies towards religious issues was provided by another document issued by the Central Committee of CPC in the early 1990s, the so-called Document 6.[5] It reiterated Document 19 but further called for more control and stricter measures to kerb any religion-related illegal activities, such as proselytising and religious fund-raising (Lavička, 2021b).

---

5   Its full title can be translated as "Notice of the Central Committee of the Communist Party of China and the State Council on Several Issues Concerning the Further Improvement of Religious Work" (关于进一步做好宗教工作若干问题的通知 *Guanyu jinyibu zuohao zongjiao gongzuo ruogan wenti de tongzhi*).

Various political statements and internal documents from this period illustrate the general atmosphere and influences surrounding the formulation of religious policies in the 1990s. But as will be shown later, their formulation is quite similar to current religious policies under Xi Jinping. For example, Luo Shuze's internal document titled "Some Hot Issues on Our Work on Religion"[6] singles out the main dangers religion poses to the Chinese government and offers recommendations for religious work. Luo says that the Chinese government has to be "vigilant against hostile international forces using religion to 'Westernise' and 'divide' [China]" (Spiegel, 1997: 65). Moreover, he also emphasises that religions must adapt to socialist society by modifying their "theology, conception, and organisation" so that believers "love the Motherland, support the leadership of the Chinese Communist Party, adhere to the socialist path, and act within the constitution and laws of the land" (Spiegel, 1997: 67). Luo also highlights the importance of government regulation and control to kerb illicit religious activities. Another essential aspect for the successful adaptation of religions to the needs of modern socialist China is to have a large cohort of religious personnel with the "correct" political consciousness to educate the undereducated devotees in rural areas (Spiegel, 1997: 68). Therefore, it is essential to promote the Marxist view of religion and atheism actively, but at the same time, any publications hurting "national and religious feelings" must be banned (Spiegel, 1997: 71).

Ye Xiaowen, from 1995–1998 the director of the Bureau of Religious Affairs of the State Council, issued another internal document. It was titled "China's Current Religious Question: Once Again an Inquiry into the Five Characteristics of Religion."[7] Ye restated the concept of five characteristics of religion, dating back to the early 1950s and drafted by the United Front Work Department of the Central Committee. These cover the long-term character, mass character, national and international character, and complex character of religion. Ye emphasised the necessity to handle all these characteristics adequately. According to this view, the government has to crack down on all activities that undermine social stability and endanger economic development. At the same time, Ye called for certain compromises and concessions when guiding religions to adapt to socialist society (Spiegel, 1997: 141). From the masses' point of view, Ye stressed that the government should recognise that there are 100 million religious believers. These people need to be educated in

---

6 An English translation of this document appears in Mickey Spiegel's *China: State Control of Religion* as Appendix 1 (Spiegel, 1997: 65–70).
7 An English translation of this document appears in Mickey Spiegel's *China: State Control of Religion* as Appendix 10 (Spiegel, 1997: 116–144).

Marxist philosophy and pulled over to "our" side instead of pushing them away (Spiegel, 1997: 142). Ye highlighted the need to follow Jiang Zemin's "three sentences"[8] about religious work to enforce CCP policies on religion, strengthen administrative control mechanisms, and adapt religions to socialist society (Potter, 2003: 323). Following these guidelines, the State Council promulgated regulations to protect "normal" religious activities from arbitrary intervention (Guo and Teng, 2012: 138).

3 Religion in China under Xi – Patient Persistence is Over

This part of the chapter shifts its attention to more recent developments under Xi Jinping's presidency. It analyses some of the essential normative texts, such as the Religious Affairs Regulations (RAR) amendment from 2017, Administrative Measures for Religious Groups (AMRG) from 2020, and the Administrative Measures for Religious Clergy (AMRC) from 2021. It also looks at the official policy narrative represented by the 2018 whitepaper on China's Policies and Practices on Protecting Freedom of Religious Belief.

The RAR had already come into effect on March 1, 2005; however, we will focus on its amendment from 2017, enforced the following year on February 1. The main idea of this part is to illustrate how the changes in official attitude towards the religious administration were written into the law during Xi's first term. The new amendment increased the number of articles from 48 to 77 and added two more chapters dedicated explicitly to religious education institutions (Ch. 3) and religious activities (Ch. 6). In its general provisions (Ch.1), the RAR reiterates some of the legal guarantees covered by the Chinese Constitution, such as freedom of religious belief and freedom not to believe in any religion (State Council, 2017: Art. 1–2). However, it adds more of a recent political vocabulary, such as the call for "raising the level of the rule of law in religious work" (提高宗教工作法治化水平 *tigao zongjiao gongzuo fazhihua shuiping*). The term *fazhihua* has been quite frequent in official documents, but hidden behind the declared increase of the rule of law are stricter regulations and constraints. Not surprisingly, in the RAR amendment, we can observe a significant increase in articles dealing with punishments, suggesting their importance in the management of religion (Lavička, 2021a: 67).

---

8 三句话 *San ju hua* – Jiang Zemin coined this term during his speech at the National United Front Work Conference in Beijing on 7 November 1993 (Jiang, 1993).

The following Article 3 was added to the new amendment to reflect new challenges for the Chinese leadership related to religion. In particular, the problem of religious extremism posed by radical Islam began to resonate in the early 2000s. The perceived threat of infiltration through religious missions was already present in Document 19. Nevertheless, the former Party Secretary of the Xinjiang Uyghur Autonomous Region (XUAR), Zhang Chunxian, said at the conference of religious leaders that "[t]here have been escalated infiltration and sabotage activities from foreign hostile forces that are disguised as religion" (Bai, 2015). And so the article calls for "stopping illegal activities, deterring extremism, resisting infiltration and cracking down on crime" (State Council, 2017: Art. 3).

Article 4 reiterates that the state protects normal religious activities. Still, at the same time, it encourages religions to become compatible with the socialist society, practice the core socialist values (社会主义核心价值观 *shehuizhuyi hexin jiazhiguan*), and "safeguard national unity, ethnic unity, religious harmony and social stability". Religion must not be used to "endanger national security, disrupt public order, impair the health of citizens, and interfere with the educational system of the State [...] or create contradictions or conflicts between different religions or within the same religion, or between citizens with religious belief and citizens with no religious belief, propagate, support or fund religious extremism, or make use of religion to undermine ethnic unity, split the country or engage in terrorist activities" (State Council, 2017: Art. 4). Article 5 states that all religions shall observe the principle of independence and self-management. However, this refers only to their independence from external foreign forces, not the actual independence, because the people's governments at all levels retain total control and make sure religious affairs are managed in the national and public interest (State Council, 2017: Art. 6).

Following a short Chapter 2 on Religious Bodies, Chapters 3–7 specify control mechanisms and restrictions on institutions of religious education (Ch. 3), religious venues (Ch. 4), religious personnel (Ch. 5), religious activities (Ch. 6), and religious property (Ch. 7). According to Article 19, religious venues include officially approved monasteries, temples, mosques and churches, and other fixed locations, meaning that other places, including private homes, are deemed illegal. The following sixteen articles define registration procedures and management of religious venues. In the early 2000s, there were numerous reports about often gigantic religious statues being built across China. However, under Xi Jinping, this situation radically changed, and more news about these statues being dismantled or demolished have appeared (SCMP, 2018). The amended RAR contains a special provision which expressly forbids the construction of giant outdoor religious statues outside the designated religious compounds, such as monasteries, temples, etc. (State Council, 2017: Art. 30).

The personnel question is essential to implement the Chinese government's religious policies effectively and reach the Party and state's objectives in spiritual work. Therefore, it has a dedicated Chapter 5 of the RAR. Particular interest is given to the selection and approval of the religious staff. Article 36 even specifies that "[t]he succession of a living Buddha of Tibetan Buddhism shall be conducted in accordance with the religious ritual and historical conventions under the guidance of Buddhist organizations, and shall be reported to the religious affairs department of the people's government at or above the provincial level or to a people's government at or above the provincial level for approval." Similarly, the selection of Catholic bishops has to be approved by the religious affairs department of the State Council (State Council, 2017: Art. 36). Without obtaining official approval, any religious activity of such a person would be illegal. The selection of Catholic bishops has caused significant disagreement between the PRC and the Holy See, the only place in Europe diplomatically recognising the Republic of China (Taiwan) and thus having no official diplomatic relations with mainland China. However, under Xi Jinping, China and the Vatican signed a provisional agreement about the appointment of bishops in 2018 and renewed it for a further two years in 2020. The exact content is unknown to the public. Still, according to some sources, the agreement gives the Pope the power of veto over the Chinese bishops' appointments, ending the existence of illicit bishops appointed by the Chinese government, but not recognised by the Vatican (Mok, 2021). The Pope has been criticised for pursuing closer ties with China, especially regarding the heightened persecution of religious minorities under Xi. Some argue it is because of the Chinese underexploited religious market opportunities (The Economist, 2020).

The religious institutions may produce and distribute internal publications. However, they must not contain content that undermines harmonious relations between citizens with religious belief and citizens with no religious belief; harmony between different religions or the internal harmony of a religion; discriminates against or humiliates citizens with religious belief or citizens with no religious belief; advocates religious extremism; or contravenes the principle of independence and self-management of religion (State Council, 2017: Art. 45). The amended RAR implements stricter control of financial matters of religious institutions and limits the private support of various donors. It is apparent when looking at Article 52 stating that "religious groups, religious education institutions, and religious activity sites are non-profit organizations"; thus, their "property and income shall be used for activities consistent with their purposes", such as public welfare and charitable undertakings

(State Council, 2017: Art. 52). However, nobody can misuse charitable activities to propagate religion (State Council, 2017: Art. 56).

The government's increased control over the financial matters of religious institutions in recent years is apparent. According to the RAR, a religious group must not accept foreign donations with attached conditions. When the amount exceeds 100,000 RMB, the religious affairs department of the local people's government at or above county level must approve it (State Council, 2017: Art. 57). Moreover, religious groups need to conduct financial audits and are subjected to inspections performed by relevant government departments (State Council, 2017: Art. 58). Chapter 7 introduces stricter punishments and fines for offences against the RAR. It also targets people "advocating, supporting, or funding religious extremism, or using religion to harm national security or public safety, undermine ethnic unity, divide the nation, or conduct terrorist activities and separatism" (State Council, 2017: Art. 63). Fines for illegal religious activities are set between 100,000 RMB and 300,000 RMB (State Council, 2017: Art. 64). Additionally, all of the illegal gains should be confiscated (State Council, 2017: Art. 65).

The 2017 amendment to the Religious Affairs Regulations expands overall control over religious affairs by the religious affairs departments, in line with Xi Jinping's increasing centralisation of power and control. The more restrictive policies on religious personnel, religious assets, and published materials are evident. Furthermore, the RAR amendment also legalises demolition of religious buildings in the name of public interest or urban planning, which is already happening across China (Cook, 2017).

The pressure directed at religious groups was further increased in early 2020 when the Administrative Measures for Religious Groups (AMRG, 宗教团体管理办法 *Zongjiao tuanti guanli banfa*) came into force. This document consists of six chapters and 41 articles that significantly increase the groups' administrative burden and decrease their already minimal autonomy. According to Article 1, these measures were created to regulate the administration of religious organisations, promote their healthy development, and actively guide religions to adapt to the socialist society (Bitter Winter, 2020: Art. 1). Article 17 reads that "[r]eligious organizations should publicize the guidelines and policies of the Communist Party of China [...] instruct and direct the clergy and religious citizens to support the rule of the Communist Party of China, support the socialist system, [and] follow the path of socialism with Chinese characteristics" (Bitter Winter, 2020: Art. 17). Moreover, according to Article 22, the religious organisations should also "provide interpretations for doctrines and canons that meet the requirements of the development and progress of modern China, and in accordance with the glorious traditional Chinese culture" (Bitter Winter, 2020: Art. 22).

On 1 May 2021, new Administrative Measures for Religious Clergy (AMRC, 宗教教职人员管理办法 *Zongjiao jiaozhi renyuan guanli banfa*) came into effect to "improve the cultivation of religious talents and protect their legal interests" (Liu and Lin, 2021). They consist of seven chapters and 52 articles. According to Massimo Introvigne, "they create an Orwellian system of surveillance and strengthen the already strict control on clergy" (Introvigne, 2021). The control mechanism is realised by creating a national database of authorised clergy. The individuals are regularly evaluated and either rewarded or punished so that compliant clergy are transformed into CCP apparatchiks (Introvigne, 2021). In Article 3, we are informed that religious clergy should love the Motherland, and support the leadership of the Chinese Communist Party and the socialist system. They should also practice the core values of socialism, adhere to the Sinicisation of religion in China, and maintain national unity, religious harmony, and social stability (Art. 3). So far, attempts to control and Sinicise religion and co-opt some religious leaders have not led to a complete containment of religious affairs. Instead, numerous religious leaders collaborating with the government were attacked or assassinated. This situation has been particularly prominent in the Xinjiang Uyghur Autonomous Region. The vice president of Xinjiang Islamic Association and imam of the Id Kah Mosque Jüme Tahir was assassinated in 2014 (SCIO, 2019: Ch. 3).

All these new regulations correspond with Xi's general attitude towards religion and the imperative of Sinicization of all parts of Chinese culture (Madsen, 2020: 20). During his speech[9] at the 19th National Congress of the CCP on 18 October 2017, Xi stated that the Party's policy is to "uphold the principle that religions in China must be Chinese in orientation," and that the Party will "provide active guidance to religions so that they can adapt themselves to socialist society" (Xinhua, 2017). Xi's thoughts were reiterated and further elaborated in the 2018 whitepaper. According to Chapter 1, adapting religions to the socialist society means subordinating them to the overall interests of the nation and Chinese people. Besides, it is necessary to ensure their support of CCP leadership and the socialist system, embracing core socialist values and integrating religious teachings and rules with Chinese culture (SCIO, 2018: Ch. 1). The increasing control and bureaucratic burden are explained as an improvement and ensuring that all activities are carried out in an orderly manner. Places of

---

9   The title of the speech was "Secure a Decisive Victory in Building a Moderately Prosperous Society in All Respects and Strive for the Great Success of Socialism with Chinese Characteristics for a New Era". It lasted for three and half hours and covers 66 pages of text.

worship have access to public services such as running water, electricity, etc. (SCIO, 2018: Ch. 3). The whitepaper praises the government for improving the living conditions of clerics. It states that thanks to the government's actions, the majority of religious personnel are covered by medical and social insurance. It also stresses that all normal religious activities and celebrations are protected by law. The same chapter also warns about the commercialisation of Buddhism and Taoism and informs about investigation carried out since 2012 (SCIO, 2018: Ch. 3) The following two chapters introduce the CCP vision on religions. Religions have to keep pace with the times and adapt to socialist society. Moreover, they also need to interpret their teachings and rules to conform to the national conditions and the Chinese context. Their teachings have to integrate patriotism, peace and unity. To show their positive role in society, religious institutions are encouraged to engage in charity activities and advocate "green development", such as an environmental form of burning incense and construction of eco-friendly temples (SCIO, 2018: Ch. 4).

4 Concluding Remarks

The Chinese government strategy towards religion did not diametrically change after Xi Jinping assumed his leadership, as some would argue. The trajectory set up during the Deng Xiaoping era and represented by Document 19 has remained the same. What is different is the speed at which China is moving towards its vision of a modern socialist state led by the scientific/atheistic Chinese Communist Party. Under Xi Jinping, the political leadership is no longer willing to wait patiently for the religions to *laihua* (来化) – 'come and be transformed', i.e., 'become civilized' (Leibold, 2007: 5; Joniak–Luthi, 2015: 27). The change of gears in religious policies is clearly visible when comparing Document 19 with current religious policies and laws. The cautious and considerably lenient attitude towards spiritual practices, especially among minorities, has changed rapidly over the decades. Under the current leadership, there is no longer a space for tolerance or special treatment inconsistent with officially proclaimed policies and laws. The reasons behind this change of tactics are numerous. However, the common denominator is the question of the legitimacy of the Chinese Communist Party. The Party's ideological emptiness following the death of Mao Zedong and the end of the Cultural Revolution was swiftly substituted with the vision of continuous economic growth and prosperity. The mantra of increasing material wealth became the main legitimising factor of the persistent leading role of the Party. However, the current slowing down of China's economic growth and rising social instability significantly undermine such a narrative.

Moreover, the Chinese leadership has learned from the bitter experiences of other socialist countries. It is, therefore, very aware that any concessions or leadership weakness could spiral into similar situations, which led to the fall of the Socialist Bloc in Europe. We now witness that the Party has to do more than reiterate its vision of increasing prosperity and harmony to remain in power. It emphasises nationalistic rhetoric and patriotism, and implements stricter and more sophisticated control of its population. Moreover, the Chinese government implements a more legalistic attitude towards the citizens and consistently punishes any deviation from the set rules.

The current administration requires a complete subordination of religions to the Communist Party leadership. The Chinese government is speeding up the Sinicisation of religions to strengthen and diversify the overall control of its citizens, all this to avoid any ideological alternative and an uncontrollable social force that could endanger or overthrow the leadership of the Communist Party. Moreover, the application of modern technologies, including artificial intelligence, and the gradual implementation of social credit systems, which can assess enormous amounts of data, make the control mechanisms more efficient but also Orwellian.

Acknowledgment

This work was supported by OP JAC Project "MSCA Fellowships at Palacký University II" no. cz.02.01.01/00/22_010/0006945 at Palacký University Olomouc, Czech Republic.

References

Bai Tiantian (2015) Xinjiang Party Chief Warns of 'Political Struggle' in Region. *Global Times*, 16 June, http://www.globaltimes.cn/content/927241.shtml, accessed 11 September 2022.

Bitter Winter (2020) English Translation of the 2019 Administrative Measures for Religious Groups. 15 January, https://bitterwinter.org/2019-administrative-measures-for-religious-groups, accessed 11 September 2022.

Central Government of the People's Republic of China (CGPRC) (2009) Zongjiao xinyang ziyou weida shijian – woguo 60 nian zongjiao gongzuo zongshu [The Great Practice of the Freedom of Religious Belief: A Summary of the 60 Year's Religious

Affairs since the Establishment of New China]. 4 September, http://www.gov.cn/jrzg/2009-09/04/content_1409389.htm, accessed 10 September 2022.

Chan, Kim-Kwong (2005) Religion in China in the Twenty-first Century: Some Scenarios. *Religion, State, and Society*, 33(2), pp. 87–119.

Chinese Communist Party Central Committee (1987) Guanyu woguo shehuizhuyi shiqi zongjiao wenti de jiben guandian he jiben zhengce [The Basic Viewpoint on the Religious Question during Our Country's Socialist Period]. In: *Shiyijie sanzhong quanhui yilai zhongyao wenxian xuandu* [Collection of Important Documents since the Third Plenum of the Eleventh Party Congress], vol. 1. Beijing: People's Publishing House, pp. 428–448.

Cook, Sarah (2017) The Battle for China's Spirit: Religious Revival, Repression, and Resistance under Xi Jinping. *A Freedom House Special Report*, February 2017, https://freedomhouse.org/sites/default/files/FH_ChinasSprit2016_FULL_FINAL_140pages_compressed.pdf, accessed 12 September 2022.

Flocruz, Jaimie A. and Joshua Cooper (1999) Inside China's Search for Its Soul: The 50th Anniversary of Mao's Revolution Finds the Nation Balancing a Rotting Ideology against a Hopeful Future. *Time*, 15(14), pp. 68–72.

Freedom House (2021) Freedom in the World 2021: China. https://freedomhouse.org/country/china/freedom-world/2021, accessed 10 September 2022.

Guo, Baogang and Chung-Chian Teng (2012) *Taiwan and the Rise of China: Cross-strait Relations in the Twenty-first Century*. Lanham: Lexington Books.

Introvigne, Massimo (2021) Enter the "Administrative Measures for Religious Clergy": Be Afraid, Be Very Afraid. 11 February, https://bitterwinter.org/enter-the-administrative-measures-for-religious-clergy, accessed 10 September 2022.

Jiang Zemin (1993) Gaodu zhongshi minzu gongzuo he zongjiao gongzuo [Pay Great Attention to Ethnic and Religious Work]. 7 November, http://www.reformdata.org/1993/1107/4263.shtml, accessed 11 September 2022.

Joniak-Luthi, Agnieszka (2015) *The Han: China's Diverse Majority*. Seattle: University of Washington Press.

Joske, Alex (2019) Reorganizing the United Front Work Department: New Structures for a New Era of Diaspora and Religious Affairs Work. 9 May, https://jamestown.org/program/reorganizing-the-united-front-work-department-new-structures-for-a-new-era-of-diaspora-and-religious-affairs-work, accessed 11 September 2022.

Lavička, Martin (2021a) Changes in Chinese Legal Narratives about Religious Affairs in Xinjiang. *Asian Ethnicity*, 22(1), pp. 61–76.

Lavička, Martin (2021b) China's Guinea Pig? Xinjiang as a Testing Ground for Religious Policies. *The China Story*, 2 July, https://www.thechinastory.org/chinas-guinea-pig-xinjiang-as-a-testing-ground-for-religious-policies, accessed 30 August 2022.

Leibold, James (2007) *Reconfiguring Chinese Nationalism: How the Qing Frontier and Its Indigenes Became Chinese*. New York: Palgrave Macmillan.

Liu Xin and Lin Xiaoyi (2021) China Issues Regulations on Religious Clergy. *Global Times*, 9 February, https://www.globaltimes.cn/page/202102/1215466.shtml, accessed 10 September 2022.

MacInnis, Donald E. (1989) *Religion in China Today: Policy and Practice*. Maryknoll, NY: Orbis Books.

Mackerras, Colin (1999) Religion and the Education of China's Minorities. In: Gerard A. Postiglione (ed.) *China's National Minority Education: Culture, Schooling, and Development*. New York: Falmer Press, pp. 23–54.

Madsen, Richard (2020) Religious Policy in China. In: Stephan Feuchtwang (ed.) *Handbook on Religion in China*. Cheltenham: Edward Elgar Publishing, pp. 17–33.

Madsen, Richard (2021) Introduction. In: Richard Madsen (ed.) *The Sinicization of Chinese Religions: From Above and Below*. Leiden: Brill, pp. 1–15.

McCleary, Rachel and Robert J. Barro (2019) *The Wealth of Religions: The Political Economy of Believing and Belonging*. Princeton: Princeton University Press.

Mok, Chit Wai John (2021) Sino-Vatican Provisional Agreement: Unresolved Issues. *The China Story*, 7 July, https://www.thechinastory.org/sino-vatican-provisional-agreement-unresolved-issues, accessed 08 September 2022.

National People's Congress (NPC) (1954) Constitution of the People's Repubic of China. *Law of China*, https://www.lawinfochina.com/display.aspx?lib=law&id=14754&CGid, accessed 10 September 2022.

National People's Congress (NPC) (1975) Constitution of the People's Repubic of China. *PKULAW*, https://www.pkulaw.com/chl/b9b88ee12f460b95bdfb.html?isFromV5=1, accessed 10 September 2022.

National People's Congress (NPC) (1978) Constitution of the People's Repubic of China. *PKULAW*, https://www.pkulaw.com/chl/c8492c76a860aeb0bdfb.html?tiao=0, accessed 10 September 2022.

National People's Congress (NPC) (1982) Constitution of the People's Repubic of China. *PKULAW*, https://www.pkulaw.com/chl/5c498812eb87061ebdfb.html?tiao=0, accessed 10 September 2022.

Potter, Pitman B. (2003) Belief in Control: Regulation of Religion in China. *The China Quarterly*, 174(June), pp. 317–337.

Ringen, Stein (2016) *The Perfect Dictatorship: China in the 21st Century*. Hong Kong: Hong Kong University Press.

Roberts, Sean R. (2018) The Biopolitics of China's "War on Terror" and the Exclusion of the Uyghurs. *Critical Asian Studies*, 50(2), pp. 232–258.

Roberts, Sean R. (2020) *The War on the Uyghurs: China's Campaign against Xinjiang's Muslims*. Manchester: Manchester University Press.

Shambaugh, David (2008) *China's Communist Party: Atrophy and Adaptation*. Berkeley: University of California Press.

South China Morning Post (SCMP) (2018) China Orders Crackdown on Large Outdoor Religious Statues to 'Prevent Commercialisation'. 26 May, https ://www.scmp.com/news/china/policies-politics/article/2147929/china-orders-crackdown-large-outdoor-religious-statues, accessed 8 September 2022.

Spiegel, Mickey (1997) *China: State Control of Religion*. London: Human Rights Watch.

State Council (2017) Zongjiao shiwu tiaoli [Religious Affairs Regulations (RAR)]. PKULAW, 25 August, http://www.pkulaw.cn/fulltext_form.aspx?Db=chl&Gid=301551, accessed 11 September 2022.

State Council Information Office (SCIO) (2018) China's Policies and Practices on Protecting Freedom of Religious Belief. 4 March, http://www.scio.gov.cn/zfbps/32832/Document/1626734/1626734.htm, accessed 12 September 2022.

State Council Information Office (SCIO) (2019) The Fight Against Terrorism and Extremism and Human Rights Protection in Xinjiang. 18 March, http://www.scio.gov.cn/zfbps/ndhf/39911/Document/1649933/1649933.htm, accessed 30 August 2022.

The Economist (2020) The Vatican faces Criticism for Pursuing Closer Ties with China. 13 September, https://www.economist.com/china/2020/09/13/the-vatican-faces-criticism-for-pursuing-closer-ties-with-china, accessed 10 September 2022.

Wenzel-Teuber, Katharina (2017) Statistics on Religions and Churches in the People's Republic of China – Update for the Year 2016. *Religions & Christianity in Today's China*, 7(2), pp. 26–53.

Xinhua (2017) Full Text of Xi Jinping's Report at 19th CPC National Congress. 3 November, http://www.xinhuanet.com/english/special/2017-11/03/c_136725942.htm, accessed 07 September 2022.

Xinhua (2018) Zhonggong Zhongyang yinfa 'Shenhua he guojia jigou gaige fang an' [The Central Committee of the Communist Party of China Issued the 'Deepening Party and State Institutional Reform Plan']. 23 March, http://www.gov.cn/zhengce/2018-03/21/content_5276191.htm#1, accessed 07 September 2022.

Yang, Fenggang (2012) *Religion in China: Survival and Revival under Communist Rule*. New York: Oxford University Press.

Yang, Fenggang (2021) Sinicization or Chinafication? Cultural Assimilation vs. Political Domestication of Christianity in China and Beyond. In: Richard Madsen (ed.) *The Sinicization of Chinese Religions: From Above and Below*. Leiden: Brill, pp. 16–43.

Yang, Xiangwen (2020) State-Run Churches in Handan City Destroyed as 'Illegal'. *Bitter Winter*, 9 February, https://bitterwinter.org/state-run-churches-in-handan-city-destroyed, accessed 10 September 2022.

CHAPTER 14

Cinema

Reconsolidation of Party-State Hegemony in a Market Economy

Chris Berry

1 Introduction

How should we understand the development of the cinema during the Xi Jinping era? If we apply a simple economic model, there is no doubt that the Chinese commercial film industry has been in a state of robust health during the Xi era. Prior to the arrival of COVID-19 in December 2019, the value of the People's Republic of China (PRC) box office grew from USD 929 million in 2012, the year Xi became General Secretary of the Chinese Communist Party (CCP), to USD 9.14 billion in 2019, overtaking the United States to become the most valuable cinema market in the world. Furthermore, whereas the 3D release of the James Cameron film *Titanic* topped the box office in 2012, in 2019 the local 3D animation film *Ne Zha* (哪吒之魔童降世 *Nezha Zhi Motong Jiangshi*), directed by Yu Yang, took the honours. This was part of a general shift towards Chinese films topping the domestic box office during the Xi era. These successes are represented in Figure 14.1 and Table 14.1 below.

Just how remarkable this economic achievement is becomes clearer if we look back to the turn of the century. Then, China's imminent entry to the World Trade Organisation (WTO) at the end of 2001 led Chinese filmmakers to speak anxiously about Hollywood as the 'wolf at the door' (Rosen, 2002). This chapter does not seek to challenge those figures or the remarkable picture of economic growth that they represent. However, this chapter does set out to build a fuller picture of the fortunes of Chinese cinema under Xi than economic statistics alone can provide.

Indeed, Xi's own comments indicate that to understand Chinese cinema through a simple revenue lens is inadequate. In 2014, Xi gave a speech at the Beijing Forum on Literature and Art in which he affirmed that 'under the conditions of the development of a socialist market economy, many cultural products must realize their value through the market'. However, he simultaneously insisted that 'compared with social benefits, economic benefits are secondary'. He further clarified that 'when two benefits and two values conflict, economic benefits must obey social benefits, and market value must obey social values'

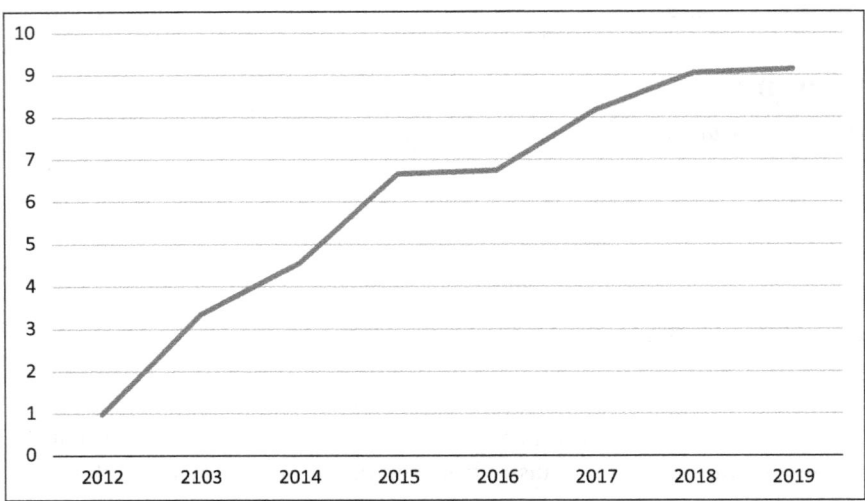

FIGURE 14.1 Annual box office, People's Republic of China in USD billions
SOURCE: BOX OFFICE MOJO, N.D.

TABLE 14.1   PRC top box office films and their country of production, 2012–2019

Year	Title	Country
2019	*Ne Zha*	China
2018	*Operation Red Sea*	China (Mainland and Hong Kong)
2017	*Wolf Warrior 2*	China
2016	*The Mermaid*	China (Mainland and Hong Kong)
2015	*Furious 7*	USA
2014	*Transformers: Age of Extinction*	USA
2013	*Journey to the West*	China (Mainland and Hong Kong)
2012	*Titanic* (3-D)	USA

(Xi, 2015).[1] As one commentator noted, these remarks are 'a potent reminder that the control of arts and culture remain in the forefront of the Chinese

---

1 My translation of: '在发展社会主义市场经济的条件下，许多文化产品要通过市场实现价值', '然而，同社会效益相比，经济效益是第二位的', and '当两个效益、两种价值发生矛盾时，经济效益要服从社会效益，市场价值要服从社会价值'.

leadership's minds' (Canaves, 2015) and a reassertion of the leading role of the Party-state.

To address cinema as an institution with 'social' as well as 'economic' benefits and values, this chapter takes a cultural studies approach, which it understands as a critical interrogation of how culture is shaped by and shapes power (Barker, 2008: 476). With this approach in mind, it starts by noting that although Xi's remarks assert the primacy of 'social values', they do not mark a return to class struggle and the command economy that we associate with the Mao era. The first section of the chapter addresses the commercial mainstream cinema. It notes that the remarkable economic growth experienced in the Xi Jinping era is the result of the policies adopted in previous years. If the challenge of those years was to save the industry in the face of the challenges of the marketplace, the challenge for the Xi government has been how to remind the industry of who is boss. This has been achieved by the withdrawal of completed and prominent films from the market, at great economic expense to producers; the disciplining of film stars by disappearing them from public view; and the promotion through cinema of the patriotic, some would say nationalistic, values that have taken the place of class struggle in legitimating the government.

A cultural studies approach to cinema as more than just the market requires that we also attend to those films that are excluded from the marketplace. One of the distinctive features of cinema in the People's Republic of China since 1989 has been the emergence and growth of a substantial independent cinema, which is examined in the second section of this chapter. The emergence of this new sector was also a consequence of marketisation, and, like the commercial cinema, it was reaching new levels of success and prominence when Xi came to power. With the commercial cinema, Xi's government has been careful to avoid killing the goose that has been laying so many golden eggs. But with the independent cinema, the government has sought to suppress it as a manifestation of the nascent civil society it decided was unacceptable. First, it damaged the infrastructure that sustained independent cinema, and then the implementation of China's first film law, the Film Industry Promotion Law in 2017, produced a decisive chilling effect.

Although reassertion of control is a key theme of the Xi era, it is important to recognise reassertion is a not a return to the past: there has been no renationalisation of the cinema industry. The market continues to produce surprises. And, at the same time as the independent cinema has been suppressed, a new art cinema has emerged within the censorship system. Characterised by a high level of cinematic literacy and invention and a retreat from any direct engagement with political and social issues, this new solipsism, as I call it, is the focus of the third and final section of this chapter.

2   The Disciplined and Patriotic Mainstream

Xi Jinping's acknowledgment of the importance of the marketplace at the same time as he asserts the even greater importance of social benefits and values is significant in two ways. On one hand, it means that his government is not turning the clock back to the era when the cinema was entirely state-owned and operated through a command economy of allocated resources and production plans. On the other hand, it dispels any lingering illusions that the introduction of the market economy is the first step towards becoming a liberal, multi-party, capitalist country. How can we see this distinctively Chinese configuration of a thriving market economy within a one-party system manifesting itself in the commercial cinema during the Xi era?

First, the Xi government has continued the fundamental economic changes of the Reform Era in the cinema. These changes introduced market principles to the running of the industry and also opened the market up to more imports. These policies date back as far as the mid-1980s, with the introduction of a system where state-owned enterprises, such as film studios and film distribution and exhibition chains, became responsible for profits and losses – in other words, the logic of the market (Zhu, 2003). Before this shift, the film industry had been entirely nationalized in the years following the establishment of the People's Republic of China. It was prioritized as an important medium for getting the Party-state's message to the masses, many of whom were illiterate. It was run on a command economy model, where resources were allocated to build the industry and annual plans determined which films would be made on what topics (Clark, 1987).

Marketization did not by itself ensure the economic success according to the logic of the marketplace that has been witnessed during the Xi era. At first, the local industry did not have the capital resources to produce high budget entertainment films or to renovate movie theatres. In an era when television was taking off, audiences were staying at home. In 1994, hoping to improve overall revenues for the industry, the government permitted the import of up to ten films on a revenue share basis. Film distribution, including the import of foreign films, was in the hands of a state monopoly, the China Film Corporation (CFC, 中国电影公司 *Zhongguo Dianying Gongsi*). Before this reform, the CFC had to raise hard currency funds through sales of Chinese films to buy the rights to import films. Now they could import major international blockbusters on the promise of a share of future revenue alone. Box revenues did improve, with the ten imports taking as much as 80 per cent of the whole box office (Zhu and Nakajima, 2010: 28–29).

However, although importing on a revenue sharing basis helped CFC, it did not help the rest of the Chinese film industry. Indeed, CFC lost much of its economic motivation to export or to promote local cinema. With entry into the WTO in 2001 holding out the prospect of further relaxation of trade barriers and more Hollywood imports, no wonder Chinese filmmakers spoke of the 'wolf at the door'. Indeed, the Chinese government has allowed the number of films imported annually on a revenue sharing basis to grow to thirty-four. However, it has never given way to Hollywood's demands for a completely open market (Davis, 2022).

Furthermore, in the years following entry to the WTO, the government also restructured the film industry and realigned interests by creating state-owned conglomerates (集团 *jituan*) that cut across the old divide between the production studios and the distribution and exhibition industries. For example, the CFC was renamed the China Film Group Corporation (CFGC, 中国电影集团公司 *Zhongguo Dianying Jituan Gongsi*) in 1999, and it incorporated the former Beijing Film Studio and other production enterprises, becoming 'vertically integrated' (Olsson, 2021). In the process, its interests were realigned again: CFGC stood to benefit from local film production as well as from imports, and especially from the films it produced itself. This change motivated it to channel its profits from the shared revenue imports into local productions. Other conglomerates had similar effects across the state-owned cinema sector by also vertically integrating production, distribution, and exhibition interests. Other reforms included the introduction of private companies into the industry.

After this restructuring, the marketized film industry was configured appropriately to spark the massive growth experienced during the Xi era. Xi's predecessors faced the challenge of saving the mainstream Chinese film industry in the face of marketization. However, his government faced the challenge of ensuring that the burgeoning industry continued to serve the Party-state above all else and did not just pander to the box office. This is the implication of Xi's comments about 'social' and 'economic' benefits. How has the Xi government exerted control?

There is an old Chinese idiom called 'killing the chicken to scare the monkey' (杀鸡儆猴 *shaji jinghou*) or, in other words, intimidation. The Xi government has directed this against both films and individuals. Taking films first, it has used the power of the Film Bureau to prevent films from being released to deter filmmakers from producing critical or, in Chinese parlance, 'sensitive' (敏感 *min'gan*) works. During the Xi years, responsibility for film censorship has shifted. When Xi came to power, the Film Bureau was part of the State Administration for Radio, Film and Television (SARFT). In 2013, SARFT was merged with the General Administration of Press and Publication (GAPP) to create the State Administration of Press, Publication, Radio, Film and Television (SAPPRFT). In 2018, SAPPRFT was abolished, and its regulatory functions were taken over by the CCP's Department of Propaganda (Buckley, 2018).

While these changes gave the CCP direct control over censorship, the basic system has remained the same. A film cannot be released in the commercial exhibition system without passing censorship. There is no classification system, so once a film has been passed, it can be seen by anyone willing to buy a ticket. The regulations concerning forbidden content are published, but they are not all very concrete or specific. For example, they contain concerns about 'undermining social stability' and 'jeopardizing social ethics' (Xu, 2017: 32). Such categories provide ample room for interpretation, creating a chilling effect that discourages producers from investing in films that risk being banned. Here, the government has been able to harness the character of a marketized economy to its advantage.

In addition to anxieties produced by the challenges of passing the basic censorship system itself, the Xi government has intervened to block and delay the release of certain high-profile works, potentially maximizing the economic losses to producers, and sending a clear 'monkey-scaring' message to everyone in the film production system. Two 2020 examples are Guan Hu's *The Eight Hundred* (八百 *Babai*) and Zhang Yimou's *One Second* (一秒钟 *Yimiao Zhong*). Both films had their 2019 film festival premieres cancelled at the last minute for unspecified 'technical reasons' and were finally released later. While *The Eight Hundred* went on to become a box office blockbuster, Zhang's film never really recovered.

The Eight Hundred depicts the last stand of a small group of valiant Chinese soldiers as the Japanese invaded Shanghai in 1937. The first Chinese film shot entirely with Imax cameras, it was a very high-budget production that reportedly took ten years to complete. The film's premiere was scheduled as the opening night film for China's only A-list film festival, the Shanghai International Film Festival, in 2019, before its last-minute withdrawal. Because the official reason was 'technical problems' we may never know what the real issue was. But surely it cannot be a coincidence that the Chinese soldiers in question were not Communists but fighting for the Nationalist (国民党 *Guomindang*) government army that the Communists later overthrew to establish the People's Republic in 1949 (Rose, 2020)?

One Second depicts an episode in the Cultural Revolution (1966–1976) where an escapee from a prison farm is desperate to watch a screening of Wu Zhaodi's 1964 film *Heroic Sons and Daughters* (英雄儿女 *Yingxiong Ernü*), because he has heard that his daughter appears for a few seconds as an extra in the film. *One Second* was scheduled to appear in competition in the 2019 Berlin International Film Festival, one of the world's most prestigious festivals. Although the repudiation of the Cultural Revolution remains uncontested, it is a topic that the government generally prefers filmmakers not to spotlight, and it was not until late 2020 that it was released in China (Ehrlich, 2021).

Second, and on a scale not pursued by previous Reform Era administrations, high-profile individuals have also been punished as an example to others. The sudden fall from grace of people like the world-famous founder of Alibaba, Jack Ma, is known internationally (McMorrow and Yu, 2021). This intimidation technique has also been used in the film industry with two major Chinese movie stars functioning as exemplary 'chickens'. First, Fan Bingbing was at the height of her fame when she appeared on the red carpet at Cannes International Film Festival in May 2018. Then, the next month, she simply disappeared from public view. She reappeared in October after three or four months of detention, having admitted tax irregularities and paid fines. On her social media, she stated, 'Without the policies of the Party and the country, without the love of the people, there is no Fan Bingbing' (Seidel, 2019).

Exactly what happened to Fan Bingbing during the period of her disappearance is not known. But a variety of forms of extra-legal detention are known to operate in the People's Republic of China, effectively disappearing people. These include what are sometimes known as 'black jails' (黑监狱 *hei jianyu*), a system of informal and unofficial imprisonment while under investigation. These are depicted in Vivian Qu's independent film *Trap Street* (水印街 *Shuiyin Jie*, 2013), which, unsurprisingly, has never been released in China. According to the United Nations Office of the High Commissioner for Human Rights (OHCHR), the CCP has since 2018 formalized a longstanding 'twin rules' (双规 *shuanggui*) process of extra-legally detaining Party members suspected of disciplinary infractions, renaming it *liuzhi* (留置) (Caster, 2019).

Although Fan Bingbing has been able to return to public life, the other high-profile example from the film industry has been less fortunate. Vicky Zhao (Zhao Wei) was not only a megastar, but also a director, producer, and businesswoman, having built a huge global investment empire with her husband, including highly publicized involvement in the French wine industry through ownership and operation of major vineyards in Bordeaux. On 27 August 2021, all films and television dramas featuring her disappeared from Chinese video streaming services, and she herself disappeared from public view. At the time of writing this chapter, there has been no official announcement of what has happened to her or why this punishment has been meted out to her, although there was a long history of prior infractions and scandals that had included accusations of being unpatriotic (Seidel, 2021).

Behind all the examples given is the Xi government's shift towards more conservative values. When work on *The Eight Hundred* began, a more conciliatory attitude towards the Nationalist army's role in resisting Japanese invasion was probably more acceptable, and the Cultural Revolution may not have been as taboo when Zhang Yimou started work on *One Second*. In 2021, another military history film, *The Battle at Lake Changjin* (长津湖 *Changjin Hu*), was released and became the top Chinese box office film of all time (Frater, 2021).

Co-directed by veteran mainland director Chen Kaige and Hong Kong directors Dante Lam (Lin Chaoxian) and Tsui Hark (Xu Ke), *The Battle at Lake Changjin* combines patriotic communist nostalgia with commercial moviemaking appeal in its depiction of a confrontation in the Korean War. *The Eight Hundred* focused on the wrong kind of Chinese – the Nationalists – failing against the old enemy – the Japanese. *The Battle at Lake Changjin* is about the right kind of Chinese heroes – Communist soldiers – winning against the odds and against the Americans. Although the Xi government is not particularly fond of Japan, it is the United States who are the current main enemy again if the rhetoric about a 'second Cold War' is to be believed. The film is the latest in a series of bellicose box office hits that also include two films focused on China's presence in Africa, *Operation Red Sea* (红海行动 *Honghai Xingdong*) from 2018, also directed by Dante Lam, and *Wolf Warrior 2* (战狼 2 *Zhanlang 2*) from 2017.

Directed by and starring Wu Jing, who also appears in *The Battle at Lake Changjin*, the *Wolf Warrior* films are the origin of China's aggressive new 'wolf warrior' diplomacy (Sullivan and Wang, 2022). As well as a strident anti-Americanism, the Wolf Warrior films display a significant disdain for the new rich. The eponymous hero is shown angrily attacking property developers who are evicting a soldier's widow and her family, for example. In this way, the films are also aligned with the crackdown on the lifestyles of celebrities like Fan Bingbing and Vicky Zhao.

3 The Death of the Independent Sector

The reconsolidation of Party-state hegemony over the cinema during Xi Jinping's rule has been felt not only in the commercial mainstream but also in another sector of the Chinese film industry – independent cinema. Like the commercial mainstream, the existence of the independent sector is dependent on marketisation. Like the commercial mainstream, it also reached unprecedented levels of stability and health in the years before Xi came to power. These were manifested in the existence of a growing infrastructure of regular screening events. However, the very existence of such a thing as independent cinema as an informal sector of the film industry and element of a nascent civil society has not been acceptable to the Xi government's democratic centralist vision. Therefore, it has moved to not simply discipline but suppress independent cinema.

This section of the chapter investigates the unique character of independent cinema in the People's Republic of China and its condition going into the Xi era. It highlights two key stages in the suppression of independent cinema. First, the government moved to destroy the infrastructure of regular screening events. Second, it implemented China's first film law in 2017, making independent film production illegal. Although no prosecutions have followed, 'independent' has become a toxic brand in the PRC and filmmakers have either left the country, stopped making films, or moved 'inside the system'.

Chinese indies are among the globally best-known examples of Chinese cinema. For instance, Jia Zhangke's first feature, *Xiao Wu* (小武, also known as *Pickpocket*, 1997) was selected for Berlin. His follow-up, *Platform* (站台 *Zhantai*, 2000) debuted in Venice, and his third film, *Unknown Pleasures* (任逍遥 *Ren Xiao Yao*, 2002), premiered at Cannes. But none of them appeared in annual film production lists and other official Chinese government data at the time. In most liberal market economies, independent cinema refers to films made outside the mainstream and often without commercial aims. These characteristics do apply to Chinese independent cinema. But Chinese independent films are also usually defined as those that have not undergone Film Bureau censorship. Films that have not passed censorship cannot be released in Chinese movie theatres. On rare occasions, they can be released on DVD, for example, if the relevant censorship body covering DVD releases passes them. But for the most part, in the eyes of the state, they do not exist (Berry, 2006).

Independent production in the People's Republic of China started at the end of the 1980s, initially with documentaries, but very quickly also included dramatic features. It was made possible by the introduction of the market economy and private enterprise. Just as some people were trying their luck as entrepreneurs outside the state-owned system in other areas of life, so too some filmmakers began making films outside the state-owned studios and television stations. Existing regulations from the command economy era did not envisage such a possibility. In the absence of any explicit prohibition, when I asked independent filmmakers about their legal status, they told me they believed their activities were legal so long as they did not attempt to show their films commercially in movie theatres without a dragon seal.

Initially, the number of films produced in this way were small, because of the high cost of production on celluloid and the low income. But the arrival of home digital video (DV) cameras in China in 1997 changed that, and it became possible to produce films with little training or money. Independent film culture rapidly grew from a small scene in which everyone knew each other to one where everyone's lists of important new films and filmmakers differed. Chinese independent cinema became a brand on the international film festival circuit. Festivals such as Hong Kong, Rotterdam, and Vancouver became well-known for showcasing these films, because their curators felt they were more exciting than the government-approved films. Tony Rayns notes that during his time at the Vancouver International Film Festival, he stopped selecting any Chinese films that were not indies (Interview, 6 August 2019).

Furthermore, an alternative screening network developed in China, consisting of various regular festivals at which independent filmmakers gathered and screened their films. In Nanjing, the China Independent Film Festival (CIFF, 中国独立影像年度展 *Zhongguo Duli Yingxiang Niandu Zhan*) was established in 2003, and rapidly became an important forum for debates about independent cinema (Yu and Wu, 2017). Also established in 2003 was the Yunnan Multi Culture Visual Festival (云之南记录影像展 *Yunzhinan Jilu Yingxiang Zhan*), generally known as Yunfest. Focused on ethnographic film, it took place in Kunming under the auspices of the Yunnan Academy of Social Sciences (Robinson and Chio, 2013: 23). Among the most prominent in a growing roster of events was the Beijing Independent Film Festival (BIFF, 北京独立电影展 *Beijing Duli Dianying Zhan*), held by the Li Xianting Film Fund in Songzhuang village outside the capital and founded in 2006. Readers of Chinese will have noticed that none of these events that called themselves 'festival' in English adopted the Chinese equivalent term, *jie* (节), but instead used the word for 'exhibition' (展 *zhan*). State regulations maintained that 'film festivals' had to be licensed by the Film Bureau, so calling the event an 'exhibition' was an effort to get round this requirement (Berry, 2009).

These festivals and other similar events constituted an infrastructure of public spaces for independent film culture in China and its 'critically engaged cinematic discourse' (Kraicer, 2011). In 2010, Hong Kong University Press published a book that I co-edited under the title *The New Chinese Documentary Movement: For the Public Record* (Berry, Lu and Rofel, 2010). The idea of 'publicness', or a space for debate and discussion autonomous of the state, runs through much of the writing on independent film culture in China. During the

1990s and 2000s, the possibility that the market economy was also creating civil society and public culture was widely entertained.

Almost by definition, independent cinema was part of this nascent critical public culture. Films that are critical of the government or expose social problems rather than simply singing the good news about the PRC struggle to pass the censors. And no filmmaker would choose not to undergo censorship if their film could pass, because passing censorship is the precondition for ticket sales. The very first film recognised as 'independent' in China was Wu Wenguang's 1990 documentary, *Bumming in Beijing* (流浪北京 *Liulang Beijing*). It followed four artists who had dropped out of the state-owned system and were trying to get by on their own, living in squalid rented accommodation conditions that the Party-state would be unlikely to want to acknowledge existed. Jia Zhangke's first film, *Xiao Wu*, mentioned above, compared a pickpocket to his former felon friend who has become an 'entrepreneur,' and most of his early films depicted a sleazy picture of the market economy in small-town China.

However, one of the hallmark shifts that has occurred under Xi Jinping is the explicit condemnation of such ideas as civil society, constitutional democracy, and other values held to be Western threats to the rule of the CCP. The notorious Document 9 issued by the CCP's General Office in 2013 communicates this perspective (ChinaFile Editors, 2013). Given the nature of independent film culture in China, it is hardly surprising that the Xi government's crackdown on critical thinking has encompassed it. The proliferation of cameras on mobile phones and so on makes it impossible to prevent people from making moving image works that are not submitted to the Film Bureau for censorship. But the government has moved against the infrastructure of events that sustained the recognition, circulation and discussion of such works as 'independent films'. Yunfest held its last edition 2013, BIFF in 2014 and CIFF held its last full Nanjing edition in 2013, continuing in name only (Nornes, 2019: 78–79).

After the dismantling of independent cinema, the Xi government consolidated its position by passing China's first film law, the Film Industry Promotion Law, which went into effect in 2017. The law is broad in its application (Zhang, 2017) and not especially directed at independent cinema. Prior to this law, the cinema industry had been guided by various 'documents' (文件 *wenjian*) issued by the Film Bureau. The existence of a Film Law, implying penalties ranging from fines to imprisonment for infringements, sent a more powerful message to the film world. Articles 13 and 17 of the new law specifically require that all film productions are registered with and approved by the Film Bureau prior to production and again prior to release (China Law Translate, 2016). Any remaining 'grey area' of doubt was removed by the law, and it became clear that independent film production and screening in China is illegal.

The 2017 Film Law had a chilling effect, and led commentators, including me, to declare that Chinese independent cinema was dead (Berry, 2017). Indeed, filmmakers who were active on the independent cinema scene have had to make some difficult choices. Many have stopped making films, like Cui Zi'en, China's most famous queer filmmaker. Others have moved out of the film world and into the art world. Wang Bing is probably the most prominent example of someone who started out in documentary and now operates almost entirely in the international art world with international funding. Others, like Ying Liang, Wen Hai, Zhu Rikun, and Zeng Jinyan, who know their films are completely unacceptable to the government, have left China, effectively exiling themselves.

Although individuals may still be making films on the quiet, and some privately owned cafes and specialised venues may slip the occasional film without a dragon seal into their screenings, 'independent' has become a toxic brand in China. Nobody says they are making 'independent films' anymore.

4 Surprise Hits in the Mainstream, New Solipsism in the Arthouse

The death of independent film as a sector of film culture and production in China under Xi Jinping is certainly a significant reassertion of Party-state control over cultural production. But it does not mean a return to the command economy. The state has not nationalised private film companies. Nor are there annual production meetings in which heads of studios are told what kinds of films to produce to help publicize new government policies. The market economy continues to operate, within the parameters produced by the Film Law and the various associated actions to enforce and consolidate Party-state control. This is a distinctive new configuration of the same fundamental power structure that has been in place since the beginning of the Reform Era. If agency is not monopolized by the Party-state, but control is reasserted, how does agency beyond the Party-state manifest itself today?

In the mainstream, it is important to acknowledge that the market can still produce surprises. The mechanisms that require Film Bureau approval of scripts and finished products, along with the threat of economic losses associated with challenging those mechanisms, ensure that no films that are critical of existing circumstances can be released, unless their criticism is in line with current government policy. But reliance on ticket sales means that the audience can still produce surprises, either by ignoring a film the Party-state has promoted or by producing surprise hits.

2021 produced an outstanding example of such a surprise box office blockbuster. The lunar new year, known in China as Spring Festival, is the country's main holiday season and prime time for new film releases. In 2021, these included *Hi, Mom* (你好，李焕英 *Ni Hao, Li Huanying*), the medium-budget debut of woman director Jia Ling. A well-known television sketch comedian, she also stars in the film as a woman who feels she has failed her mother. Travelling back in time, she attempts to find her mother a better husband so that she will avoid the disappointments to come. Excellent word of mouth led to sustained box office success that far outstripped expectations, extending the film's release into the May Day holidays. With revenues of 5.4 billion Chinese *yuan* (approximately USD 838 million), it became the third highest-grossing Chinese film of all time, behind only *Wolf Warrior 2* and *Lake Changjin*. It also became the most successful film by a woman director anywhere in the world, overtaking Patty Jenkins's 2017 *Wonder Woman* (Davis, 2021).

As a mainstream film with a dragon seal produced in the Xi Jinping era, it goes almost without saying that *Hi, Mom* is not critical of the government in any way. But it is also notable that *Hi, Mom* is not a bellicose film about conflicts with the West. Rather than going back to an episode like the Korean War, the lead character is transported back in time to 1981, the beginning of the Deng Xiaoping's Reform Era, when China was beginning to open up to the outside world and owning consumer goods like a television set was becoming a real possibility. This configuration is perfectly acceptable to the current government, because the Reform Era can be seen as the foundation of Xi's own 'China Dream' vision of material plenty for all. But the choice of time and setting also suggests a nostalgia for a time when not only the nightmarish class struggle of the Cultural Revolution decade (1966–1976) had been laid to rest but also China was building bridges with the rest of the world rather than burning them.

As well as market-driven surprises like *Hi, Mom* in the mainstream, China's post-Film Law cinema industry has seen the tentative development of a sector to take the place of the suppressed independent cinema, but within the system rather than outside it. This is the realm of the art film (艺术片 *yishupian*). Like independent films, art films in China are more formally and thematically experimental, and less driven by the quest for box office profits. But unlike independent films, Chinese art films are submitted for censorship and in possession of a dragon seal. Just as Wu Wenguang's 1990 documentary *Bumming in Beijing* sparked awareness of independent cinema in China, Bi Gan's *Kaili Blues* (路边野餐 *Lubian Yecan*) made the world aware of Chinese art cinema when it premiered at the Locarno International Film Festival in 2015 and won the Best Emerging Director award.

Kaili Blues predates the 2017 Film Industry Promotion Law and therefore reminds us that Chinese art cinema has deep roots. Films that prioritized neither profit nor promotion of government policy can be traced back to the emergence of auteur cinema in China in the 1980s, associated most strongly with the so-called Fifth Generation of filmmakers. Graduates of the Beijing Film Academy in 1982, they were the first generation of Chinese filmmakers to be exposed to Italian Neo-Realism, the French New Wave, and the other elements making up the foundations of the international art cinema movement in the post-World War Two era (Ni, 2003).

However, in the new century, art cinema had become associated with independent directors whose international exposure and successes placed them under pressure to submit their films for censorship, or to go from underground to above ground. As mentioned above, the best-known example is probably Jia Zhangke, whose first three films, *Xiao Wu*, *Platform*, and *Unknown Pleasures* were also all independent films. After their international festival successes, he was called in to a meeting with the Film Bureau, and his next film, *The World* (世界 *Shijie*, 2004), was his first film to appear with a dragon seal (Interview with Tony Rayns, 16 August 2019). Other filmmakers who had started out making films independently in the 1990s, such as Zhang Yuan and Wang Xiaoshuai, had already gone through similar experiences.

Another example of a filmmaker who, like Bi Gan, has followed the art film model and got dragon seals from his very first film on would be Pema Tseden, who became the first Tibetan feature film director with his debut film *The Silent Holy Stones* (静静的玛尼石 *Jingjing de Manishi*, རང་རྒྱལ་གྱི་མ་ཎི་རྡོ་འབུམ། *Lhang Jags Kyi Ma Ni Rdo 'Bum*) in 2002. Anything to do with Tibet is politically sensitive in China, and so it is inconceivable that the government would permit a Tibetan director to make feature films without submitting them to the censorship authorities.

However, what has changed for Chinese art films during the Xi era is the intolerance of any critical engagement with social issues. All the pre-2012 films cited above could be said to touch on social issues of various kinds, but within tolerated parameters at the time. Jia Zhangke's *The World* depicts the travails of internal migrants and their thwarted aspirations, which is not so far removed from his earlier, underground films. Pema Tseden's films show the impact of modernity on traditional culture, but without necessarily directing blame or even suggesting that this is anything other than a sad necessity. *The Silent Holy Stones*, for example, follows a child lama who should devote himself to religious life but is also drawn to television cartoons and martial arts videos.

With *Kaili Blues* and the new arts cinema of the Xi era, the focus is less on social issues than on states of mind, the apprehension of time, distinguishing dream from memory, and so forth. The main character is a small-town doctor. Trying to find his son, he enters a train tunnel to a place called Dangmai, where reality and dream get mixed together, along with past, present, and future. A formally highly sophisticated exploration of the mind and subjective experience characterises much of the new art cinema of China. For example, in Qiu Sheng's *Suburban Birds* (郊区的鸟 *Jiaoqu de Niao*, 2018), a surveyor investigating subsidence in the suburbs of Shanghai crosses paths with his own past come to life in the grounds of a primary school. In Zhu Xin's *Vanishing Days* (漫游 *Manyou*, 2018), a teenager drifts in and out of the summer haze, listening to her mother and aunt's stories and slowly losing track of what is real and what is imagined as objects disappear and reappear in unexplained ways. As this beautiful and mesmerizing cinema withdraws from the social, Chinese art cinema in the Xi Jinping era seems to be pursuing a new solipsism. In an age of growing restrictions, such a retreat is perhaps the only safe and sensible way to keep working.

5   Conclusion

The Chinese title of *Kaili Blues* means 'Roadside Picnic,' the title of the Strugatsky Brothers novel on which the Russian filmmaker Andrei Tarkovsky based his 1979 film *Stalker* (Xiao and Andrew, 2019). Perhaps the link between Bi Gan and Tarkovsky is more than just a question of personal taste. If we understand cultural configurations as shaped by power, there are some parallels between the Leonid Brezhnev era and the Xi Jinping era. In both cases, a waning of faith in the socialist cause following the death of Joseph Stalin in the Soviet case and Mao Zedong in the Chinese case and the revelations that followed led to a relaxation of central control that allowed youth culture, consumer culture, and foreign cultural imports – so long as they did not challenge the power of the Party-state. In these circumstances, a solipsistic art cinema of high formalist explorations becomes a logical outlet for creative energy and passion.

But where the Xi era and the Brezhnev era differ is in their economic models. While the Soviet Union never moved away from the command economy and feared that the market economy would destroy their system, Xi's China has not only permitted but also harnessed the market economy. In the case of the mainstream cinema, this embrace of the market has not simply meant the emergence of a box office-driven cinema based on genres and stars. Through a careful disciplining that has reminded all involved of the dependence of their industry on the Party-state, a burgeoning commercial cinema that serves the Party-state rather than challenges it has been established.

Acknowledgement

Some of the research cited in this essay was produced as part of the UK Arts and Humanities Research Council (AHRC)-funded project AH/S001778/1, 'Independent Cinema in China 1990–2017: State, Market and Film Culture'. I am grateful for the support of the AHRC.

References

Barker, Chris (2008) *Cultural Studies: Theory and Practice*. London: Sage.

Berry, Chris (2006) Independently Chinese: Duan Jinchuan, Jiang Yue and Chinese Documentary. In: Paul Pickowicz and Yingjin Zhang (eds.) *From Underground to Independent: Alternative Film Culture in Contemporary China*. Lanham: Rowman and Littlefield, pp. 102–122.

Berry, Chris (2009) When Is a Film Festival Not a Festival? The 6th China Independent Film Festival. *Senses of Cinema*, 53, https://www.sensesofcinema.com/2009/festival-reports/when-is-a-film-festival-not-a-festival-the-6th-china-independent-film-festival/, accessed 27 January 2024.

Berry, Chris (2017) The Death of Chinese Independent Cinema. *The Asia Dialogue*, 3 July, https://theasiadialogue.com/2017/07/03/the-death-of-chinese-independent-cinema/, accessed 2 February 2023.

Berry, Chris, Lu Xinyu and Lisa Rofel (eds.) (2010) *The New Chinese Documentary Film Movement: For the Public Record*. Hong Kong: Hong Kong University Press.

Box Office Mojo (n.d.), https://boxofficemojo.com/year/?area=cn, accessed 26 December 2021.

Buckley, Chris (2018) China Gives Communist Party More Control Over Policy and Media. *New York Times*, 21 March, https://www.nytimes.com/2018/03/21/world/asia/china-communist-party-xi-jinping.html, accessed 27 January 2024.

Canaves, Sky (2015) Chinese President's Speech on the Arts: The Hollywood Connection. *China Film Insider*, 20 October, https://chinafilminsider.com/chinese-presidents-speech-on-the-arts-the-hollywood-connection/, accessed 27 January 2024.

Caster, Michael (2019) Systematizing Human Rights Violations. *Made in China Journal*, 4(3), https://madeinchinajournal.com/2019/10/25/systematising-human-rights-violations/, accessed 27 January 2024.

China Law Translate (2016) Film Industry Promotion Law 2016. 7 November, https://www.chinalawtranslate.com/en/film-industry-promotion-law-2016/, accessed 27 January 2024.

ChinaFile Editors (2013) Document 9: A ChinaFile Translation. 8 November, https://www.chinafile.com/document-9-chinafile-translation, accessed 27 January 2024.

Clark, Paul (1987) *Chinese Cinema: Culture and Politics Since 1949*. New York: Cambridge University Press.

Davis, Rebecca (2021) Move Over, Patty Jenkins: How China's Jia Ling Became the World's Highest-Grossing Female Director. *Variety*, 14 March, https://variety.com/2021/film/news/jia-ling-world-top-female-director-1234973045/, accessed 27 January 2024.

Davis, Rebecca (2022) By the Numbers: Foreign Films Squeezed in China Film Market. *Variety*, 22 June, https://variety.com/2022/film/news/foreign-titles-squeezed-in-china-film-market-1235151950/, accessed 27 January 2024.

Ehrlich, David (2021) 'One Second' Review: Zhang Yimou's Ode to the Power of Cinema Finally Sees the Light of Day. *IndieWire*, 18 September, https://www.indiewire.com/2021/09/one-second-review-zhang-yimou-1234665559/, accessed 27 January 2024.

Frater, Patrick (2021) 'Battle at Lake Changjin' Breaks China's All-Time Box Office Record. *Variety*, 24 November, https://variety.com/2021/film/asia/china-all-time-box-office-record-battle-at-lake-changjin-1235119687/, accessed 27 January 2024.

Kraicer, Shelly (2011) Fall Festival Report, Part Two: Under Save Cover, A Fierce Debate. *dGenerate Films*, 7 December, https://www.dgeneratefilms.com/post/shelly-on-film-fall-festival-report-part-two-under-safe-cover-a-fierce-debate, accessed 27 January 2024.

McMorrow, Ryan and Sun Yu (2021) The Vanishing Billionaire: How Jack Ma Fell Foul of Xi Jinping. *Financial Times*, 15 April, https://www.ft.com/content/1fe0559f-de6d-490e-b312-abba0181da1f, accessed 27 January 2024.

Ni Zhen (2003) *Memoirs from the Beijing Film Academy: The Genesis of China's Fifth Generation*. Translated by Chris Berry. Durham: Duke University Press.

Nornes, Markus (2019) Filmless Festivals and Dragon Seals: Independent Cinema in China. *Film Quarterly*, 72(3), pp. 78–86.

Olsson, Carlo P. (2021) How China Is Aligning Its Films with New Markets and Partners: China Film Group. *Filmpulse*, 18 April, https://filmpulse.info/china-film-group-co-production-corporation/, accessed 27 January 2024.

Robinson, Luke and Jenny Chio (2013) Making Space for Chinese Independent Documentary: The Case of Yunfest 2011. *Journal of Chinese Cinemas*, 7(1), pp. 21–40.

Rose, Steve (2020) The Eight Hundred: How China's Blockbusters Became a New Political Battleground. *The Guardian*, 18 September, https://www.theguardian.com/film/2020/sep/18/the-eight-hundred-how-chinas-blockbusters-became-a-new-political-battleground, accessed 27 January 2024.

Rosen, Stan (2002) The Wolf at the Door: Hollywood and the Film Market in China. In: Eric J. Heikkila and Rafael Pizarro (eds.) *Southern California and the World.* Westport, CT: Praeger, pp. 49–78.

Seidel, Jamie (2019) Chilling Story Behind Fan Bingbing's Disappearance. *News.Com.Au,* 11 August, https://www.news.com.au/entertainment/celebrity-life/chilling-story-behind-fan-bingbings-disappearance/news-story/58fc11758fe171e8fb9c36eb54c5831d, accessed 27 January 2024.

Seidel, Jamie (2021) China Erases Billionaire Actress Zhao Wei from History. *News.Com.Au,* 31 August, https://www.news.com.au/technology/online/internet/china-erases-billionaire-actress-zhao-wei-from-history/news-story/94100f6569377078cfeee411f5fc3538, accessed 27 January 2024.

Sullivan, Jonathan and Weixiang Wang (2022) China's 'Wolf Warrior Diplomacy': The Interaction of Formal Diplomacy and Cyber-Nationalism. *Journal of Current Chinese Affairs,* 52(1), pp. 68–88. DOI:10.1177/18681026221079841.

Xi Jinping (2015) Zai Wenyi Gongzuohui shang de Jianghua [Speech at the Forum on Literature and the Arts]. *Xinhua Wang,* 14 October, http://www.xinhuanet.com//politics/2015-10/14/c_1116825558.htm, accessed 27 January 2024.

Xiao Jiwei and Dudley Andrew (2019) Poetics and the Periphery: The Journey of *Kaili Blues. Cineaste,* 44(3), https://www.cineaste.com/summer2019/poetics-and-periphery-journey-of-kaili-blues, accessed 15 May 2024.

Xu Shuo (2017) *The Curious Case of Chinese Film Censorship: An Analysis of the Film Administration Regulations.* Unpublished Master of Arts thesis. Eugene: University of Oregon.

Yu, Sabrina Qiong and Lydia Dan Wu (2017) The China Independent Film Festival and Chinese Independent Film Festivals: Self-Legitimization and Institutionalization. In: Chris Berry and Luke Robinson (eds.) *Chinese Film Festivals: Sites of Translation.* New York: Palgrave Macmillan, pp. 169–191.

Zhang, Rebecca Xiaomeng (2017) In Light of China's Film Industry Promotion Law: Implications for Cross-Border Transactions between China and the US in the Film Industry. *Northwestern Journal of International Law & Business,* 38(1), pp. 161–185.

Zhu Ying (2003) *Chinese Cinema During the Era of Reform: The Ingenuity of the System.* Westport, CT: Praeger.

Zhu Ying and Seio Nakajima (2010) The Evolution of Chinese Film as an Industry. In: Ying Zhu and Stanley Rosen (eds.) *Art, Politics and Commerce in Chinese Cinema.* Hong Kong: Hong Kong University Press, pp. 17–34.

CHAPTER 15

Between Art and Social Responsibility
The Politics of Music in the Xi Jinping Era

Hanna Kupś

1   Introduction

Deeply rooted in past practices, the idea of looking at art through the prism of ideologically enhanced lenses attracted the Chinese Communist Party (CCP) from the beginning of its activity. The political adaptability of music had been frequently promoted by the leaders of the Party, including Mao Zedong (1893–1976), who, in the Gutian Resolutions of 1929, advocated the establishment of propaganda teams and soldiers' clubs, as well as the writing and collecting of revolutionary songs (Judd, 1983: 130–131 as cited in Gong, 2008: 62). With the calls of Lü Ji (1909–2002) for the establishment of "new music" in 1936, art had been recognized as a weapon to be actively used in the process of political and social engineering, potentially helpful in liberating the masses (Hung, 1996: 906; Lü, 1936: 299, 301 as cited in Hung, 1996: 906). The notion found further development in Mao's Talks at the Yan'an Forum on Literature and Art (延安文艺座谈会 *Yan'an Wenyi Zuotanhui*) in 1942, which reaffirmed culture's subservience to the CCP and decided its fate for a long time to come. As successful as the Party was in previous artistic endeavors, it is no surprise that its allegiance to political music has continued into the twenty-first century. Soon after his assumption of the leadership, Xi Jinping (1953–) delivered his own recommendations for the desired development of art and literature, fusing past cultural policies with strategies better adapted to the challenges of the new period. The colorful videos and catchy tunes of propaganda songs are to attract the new generation of local and international audiences. The Party's endeavors, however, are not limited to the production of new content, as it aims to limit forms of art counterproductive to its interests. This chapter draws upon news reports and scholarship concerning the political use of music in China in an attempt to summarize the main tendencies and strategies of the CCP concerning music, as the country nears the end of the first decade of Xi Jinping's rule. Divided into three parts, it begins with an outline of Xi Jinping's art theory presented at the Beijing Forum on Literature and Art (北京文艺工作座谈会 *Beijing Wenyi Gongzuo Zuotanhui*) in 2014. The description is followed by an analysis of manifestations of political influence on music presented in two subchapters, the first covering active efforts of the Chinese authorities in the dissemination of propaganda, and the second devoted to the Party's restrictions of undesirable artists and forms of art.

2   The Xi Jinping's Theory of Literature and Art

In 2012 and 2013, the shift in the leadership of the CCP and China marked the beginning of a change of course in the Party's approach to art and literature. While the period of Xi Jinping's predecessors, Jiang Zemin (1926–2022) and Hu Jintao (1942–), can be described as one of "relative freedom from the tight ideological and political straitjacket of the CCP" (Yang and Jiang, 2020: 5), in the second decade of the twenty-first century its policy on art is often thought of as more reminiscent of the guidelines of the Mao era. The comparison can seem especially strong when analyzing the form and content of the speech made by Xi Jinping during the Forum on Literature and Art in Beijing. Delivered on October 15, 2014, more than seventy years after the Yan'an Talks, the address met with positive coverage in Chinese media, which informed of the enthusiastic reception of the recommendations made by Xi in artistic and academic circles.[1] Interestingly, however, and similarly to Mao's art theory, the official transcript of the lecture in Beijing was published with a notable, although unexplained, one-year delay. As noted by Federica Mirra, the content of the summary released in the media in October 2014 and the official transcript of 2015 reveal certain discrepancies, and the postponement may be attributed to the need for an evaluation of the people's response and the incorporation of potential amendments (Mirra, 2016: 29–30).

Xi Jinping's recommendations for the future direction of artistic endeavors are organized around five interrelated topics.[2] The first part explains the necessity of cultural growth, including the connection between cultural prosperity and the realization of the great rejuvenation of the Chinese nation. Xi stated that throughout the ages China's culture has been of vital importance to the survival and development of the nation, as well as a deciding factor in attaining a position and influence across the globe. As in the case of numerous foreign artists and writers, China's creations, too, contributed to the progress of both

---

1   For example, prof. Fan Ceng of Peking University created a series of poems in celebration of Xi Jinping's speech at the Forum on Literature and Art in Beijing (Xinlang wang, 2014).
2   The following account of the artistic guidelines presented by Xi Jinping in Beijing draws upon the official version of the speech (see Xinhua wang, 2015b).

Chinese and world civilizations, which adds to the national confidence, its revitalization ability, common sentiments, values, ideals, and consciousness. Consequently, as the great revival of the Chinese nation requires enormous material and spiritual contributions, without the positive example of modern culture the state and its people will not be able to rise above other countries of the world. The role of national culture has thus been identified by Xi as pivotal in the efforts to implement reforms introduced during the Third Plenum of the 18th National Congress (i.e., construction of socialism with Chinese characteristics, Two Centenaries, and the Chinese Dream) (Xinhua wang, 2015b).

Subsequently, the attention of the General Secretary focuses on the quality of the artistic expression and the social responsibility that rest on the shoulders of Chinese artists. Literature and art are considered to be indicators of the creativity of a whole nation. It is suggested that works of art should promote the contemporary system of Chinese values, the spirit of Chinese culture, aesthetic pursuits, ideology, artistry and enjoyability. Since the times of China's Reform and Opening-up (initiated in 1978), many authors have not, however, lived up to the expectations of the people. The sheer number of works do not translate into a high standard, as some of them "ridicule the sublime, distort classics, subvert history, defame Chinese masses and heroes, confuse right and wrong, good and evil, ugliness and beauty, as well as exaggerate the dark side of society" (Xinhua wang, 2015b). Works of low quality, described as "ready source of money", "ecstasy" or even "cultural 'trash'", represent a warning against losing one's way in the realities of the market economy. Xi sees the role of artists as of noble heralds, praising appropriate attitudes and reflecting the spirit of Chinese culture. A fine creation is supposed to reflect high ideological, artistic, and creative standards. Only then will it win the approval and the appreciation of the people. The rule encompasses both traditional and modern means of communication. Aware of the number, activity, and influence of young artists on the internet, Xi recommends their mobilization to promote socialist art to a wider audience (Xinhua wang, 2015b).

The subservience of art to the needs of the many constitutes the focal point of the third part of Xi Jinping's art theory. It states that the people cannot do without art, and although the material needs of the population are a priority, it is the spiritual culture, an inherent element of civilization, that distinguishes humans from animals. Servitude to the masses and the socialist cause are thus the key task assigned to art by the Party. Artistic creation should meet the current demands and challenges, and, with increasing international attention on China, accommodate the need to represent the Chinese point of view across the world. On the other hand, it should be remembered that art cannot exist in isolation from society. Being both the source and recipients of artistic creation, people are considered to be more than just an abstract symbol. Consequently, knowledge and inspiration should be drawn from the experience of entire generations and cannot be replaced by the feelings of individual persons. The search for the right message requires from artists a deep sympathy or even love for their topic. The form and technique used in the process of artistic creation are secondary to the promoted content. Not devoid of negative qualities, society needs to be educated morally and be developed in a positive, hopeful way. Implicit in art, ethical guidance is thus a priority over the material benefits for the creator. An outstanding work of art should be able to attain success in the artistic, ideological, and market fields. If they are in conflict with each other, the artist is expected to sacrifice financial gain in favor of promoting a valuable, socially responsible message (Xinhua wang, 2015b).

The fourth paragraph of the General Secretary's speech elaborates on the need for the cultivation of core socialist values by means of artistic creation. As the binder of the entire nation, principles of that kind are seen as an ethical and ideological keystone, necessary for the healthy and proper development of the Chinese society. This is particularly important in modern times, which Xi Jinping sees as threatened by the progressive decline of morality. To avoid further spiritual decay, core socialist values should be given publicity, for example, in the course of education, through cultural influences or by the systemic guarantees. In this context, art is considered to be a formative force capable of igniting constructive social attitudes, among which patriotism, search for truth, goodness, and beauty, as well as the reverence of tradition are to be of the most beneficial nature. Accordingly, it is in the hands of cultural workers (文艺工作者 *wenyi gongzuozhe*) that lay the responsibility of presenting the Chinese perspective and aesthetics. The turn to Chinese heritage does not, however, mean an indiscriminative implementation of past practices or isolation from Western culture but only more selective use of it determined by the current needs of the nation. Xi underlined that such practices, exemplified, among others, by Lu Xun's literature, had already taken place in the course of Chinese history and contributed to the growth of the local culture. The fear of international competition is thus unwarranted, as it can be conducive to the high quality and standard of Chinese artistic creations (Xinhua wang, 2015b).

The final part of Xi Jinping's speech, devoted to the supervision of art and its creators, identifies the Party as the fundamental guarantor of the development of socialist art. The strengthening and improvement of the CCP's artistic guidance requires an appropriate cultural leadership which is conscious of the prominent role of cultural workers and the rules governing the artistic process but at the same time possesses an appropriate moral compass preventing the transcension of the ideologically acceptable boundaries. With the traditional creations under control, the development of effective, updated measures of management is deemed necessary in the case of modern cultural production and dissemination. As the state cannot afford the promotion of harmful cultural works, it is necessary to develop an appropriate system of artistic supervision and criticism that will nip such dangers in the bud, while simultaneously allowing for the healthy progress of art in China (Xinhua wang, 2015b).

The art theory presented by Xi Jinping at the Beijing Forum derives from the deeply rooted confidence in the social applicability of art in China. The success of the Chinese Dream, as well as the attainment of the great rejuvenation of the Chinese nation, is perceived as interrelated with the influence exercised on the masses by culture and its media, focus on the people, and reaffirmation of the Party's leadership. While the parallels in the artistic thoughts of both Great Helmsmen are undeniable,[3] it is important to note that new policies presented by the current General Secretary are not simply derivative. The art theory of Xi Jinping constitutes instead an updated set of recommendations for artistic creation, adjusted to the requirements and challenges of the present. In Xi's cultural policy, as summarized by Yang Jiangang and Jiang Gongyan, the adhesion to the Marxist doctrine is interwoven with the discerned need for balance between ideology, artistry, and enjoyability. Artistic efforts are focused on the strengthening of cultural confidence and security, and cultural exchanges with the outside world are encouraged by the Party. The development of Chinese culture is also powered by research into humanities and social sciences, which has been stimulated by an increase in funding (Yang and Jiang, 2020: 6–7). Apart from that, as noted by Wai-Chung Ho, the promotion of Confucianism in the General Secretary's speeches is in direct opposition to the approach of the Mao era (Ho, 2021: 56). The art theory of Xi Jinping can thus be seen as an amalgam of past cultural policies, including Mao's and Deng Xiaoping's (1904–1997), which, augmented by new, original solutions, form the foundation of China's soft power, aimed at both national and international audiences.

3 Politics in Chinese Music

3.1 *The Fostering of Appropriate Values and Attitudes*

While Xi Jinping's art theory pertains to art and literature in general, its scope encompasses music and musical activities. Soon after the Beijing Forum,

---

3 For a more detailed summary of the common denominators in Mao Zedong's and Xi Jinping's art theory, see Ma, 2018.

the Party encouraged the composition of songs and poems that promoted "democracy", "equality", "justice", "freedom" and other core socialist values,[4] also to be included in textbooks on Chinese history and morality (Agence France-Presse, 2014). Subsequent reports from the Chinese media informed of the incorporation of the above principles into the curricula of elementary and middle schools in Beijing (Xinlang jiaoyu, 2014), and in Sichuan the song called "Centennial Promise" (2014) has been added into the provincial teaching materials of 2015 for the third and fifth grades of elementary school, as well as the first and the second grades of junior high (Xinhua she, 2014). Fostering correct social attitudes can be described as one of the main points of attention for the Chinese authorities, and the core socialist values are advocated outside of the education system as well. As noted by Ho, "the campaign [...] is conducted in all major cities through recitation sessions, singing, and dancing in the mainland" (Ho, 2018b: 235). Ensured by the Party, the provision of prime-time in television and radio, as well as more space in newspapers, is to guarantee publicity for favorable standards (Ho, 2021: 70). Musical bands such as 56 Flowers[5] promote red songs about the Chinese nation, socialist regime, and its core values (Guo, 2016). Drawing upon popular trends, they try to entice younger audiences to abide by the advocated code of behavior. Apart from that, the strategy to foster positive social attitudes can be observed in the form of musical pieces endorsing qualities epitomized by outstanding individuals. In 2016, a rap song called "Marx Is a Post 90s" (2016)[6] was posted on the social media account of the Communist Youth League, and quickly went viral (Fan, 2016; Gao, 2016). Although the author of the song, Zhuo Sinna, admitted to never having read Marx's works (as reported by Fan, 2016), the German philosopher was described as "dear" and compared to "Venus" or "lone boat moving between the mountains, and in that way fighting for the truth". Said to "no longer be plan B", Marxism succeeded in changing the perspective of a lyrical ego, previously uninterested in the ideology (From China, 2016).

While "Marx Is a Post 90s" can be seen as a part of broader efforts to spread the appeal of the philosopher and his ideology to Chinese youth,[7] it is worth

---

4   The inclusion of core socialist values in the overall education plan was announced by the CCP in December 2013 (Ho, 2018b: 234).
5   Chinese: 五十六朵花 Wushiliu duo hua. The girl band consists of 56 members representing 56 different ethnic groups in China (Guo, 2016).
6   The music video is available at: https://www.youtube.com/watch?v=jN2UBLb7U7o, accessed 22 December 2021.
7   For example, in 2019 the Propaganda Department of the Communist Youth League and CCP's Central Office for the Research and Construction of Marxist Theory adapted Karl Marx's life into seven-episode anime "The Leader" (Baptista, 2019).

noting that the CCP is careful in its search for the appropriate role models. Widely reported by the media, the existence of numerous paeans to the General Secretary, Xi Jinping, is a part of a primarily bottom-down movement, and is not indiscriminately accepted by the Party. Songs, such as "Xi Dada loves Peng Mama" (2014)[8] and "Everyone Brags About Xi Dada" (2015)[9] paint a picture of a benevolent yet strong leader who "dares to fight the tigers no matter how big they are" (as in the lyrics of "Xi Dada Loves Peng Mama", Gu Taishi, 2014), and "is equipped in both military and civil skills" (as in "Everyone Brags About Xi Dada", Bingruo Migan, 2018). At the same time, they often underline Xi's relatability and put his positive traits in the context of everyday life (i.e., depicting his as a good, loving husband or an unassuming citizen, waiting patiently for his turn in a baozi (steamed stuffed bun) stand):

Lyrics of "The Baozi Stand" (2014), a song by Wu Songjin and Zou Dangrong, translated by the Author (source: Jian xing jian zhi, 2014)[10]

Baozi stand, baozi stand
Let me tell you, that on a certain day before this New Year's Day
I went into that baozi stand for a lunch
When I was standing in line, behind me stepped one man…
He smiled faintly, and waved his hand
And he still stepped behind me, at the end of the line
He ordered a combo meal, only twenty-one yuan
He got a baozi with pork and onion, and one with mustard greens and stir-fried liver
He stood with us in a great line, and paid the bill himself
He held the tray with both hands, and he moved towards me
And where did he sit?
Gee! Dear all, dear all!
What a coincidence! He sat right by me!

---

8   The music video is available at: https://www.youtube.com/watch?v=Sz36EnT1jfg, accessed 22 December 2021.
9   The music video is available at: https://www.youtube.com/watch?v=30DCb2xlRKY, accessed 22 December 2021.
10   The song commemorated Xi Jinping's visit to a baozi stand in Beijing in 2013, see BBC News, 2013b.

In some cases, musical praise for Xi Jinping reveals similarities to the propaganda pieces from times past. The echo of former creations could be heard in "The East is Red Again" (2016)[11] or "To Follow You is to Follow the Sun" (2017).[12] If the former simply paraphrased the revolutionary classic, the latter emulated both the style and the motives distinctive of the period, such as the supernatural attributes of the Chairman and his comparison to the sun (see Xin Zhongguo pindao, 2017; Ziyou shijie xinwen lianbo, 2017). Contrary to the past, however, the digital era allows for a more critical reception of the leader's eulogies. While some songs are met with a generally positive response, others, such as "Never Forgetting the Kindness of the General Secretary Xi" (2019), are described as the "low-end redness" (低级红 *diji hong*) and "high-end darkness" (高级黑 *gaoji hei*) (Da Jiyuan, 2019) (i.e., excessive applause or an indirect, sophisticated attack on the CCP and its ideology, respectively). As observed by Yin Liangen and Terry Flew, the CCP seems to allow only the songs resulting from spontaneous netizen behavior, as they do not bear a negative political influence (Yin and Flew, 2017: 20). Similar efforts of the local authorities and central media are, in contrast, generally forbidden or thwarted (Yin and Flew, 2017: 28–29). The lack of state-driven support, among others, has made researchers doubtful of the durability of Xi Jinping's personality cult (Yin and Flew, 2017: 30), the topic often raised in connection with the songs in praise of the General Secretary. On the other hand, the CCP's references to Xi as the "helmsman" or "people's leader" (Tian, 2021) may be the proof of the opposite tendency.

In its encouragement of positive social attitudes, the government agenda often focuses on fostering collective hopes and experiences. "Our Dream Shall Come True" (2021),[13] a theme song for the documentary series "Making a New China",[14] commemorates, for example, the hundredth anniversary of the CCP. The lyrics remind us of past grievances and accentuate future goals to the images depicting pivotal events, accomplishments, and persons of Chinese history on one hand, and normal people of various ethnicities on the other (see CGTN, 2021). While the CCP centenary remains probably unrivaled in the

---

11   The music video is available at: https://www.youtube.com/watch?v=8krIYuJopwA, accessed 22 December 2021.

12   The music video is available at: https://www.youtube.com/watch?v=CK_1tYyJ-aE, accessed 22 December 2021.

13   Chinese: 终达所愿 *Zhongda suoyuan*. The music video is available at: https://news.cgtn.com/news/2021-06-28/Theme-song-for-Making-a-New-China-Our-Dream-Shall-Come-True--11sQZJqvg2Y/index.html, accessed 22 December 2021.

14   Chinese: 敢教日月换新天 *Ganjiao riyue huan xin tian*, a 24-episode documentary series directed by Yan Dong. Produced and distributed by China Media Group (中央广播电视总台 *Zhongyang Guangbo Dianshi Zongtai*) (Baidu Baike, n.d.).

grandeur of musical celebration, similar efforts have adorned various anniversaries connected to the state and the Party in the past. Patriotic songs, such as "We Walk on the Great Road" (1962), and "Ode to the Motherland" (1950), as well as more modern additions, including "Love Each Other" (2009) and "A Man Should Stand Strong" (1991) were, for example, performed during the gala celebrating the 70th anniversary of the founding of the PRC (China Plus, 2019).

English subtitles in the music video of "Our Dream Shall Come True", a song by Zhu Hai and He Muyang (CGTN, 2021).

From dark night to daybreak	From poverty to prosperity
It's been a long journey	To greatness and glory
A million steps of faith	Countless endeavors, countless
Dotting out the New China	sacrifices
From poverty to prosperity	Made for the people's well-being
To greatness and glory	With all our faithfulness
Countless endeavors, countless sacrifices	We are standing at a brand-new
Made for the people's well-being	starting point
Rock-solid in our faith	Our aspirations remain, so does
We fear no reaching for the stars	our devotion
Come rain or shine, we'll keep sailing on	After a century of striving we're
With the entire Chinese nation, for a	moving forward
better tomorrow	Our dream shall come true

The common Chinese identity is also being reasserted around the anthem. In 2017 the Standing Committee of the National People's Congress of the CCP approved the National Anthem Law (see Zhonghua Renmin Gongheguo Zhongyang Renmin Zhengfu, 2017), which states that the national song is to be respected and its dignity protected by all citizens and organizations (§3 of Zhonghua Renmin Gongheguo Zhongyang Renmin Zhengfu, 2017). The law ensures the performance of the anthem at various official political gatherings and significant sports events (§4 of Zhonghua Renmin Gongheguo Zhongyang Renmin Zhengfu, 2017). At the same time, it restricts its use in commercials or as a trademark, during inappropriate situations, such as funerals, or as background music in public places (§8 of Zhonghua Renmin Gongheguo Zhongyang Renmin Zhengfu, 2017). Malicious modifications to the lyrics or melody, distorted or derogatory performances, as well as other insults to the anthem in public are considered criminal offenses, with the penalty of detention of up to 15 days (§15 of Zhonghua Renmin Gongheguo Zhongyang Renmin Zhengfu, 2017). On November 4, 2017, the punishment for offending the anthem was extended to include deprivation of political rights, criminal detention, and imprisonment of up to three years for serious acts of disrespect (Xinhuanet, 2017). The authorities are vigilant in their efforts to protect the dignity of the anthem. In 2018 a Chinese live-streaming celebrity Yang Kaili (also known as Li Ge) was confined for five days after briefly singing the national song and flailing her arms around at the same time. The platform she had used, Huya (虎牙), subsequently took down the controversial video and banned her channel (BBC News, 2018). It should be noted that the November amendment also inserted the regulations into the Annex III of the Hong Kong Basic Law and required them to be implemented by local promulgation or legislation (The Legislative Council of the Hong Kong Special Administrative Region of the People's Republic of China, n.d. as cited in Yu, 2018: 79). Among protests, the bill was passed after approximately two and a half years. Signed by Carrie Lam, the Chief Executive of Hong Kong, on June 11, 2020, the National Anthem Ordinance came into effect the next day (The Government of the Hong Kong Special Administrative Region, 2020). In July 2021, Hong Kong police arrested a man who had allegedly booed the Chinese anthem in a shopping mall while watching the broadcast of the medal award ceremony where fencer Edgar Cheung received the Olympic gold. The punishment for violation of the ordinance in Hong Kong includes a fine of up to HKD 50,000 (USD 6,432) and as much as three years of imprisonment (Baigorri et al., 2021).

3.2 *The Promotion of Governmental Campaigns*

The musicality of Chinese politics can be observed in the promotion of specific governmental campaigns, events, and institutions. Songs, such as "The 13 What" (2015)[15] and "Two Sessions: To the World from China" (2019)[16] are forthcoming in their explanation of the fundamental meaning of the Thirteenth Five Year Plan and in praise of the annual plenary session of the National People's Congress and the Chinese People's Political Consultative Conference, respectively (see CGTN America, 2015; and The China Project, 2019). In some cases, the dissemination of the intended message is not as direct. For example, "Live

---

15   The music video is available at: https://www.youtube.com/watch?v=LhLrHCKMqyM, accessed 22 December 2021.
16   The music video is available at: https://www.youtube.com/watch?v=a5rvO5e-rik, accessed 22 December 2021.

Up to Your Word" (2019)[17] alludes to the controversial Social Credit System, giving advice on how to be a trustworthy citizen without specifically mentioning the program (KarRoy Kai Yuan pindao TF Boys Wang Junkai X Wang Yuan, 2019). Dedication to public safety on the internet resounds also in the lyrics of "The Mind and Spirit of Cyberspace Security" (2015) (see ProPublica, 2015).[18] According to Emily Rauhala, the anthem of the Cyberspace Administration of China is, however, "a rousing choral tribute to the Chinese system of online surveillance and censorship known as the Great Firewall and the government department behind it" (Rauhala, 2015).

English subtitles in the music video of "The 13 What", a song by the Road to Rejuvenation Studios (CGTN America, 2015).

[...]	But it's not over yet!
Every five years in China, man	When the plan comes out, the work's
They make a new development plan!	not done.
The time has come for number 13.	In fact, it's really just begun!
The 十三五![19] That's what it means!	Because every province, county,
[...]	city, too,
[Chorus]:	Have got to figure out what they're
If you wanna know what China's	gonna do.
gonna do,	Whoa!
Best pay attention to the 十三五!	That's a lot to do!
The 十三五!	I know!
The 十三五!	Hey, what's it called again?
The 十三 what?	The 十三五!
The 十三五!	[...]
[...]	

A group of musical pieces advertises the flagship projects of the General Secretary himself. In addition to the songs mentioned above, references to the Chinese Dream are disseminated on Chinese TV and online in talent shows, singing contests, or by individual artists. In celebration of the 65th anniversary of the PRC, the government also promoted 20 songs related to the concept

---

17   The music video is available at: https://www.youtube.com/watch?v=mY9gKv3eNqE&t=62s, accessed 22 December 2021.
18   The music video is available at https://www.youtube.com/watch?v=kbBKPqOh6DU, accessed 22 December 2021.
19   十三五 *shisan wu* is a Chinese abbreviation of the Thirteen Five Year Plan.

(Ho, 2018b: 71). The Belt and Road Initiative, a global infrastructure development strategy, is proclaimed in songs such as "The Belt and Road is How" (2017),[20] "The Belt and Road, Sing Along" (2017),[21] or "I'd Like to Build the World a Road" (2018)[22] (see New China TV, 2017a; New China TV, 2017b; Block Making Machine Supplier, 2018, respectively). The Four-pronged Comprehensive Strategy, a list of four ideological directives including the attainment of a moderately prosperous society, the deepening of the reforms, the advancement of the rule of law, and the strengthening of strict Party governance (The State Council. The People's Republic of China, 2017), are the theme of the "Four Comprehensives" (2016) (see New China TV, 2016).[23] The second anniversary of the Central Leading Group for Comprehensively Deepening Reforms, a body led by the General Secretary, was celebrated in the song "The Reform Group is Two Years Old" (2015) (see Vernon D, 2015).[24]

English subtitles of the chorus of the "Four Comprehensives" (author not credited, song produced by Xinhua All Media Service) (New China TV, 2016).

[Chorus]: Follow me, Four Comprehensives, Four Comprehensives,
prosperity is the goal.
Follow me, Four Comprehensives, Four Comprehensives,
reform is the drive.
Follow me, Four Comprehensives, Four Comprehensives,
rule of law is the guarantee.
Follow me, Four Comprehensives, Four Comprehensives,
Party building is the key.

Propaganda songs are often disseminated by the state-controlled media, which can also be involved in the creation of pro-government music, as in the case of "I'd Like to Build the World a Road", which was put together by People's

---

20   The music video is available at: https://www.youtube.com/watch?v=MolJc3PMNIg, accessed 22 December 2021.
21   The music video is available at: https://www.youtube.com/watch?v=98RNh7rwyf8, accessed 22 December 2021.
22   The music video is available at: https://www.youtube.com/watch?v=LLm2m9Sw8ZA, accessed 22 December 2021.
23   The music video is available at: https://www.youtube.com/watch?v=E8v8ZeTKaAA, accessed 22 December 2021.
24   The music video is available at: https://www.youtube.com/watch?v=xhU8C5RCbBs, accessed 22 December 2021.

Daily (McGill, 2018) and "Two Sessions: To the World from China", which was co-produced by Xinhuanet (Xinhuanet, 2019). Some videos, including "The 13 What", can be attributed to the Road to Rejuvenation Studios (~The Studio on Fuxing Road), a production company with "a sophisticated, tailored approach to public relations, involving a skilled team of producers, marketers, directors, artists, writers, and voice talent" (Stember, 2016: 8), and, based on the inquires by Matthew Robertson for the Epoch Times, "at least some of this process [...] being outsourced to private firms outside of China" (Stember, 2016: 8). The visual and audio content of music videos seems to indicate that they are primarily targeted at younger audiences. Catchy tunes of pop or hip-hop songs, as well as colorful animations or videos depicting children or youth, soften the promoted message and are presumably designed to construct a more friendly or "cool" image of Chinese politics. Correspondingly, the choice of English for the lyrics and captions of some of the music videos is presumably not accidental, which suggests that the musical soft power is directed, at least in part, internationally. The success of these songs among the intended groups is, however, difficult to measure. While, according to Christina Zhou, "Live Up to Your Word" met with a positive reception from Chinese netizens (Zhou, 2019), most news reports encountered in the course of this research informed of mixed or antagonistic reactions (e.g., Phillips, 2015b; and RFI, 2015). Foreign observers are also typically critical. In the 2018 episode of late-night HBO show *Last Week Tonight*, comedian John Oliver presented a parody of the song "The Belt and Road is How" (Hong Wrong, 2018), and, as a result, was subsequently censored on the Chinese internet (Dillet, 2018).

4   Music in Chinese Politics

The suppression of sensitive content in art is not limited to Xi Jinping's administration and the PRC, as the control of both artists and their creations has been widely recognized to have a long tradition in various countries, periods and contexts around the world. In recent years, however, numerous observers (e.g., Holmes, 2021; Singh, 2018 or Xu and Albert, 2017) have warned of the increasing censorship in China. The internet era brought along careful monitoring of uploaded musical products. Hon-Lun Yang observes that while "circumstantial" at times (p. 172), the rationale behind imposing restrictions include illegal music sharing and piracy, satirical or cynical takes on social mores, descriptions of the [negative] experiences of the people (老百姓 *laobaixing*), and politically sensitive content (Yang, 2020: 172–173), i.e., "songs seen as spreading subversive messages or as posing a threat to national security, as well as hindrance to social harmony" (Yang, 2020: 173). The regulatory measures of the media and the internet are currently imposed by the National Radio and Television Administration (NRTA),[25] an organization directly under the Propaganda Department of the Central Committee of the CCP[26] (Ho, 2018a as cited in Amar, 2020: 26–27). With the NRTA controlling the publication and distribution of the cultural products, live music and live venues are supervised by the Ministry of Culture and Tourism (文化和旅游部 *Wenhua he Lüyou Bu*), and various local cultural bureaus (Feng, 2019 as cited in Amar, 2020: 27). The authorities have, thus, a casting "vote" in the legal dissemination of music, at the same time being the cause of the self-censorship of the Chinese artists (Amar, 2020: 27–28). In an effort to make the cultural policy more efficient, the PRC co-opts celebrities from "outside the system", who then receive numerous advantages for their support (Xu and Yang, 2021: 211). Failure to comply with the promoted message and attitudes can, however, have dire consequences, including a long-lasting ban of a celebrity, accompanied by the practice of "naming and shaming" in the state media (Xu and Yang, 2021: 205–206). Professional associations that emerged after the General Secretary's speech in 2014 guard the spirit of the art through self-discipline and self-education campaigns, their efforts reinforced by various new laws and notices released by governmental organizations (Xu and Yang, 2021: 207–208). The Party is exerting control over increasingly larger domains: starting October 1, 2021, songs with undesirable content have been removed from karaoke venues, further restricting citizens' access to music not in line with the Party's policy (Tan, 2021).

4.1 *The Flexibility of the Regulatory Measures*

The Party's attitude toward music can vary depending on the message presented within its means, a tendency best exemplified in recent years by developments in hip-hop. While the history of the musical style can be traced back to the 1990s in China (Sullivan and Zhao, 2021 as cited in Nie, 2021: 4), only recently did it gain momentum, attracting wider attention thanks to the online show *The Rap of China* (中国有嘻哈 *Zhongguo you xi-ha*) (Nie, 2021: 5). Thought to be an aftermath of an "edge ball" strategy, a practice that "draws

---

25 Chinese: 国家广播电视总局 *Guojia Guangbo Dianshi Zongju*. Formerly known as State Administration of Press, Publication, Radio, Film and Television (SAPPRFT, 国家新闻出版广电总局 *Guojia Xinwen Chuban Guang Dian Zongju*, 2013–2018) and State Administration of Radio, Film, and Television (SARFT, 国家广播电影电视总局 *Guojia Guangbo Dianying Dianshi Zongju*, 1998–2013).

26 Chinese: 中共中央宣传部 *Zhonggong Zhongyang Xuanchuanbu*. Also known as the Publicity Department of the Central Committee of the CCP.

viewers by being at the "edges" of content likely to attract governmental censorship" (Flew et al., 2019: 99), the program received the highest rating in China in 2017, with 3 billion hits in total for the first season (Wan, 2017 as cited in Flew et al., 2019: 100). The success of the show cannot be equated, however, with the general acceptance of hip-hop culture by the CCP, as both before its release and afterward did it suffer from the imposed restrictions. In 2015 the Ministry of Culture blacklisted 120 songs with content promoting "obscenity, violence, abetment or harming social ethics", demanding they be taken down by the internet culture providers, under the threat of being strictly investigated and prosecuted (Xinhua wang, 2015a). As summarized by Nathanel Amar, the ban encompassed mainly hip-hop bands from China, Taiwan, and Hong Kong. Contrary to the overtones of the announced regulations, its effects were, however, not long-lasting, and in some cases they even contributed to the popularization of the indicated artists (Amar, 2020: 30). More consequential in their nature were constrictions imposed three years later. In 2018, Gao Changli, director of the SAPPRFT Administration's Publicity Department, announced "four definitely dont's" (四个绝对不用 *si ge juedui bu yong*) (i.e., standards for inviting guests to the television and radio programs). The regulation stated specifically that guests with tattoos, or those involved in the hip-hop culture, subcultures (non-mainstream cultures), and decadent (dispirited) cultures should also be excluded (Xinlang yule, 2018). As in the case of GAI, VaVa, and PG One (Liu, 2018), the ban affected individual musicians and bands. The impact of the censorship was visible across the entirety of the genre as well, with the differences appearing in both the sound and lyrics of hip-hop songs, especially high-profile ones, after its enactment (Nie, 2021: 12). *The Rap of China* returned, surprisingly, for a second season in 2018, and later for a third (2019) and fourth (2020). As noted by Terry Flew et al., however, during the second season it underwent certain changes, including "rebranding and rebuilding [of its] value", as well as internationalization, making it potentially less politically sensitive (Flew et al., 2019: 101).

The scrutiny of the Chinese authorities does not pertain to all manifestations of hip-hop culture, however. Music and artists representing values and attitudes along the lines of the propagated politics are not only acceptable but even promoted by the Party. As shown through examples of music video advertising campaigns and initiatives significant to the government and the General Secretary, the CCP intentionally utilizes hip-hop for their own ends. Approval can also be granted to creations not directly produced by the state. A particularly recognizable supporter of the Chinese cause is, for example, CD Rev (Chengdu Revolution or 天府事变 *Tianfu Shibian*). A group of gangsta rappers from Chengdu was formed on the National Day of the PRC in 2015 (Phillips,

2016) and has since released a number of nationalistic songs in English and Chinese commenting on current political circumstances or figures, including "This is China" (2016),[27] "No THAAD" (2017)[28] and "Mr. Virus" (2020).[29] CD Rev often collaborates with the Communist Youth League, which, despite the ban imposed in 2015, displayed tolerance towards the vulgarity of the groups' early creations, such as "The Force of Red" (2016) (Phillips, 2016). While the connection to the Party and the pro-government message of the CD Rev songs puts the sincerity of their efforts in doubt, as pointed out by Sheng Zou, "it is simplistic to reduce them to hired agents of the state and to neglect the complexity of the process of interpellation and the spontaneity of patriotism as a popular sentiment" (Zou, 2019: 185). Wai-Chung Ho observes that patriotism is strong in many Chinese rappers, who publicly and creatively expressed their support for the Chinese authorities and Hong Kong police during the pro-democracy protests in 2019 (Ho, 2021: 80). Similarly, to honor the 100th anniversary of the founding of the CCP, a hundred Chinese rappers expressed their love for the country in the 15-minute song "100%" (Global Times, 2021). No matter the incentive, the patriotic spirit of hip-hop seems to have won the approval of the CCP and will probably adorn state messages in times to come.

4.2 The Restrictions Placed on Foreign Music

It is important to note that the scope of restrictions exceeds local art and encompasses music from all territories of Greater China. Songs by supporters of the Hong Kong protests, such as Albert Leung, are unavailable in Chinese online music stores (Yang, 2019). Hong Kong pro-democracy singers, including Denise Ho and Anthony Wong, as well as Jacky Cheung, whose song referred to the Tiananmen Square crackdown (1989), had their creations removed from Apple Music's China service (Chan, 2019), with the company subsequently facing criticism from members of the American Congress and Human Rights Watch's China Director (Owen, 2019). Symbolic of the movement, the song "Do You Hear the People Sing" from *Les Misérables* was removed from the soundtrack albums on Chinese streaming sites (Rahim, 2019). Similarly, "Glory to Hong Kong" , the unofficial anthem of the protesters, was banned from being played, sung or broadcast in Hong Kong schools (Davidson, 2020). Moreover, political reasons

---

27   The video is available at: https://www.youtube.com/watch?v=bpRJN6Pa_DE, accessed 22 December 2021.
28   The video is available at: https://www.youtube.com/watch?v=9ponQdvHOOo, accessed 22 December 2021.
29   The video is available at: https://weibo.com/tv/show/1034:4493565884039193?from=old_pc_videoshow, accessed 22 December 2021.

are listed behind cancellations of concerts by a number of Western artists. Performances by Maroon 5 in 2015, Bon Jovi in 2015 and Selena Gomez in 2016 likely fell through because of their associations with the Dalai Lama (Phillips, 2015a; BBC News, 2015; NZ Herald, 2016). Likewise, after lifting of a three-year ban in 2014 (Shadbolt, 2014), Chinese authorities once again disallowed Lady Gaga's music because of her meeting with the Tibetan spiritual leader in 2016 (Lynch, 2016). A perceived support of Tibet is not the only reason for banning a foreign star. In 2017, Katy Perry was denied entry to China as a result of a 2015 concert in Taipei, where she wore a dress with sunflowers and waved the Taiwanese flag (Smith and Coleman, 2017). Apart from that, the critique of Chinese state policy, as well as ending of the partnership with Huawei, resulted in the music of Zara Larsson being removed from Apple Music in China in 2020 (Stassen, 2020). Not all activity of foreign artists, even of a potentially sensitive nature, meets a backlash from the Chinese authorities. Taylor Swift performed a concert in Shanghai in 2015, even though commentators (e.g., Yan, 2015) expected censorship over the name of a tour ("1989") and initials of a singer, both of which could be interpreted as references to the June Fourth Incident. In some cases, bands that could be seen as opposing the values and attitudes promoted by the PRC, are allowed to perform after the exclusion of certain songs or lyrics, as shown during the concerts of metal and rock bands, such as Metallica in 2013 (Pasbani, 2013), the Rolling Stones in 2014 (Stubbs, 2014), and Megadeth in 2015 (Putz, 2015). On the other hand, it should be noted that the Party is not averse to cooperating with certain foreign artists. CCTV's Spring Gala welcomed, for example, the performances of Celine Dion in 2013 (BBC News, 2013a) and Andrea and Matteo Bocelli in 2021 (Kelly, 2021).

The impact of Chinese politics on music is also evident in the case of Hallyu. Korean popular culture appeared in China in the 1990s as a result of the normalization of bilateral relations between South Korea and the PRC (Sun and Liew, 2019: 424). Since the early period, it enjoyed the endorsement of the Chinese state (Chen, 2016: 5), as the connection between the two countries, reflected in the traditional Confucian values resounding in the Korean television dramas, corresponded to the cultural policy of the Chinese government and was compatible with the CCP's ideology of the Hu Jintao era (Chen, 2016: 7). While Hallyu quickly gained a lot of attention, the consumer response to the Korean cultural products was not unequivocally positive. Focused on different aspects of the disseminated content, the apprehension towards Hallyu did not concern politics until 2007, when the antipathy toward Korean culture had been amplified by a series of incidents, starting with the claim that "Mount Paektu is our territory" presented on signboards by South-Korean athletes during the Sixth Asian Winter Games (Chen, 2016: 11). From 2010 territorial disputes further reinforced the nationalistic animosity toward Korea among Chinese citizens (Chen, 2016: 14). Tensions involving Hallyu remain active in China in Xi Jinping's era, as fans judge not only idols' artistry, but also their political stances. The impact, however, is not limited to South Korean and Chinese affairs. The transnational character of K-pop's influence can be observed in the "Tzuyu Scandal",[30] and, on a lesser scale, in the objection to the ruling of the Hague Tribunal voiced by Chinese K-pop celebrities.[31] As noted by Olga Fedorenko, the avoidance of divisive issues does not guarantee disentanglement from geopolitical matters. The deployment of the American anti-missile system (Terminal High Altitude Area Defense, THAAD) by South Korea amid protests from the Chinese government resulted in the cancelation and postponement of a number of K-pop events and productions in China, as well as a drop in the value of Korean entertainment company stock (Fedorenko, 2017: 511; Song, 2016 as cited in Fedorenko 2017: 511). The unofficial ban on Hallyu has continued in recent years, including denial of visa applications for K-pop artists, as well as blockage of television shows and music on streaming services (Baptista, 2020). While restrictions still impact the K-pop industry in China, media reports inform of the gradual easing of Hallyu suppression, exemplified by the signing of endorsement deals by K-pop stars Lisa and G-Dragon (Yim, 2020), the Chinese invitation of the latter to appear in the *We Are The World* online concert (Sunio, 2020), and, most notably, in the recent cooperation signed between China Central Television (CCTV) and the Korean Broadcasting System (KBS) (Davis, 2021). At the same time, the tendency to follow and react to K-pop celebrities' politically tinged comments has not changed. For example, a remark made by BTS leader RM concerning shared "history of pain" by American and Korean soldiers during the 1950–1953 war

---

30   In November 2015, Taiwanese artist Chou Tzuyu, a member of popular K-pop group TWICE, created great controversy in the PRC when she waved a Republic of China (Taiwan) flag on one of the episodes of a Korean TV show *My Little Television*. With the canceled performances of TWICE and other artists in China and overall significant impact on the business of JYP, one of the biggest Korean management companies, the firm's founder released a series of official apologies, followed by a video in which Chou Tzuyu herself expressed regret and reaffirmed her belief in One China policy. The recording, in turn, inflamed public opinion in Taiwan, even affecting the presidential election of 2016 (Ahn and Lin, 2018: 159–160).

31   After the unfavorable verdict of the Hague Tribunal in 2016 ruling against China in the dispute concerning the Spratly Islands in the South China Sea, Chinese K-pop celebrities, including Zhou Mi, Lay, Victoria Song, Fei, and Jia defended Chinese claims by reposting a Chinese nationalistic poster from People's Daily on their Sina Weibo accounts. The action was met with the support of Chinese netizens and a backlash from fans from the Philippines, Vietnam, Malaysia, Indonesia, and Brunei (Tan, 2016).

enraged Chinese netizens and resulted in the disappearance of adverts promoting Samsung and other companies' products that featured members of the group from Chinese websites and social media platforms (BBC News, 2020).

5 Conclusion

Xi Jinping's policy towards music and art draws upon the CCP's strategies devised since its formation. It should not be, however, understood as simply a passive continuation of previous tendencies, as it actively adjusts to new challenges, audiences and tastes. The 2014 Beijing Forum on Literature and Art recognized the necessity of continued cultural development, as well as its relevance in the attainment of the Chinese Dream and great rejuvenation of the Chinese nation. The promotion of governmental strategies and campaigns, both within and outside China, thus constitute prominent goals of the propaganda music disseminated across the state media (e.g., "The 13 What" and "Four Comprehensives"). Chinese art is to reflect a high ideological, artistic and creative standard, and utilize them in the dissemination of Chinese principles. As an effect, core socialist values, such as "democracy" and "equality", are promoted at various stages of education, as well as in homes, through television and radio. Ethical guidance of the Party includes fostering of patriotism and unity. Collective experiences, grievances and hopes are accentuated in the lyrics of songs performed or created for various celebrations, including the CCP centenary in 2021. At the same time, the National Anthem Law ensures the protection of and respect for the national song, even among those citizens of Hong Kong, who dispute the rule of the CCP over the territory. As an overseer of the entirety of the artistic process, the Party is vigilant in its control of the musical domain. The suppression of sensitive content is updated to include all kinds of publications and distribution channels, and the Party is the sole decision-maker with regards to the legality of musical products. While the CCP tends to cooperate with the musicians from outside the system to promote desired content, the departure from the designated message, both in the lyrics of the songs and in the private lives of the artists, may result in a ban or thwart of their profits to discourage future resistance or lack of cooperation. The CCP's control of music is far-reaching. It encompasses entire genres, individual artists and normal people alike. Significantly, in recent years the censorship has often exceeded the borders of the local Chinese market to involve foreign artists and music devoid of direct connection to the politics of the Chinese government. It should be noted that the above tendencies and examples do not exhaust the entirety of the political use of music in China. The limitations placed on the chapter have impeded the examination of various significant phenomena, including developments in military music, local initiatives or music policy in Xinjiang, which can each be developed into a form of separate analysis. As a reflection of the CCP's ideology, the politics of music in China ought to be recognized for its considerable research potential. It contributes to the understanding of the most recent history of Chinese music, shedding light on motives that lay behind a part of its creations.

Bibliography

Agence France-Presse (2014) Communist Beijing Brings 'Freedom' to Classes Via Songs: Report. *NDTV World*, 5 November, https://www.ndtv.com/world-news/communist-beijing-brings-freedom-to-classes-via-songs-report-689289, accessed 22 December 2021.

Ahn, Ji-Hyun and Tien-wen Lin (2018) The politics of apology: The 'Tzuyu Scandal' and transnational dynamics of K-pop. *The International Communication Gazette*, 81(2), pp. 158–175.

Amar, Nathanel (2020) Navigating and Circumventing (Self)censorship in the Chinese Music Scene. *China Perspectives*, 2020(2), pp. 25–33.

Baidu Baike (n.d.) Gan jiao riyue huan xin tian (2021 nian Zhongyang Guangbo Dianshi Zongtai tuichu de wenxian zhuantipian) ["Making a New China" (The 2021 documentary series released by China Media Group)]. https://baike.baidu.com/item/%E6%95%A2%E6%95%99%E6%97%A5%E6%9C%88%E6%8D%A2%E6%96%B0%E5%A4%A9/57291531, accessed 22 December 2021.

Baigorri, Manuel, Natalie Lung and Kari Soo Lindberg (2021) Hong Kong Arrests Man Over Booing China Anthem at Event for Olympics Win. *Bloomberg*, 30 June, www.bloomberg.com/news/articles/2021-07-30/hong-kong-arrests-man-over-booing-china-anthem-at-olympics-event, accessed 22 December 2021.

Baptista, Eduardo (2019) Romantic Karl Marx anime targets new generation of Chinese communists. *CNN*, 25 January, https://edition.cnn.com/2019/01/25/asia/china-marx-anime-intl/index.html, accessed 28 December 2021.

Baptista, Eduardo (2020) What happens when South Korea's K-pop meet the Communist Party of China? *South China Morning Post*, 15 November, https://www.scmp.com/news/china/diplomacy/article/3109904/what-happens-when-south-koreas-k-pop-meets-communist-party, accessed 22 December 2021.

BBC News (2013a) Celine Dion sings in Mandarin for state TV's New Year Gala show. 10 February, https://www.bbc.com/news/av/world-asia-21401187, accessed 22 December 2021.

BBC News (2013b) Chinese President Xi Jinping buys normal steamed bun. 30 December, https://www.bbc.com/news/av/world-asia-china-25548614, accessed 22 December 2021.

BBC News (2015) Bon Jovi's first gigs in China cancelled by officials. 8 September, https://www.bbc.com/news/entertainment-arts-34184537, accessed 22 December 2021.

BBC News (2018) Yang Kaili: China live-streamer detained for 'insulting' national anthem. 15 October, https://www.bbc.com/news/world-asia-china-45859650, accessed 22 December 2021.

BBC News (2020) BTS in trouble in China over Korean War comments. 13 October, https://www.bbc.com/news/world-asia-54513408, accessed 22 December 2021.

Bingruo Migan (2018) Xi Jinping you yi shenqu《Xi Dada, renren kua》["Everyone Brags About Xi Dada" – Another Eulogy of Xi Jinping]. *YouTube*, 1 November, https://www.youtube.com/watch?v=30DCb2xlRKY, accessed 22 December 2021.

Block Making Machine Supplier (2018) I'd like to build the world a road. OBOR. The belt and road. *YouTube*, 8 October, https://www.youtube.com/watch?v=LLm2m9Sw8ZA, accessed 22 December 2021.

CGTN (2021) Theme song for documentary series 'Making a New China': 'Our Dream Shall Come True'. 28 June, https://news.cgtn.com/news/2021-06-28/Theme-song-for-Making-a-New-China-Our-Dream-Shall-Come-True--11sQZJqvg2Y/index.html, accessed 22 December 2021.

CGTN America (2015) Shisanwu zhi Ge The 13 WHAT – A song about China's 13th 5-year plan. *YouTube*, 27 October, https://www.youtube.com/watch?v=LhLrHCKMqyM, accessed 22 December 2021.

Chan, Holmes (2019) Apple Music in China removes Jacky Cheung song with reference to Tiananmen massacre. *Hong Kong Free Press*, 9 April, https://hongkongfp.com/2019/04/09/apple-music-china-removes-jacky-cheung-song-reference-tiananmen-massacre/, accessed 22 December 2021.

Chen, Lu (2016) The emergence of the anti-Hallyu movement in China. *Media, Culture & Society*, pp. 1–17.

China Plus (2019) [Live Updates] Gala celebrating 70th anniversary of PRC's founding. 1 October, http://chinaplus.cri.cn/newslive/2019/287/index.html, accessed 22 December 2021.

Da Jiyuan (2019) Xi Jinping Liang Hui zao "diji hong, gaoji hei" yi shou hongge bei su shan [The red song describing Two Congresses of Xi Jinping as "low-end redness" and "high-end darkness" removed quickly]. *The Epoch Times*, 10 March, https://www.epochtimes.com/gb/19/3/10/n11102281.htm, accessed 22 December 2021.

Davidson, Helen (2020) Protest anthem banned in Hong Kong schools as new security office opens. *The Guardian*, 8 July, https://www.theguardian.com/world/2020/jul/08/protest-anthem-banned-in-hong-kong-schools-as-new-security-office-opens, accessed 22 December 2021.

Davis, Rebecca (2021) China's CCTV and Korea's KBS Sign Agreement, Potentially Signaling End to Content Ban. *Variety*, 22 February, https://variety.com/2021/film/news/cctv-kbs-partnership-1234912919/, accessed 22 December 2021.

Dillet, Romain (2018) John Oliver is erased from Chinese internet following segment on China. *TechCrunch+*, 25 June, https://techcrunch.com/2018/06/25/john-oliver-is-erased-from-chinese-internet-following-segment-on-china/?guce_referrer=aHR0cHM6Ly93d3cuZ29vZ2xlLmNvbS8&guce_referrer_sig=AQAAAF-qVRCf-T6iKjHomSybuIvr31VUXRfF3Ap_DTwFzaNNc2ox8iFXsWjGL1sWNpuE0HkYzcf-5ub3KaWZfIIMz8HYNWqrrGKoDznmFJwfHlvNJdDUtwKuoBa924XAylX6HzH-N1v0o7kFaLbXjpxGr7OvuW6pb8KokAWG4ri-AjV9w_&guccounter=2, accessed 22 December 2021.

Fan Yiying (2016) Hip Song Gives Karl Marx Good Rap. *Sixth Tone*, 29 March, https://www.sixthtone.com/news/658/hip-song-gives-karl-marx-good-rap, accessed 22 December 2021.

Fedorenko, Olga (2017) Korean-Wave celebrities between global capital and regional nationalisms. *Inter-Asia Cultural Studies*, 18(4), pp. 498–517.

Feng, Jiayun (2019) Inside China's ever-evolving censorship apparatus. *SupChina*, 23 August, https://signal.supchina.com/inside-chinas-ever-evolving-censorship-apparatus/.

Flew, Terry, Mark Ryan and Chunmeizi Su (2019) Culture, communication and hybridity: The case of The Rap in China. *Journal of Multicultural Discourses*, 14(2), pp. 93–106.

From China (2016) Marx is post 90's (Hip-Hop song of Karl Marx, founder of communism). *YouTube*, 1 June, https://www.youtube.com/watch?v=jN2UBLb7U7o, accessed 22 December 2021.

Gao Yinan (2016) New Viral Song Proves Ongoing Relevance of Karl Marx Among Youth. *People's Daily Online*, 25 May, http://en.people.cn/n3/2016/0525/c90000-9063036.html, accessed 22 December 2021.

Global Times (2021) 100 Chinese rappers celebrate centenary of CPC with patriotic cipher. 22 June, https://www.globaltimes.cn/page/202106/1226804.shtml, accessed 22 December 2021.

Gong, Hong-Yu (2008) Music, Nationalism and the Search for Modernity in China, 1911–1949. *New Zealand Journal of Asian Studies*, 10(2), pp. 38–69.

Gu Taishi (2014) Yu Runze Xu An 《Xi Dada aizhe Peng Mama》 yuanban MV [The Original MV of the "Xi Dada loves Peng Mama" by Yu Runze and Xu An]. *YouTube*, 18 November, https://www.youtube.com/watch?v=Sz36EnT1jfg, accessed 22 December 2021.

Guo, Diandian (2016) 56 Flowers: The All-Girl Group Promoting Socialist Values. *What's on Weibo*, 13 May, https://www.whatsonweibo.com/56-flowers/, accessed 22 December 2021.

Ho, Pang-Chie (2018a) Goodbye, SAPPRFT (But not Chinese censorship). *SupChina*, 21 March, https://supchina.com/2018/03/21/goodbye-sapprft-but-not-chinese-cen sorship/.

Ho, Wai-Chung (2018b) *Culture, Music Education, and the Chinese Dream in Mainland China*. Singapore: Springer.

Ho, Wai-Chung (2021) *Globalization, Nationalism, and Music Education in the Twenty-First Century in Greater China*. Amsterdam: Amsterdam University Press.

Holmes, Oliver (2021) No cults, no politics, no ghouls: how China censors the video game world. *The Guardian*, 15 July, https://www.theguardian.com/news/2021/jul/15/china-video-game-censorship-tencent-netease-blizzard, accessed 22 December 2021.

Hong Wrong (2018) Video: Comedian John Oliver writes a 'cuddly propaganda' song for China's Xi Jinping. *Hong Kong Free Press*, 18 June, https://hongkongfp.com/2018/06/18/video-comedian-jon-oliver-writes-cuddly-propaganda-song-chinas-xi-jinping/, accessed 22 December 2021.

Hung, Chang-Tai (1996) The Politics of Songs: Myths and Symbols in the Chinese Communist War Music, 1937–1949. *Modern Asian Studies. Special Issue: War in Modern China (Oct., 1996)*, 30(4), pp. 901–929.

Jian xing jian zhi (2014) Wu Lingjin Baozi Pu geci quanwen Baozi Ge zan zhuxi chuan Gong Linna deng huo jiang yanchang [The full text of "The Baozi Stand" by Wu Lingjin. "The Baozi Stand" song to be performed by Gong Linna]. *52FuQing.com*, 23 January, https://www.52fuqing.com/newsshow-314581.html, accessed 22 December 2021.

Judd, Ellen R. (1983) Revolutionary Drama and Song in the Jiangxi Soviet. *Modern China*, 9(1), pp. 127–60.

KarRoy Kai Yuan pindao TF Boys Wang Junkai X Wang Yuan (2019) 【TFBOYS Wang Yuan Roy】Chengxin dianliang Zhongguo《Shuodao zuodao》MV shang xian【KarRoy Kai Yuan pindao】[【TFBOYS Wang Yuan Roy】Light up China with honesty. "Live Up to Your Word" MV is online【KarRoy Kai Yuan channel】]. *YouTube*, 22 April, https://www.youtube.com/watch?v=mY9gKv3eNqE&t=62s, accessed 22 December 2021.

Kelly, Sharon (2021) Watch Andrea And Matteo Bocelli's Spring Festival Gala Performance. 12 February, https://www.udiscovermusic.com/classical-news/andrea-and-matteo-bocelli-spring-festival-gala/, accessed 22 December 2021.

Liu, Marian (2018) Hatin' on hip hop: China's rap scene frustrated by crackdown. *CNN*, 29 March, https://edition.cnn.com/2018/03/29/asia/hip-hop-china-intl/index.html, accessed 22 December 2021.

Lü, Ji (1936) Zhongguo xin yinyue de zhanwang [The outlook of China's new music]. *Guangming [The light]*, 1(5), pp. n.d.

Lynch, John (2016) Why Lady Gaga was just banned from China. *Business Insider*, 29 June, https://www.businessinsider.com/why-lady-gaga-was-banned-from-china-2016-6?IR=T, accessed 22 December 2021.

Ma Yue (2018) Discussing Xi Jinping's Inheritance and Development of Mao Zedong's Literary Thought – Based on a comparative research of Xi Jinping and Mao Zedong's talk at the forum on literature and art. *Advances in Social Science, Education and Humanities Research*, 204, pp. 555–560.

McGill, Bobby (2018) 'I'd Like to Build the World a Road' – China Pitches Trade Initiative with Cover of Iconic Coke Ad. *Branding in Asia*, 10 September, https://www.brandinginasia.com/china-cover-classic-coke-ad/, accessed 22 December 2021.

Mirra, Federica (2016) *Art Theory in Xi Jinping's Policy*. MA Thesis. Leiden: Leiden University.

New China TV (2016) China's national strategy in a rap song. *YouTube*, 2 February, https://www.youtube.com/watch?v=E8v8ZeTKaAA, accessed 22 December 2021.

New China TV (2017a) Music Video: The Belt and Road is How. *YouTube*, 10 May, https://www.youtube.com/watch?v=MolJc3PMNIg, accessed 22 December 2022.

New China TV (2017b) Music Video: The Belt and Road, Sing Along Yi dai yi lu quan qiu chang. *YouTube*, 14 May, https://www.youtube.com/watch?v=98RNh7rwyf8, accessed 22 December 2021.

Nie, Ke (2021) Disperse and preserve the perverse: computing how hip-hop censorship changed popular music genres in China. *Poetics*, 88, pp. 1–16.

NZ Herald (2016) Dalai Lama gets Selena Gomez banned from China. 20 April, https://www.nzherald.co.nz/entertainment/dalai-lama-gets-selena-gomez-banned-from-china/2EDWS25BJ2PZ7L6YFM27I6BWJI/, accessed 22 December 2021.

Owen, Malcolm (2019) US lawmakers attack Apple for song takedowns in Chinese government censorship effort. *Apple Insider*, 12 April, https://appleinsider.com/articles/19/04/12/us-lawmakers-attack-apple-for-song-takedowns-in-chinese-government-censorship-effort, accessed 22 December 2021.

Pasbani, Robert (2013) Chinese Government Didn't Allow METALLICA To Play "Master Of Puppets" At Shanghai Shows. *Metal Injection*, 25 September, https://metalinjection.net/news/chinese-government-didnt-allow-metallica-play-master-puppets-shanghai-shows, accessed 22 December 2021.

Phillips, Tom (2015a) Maroon 5 Dalai Lama tweet may have led to cancelled China concerts. *The Guardian*, 17 July, https://www.theguardian.com/music/2015/jul/17/maroon-5-dalai-lama-tweet-may-have-led-to-cancelled-china-concerts, accessed 22 December 2021.

Phillips, Tom (2015b) 'Rule the party strictly!': Chinese president 'Big Daddy Xi' makes rap debut. *The Guardian*, 29 December, https://www.theguardian.com/world/2015/dec/29/rule-the-party-strictly-chinese-president-big-daddy-xi-makes-rap-debut, accessed 22 December 2021.

Phillips, Tom (2016) Chinese officials hire gangsta rappers to boost China's image abroad. *The Guardian*, 30 June, https://www.theguardian.com/world/2016/jun/30/chinese-officials-hire-gangsta-rappers-to-boost-chinas-image-abroad, accessed 22 December 2021.

ProPublica (2015) China's Internet Censorship Agency Has Its Own Anthem And We Translated It. *YouTube*, 12 February, https://www.youtube.com/watch?v=kbBKPqOh6DU, accessed 22 December 2021.

Putz, Catherine (2015) Megadeth's First Show in China Censored. *The Diplomat*, 9 October, https://thediplomat.com/2015/10/megadeths-first-show-in-china-censored/, accessed 22 December 2021.

Rahim, Zamira (2019) The song from Les Miserables that has become a protest anthem in Hong Kong. *The Independent*, 18 September, https://www.independent.co.uk/arts-entertainment/music/features/les-miserables-hong-kong-protests-do-you-hear-the-people-sing-musical-a9081401.html, accessed 22 December 2021.

Rauhala, Emily (2015) Watch China's Creepy Musical Tribute to Its Online Censors. *Time*, 12 February, https://time.com/3706622/china-online-censorship-song-great-firewall/, accessed 22 December 2021.

RFI (2015) Chinese state TV fights for Xi's right to rule via rap. *Radio France Internationale*, 30 December, https://www.rfi.fr/en/chinese-state-tv-fights-xis-right-rule-rap, accessed 22 December 2021.

Shadbolt, Peter (2014) After three years on the blacklist, China lifts gag on Lady Gaga. *CNN*, 21 January, https://edition.cnn.com/2014/01/21/world/asia/china-lady-gaga-ban/index.html, accessed 22 December 2021.

Singh, Gunjan (2018) Increasing nationalism and censorship under Xi Jinping. *Asia Times*, 12 August, https://asiatimes.com/2018/08/increasing-nationalism-and-censorship-under-xi-jinping/, accessed 22 December 2021.

Smith, Emily and Oli Coleman (2017) Katy Perry banned from China as Victoria's Secret Fashion Show continues to crumble. *Page Six*, 16 November, https://pagesix.com/2017/11/16/katy-perry-banned-from-china-as-victorias-secret-fashion-show-continues-to-crumble/, accessed 22 December 2021.

Song, Jung-a (2016) Seoul Missile Move Sparks Fears for Pop Culture Exports to China. *Financial Times*, 8 August, http://www.ft.com/cms/s/0/2fea068e-5d48-11e6-bb77-a121aa8abd95.html#axzz4Gwr3UZw4.

Stassen, Murray (2020) Zara Larsson music pulled from Apple Music in China following criticism of state (report). *Music Business Worldwide*, 10 August, https://www.musicbusinessworldwide.com/zara-larsson-music-pulled-from-apple-music-in-china-following-criticism-of-state-report/, accessed 22 December 2021.

Stember, Nick (2016) The Road to Rejuvenation: The Animated Xi Jinping. In: Glora Davies, Jeremy Goldkorn and Luigi Tomba (eds.) *Pollution*. Acton: Australian National University Press, pp. 5–10.

Stubbs, Dan (2014) The Rolling Stones return to China, with setlist reflecting government censorship. *NME*, 13 March, https://www.nme.com/news/music/the-rolling-stones-114-1246866, accessed 22 December 2021.

Sullivan, Johnatan and Yupei Zhao (2021) Rappers as Knights-Errant: Classic Allusions in the Mainstreaming of Chinese Rap. *Popular Music and Society*, 44(3), pp. 274–291.

Sun, Meicheng and Kai Khiun Liew (2019) Analog Hallyu: Historicizing K-pop formations in China. *Global Media and China*, 4(4), pp. 419–436.

Sunio, Patti (2020) K-pop in China – does G-Dragon's Nongfu Spring deal signal the end of Beijing's unofficial ban on Korean entertainment? *South China Morning Post*, 1 June, https://www.scmp.com/magazines/style/news-trends/article/3086925/k-pop-china-does-g-dragons-nongfu-spring-deal-signal, accessed 22 December 2021.

Tan Kee Yun (2016) Fans angry after Chinese K-pop stars display patriotism. *The New Paper*, 15 July, https://www.tnp.sg/news/world/fans-angry-after-chinese-k-pop-stars-display-patriotism, accessed 22 December 2021.

Tan, Yvette (2021) China to ban karaoke songs with 'illegal content'. *BBC News*, 11 August, https://www.bbc.com/news/world-asia-china-58168638, accessed 22 December 2021.

The China Project (2019) Two Sessions: A rap song extolling China's annual policy meeting. *Youtube*, 4 March, https://www.youtube.com/watch?v=a5rvO5e-rik, accessed 22 December 2021.

The Government of the Hong Kong Special Administrative Region (2020). CE signs National Anthem Ordinance (with photos). 11 June, https://www.info.gov.hk/gia/general/202006/11/P2020061100793.htm, accessed 22 December 2021.

The Legislative Council of the Hong Kong Special Administrative Region of the People's Republic of China (n.d.) Applying National Laws in Hong Kong. https://www.legco.gov.hk/researchpublications/english/essentials-1516ise07-applying-national-laws-in-hong-kong.htm.

The State Council. The People's Republic of China (2017) To revive China, Xi holds high banner of socialism with Chinese characteristics. 28 July, http://english.www.gov.cn/news/top_news/2017/09/28/content_281475890831923.htm, accessed 22 December 2021.

Tian, Yew Lun (2021) China's Communist Party hails President Xi as 'helmsman'. *Reuters*, 12 November, https://www.reuters.com/world/china/president-xi-is-helmsman-chinas-rejuvenation-says-party-official-2021-11-12/, accessed 28 December 2021.

Vernon D (2015) CCTV Communist Corruption Rap feat President Xi JinPing. *YouTube*, 28 December, https://www.youtube.com/watch?v=xhU8C5RCbBs, accessed 22 December 2021.

Wan Xu (2017) Wangluo zizhi yinyuelei xuan xiu jiemu 《Zhongguo you xi-ha》de chenggong yinsu fenxi [An analysis of the success factors of the self-made variety show "The Rap of China"]. *Collection*, 11(46), pp. n.d.

Xin Zhongguo pindao (2017) Aiguo xin hongge: 《Dongfang you hong》 [New patriotic red song: "The East is Red Again"]. *YouTube*, 28 October, https://www.youtube.com/watch?v=8krIYuJopwA, accessed 22 December 2021.

Xinhua she (2014) Shehuizhuyi hexin jiazhiguan gequ bianru Sichuan zhong- xiaoxue jiaocai [Songs about core socialist values included in the teaching materials of elementary schools and high schools in Sichuan]. 31 December, https://news.sina.com.cn/c/2014-12-31/181631349770.shtml?cre=sinapc, accessed 22 December 2021.

Xinhua wang (2015a) Wenhua Bu gongbu wangluo yinyue chanpin "hei mingdan" tigongzhe jiang yifa chachu [The Ministry of Culture announces the "black list" of internet music products, those who provide them will be prosecuted in accordance with Chinese law]. 10 August, http://www.xinhuanet.com/politics/2015-08/10/c_111 6205562.htm, accessed 22 December 2021.

Xinhua wang (2015b) (Shouquan fabu) Xi Jinping: zai Wenyi Gongzuo Zuotanhui shang de jianghua [(The authorized announcement) Xi Jinping: speech at the Beijing Forum on Literature and Art]. 14 October, http://www.xinhuanet.com//polit ics/2015-10/14/c_1116825558.htm, accessed 03 November 2021.

Xinhuanet (2017) Disrespecting national anthem to get criminal punishment. 4 November, http://www.xinhuanet.com//english/2017-11/04/c_136728106.htm, accessed 10 December 2021.

Xinhuanet (2019) MV: "Two sessions": To the world, From China. 3 March, http://www.xinhuanet.com/english/2019-03/03/c_137864806.htm?fbclid=IwAR0XSzR6Bfhc YiNy5AzZKMyk_5s-QRZLdDNYRp_ZK7I4qEIpo8MXwhqkjKI#0-twi-1-63012-72502 27817ecdff034dc9540e6c76667, accessed 2 December 2021.

Xinlang jiaoyu (2014) Shehuizhuyi hexin jiazhiguan jiaoyu rongjin zhong- xiaoxue ketang [The core socialist values enter the classrooms of elementary schools and high Schools]. 13 November, http://edu.sina.com.cn/zxx/2014-11-13/1824443 342.shtml, accessed 22 December 2021.

Xinlang wang (2014) Bei Da jiaoshou Fan Ceng deng zuo shi 9 shou he Xi Jinping Wenyi Zuotanhui jianghua [Fan Ceng, the professor at the Beijing University composed nine poems congratulating Xi Jinping on the Beijing Forum on Literature and Art]. 27 October, http://news.sina.com.cn/c/2014-10-27/133431051094.shtml, accessed 22 December 2021.

Xinlang yule (2018) Zongju tichu jiemu jiabin biaozhun: Gediao di wenshen xiha Wenhua Bu yong [The Headquarters put forward standards for guest of the shows: low morality, tattoos, hip-hop culture to be excluded]. 19 January, http://ent.sina.com.cn/tv/zy/2018-01-19/doc-ifyquptv7935320.shtml, accessed 22 December 2021.

Xu, Beina and Eleanor Albert (2017) Media Censorship in China. *Council on Foreign Relations*, 17 February, https://www.cfr.org/backgrounder/media-censorship-china, 22 December 2021.

Xu, Jian and Ling Yang (2021) Governing entertainment celebrities in China: practices, policies and politics (2005–2020). *Celebrity Studies*, 12(2), pp. 202–218.

Yan, Sophia (2015) Why Swift may have to tailor her 1989 tour for China. *CNN Money*, 22 July, https://money.cnn.com/2015/07/22/news/taylor-swift-1989-china/index.html, accessed 22 December 2021.

Yang, Hon-Lun (2020) Songs of the Outcast: Popular Music, Class, and Censorship in the PRC. In: Ian Peddie (ed.) *The Bloomsbury Handbook of Popular Music and Social Class*. New York: Bloomsbury Academic, pp. 161–182.

Yang Jiangang and Jiang Gongyan (2020) Reflections on Political Policies and Statements in Arts and Literature in PRC. *CLCWeb: Comparative Literature and Culture*, 22(5), pp. 1–9.

Yang, Sophia (2019) China scraps over 3,000 songs by HK lyricist Albert Leung for his speech in Taiwan: report. *Taiwan News*, 23 November, https://www.taiwannews.com.tw/en/news/3823249, accessed 22 December 2021.

Yim Hyun-su (2020) Don't be too optimistic about lifting of K-pop ban in China: experts. *The Korea Herald*, 21 May, http://www.koreaherald.com/view.php?ud=20200521000711, accessed 22 December 2021.

Yin Liangen and Terry Flew (2017) Xi Dada loves Peng Mama: Digital Culture and the Return of Charismatic Authority In China. *Conference Papers – International Communication Association*, pp. 1–42.

Yu, Ting-Fai (2018) Contextualising the National Anthem Law in Mainland China and Hong Kong: Football as a Field of Political Contention. *China Perspectives*, 2018(3), pp. 79–82.

Zhonghua Renmin Gongheguo Zhongyang Renmin Zhengfu (2017) Zhonghua Renmin Gongheguo Guoge Fa [The National Anthem Law of the People's Republic of China]. *Xinhua she*, 4 September, https://www.gov.cn/guoqing/2017-09/04/content_5222515.htm, accessed 28 December 2012.

Zhou, Christina (2019) China's new propaganda music video celebrates trustworthiness and the Social Credit System. *ABC News*, 8 May, https://www.abc.net.au/news/2019-05-08/beijing-makes-music-video-promoting-the-social-credit-system/11088402, accessed 22 December 2021.

Ziyou shijie xinwen lianbo (2017) Gequ 《Genzhe ni jiu shi genzhe na taiyang》gesong Xi Jinping ["To Follow You is to Follow the Sun" – The song praising Xi Jinping]. *YouTube*, 21 November, https://www.youtube.com/watch?v=CK_1tYyJ-aE, accessed 22 December 2021.

Zou, Sheng (2019), When nationalism meets hip-hop: aestheticized politics of ideotainment in China. *Communication and Critical/Cultural Studies*, 16(3), pp. 178–195.

CHAPTER 16

Community of Common Language
The Last Decade in the Advancement of Putonghua

Kamil Burkiewicz

L'Impartial Tientsin (大公报 *Dagong Bao*), a Chinese newspaper founded in 1902, was an engaged witness to socio-political movements and radical changes during the very last years of Manchu Qing Dynasty's reign (1644–1912) and the following decades. In one of its issues from October 1903, the periodical presented a collection of humorous curiosities that occurred in the course of provincial level civil service exam known as *xiangshi* (乡试). One of them concerned an examinee who, apparently firmly attached to traditional education, misinterpreted the term Guowen (国文), lit. 'National Language', as Manchu language (Wang, 2019: 442). While for reform-oriented intellectuals of the time Guowen or the roughly synonymous Guoyu (国语), redefined as the concept of a nationwide standard language, had already been recognised as an essential element for building a modern state and fostering a sense of national community among Chinese people, its older meaning, associating Guoyu with the language of a ruling regime, was still in use within conservative circles and imperial administration.[1] Nowadays, after over a century since the recalled anecdote took place, such connotation is, however, by all means incompatible with the present political and linguistic situation in China. Or is it?

Putonghua (普通话), lit. 'Common Speech', in Western linguistic discourse often referred to as Modern Standard Chinese or Standard Mandarin, holds the status of the nationwide language in the People's Republic of China. Despite existing differences in nomenclature, its actual ideological and formational roots clearly stem from Guoyu – arduously defined and shaped during the National Language Movement (国语运动 *Guoyu Yundong*) in the first half of the 20th century, that is, before the Chinese Communists seizure of power. Being progressively increased through decades of intensive promotion,

---

1 Guoyu has also non-linguistic connotations, like the title of an ancient Chinese text usually translated as *Discourses of the States*, which are irrelevant to the topic of this chapter. The meaning of "ruling dynasty's language" came into use long before the Manchu period and can be traced back as early as the period of Northern Wei (北魏, 386–534), when another non-Han Chinese regime controlled vast portions of today's northern China (Gu, n.d.).

according to data provided by the PRC's Ministry of Education, the penetration rate of Putonghua among China's population has exceeded 80% in 2020 (Jiaoyu Bu, 2021a). Despite the actual level of proficiency of its speakers, which strongly varies regionally and socially (Zhao and Liu, 2021: 885), the linguistic unification (语言统一 *yuyan tongyi*) of the country seems to be quite well advanced and relatively close to completion. The progress achieved so far is considerable especially when confronted with voices of sceptical criticism heard from many scholars a century ago at the very initial stages of the process, including Hu Shi's statement claiming "It will never be possible not even in one thousand years!" (Ouyang, 1998: 129). The present Chinese administration is, however, far from considering the heretofore achievements as a premise to demote further language reforms as part of national priorities. Quite the contrary, intensive arrangements in this area have been launched recently and more are set out in the outline of the 14th Five-Year Plan, marking a new phase of Putonghua promotion and codification. Their ultimate goal is, judging from observed tendencies, integral to a broader policy context – the systematic building of a homogeneous and cohesive society, made up of a community that not only speaks the 'Common Speech', but also shares a common discourse and attitudes.

This chapter aims at a brief investigation of political, ideological and linguistic aspects of Putonghua in the past decade, shaped by Xi Jinping's ascendency to the helm and successive accumulation of power, as well as possible trends for the near future. The ongoing language policy appears to remain an important element of further strengthening of the country's integrity, national pride and position in the world. Therefore, the current state of the language that went through over a century of refinement and continues its development under Xi's presidency is undoubtedly worth an overall study. The discussed issues are organised into three main sections, followed by a short conclusion. The initial content covers selective exploration of the historical roots and the circumstances of the legal establishment of Putonghua (Section 1), providing necessary background for an overview of the imposed language policy and ideology (Section 2). Since the PRC's government, irrespective of its revolutionary origins and self-proclaimed principles, is actually directly following or adapting some ideas inherited from the Republic of China and imperial period, the present state cannot be discussed without reference to the past. Finally, in order to complete a comprehensive picture of the subject matter, characteristics of the still continuing standardization processes are discussed (Section 3).

1 The Origins of Putonghua and the Initial Stages of Its Promotion

Late Qing Dynasty writer and educator Wu Rulun (1840–1903) in his 1902 published account "Records on a Tour to the East" (东游丛录 *Dong You Cong Lu*) made observations on the status of Tokyo dialect in Japan and referred to it as *putongyu* (普通语), i.e., 'common language'. A few years later, the term *putonghua* appeared in Zhu Wenxiong's (1883–1961) "New Alphabet of Jiangsu" (江苏新字母 *Jiangsu Xin Zimu*, 1906) in the context of "commonly used speeches in respective provinces" (Li, 2003: 2). The first instances of using a similar or the exact form of the term that several decades later eventually became the name of the nationwide language standard in China were, however, quite rare in Chinese literature of the period. Most of the proponents of language reforms applied the word 'Guoyu' when debating various ideas on how the national standard should be codified.

1.1 The National Language Movement

At the very beginnings of language reform initiatives that started to emerge throughout the final decade of the 19th century the spotlight was specifically put on the common problem of illiteracy within Chinese population. Many progressive individuals blamed the traditional sinographic writing system. Lu Gangzhang (1854–1928) claimed that the rate of literacy in Europe and America was very high "all because they use writing systems based on *qieyin*[2] characters" (Lu, 1892: 4). Although initially not attracting particular attention, phonological differences among Chinese topolects soon became one of the focuses of the reform debate. A pressing need for establishing a nationwide pronunciation norm has also been addressed by some regional officials, like Lin Lucun (1879–1919), who advocated for the promotion of Lu Gangzhang's phonetic script with standard pronunciation based on Beijing dialect of Mandarin that will "unite hearts of people within the Four Seas[3]" (Li, 1896: 5–6). Besides the

---

2 *Qieyin* (切音) – a method of phonetic notation corresponding to the traditional *fanqie* (反切) system, in which phonetic values of sinograms were divided into initials and finals represented respectively by corresponding attributes of other two sinograms. The publication of Lu Gangzhang's system, made of 37 symbols denoting initials, non-nasal finals and nasal finals, initiated a wave of other alphabets and syllabaries proposals, like Wu Zhihui's (1865–1953) "Bean-Sprout Alphabet" (豆芽字母 *Douya Zimu*, 1895) and Cai Xiyong's (1850–1896) "Phonetic Quick Script" (传音快字 *Chuanyin Kuaizi*, 1896). Some of them were intended to replace the sinographic writing system, while others were meant to serve as educational aids for the illiterate. These efforts came to be collectively known as the Qieyinzi Movement (切音字运动 *Qieyinzi Yundong*, 1892–1911), considered as an initial stage of the National Language Movement.

3 The Four Seas (四海 *Si Hai*) – metaphorical expression for boundaries of ancient China.

original aim of improving literacy rates, the projected language reforms and policies thus came to be recognised as an important catalyst of national identity formation. Such perspective stimulated the increasing popularity of the term Guoyu – the 'National Language' emerged in texts from various fields, including common schooling, in the context of which Chen Duxiu (1879–1942) fervently urged: "If we do not take Guoyu [education] seriously, what kind of nation are we going to be?" (1904: 42).

At the turn of the 19th and 20th centuries, the slogan of language unification at the national level assumed a prominent place in the reformist discourse. Regarding the question of what the basis of Guoyu should be, Northern Mandarin,[4] particularly the Beijing dialect, for many seemed a natural choice. The eminent socio-political status of the capital's speech was one of the main reasons for which, as stated in *L'Impartial Tientsin* in 1910, it received "acquiescent support from all of today's proponents of the language unification" (Wang, 2019: 302).[5] The Qing's imperial administration eventually acknowledged and adapted to the trend by issuing the "Approaches to the Unification of the National Language" (统一国语办法案 *Tongyi Guoyu Banfa An*) the next year. The document confirmed the status of the Beijing speech, though some phonological features of other Chinese varieties, like the checked tone,[6] were also to be included in the planned standard (Li, 2003: 3).

The fate of the act was doomed with the abrupt collapse of the Manchu regime a few months later. The conceptual approach that it set out, however, found a direct continuation in the newly established Republic of China. The Conference on the Unification of Pronunciation (读音统一会 *Duyin Tongyi*

---

4 Mandarin (官话 *Guanhua*), a group of related varieties of Chinese natively spoken in northern and southeastern China, among which the variant present in the area of Nanjing and later the dialect of Beijing contributed to the formation of a koine used by members of the imperial administration in oral communication, hence the Chinese name Guanhua lit. meaning 'officials' language'. The knowledge of the koine was not, however, limited to officials only. Newcomers to the capital region pursuing a career in the imperial cadres often learned Guanhua from their local servants (Sun, 1983: 588).

5 In fact, there were some critical voices against the adoption of the Beijing dialect, mostly raised by speakers of Southern Mandarin varieties. Wu Zhihui made a clear distinction between the proper Guanhua and "the speech from Yan" (燕, an old name for the region of Beijing), which "if used as the standard, would make Beijing barbarians [...] go abroad and teach their strange barking-like noise as Guanhua, uglifying the image of China" (Wu, 1927: 90). This and similar opinions carried strong ethnic connotations – the said "barbarians" referred to the Manchurians and other nationalities of northern origins.

6 Checked tone (入声 *rusheng*, 'entering tone') occurs exclusively in syllables that end in a stop consonant or a glottal stop. Although not present in the majority of Mandarin varieties, it remains a valid feature in the south-eastern branches of Chinese.

Hui) was formally opened on 15th February 1913 and continued its work for more than three months. The assembled delegates, among whom were personas already widely known in intellectual circles and those whose careers were yet to fully blossom, like Zhou Shuren,[7] ultimately manged to vote through standardized phonetic values for several thousand sinograms and a set of symbols for their notation, named as Zhuyin Zimu[8] (Li, 1934: 57). The actual attempt to implement the therefore codified Guoyu was due to domestic political turmoil postponed until 1919,[9] when the first dedicated dictionaries were officially released (Wang, 2019: 318). Unfortunately, the inclusiveness of the standard, which while being based on the Beijing speech, also comprised some characteristics of other dialects, aroused wide criticism for its artificiality. Many argued that "Guoyu became a castle in the air by taking a little from the east and a little from the west" (Wang, 2019: 326) – the resulting lack of native speakers and insufficient teaching resources have substantially hampered the implementation process.

The evident failure of the standardization efforts undertaken so far has reinforced the arguments of those who, instead of dialectal inclusiveness, advocated for the exclusive adoption of the speech of the capital city. Even some declared critics of the latter have gradually changed their attitude. Qian Xuantong (1887–1939) eventually admitted that "Guoyu should be built on a living language, precisely the Beijing speech [...], whose standard is easy to define" (Qian, 1926: 15). Consequently, after the decision of the Ministry of Education "A Glossary of Frequently Used Characters with Their National Pronunciation" (国音常用字汇 *Guoyin Changyong Zihui*) was published in 1932. The thus presented revised model of Guoyu did not include the checked tone as well as all other phonetic features non-existent in the capital's dialect (Li, 1934: 263–265).

Meanwhile a new opposition emerged against the centrally imposed language standard. For the Chinese communists Guoyu was yet another tool of

---

7 Zhou Shuren (1881–1936), better known under his literary double Lu Xun, was one of the most prominent authors that contributed to the creation of modern Chinese literature written in the vernacular (cf. footnote 9).

8 The original set of Zhuyin Zimu (注音字母 'Phonetic Notation Alphabet') later underwent a number of complementary modifications. Renamed as Zhuyin Fuhao (注音符号 'Phonetic Notation Symbols') in 1932, it remains in use in the education system of the Republic of China in Taiwan.

9 These turbulent years also witnessed crucial social and cultural transformations instigated by the New Culture Movement (新文化運動 *Xin Wenhua Yundong*) and since 1919 the May Fourth Movement (五四运动 *Wu Si Yundong*), an important component of which was the development and promotion of Baihuawen (白话文 'Vernacular Writing'), also known as Standard Written Chinese.

oppression and forced assimilation of ethnicities in the multi-cultural society (Qu, 1989: 169). Qu Qiubai (1899–1935), one of the leaders of the then Left Wing Culture Movement (左翼文化运动 *Zuoyi Wenhua Yundong*), passionately advocated for the use of the term Putonghua instead of Guoyu. In his view, apparently deeply influenced by Nikolai Marr's idea of the class-nature of language, the 'Common Speech' was to be forged naturally through daily communication within proletarian masses, especially in highly industrialised and modern urban centres like Shanghai. Nevertheless, Qu also assumed that regional Chinese varieties, both spoken and written, would remain in use (Qu, 1989: 16–17).

1.2 The First Period of Putonghua Legislative Installation and Promotion

Although the first years after the proclamation of the People's Republic in 1949 were marked by struggles to consolidate the new state's integrity, severe internal and external challenges did not completely impede the debate on language policy. Some of its participants followed the tracks of Qu Qiubai's thinking and supported the idea of Putonghua as "a language coined in harbour docks, public institutions, factories, universities, among People's Liberation Army troops" (Liu, 1953: 16). On the other hand, troublesome political connotations made the term Guoyu gradually disappear from the discourse. Even one of the most prominent supporters of the 'National Language', Li Jinxi (1890–1978), eventually condemned it as historically inaccurate (Li and Liu, 1955: 12). Under the guise of nomenclature, however, the conceptual basis of Guoyu has apparently remained prevalent. The Chinese state, in the person of the Minister of Education, concluded the debate with a report titled "Unswervingly Promote Putonghua with Phonetic Features Standardized on the Beijing Dialect" (Zhang, 1955). The document initiated a series of legislative actions finalised with the promulgation of the "State Council Instructions on the Promotion of Putonghua" in 1956. Besides the already defined pronunciation basis of the 'Common Speech', the instructions also specified Mandarin dialects as the source of its lexicon and model works in Baihuawen as determinants of grammar norms (Zhou, 1956).

The actual promotion of Putonghua, conducted along with the introduction of Hanyu Pinyin,[10] did not fulfil the ambitious goals it was meant to achieve in the following few years. Instead of the expected proliferation of Putonghua in

---

10   Hanyu Pinyin (汉语拼音), the official romanization system for Modern Standard Chinese, was designed as a tool to facilitate the teaching of Putonghua and phonetic notation of Chinese characters. Despite earlier postulates for a complete replacement of sinographs with an alphabet, raised among others by Qu Qiubai in the 1930s, the PRC authorities chose to establish the standard writing system based on simplified Chinese characters (简化字 *jianhuazi*).

primary, secondary and higher schools across the country, except for regions inhabited by ethnic minorities, as well as all other public spheres (Zhou, 1956), the campaign was soon disturbed by new socio-economic policies, with the Great Leap Forward at the forefront. As a result, no tangible progress was achieved during the next two decades.

2 The Development of the Current Language Policy and Ideology

The change of political climate and extensive reforms undertaken in China at the turn of the 1970s and 1980s enabled a more systematic and thorough approach to the popularization of Putonghua. The policy of language unification, just like in the late 19th century, was once again recognised as one of the crucial factors in stimulating the country's socio-economic development. During the subsequent decades, however, especially after Xi Jinping's appointment as the paramount leader, its principles seemingly underwent a shift in ideological accents.

2.1 *The Period before Xi Jinping*

The strong commitment to intensify efforts towards improving Standard Mandarin acquisition among Chinese population was embedded in the PRC Constitution of 1982, the first one that defined Putonghua as the nationwide-promoted language (Article 19).[11] In terms of drafting a concrete promotion strategy, the leading role was entrusted to the National Working Committee on Language and Script (国家语言文字工作委员会 *Guojia Yuyan Wenzi Gongzuo Weiyuanhui*), reconstituted in 1985 from the previous Committee for Chinese Writing Reform (中国文字改革委员会 *Zhongguo Wenzi Gaige Weiyuanhui*). Soon after that a new set of dedicated guidelines came out in 1986. From then on further refinement and enforcement of the national language standard and the corresponding writing system, deemed crucial to the development of the state's economy, culture, education and science, was to be realized through the imposition of Putonghua as the language of instruction in all schools across

---

11   For the full text of the PRC's Constitution, see the Chinese Central Government's official website: <http://www.gov.cn/guoqing/2018-03/22/content_5276318.htm>. Apart from the promotion of Putonghua, the Constitution also provides a legal guarantee of freedom to use native languages and corresponding writing systems (Article 1). Furthermore, all administrative units conferred with the status of 'autonomy' are empowered to establish their own rules concerning the presence of local tongues and cultures in public life (Article 121).

the country, the working language of government and administration, as well as the language used in all kinds of broadcasting media and other public domains (Klöter, 2021: 113). The execution of these guidelines required the creation of a system of language competences evaluation – Putonghua Proficiency Test (普通话水平测试 *Putonghua Shuiping Ceshi*), which started to be implemented in 1995 and gradually became a mandatory prerequisite for media presenters, actors, teachers, civil service employees and other public sector workers (Jiaoyu Bu, 2021b). In order to ensure proper social reception, the strengthened language policy was accompanied by comprehensive propaganda measures, inter alia, by establishing the National Putonghua Promotion Week (全国推广普通话宣传周 *Quanguo Tuiguang Putonghua Xuanchuan Zhou*), organised annually in September since 1998.

The above outlined promotion objectives were reconfirmed and detailed in the "Law of the People's Republic of China on the Nationwide Language and Script", adopted by the Standing Committee of the National's People's Congress in 2000. Although the presence of Chinese varieties other than Putonghua in mass media, publications and similar public channels of communication was strictly restricted to a few specific circumstances (Quanguo Renda Changweihui, 2000), the penetration rate of the 'Common Speech' by 2004 reached the disappointing level of 53.06 percent (Wang, 2015: 85). The subsequent efforts were therefore intensified by a more rigorous execution and evaluation of the policy, especially in the south-eastern regions known for the vivid use of local dialects (Klöter, 2021: 114). Significant progress has been demonstrated through the data collected in 2013, according to which 70 percent of the population were able to communicate in Putonghua, however, mostly at a low level of proficiency (Wang, 2015: 86).

2.2 *The Xi Jinping Era*

The premises of the considerable shift in ideological accents of the language policy that followed Xi Jinping's ascendancy to power could be seen in numerous domestic publications in the late 2000s and early 2010s. Their authors warned of the alleged negative impact on Chinese language and native way of thinking exerted by Western languages, especially English, and culturally alien discourse. The 'crisis of Chinese' (汉语危机 *Hanyu weiji*) was supposed to be caused by "frantic enthusiasm" towards learning foreign languages, observed both within the state system of education and private tutoring institutions, deteriorating the mother tongue skills of the younger generation (Fu, 2012). Furthermore, external linguistic influences were considered to have endangered the domestic literary heritage (Yue, 2007), while the ideology present in Western discourse was found to have permeated Chinese discourse, making the

Chinese people perceive the surrounding reality through imported concepts and terms, rather than values derived from Confucian and other indigenous traditions (Zhang, 2004). Faced with new internal and external challenges of the second decade of the 21st century, the country's central authorities have apparently acknowledged the problem by initiating countermeasures with the aim of maintaining decisive control over the course of public debate and general attitudes among society. The ongoing language policy, although officially still concentrated on stimulating economic growth and social development, seems to be an important part of them. It is therefore an admissible assertion that the promotion of Putonghua has recently entered a new period.[12]

A proper understating of the ideological core of this new period requires a broader look from an overall perspective of strategic policies and corresponding slogans introduced since the 18th National Congress of the Chinese Communist Party in 2012. Xi Jinping, the then newly appointed Party's General Secretary, inaugurated his leadership with the launch of 'Chinese Dream' (中国梦 *Zhongguo Meng*) discourse, ambiguously defined as the common strive for 'the great rejuvenation of the Chinese nation' (中华民族伟大复兴 *Zhonghua minzu weida fuxing*). The path to the realization of the dream has been set by the incorporation of "Xi Jinping thought on socialism with Chinese characteristics for a new era" (习近平新时代中国特色社会主义思想 *Xi Jinping xin shidai Zhongguo tese shehui zhuyi sixiang*) into the Constitution of the CCP in 2017 and the Constitution of the PRC in the following year. The therein outlined further development of China is inextricably linked with the doctrine of the 'four matters of confidence' (四个自信 *si ge zixin*), calling the Chinese people to strengthen their confidence in the socialist path, guiding theories, political system and culture. The fourth of these confidences[13] refers to an outright affirmation of China's own culture being fundamental to the present national order and identity, and therefore ensuring the independence from servile imitation of foreign models (Li, 2020: 8). In the context of the aforementioned 'crisis of Chinese', the intensification of promotion, protection and standardization of Putonghua becomes even more imperative, because the

---

12 The hereby proposed distinction of a new period in Putonghua promotion actually fit into the narrative of Xi's leadership, focused on emphasizing the epochal character of the undergoing transformation. The latest example is the "Third Resolution on History" (第三个历史决议 *Di-san ge Lishi Jueyi*). The document, released by the Standing Committee of the CCP in November 2021, stresses Xi's position as the core of the Party and his leading role in moving China into a new era.

13 The doctrine was originally proposed by the CCP's former General Secretary Hu Jintao (1942-) in the form of the 'three matters of confidence'. The element of cultural confidence was added by Xi Jinping in 2014.

'Common Speech', as Xi has pointed out, serves as "the important carrier of culture, which constitutes the soul of the country" and helps to "forge the Chinese nation's community consciousness"[14] (Wang, 2020: 6). The implication behind these narratives is that Putonghua plays an integral part in consolidating the integrity of the country under the CCP. It is the fundamental medium of communication between the state and the governed population, used to shape a particular cultural framework[15] and guide expected behaviours and attitudes.

Having specified the socio-political significance of Putonghua, it comes without surprise that the proliferation rate of Standard Mandarin, which at the beginning of Xi Jinping's tenure reached the level of 70 percent (Wang, 2015: 85), was found far from satisfactory and called for further enhancement. Consequently, the rhetoric of propaganda started to concentrate on emphasizing the close dependence between language policy and the realization of 'Chinese Dream'. The motto of the 17th National Putonghua Promotion Week in 2014, organised under a new expanded format abundant in various promotional activities at the nationwide and regional levels, claimed that "speaking good Putonghua will make everyone's dream come true" (说好普通话圆梦你我他 *Shuo hao Putonghua yuanmeng ni wo ta*) (Xu, 2021: 226). A few years later, during the 21st edition of the week, the necessity of acquiring proper language proficiency was also directly linked with patriotism, expected to be verbalised by "using Putonghua to chant the seventieth anniversary of the founding of the People's Republic of China and using standardized characters to write patriotic feelings" (普通话诵七十华诞，规范字书爱国情怀 *Putonghua song qishi Hua dan, guifan zi shu aiguo qinghuai*) (Xu, 2021: 227).

Along with the intensified agitation campaign, new institutional and legislative initiatives came in response to the goals set out in the PRC's 13th Five-Year Plan (2016–2020), aimed at achieving "substantial proliferation of the national standard across the whole country" (Jiaoyu Bu and Guojia Yuwei,

---

14 *Zhonghua minzu* (中华民族), lit. 'Chinese nation', is a term related to the concept of one multi-ethnic Chinese nation state with a common national identity. Having been forged at the beginning of the 20th century and utilized by the government of the Republic of China, the term was rejected during the Mao Zedong's era and reincorporated into the official discourse after his death, when the narrative of a multi-national communist statehood was gradually renounced.

15 Along with the recognition of Putonghua being a carrier of culture, those who do not speak the 'Common Speech' or their proficiency level is low are often openly or implicitly considered uncultured and uncivilized – such suggestion can be found for example in the popular slogan "Speak Putonghua, write standardized characters, and be a civilized person" (说普通话，写规范字，做文明人 *Shuo Putonghua, xie guifan zi, zuo wenming ren*).

2016). Since the official data showed that "the ratio of Putonghua speakers in most major cities exceeded 90 percent", while "in many rural areas barely reached about 40 percent and even less within districts inhabited by non-Han nationalities" (Jiaoyu Bu and Guojia Yuwei, 2017), the main focus was laid on less urbanized rural regions in the west of China. Wealthier and better developed municipalities have been obliged to provide infrastructural and organisational support in the program of enhancing Putonghua teaching, including the development of language courses, textbooks and other educational materials tailored for various groups such as local administration cadres and young farmers. Preschool and school-age youth, especially from minority nationalities, seemed the object of particular concern as the system of obligatory education remained "the main front and channel for the spread of Putonghua". More qualified teachers were to be employed in schools and kindergartens, with the latter envisaged as facilities responsible for "cultivating interest in reading and enabling children to conduct basic communication in Standard Mandarin" (Jiaoyu Bu and Guojia Yuwei, 2016).

Although the directives announced by the Ministry of Education contained provisions on bilingual education[16] and systemic protection of indigenous languages and writing systems, inter alia, through dedicated research programs and the use of advanced technologies to build electronic language resources (Jiaoyu Bu and Guojia Yuwei, 2016), the actual course of educational policy, as seen from both unofficial and official decisions carried out by regional authorities, tends towards gradual replacement of minorities languages with Putonghua. The presence of teaching materials in local languages is being systematically diminished in favour of centrally unified textbooks, if not completely eliminated. Such practices can be observed in large minority areas like Tibet, Xinjiang and more recently in Inner Mongolia (Neimenggu Zizhiqu Jiaoyu Ting, 2020), as well as less populous ethnic communities in the southwestern provinces.[17] The

---

16   Bilingual education (双语教育 *shuangyu jiaoyu*), i.e., the complementary use of Putonghua and native languages of respective minority nationalities in schools, was officially implemented by the people's governments of all provinces and autonomous regions in 2010 after the announcement of the "Outline of China's National Plan for Medium and Long-term Education Reform and Development" (国家中长期教育改革和发展规划纲要 *Guojia Zhongchangqi Jiaoyu Gaige he Fazhan Guihua Gangyao*).

17   According to this author's personal experience, based on his own field research and publications on the language and culture of the Sui (水 *Shui*) people, the southwestern minorities possess very limited and uneven access to formal education in the indigenous languages. With a population of approximately 400,000 people living mainly in Guizhou Province, the Sui have only a few local schools providing Sui language and culture classes. Moreover, most of the content of the dedicated textbooks is written in Mandarin, as in the case of *A Reader on the Sui Culture for Primary School* (水族文化进校园读本 *Shuizu*

dominant official explanation for the ongoing processes appeals to the need of improving minorities' position on the state labour market and consequently their economic condition – the need which itself is generally uncontested among members of those communities. There is however at least one more clearly articulated agenda, though much less pronounced, behind the promotion of Standard Mandarin, and the cultural system it represents as well, with the objective of "reducing factors causing instability"[18] (HRW, 2020). This kind of rhetoric shows that the alleged threats attributed to the 'crisis of Chinese' may be identified not only within external, but also, if not mainly, internal factors, wherein citizens not subjected to Putonghua education are perceived as potential instigators of social disorder and disintegration.

The realisation of all goals set out in the 13th Five-Year Plan was announced to be successfully completed. Since the popularization rate of the 'Common Speech' reached the expected value of 80,72 percent (Jiaoyu Bu, 2021b), the new aim of 85 percent was incorporated into the 14th Five-Year Plan (2021–2025). Following the path of the previous period, the current framework continues to concentrate on school and preschool children. In accordance with the spirit of the phrase "education in the revolutionary tradition must start during childhood" (革命传统教育要从娃娃抓起 *geming chuantong jiaoyu yao cong wawa zhua qi*), articulated by Xi Jinping in 2016 and then widely promoted, the new education campaign is conducted under the slogan "united sounds of children's language" (童语同音 *tongyu tongyin*). Its ambitious objective is to provide kindergarten care and associated services to all children living in rural aeras across the country, with particular emphasis on the 'three regions and three prefectures'.[19] These institutions, staffed by qualified teachers from more developed regions, will ensure initial acquisition of Putonghua as a competence needed for more effective school education. However, considering

---

Wenhua Jin Xiaoyuan Duben, 2007). The dynamic of Putonghua popularization within such communities is especially evident. While in the late 1980s and 1990s, the level of Chinese language acquisition among Sui children was deemed insufficient and viewed as one of the major challenges of public education in the region (Zhang and Chen, 1989), now, young people constitute the main segment of society that is most open to Chinese language influences.

18   Instability, orig. *bu wending* (不稳定), is a euphemism for political disturbance, closely related to another term, *weiwen* (维稳 'stability maintenance'), covering all measures taken by the state organs for reasons of ensuring public security and the present governmental authority.

19   'Three regions and three prefectures' (三州三区 *san zhou san qu*) is a geographical term coined in 2018 and refers to deeply impoverished areas of China, including the whole Tibet, four districts in Xinjiang, as well as minority regions in Sichuan, Gansu and Yunnan Provinces.

one of the main postulates of the campaign states that preschool children are to be accustomed to "think in Putonghua" (Jiaoyu Bu, 2021c), the intentioned agenda apparently goes beyond the sole improvement of educational opportunities and aims at cultural assimilation through language assimilation.

3 The Ongoing Further Standardization of Putonghua and Its Social Reception

While the initial stages of the National Language Movement and the corresponding efforts to establish a nationwide language standard, as discussed earlier in the chapter (Section 1), were intended to be part of necessary measures in order to rejuvenate, modernize and to a certain extent also Westernize post-imperial China, the current tendencies both in the promotion and further standardization of Putonghua are clearly directed towards increasing resistance against external influences brought by globalization, enhancing traditional culture and spiritual heritage of the imperial past.[20] The need for protection of the 'Common Speech' as a carrier of these values, signalled in articles on the 'crisis of Chinese', has been recognised within governmental circles and directly reflected in legal regulations. A prominent example of such regulations is the "Notice Concerning the Normative Use of the National Common Spoken and Written Language in Radio and Television Programmes and Advertising" issued by the National Radio and Television Administration. The document, besides the prohibition of indiscriminate use of foreign words and popular phrases originating from Internet slang, puts a special focus on inappropriate modifications of historically shaped idiomatic expressions or imitations of their structures in order to create new ones – the practice that "goes against the promotion of the spirit of traditional Chinese culture" (Guojia Xinwen Chuban Guang Dian Zongju, 2014). The overall attitude of the PRC's authorities towards the standardization and maintenance of Putonghua,

---

20   Numerous references to classical literature and culture constitute an important part of the current state ideology, but even in the earlier history of Chinese communism, when they were officially condemned as despicable remnants of the feudal order, radical revolutionary rhetoric was in fact deeply influenced by concepts derived from, inter alia, Confucian classics. For example, motifs of self-reflection (自我反省 *ziwo fanxing*) and self-criticism (自我批评 *ziwo piping*) appeared in Confucius's *Analects* as essential practices for shaping the moral integrity of a nobleman (君子 *junzi*), and in communist leaders' rhetoric emerged as determinants of a good communist – cf. *How to be a Good Communist* (论共产党员的修养 *Lun Gongchandangyuan de Xiuyang*, 1939) by Liu Shaoqi (1898–1969) (Lu, 2004: 44–45).

as can be seen considerably conservative, highly regulated and biased against external influences, is therefore coherent with the omnipresent narrative of the 'Chinese characteristic' (中国特色 *Zhongguo tese*), highlighting civilizational and cultural uniqueness of the present China.

3.1   Standardization and Normalization in the Last Decade

In 1956, when the PRC's authorities promulgated the promotion of the nationwide language standard, the only aspect of Putonghua actually subjected to precise and strict codification was its phonological system (Norman, 1988: 138). The then established pronunciation norms remained virtually intact to the present day, resisting any influences of regional Chinese varieties or foreign languages.[21] Other aspects, like vocabulary and grammar, which were only roughly defined as based respectively on Northern Mandarin and model literary works, became objects of further systematisation which, along with modifications applied to the sinographic writing system, is still in process.

Standardization and normalization efforts undertaken by official institutions during Xi Jinping's era are manifested mainly through regulations concerning lexical norms and to a lesser extent also phonetic values of some of the Chinese characters. The latter emerged in the form of the draft of the revised "Table of Approved Pronunciation Variants of Polyphonic Characters in Putonghua" (普通话异读词审音表 *Putonghua Yiduci Shen Yin Biao*), originally published in 1985 (Jiaoyu Bu, 2016).[22] In the context of the language ideology and policy, discussed in the previous section, seemingly more meaningful than minor changes within sinograms and their phonetic values is the codification of the Putonghua lexicon. The most authoritative publication in the field is *The Contemporary Chinese Dictionary* (现代汉语词典 *Xiandai Hanyu Cidian*), meant to serve as a standard reference guide on the form, pronunciation,

---

21   The rigid rules of pronunciation in Standard Mandarin do not prevent, however, the existence of the so-called 'Popular Putonghua' (大众普通话 *Dazhong Putonghua*), which according to Yao is actually spoken by ordinary people and comprises various elements of nonstandard pronunciation (1998: 1–2). The most common deviations from the standard include, for example, the substitution of retroflex initials [tʂ], [tʂh] and [ʂ] for alveolar initials [ts], [tsh] and [s], as well as the omission of [ɹ] sound suffix.

22   Since its publication in 2016, the draft has provoked many negative responses and thus has not yet been officially promulgated, however, has already been partly incorporated into dictionaries and educational materials. Critics argue that the proposed changes will elevate common mispronunciations to the status of a valid norm, like the word *tieji* (铁骑 'armoured warhorse') frequently mispronounced as *tieqi* (Gui, 2019). Not only ordinary people struggle with the complexity of polyphonic characters, Xi Jinping is also known for numerous mispronunciations in his speeches (Mair, 2018).

meaning and usage of words and phrasal expressions. Since its first edition, which was presented in 1979 as a result of compilation works initiated in the mid-1950s (Gottlieb and Chen, 2001: 67), the dictionary has had seven editions so far with the last one published in 2016 and containing ca. seventy thousand entries.

Similarly to the previous versions, the seventh edition came out with a set of new or expanded entries. Among 376 words and phrases that were not included in the sixth edition from 2012, several distinct categories can be clearly distinguished based on thematic and origin criteria. One of them concerns late technologies and electronic devices (for example: 充电宝 *chongdian bao* 'power bank', 大数据 *da shuju* 'big data', 电商 *dianshang* 'e-commerce', 二维码 *erweima* 'QR code'). Another one comprises terms in the field of economics (for example: 创投 *chuangtou* 'venture capital investment', 减持 *jianchi* 'stock underweight'). Despite legal regulations mentioned at the beginning of this section, new entries also include a small portion of expressions that originate from Internet slang (拉黑 *lahei* 'to blacklist somebody', 泪奔 *leiben* 'burst with tears', 拍砖 *paizhuan* 'to throw a brick against somebody, to scold', 刷屏 *shuaping* 'message flooding', 学霸 *xueba* 'extremely proficient student'). Most words of the above categories, especially the ones invented by Internet communities, have been in wide use for a considerable period of time – at least one or two decades. From the compilers' perspective, taking into consideration only those expressions which proved to be well rooted in the language, not a short-lived and contextually limited phenomenon, is undoubtedly reasonable. There is, however, one other category of new entries collected according to apparently different criteria.

A large portion of appended terms is related to the CCP government, both its history and the newest political concepts and slogans formulated within a few years prior to the publication of the dictionary. The former (for example: 建党 *jian Dang* 'the founding of the Party', 新中国 *Xin Zhongguo* 'New China') are much less numerous than the latter, mostly phrasal expressions (八项规定 *ba xiang guiding* 'the eight-point regulation', 两个一百年 *liang ge yibai nian* 'the two centenaries', 社会主义核心价值观 *shehui zhuyi hexin jiazhiguan* 'the core socialist values', 四个全面 *si ge quanmian* 'the four comprehensives'). The long existing polysemic word of dialectal origin, *dada* (大大), usually denoting 'father' or 'elder', appears as a specific case – it has only recently won recognition by the dictionary when it began to be used as a popular reference to Xi Jinping. 'Papa Xi' himself also contributed to the lexical standard, since the new entries comprise expressions from his numerous speeches and political initiatives. Among them are proverbs and quotes taken from classic literature (打铁还需自身硬 *datie hai xu zishen ying* 'to forge iron one must be strong', 行百里者半九十, *xing bai li zhe ban jiushi* 'ninety *li* is half of a hundred *li* journey'), as well as his supposedly own inventions (钉钉子精神 *ding dingzi jingshen* 'spirit of driving nails').

The above instances show that the methods of adding new lexical units to normative dictionaries may vary depending on words origins and the current context. The imposed language standard is therefore to a certain extent, at least lexically, shaped by the political agenda.

3.2   Social Reception

The overzealous enthusiasm, manifested on various levels of administration, towards protection of language purity sometimes may lead to sudden eruption of discontent among regional communities. Shanghai authorities have experienced such a backlash in 2018 after their decision to eradicate nonstandard vocabulary from primary-school textbooks. As a result, a popular in the southern part of the country kinship term *waipo* (外婆 'maternal grandma'), in *The Contemporary Chinese Dictionary* labelled as dialectal, was replaced with *laolao* (姥姥) – a word of the same meaning but northern origin. Under the pressure of strongly negative public response, however, the change was eventually reverted (Yao, 2018).

Unfortunately, this is one of few examples when people's regional attachment and concerns over the condition of locally used Chinese varieties were heard by decision makers. Several protests against the supremacy of Putonghua and the continuing marginalization of local linguistic heritage had already taken place before Xi Jinping ascended to power. One of the most noticeable was instigated in 2010 in the southern metropolis of Guangzhou, after the government's decision to reduce Cantonese content broadcasted on provincial radio and television stations. The street manifestations were accompanied by feverish online discussions in which netizens argued that despite the dominant narrative, "Cantonese is not [merely] a dialect" (Li and Tong, 2021: 157–158). People's loudly articulated postulates did not, however, prompt the establishment of any mechanism of systemic protection of Chinese topolects, even a questionable one – as in the case of languages of ethnic minorities. Although the Ministry of Education allows to include a limited amount of locally oriented subjects in the curricula for compulsory education, only a few regional authorities actually introduced some non-Mandarin content into teaching syllabuses, though only in the form of folk songs and other folklore creations (Zhou, 2019: 77). Similarly, the "China Language Resources Protection Project" (中国语言资源保护工程 *Zhongguo Yuyan Ziyuan Baohu Gongcheng*), launched in 2015 to develop a comprehensive resource database for both Chinese dialects and minorities languages (Jiaoyu Bu and Guojia Yuwei, 2016), gives the impression of being aimed at archiving rather than preserving living languages.

Despite voices warning of the gradual loss of linguistic heritage and regional identity, coming largely from historically non-Mandarin-speaking areas, the proliferation of Putonghua and its growing hegemonic status meet with strong support from various social groups. From the perspective of individuals belonging to these groups, the 'Common Speech' is often associated with social advancement, modernity and emancipation. Women living in large urban centres, like traditionally Wu Chinese speaking Shanghai, are more enthusiastic towards using Putonghua in a wide range of contexts and environments than men, representing comparably more conservative attitudes (Xu, 2021: 93). The nationwide language standard hence appears as an accelerator of the shift from a patriarchal society, wherein Putonghua can help female citizens to improve their social status. Another group that in a similar way seeks for acceptance and recognition comprises rural migrant workers, both of Han and other ethnicities, for whom the acquisition of Putonghua allows for better employment, as well as integration with urban communities they come to work in (Fu, 2021: 141–142). Apart from individual aspirations and interests, a substantial part of Chinese society strongly believes, whether because of the ubiquitous propaganda or other reasons, that Putonghua is an inevitable symbol of the country's modernity and rise to global superpower. The acceptance of the language ideology and its consequences becomes therefore a matter of patriotism.

4   Conclusion

The ideology behind the ongoing promotion and standardization of Putonghua to a certain extent constitutes a continuation of postulates put forward by the National Language Movement. Just like over a century ago, the nationwide language standard is meant to play a very important role in integrating society, building community identity and pride, and consequently increasing the country's development potential. Unlike the then outlined aims, however, Putonghua emerges also as a means of vertical governance enforced by the CCP over China's population. It comprises, therefore, both the function that the Guoyu of Manchu-ruled Qing dynasty once had, being the language of the ruling regime – as mentioned at the very beginning of this chapter, as well as a medium through which particular national-civic consciousness, system of values and worldview are effectively communicated to the masses.

As the effectiveness of vertical governance is inevitably inversely proportional to the degree of horizontal diversity, the further deepening of the processes of uniformity and homogenization among Chinese society becomes one of the major conditions for the strengthening of the CCP's supremacy. Hence, irrespective of 'Papa Xi' and other Chinese leaders' personal attitudes towards the abundant linguistic heritage still present within PRC's borders, the ongoing policies will definitely not noticeably contribute to sustain its vitality. Quite the opposite, despite the actual origin of Putonghua, the role of the 'Common Speech' as the carrier of tradition will be consistently emphasized, and consequently so will the need of keeping it pure from external influences.

References

Chen Duxiu 陈独秀 (1904) Guoyu Jiaoyu 国语教育 [Guoyu Education]. In: Ren Jianshu 任建树 (ed.) (2009) *Chen Duxiu Zhuzuo Xuanbian Di-yi Juan* 陈独秀著作选编第一卷 [Collected Works of Chen Duxiu, Vol. 1]. Shanghai 上海: Shanghai Renmin Chubanshe 上海人民出版社, pp. 42–43.

Fu Lianlian 傅连连 (2012) Qiantan Hanyu zai Waiyu Xuexi Zhong de Shentou yu Zhongguo Hanyu Weiji 浅谈汉语在外语学习中的渗透与中国汉语危机 [The Infiltration of Chinese in Foreign Language Learning and the Crisis of Chinese in China]. *Changchun Ligong Daxue Xuebao* 长春理工大学学报, 12, pp. 186–187.

Fu Yirong 付义荣 (2021) Survey of the State of Language Among New and Earlier Rural Migrant Workers. In: Li Wei 李嵬 (ed.) *The Language Situation in China Volume 8*. Berlin/Boston: De Gruyter Mouton, pp. 129–144.

Gottlieb, Nanette and Ping Chen (2001) *Language Planning and Language Policy: East Asian Perspectives*. Richmond: Curzon Press.

Gu Yanwu 顾炎武 (n.d.) *Rizhi Lu* 日知录 [Record of Daily Study]. Reprint (2011), https://ctext.org/wiki.pl?if=en&chapter=481462#p32, accessed 17 January 2022.

Gui Conglu 桂从路 (2019) Gengxu Hanzi Yinyun zhi Mei 赓续汉字音韵之美 [The Continuous Beauty of the Chinese Characters Phonology]. *Renmin Ribao* 人民日报, 25 February, p. 5.

Guojia Xinwen Chuban Guang Dian Zongju 国家新闻出版广电总局 (2014) Guanyu Guangbo Dianshi Jiemu he Guanggao Zhong Guifan Shiyong Guojia Tongyong Yuyan Wenzi de Tongzhi 关于广播电视节目和广告中规范使用国家通用语言文字的通知 [Notice Concerning the Normative Use of the National Common Spoken and Written Language in Radio and Television Programmes and Advertising]. 27 November, http://www.nrta.gov.cn/art/2014/11/27/art_31_747.html, accessed 13 January 2022.

HRW Humans Rights Watch (2020) China's 'Bilingual Education' Policy in Tibet. 4 March, https://www.hrw.org/report/2020/03/04/chinas-bilingual-education-policy-tibet/tibetan-medium-schooling-under-threat, accessed 25 February 2022.

Jiaoyu Bu 教育部 (2016)《Putonghua Yiduci Shen Yin Biao Xiuding Gao》Zhengqiu Yijian Gonggao《普通话异读词审音表修订稿》征求意见公告 [Announcement on Solicitation of Opinions on the "Draft of the Revised Table of Approved Variant Pronunciations of Polyphonic Characters in Putonghua"]. 6 June, http://www.moe.gov.cn/jyb_xwfb/s248/201606/t20160606_248272.html, accessed 4 March 2022.

Jiaoyu Bu 教育部 (2021a) Quanguo Fanwei nei Putonghua Jilü Dadao 80.72% 全国范围内普通话普及率达到80.72% [The Nationwide Penetration Rate of Putonghua Reached 80.72%]. 2 June, http://www.moe.gov.cn/fbh/live/2021/53486/mtbd/202106/t20210602_535129.html, accessed 15 December 2021.

Jiaoyu Bu 教育部 (2021b) Putonghua Shuiping Ceshi Guanli Guiding 普通话水平测试管理规定 [Management Regulations of the Putonghua Proficiency Test]. 27 November, http://www.gov.cn/zhengce/zhengceku/2021-12/09/content_5659561.htm, accessed 13 January 2022.

Jiaoyu Bu 教育部 (2021c) Tongyu Tongyin: Zhulao You'er Putonghua Jichu 童语同音：筑牢幼儿普通话基础 [Unified Sound of Children's Language: Building a Solid Foundation for Children to Speak Putonghua]. 17 October, http://www.moe.gov.cn/jyb_xwfb/s5147/202110/t20211018573160.html, accessed 5 February 2022.

Jiaoyu Bu 教育部 and Guojia Yuwei 国家语委 (2016) Jiaoyu Bu Guojia Yuwei Guanyu Yinfa《Guojia Yuyan Wenzi Shiye "Shisan Wu" Fazhan Guihua》de Tongzhi 教育部国家语委关于印发《国家语言文字事业"十三五"发展规划》的通知 [The Notification of the Ministry of Education and the National Working Committee on Language and Script Concerning the Publication of the *"13th Five-Year Plan" for the Development of the National Languages and Scripts*]. http://www.gov.cn/gongbao/content/2017/content_5194901.htm, accessed 23 December 2021.

Jiaoyu Bu 教育部 and Guojia Yuwei 国家语委 (2017) Jiaoyu Bu Guojia Yuwei Guanyu Kaizhan Putonghua Jiben Puji ji Xianyu Yanshou Gongzuo de Tongzhi 教育部国家语委关于开展普通话基本普及县域验收工作的通知 [The Notification of the Ministry of Education and the National Working Committee on Language and Script Concerning the Realization of the Basic Proliferation of Putonghua and Verification Works on the County Level]. http://www.moe.gov.cn/srcsite/A18/s7066/201704/t20170401_301699.html, accessed 23 December 2021.

Klöter, Henning (2021) One Legacy, Two Legislations: Language Policies on the Two Sides of the Taiwan Strait. In: Henning Klöter and Mårten Söderblom Saarela (eds.) *Language Diversity in the Sinophone World*. New York and London: Routledge, pp. 101–121.

Li, David C.S. and Choi-lan Tong (2021) A Tale of Two Special Administrative Regions: The State of Multilingualism in Hong Kong and Macao. In: Henning Klöter and Mårten Söderblom Saarela (eds.) *Language Diversity in the Sinophone World*. New York and London: Routledge, pp. 142–163.

Li Jiesan (1896) *Minqiang Kuaizi* 闽腔快字 [Shorthand Script for Min Speech]. Wuchang 武昌: (n.d.).

Li Jinxi 黎锦熙 (1934) *Guoyu Yundong Shigang* 国语运动史纲 [An Outline of History of the National Language Movement]. Shanghai 上海: Shangwu Yinshu Guan 商务印书馆.

Li Jinxi 黎锦熙 and Liu Shiru 刘世儒 (1955) Cong Hanyu Fazhan Guocheng Shuo dao Hanyu Guifanhua 从汉语发展过程说到汉语规范化 [From the Process of Chinese Language Development to its Standardization]. *Zhongguo Yuwen* 中国语文, 9, p. 12.

Li Junru 李君如 (2020) Xianzhu Youshi Zhujiu 'Si ge Zixin' 显著优势铸就'四个自信' [Outstanding Advantages Cast the 'Four Matters of Confidence']. *Renmin Ribao* 人民日报, 7 January, p. 8.

Li Yuming 李宇明 (2003) Qing Mo Wenzi Gaigejia Lun Yuyan Tongyi 清末文字改革家论语言统一 [Late Qing Script Reformers' Views on Language Unification]. *Jiaoyu yu Yanjiu* 教育与研究, 3, pp. 1–11.

Liu Jin 刘进 (1953) Tan Minzu Gongtongyu 谈民族共同语 [Discussion on the National Common Language]. *Zhongguo Yuwen* 中国语文, 12, pp. 16–17.

Lu Gangzhang 卢戆章 (1892) *Yi Mu Liaoran Chujie* 一目了然初阶 [First Steps in Being Able to Understand at a Glance]. Xiamen 厦门: Wu Qi Ding Bei Wen Zhai 五崎顶倍文斋.

Lu, Xing (2004) *Rhetoric of the Chinese Cultural Revolution: Impacts on Chinese Thought, Culture, and Communication*. Columbia: University of South Carolina Press.

Mair, Victor (2018) Xi Jinping's Reading Errors Multiply. *Language Log*, 28 December, https://languagelog.ldc.upenn.edu/nll/?p=41265, accessed 5 March 2022.

Neimenggu Zizhiqu Jiaoyu Ting 内蒙古自治区教育厅 (2020) Nei Menggu Zizhiqu Jiaoyu Ting Shiyong Guojia Tongbian Jiaocai "You Wen Bi Da" 内蒙古自治区教育厅使用国家统编教材"有问必答" ["Questions that Must Be Answered" Concerning the Use of the Standardized Textbooks by the Education Department of Inner Mongolia Autonomous Region]. http://jyj.nmg.gov.cn/zwgk/cjd/202103/t20210302_989184.html, accessed 18 December 2021.

Norman, Jerry (1988) *Chinese*. Cambridge: Cambridge University Press.

Ouyang Zhe 欧阳哲 (ed.) (1998) *Hu Shi Wenji 8* 胡适文集8 [Collected Works of Hu Shi, Vol. 8]. Beijing 北京: Beijing Daxue Chubanshe 北京大学出版社.

Qian Xuantong 钱玄同 (1926) Xu Si 序四 [Preface Four]. In: *Gu Jiegang Minsu Lunwen Ji Juan Yi* 顾颉刚民俗论文集卷一 [Collection of Gu Jiegang's Essays on Folklore, Vol. 1] (2011). Beijing 北京: Zhonghua Shuju 中华书局, pp. 12–21.

Qu Qiubai 瞿秋白 (1989) *Qu Qiubai Wenji: Wenxue Bian Di-san Juan* 瞿秋白文集：文学篇第三卷 [Collected Works of Qu Qiubai: Literature Series, Vol. 3]. Beijing 北京: Renmin Wenxue Chubanshe 人民文学出版社.

Quanguo Renda Changweihui 全国人大常委会 (2000) Zhonghua Renmin Gongheguo Guojia Tongyong Yuyan Wenzi Fa 中华人民共和国国家通用语言文字法 [Law of the People's Republic of China on the Nationwide Language and Script]. http://www.gov.cn/ziliao/flfg/2005-08/31/ content_27920.htm, accessed 18 November 2021.

Sun Baoxuan 孙宝瑄 (1983) *Wang Shan Lu Riji* 忘山庐日记 [A Diary from the Wang Shan Studio]. Shanghai 上海: Guji Chubanshe 古籍出版社.

Wang Chen 王晨 (2020) Jin Yi Bu Guanche Shishi Guojia Tongyong Yuyan Wenzi Fa Zhulao Zhonghua Minzu Gongtongti Yishi 进一步贯彻实施国家通用语言文字法 铸牢中华民族共同体意识 [Further Implementation of the Law on the Nationwide Language and Script to Forge the Chinese Nation's Community Consciousness]. *Renmin Ribao* 人民日报, 11 November, p. 6.

Wang Dongjie 王东杰 (2019) *Sheng Ru Xin Tong: Guoyu Yundong yu Xiandai Zhongguo* 声入心通：国语运动与现代中国 [Sound Permeating Trough Mind: The National Language Movement and Modern China]. Beijing 北京：Beijing Shifan Daxue Chubanshe 北京师范大学出版社.

Wang Shikai 王世凯 (2015) *Yuyan Zhengce Lilun yu Shiwu* 语言政策理论与实务 [The Theory and Practice of Language Policy]. Beijing 北京: Zhongguo Shehui Kexue Chubanshe 中国社会科学出版社.

Wu Zhihui 吴稚晖 (1927) *Wu Zhihui Quanji Juan Er* 吴稚晖全集卷二 [Collected Works of Wu Zhihui, Vol. 2]. Shanghai 上海: Qunzhong Tushu Gongsi 群众图书公司.

Xu, Fang (2021) *Silencing Shanghai: Language and Identity in Urban China*. Lanham: Lexington Books.

Yao Dehuai 姚德怀 (1998) Guifan Putonghua yu Dazhong Putonghua 规范普通话与大众普通话 [Standard Putonghua and Popular Putonghua]. *Yuwen Jianshe Tongxun* 语文建设通讯, 57, pp. 1–12.

Yao Quangui 姚权贵 (2018) Laolao Hao Haishi Waipo Hao? 姥姥好还是外婆好？[Which One Is Better, *Laolao* or *Waipo*?]. *Yuwen Jianshe* 语文建设, 9, pp. 68–70.

Yue Jianyi 岳建一 (2007) Kuitong Hanyu Weiji 愧痛汉语危机 [Painful Shame About the Crisis of Chinese]. *Shehui Kexue Luntan* 社会科学论坛, 6, pp. 149–158.

Zhang Honglin 张洪林 and Chen Yingshu 陈应枢 (1989) Shuizu Diqu Shuxue Jiaoxue Yuyan Wenti ji Duice 水族地区数学教学语言问题及对策 [Linguistic Problems and Countermeasures on Mathematics Teaching in Areas Inhabited by the Sui Ethnic Group]. *Guizhou Shida Ziran Kexue Zhuanji* 贵州师大自然科学专集, 1 (10), pp. 71–75.

Zhang Weizhong 张卫中 (2004) 20 Shiji Chu de Hanyu de Ouhua yu Wenxue de Biange 20 世纪初汉语的欧化与文学的变革 [The Europeanization of Chinese and the Reform of Chinese Literature in the Early 20th Century]. *Wenxue Zhengming* 文学争鸣, 3, pp. 38–34.

Zhang Xiruo 张奚若 (1955) Dali Tuiguang yi Beijing Yuyin wei Biaozhun Yin de Putonghua 大力推广以北京语音为标准音的普通话 [Unswervingly Promote Putonghua with Phonetic Features Standardized on the Beijing Dialect]. *Jiangsu Jiaoyu* 江苏教育, 24, pp. 7–9.

Zhao, Hui and Hong Liu (2021) (Standard) Language Ideology and Regional Putonghua in Chinese Social Media: A View from Weibo. *Journal of Multilingual and Multicultural Development*, 42, pp. 882–896.

Zhongguo Shehui Kexueyuan Yuyan Yanjiuso Cidian Bianjishi 中国社会科学院语言研究所词典编辑室 (2016) *Xiandai Hanyu Cidian Di 7 Ban* 现代汉语词典第7版 [The Contemporary Chinese Dictionary, 7th Edition]. Beijing 北京: Shangwu Yinshu Guan 商务印书馆.

Zhou Enlai 周恩来 (1956) Guowu Yuan Guanyu Tuiguang Putonghua de Zhishi 国务院关于推广普通话的指示 [State Council Instructions on the Promotion of Putonghua]. 02 August, http://www.gov.cn/test/2005-08/02/content19132.htm, accessed 23 November 2021.

Zhou Minglang (2019) *Language Ideology and Order in Rising China*. London and New York: Palgrave Macmillan.

PART 5

Foreign Policy Dimensions

CHAPTER 17

China's Belt and Road Initiative as Xi's Personal Legacy Project

Konstantinas Andrijauskas

Less than a year into his tenure as the General Secretary of the Chinese Communist Party (CCP) and roughly half a year after becoming the President of the People's Republic of China (PRC), Xi Jinping proclaimed what later came to be known as the One Belt One Road or Belt and Road Initiative (BRI, also known as B&R; 一带一路 *yidai yilu*).[1] Rather unusually for the domestic-focused Chinese leadership, the BRI's two corresponding components – the terrestrial Silk Road Economic Belt (丝绸之路经济带 *Sichou zhilu jingji dai*) and the 21st Century Maritime Silk Road (21世纪海上丝绸之路 *21 shiji haishang sichou zhilu*) – were first unveiled abroad during Xi's trips to neighbouring Kazakhstan and Indonesia in September and October 2013 respectively. Since then China's most ambitious foreign policy megaproject ever has acquired a life of its own by rapidly becoming a key factor in the country's international conduct in general and Xi's qualitatively novel political era in particular.

As a result, a cottage industry of more and less academic publications on the BRI emerged both in China and abroad. Numerous books and articles scrutinised the initiative's key features, aims and targets on both domestic and international levels of analysis and ranging from purely economic to essentially (geo-)political research approaches. In the latter case, prominent foreign China watchers called the BRI part economic programme for Chinese industry, part global infrastructure project, but foremost, a geo-strategic vision for a new world order determined by Beijing (Strittmatter, 2019); an expression of China's new grand strategy of socialising and integrating Asia, Europe, the Middle East and Africa into a Sinocentric physical network and by extension a normative community (Callahan, 2016); or even "nothing less than the rebranding of China's entire foreign policy, in all its complexity" (Millward, 2018). Hence, the BRI should be viewed within the larger framework of Beijing's more proactive

---

1   For the sake of convenience, 'initiative' will be used throughout the chapter to designate the BRI, although such a term does not adequately represent its design, ambition or practical implementation thus far.

engagement with the outside world, associated with Xi's directive of 'striving for achievement' (奋发有为 *fenfa youwei*) that curiously appeared at a roughly similar time to his proposal for the two new silk roads, and the long-term goal of creating the so-called 'community of common destiny for mankind' (人类命运共同体 *renlei mingyun gongtongti*) (Rolland, 2017), or globalisation with Chinese characteristics.

Although Xi's personal touch and political investment into the BRI has been widely recognised, the actual implications of such interrelationship largely escaped academic scrutiny. This chapter therefore amounts to a qualitative case study of the initiative's conceptual and thematic evolution as well as a concise assessment of its implementation some eight years later, with particular focus on Xi's self-designated or officially attributed rhetorical and practical role in this process. Such an endeavour is timely considering that the Chinese authorities had previously announced the completion of the BRI's first stage by 2021, the CCP's 100th anniversary, tellingly coinciding with a pledge to establish a 'moderately prosperous society' (小康社会 *xiaokang shehui*) and so accomplish the first of the two 'centennial goals' (两个一百年奋斗目标 *liang ge yibai nian fendou mubiao*). It would also allow for at least tentative account of the impact that the ongoing COVID-19 pandemic has had on its actual roll-out worldwide.

Based on careful contextual examination of relevant primary and secondary textual sources, including selective methodological application of narrative analysis in the former case, this chapter first provides a necessary background discussion about the actual definition of the BRI, which is a way more complex and significant topic than might initially seem, particularly considering Xi's alleged authorship and appropriation of it. Then follows a concise assessment of the BRI's practical implementation as of the mid-2022 with a special focus on overall evidence as opposed to separate case studies that would either highlight its progress or, to the contrary, expose its weaknesses. Xi's role at this stage predictably amounts to being careful enough in claiming the real or imagined victories associated with the BRI, while distancing from an increasing amount of problems and obstacles in its actual execution abroad. As the initiative does indeed represent the key legacy project by China's most powerful leader since Mao Zedong, it is considered too big and important to fail and therefore would remain a feature of Beijing's domestic and foreign policy making throughout the rest of Xi's tenure and most probably much beyond.

1 Xi's Input during the BRI's Initial Stages

Despite clearly unprecedented ambitions voiced by Xi in the two seminal 2013 speeches, the exact official description of the would-be BRI had to await for several years and other messengers, but nevertheless remained a widely contested topic. Luckily, the base working definition that everyone would probably agree upon was provided by what approximates to the initiative's official website:

> The B&R [...] is a development strategy and framework, proposed by Chinese President Xi Jinping that focuses on connectivity and cooperation among countries primarily between China and the rest of Eurasia, which consists of two main components, the land-based 'Silk Road Economic Belt' and oceangoing 'Maritime Silk Road'.
> Belt and Road Portal, 2016

Quite remarkably, even such a short passage clearly exemplifies this chapter's key topic, namely an intimate connection between the BRI and China's current leader. As a matter of fact, the association has become so complete that the initiative's prior intellectual origins are often forgotten. The primary question about its actual authorship is therefore more pertinent than might seem today. Somewhat similarly to Xi's adoption of another adage, the 'Chinese Dream' (中国梦 *Zhongguo Meng*), that also came to define his tenure and derived from previous academic sources, most notably Liu Mingfu's eponymous nationalist book (2015), the BRI can be particularly traced to a short article published just three weeks before the start of the watershed 18th CCP National Congress. Its author Wang Jisi (2012), one of the most respected Chinese international relations scholars, argued for his country's geostrategic march towards the Eurasian west largely in response to the contemporaneous 'strategic rebalancing' initiated by the then American government. Xi's proclamation of the terrestrial 'Silk Road Economic Belt' less than a year later amounted to a tacit overall agreement with Wang's programme,[2] while notable additions to it, most significantly the actual 'Maritime Silk Road', implied the new leader's personal input.

---

2 Admittedly, Wang's ideas were not entirely new either. Knowledgeable authors (Rolland, 2017: 117–118) particularly cite the outspoken general Liu Yazhou (2007) who proposed a similar programme as early as 2001 in the wake of 9/11 and allegedly turned to be rather close to Xi.

The impact of another Wang was probably even more important. Indeed, considering his utmost influence on China's ideological work and related grand designs, it was natural to expect that Wang Huning, the philosopher-king behind Xi, would take a major part in actually translating an essentially academic proposal into a more elaborate policy-making one (though admittedly with notable Chinese characteristics), similarly to his alleged previous role in formulating 'Three Represents' (三个代表 *san ge daibiao*) and 'Scientific Development' (科学发展 *kexue fazhan*) theories, associated with Jiang Zemin and Hu Jintao tenures respectively, as well as the above-mentioned contemporary 'Chinese Dream'. The allegation about Wang's contribution has been particularly strengthened when he became the first deputy head of the new Leading Group for Promoting the Belt and Road Initiative (国家推进"一带一路"建设工作领导小组 *Guojia tuijin "yidai yilu" jianshe gongzuo lingdao xiaozu*) created under the State Council in 2015. In appreciation of his decades-long loyal service to the Party and particularly his defining theoretical contribution during the Xi era, characteristically low profile Wang was finally elevated to the CCP's top-seven Politburo Standing Committee in autumn 2017 (Maçães, 2019: 39–40). Kerry Brown, a prominent British sinologist, perceptively noted that this marked the first time that an international relations scholar without usual administrative experience in the regions was elevated to such heights, and therefore clearly indicated the significance of China's global role for Xi's administration (2018: 75).[3]

Nobody, however, should question Xi's ultimate authorship of the BRI, especially considering that adopting certain theoretical suggestions from below is something natural and even expected from the political leadership both within China and abroad.[4] Notably, Xi tactically solidified such a personal association by invoking his own biographical details. Although born in Beijing, he is a son of Xi Zhongxun, a major CCP figure known for relative moderation and particular influence during the first two decades of the reform era,[5] and therefore descends through his father from Shaanxi, a poor northern inland province but also a key region in the history of China, both imperial and revolutionary.

---

3 According to one of the most respected American China watchers, Wang retained his unusually long influence as a key foreign policy advisor, accompanying all of the three paramount leaders to meetings with their counterparts from abroad, including during the trips overseas (Shambaugh, 2021).

4 Tellingly, a series of interviews conducted with various Chinese stakeholders by one researcher showed a clear willingness to claim the title of being the initial proposer of the would-be BRI (Ye, 2020: 4).

5 Xi Zhongxun was sometimes considered one of the so-called 'Eight Elders' or 'Immortals' who wielded huge influence over Chinese politics in the last two decades of the 20th century.

Xi the son now famously 'returned' to his ancestral homeplace as a 'sent-down youth' during the Cultural Revolution where he stayed for half a decade before being allowed to get back to the capital in the mid-1970s. During his lengthy rise to power outside of Beijing (1982–2007), he spent some 17 years in Fujian (1985–2002), a southern maritime province traditionally associated with entrepreneurial outlook and relatively outward orientation, including towards neighbouring Taiwan and the global Chinese diaspora.[6]

Hence, it was hardly a coincidence that the Belt and Road apparently took the cities of Xi'an and Quanzhou as their two respective starting points. Besides being traditionally associated with terrestrial and maritime components of the Silk Road, they also hinted at Xi's lengthy tenures in Shaanxi and Fujian respectively.[7] Such personal connection has been established since the actual proclamation of the initiative's terrestrial 'Belt' when Xi called the former his 'home province' in an often-quoted passage from the seminal speech (2013a) delivered in the Kazakhstani capital.[8] A series of rather opaque maps published by the Chinese media outlets consolidated these geopolitical imaginaries (Mayer and Balázs, 2018) and by extension Xi's paramount role as well. In spring 2015 the authorities in Beijing finally released the first exhaustive official document on the BRI with its described aim being the following:

> to promote the connectivity of Asian, European and African continents and their adjacent seas, establish and strengthen partnerships among the countries along the Belt and Road, set up all-dimensional, multi-tiered and composite connectivity networks, and realize diversified, independent, balanced and sustainable development in these countries.
> PRC State Council, 2015

As is customary in China, members of the academia also joined the efforts to interpret and popularise the leadership's latest policy programme. Wang Yiwei, another celebrated international relations scholar, in his self-described first Chinese book to explain the BRI from the perspective of this discipline called the initiative a "Eurasian transport network, an integrated, three-dimensional and interconnected system that is composed of railways, highways, aviation,

---

6 Xi would subsequently call Fujian his 'second home' (Shambaugh, 2021).
7 The fact that Xi spent most of that time in other locations within those provinces is less relevant.
8 In that same passage Xi equated himself with Zhang Qian, a legendary Chinese envoy who reached Central Asia on behalf of his native Han dynasty and therefore came to be associated with what would centuries later acquire the name of the Silk Road.

navigation, oil and gas pipelines, transmission lines and communication networks" (Wang, 2016: 2). According to one of the most respected American China watchers, her prominent Chinese counterparts do indeed recognise that the BRI stems precisely from Xi's desire to contribute to his historical legacy while performing the country's 'third revolution' (Economy, 2018: 196) after the two conducted by the victorious founding father of the People's Republic, Mao Zedong, and the architect of the country's economic reforms, Deng Xiaoping.[9]

The BRI should therefore be viewed within the larger framework of Xi's remarkable personalisation of political power,[10] unprecedented since Deng if not Mao. For the current Chinese leader, tellingly nicknamed 'the chairman of everything' (Saich, 2021), 'CEO, China' (Brown, 2016) or simply a 'modern emperor' (Shambaugh, 2021) due to his especially authoritarian hands-on approach and effective attack on decades-long Dengist consensus advocating for a certain distance between the CCP and the state and society, the initiative serves as an important legitimising tool, and the relationship is that of reinforcing each other. This became particularly apparent in a series of events throughout the fateful 2017. To begin with, the first Belt and Road Forum for International Cooperation was conducted in mid-May where Xi addressed the alleged nearly thirty fellow heads of state and delegates from over 130 countries and 70 international organisations by notably calling the initiative 'a project of the century' (Hillman, 2020: 3).

During the 19th CCP National Congress held only five months later Xi was not only reconfirmed as the Party's leader, but also strengthened his apparent ambitions to stay in full power beyond the supposed deadline in 2022 by preventing the rise of any potential designated successor and setting the stage for the abolishment of term limits for his presidency that would come in effect the following year. One of the most indicative additional outcomes of the Congress was the inclusion of the BRI into the Party's Constitution, its defining statute,[11] along with the current leadership's ideological programme, the Xi Jinping Thought (习近平思想 *Xi Jinping sixiang*). As was correctly noted by some of the most prolific foreign researchers of the BRI itself, this move meant

---

9 The implicitly promoted view about the relationship between the PRC's three paramount leaders is exemplified by the increasingly widespread Chinese saying that under Mao they stood up (站起来 *zhan qilai*), under Deng became rich (富起来 *fu qilai*), and under Xi got strong (强起来 *qiang qilai*) (Shambaugh, 2021).
10 Also at the cost of the CCP's own collective leadership (集体领导 *jiti lingdao*) (Li, 2016: 1).
11 The BRI had been previously included into the party-state's other key documents, including the two latest five-year plans and the 'Made in China 2025' national strategic plan for industrial policy (Dillon, 2021: 144).

that the initiative would become nearly impossible to abandon (Maçães, 2019), and therefore could be expected to shape China's policies for decades to come (Miller, 2019), extending way beyond Xi's own tenure and lifetime (Hillman, 2020), and as a result, clearly conforming to what is expected from a true political legacy project. Indeed, if there was any more exact deadline for the BRI's whole completion hinted at all, it usually set the target at the distant and highly symbolic 2049, the 100th anniversary of the PRC that would mark the delivery of full Chinese style modernity, the second of the two 'centennial goals' (Brown and Tsimonis, 2017).

Certainly, the initiative's precious service to Xi derives not only from its projection towards a faraway future but it's supposed origins in an even more remote past. Besides implying his political power, the appellation of China's 'new emperor' appears as pertinent considering that Xi is a particularly suitable representative of the CCP's legitimising turn since the end of the Cold War towards the country's remarkably rich history and culture.[12] The Silk Road, despite its well-known intrinsic ambiguities and recent essentially Western conceptual origins (Hansen, 2012), remains an emphatically benign, supposedly universal and perhaps most iconic example of long distance exchange. It hints at China's alleged peaceful and non-hegemonic character but also at its two-millennia old and mutually beneficial engagement with the rest of the Eurasian landmass and even beyond in the Eastern hemisphere, including insular Southeast Asia and East Africa. More subtly, the Silk Road narrative evokes memories of the Middle Empire's historical greatness and ostensibly natural primacy in global affairs. A representative of another key nation at the outset of globalisation, the Portuguese scholar Bruno Maçães, perceptively noted that the Silk Road's reference to a world before European hegemony when China was both the centre of the global economy and a technological powerhouse, including because of its control of silk production secrets, implied an invitation to get back to the usual international order (Maçães, 2019: 23–24) after a historically rather short Western interregnum. This call was particularly directed at supposedly more receptive audiences in countries that shared Chinese nostalgia about pre-modern imperial greatness (Mayer, 2018), such as India, Iran, Mongolia, Turkey, the bigger Central Asian -stans or partially Russia.

It was none other than Xi who actually became the principal messenger of the BRI abroad. Indeed, during the first several years of the initiative's existence all major statements related to it had been made by Xi himself (Rolland,

---

12   As noted by Brown, Xi's *magnum opus* and itself an important sign to his personalisation of power, *The Governance of China*, contains far more references to Chinese imperial past than to Mao or Karl Marx (2017: 29).

2017: 48). Often called the Chinese 'storyteller-in-chief' (Brown, 2018), he was the one to now famously urge diplomats and other stakeholders to "tell China's story well" (对外讲好中国故事 *duiwai jiang hao Zhongguo gushi*). In a remarkable fashion, Xi did so himself while visiting the Chinese record-breaking nearly 70 countries representing all of the inhabited continents on more than 40 trips abroad between 2012 and the start of the pandemic in 2020 (Shambaugh, 2021). The BRI has been emphatically promoted in these bilateral and multilateral settings. Perhaps most famously in the latter case, Xi (2017) advocated for his signature megaproject during a keynote speech at the 2017 Davos World Economic Forum where the concluding BRI references were widely interpreted as the clearest material manifestation of China's new and uncharacteristically bold pledge to lead economic globalisation in the context of then upcoming relatively isolationist Donald Trump administration in the US.

2 Defining the BRI

It was arguably the 2017 acknowledgement that provided a necessary missing link in more serious attempts to define the BRI. Hence, the megaproject reflects not only China's switch towards a more active foreign policy strategy, aimed at shaping its external environment rather than merely adapting to it, but also the country's sheer transformation from a regional into a genuine global power (Mações, 2019). The BRI rapidly became the most clear-cut example of China's multilateral contributions – one of the two main characteristics of Xi's foreign policy along with unilateral assertiveness (Shambaugh, 2021). Its strategic design amounts to what a perceptive scholar defined as 'institutional realism with Chinese characteristics' that aimed at maximising national interests through building international institutions in order to ensure other countries' structural reliance on China and to bolster the party-state's legitimacy in its bid to assume global leadership (Shen, 2018: 399). Hence, along with a plethora of related Chinese institutions, the BRI is a key example of a 'parallel order' to that established by the West in general and the US in particular largely throughout the Cold War era (Stuenkel, 2016).

The functional basis of the BRI is broadly defined as physical infrastructure, something that China itself excelled in and therefore could realistically hope to use in its economic relations with the rest of the world. Indeed, closely following a popular local saying that in order to get rich one has to build roads (要想富先修路 *yao xiang fu xian xiu lu*), infrastructure construction has become the 'Chinese solution' in terms of boosting domestic economic growth and promoting regional development and integration throughout the post-Maoist reform era (Xing, 2019: 14), particularly as a stimulating response to major international financial crises. Its role as China's principal 'public good' to be offered abroad has been solidified by the creation of the Beijing-based Asian Infrastructure Investment Bank, first proposed by Xi in his landmark Jakarta speech (2013b) and widely interpreted as yet another parallel institution of global economic governance and the most explicit organisational manifestation of the BRI.

What was arguably needed in order to attract attention abroad was the original initiative's expansion on thematic and especially financial terms. In the latter case, the Chinese leadership started with the announcement of the USD 40 billion Silk Road Fund in late 2014 and a pledge of USD 46 billion for the China–Pakistan Economic Corridor (CPEC), widely considered to be a flagship programme of the BRI. Beijing's vaguely-stated overall financial commitments to the initiative would eventually balloon to some USD 1 trillion (Hillman, 2020: 3). In the case of thematic scope, the BRI's progression has followed Xi's seminal remark about the Belt's five main linking dimensions which stated that policy coordination and infrastructure connectivity should also be joined by unimpeded trade, financial integration and people-to-people exchanges. As was astutely observed by Maçães, the seemingly clumsy use of the 'belt' term in order to describe the initiative's terrestrial part actually made a lot of sense, since its six original constituent economic corridors were not designed as simple transport connections but implied spaces of deeper economic integration, including fragmentation of production chains across different geographies and local comparative advantages. In a somewhat counter-intuitive fashion, the 'road' designation for the BRI's maritime component is also fitting because it merely aims to connect the end points across several oceans (Maçães, 2019: 52–53), an obviously less transformative, yet still ambitious task.

Besides the flagship CPEC, the Belt was eventually designed to be composed of five other 'economic corridors', namely the spinal New Eurasian Land Bridge (NELB) through Kazakhstan and Russia to Western Europe, the China–Mongolia–Russia and the China–Central Asia–West Asia economic corridors north and south of the NELB respectively, and the China–Indochina Peninsula and the Bangladesh–China–India–Myanmar economic corridors correspondingly branching out to Southeast and South Asia. Since the latter's status has become by far the most ambiguous largely due to India's increasing scepticism (see below), the so-called Nepal–China Trans-Himalayan Multi-dimensional Connectivity Network seems to have largely supplanted it since 2019 (Engh, 2021). Such 'corridorisation' is used by Beijing in order to organise and integrate territory in a qualitatively different fashion than the more usual means associated with regions or nation states, and would lead to a system of Chinese-style industrial parks and free trade zones far away beyond its borders (Mayer, 2018).

To sum up, perfectly consistent with what is to be expected from grand strategic designs, the BRI pursues an impressive list of various political, economic and strategic goals, helpfully summarised in perhaps the most meticulous early account of the initiative by Nadège Rolland. Besides serving as a legitimising and strengthening device for the current Chinese leadership, a political objective most relevant for this chapter, in economic terms the BRI aims to address many of China's especially pressing problems without fundamentally altering its development model, namely further stimulate growth; utilise its overcapacity in construction materials and basic industries; employ some of its impressively accumulated foreign reserves; widen the access to foreign markets for its companies, particularly state-owned enterprises; contribute to the internationalisation of the Chinese currency, the Renminbi (Rolland, 2017); and export some of its low value-added manufacturing overseas (Arduino and Gong, 2018).

In the political-strategic domain, the BRI strives to enhance security in China's periphery, both within and beyond its borders; ensure uninterrupted supply of strategic resources; transform increased economic dependence into larger political influence abroad, with the middle-term focus on the strengthening of Chinese strategic depth and hedging against possible disruptions to maritime supply (the so-called 'Malacca dilemma') as well as other alleged challenges mostly posed by the US; and, last but not least, the particularly contentious long-term objective of creating a Sinocentric order in Eurasia (Rolland, 2017) with further expansion possibilities to the rest of the Eastern hemisphere and even the whole world. It is obviously the political-strategic component that has produced most of resistance to the BRI abroad.

3 Assessing the Interim Accomplishments

As of the mid-2022, eight full years have passed since the BRI's official proclamation. Considering that the initiative's primary stage therefore should have been allegedly completed in coincidence with the first of the two so-called 'centennial goals',[13] the assessment of its practical implementation seems to be

---

13 Xi himself declared that China had finally eliminated 'absolute poverty' by the 100th anniversary of the CCP, therefore resulting in a 'moderately prosperous society' (Shambaugh, 2021).

a particularly timely endeavour. Judging from the actions by the authorities in Beijing, the BRI's whole eight-year period of existence, itself an auspicious time frame for the Chinese,[14] can be roughly divided into three principal stages: preparatory (from its proclamation in 2013 to more explicit formulation in 2015), full and particularly enthusiastic domestic embrace (to its complete inclusion into the party-state's institutional and ideological system in 2017), and more critical reappraisal since 2018. Xi has been leading the process throughout all of these stages and the corresponding shifts that marked them, with the latest alteration widely and correctly considered as especially telling.

Barely half a year after explicitly denying that the BRI was a plot of China at the Boao Forum in April 2018, Xi called for moving from the initiative's metaphorical comparison to *xieyi* (写意), a traditional Chinese painting style which used broad brush strokes, to that of *gongbi* (工笔), a realistic technique associated with meticulous paintings, during his speech marking its fifth anniversary. This reference was interpreted as an acknowledgement of the fact that many details still had to be worked out (Hillman, 2020), or even a tacit call to scale back the whole endeavour (McGregor, 2019). In any case, it essentially amounted to a recognition that the BRI's allegedly conscious vague, flexible and multi-dimensional nature, often compared to defining principles of Daoist thought, came to be increasingly perceived as its weakness instead of a strength. The same fuzzy characteristics have naturally made the assessment of its practical short-to-medium term results a trying and contentious affair.

One way of pursuing this has to do with the number of key foreign actors that actually joined the BRI. In terms of the interest expressed abroad, the initiative long seemed to be a success. As has been noted above, the first BRI international cooperation forum held in 2017 allegedly attracted almost 30 heads of state and delegates from over 130 countries and 70 international organisations. However, although the follow-up forum organised two years later succeeded in gathering an even larger amount of foreign highest-level representatives, continuing neglect by many significant Eurasian countries, most notably India, Japan and all of the European members of the G7 save Italy (*The Diplomat*, 2019), hinted at a fair amount of scepticism. As regards the actual international commitments, Xi himself stated that more than 150 countries and international organisations had signed agreements on the BRI cooperation with China by the time of his keynote speech opening the second forum in April, 2019 (Xi, 2019).[15] Nevertheless, the respective memoranda

---

14   Eight is considered a lucky number in Chinese culture.
15   The Chinese Foreign Minister Wang Yi specified that 123 countries and 29 international organisations had signed on it in one way or another (Wang, 2019).

of understanding, the most usual of such documents, are legally non-binding by nature and have not necessarily resulted in anything practical or even prevented certain bilateral relationships with China from worsening to rarely seen levels, as has been shown by Lithuania.[16]

Holding the BRI fora in 2017 and 2019 suggested that these would become regular events conducted on biannual basis, but the mid-2021 iteration tellingly lacked of previous pomp in terms of its geographical scope (targeting the Asia–Pacific without no Africans, Europeans or even Russians being present), the number and rank of attendees (29 country representatives of mostly ministerial level), the method (virtual instead of in-person), and, most importantly for the purposes of this chapter, the official host being China's Foreign Minister Wang Yi, with Xi merely delivering a written address. Always committed to the principle of making a virtue out of necessity, Beijing attempted to offset this downgrade by proposing two new BRI-themed 'partnerships' of particularly pressing significance across the globe, namely on COVID-19 vaccines cooperation and green development (Tiezzi, 2021), which joined previous efforts to conceptually expand the initiative by the Polar and Digital Silk Roads. Although any mention of the BRI was curiously absent in Xi's September 2021 remote speech to the UN General Assembly that proposed a qualitatively novel 'Global Development Initiative' (Xi, 2021a), his continuing commitment to the original mega-project was stressed again during an online address at the G20 Rome Summit a month later (Xi, 2021b). It seems safe to conclude at this point that such lowering of the BRI's profile had a lot to do with China's more explicit recognition of numerous obstacles to its implementation.

According to Rolland, throughout the first several years of the initiative's existence the Chinese experts themselves had identified four main challenges faced by it, namely Beijing's lack of experience in Eurasia's complex environment, external security risks that could draw China into local quagmires, questionable economic viability, and misgivings of great powers and smaller recipient countries (Rolland, 2017: 153), the latter apparently being the most significant as of this writing (see below). Leading foreign experts of Chinese politics have summarised key criticisms of the BRI abroad that include accusations of more or less deliberate acquisitions of sovereign assets to compensate for debt repayments that small recipient countries cannot meet ('debt trap diplomacy'); often exclusive use of Chinese labour instead of the local one; environmental damage (including de facto 'export of pollution', most

---

16   At the time of this writing, Sino-Lithuanian relations have reached a crisis point rarely seen in Chinese foreign policy making since the end of the Cold War.

notoriously by building coal power plants); implementation of low-quality and even unnecessary projects ('white elephants'); stress on infrastructure that exploits the target countries' raw materials in China's benefit (economic neo-imperialism); and, last but not least, ancillary corruption (Shambaugh, 2021) and its adverse effects not only for recipients' financial stability and transparency but also general quality of governance, rule of law and even democratic credentials or mere aspirations.

Another possible way to assess the BRI's implementation thus far has to do with financial and project-based outcomes but suffers from the same challenges associated with its fuzzy, flexible and ongoing long-term characteristics. As has been correctly noted by numerous commentators, a fair share of the projects now associated with the initiative have been planned for years and often predate 2013. Since the whole affair is intimately tied to Xi's reputation, many riskier endeavours may have been taken in order to meet political objectives without much underlying economic viability and potential (Saich, 2021: 424–425). Hence, despite outlandish claims about the BRI's overall financial burden passing USD 1 trillion or rather precisely because of them, China itself may be hugely overreaching (Hillman, 2020) with all of the possible negative repercussions for both the party-state and its current leader.

As the initiative's widely recognised flagship, the CPEC is particularly telling of many of its key characteristics and practical achievements but also inherent flaws. Although first mentioned by China's premier Li Keqiang several months before the proclamation of the BRI, it acquired Xi's personal stamp during his April 2015 visit to Pakistan when their bilateral 'all-weather' relationship, perhaps the closest for Beijing of all, was strengthened further. Since then this corridor has rapidly expanded on paper to a couple of hundred transportation, energy and digital infrastructure projects (Rolland, 2017: 77–78) as well as the alleged total commitment of USD 100 billion but only a fraction of that has been delivered (Hillman, 2020) even despite providing an example of the most active BRI-related construction on the ground. As perceptively noted by one of the foremost American thinkers on geostrategy, the CPEC is crucial for Beijing's goal to join the terrestrial and maritime components of the initiative (Kaplan, 2018), but it might as well become an economic and security quagmire and even import instability to China itself. Indeed, many of the CPEC's constituent projects are implemented in particularly sensitive parts of Pakistan, mired by separatism, religious extremism, international disputes or a combination of all of these. In addition, New Delhi's scepticism about the whole BRI has a lot to do with the acknowledgement that the CPEC strengthens Sino-Pakistani control over their respective parts of disputed Kashmir and contributes to India's perceived strategic encirclement, metaphorically called the 'string of pearls', as is particularly evident in the Chinese development of the Gwadar deep water seaport, itself a flagship.

Some of the BRI's other key corridors seem to have been particularly threatened by the global health crisis and rising general economic and socio-political instability across much of the world, including those target countries that are important or even essential for its success. Although China's merchandise trade with and non-financial overseas direct investment into what it considers to be the initiative's members continued to expand throughout the first rough year of the pandemic, the contract value of construction projects decreased by 1% to USD 46.5 billion year on year in the first half of 2021 (Economist Intelligence Unit, 2021). Even more significantly, throughout this same time frame potential problems for the BRI's implementation were clearly exposed due to the ongoing political crisis in Belarus since August 2020, Myanmar's military coup d'état in February 2021, the Taliban's takeover of Afghanistan in August 2021, Kazakhstan's violent protests in January 2022, and most crucially Russia's full-scale invasion of Ukraine since late February 2022. Indeed, much of Eurasia hardly seems ripe for any integration today, while the BRI's two key terrestrial corridors through the post-Soviet space are almost fully and potentially indefinitely put on hold as China's principal strategic partners in Eastern Europe (Russia and Belarus vs. Ukraine and Poland) find themselves on different sides of the entire continent's largest military conflict since the Second World War.

Almost as telling and important has been intensified resistance to the BRI by major Western powers that occurred in the backdrop of clearly worsening relationships with China. Throughout the initial years of the initiative's existence the US perceived it as relatively modest in terms of practical goals and outcomes, notwithstanding often outlandish claims. In a series of interviews on this topic conducted by the author in spring 2017,[17] several American scholars suggested that Washington should allow Beijing to proceed uninterrupted with the BRI because in the case of success it would contribute to stabilisation of Central Eurasia, a goal shared with their own country, while in the case of failure China would be the one to put a blame on by the target countries and the rest of international community.

Since Joe Biden stepped into the White House, however, growing American recognition of the BRI's 'parallel' characteristics has acquired more visible shape characterised by resistance through the two interrelated means of global governance and alliances, themselves trademarks of the new presidency particularly in comparison to its immediate predecessor. As a result, Washington

---

17 Interviews were conducted as part of the author's Fulbright scholar program.

strengthened its previous pledge for the 'free and open Indo-Pacific', a concept conveniently borrowed from Tokyo (Maçães, 2019: 125), not only by deepening earlier (the Quad)[18] and initiating new (AUKUS)[19] multilateral security arrangements, but also being the apparent mastermind behind the G7's Build Back Better World (B3W) infrastructure-focused initiative, a thinly veiled rival to the BRI. Considering that three members of the latter group are also key EU states, one could not escape the conclusion about the whole union's position on the Chinese initiative, especially telling in Italy's apparent shift on the matter. As if to confirm this, in late 2021 the EU introduced its Global Gateway initiative, a self-described new infrastructure-based strategy with plans to mobilise up to €300 billion of investments (European Commission, 2021).

Even smaller EU member-states have been increasingly cooperating on connectivity with blessings coming from both Brussels and Washington, as is especially evident in the Three Seas Initiative uniting twelve countries from the Baltic Sea in the north to the Mediterranean and Black seas in the south (Three Seas Initiative, 2021), and presenting a partial alternative to both the BRI and the Beijing-led but increasingly moribund 16+1[20] cooperation framework. The initiative's success is therefore by no means assured, particularly in the democratic part of Eurasia.

4   Conclusions

As the Belt and Road approaches decadal anniversary, one can safely conclude that it is by far the most ambitious international scheme any modern Chinese governing regime has ever designed. The whole initiative's intimate association with Xi Jinping is hence even more striking. Although its intellectual origins are elsewhere, China's most powerful leader in decades is the BRI's undisputable author, principal propagator and the main beneficiary. The connection between the two has become so complete that merely calling it Xi's personal pet project would amount to a major understatement. As a matter of fact, they are clearly reinforcing one another. Ever since the original proclamation of the terrestrial 'Belt' in September 2013, Xi has solidified his role as the BRI's foremost representative and messenger by tactically invoking positive

---

18   The Quadrilateral Security Dialogue between the US, Australia, Japan and India, established in 2007 and revived in 2017.
19   A trilateral security pact between the US, UK and Australia, announced in September 2020.
20   Officially the framework of Cooperation between China and Central and Eastern European Countries (China–CEEC), established in 2012.

historical parallels from immemorial times of China's imperial greatness and much more recent personal biography, but also presenting a vision for the nation's future up to the mid-21st century. The initiative is designed to outlast Xi's own tenure at the helm of Chinese politics, that would likely coincide with his lifetime, and therefore amounts to what is expected from a true legacy project.

Arguably these defining traits of the BRI allow one to better comprehend its development up to this point and future prospects as well. Tellingly, Xi has been the principal figure behind the initiative throughout all of its three apparent stages defined thus far, though a more critical reappraisal of the whole endeavour taking place since 2018 has proceeded in the backdrop of a certain personal distancing from an increasing amount of problems and obstacles in its actual implementation abroad. Always eager to claim real or imagined victories, he had indeed succeeded in achieving one of his key objectives by then, namely firm inclusion of the BRI into the party-state's political, economic and ideological structure, providing the new basis for the whole country's long-term grand strategy of international conduct. This obviously revealed its crucial but surprisingly neglected function of effectively being a legitimising and strengthening device for the current Chinese leadership in general and Xi in particular. On the latter account, it provides an extra tacit rationale for the widely expected extension of his tenure beyond 2022.

However, the BRI's remarkably close association with Xi has already contributed to some of its key problems. Too big to fail and too personal to be criticised domestically, the initiative has effectively become a catch-all term, and despite a certain review throughout these last several years, there is no sign that this trend would stop and an increasing number of its design flaws and structural inefficiencies would be genuinely addressed. It seems that the Chinese leadership and the BRI would either prevail or fail *together*, and the ultimate settlement of this dilemma is conveniently placed some three decades away. In the meantime, this 'project of the century' will surely remain a significant if not defining feature of Beijing's domestic and foreign policies. Luckily for Xi, the BRI seems to have been internalised within the country to such a degree that even major setbacks abroad would not question its alleged quintessential value for China's comprehensive domestic development. And the setbacks will surely be many.

References

Arduino, Alessandro and Xue Gong (2018) Introduction. In: Alessandro Arduino and Xue Gong (eds.) *Securing the Belt and Road Initiative: Risk Assessment, Private Security and Special Insurances along the New Wave of Chinese Outbound Investments.* Singapore: Springer Nation, pp. 3–14.

Belt and Road Portal (2016) What is "Belt and Road" initiative?, 22 October, https://eng.yidaiyilu.gov.cn/ghsl/cjwd/2757.htm, accessed 10 November 2021.

Brown, Kerry (2016) *CEO, China: The Rise of Xi Jinping.* London–New York: I.B.Tauris.

Brown, Kerry (2017) *China's World : What Does China Want?* London–New York: I.B. Tauris.

Brown, Kerry (2018) *The World According to Xi: Everything You Need to Know About New China.* London–New York: I.B.Tauris.

Brown, Kerry and Konstantinos Tsimonis (2017) The Future of the Chinese Communist Party. In: Willy Wo-Lap Lam (ed.) *Routledge Handbook of the Chinese Communist Party.* Oxon, New York: Routledge, pp. 335–351.

Callahan, William (2016) China's Belt and Road Initiative and the New Eurasian Order. Norwegian Institute of International Affairs, *Policy Brief,* 22, pp. 1–4.

Dillon, Michael (2021) *China in the Age of Xi Jinping.* Oxon–New York: Routledge.

Diplomat, the (2019) Second Belt and Road Forum Top-Level Attendees, 27 April, https://thediplomat.com/2019/04/second-belt-and-road-forum-top-level-attendees/, accessed 10 December 2021.

Economist Intelligence Unit (2021) Belt and Road Quarterly: Q2 2021, 28 July, https://www.eiu.com/n/belt-and-road-quarterly-q2-2021/, accessed 8 December 2021.

Economy, Elizabeth C. (2018) *The Third Revolution: Xi Jinping and the New Chinese State.* New York: Oxford University Press.

Engh, Sunniva (2021) India's China Policy under Modi: Growing Co-operation, Enduring Disagreement, Increasing Rivalry. In: Jo Inge Bekkevold and S. Kalyanaram (eds.) *India's Great Power Politics: Managing China's Rise.* Oxon–New York: Routledge, pp. 75–99.

European Commission (2021) Global Gateway: up to €300 billion for the European Union's strategy to boost sustainable links around the world, 1 December, https://ec.europa.eu/commission/presscorner/detail/en/ip_21_6433, accessed 19 June 2022.

Hansen, Valerie (2012) *The Silk Road: A New History.* Oxford–New York: Oxford University Press.

Hillman, Jonathan E. (2020) *The Emperor's New Road: China and the Project of the Century.* New Haven–London: Yale University Press.

Kaplan, Robert D. (2018) *The Return of Marco Polo's World: War, Strategy, and American Interests in the Twenty-first Century.* New York: Random House.

Li, Cheng (2016) *Chinese Politics in the Xi Jinping Era: Reassessing Collective Leadership.* Washington, D.C.: Brookings Institution Press.

Liu Mingfu (2015) *The China Dream: Great Power Thinking & Strategic Posture in the Post-American Era.* New York: CN Time Books.

Liu Yazhou (2007) The Grand National Strategy. *Chinese Law & Government,* 40(2), pp. 13–36.

Mações, Bruno (2019) *Belt and Road: A Chinese World Order.* London: Hurst & Company.

Mayer, Maximilian (2018) China's Rise as Eurasian Power: The Revival of the Silk Road and Its Consequences. In: Maximilian Mayer (ed.) *Rethinking the Silk Road: China's Belt and Road Initiative and Emerging Eurasian Relations.* Singapore: Palgrave Macmillan, pp. 1–42.

Mayer, Maximilian and Dániel Balázs (2018) Modern Silk Road Imaginaries and the Co-production of Space. In: Maximilian Mayer (ed.) *Rethinking the Silk Road: China's Belt and Road Initiative and Emerging Eurasian Relations.* Singapore: Palgrave Macmillan, pp. 205–226.

McGregor, Richard (2019) *Xi Jinping: The Backlash.* Penguin.

Miller, Tom (2019) *China's Asia Dream: Empire Building along the New Silk Road.* 2nd edition. London: Zed Books.

Millward, James A. (2018) Is China a Colonial Power? *The New York Times,* 4 May, https://www.nytimes.com/2018/05/04/opinion/sunday/china-colonial-power-jinping.html, accessed 16 November 2021.

PRC State Council, the (2015) Vision and Actions on Jointly Building Silk Road Economic Belt and 21st Century Maritime Silk Road. *Belt and Road Forum for International Cooperation,* 10 April 2017, http://2017.beltandroadforum.org/english/n100/2017/0410/c22-45.html, accessed 22 November 2021.

Rolland, Nadège (2017) *China's Eurasian Century? Political and Strategic Implications of the Belt and Road Initiative.* Seattle–Washington, D.C.: The National Bureau of Asian Research.

Saich, Tony (2021) *From Rebel to Ruler: One Hundred Years of the Chinese Communist Party.* Cambridge: The Belknap Press of Harvard University Press.

Shambaugh, David (2021) *China's Leaders from Mao to Now.* Cambridge, Medford: Polity.

Shen, Simon (2018) China and the World: From the Chinese Dream to the Chinese World Order. In: Willy Wo-Lap Lam (ed.) *Routledge Handbook of the Chinese Communist Party.* Oxon, New York: Routledge, pp. 391–405.

Strittmatter, Kai (2019) *We Have Been Harmonised: Life in China's Surveillance State.* London: Old Street Publishing.

Stuenkel, Oliver (2016) *Post-Western World: How Emerging Powers Are Remaking the World Order.* Cambridge, Malden: Polity Press.

Three Seas Initiative (2021) Three Seas Story, https://3seas.eu/about/threeseasstory, accessed 29 December, 2021.

Tiezzi, Shannon (2021) China Holds Slimmed-Down Belt and Road Conference. *The Diplomat,* 25 June, https://thediplomat.com/2021/06/china-holds-slimmed-down-belt-and-road-conference/, accessed 16 December 2021.

Wang Jisi (2012) "Xi jin", Zhongguo diyuan zhanlue de zai pingheng. *Huanqiu shibao,* 17 October, https://opinion.huanqiu.com/article/9CaKrnJxoLS, accessed 11 November 2021.

Wang Yi (2019) Wang Yi: Evaluation of the Belt and Road Initiative (BRI) Should Be Based on Facts. *The Second Belt and Road Forum for International Cooperation,* 19 April, http://www.beltandroadforum.org/english/n100/2019/0427/c22-1292.html, accessed 5 December 2021.

Wang Yiwei (2016) *The Belt and Road Initiative: What Will China Offer the World in Its Rise.* Beijing: New World Press.

Xi Jinping (2013a) Promote Friendship between Our People and Work Together to Build a Bright Future. Speech at the Nazarbayev University, Astana, Kazakhstan. *Embassy of the PRC in Belgium,* 7 September, https://www.fmprc.gov.cn/ce/cebel/eng/zxxx/t1078088.htm, accessed 10 November 2021.

Xi Jinping (2013b) Speech to the Indonesian Parliament, Jakarta, Indonesia. *ASEAN–China Centre,* 2 October, http://www.asean-china-center.org/english/2013-10/03/c_133062675.htm, accessed 10 November 2021.

Xi Jinping (2017) Jointly Shoulder Responsibility of Our Times, Promote Global Growth. Keynote Speech at the World Economic Forum, Davos, Switzerland. *CGTN,* 17 January, https://america.cgtn.com/2017/01/17/full-text-of-xi-jinping-keynote-at-the-world-economic-forum, 20 December 2021.

Xi Jinping (2019) Working Together to Deliver a Brighter Future for Belt and Road Cooperation. Keynote Speech at the Second Belt and Road Forum for International Cooperation, Beijing, China. *The Second Belt and Road Forum for International Cooperation,* 26 April, http://www.beltandroadforum.org/english/n100/2019/0426/c22-1266.html, accessed 10 December 2021.

Xi Jinping (2021a) Bolstering Confidence and Jointly Overcoming Difficulties to Build a Better World. Statement at the United Nations General Assembly. *Xinhua,* 21 September, http://www.news.cn/english/2021-09/22/c_1310201230.htm, accessed 22 December 2021.

Xi Jinping (2021b) Acting in Solidarity for a Shared Future. Remarks at the 16th G20 Leaders' Summit. *Qiushi,* 30 October, http://en.qstheory.cn/2021-10/31/c_675913.htm, accessed 22 December 2021.

Xing, Li (2019) China's Pursuit of the "One Belt One Road" Initiative: A New World Order with Chinese Characteristics? In: Li Xing (ed.) *Mapping China's 'One Belt One Road' Initiative.* Cham: Palgrave Macmillan, pp. 1–27.

Ye, Min (2020) *The Belt Road and Beyond: State-Mobilized Globalization in China: 1998–2018.* Cambridge: Cambridge University Press.

CHAPTER 18

Chinese 'Security' in the Xi Era

David A. Welch

China is firm in upholding its core interests which include the following: state sovereignty, national security, territorial integrity and national reunification, China's political system established by the Constitution and overall social stability, and the basic safeguards for ensuring sustainable economic and social development.
State Council of the People's Republic of China, 2011

∵

Analysts generally agree that the Xi Jinping era represents an important break from past Chinese foreign policy practice. Under Xi, China has grown bolder and more assertive across the full range of foreign policy domains – strategic, economic, and diplomatic. We have seen, for example, a dramatic acceleration in the expansion and modernization of Chinese military power, most notably with respect to the creation of a blue-water navy and the establishment of China's first overseas military base in Djibouti (Poulin, 2016). We have also seen a dramatically increased presence in the South China Sea; unprecedentedly alarming rhetoric over the future of Taiwan; a bold geostrategic push into Central Asia, Africa, and even Europe in the form of the Belt and Road Initiative (BRI); and governance innovations such as the Asian Infrastructure Investment Bank (AIIB). We have also seen stepped-up efforts to control the global narrative on China, to position China as an indispensable supplier of communications technology, and to enhance China's cyber warfare capabilities. Finally, we have seen a willingness to break with diplomatic protocol, most notably in the form of 'wolf-warrior diplomacy' (Chang-Liao, 2022). These all stand in stark contrast to China's relatively passive approach to foreign policy under previous leaders. Mao Zedong and his immediate successors were certainly willing to use military force to protect proximate interests, most notably maintaining North Korea as a buffer against American encroachment in the Korean War (1950–1953); asserting territorial claims against India in the Himalayas (1962), the Soviet Union on the Amur River (1969), and Vietnam in the Paracel Islands

(1974); and chastising Vietnam for its intervention in Cambodia (1979). Mao, of course, was also famously enthusiastic about the cause of communist revolution elsewhere (Lüthi, 2020: 117–137). But for the most part, Chinese leaders concentrated their efforts on domestic objectives – fighting poverty, promoting economic development, and consolidating Communist Party rule – for which they considered a degree of decorum and good international citizenship instrumentally valuable.

The question naturally arises whether Chinese foreign policy under Xi is better understood as a simple function of rising Chinese power or a reflection of Xi himself. Scholars with a broadly 'Realist' understanding of International Relations stress the former (e.g. Mearsheimer, 2010). In this chapter, I stress the latter. I do so not because I wish to deny the natural tendency for states to seek to assert themselves on the world stage when their relative power increases, but rather because the *ways* in which China has been asserting itself, when viewed in conjunction with important trends and developments in Chinese domestic affairs, fit better with a narrative that stresses the paramount importance of Xi's worldview. Put another way, it is difficult to imagine that if a leader such as Deng Xiaoping, Zhao Ziyang, Jiang Zemin, or Hu Jintao was in charge in China today, China's foreign policy would closely resemble Xi's.

1   Xi Jinping's Thought

By 'Xi Jinping's Thought,' I do not mean in this section the canonical 14-point set of policy precepts known as 'Xi Jinping Thought' incorporated into the Constitution of the Chinese Communist Party in the 19th National Congress. I mean instead the basic worldview that those precepts are intended to serve (Peters, 2017). What does Xi care most about? What does he want? What does he fear?

It is, of course, difficult to reconstruct a leader's worldview accurately at the best of times, particularly from a distance. In the case of Xi, we are further hampered by the lack of a quality biography. Inferences based on fragmentary, largely anecdotal evidence from his early childhood and subsequent rise through the party ranks are of limited value precisely because they stress a high degree of caution and pragmatism seemingly intended primarily to help him keep his head down and avoid making enemies so as to enable him to realize what was clearly a significant ambition (Torigian, 2018). Small wonder that, having risen, Xi appears in many respects to have thrown that caution to the wind, revealing himself, as one prominent scholar has put it, as an 'autocratic, muscular-nationalist, order-obsessed strongman' (Wasserstrom, 2021).

Important clues to Xi's worldview may be found both in his image management and in the content of his policies and actions. With respect to the former, there is no question but that Xi has sought to position himself as second to none in the pantheon of Chinese heroes (Esarey, 2021). He has encouraged adulation and embraced the title 'People's Leader,' held previously only by Mao. He has also cultivated a cult of personality combining paternal and messianic archetypes while systematically promoting a narrative suggesting that corresponding perceptions of him are genuine, heartfelt, and organic – expressing the genuine love of the Chinese people – rather than deliberately cultivated. Indeed, denying the manufacture of a cult of personality is an important part of that very manufacturing process.

Acutely sensitive to slights, Xi has attuned China's impressive censorship apparatus to scrub not only any remotely critical comment on his policies, personality, or personal or family circumstances, but also any reference whatsoever to Winnie-the-Pooh (Repnikova, 2019).

Perhaps most significantly, Xi has systematically attempted to neutralize real or potential threats to his position – in part through an energetic anticorruption campaign launched in 2013 (Wang and Zeng, 2016) – and has succeeded in removing presidential term limits, potentially cementing his position indefinitely. At the same time, he has sought to promote masculine virtues throughout Chinese society – much to the detriment of gender equality (Mitter, 2021; Gao, 2021) – and a conception of Chinese thriving that cannot be disentangled from his personal leadership and future legacy.

The overall picture that emerges, then, is of a leader with high self-efficacy, powerful alpha male tendencies, a hypermasculine streak, and a penchant for control. Whether these reflect ego gratification needs or genuine conviction about what is in the best interest of China is an open question. Both can operate at the same time. It is important to note, of course, that while the degree of internal control Xi enjoys is certainly impressive, it is not necessarily absolute. The Chinese state is famously bureaucratic, and this, combined with regional political pressures and subterranean factional tensions, imposes upon any Chinese leader the need to indulge and gratify other players from time to time (Lai and Kang, 2014; Wong, 2018). Nevertheless, it seems evident that Xi's number one priority is to remain in power.

Remaining in power in China depends upon continued Communist Party rule, which depends in turn upon both an absence of alternatives and generalized social deference. In the early decades of the People's Republic (PRC), the legitimacy of the Party rested upon a combination of anti-imperialism, communist ideology, and poverty reduction. Over time, these pillars began to weaken. Anti-imperialism requires bogeys, but normalized relations with wartime enemies and the return of Hong Kong largely deprived the regime of its best (although state cultural policy, primarily through television and film, energetically tries to keep memories of the Japanese occupation, the Korean War, and the Vietnam War alive, with at least some success; Naftali, 2018). Deng's economic reforms put China firmly on the path of state capitalism and resulted also in egregious wealth and income inequalities inconsistent with communist principles. Xi himself has recently declared 'complete victory' in eradicating extreme poverty (Xinhua, 2021). Accordingly, the legitimacy of the Party rests today on two new pillars: (1) high year-over-year economic growth rates; and (2) defending China's sovereignty, territorial integrity, and international standing – the last of which is perhaps best understood in terms of national honour.

Xi has done an exceptional job of preventing the rise of political alternatives, real or imagined. Through co-optation, neutralization, or outright crackdown, he has taken aim at separatist movements, so-called terrorists, democracy activists, human rights activists, organized religions, and even the Falun Gong. The most egregious examples of these efforts are the ongoing industrial-scale cultural genocide of Uyghurs and other Muslims in Xinjiang, which involves mass incarceration, forced labour, forced sterilization, and other similar horrors (Ala, 2021); the largely successful stamping out of liberal democracy in Hong Kong following the passage of a now-notorious 2020 national security law (one that violated China's commitment not to interfere in Hong Kong's affairs until 2047); and systematic efforts to Sinicize not only Xinjiang, but also Tibet (Cheng, 2021). In addition, by taking the fight against the regime's critics and opponents abroad, Xi has embraced exactly the kind of flagrant interference in the domestic affairs of other states that he decries when outsiders criticize China. The overall impression that this pattern of behaviour leaves is one of paranoia. Not surprisingly, China famously spends more on domestic security and internal control than it does on protection against external foes (Zenz, 2018).

No doubt part of this paranoia is a function of the fact that the prospects of maintaining high year-over-year economic growth rates are dim and getting dimmer. China is already experiencing water shortages, energy shortages, commodity shortages, and desertification. Soon it will begin experiencing land loss due to sea level rise. Moreover, China's demographic profile is inauspicious. With one of the world's most rapidly aging populations and an extremely low birth rate, in 15 to 25 years China will not have a working-age population adequate to support the elderly. As a middle-income country, China is not well-positioned to create and maintain an expensive social safety net and the range of medical services that an elderly population requires.

Indeed, one interpretation of the BRI, discussed in the previous chapter, is that it is Xi Jinping's Hail Mary attempt to maintain high annual growth rates by dramatically increasing demand for, and reducing the costs of, Chinese exports (Welch, 2020).

This leaves the defence of China's sovereignty, territorial integrity, and national honour as the most robust pillar of Communist Party legitimacy today. Recognizing this renders intelligible every single aspect of Chinese foreign and security policy under Xi Jinping.

2 Sovereignty and Territorial Integrity

China has active territorial disputes with Japan, India, Vietnam, Malaysia, the Philippines, and Bhutan. In addition, China has active maritime disputes with South Korea, Japan, Vietnam, Malaysia, the Philippines, Brunei, and possibly, but somewhat ambiguously, Indonesia (Strangio, 2021). These disputes play an outsized role in China's foreign policy because they implicate sovereignty. I will address each – some at greater length than others – in a moment; but I would like to begin with what China calls its 'most sensitive core interest,' i.e., Taiwan.

2.1 *Taiwan*

The broad outlines of the Taiwan issue are probably familiar to readers of this book: Beijing considers Taiwan a renegade province that must be brought back under its control for the country to be complete.

Taiwan remains outside Beijing's control as a legacy of the technically-still-unfinished Chinese Civil War. In 1949, the Nationalist president of the Republic of China (ROC), Chiang Kai-shek, fled with his remaining forces to the safety of Taiwan and various minor islands where he enjoyed the protection of the US military. Although Chiang was a classic authoritarian leader, over the years Taiwan liberalized and democratized and has blossomed into a wealthy, thriving, de facto independent state whose people increasingly identify only as Taiwanese (see Figure 18.1) and who have almost entirely lost interest in what Beijing calls 'reunification' (Everington, 2021). Although relatively few countries today have formal diplomatic relations with Taipei, most countries that have formal diplomatic relations with Beijing – such as the United States and Japan – have the functional equivalent and merely 'take note' of Beijing's claim to Taiwan, rather than endorse it.

From both a legal and moral point of view, Beijing's claim to Taiwan is weak. Taiwan was only ruled by mainland China for approximately 200 years – a very brief period of time, when seen against the background of China's long history

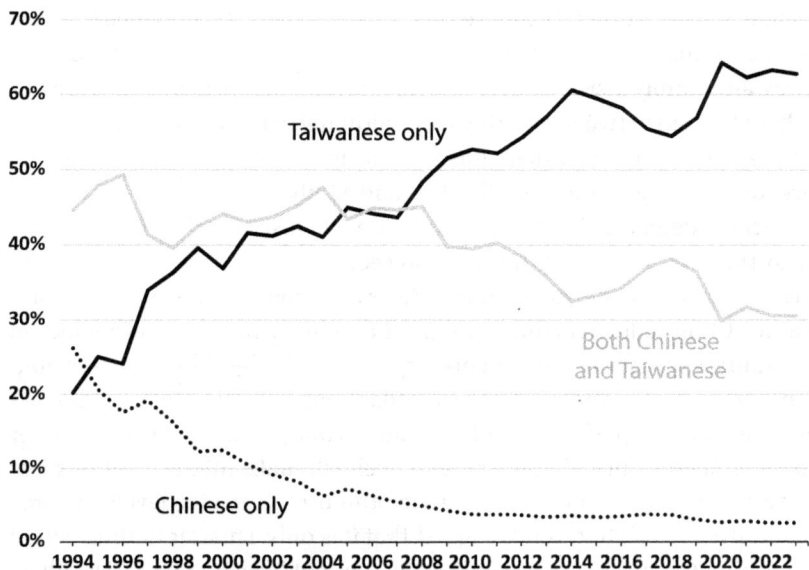

FIGURE 18.1 How do people in Taiwan identify?
SOURCE: NATIONAL CHENGCHI UNIVERSITY ELECTION STUDY CENTER 2021

(Manthorpe, 2009). The Qing Dynasty ceded Taiwan to Japan at the conclusion of the Sino-Japanese war in 1895, and in 1945 Japan returned it to the Qing Dynasty's successor, the Republic of China, in whose hands it remains. Taiwanese leaders routinely and correctly note that Taiwan has never been part of the People's Republic of China. Certainly from the perspective of the principle of self-determination, Taiwan has every right to determine its own political fate, particularly in view of the fact that the Qing Dynasty's rule over Taiwan was essentially settler-colonial.

There is no denying, however, the passion and sincerity of mainland Chinese claims to Taiwan, weak though they may be. Both Chinese elites and the general Chinese public have been socialized into believing that Taiwan is an inherent part of China. Conceptions of unredeemed entitlement trigger the sense of injustice, an exceptionally powerful moral emotion that, when inflamed, has particular effects on decision-making, such as increased stridency and risk-taking and a decreased willingness to compromise. Only the categorical satisfaction of a perceived injustice will assuage it (Welch, 2017a). It is therefore not surprising that Beijing maintains a firm and consistent line that a Taiwanese declaration of independence would cross a 'red line' triggering 'drastic measures' (Woo and Lee, 2021).

This line has been official Chinese policy for decades, but previous Chinese leaders maintained studied ambiguity about what would constitute 'drastic measures' and simply insisted upon 'eventual' reunification. Under Xi, the messaging has changed in two interesting ways, although with ups and downs: first, Beijing has clearly signalled that 'drastic measures' would potentially include military force; second, Chinese officials – and Xi himself – have from time to time evinced a degree of urgency and impatience, insisting that Taiwan must return to the motherland 'within the foreseeable future' (Buckley, 2018). To some extent this new messaging may reflect a changing balance of capabilities. Earlier Chinese leaders did not have the military tools to make good on explicit military threats. It is still an open question whether China has the ability to invade, conquer, and hold Taiwan today, particularly in light of Russia's recent poor military performance in Ukraine. Analysts are split on whether Moscow's difficulties bringing Ukraine to heel will make military options less attractive for Beijing or merely incentivize the use of greater levels of force (Lin and Culver, 2022). But trends suggest that it is only a matter of time before China acquires the necessary capability if it does not have it already (Davidson and Borger, 2021). It is clear that China's military modernization and expansion have been designed in significant part with Taiwan in mind, and it is difficult to avoid the impression that Xi sees Taiwan as a legacy issue, in which case he might very well be willing to gamble to take it. For this reason, Taiwan is at present the most dangerous flashpoint in East Asia – and possibly in the world.

2.2   *The South China Sea*

By far the most complex diplomatic challenge China faces is in the South China Sea – an enormously important body of water both economically and strategically where China finds itself dealing with multiple overlapping territorial and maritime claims.

Chinese policy in the South China Sea is generally not well-understood (Raymond and Welch, 2022). The dominant narrative internationally is that China has been behaving as an expansionistic aggressor, bullying rival claimants on the basis of transparently insupportable legal claims. It is true that China's public interpretation of its legal entitlements is insupportable (Dupuy and Dupuy, 2017). But Chinese leaders are aware of this. They simply find themselves unable to do anything about it. Justifying these statements will require me to do some careful unpacking.

It is important to recognize that, until relatively recently, the South China Sea was effectively a regional commons. Sailors navigated it and fishermen fished it more or less at will. Littoral authorities did not bother to stake legal claims of various kinds, largely because Westphalian principles of sovereign territoriality and practices of strict border demarcation had not yet arrived in Southeast Asia. This changed during postwar decolonization. Newly-independent states took pains to establish their Westphalian bona fides in part by staking out highly specific maritime and territorial claims (Hayton, 2014).

The Republic of China imagined itself the rightful owner of all the territorial features in the South China Sea and published maps denoting this by means of an eleven-dashed line (Chung, 2016). When the Communists drove the Nationalists from the mainland, Beijing embraced the Republic of China's claims, but dropped two dashes from the eleven-dashed line after concluding a maritime boundary agreement with Vietnam in the Gulf of Tonkin. Problematically, however, Beijing never stated clearly that it regarded the now-famous Nine-Dashed Line merely as a cartographic convenience delineating territorial claims, occasionally giving the impression that it was intended to denote a maritime claim as well. If indeed Beijing did intend it to mark out a maritime claim, it would effectively be asserting that the South China Sea is a Chinese lake.

Despite Beijing's bold claims, the People's Republic of China did not, in fact, physically control anything until the 1970s. The first permanent garrison in the South China Sea was established by Taiwan on Itu Aba (Taiping Island) – the largest of the Spratly Islands – in 1956. In 1974, as the Vietnam War drew to an end and it became clear that the US Navy presence in the South China Sea would diminish, Beijing seized control of the Paracel Islands. In the late 1980s, China, Vietnam, Malaysia, and the Philippines scrambled to establish outposts in the Spratly Islands. Finally, in 2012 China added Scarborough Shoal to its portfolio of controlled features after reneging on a mutual-withdrawal deal with Manila in a move that Philippine President Benigno Aquino compared at the time to Adolf Hitler's 1939 annexation of Czechoslovakia (Bradsher, 2014).

Today, only China and Taiwan claim all of the territorial features in the South China Sea. Vietnam claims the Paracels; the Philippines claims Scarborough Shoal; and Malaysia, Vietnam, and the Philippines each claim some of the Spratlys. No territorial feature, in short, is uncontested.

What of maritime claims? It is important to note that all of the South China Sea claimants are either signatories to the United Nations Convention on the Law of the Sea (UNCLOS) or – in the case of Taiwan, which is not formally party owing to its lack of UN membership – recognize it as binding customary law.[1] The chief purpose of UNCLOS was to replace a veritable cacophony

---

1   While the United States is also not party to UNCLOS, the official American position, too, is that most of the provisions of UNCLOS now have the status of customary international law (Almond, 2017).

of principles governing maritime claims with a single, consistent set. China, however, never updated its domestic law to render it consistent with UNCLOS and continued to assert 'historical' claims to 'relevant' waters 'adjacent' to territorial features. As these terms have no legal meaning under international law, exactly what China claims is ambiguous. The general perception, however, is that China 'claims virtually the entire South China Sea' (Mastro, 2021).

Beginning in 2012, assertive nationalists in the People's Liberation Army and other state security organs began winning internal bureaucratic battles against more cautious internationalists in the foreign ministry, ushering in a brief period of reckless unilateralism that saw, in addition to the seizure of Scarborough Shoal, (1) a rapid and dramatic artificial island building program in the Spratlys, beginning in 2013, that transformed China's meagre holdings there into formidable military outposts (Asia Maritime Transparency Initiative, n.d.); (2) the declaration of an Air Defense Identification Zone in the East China Sea on November 24, 2013 (Rinehart and Elias, 2015); and (3) the deployment of an oil platform on May 2, 2014, to waters claimed by Hanoi – despite 'a longstanding pledge to avoid placing rigs in disputed areas' (Morton, 2016: 924) – triggering a furious reaction in Vietnam and fatal high-seas confrontations between Chinese and Vietnamese vessels. Just as the internationalists worried, these moves generated fear and distrust abroad, cultivated an image of China as an expansionistic aggressor, and triggered balancing behaviour.

Most significantly, China's turn to assertive nationalism prompted Manila to launch a case under UNCLOS that invalidated almost all of what the international community understood to be China's maritime claims. In July 2016, the Arbitral Tribunal hearing *Philippines v. China* declared China's Nine-Dashed Line 'of no legal status or effect,' invalidated its historical waters claims, and – perhaps most importantly – found that as no Spratly 'islands' were, in fact, 'islands' under UNCLOS, merely 'rocks' or low-tide elevations (LTEs), none was entitled to a 200-n.m. Exclusive Economic Zone (EEZ). This had the immediate effect of simplifying overlapping maritime claims considerably. As a result, the only EEZ that China can possibly claim extends 200 n.m. from Hainan Island (and possibly also from the Paracels Islands *if* the Paracels are, in fact, rightfully China's *and* if they qualify as 'islands' rather than 'rocks' – a question that the Arbitral Tribunal did not address). It also means that China's artificial island at Mischief Reef falls solely under Manila's jurisdiction (Permanent Court of Arbitration, 2016). While China declared the Arbitral Tribunal ruling 'null and void,' Beijing was fortunate that incoming Filipino president Rodrigo Duterte opted to pocket Manila's win in return for promises of economic concessions (Regencia, 2021).

While the currently dominant 'aggressive China' narrative was generally accurate for the period 2012–2016, Beijing has since largely complied with the arbitral award even while refusing to acknowledge it (Welch, 2017b; Hayton, 2017; Welch and Logendrarajah, 2019; Raymond and Welch, 2022). The point of this new policy of 'stealthy compliance' is to pretend to a mobilized, nationalistic domestic audience that China has lost nothing while technically avoiding outlawry. Simultaneously, China has also sought to change the channel, attempting to engage rival claimants in maritime cooperation and joint development. But it has also signaled aggressively to dissuade rival claimants from taking any action, such as exploring for oil in their own EEZs, that would force Beijing to choose between admitting legal defeat in *Philippines v. China* and visibly violating the terms of the award. Small wonder that the international audience has generally not noticed China's new tack.

Whether Beijing's delicate balancing act is sustainable over the long run remains to be seen. The most significant Sword of Damocles hanging over Beijing's head is the prospect of Manila issuing an eviction notice for Mischief Reef. This would force China off its tightrope. Given that the domestic legitimacy of the regime now rests largely on its capacity to defend what it and hundreds of millions of Chinese consider to be China's territorial integrity, sovereign rights, and national honour, the smart money would bet on China choosing overt outlawry over compliance. Indeed, there are ominous signs that assertive nationalists may once again be gaining the upper hand in internal policy debates given the lack of traction stealthy compliance has had in promoting Chinese interests (Raymond and Welch, 2022).

2.3   The East China Sea

China is involved in two disputes in the East China Sea, both with Japan, but, complicating matters somewhat, in one significant respect also with Taiwan.

The more straightforward of the two disputes is strictly a maritime dispute. China and Japan have overlapping EEZ claims just to the west of the Okinawa Trough on what is the extreme eastern edge of China's continental shelf. The area involved is relatively small, and while it is rich with natural gas, oceanic topography makes it impossible for Japan to exploit it in any case. The disputed area is under effective Chinese control and is home to currently-productive gas fields (Manicom, 2014). While Tokyo insists on maintaining its claim, the dispute is, in fact, at present merely rhetorical and diplomatic, and therefore under tolerably good regulation. Accordingly, it rarely makes headlines.

The more serious dispute is primarily territorial but has a maritime dimension as well. At stake are the Senkaku Islands (known as the Diaoyu Islands in China), which are administered by Japan but claimed also by China and

Taiwan. While the history of the islands is long, complicated, and somewhat obscure, it is likely that if the dispute went to adjudication Japan's claim would prevail, quite simply because neither the PRC nor the ROC has maintained its claim consistently. Through official publications and communications, Beijing and Taipei have both tacitly or explicitly acknowledged Japanese sovereignty from time to time.[2] According to the legal doctrine of estoppel, this is tantamount to renunciation. But, once again, the dispute has taken on a symbolic importance far outstripping the material or strategic value of the islands, and public passions run high, driven by sincere convictions on all sides of the justice of each country's claim.

Most analysts would describe the Senkaku dispute as stable but dangerous, owing to the almost daily risk of inadvertent conflict between Chinese and Japanese ships and aircraft. The recent passage of a law authorizing the Chinese Coast Guard to use force in defence of maritime and territorial claims has certainly heightened anxieties (Ngyuen, 2021). But the dispute has become somewhat ritualized and it is difficult to see any advantage to either side of rocking the proverbial boat. It is a useful lightning rod, however, for Chinese authorities who might wish to redirect domestic discontent by keeping the flame of grievance against Japan alive (He, 2012).

2.4 *The Himalayan Frontier*

Among the oddest territorial disputes in the world are those between India and China along the Himalayan frontier (Mansingh, 2011; Raju, 2020). These involve a series of uninhabited or sparsely inhabited remote areas neither particularly accessible nor particularly valuable strategically or economically. As is the case with many territorial disputes, however, they have taken on outsized symbolic importance.

The primary areas under dispute are the Aksai Chin, claimed by India but controlled by China, and lands to the south of the McMahon line in Arunachal Pradesh, claimed by China but controlled by India. Various smaller areas along what is clearly an ill-defined border are also contested. These disputes have erupted into major war only once, in 1962, won decisively by China, but skirmishes and standoffs are quite common. The most recent conflicts occurred in 2020 and 2021 along the Line of Actual Control in Ladakh, primarily at Pangong Lake and in the Galwan Valley, but there have been skirmishes elsewhere as well, including in the vicinity of Sikkim. Typically, these skirmishes are set off by attempts on one side or the other to improve infrastructure, primarily in the

---

2 Miyoshi, 2018; but cf. Su, 2005, which ignores the latter point.

form of roads. The potential for escalation is limited to a significant degree by the remoteness and inhospitableness of the theatre of operations itself; but neither India nor China perceives a significant advantage in escalation. That plus a long history of crisis management efforts helps keep the disputes under relatively good regulation.

China also has a relatively minor territorial dispute with Bhutan in the Doklam Plateau, but recently has been building roads and villages in the area uncharacteristically assertively (Barnett, 2021). This would seem to indicate a willingness to act unilaterally despite reputational costs that has occasionally marked Xi's foreign policy in other areas as well.

3 Narrative Management

So much for 'core interests' and maritime and territory disputes. We move next to one of the most interesting aspects of Chinese security policy under Xi Jinping: its unprecedented emphasis on attempts to manage the global narrative on China (Yang, 2021).

While all great powers have engaged in propaganda efforts of one kind or another throughout history, no country has embarked upon such an energetic and systematic campaign to project, promote, and defend a particular global image and to deflect criticism, often by attempting to redirect it to foreign targets. To this end, China enlists both its extensive diaspora community and, increasingly, social media (Cadell, 2021). Beijing actively seeks to shut down or, if this is not possible, overwhelm with positive messaging criticism of such things as China's human rights violations, environmental record, official corruption, interference with Hong Kong's autonomy, predatory overseas lending practices, mercantilist business practices, strategic overseas investments, the intimate relationship between state security and intelligence organs on the one hand and state owned enterprises (SOEs) or nominally-privately-owned telecommunications companies on the other, and a host of other hot-button issues. These efforts are richly ironic in at least three respects: first, one of the main theatres of operation for Chinese narrative management efforts is in cyberspace, where China makes extensive use of bots and fake accounts on social media platforms that are banned in China, such as Facebook and Twitter; second, as I mentioned in the introduction, these efforts involve interference in the domestic affairs of other states of the kind that China rails against as part of its narrative management efforts; and third – in what is perhaps the most meta of the ironies involved – among the things China's narrative management efforts target is criticism of China's narrative management efforts.

The primary objective of Chinese narrative management efforts is to burnish both Xi's personal image and that of the Communist Party as reliable stewards and defenders – indeed, the *only* reliable stewards and defenders – of Chinese national interests. Once again, the ultimate target here is the domestic audience, and the chief goals are to prevent (1) criticism of, or dissatisfaction with, either Xi or the Party, and (2) flirtation with liberal democratic ideals (Jia, 2019).

Whether China's narrative management efforts do, in fact, contribute to Chinese security is an open question (Tsang and Cheung, 2021). In certain respects, it would appear to be backfiring badly. China's often ham-handed messaging has without question contributed to the recent dramatic decline in China's international reputation (Silver et al., 2020). On the other hand, by maintaining such tight control over the domestic information environment, the regime seems to be able to prevent international criticism from stimulating much in the way of domestic criticism. Indeed, when there is leakage to the domestic sphere, the regime often seems able to exploit it as a way of cultivating a rally-'round-the-flag effect. The recent Peng Shuai affair may be a rare exception. It is possible that by coming down hard on a prominent tennis star for implicating a senior Communist Party member in a shocking #MeToo story, the regime may have damaged its own image (Lau, 2021). Similarly, Xi's stringent 'zero-COVID' policy and the resultant highly-unpopular lockdowns in Shanghai and Beijing have clearly fanned the flames of internal opposition (Gan, 2022). In both cases, international criticism played an important role in stimulating domestic criticism.

4   Coercive Diplomacy

From time to time, China responds to slights or perceived threats in a straightforwardly coercive manner. Again, this is not unusual Great Power behaviour, historically speaking, but in certain respects China's approach is curiously anachronistic. China's response to Canada's arrest and trial of Huawei Chief Financial Officer Meng Wanzhou on a US extradition warrant on December 1, 2018, is particularly notable in this regard. Nine days later, China countered by arresting Canadian citizens Michael Kovrig and Michael Spavor – the 'Two Michaels' – on trumped-up national security charges, releasing them within hours of Meng's release on September 24, 2021. Taking hostages as bargaining chips is an archaic practice, and the only countries that have embraced it in recent times have been China, North Korea, Venezuela, Turkey, and Iran (Gilbert and Rivard Piché, 2021/2022). If it were possible to provide a non-arbitrary definition of 'rogue-state' behaviour, hostage diplomacy would certainly qualify.

More often, however, China makes use of traditional carrots and sticks. Prime examples of the former include China's use of economic incentives to poach Taiwan's few remaining diplomatic allies (Shattuck, 2020). Prime examples of the latter include Beijing's responses to Australian Prime Minister Scott Morrison's May 2020 call for a robust investigation into the origins of COVID-19 and other measures taken by Canberra to protect Australia from undue influence of the kind associated with Chinese narrative management efforts: e.g., punishing tariffs, 'anti-dumping' measures, travel warnings for Chinese citizens thinking about visiting or studying in Australia, and a barrage of cyberattacks.

It is difficult to know how effective Chinese coercive diplomacy is on balance. Beijing has certainly succeeded in buying diplomatic recognition in a number of states as part of its efforts to isolate Taiwan. Neither hostage diplomacy nor economic coercion in the cases of Canada and Australia appear to have achieved their immediate goals, but it is difficult to know how many times veiled or implicit threats may have deterred action of the kind that Beijing disapproves. It is possible that China has made use of explicit threats with plausible deniability; for example, Filipino president Rodrigo Duterte has reportedly claimed that, in a private exchange in 2017, Xi threatened war if the Philippines proceeded with plans to drill for oil in a South China Sea block that falls squarely within the Philippines' own EEZ (Mogato, 2017). One thing that does seem tolerably clear, however, is that Chinese coercive diplomacy tends to work at cross purposes with Chinese narrative management efforts. It is difficult to look benign when the world sees you playing dirty. It seems likely, however, that – unlike narrative management efforts – coercive diplomacy is largely ad hoc and reactive rather than forward-looking and strategic. It is also entirely possible that the two spring from somewhat different bureaucratic sources (Lai and Kang, 2014).

5 China and 'International Order'

A key but often underappreciated element of security policy is cultivating and maintaining a congenial regional and global milieu (Goddard and Nexon, 2016). This is where the concept of 'international order' figures.

Much has been said or written recently of the so-called Chinese threat to international order (e.g., Doshi, 2021). Here I would like to push back on that idea and suggest that China largely benefits from – and knows that it benefits from – the current international order, and that while it would like to see what it considers suitable adjustments, these are better understood as marginal than revisionist or revolutionary. China has no grand design for a radical alternative.

It is important, first, to specify what I mean by 'international order.' Generically, what I have in mind are the fundamental rules, norms, and institutions of global governance specifying who or what has standing as actors, how they are to relate to each other, how they are to conduct joint business, and how they are to resolve disputes (Raymond, 2019: 27–36). We frequently hear the phrases 'rules-based international order' (RBIO, sometimes rendered RBO for 'rules-based order') and 'liberal international order' (LIO), although relatively few people define and distinguish these rigorously (Scott, 2021). Arguably, this is not possible; these are contested and contestable concepts put primarily to rhetorical and political rather than analytical use (Martel, 2022). But for my part, I think it is possible and desirable to provide at least a rough distinction.

Key elements of the current RBIO, I would argue, include sovereign territoriality, the fundamental principles of the UN Charter, various bodies and branches of international law, the mechanisms and institutions of conflict resolution sanctioned by these, and various core legal principles such as *pacta sunt servanda* ('agreements will be kept'). This is not necessarily an exhaustive list, but it points to the constitutive and regulative rules that facilitate orderly interaction. Different eras of human history have seen different sets of constitutive and regulative rules, some of them richer or better defined than others, but it is difficult to find clear examples of epochs in which it would have made no sense whatsoever to say that there was a rules-based international order of some kind.

The LIO, in contrast, is a historically contingent set of additional institutions, rules, norms, and principles negotiated at the close of World War II that were largely intended to avoid a replay of pathological interwar dynamics. The LIO includes the Bretton Woods institutions (the General Agreement on Tariffs and Trade [GATT; later the World Trade Organization, or WTO], the International Monetary Fund [IMF], and the World Bank); specific provisions for the protection of vulnerable groups and individuals as articulated in various human rights instruments; and the principles of what John Ruggie called 'embedded liberalism,' a compromise that permitted states a degree of economic protection for the purpose of maintaining social safety nets while promoting generally free movement of goods (Ruggie, 1982). It is important to note that the LIO has evolved over the years. Newer features include the relatively free movement of capital and the doctrine of the Responsibility to Protect (R2P). An important principle that has largely fallen into disuse, owing to asymptotic decolonization and the consolidation of state borders, is self-determination of peoples.

China under Xi has shown no appetite for revising the current RBIO. Rhetorically, at least, China is among the most vocal defenders of the principle of state sovereignty (although the notion of sovereignty that China champions is somewhat archaic; Paris, 2020) and its correlate, the principle of non-interference in the internal affairs of other states. While it is true that it honours these in the breach in pursuit of Chinese interests, those interests themselves – particularly certain 'core' interests – are very much articulated in the language of those same principles. Similarly, China is an active participant in the UN system where it is generally cooperative and constructive and only occasionally obstructive (less obstructive than Russia, certainly, and arguably less obstructive than the United States; see, e.g., Figure 18.2). Finally, with the sole striking exceptions of its awkward, *sui generis* legal position on the South China Sea and its unconventional interpretation of certain UNCLOS provisions,³ China is also a major beneficiary and supporter of international law as a source of stability and predictability in international affairs.

China is somewhat less committed to the LIO, but, again, has given no indication of a desire to overthrow it wholesale. It has certainly expressed a degree of frustration with the increasingly anachronistic distribution of (legitimate) power (i.e., authority) in the Bretton Woods institutions – the creation of the AIIB is perhaps the most obvious expression of this – but it has benefited enormously from the relatively open global trade regime that the LIO has enabled. Indeed, it is highly dependent upon it. Less palatable to China are the classical liberal values that inform other aspects of the LIO such as the global human rights regime, R2P, and the principle of self-determination. Indeed, these values are threats to Communist Party rule. But rather than attempt to uproot them, Beijing appears content to manage them, primarily by wielding as shields the principle of non-interference and, selectively, its UN Security Council veto.

Three things in particular appear to give China's neighbours and other Great Powers pause about Beijing's commitment to the current international order however one conceives it. The first is China's behaviour in the South China Sea, which is universally interpreted as revisionist. The second is the increasingly prevalent use of the concept of *Tianxia* (天下) in Chinese International Relations theory and foreign policy discourse, often interpreted as code for Chinese domination (Shiu, 2020). The third is China's ancient history as the

---

3 The most important of these is China's insistence that UNCLOS permits coastal states to regulate other countries' military activities in the EEZ (Pedrozo, 2014).

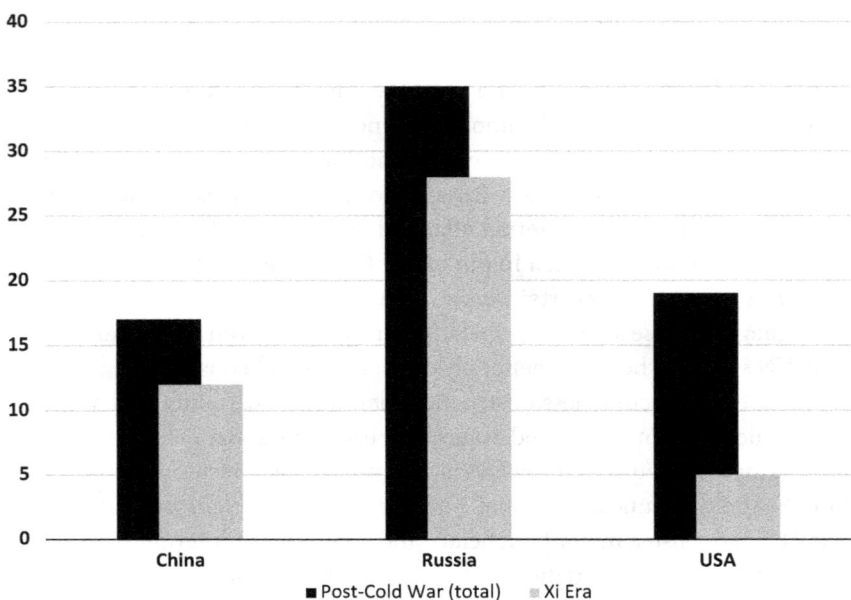

FIGURE 18.2 UN Security Council vetoes
SOURCE: UNITED NATIONS 2021

preeminent power in East Asia, at least since the beginning of the Middle Kingdom period, grounded in a sense of civilizational superiority and noblesse oblige toward weaker 'barbarian' neighbours. The latter two are closely connected, and Xi's rhetoric about such things as 'the Chinese Dream' and 'a new model of major power relations' – widely interpreted as a spheres-of-influence proposal requiring the United States to withdraw from the Western Pacific – evoke fear of China desiring to reconstitute a regional hierarchic tributary system of the kind that it presided over centuries ago (Sasse, 2020).

There is no doubt that such a system would gratify China's self-concept not only as a country worthy of preeminence, but also as one that has been victimized and humiliated for more than 100 years by other Great Powers, some of whom genuinely qualify as 'barbarian' in China's eyes. Xi, like the vast majority of Chinese, unquestionably believes that it is time for China to take its rightful place among the top tier of global powers. But path dependencies being what they are, there is no plausible way for China to relive its past glory. No one else would put up with it. Moreover, given China's success under current arrangements, any radical attempt to revise them would represent the kind of risk acceptance in the domain of gains that Prospect Theory tells us is extremely unlikely (Kahneman and Tversky, 1979). Finally, as I have argued elsewhere,

China is simply not in a position to exercise the kind of preeminence that its neighbours fear. Instead, it is likely soon to peak (Welch, 2020). China faces serious limits to growth, and the very challenges that represent long-term threats to Communist Party rule also represent deterrents to overreach. Xi Jinping's largely pragmatic approach to international order reflects this.

6 Conclusion

With only rare exceptions (such as China's legal position on the South China Sea and angry knee-jerk reactions to various international developments), Chinese security policy under Xi Jinping can be seen as remarkably logical and coherent – but only through an analytical lens that stresses Xi's personal obsession with power and control. The primary alternative lens – Realism – cannot account for what would otherwise appear to be deep irrationalities in the pursuit of goals that are fundamental from a Realist perspective. No prudent Realist leader would willingly alienate the international community and trigger balancing behaviour by threatening Taiwan, pushing an insupportable line on the South China Sea, ignoring China's commitment to respect Hong Kong's autonomy, turning a deaf ear to outrage over cultural genocide and human rights abuses in Xinjiang, and meddling in the internal affairs of other states in a self-defeating effort to control the global narrative. China is a country with significant hard-power capability, but far less hard-power capability than is required to shove things down other countries' throats. It has essentially no soft-power capability whatsoever and has squandered opportunities to enhance it even as the United States was busily squandering its own during the presidency of Donald J. Trump. Finally, China has only one (informal) ally – North Korea, more liability than an asset – and no true friends.

A leader attempting to navigate the challenges of a peaceful rise would play things very differently – arguably, much the same way Deng did, internalizing the complex wisdom of Sun Tzu and deftly turning challenges into opportunities. Xi is a very different kind of ruler, but not because of any lack of knowledge or intellect. Xi simply has one (and *only* one) priority, to which all else must be considered subordinate: maintaining power and exercising control.

It is important to note that this way of understanding Chinese security policy does not necessarily pathologize Xi. There is no particular need to leap to a diagnosis of malignant narcissism or sociopathy. As I noted earlier, it is entirely possible that Xi sincerely believes that he is the only person who can successfully manage China's rise and that his open-ended personal rule is a necessary condition for realizing 'the Chinese Dream.' His motives, in short, may well be other-regarding, at least to a certain extent, and he may truly imagine his future place in history in that light. But at the end of the day this makes no meaningful difference. Chinese security policy is and will continue to be Xi Jinping's security policy until and unless some combination of mistakes, internal stresses, and/or external pressures brings the whole edifice tumbling down.

References

Ala, Mamtimin (2021) *Worse Than Death: Reflections on the Uyghur Genocide*. Lanham, MD: Hamilton Books.

Almond, Roncevert Ganon (2017) US Ratification of the Law of the Sea Convention. *The Diplomat*, 24 May, https://thediplomat.com/2017/05/u-s-ratification-of-the-law-of-the-sea-convention/, accessed 31 January 2024.

Asia Maritime Transparency Initiative (n.d.) China Island Tracker. *Center for Strategic and International Studies*, https://amti.csis.org/island-tracker/china/, accessed 31 January 2024.

Barnett, Robert (2021) China Is Building Entire Villages in Another Country's Territory. *Foreign Policy*, 7 May, https://foreignpolicy.com/2021/05/07/china-bhutan-border-villages-security-forces/, accessed 31 January 2024.

Bradsher, Keith (2014) Philippine Leader Sounds Alarm on China. *The New York Times*, 4 February, https://www.nytimes.com/2014/02/05/world/asia/philippine-leader-urges-international-help-in-resisting-chinas-sea-claims.html, accessed 31 January 2024.

Buckley, Chris (2018) China's New 'Helmsman' Offers a Strident Nationalist Message. *The New York Times*, 20 March, https://www.nytimes.com/2018/03/20/world/asia/china-xi-jinping-helmsman-congress.html, accessed 31 January 2024.

Cadell, Cate (2021) China Harvests Masses of Data on Western Targets, Documents Show. *The Washington Post*, 31 December, https://www.washingtonpost.com/national-security/china-harvests-masses-of-data-on-western-targets-documents-show/2021/12/31/3981ce9c-538e-11ec-8927-c396fa861a71_story.html, accessed 31 January 2024.

Chang-Liao, Nien-chung (2022) Why Have Chinese Diplomats Become So Aggressive? *Survival*, 64(1), pp. 179–190.

Cheng, Fangyi (2021) The Evolution of 'Sinicisation'. *Journal of the Royal Asiatic Society*, 31(2), pp. 321–342.

Chung, Chris P. C. (2016) Drawing the U-Shaped Line: China's Claim in the South China Sea, 1946–1974. *Modern China*, 42(1), pp. 38–72.

Davidson, Helen and Julian Borger (2021) China Could Mount Full-Scale Invasion by 2025, Taiwan Defence Minister Says. *The Guardian,* 6 October, https://www.theguardian.com/world/2021/oct/06/biden-says-he-and-chinas-xi-have-agreed-to-abide-by-taiwan-agreement, accessed 31 January 2024.

Doshi, Rosh (2021) *The Long Game: China's Grand Strategy and the Displacement of American Order.* Oxford: Oxford University Press.

Dupuy, Florian and Pierre-Marie Dupuy (2017) A Legal Analysis of China's Historic Rights Claim in the South China Sea. *American Journal of International Law,* 107(1), pp. 124–141.

Esarey, Ashley (2021) Propaganda as a Lens for Assessing Xi Jinping's Leadership. *Journal of Contemporary China,* 30(132), pp. 888–901.

Everington, Keoni (2021) 72.5% of Taiwanese Willing to Fight against Chinese Invasion. *Taiwan News,* 30 December, https://www.taiwannews.com.tw/en/news/4393119, accessed 31 January 2024.

Gan, Nectar (2022) Xi Jinping Sends Warning to Anyone Who Questions China's Zero-COVID Policy. *CNN,* 6 May, https://www.cnn.com/2022/05/06/china/china-xi-pbsc-zero-covid-intl-hnk/index.html, accessed 31 January 2024.

Gao, Helen (2021) China's Ban on 'Sissy Men' Is Bound to Backfire. *The New York Times,* 31 December, https://www.nytimes.com/2021/12/31/opinion/china-masculinity.html, accessed 31 January 2024.

Gilbert, Danielle, and Gaëlle Rivard Piché (2021/2022) Caught between Giants: Hostage Diplomacy and Negotiation Strategy for Middle Powers. *Texas National Security Review,* 5(1), pp. 11–32.

Goddard, Stacie E. and Daniel H. Nexon (2016) The Dynamics of Power Politics: A Framework for Analysis. *Journal of Global Security Studies,* 1(1), pp. 4–18.

Hayton, Bill (2014) *The South China Sea: The Struggle for Power in Asia.* New Haven, CT: Yale University Press.

Hayton, Bill (2017) Denounce but Comply: China's Response to the South China Sea Arbitration Ruling. *Georgetown Journal of International Affairs,* 18(2), pp. 104–111.

He, Yinan (2012) Nationalism and the China-Japan Island Disputes. *Asia Unbound,* 18 September, https://www.cfr.org/blog/nationalism-and-china-japan-island-disputes, accessed 31 January 2024.

Jia, Lianrui (2019) What Public and Whose Opinion? A Study of Chinese Online Public Opinion Analysis. *Communication and the Public,* 4(1), pp. 21–34.

Kahneman, Daniel and Amos Tversky (1979) Prospect Theory: An Analysis of Decisions under Risk. *Econometrica,* 47(2), pp. 263–291.

Lai, Hongyi and Su-Jeong Kang (2014) Domestic Bureaucratic Politics and Chinese Foreign Policy. *Journal of Contemporary China,* 23(86), pp. 294–313.

Lau, Jessie (2021) Why Tennis Star Peng Shuai's #Metoo Allegation is Such a Threat to China's Leaders. *New Statesman,* 23 November, https://www.newstatesman.com/world/2021/11/why-tennis-star-peng-shuais-metoo-allegation-is-such-a-threat-to-chinas-leaders, accessed 31 January 2024.

Lin, Bonnie and John Culver (2022) China's Taiwan Invasion Plans May Get Faster and Deadlier. *Foreign Policy,* 19 April, https://foreignpolicy.com/2022/04/19/china-invasion-ukraine-taiwan/, accessed 31 January 2024.

Lüthi, Lorenz M. (2020) *Cold Wars: Asia, the Middle East, Europe.* Cambridge: Cambridge University Press.

Manicom, James (2014) *Bridging Trouble Waters: China, Japan, and Maritime Order in the East China Sea.* Washington, DC: Georgetown University Press.

Mansingh, Surjit (2011) India and China Today and Tomorrow. *The International Spectator,* 46(2), pp. 41–55.

Manthorpe, Jonathan (2009) *Forbidden Nation: A History of Taiwan.* New York: St. Martin's Griffin.

Martel, Stéphanie (2022) *Enacting the Security Community: Asean's Never-Ending Story.* Stanford, CA: Stanford University Press.

Mastro, Oriana Skylar (2021) How China is Bending the Rules in the South China Sea. *The Interpreter. The Lowy Institute,* 17 February, https://www.lowyinstitute.org/the-interpreter/how-china-bending-rules-south-china-sea, accessed 31 January 2024.

Mearsheimer, John J. (2010) The Gathering Storm: China's Challenge to US Power in Asia. *Chinese Journal of International Politics,* 3(4), pp. 381–396.

Mitter, Rana (2021) The Super-Rich, 'Sissy Boys', Celebs – All Targets in Xi's Bid to End Cultural Difference. *The Guardian,* 5 September, https://www.theguardian.com/commentisfree/2021/sep/05/super-rich-sissy-boys-celebs-all-targets-in-xis-bid-to-end-cultural-difference, accessed 31 January 2024.

Miyoshi, Masahiro (2018) Protest and Acquiescence in Territorial Acquisition: In Relation to the Senkaku Islands. *OPRI Center of Island Studies,* Last Modified 1 May, https://www.spf.org/islandstudies/research/a00019r.html, accessed 31 January 2024.

Mogato, Manuel (2017) Duterte Says China's Xi Threatened War If Philippines Drills for Oil. *Reuters,* 19 May, https://www.reuters.com/article/us-southchinasea-philippines-china/duterte-says-chinas-xi-threatened-war-if-philippines-drills-for-oil-idUSKCN18F1DJ, accessed 31 January 2024.

Morton, Katherine (2016) China's Ambition in the South China Sea: Is a Legitimate Maritime Order Possible? *International Affairs,* 92(4), pp. 909–940.

Naftali, Orna (2018) 'These War Dramas Are Like Cartoons': Education, Media Consumption, and Chinese Youth Attitudes Towards Japan. *Journal of Contemporary China,* 27(113), pp. 703–718.

National Chengchi University Election Study Center (2021) Taiwanese/Chinese Identity (1992/06–2021/06). *Election Study Center, National Chengchi University,*

Last Modified 20 July, https://esc.nccu.edu.tw/PageDoc/Detail?fid=7800&id=6961, accessed 31 January 2024.

Ngyuen, Thanh Trung (2021) How China's Coast Guard Law Has Changed the Regional Security Structure. *Asia Maritime Transparency Initiative,* Last Modified 12 April, https://amti.csis.org/how-chinas-coast-guard-law-has-changed-the-regional-security-structure/, accessed 31 January 2024.

Paris, Roland (2020) The Right to Dominate: How Old Ideas About Sovereignty Pose New Challenges for World Order. *International Organization,* 74(3), pp. 453–489.

Pedrozo, Raul (2014) Military Activities in the Exclusive Economic Zone: East Asia Focus. *International Law Studies,* 90, pp. 515–543.

Permanent Court of Arbitration (2016) *Award, Philippines v. China (Case No. 2013–19).* The Hague: Permanent Court of Arbitration, https://pcacases.com/web/sendAttach/2086, accessed 31 January 2024.

Peters, Michael A. (2017) The Chinese Dream: Xi Jinping Thought on Socialism with Chinese Characteristics for a New Era. *Educational Philosophy and Theory,* 49(14), pp. 1299–1304.

Poulin, Andrew (2016) Going Blue: The Transformation of China's Navy. *The Diplomat,* 15 April, https://thediplomat.com/2016/04/going-blue-the-transformation-of-chinas-navy/, accessed 31 January 2024.

Raju, K. D. (2020) Doklam and Beyond: Revisiting the India-China Territorial Disputes: An International Law Perspective. *India Review,* 19(1), pp. 85–105.

Raymond, Mark (2019) *Social Practices of Rule Making in International Politics.* New York: Oxford University Press.

Raymond, Mark and David A. Welch (2022) What's Really Going on in the South China Sea? *Journal of Current Southeast Asian Affairs,* 41(2), pp. 214–239.

Regencia, Ted (2021) Is Duterte Squandering the Hague Victory to Appease Beijing? *Al Jazeera,* 12 July, https://www.aljazeera.com/news/2021/7/12/south-china-sea-nine-dash-line-ruling, accessed 31 January 2024.

Repnikova, Maria (2019) Media Politics under Xi: Shifts and Continuities. *SAIS Review of International Affairs,* 38(2), pp. 55–67.

Rinehart, Ian E. and Bart Elias (2015) *China's Air Defense Identification Zone (ADIZ).* Washington, DC: Congressional Research Service, https://fas.org/sgp/crs/row/R43894.pdf, accessed 31 January 2024.

Ruggie, John Gerard (1982) International Regimes, Transactions, and Change: Embedded Liberalism in the Postwar Economic Order. *International Organization,* 36(2), pp. 379–415.

Sasse, Ben (2020) The Responsibility to Counter China's Ambitions Falls to Us. *The Atlantic,* 26 January, https://www.theatlantic.com/ideas/archive/2020/01/china-sasse/605074/, accessed 31 January 2024.

Scott, Ben (2021) Rules-Based Order: What's in a Name? *The Interpreter. The Lowy Institute,* 30 June, https://www.lowyinstitute.org/the-interpreter/rules-based-order-what-s-name, accessed 31 January 2024.

Shattuck, Thomas J. (2020) The Race to Zero? China's Poaching of Taiwan's Diplomatic Allies. *Orbis,* 64(2), pp. 334–352.

Shiu, Sin Por (2020) Tianxia: China's Concept of International Order. *Global Asia,* 15(2), pp. 44–50, https://www.globalasia.org/v15no2/cover/tianxia-chinas-concept-of-international-order_shiu-sin-por, accessed 31 January 2024.

Silver, Laura, Kat Devlin, and Christine Huang (2020) Unfavorable Views of China Reach Historic Highs in Many Countries. *Pew Research Center,* Last Modified 6 October, https://www.pewresearch.org/global/2020/10/06/unfavorable-views-of-china-reach-historic-highs-in-many-countries/, accessed 31 January 2024.

State Council of the People's Republic of China (2011) China's Peaceful Development, http://english.www.gov.cn/archive/white_paper/2014/09/09/content_281474986284646.htm, accessed 31 January 2024.

Strangio, Sebastian (2021) China Demanded Halt to Indonesian Drilling near Natuna Islands: Report. *The Diplomat,* 2 December, https://thediplomat.com/2021/12/china-demanded-halt-to-indonesian-drilling-near-natuna-islands-report/, accessed 31 January 2024.

Su, Steven Wei (2005) The Territorial Dispute over the Tiaoyu/Senkaku Islands: An Update. *Ocean Development & International Law,* 36(1), pp. 45–61.

Torigian, Joseph (2018) Historical Legacies and Leaders' Worldviews. *China Perspectives,* (1/2), zapp. 7–15.

Tsang, Steve and Olivia Cheung (2021) Has Xi Jinping Made China's Political System More Resilient and Enduring? *Third World Quarterly,* 43(1), pp. 1–19.

United Nations (2021) Security Council – Veto List. *Dag Hammarskjöld Library,* https://research.un.org/en/docs/sc/quick, accessed 31 January 2024.

Wang, Zhengxu and Jinghan Zeng (2016) Xi Jinping: The Game Changer of Chinese Elite Politics? *Contemporary Politics,* 22(4), pp. 469–486.

Wasserstrom, Jeffrey (2021) Why Are There No Biographies of Xi Jinping? *The Atlantic,* 30 January, https://www.theatlantic.com/international/archive/2021/01/xi-jinping-china-biography/617852/, accessed 31 January 2024.

Welch, David A. (2017a) The Justice Motive in East Asia's Territorial Disputes. *Group Decision and Negotiation,* 26(1), pp. 71–92.

Welch, David A. (2017b) Philippines v. China One Year Later: A Surprising Compliance from Beijing. *The Globe and Mail,* 12 July, https://www.theglobeandmail.com/opinion/philippines-v-china-one-year-later-a-surprising-compliance-from-beijing/article35660244/, accessed 31 January 2024.

Welch, David A. (2020) China, the United States, and 'Thucydides's Trap'. In: Huiyun Feng and Kai He (eds.) *China's Challenges and International Order Transition: Beyond 'Thucydides's Trap'*. Ann Arbor: University of Michigan Press, pp. 47–70.

Welch, David A. and Kobi Logendrarajah (2019) Is China Still an Outlaw in the South China Sea? *Open Canada*, 29 July, https://www.opencanada.org/features/china-still-outlaw-south-china-sea/, accessed 31 January 2024.

Wong, Audrye (2018) More Than Peripheral: How Provinces Influence China's Foreign Policy. *The China Quarterly*, 235, pp. 735–757.

Woo, Ryan and Yimou Lee (2021) China Warns of 'Drastic Measures' If Taiwan Provokes on Independence. *Reuters*, 29 December, https://www.reuters.com/world/china/china-warns-drastic-measures-if-taiwan-provokes-independence-2021-12-29/, accessed 31 January 2024.

Xinhua (2021) Xi Declares 'Complete Victory' in Eradicating Absolute Poverty in China. *Xinhua*, 26 February, http://www.xinhuanet.com/english/2021-02/26/c_139767705.htm, accessed 31 January 2024.

Yang, Yi Edward (2021) China's Strategic Narratives in Global Governance Reform under Xi Jinping. *Journal of Contemporary China*, 30(128), pp. 299–313.

Zenz, Adrian (2018) China's Domestic Security Spending: An Analysis of Available Data. *China Brief*, 18(4), pp. 5–11.

CHAPTER 19

China's Space Program and Its Quest for Superpowerhood

Goals, Strategies, Perception of Challenges

Michał Dahl, Hanna Kupś and Maciej Szatkowski

One of the most momentous consequences of the ongoing process of Chinese transformation is that the People's Republic of China (PRC) has been promoted to the group of key actors in the international arena (see, e.g., Cao, 2009; Hameiri and Jones, 2015). From the Chinese perspective this phenomenon is not perceived as a promotion, but rather as a return to the position that China – an ancient civilization – used to hold for centuries. The fact, hovever, is that in more than 70 years of the PRC's history there has been no period in which the state was able to significantly influence the shape of the global order to the same extent as today. The course of the Chinese transformation process is the result of strategies implemented by successive generations of leaders, represented by Xi Jinping and Li Keqiang. Under Xi's leadership, China started openly questioning the world order that emerged after the collapse of the Cold War's bipolar system, based on the unquestionable domination of the United States.[1] Even though the implementation of the "two centenary goals" (两个一百年 *liangge yibai nian*), necessary to accomplish the "great rejuvenation of the Chinese nation" (中华民族伟大复兴 *Zhonghua minzu weida fuxing*), relates primarily to the domestic needs, these two goals also aim at confirming the status of China as a world superpower.[2]

Nowadays the competition between the major powers manifests itself not only in rather conventional rivalry for economic assets or strategic military advantage but also in the field of power engineering, transportation, and advanced information technologies. It also includes domination in space – a

---

1 It is worth mentioning that China's positioning on the international arena remains a subject of lively debate. To provide an example, the current increasingly assertive policy of Beijing contrasts with Deng Xiaoping's famous low-profile approach and belief that the country "should never seek a leadership position" (绝不当头 *juebu dangtou*) in the developing world (Deng, n.d.: 363 as cited in Pu, 2017: 147).
2 Despite the real potential currently held by China on the world stage, academicians still refer to the country as a "rising" or "emerging" superpower (see Masood, 2019; Pu, 2017).

sphere that is related to all of the above-mentioned fields as it reflects the technological advancement of a given country. The strategic importance of space has also been noticed by Chinese decision-makers, and it has been reflected both in political manifestos (e.g., by Xi Jinping referring to the space exploration as the "Space Dream", 航天梦 *hangtian meng*), and specific strategies, such as "Made in China 2025" (see Xinhuanet, 2017 and Institute for Security & Development Policy, 2018 respectively).

The cosmos is becoming a symbolic, but also a strategic area that is given more and more prominence in the political and media discourse, as well as to a certain extent – in the academic debate. Authors often refer to the Cold War space race, describing the current situation, in particular the Sino-American rivalry, as the space race 2.0. (see Chizea, Chichebe, and EseOghene, 2019; Drozhashchikh, 2019). Yet despite a number of similarities, most notably the implementation of ambitious space exploration programs, the present situation is fundamentally different. Understanding this difference is essential to comprehending the nature of Chinese involvement in space and – in a broader context – the dynamics of the evolution of the contemporary international order, including the significant role of China in shaping it.

This chapter aims to prove that although the actions of the fifth generation of leaders did not inaugurate the Chinese space program, they still represent a completely new quality, motivated by various premises. Benefits in the fields of economy and security remain the most important reasons for running China's space exploration program, but they are meant to be achieved in a significantly different dimension than during the Cold War. China's role in the new competition differs as well. By drawing on the methodology used in political science research, mainly discourse analysis, supported by qualitative content analysis of selected documents, political manifestos and reports prepared by think tanks, as well as quantitative analysis of statistical data, the authors aim to present how PRC decision-makers treat space competition, why they engage in it, and what their goals and strategies are to achieve the latter. An important research problem is also to identify the challenges to the Chinese space program, including the plans and potential of Beijing's strategic rivals.

The 70th anniversary of the proclamation of the People's Republic of China celebrated on 1 October 2019 seems to have been a significant turning point for China's development, including its space program. Currently, rivalry in space is another arena of competition between great powers, primarily – but not only – the US and the PRC. Although the possibility of escalation has been already mentioned at the very beginning of the 21st century (Martel and Yoshihara, 2003: 19), a new impetus came first after China's successful launch of an antisatellite system in 2007 (the consequences of this have been often called a "space tsunami", Lele, 2013: 22) and then after the implementation of Xi Jinping's foreign policy strategy in the post-2013 period. As both dates are related to unilateral Chinese actions which have serious global implications, referring to Chinese sources is of great importance for the analysis. Supplementing the analysis with the aforementioned comparative element will enable the authors to draw conclusions about the nature and future of the Chinese space program as well as about the broader aspects of China's status in the global arena.

1 China and the Conquest of Space – Historical Context and Selected Milestones

The launch of Sputnik 1 – the Earth's first artificial satellite – on 4 October 1957, followed by sending Explorer 1 into the orbit on 31 January 1958, is considered an event that started a long-lasting competition for domination in space (Seedhouse, 2010: xiii). The so-called Space Race was dominated by actions undertaken by the United States and the Soviet Union, and the struggle for space supremacy was in line with the dynamics of Cold War rivalry. At that time countries such as South Korea, Singapore, India and Israel were also working intensively on developing relevant technologies, but their progress could not be compared to the achievements of Japan during that period (Lele, 2013: 13).

The government of the PRC has also worked on the implementation of development programs, but "the international media's attention to China's space program has been sporadic and sometimes patronizing" (Seedhouse, 2010: xiii). In fact, China joined the space race from the very beginning, and while the country did not have sufficient potential to play a significant role in the Cold War power rivalry, its commitment and achievements should not be overlooked. The history of China's space program provides an interesting case study of a transition country where ambitions are confronted with opportunities. The structure of this chapter makes it impossible to present in detail all stages of the Chinese space program, so it focuses only on selected events of symbolic and/or strategic significance. More information on these issues can be found in the works cited in this semi-chapter.

The inauguration of the Chinese space program in the 1950s was directly influenced by the country's ties with the Soviet Union. The symbolic beginning of the program was the appointment of renowned engineer and scientist Qian

Xuesen[3] as the head of the Fifth Academy of Ministry of Defense (established in 1956), after his return from the US (Drozhashchikh, 2018: 176). According to the strategy implemented by the country's leader Mao Zedong, scientists were to focus on two programs that were both strategic and prestigious – developing satellite launching technology and working on missile capability. With technical assistance from the Soviet Union, China's first satellite was successfully launched in 1970. After tests of ballistic missiles Dong Feng-2 and Dong Feng-3, the progress achieved with Dong Feng-4 was used to construct Chang Zheng-1 carrier rocket, which placed the communication satellite Dong Fang Hong-1 on the orbit (Drozhashchikh, 2018: 176).

According to Roger Handberg, prior to the successful demonstration of the capability to launch ballistic missiles in the late 1960s, China "did not truly have a space program" (Handberg, 2012: 251). Despite the achievement of the assumed strategic goals, subordinated to developing technologies for the production and delivery of weapons of mass destruction, the first decades of the Chinese nuclear program are characterized by stagnation. The reasons for this state of affairs should be ascribed not so much to the lack of appropriate financing as to political perturbations and relative technological underdevelopment (Drozhashchikh, 2018: 176; Handberg, 2012: 250).

A significant increase in the pace of the development of the PRC's space program can be associated with the implementation of Deng Xiaoping's Reform and Opening-Up (改革开放 *gaige kaifang*). In the following years China intensified its activities related to launching communication satellites used for military purposes. The country also worked on preparing its first manned space mission. The goal was accomplished in 2003 (Shenzhou V), based on experiences gained from launching unmanned spacecrafts: Shenzhou I (1999), Shenzhou II (2001) and Shenzhou III (2002) (Goswami, 2018: 76; People's Daily Online, 2003a, 2003b as cited in Goswami, 2018: 76). The success of Shenzhou V's mission secured China's status as the third nation that managed to send an astronaut into the Earth's orbit. Considering the uniqueness of the event, China joining the group of world pioneers of cosmonautics can be regarded as a milestone in human history. Some scholars see the accomplishment "as the event that launched a new space race" (Seedhouse, 2010: XII).

---

3   As he is considered "the father of China's space program", Qian Xuesen's extraordinary curriculum places him as one of the most accomplished aerospace engineers in the world's history, a man who not only contributed to the development of China's space program, but also – prior to leaving the United States in 1955 – to American nuclear weapon program (e.g., by his involvement in the Manhattan Project during World War II). For more about Qian Xuesen, his accomplishments and place in Chinese history, see: Wang, 2011.

On 11 January 2007 China conducted an anti-satellite missile (ASAT) test. By successfully destroying its own weather satellite, the PRC became the third country (besides the US and Russia) to have such capabilities (Awan and Javaid, 2020: 89). The repercussions of that event were serious and led to a change in the nature of the actors' involvement in space competition. While recognizing the successful ASAT test as the start of a new space race is debatable, as is granting such status to the launch of a manned spacecraft in 2003, the event can be regarded as one that led to weaponization of space and as a turn to a military-led direction (Banarjee, 2008 as cited in Moltz, 2011b: 35). The 2010s witnessed other important milestones of the Chinese space program, e.g., orbiting unmanned spacecraft around the Moon, landing a rover on the Moon's surface (both in 2010); testing the exoatmospheric vehicle Dong Neng-3, designed to ram and destroy satellites (2015); launching space labs Tiangong 1 and Tiangong 2 (2011 and 2016, respectively); and building Tianzhou cargo spacecraft "capable of on-orbit refueling that extends access and logistics lines" (Goswami, 2018: 76).

Handberg proposed an interesting division of Chinese space policy and strategy into four separate phases: 1. association of space with the military; 2. economic and technological development (starting with the ascension of Deng Xiaoping as the PRC's leader in 1977); 3. movement toward normalization (starting with the later stages of Deng's leadership); 4. normalcy (post-2003 period associated with the definition of the goals of the Chinese space program and its significance for China's international position, as set out in the pages of a series of white papers on space policy) (Handberg, 2012: 250–258). The distinction between the above-mentioned stages allows accurate presentation of the evolving approach of the PRC authorities to the competition in space, and illustrates the dynamics of involvement in space exploration projects.

2   Space Race 2.0?

In the context of the nature and evolution of the Chinese space program, especially during the 2010s, it is worth commenting on the validity of using the term "Space Race 2.0". Although the very meaning of the concept is intuitively understood as the comparison of the contemporary space rivalry between China and the United States with the US-Soviet Union Cold War rivalry, doubts arise as to how legitimate it is to compare both situations. James Clay Moltz undermines the legitimacy of the "2.0" indicator, pointing to the fact that the present situation is quite different. Firstly, rather than bipolar, the current international system involves interactions of multiple great powers;

secondly, unlike during the Cold War period, the current military threats are not restrained by any arms-control process; thirdly, thanks to globalization, contemporary states have much closer ties to each other (political, economic, cultural, etc.) than in the past decades; and finally, over the last 50 years there has been a significant increase in scientific knowledge regarding the implications of potential rivalry in space (Moltz, 2011b: 13–14).

Similar doubts can be raised while analyzing the term "space race". Even though it is widely used in political, media and academic circles, citing it without being aware of the differences between the Cold War and the contemporary reality might lead to misunderstandings. John M. Logsdon – one of the most persistent opponents of calling the Sino-American rivalry a "new space race" – rightly notes that unlike the Cold War competition, "[i]t is not driven by schedule or deadlines or by seeking a specific goal. Rather, it is an ongoing, high-stakes competition for space achievements and innovative approaches to accomplishing them. Both countries are setting out space plans that reflect their own interests and aspirations rather than the quest to be the 'first'" (Logsdon, 2019). Furthermore, the clear division into two hostile blocks, established during the Cold War, is unlike the present situation. It is true that Sino-American rivalry has been gaining momentum as the 2010s have progressed, yet it is also true that the intensity of rivalry decreases markedly when we consider rather developmentally-oriented countries such as Malaysia or Thailand (Moltz, 2011b: 7). There is a group of the so-called "uninvolved" states that have different aspirations, and – unlike during the original space race – they have not been forced to pick one side of the ongoing competition among superpowers. As the decades passed, the center of gravity of the space competition has shifted markedly. It is significant that in the new configuration the place of the Soviet Union as the main opponent of American leadership was taken by China – an Asian power. Compared with the Western world, Asian countries have achieved much greater progress in their space programs within a relatively short time. China, Japan, India and South Korea remain leaders in this regard, but the ambitions and achievements of countries such as Malaysia, Indonesia, the Philippines, Thailand, North Korea, Pakistan and Vietnam also deserve attention (Moltz, 2011b: 14–15).

As John Hickman points out, some see the fact that the United States won the "only possible" space race with the Apollo program as an argument strong enough to deny that the US and China are currently involved in the space race (see a quote from Bernice Johnson in Foust, 2019 as cited in Hickman, 2019: 179). He also denies the allegations that the two rivalries are of a different nature, arguing that the events of the future cannot fully repeat those that occurred in the past. According to Hickman, "[j]ust as no two arms races or humanitarian crises need to be alike in intensity to bear their categorical designations, so too space races need not be alike in their goals or intensity to be called space races" (Hickman, 2019: 179).

The above-formulated thesis is justified at the level of political manifestos, which are inherent elements of political practice. This allows to conclude that although the rivalry in the compared periods differs in many respects, the fact of its occurrence remains the same. In this context, the analysis of Chinese political discourse is particularly interesting as it allows tracing how the approach of decision-makers to competition in space has been changing. Currently, competitive rhetoric appears, inter alia, in the statements of the management of the China National Space Administration (CNSA), while further development goals were presented, for example, by its Director Zhang Kejian in 2019 (Yurou, 2019 and David, 2019 as cited in Hickman, 2019: 179).

3   China's Perception of Space and Main Reasons for Engagement in the Space Conquest

As already mentioned, the Chinese space program was launched in the 1950s with three basic goals: ensuring the economic development of the country, expanding the potential of the defense sector and – related to the first two elements – strengthening the national potential and indigenous capabilities (Wu, 2008 as cited in Awan and Javaid, 2020: 94). Implementation of each of those elements was significantly influenced by the PRC joining the space competition relatively late, with "joining" understood not in the declarative aspect, but as a consistent pursuit of the set goals. This enabled China – like other latecomers to the space program – to use a number of ready-made technological solutions developed during the Cold War. The latecomers were able to skip first-generation systems and focus on working to achieve capabilities not seen in the US-Soviet rivalry (Moltz, 2011b: 24). This fact played an important role both in China's decision to join the Cold War space rivalry (facilitated by close ties with the Soviet Union) and in the pursuit of Beijing's international ambitions after the collapse of the bipolar system (drawing on ready-made solutions).

Due to close ties among state institutions, the implementation of the space program is extremely important also for the functioning of the People's Liberation Army. In the face of the decreasing potential difference between the two main actors – the current superpower and the power contending its status – the issue of economic and technological potential takes on a new meaning compared to the Cold War situation. The strategic Sino-American rivalry in the 2010s has been gradually increasing in intensity, which is not without significance for the Chinese perception of national, regional and global security.[4] The reasons for current Chinese involvement in space competition have been aptly presented by Wang Xiji, the designer of the space launch vehicle Chinese Long March (Chang Zheng). According to Wang, "if it [China – M.D.] did not act quickly, other countries, in particular the US and Japan, would take the lead and occupy strategically important locations in space" (Chen, 2011 as cited in Goswami, 2018: 77). In other words, it seems that Chinese participation in space rivalry is not so much a question of ambition as a necessity in the pursuit of the national interest. The involvement seems difficult to avoid also in the context of progressive militarization of outer space, which is considered a novelty in international relations, with consequences that are difficult to predict.[5]

Significant factors supporting Chinese space ambitions are the hard-to-measure elements that make up Chinese soft power. While the importance of these factors should not be overstated, they appear frequently in Chinese political manifestos as well as – though to a lesser extent – official documents. Examples that illustrate the role of symbolism accompanying the implementation of space strategy are the naming of national technological achievements (e.g., already mentioned Long March rockets that refer to an important historical event from the Chinese Civil War period) and locating infrastructure (e.g., establishing one of the centers for storing lunar samples in Shaoshan, Mao Zedong's hometown) (Xinhuanet, 2019b). Aside from the obvious benefits that successes in high-tech rivalry have for China's international image, they can also be used to promote China's development model, including "socialism with Chinese characteristics" (中国特色社会主义 *Zhongguo tese shehuizhuyi*) (Drozhashchikh, 2018: 184; Lewis, 2018).

The intensification of China's efforts to gain a space advantage has been strongly endorsed by the country's leadership. A more specific version of the Chinese "Space Dream" is "the dream of space flight" (飞天梦 *feitian meng*), intended by Xi Jinping to enable "realizing the Chinese people's mighty dream of national rejuvenation" (Zhongguo Xinwen Wang, 2013 and Hangtian meng yu Zhongguo meng, 2013 as cited in Pollpeter et al., 2015: 7).[6] Xi's statements

---

4   Discussions about the inevitability of a confrontation with the United States began in China after the 2008 financial crisis, taking a new turn after the Barack Obama administration's inauguration of the "Pivot to Asia" strategy in 2011 and following foreign policy actions undertaken by Donald Trump's administration (Zhao, 2019: 393).
5   For more about the militarization of space, see Anantatmula, 2013.
6   An interesting evidence of the importance of the space for the country's long-term development is declaring April 24 as "Space Day". Celebrated since 2016, Space Day is considered "a window for the Chinese public and the world to get a better understanding of China's aerospace progress"(Xinhuanet, 2019a).

are based on a strong belief that the development of the high-tech sector is crucial for the development of China itself. The ability to effectively influence space is not only an expression of the country's technological advancement but also a stimulator of its economic, scientific and military potential, which in turn translates into real opportunities to strengthen the national power (Wu, 2013 as cited in Pollpeter et al., 2015: 7).

In the case of the space program, the relatively general program slogans of the Chinese political leadership were substantiated in the subsequent white papers on China's space activities. Each consecutive report (e.g., from 2001, 2006 and 2011) includes a section dedicated to the vision of Chinese involvement in space. The most recent white paper on China's space activities was published by the Information Office of the State Council on 27 December 2016. Before presenting four general principles of the PRC's space industry development (innovative, coordinated, peaceful, and open), the document states that the main goals of the country's space activity are:

> To build China into a space power in all respects, with the capabilities to make innovations independently, to make scientific discovery and research at the cutting edge, to promote strong and sustained economic and social development, to effectively and reliably guarantee national security, to exercise sound and efficient governance, and to carry out mutually beneficial international exchanges and cooperation; to have an advanced and open space science and technology industry, stable and reliable space infrastructure, pioneering and innovative professionals, and a rich and profound space spirit; to provide strong support for the realization of the Chinese Dream of the renewal of the Chinese nation, and make positive contributions to human civilization and progress.
> THE STATE COUNCIL OF THE PEOPLE'S REPUBLIC OF CHINA, 2016

More realistic and less wishful interpretations of space rivalry goals are usually presented in the defense white papers. To provide an example, China's 2015 Defense White Paper directly emphasizes the aspects of rivalry, portraying the space as "commanding height in international strategic competition" (People's Republic of China Information Office of the State Council, 2015 as cited in Cordesman, 2016: 3). This concept has been detailed in the latest defense strategy of July 2019. "Safeguarding Interests in Major Security Fields" (including outer space) has been identified as one of the missions of China's military in the new era. According to the PRC's leadership,

> Outer space is a critical domain in international strategic competition. Outer space security provides strategic assurance for national and social development. In the interest of the peaceful use of outer space, China actively participates in international space cooperation, develops relevant technologies and capabilities, advances holistic management of space-based information resources, strengthens space situation awareness, safeguards space assets, and enhances the capacity to safely enter, exit and openly use outer space.
>
> THE STATE COUNCIL INFORMATION OFFICE OF THE PEOPLE'S REPUBLIC OF CHINA, 2019

The narrative presented in the document is a response to the change in the directions of American foreign policy expressed in American documents on security and defense (2017 and 2018, respectively). In the eyes of Chinese decision-makers, Beijing's actions in the international arena do not pose a threat to the world order; on the contrary, they can be portrayed as just and peaceful. Similarly, activities carried out by the PRC in space, which is recognized as one of the areas of international strategic competition that are threatened by Washington's unilateral actions, also fulfill criteria of peaceful policies. On the other hand, the US has been presented as an "aggressive power" (Cordesman, 2019).

4 China's Space Technologies and Programs

Ajey Lele proposes a list of major programs that have laid a foundation for the development of China's science & technology infrastructure, including the capacity for space exploration. These programs include:

- National High-Tech R&D Development Program (National 863 Program; 国家高技术研究发展计划 *Guojia gao jishu yanjiu fazhan jihua*) – established in 1986, aimed at promoting and stimulating the development of advanced technologies;
- Program 211 (211 工程 *eryaoyao gongcheng*) – established in 1995, aimed at strengthening the excellence of domestic universities in colleges, with the priority given to institutions contributing towards the development of key disciplines;
- National Basic Research Program of China (National 973 Program; 国家重点基础研究发展计划 *Guojia zhongdian jichu yanjiu fazhan jihua*) – established in 1997, aimed at developing basic research and fostering outstanding scientists;

- National Key Technologies R&D Program (国家重点技术研发计划 *Guojia zhongdian jishu yanfa jihua*) – established in 2014, aimed at providing support to research and development, for example, in areas of sustainable development, people's livelihood, agriculture and energy (60 years of progress in Science and Technology, n.d. as cited in: Lele, 2013: 16).

A particular feature of the Chinese space program is that it contributes to political, economic, and even social and cultural areas. The main categories of Beijing's space activities, as classified by Dennis C. Shea, are: 1. Launching services and export of satellites; 2. Development of technologies that allow satellite application; 3. Human spaceflight; 4. Exploration of space; and 5. International efforts for space cooperation (Shea, 2016: 3). Just listing the areas of technological involvement makes it impossible to position China against the entities participating in the space competition for which the indicated areas may be formulated in a similar way. Only the analysis of specific programs, both those implemented over the past decades and those still being implemented, offers a chance to evaluate the achievements of Chinese space research. In a report prepared for the US-China Economic and Security Review Commission, the following areas/projects were named as achievements of PRC's space development: human spaceflights (missions of Shenzhou and Tiangong spacecraft), Shenzhou Space Capsule, Tiangong-1 Space Station, long-term space station, lunar exploration program (Chang'e spacecraft), manned lunar missions, Mars exploration project, Earth remote sensing (satellites Gaofen, Yaogan, Haiyang, Huanjing, Tianhui, Ziyuan, and Fengyun), satellite navigation, communication satellites, launch vehicles (e.g., Long March), and counterspace technologies (Pollpeter et al., 2015: 45–93).

The volume of this chapter does not allow for a precise description of each of the programs mentioned above. It is worth noting, however, that each of them is a serious contribution to the development of Chinese (and not only Chinese) space research, as evidenced by the fact that it was listed in a report prepared by an American institution. The public interest is especially aroused by the most ambitious, pioneering projects that could change the nature of space competition. These certainly include projects such as shuttles powered by nuclear energy (by 2040, enabling mining space-based resources), reusable launch vehicles (by 2035), establishing a manned space station (by 2020–2022), establishing a space solar power station (by 2050), and landing on Mars (Goswami, 2018: 76; Tian, 2017 and People's Daily Online, 2017 as cited in Goswami, 2018: 76). Regarding the latter, on 23 July 2020 a Chinese Long March-5 rocket launched successfully from Hainan island, beginning Tianwen-1 mission, the country's first attempt to land on the Red Planet (Mallapaty, 2020). The craft's arrival at the destination in May 2021 has positioned China as the third country to successfully execute a soft landing on Mars.

The analysis of programs implemented by China as part of space exploration allows defining several features that characterize the contemporary, post-Cold War strategy of the PRC towards space. These elements include concentrated effort (prioritization, indigenous research), methodological approach (long-term, deliberate goals), civil-military integration, and lack of transparency (Shea, 2016: 1–2). They make up the Chinese *sui generis* system, which has the potential to redefine the nature of space competition, instead of merely reacting to the actions of other participants of the rivalry, primarily the US.

5   Challenges to the Success of China's Space Program

Despite the ambitious design of Chinese space program, there are many factors that can disrupt or prevent their implementation, also in a relatively short term. Firstly, it is not certain whether China (as well as other players in the space competition) will be able to maintain the pace of implementing new solutions. In this context, the pressure to increase spending on armaments may prove problematic, while the state budget must enable China to respond to challenges related to social problems or supporting entrepreneurship (Moltz, 2011b: 6). It may turn out that in the face of the post-pandemic recovery, the budget of the Chinese space program will be reduced, which may – but does not have to – affect Beijing's competitiveness in comparison to the American program.

Secondly, it should be noted that although the Chinese side does not publish the full data on the space program budget, it is estimated to be much smaller than the budget allocated by Americans. For example, in the years 2015–2016, the value of Chinese and American annual expenditures remained at 1:3 ratio of approximately USD 6 billion to USD 18.5 billion, respectively (Hunt and McKenzie, 2015, NASA FY 2016 Budget Request, n.d. as cited in Goswami, 2018: 77). On the other hand, the Chinese side compensates for lower expenses with labor force that is much cheaper than in the United States and with lower costs of services (related to the institutional foundation of the program) (Goswami, 2018: 77). Taking into account the dynamic development of the Chinese economy, it is difficult to predict how long the above-mentioned advantage will persist.

Thirdly, it is unclear what form the competition for influence in outer space will take. Will there be two hostile camps in the long run, comparable to the Cold War rivalry, or will the spheres of influence be outlined in a completely different way? Is "cooperative exploration" of outer space possible, based on the mechanisms of globalization and the desire to ensure the welfare of societies, or does international rivalry have such a high escalating potential that its peaceful regulation is unlikely? (Moltz, 2011b: 6). One should also not exclude a scenario in which the competition will escalate to such an extent that it will lead to an actual arms race, which may result in a global conflict. The observed progressive militarization of space and the nature of the Sino-American rivalry in other areas (including diplomatic and economic) makes the above thesis more and more probable (Anantatmula, 2013; Campbell and Sullivan, 2019).

Another challenge to the success of China's space program is the presence and behavior of other actors in the competition. In the bipolar period the identification of countries participating in the space race was simple; nowadays, according to various criteria, more than 35 countries have the possibilities of effectively influencing space (Awan and Javaid, 2020: 97). However, capabilities to independently launch spacecrafts have so far been achieved by nine states: China, India, Iran, Israel, Japan, North Korea, Russia, South Korea and the US, as well as by the European Space Agency (US Department of Defense, 2018). On the one hand, this may accelerate the integration processes and provide China certain benefits, including cooperation with countries with developed, developing, or limited space capabilities. Besides tight cooperation with its most prominent partner Russia, Beijing has established cooperation through different frameworks, for example, with Iran, Peru, Pakistan, and Mongolia (Drozhashchikh, 2018: 182). Looking at specific programs, an example of a successful and beneficial cooperation for China is the export of satellites to countries such as Belarus, Bolivia, Laos, Nigeria, Pakistan, Sri Lanka and Venezuela (Pollpeter et al., 2015: 22).

On the other hand, the growing number of space competition participants may weaken the PRC's ability to project power. While the prospect of changing the nature of Sino-American relations in space from rivalry to constructive cooperation seems unlikely at present, the real threat to Beijing's national interest seems to be the increase in American potential consisting in the support of American initiatives by third states joining the rivalry. Depending on the development of the dynamics of space competition in the long term, India, Japan and South Korea, as well as Australia, may turn out to be China's adversaries with a significant potential. In the last case, the situation is interesting because the ambition of the Canberra authorities is only to build sovereign space capabilities, which makes Australia a potential market for already developed space technologies (see Davis, 2020; Moltz, 2011a; Prentice and Waite, 2020).

6   Summary and Conclusions

The space race, understood as competition for advantage in space, is not a new phenomenon and dates back to the Cold War rivalry between two powers. The space rivalry presented in this article involves a broader spectrum of entities, and the dynamics of their relationships are also different. Noting the significant progress that the PRC has made since joining the space competition, it should also be emphasized that Chinese participation in the competition is not free from challenges. While the success of China's space flight programs and ambitious plans to build a space station and explore Mars has led some analysts to a conclusion that "the rise of China's space program may represent the 'Sputnik shock' all over again" (Seedhouse, 2010: xiii) the actual situation seems much more complex.

Relations between countries involved in space rivalry constitute one of the least studied and, at the same time, one of the most dynamic problems of contemporary international relations. Back in 2013, Lele believed that there are "no definitive trends of immediate confrontations in space" (Lele, 2013: 3), and only a year earlier Handberg formulated a thesis about China's participation in space competition, according to which "essentially it is racing alone" (Handberg, 2012: 249). Several years later, Lele's assessment seems less unambiguous, while Handberg's comment is no longer true (though it was questionable from the very beginning). In his analysis Kevin Pollpeter stated that "[t]he emerging competition is characterized by an action-reaction dynamic in which both the United States and China are developing new operational concepts, establishing new organizations to lead space operations, investing in long-range ASMs, and developing operationally responsive capabilities to deny each other the use of space" (Pollpeter, 2017: 2). Although the author's diagnosis that Beijing and Washington use new operational concepts and implement new projects seems correct, the thesis about "action-reaction" seems doubtful. When analyzing the recent successes of Chinese cosmonautics, being a part of consistently implemented "Space Dream", one can get the impression that Beijing's actions are less and less responsive and increasingly proactive. The final confirmation of this thesis was, for example, the success of the Tianwen-1 mission. As it became a fact, Sino-US relations found themselves in a new phase, not only in the sphere of space exploration.

While the space program is neither the sole nor the most important component of China's superpowerhood, it is a significant area, both in terms of tangible economic benefits, security issues, and symbolism. Thanks to investments in technologies – implemented consistently over the years – the completion of the current programs may accelerate China's economic development and thus its promotion to the superpower status. While it is difficult to predict the directions of change in the nature of space competition, China's ambitions are likely to be fulfilled (cf. Cordesman, 2016: 3; Goswami, 2018: 90). Thanks to the system of international ties (much more extensive than during the Cold War), PRC's potential to influence international relations and their dynamics is significant. The success of the Chinese space program will not only affect the dynamics of modern space competition (rivalry rather than "space race 2.0"), but it will also significantly determine Beijing's position in the international arena.

References

60 years of progress in Science and Technology (n.d.), http://www.china.org.cn/china/60th science and technology/2009-9/11/content 18510361.htm.

Anantatmula, Vishnu (2013) US Initiative to Place Weapons in Space: The Catalyst for a Space-Based Arms Race with China and Russia. *Astropolitics. The International Journal of Space Politics & Policy,* 11(3), pp. 132–155.

Awan, Fazal Abbas and Umbreen Javaid (2020) Space Militarization Race among China-Russia and USA: Implications for South Asia. *A Research Journal of South Asian Studies,* 35(1), pp. 87–100.

Banarjee, Dipankar (2008) Indian Perspectives on Space Security. In: John M. Logsdon and James Clay Moltz (eds.) *Collective Security in Space: Asian Perspectives.* Washington, D.C.: Space Policy Institute, George Washington University, pp. 120–130.

Campbell, Kurt M. and Jake Sullivan (2019) Competition Without Catastrophe: How America Can Both Challenge and Coexist With China. *Foreign Affairs,* 1 August, https://www.foreignaffairs.com/articles/china/competition-with-china-without-catastrophe, accessed 2 February 2024.

Cao Fangjun (2009) Modernization Theory and China's Road to Modernization. *Chinese Studies in History,* 43(1), pp. 7–16.

Chen, Stephen (2011) China's Space Agency Looks to Capture Sun's Power, 3 September, http://billionyearplan.blogspot.com/2011/09/china-space-agency-looks-to-capture.html.

Chizea, Francis, Akachukwu Chichebe, and Ovie EseOghene (2019) Evolving Role of Space Actors: from Space race 1.0 to 2.0 and a Model for Developing Economies. *International Journal of Scientific & Engineering Research,* 10(6), pp. 149–153.

Cordesman, Anthony H. (2016) Chinese Space Strategy and Developments. *Center for Strategic & International Studies,* 19 August, https://www.csis.org/analysis/china-space-strategy-and-developments, accessed 2 February 2024.

Cordesman, Anthony H. (2019) China's New 2019 Defense White Paper. *Center for Strategic & International Studies,* 24 July, https://www.csis.org/analysis/chinas-new-2019-defense-white-paper, accessed 2 February 2024.

David, Leonard (2019) China Details Future Moon Plans, Including Polar Research Station. *Space.com,* 15 January, https://www.space.com/43000-china-moon-exploration-plans-research-base.html.

Davis, Malcolm (2020) The Dragon and Eagle meet in Space – Astropolitical Competition in the 21st Century, and Where Australia Sits. *Peer-reviewed Conference Paper US Naval War College and East Asia Security Centre Conference "Between Scylla and Charybdis: Is there a Middle Path for Middle Powers in the Indo-Pacific Region?",* https://easc.scholasticahq.com/article/14160.pdf, accessed 2 February 2024.

Deng Xiaoping (n.d.) Shanyu liyong shiji jingji jiejue fazhan wenti [Use World Economy to Solve Development Problems]. In: *Selected Works of Deng Xiaoping-Volume 3,* pp. n.d.

Drozhashchikh, Evgeniia (2018) China's National Space Program and the "China Dream". *Astropolitics,* 16(3), pp. 175–186.

Drozhashchikh, Evgeniia (2019) Space Race 2.0. Shifting to Asia. *Religiski-filozofiski raksti,* XXVI(2), pp. 258–281.

Foust, Jeff (2019) House Committee Presses Bridenstine for Details on Moon Plan. *The Space Review,* 2 April.

Goswami, Namrata (2018) China in Space: Ambitions and Possible Conflict. *Strategic Studies Quarterly,* 12(1), pp. 74–97.

Hameiri, Shahar and Lee Jones (2015) Rising powers and state transformation: The case of China. *European Journal of International Relations,* 22(1), pp. 72–98.

Handberg, Roger (2012) China's space strategy and policy evolution. In: Eligar Sadeh (ed.) *Space Strategy in the 21st Century: Theory and Policy.* London–New York: Routledge, pp. 249–262.

Hangtian meng yu Zhongguo meng [The Space Dream and the China Dream] (2013). *Zhongguo Hangtian Bao* [*China Space News*], July 31, pp. n.d.

Hickman, John (2019) Research Viewpoint: International Relations and the Second Space Race Between the United States and China. *Astropolitics,* 17(3), pp. 178–190.

Hunt, Katie and David McKenzie (2015) China: The Next Space Super Power? *CNN,* May, http://edition.cnn.com/interactive/2015/05/world/china-space/.

Institute for Security & Development Policy (2018) Made in China 2025, June, https://isdp.eu/content/uploads/2018/06/Made-in-China-Backgrounder.pdf, accessed 2 February 2024.

Lele, Ajey (2013) *Asian Space Race: Rhetoric or Reality?* Heidelberg–New York–Dordrecht–London: Springer.

Lewis, James Andrew (2018) Technological Competition and China. *Center for Strategic & International Studies,* 30 November, https://www.csis.org/analysis/technological-competition-and-china, accessed 2 February 2024.

Logsdon, John M. (2019) There is no space race. *Aerospace America,* April, https://aerospaceamerica.aiaa.org/departments/there-is-no-space-race/, accessed 2 February 2024.

Mallapaty, Smriti (2020) China's successful launch of Mars mission seals global era in deep-space exploration. *Nature,* 23 July, https://www.nature.com/articles/d41586-020-02187-7, accessed 2 February 2024.

Martel, William C. and Toshi Yoshihara (2003) Averting a Sino-US space race. *The Washington Quarterly,* 26(4), pp. 19–35.

Masood, Ehsan (2019) All roads lead to China. China's modern-day silk routes are reshaping science around the globe. *Nature,* 569, pp. 20–23.

Moltz, James Clay (2011a) Asia's space race. *Nature,* 480, pp. 171–173.

Moltz, James Clay (2011b) *Asia's Space Race. National Motivations, Regional Rivalries, and International Risks.* New York: Columbia University Press.

NASA FY 2016 Budget Request (n.d.) *NASA.gov,* https://www.nasa.gov/sites/default/files/files/Agency_Fact_Sheet_FY_2016.pdf.

People's Daily Online (2003a) China's Four Unmanned Spaceflights, 12 October, http://en.people.cn/200310/12/print20031012_125814.html.

People's Daily Online (2003b) China Successfully Launches its First Manned Spacecraft, 16 October, http://en.people.cn/200310/15/eng20031015_126043.shtml.

People's Daily Online (2017) China to Achieve 'Major Breakthrough' in Nuclear-Powered Space Shuttle Around 2040: Report, 17 November, http://en.people.cn/n3/2017/1117/c90000-9293719.html.

People's Republic of China Information Office of the State Council (2015) China's Military Strategy. *Xinhua,* 26 May, http://eng.mod.gov.cn/DefenseNews/2015-05/26/content_4586748.htm.

Pollpeter, Kevin (2017) The US-China Reconnaissance-Strike Competition: Anti-Ship Missiles. Space, and Counterspace. *The Study of Innovation and Technology in China Research Brief,* https://ideas.repec.org/p/cdl/globco/qt4s99s9rs.html, accessed 2 February 2024.

Pollpeter, Kevin, Eric Anderson, Jordan Wilson, and Fan Yang (2015) China Dream, Space Dream. China's Progress in Space Technologies and Implications for the United States. *US-China Economic and Security Review Commission,* 2 March, https://www.uscc.gov/research/china-dream-space-dream-chinas-progress-space-technologies-and-implications-united-states, accessed 2 February 2024.

Prentice, Paul and Nathan Waite (2020) Combining Competition and Cooperation: A Guide to US Space Relations. *Liberty University Journal of Statesmanship & Public Policy,* 1(1), Article 6, pp. 1–8.

Pu Xiaoyu (2017) Controversial Identity of a Rising China. *The Chinese Journal of International Politics*, 10(2), pp. 131–149.

Seedhouse, Erik (2010) *The New Space Race: China vs. the United States*. Berlin–Heidelberg–New York: Springer (in association with Praxis Publishing).

Shea, Dennis C. (2016) Testimony before the House Space, Science, and Technology Committee, Subcommittee on Space Hearing on "Are We Losing the Space Race to China?". *US–China Economic and Security Review Commission*, 27 September, https://www.uscc.gov/sites/default/files/Shea_House%20Space,%20Science,%20 and%20Technology%20Committee%20Testimony_092716.pdf, accessed 2 February 2024.

The State Council of the People's Republic of China (2016) Full text of white paper on China's space activities in 2016, updated: 28 December, http://english.www.gov.cn/archive/white_paper/2016/12/28/content_281475527159496.htm, accessed 2 February 2024.

The State Council Information Office of the People's Republic of China (2019) *China's National Defense in the New Era*. Beijing: Foreign Languages Press, http://english.scio.gov.cn/node_8013506.html, accessed 2 February 2024.

Tian He (2017) China Sees 'Breakthrough' in Nuclear-Powered Space Shuttles by 2040. *Global Times*, 17 November, http://www.globaltimes.cn/content/1075834.shtml.

US Department of Defense (2018) Competing in Space. *National Air and Space Intelligence Center*, December, https://media.defense.gov/2019/Jan/16/2002080 386/-1/-1/1/190115-F-NV711-0002.PDF, accessed 2 February 2024.

Wang Ning (2011) The Making of an Intellectual Hero: Chinese Narratives of Qian Xuesen. *The China Quarterly*, 206, pp. 352–371.

Wu Chunsi (2008) China's Outer Space Activities: Motivations, Goals and Policy. *Strategic Analysis*, 32(4), pp. 621–636.

Wu Weiqiang (2013) Qiantan Hangtian Qiangguo Pingjia Tixi Yanjiu [A Brief Discussion on Research on the Analysis of Strong Space Power Evaluation System]. *Hangtian Gongye Guanli [Space Industry Management]*, 3, pp. n.d.

Xinhuanet (2017) Backgrounder: Xi Jinping's vision for China's space development, 24 April, http://www.xinhuanet.com/english/2017-04/24/c_136232642.htm, accessed 2 February 2024.

Xinhuanet (2019a) China marks Space Day, 24 April, http://www.xinhuanet.com/english/2019-04/24/c_138005949_2.htm, accessed 2 February 2024.

Xinhuanet (2019b) China to build scientific research station on Moon's south pole, 24 April, http://www.xinhuanet.com/english/2019-04/24/c_138004666.htm, accessed 2 February 2024.

Yurou (ed.) (2019) China to Build Scientific Research Station on Moon's South Pole. *Xinhua*, 24 April, http://www.xinhuanet.com/english/2019-04/24/c_138004666.htm.

Zhao Minghao (2019) Is a New Cold War Inevitable? Chinese Perspectives on US–China Strategic Competition. *The Chinese Journal of International Politics,* 12(3), pp. 371–394.

Zhongguo Xinwen Wang (2013) "Xi Jinping" tian di tonghua "jidong Zhongguo feitian meng" [Xi Jinping: 'Space to Earth Communications' Encourages China's Dream of Spaceflight], 25 June, http://www.chinanews.com/gj/2013/06-25/4964690.shtml.

CHAPTER 20

China's Rise to the Global Sports Power

Vic Yu Wai Li and Marcus P. Chu

1   Introduction

Since Xi Jinping took the helm of the Communist Party of China (CPC) in November 2012 (and became China's president in March 2013), he has articulated his vision of transforming China into a moderately prosperous society (小康社会 *xiaokang shehui*) and intertwined it with his 'China Dream' (中国梦 *Zhongguo Meng*) of bringing about a great renewal of the Chinse nation.

A sports enthusiast himself, Xi Jinping has paid particular attention to China's sporting development. Early on in his first administration, sports development was elevated to an important domestic and foreign policy agenda item that has driven the country's ambition of becoming a 'strong sports power' (体育强国 *tiyu qiangguo*) (Qiushi, 2021). The government stepped up efforts to promote sporting activities amongst the public and reform the country's training for professional athletes. This was crucial to sustaining the leading performances of Chinese athletes in international sporting competitions (Chen, 2018). Xi's administration has also been determined to build on the experience of successfully bidding for and hosting the 2008 Olympics and establish China as a hub of global sports events.

There are notable evidences of these endeavors. China has won the hosting rights for a dozen major international sporting events in less than a decade, breaking the records of every previous administration and achieving what no other country could easily manage. We analyze this enviable trend in this chapter and argue that China's remarkable activism in bidding for and hosting international sporting events has been driven by several motives and has been shaped by Xi's evolving domestic and foreign policy agendas.

For China as a nation, successfully bidding for global sporting events is seen as reinforcing the perception that the nation is on the way to becoming a leading power. This would be testimonials to the actualization of Xi's encompassing vision of steering China toward 'national rejuvenation' (中华民族伟大复兴 *Zhonghua Minzu Weida Fuxing*), which help reinforce the legitimacy of Xi as CPC and China's supreme leader, and burnish Xi's image as the most powerful leader of a global rising power (Shambaugh, 2021).

Preparing for and hosting sporting events also affords invaluable opportunities for Beijing to promote China's leadership status within Asia. China has attempted to win the hearts and minds of both athletes and professional organizations – a major pillar of the country's cultural diplomacy through not just people-to-people exchanges during the preparations and hosting of sporting games, but also by inviting foreign media organizations to cover the events and broadcasting stories via China's international media network that has grown considerable in scale since the 2010s (Preuss and Alfs, 2011; Kalathil, 2017). All these, Beijing believed, would help foster the nation's soft power in the region.

Bidding for international sporting games has also served important domestic political and economic goals of Xi's regime. By using the processes associated with bidding for and hosting sporting games, Beijing has attempted to undermine the international standing of Taiwan and consolidated the central government's control over local authorities. China's quests to stage global sporting events are also derivatives of Xi's enthusiasm for sporting games.

We illustrate these considerations of Xi's administration across multiple bidding episodes. The bids for the 2022 Winter Olympics and two other international sporting events are indicative of Beijing's pursuit of national rejuvenation and projection of a strongman image of Xi at home and worldwide. The success of bringing three Asian multi-sports games to China in the early 2020s was linked to the quest for regional leadership by the Xi's administrations. China's quest for the 2020 Summer Gymnasiade reveals how bidding for sporting events was used against the Taiwanese authorities. Xi's preponderance over local authorities is illustrated by the successive bids of Chengdu, the provincial capital of Sichuan, for three sets of games in 2018. Finally, the 'Football Dream' (足球梦 *Zuqiu Meng*) of Xi is evidenced in China's bids for two international football tournaments in 2019 that would pave the way for a future bid to host the World Cup.

2   National Rejuvenation and Regime legitimacy

As Xi Jinping completed his take-over of the CPC and the Chinese state in March 2013, he swiftly centralized his grip of the Party leadership lineup and the military through personnel reshuffling and nationwide anti-corruption campaigning. He also took more proactive foreign policy initiatives and championed the Belt and Road Initiative (BRI), an integral part of which involved capitalizing on global sporting events as platforms for promoting cultural changes between China and the Belt and Road countries (Singh and Winter, 2019).

These diverse initiatives did more than strengthen Xi's standing within China and the wider world. They were also meant to demonstrate that Xi Jinping was capable of driving China toward national rejuvenation. Given the appeal and reach of global sporting games to both domestic and international audiences and the extensive experience China has acquired in bidding for and staging global sporting games such as the Olympics, the Xi administration regarded hosting international sporting games to be a principal element that would vividly display China's rising prowess and help boost Xi Jinping's legitimacy and standing within the Chinese party-state. These considerations were behind Xi's government's biddings for the 2022 Winter Olympics, the 2019 International Basketball Association (FIBA) World Cup, and the 2019 Military World Games.

Among the three, successful bid for the Winter Olympic Games was particularly important, since this would make Beijing the only city in the world to stage both the summer (2008, Beijing) and winter editions of the Olympics (China Global Television Network, 2021). In November 2013, the Beijing municipal government unveiled its intention to bid for the 2022 Winter Olympics together with Zhangjiakou, a city bordering the capital. Almaty of Kazakhstan, Lviv of Ukraine, Oslo of Norway, Stockholm of Sweden, and Cracow of Poland all submitted their own applications to the International Olympic Committee (IOC). The Chinese media, however, was skeptical of Beijing's chances of winning the bid and considered that the city would be more ready for the contest to host the 2026 Winter Games due to the lack of experience of staging winter sport events, the low popularity of winter sports in China and the uncertain supply of natural snow and poor air quality in the Beijing area (Beijing Youth Daily, 2013; Liaoning Daily, 2013; Nanjing Daily, 2013). The IOC also appeared reluctant to grant the hosting rights of two consecutive Winter Olympics to East Asian countries, after Pyeongchang, South Korea, had won the 2018 Winter Olympics hosting right.

However, these disadvantages did little to dissuade Beijing and Zhangjiakou's pursuit of the 2022 Winter Games given Xi and his administration's support behind the bid and determination to boost its sense of national greatness by bringing the Winter Olympics to China. In view of the earlier defeat of Harbin to bid for the 2010 Winter Olympics under the Jiang Zemin administration in 2002, Xi regarded the victory of Beijing over the aspiring European cities in the bidding contest of the 2022 games under his leadership as an important way to show that his administration was more competent than the previous governments. A successful 2022 Winter Olympics would also be a symbolic milestone that coincided with Xi's ten-year anniversary of ruling of the country.

A series of events helped China's odds. The Ukraine-Russia military conflict forced Lviv to discontinue its application (Mitchell, 2014). Stockholm, Cracow, and Oslo also withdrew their applications due to widespread domestic disapproval (Wilson, 2014; Payne, 2014; Zinser, 2014). This left Beijing in a head-on contest with Almaty, the host city of the 2017 Winter Universiade. To win the IOC's support, Beijing and Zhangjiakou jointly announced lavish plans to improve the cities' air quality and ensure a sufficient supply of artificial snow if necessary (Beijing Daily, 2015a; 2015b).

Xi also promised to the senior executives of the IOC and other international sporting organizations that his administration would mobilize over 300 million Chinese nationals to participate in various winter sports if the 2022 Winter Olympics were staged in China (People's Daily, 2014; 2015). This helped deflect criticism of a lack of Chinese public understanding and participation in winter sports and galvanized the campaign to promote mass sport in the country. Xi's intervention clearly helped Beijing and Zhangjiakou. The IOC granted the hosting rights of the 2022 Games to China in July 2015.

Like the bidding for the 2022 Winter Games, China's jockeying for the 2019 FIBA World Cup was motivated by its quest to demonstrate continuing progress toward national rejuvenation. Since the early days of reform, Beijing had been eager to raise China's profile in global basketball but had met major hurdles when trying to build competitive national teams and establish a professional domestic league to support the larger national goal (Houlihan, Tan and Green, 2010).

Since Xi and his administration was determined to bring the basketball tournament to China, various initiatives that aimed to overcome these challenges were rolled out in the 2010s (Huang and Hong, 2015). Xiao Tian, a senior Chinese sports official, was nominated by Beijing as one of the FIBA Vice Presidents (International Basketball Federation, 2014). This greatly reassured the Chinese basketball association of their prospects of organizing a FIBA event. Accordingly, the Chinese Basketball Association (CBA) put forward a proposal to the central authorities whereby Beijing would co-host the 2019 FIBA World Cup with seven other Chinese cities that had either been previous hosts of international sporting events or were localities with vibrant basketball activities. These included Wuhan, Nanjing (host of the 2014 Summer Youth Olympics), Guangzhou (host of the 2010 Asian Games), Shenzhen (host of the 2011 Summer Universiade), Suzhou (host of the 2002 FIBA World Championship for Women), Dongguan (the national basketball city of China), and Foshan (a city of Guangdong province with a strong basketball tradition). Xi's administration promptly approved the CBA's plans and encouraged it to apply to FIBA.

In the view of the central authorities, the holding of the 2019 FIBA World Cup in China could be leveraged to celebrate the communist regime's 70th anniversary and demonstrate China's breakthrough in the global basketball circuit that had been previously dominated by Western powers and athletes. As China's cities ramped up their bidding campaigns, the national basketball associations of France, Germany, the Philippines, Qatar, and Turkey also informed FIBA of their interest in staging the event.

To Xi's administration, this 'multinational competition' was reminiscent of the defeat of Beijing, Hangzhou, Suzhou, Shenyang, and Qingdao in 2009 by five Spanish cities (Madrid, Barcelona, and three other cities) in the bidding contest to host the 2014 FIBA World Cup that occurred during Hu Jintao's administration. To avoid another embarrassing defeat, Xi and his sports officials deemed that winning the hosting rights of the 2019 FIBA World Cup was imperative, as a failure under Xi's leadership might embarrass his leadership standing to steer the bidding campaign.

To be sure, the bid was somewhat overshadowed by a bribery probe of a senior sports official in June 2015, which led to fears that China would lose the FIBA bidding contest (Blanchard, 2015). China's odds, however, were improved after France, Germany, Qatar, and Turkey dropped their applications. Beijing also used Yao Ming, a globally renowned NBA player, in its lobbying and publicity endeavors at FIBA (Helin, 2015). The concerted publicity efforts of Beijing and Yao paid off. Beijing and its co-hosting cities became the frontrunner during the latter stages of the 2019 FIBA World Cup bidding contest. Most of the FIBA executive committee members cast their votes for the Chinese cities over their Filipino rivals due to the clear infrastructural advantages of China and Beijing and other cities very staunch insistence that they would make every possible effort to host a successful FIBA World Cup.

When the bidding contest for the Winter Games was under way in 2014, Xi's regime was challenged by a confidence crisis from within the military. Xu Caihou, a former CPC Central Military Commission (CMC) Vice Chairman and Politburo member, was arrested as part of a corruption investigation, together with other active and retired senior officers. The scandal, widely reported in both the local and international media, gravely tarnished the image of the Chinese military, and led to serious doubts about Chinese troops' ability to support national rejuvenation (Tiezzi, 2014).

Xi's administration sought to capitalize on another bid for an international sporting event as part of the endeavors to restore confidence in and public images of China's military. To Beijing's favor, senior figures from the international sporting community viewed China's readiness to host international sporting games for the world's militaries. Among them, Abdulhakim Al-Shino, the International Military Sports Council (CISM) president and a colonel in Bahrain's armed forces, explicitly recommended that the 2019 Military World Games be hosted in Wuhan, capital city of Hubei in central China (Wuhan Evening News, 2015). This presented an invaluable opportunity for Xi's administration to advance the bidding campaign of the Military World Games in order to display how the military had transformed into a modern institution, much like its foreign counterparts, under Xi's leadership, and to downplay the adverse impacts on the Chinese military's images following the scandal. Beijing calculated that the games would highlight the physical competence of the Chinese soldier athletes by them winning medals at the global sporting event and restore public confidence in Chinese war-fighting capabilities. Hosting the Military World Games in 2019 in China would also coincide with the communist regime's 70th anniversary, further strengthening Xi's supreme authority within the Party and over the military.

Already favored by CISM, these factors boosted China's bid for the games and improved the odds of Wuhan. With Xi Jinping assuming the top military post as CMC Chairperson, the original bidding proposal of Wuhan for the 2019 Military Games, once shelved by the CMC, was revived and the city gained the support of both the central government and the party (Chu, 2021: 132). Subsequently, with the approval of the CMC, Wuhan formally put forwards its application in May 2015 and met no competitor. The city quickly obtained the hosting rights in the same month (Wenweipo, 2017).

3   Quest for Regional Leadership

Pursuits to host international sporting events in Xi's first two administrations were also motivated by a somewhat different but equally important consideration to enhance China's soft power through hosting sporting games. The bidding contests for the 2022 Asian Games, the 2020 Asian Beach Games, and the 2021 Asian Youth Games were driven by Beijing's intents to demonstrate its leadership in the region and to rally support for its flagship geo-economic initiative. Specifically, in hosting multiple sporting games for Asian nations, China attempted to consolidate its engagement and deepen the connections with participating athletes and nations and reinforce socio-cultural supports along the Belt and Road countries for the China-led BRI.

Among the three games, the Asian Games has been the largest Asia-wide multi-sports event China was familiar to given its experience of going through the bidding processes of the 1990 Beijing and 2010 Guangzhou games that defeated its competitors and won global acclaims of staging the two games with great successes (Chu, 2013). However, China's third hosting of the Games in Hangzhou in 2022 was exceptional – it entered the bidding without any rivals because other Asian countries had found the burden of hosting international sporting events financially challenging. Hanoi, Vietnam's capital city, discontinued its preparations to host the 2019 18th Asian Games due to the considerable burden the city anticipated to incur in April 2014 (Reuters, 2014). While the Olympic Council of Asia (OCA) promptly found alternative hosts in Indonesia's Jakarta and Palembang, the episodes discouraged other interested cities in Asia from participating in the bidding process.

By contrast, Beijing and China's local governments remained very proactive. As the OCA was looking for a host city of the 19th Asian Games in 2023, the Zhejiang provincial government informed Beijing of its intention that Hangzhou submit a bidding proposal (Qi, 2021). Xi subsequently extended his staunch support because hosting the Asian Games, the largest and most prestigious sporting event in Asia, to Hangzhou would consolidate China's influence in the Asian sporting community and underline that it had become a strong sporting power in the region.

In addition, having Hangzhou lead the bidding would help promote Xi's political network by advancing the career of Zhejiang governor, Li Qiang, a political protégé of Xi Jinping. To retain strong influence within the Party, it would be important for Xi to ensure that his preferred allies building up strong enough track records within the party-state so that they would take up higher positions to support and consolidate Xi's long-term ruling. As such, Xi introduced several measures benefitting Zhejiang's bidding for the Asian Games that helped burnish the performance and credentials of Li Qiang, who was marked for higher positions (and became China's Premier in March 2023).

With such political calculus, China remained committed to its Asian Games bid even after the OCA's decision to move forward the 19th Asian Games a whole year to 2022 (Rutherford, 2014).[1] China's central authorities asked Hangzhou to revise its application for the 2022 Games, since this would showcase China's willingness to shoulder responsibilities in Asian sporting affairs whereas other aspiring Asian cities aborted their plans due to the reduced available time to prepare for the sporting event (Qi, 2021). Hangzhou's bidding package for the 2022 Asian Games was submitted to the OCA on August 16th, 2015, and was the only applicant.

---

1 The OCA maintained such an arrangement since the 18th Asian Games had been held in 2018, instead of 2019. The Indonesian authorities requested to stage the games in 2018 in order to avoid running the regional sporting events alongside the Indonesian general election in 2019.

As in the Beijing bid for the 2022 Winter Olympic Games, Xi stressed that his administration would spare nothing to support Hangzhou's bid for the Asian Games. At his meeting with OCA president, Ahmad Al-Fahad Al-Sabah, in late August 2015 he stressed that the city would make the 2022 Asian Games an enormous success (Xinhua, 2015). This evidently consolidated the support of OCA executives and members for China's third bid for the Asian Games. Hangzhou was given the hosting rights in September 2015.

To expand the engagements with the Asian sporting associations and athletes, Xi's administration also gave enthusiastic support to the OCA's multi-sports events by agreeing to host smaller events for specific disciplines and athletic groups in addition to the larger Asian Games. In the case of the 2020 Asian Beach Games, Xi and his administration has in effect appointed Sanya of Hainan Province to be the sole candidate to submit a hosting bid in 2018 after the OCA President had found that there were no other interested Asian cities and appealed in person to Xi for help (Xinhua, 2017; 2018a).

China also took up the leadership role in salvaging the 2021 Asian Youth Games by having Shantou of Guangdong Province to enter the bidding for the game's hosting right as the sole candidate city in 2019. The OCA again turned to China after the 2017 edition of the Youth Games initially slated to take place in Sri Lanka was cancelled in 2015 due to political interference in the country's National Olympic Committee and the withdrawal of Jakarta, the line-up replacement in 2016 (Etchells, 2015; Xinhua, 2019a). While these caused great disappointment among the youth athletes and sporting associations in the region (Butler, 2016), China had emerged as a more reliable and resourceful partner that would ensure successful hosting of multi-sports events.

To China's foreign policy and sports officials, taking up the hosting duties of the various pan-Asian sporting events not only demonstrated China's leadership of Asia's sport development, it also further promoted the country's image as a responsible great power in the region. More importantly, these sporting events would serve as invaluable opportunities to win the hearts and minds of thousands of Asian athletes and officials that was regarded as particularly important to the longer-term success of BRI that involved extensive inflows of China's capitals in hundreds of investment projects. Despite their potential economic benefits, China's expanding influence had resulted in some dissatisfactions among local populations and concerns of the eventual political-economic dependence on China. Some project host governments had even decided to suspend BRI projects as a result (e.g., Kynge, 2018; Yamada and Palma, 2018). Therefore, the staging of Asia-wide sporting events was seen by Beijing as affording an invaluable chance not just to showcase China's world-class stadiums and urban infrastructure but also to engage in people-to-people diplomacy that might assuage the concerns of Asian partners about the BRI's adverse impacts on the local societies.

4 The Cross-Strait Power Play

No political agenda was more critical to Xi's administration than cross-strait relations. Despite the warming ties between Beijing and Taipei during the Kuomintang administration of Ma Ying-jeou between 2008 and 2016, the victory of Tsai Ing-wen, a Democratic Progressive Party (DPP) candidate, in 2016 elections resulted in considerable degrading of cross-strait dynamics. Unlike her predecessor, Tsai refused to embrace the 1992 Consensus that acknowledged the two territories across the strait both belonged to China (while leaving some room for respective interpretations of the One China principle).

More alarming to Beijing was the fact that Tsai had been a vocal politician known for her pro-independence views (Wu, 2016). Under her administration, Taiwan strengthened relations with the US and strived to expand its engagements with, and visibility in, international governmental and non-governmental organizations (Chin and Hutzler, 2016; Yoon and Wu, 2017). In the global sporting arena, Tsai's administration also pushed for a referendum which would allow for Taiwanese athletes to take part in the 2020 Tokyo Olympics under the name of 'Taiwan' instead of 'Chinese Taipei' (Aspinwall, 2018).

Accordingly, it was imperative for Beijing to 'penalize' a renegade Taiwan because Tsai and her administration had breached the One China principle and complicated the realization of full national unification (i.e., Taiwan returning to the China's sovereign rule). Chinese diplomats squeezed Taiwan's international space by breaking the island's diplomatic ties with São Tomé and Príncipe and Panama in 2016 and 2017, respectively (Wu and Blanchard, 2016; Moreno and Wen, 2017). Beijing was able to have international organizations such as the World Health Organization, in which Taiwan had previously participated in an observer capacity, ban the island's officials from attending after Tsai took office in May 2016 (Lampert and Wu, 2016; Taipei Times, 2016; Miles, 2017). As a clear expression of Beijing's displeasure toward Tsai's government, Chinese athletes undertook a semi-boycott of the Taipei 2017 Summer Universiade, refusing to take part in team sports (Bardenhagen, 2017; Ellis and Sung, 2017).

To narrow down the space of Taiwan's involvement in global sporting activities, Xi and his administration decided to support Jinjiang, a county-level city in Fujian province best known for being a manufacturing hub of sneakers, in its proposal to host the 2020 Summer Gymnasiade in late 2017. Evidently,

Beijing was aware of the lack of familiarity of the county-level city within the global sporting community. Nevertheless, it remained committed to backing Jinjiang in order to foil the bid of Taoyuan, a city adjacent to Taipei that was led by a DPP mayor seeking to gain global recognition of the city as an international hub of social-cultural exchanges.

However, the International School Sport Federation (ISF), the governing organization of Gymnasiade, viewed Taiwan very favorably as a potential host of the games. The ISF president even discussed with Taiwan's vice president the possibility of Taiwan hosting the 2020 Games during an official visit in 2016, prior to commencement of the official bidding for the games and the site visits of competing cities (International School Sports Federation, 2016; 2017; Sports Administration, Ministry of Education of the Republic of China (Taiwan), 2016). To boost its odds, Taoyuan promised that it would provide royalties of EUR 1 million to the ISF, subsidize delegations from emerging economies, and spend NTD 10 million on stadium renovations, among other financial support of the ISF and participating athletes (Chu, 2022).

The ISF pro-Taiwan gesture clearly irritated Beijing and triggered countermeasures. To outmaneuver Taoyuan, and with the financial guarantees of the Beijing central and Fujian provincial governments, Jinjiang announced that it would provide royalties of EUR 2 million, waive the living costs of all participant athletes, cover the full flight costs of any delegation from the 30 poorest countries as well as 80 percent of the flight costs of every other delegation, offer scholarships to 400 ISF-recommended students between 2017 and 2020, spend over CNY 1.7 billion on stadium building and renovations, and encourage mainland Chinese business enterprises to co-operate with the ISF. The Chinese authorities also promised that it would facilitate 85 million Chinese secondary school students to participate in sports activities if Jinjiang won the 2020 Gymnasiade hosting rights (Chu, 2022). The very generous offer of Beijing and the Chinese authorities' high-key promise eventually cumulated in the landslide victory of Jinjiang in October 2017.

5 Xi's Preponderance over Local China

In addition to the foreign policy and cross-strait agendas discussed, Xi also sought to consolidate his preponderance over China's party-state hierarchy as his administration entered its second term in late 2017. As an important part of such effort, the 'Thought on Socialism with Chinese Characteristics for a New Era' was incorporated into the CPC constitution during the 19th CPC National Congress of October 2017 and became an ideological footprint that would define his leadership of the party-state at both the central and local levels. On the same occasion, Xi Jinping also emphasized the importance of accelerating China's transformation into a strong sporting power, among other social-economic agendas that would define his political legacy (Xi, 2017).

These moves have set the stage for Xi and his administration to reinforce, if not impose, their agendas over the local authorities. Among the several inspection trips Xi and his entourage made, Xi instructed local officials to thoroughly follow his policy guidance delivered by the Party Congress during a high-profile visit to Sichuan province a few weeks before the 2018 National People's Congress that was slated to make possible Xi's indefinite rule (Buckley and Bradsher, 2018; Xinhua, 2018b). To toe the line with Xi's mandate, Sichuan officials decided to transform Chengdu, the provincial capital that hosted the 2019 World Police and Fire Games, into a 'World City of Sporting Events' (世界赛事名城 *Shijie Saishi Mingcheng*) in the local government's policy agenda (Huaao Xing Kong, 2020).

This was followed by a flurry of bidding attempts launched by Chengdu between 2017 and 2019. Bids were announced for the 2021 Summer Universiade, the 2022 World Table Tennis Championships, and the 2025 World Games. In the second half of 2018, Chengdu submitted its plans to host the 2021 Summer Universiade and the 2022 World Table Tennis Championships to the Sichuan provincial and Chinese central governments. The city's moves were expected to appeal to the Xi's administration due to the high chance of succeeding in the bidding exercises following the dropping out of all competing hosting cities that once showed interest in hosting the 2021 Summer Universiade. To salvage the games for university student athletes by proactively looking for an alternative host, the International University Sports Federation (FISU), the organizing authority of Universiade, had invited the two Koreas to co-host this event in late 2018 but was dismissed by both Korean authorities due to the uncertain situation in the peninsula (Pavitt, 2017; Korean Broadcasting System, 2018).

Chengdu's interest therefore had saved the sporting body from the embarrassing arrangement of cancelling the 2021 games. Backed by both the Beijing and Sichuan authorities, Chengdu presented its application to host the 2021 Summer Universiade and the FISU issued a preliminary hosting contract with the Chinese city before its investigation trip scheduled for January 2019 (Palmer, 2018).

The enthusiasm of Chengdu to brand itself as a busy hub of international sporting events and to demonstrate its adherence to Xi's mandates did not end there. As it was sealing the hosting agreement with FISU, both provincial and city leaders wasted little time preparing to bid for other international sporting games. Chengdu tendered its application for the 2022 World Table

Tennis Championships to the International Table Tennis Federation (ITTF) at the end of December 2018, just two weeks after signing a contract with FISU (China Daily, 2019). Although ITTF's executives also received proposals from Lisbon, Portugal and Kitakyushu, Japan, the sporting organization chose the Chinese city to host the tournament. This was not just because of the constant enthusiasm of the Chinese public in table tennis competitions, more importantly, the backing of both the Chinese central and Sichuan provincial authorities to a successful staging of the games was also pivotal to assuring the ITTF that the Chengdu-hosted game would be a very successful one (Sohu, 2019; Rowbottom, 2019).

The city became aware of another opportunity while the bidding competition for the 2022 World Table Tennis Championships was taking place. As in the bidding for the 2021 Summer Universiade, the Chengdu authorities was aware of difficulties of the International World Games Association (IWGA) in identifying a host for the 2025 World Games, an international sporting event comprised of sporting disciplines not contested at the Olympics. To seize upon the opportunity, the Chengdu government promptly expressed its interest to IWGA in taking up the hosting rights. The IWGA executives were very satisfied with the city's sports-related infrastructure during its inspection trips and described Chengdu as one of the 'most forward-looking and dynamic cities in China.' The city was quickly awarded the hosting rights to the 2025 World Games in May 2019. With three victories of bidding for the hosting rights of sporting games in less than a year, local officials of Chengdu and their provincial counterparts have effectively demonstrated how they have adhered to Xi Jinping's guidance and translated it into tangible successes (Mackay, 2019; Pavitt, 2019a).

6   Actualizing Xi's Football Dream

Differently from most of the multi-sport games highlighted in the preceding sections, China's bids for the 2021 FIFA Club World Cup and 2023 AFC Asian Cup involved a single sport and were seen as an integral part of Xi Jinping's 'football dream' that serve to promote his own standing in the country and to promote China's sporting power in a longer term (Sullivan, Chadwick and Gow, 2019).

Like table tennis and badminton, football is a popular sport in China. However, the influence of China in the international football community is much lower than that of other sports due to the relatively laggard development of Chinese football (talent development and industry practice, for example) at the various governmental levels. This had resulted in a disappointing performance of the country's national team in international competition. Xi, an enthusiastic football fan, believed that reversing the situation could be an essential piece in China's transformation into a strong sports power, and consolidate public confidence in his role in steering the country toward national rejuvenation (Yao, 2014; White, 2018).

To actualize his vision, he had outlined a three-stage plan of realizing China's football dream in 2011 well before assuming the top party-state positions. According to the plan, China should first qualify for a World Cup, then strive to host the tournament before finally winning the title (Duerden, 2021). Although the Chinese national football team lost all of its matches in the Korea-Japan World Cup of 2002, it showed that China's players had the potential to compete at the highest level of global football games. This in effect ensured that football development would remain an important goal of the country under Xi's leadership. In Xi's own words, 'China's football dream looks far away but we cannot stop' (China Daily, 2014).

Accordingly, in March 2015, Xi's administration issued a plan outlining how football development should proceed. Aside from detailing the reform of the football associations and industry, the plan highlighted China's ambition to host a Fédération Internationale de Football Association (FIFA) World Cup in the future (State Council of People's Republic of China, 2015). The Chinese Football Association (CFA), the government-sponsored industry body with the responsibility of managing football affairs in the country, echoed Beijing's view and decided that China should apply to host the 2023 Asian Football Confederation (AFC) Asian Cup.

Since the games are the most prestigious football tournament in Asia, the CFA believed that hosting the event in China would increase the country's standing among other nations potentially competing to host the 2030 or 2034 FIFA World Cups (Chu, 2021: 50). This idea was quickly endorsed and backed by Xi's administration. The CFA's bid for the Asian Cup was also helped by the withdrawal of other opponents, as they shifted their priorities to international football games (Pavitt, 2019b). As a result, China was selected as the sole applicant to host 2023 AFC Asian Cup in June 2019 (Morgan, 2019a).

In what would bring Xi's football dream a step closer to reality, China's sports officials identified another opportunity to stage an international football competition while they were expecting the AFC's decision for the 2023 Asian Cup. Specifically, Beijing took the opportunities following FIFA's decision to increase the number of participant teams in the FIFA Club World Cup (upped from seven to 24, from the 2021 tournament onward), which had previously been dominated by teams from Europe and South America. In line with the

FIFA's agenda to make the games more inclusive of Asian and African teams and have the event staged beyond regular host countries like Brazil and Spain, the CFA has decided to compete for the 2021 Club World Cup and was quickly welcomed by FIFA (Associated Press, 2017; Press Association, 2019).

For the CFA and Beijing authorities, hosting the FIFA Club World Cup would constitute invaluable experience of staging truly international football games, and pave the way for future bids for the World Cup – the blue-ribbon football event China had been eyeing. Although FIFA President Gianni Infantino was receptive to China's commitment to host the 2021 Club World Cup, strained US-China relations (aggravated by the trade war and human rights practices) resulted in calls for a boycott from US Congressmen and pressure on FIFA not to grant the 2021 FIFA Club World Cup to China (Scott, 2019).

To Beijing's pleasure, Infantino and his FIFA colleagues did not heed the American's appeals and granted China the hosting rights in October 2019 (Morgan, 2019b). This followed China's successful pursuit of the hosting rights for the 2023 Asian Cup. In an effort to rally public and local governments' support for football games, the CFA announced that Shanghai, Tianjin, Guangzhou, Wuhan, Shenyang, Jinan, Hangzhou, and Dalian would be the host cities of the 2021 FIFA Club World Cup, and the matches of the AFC Asian Cup would be staged in Beijing, Tianjin, Shanghai, Chongqing, Chengdu, Xi'an, Dalian, Qingdao, Xiamen, and Suzhou (Xinhua, 2019b).

The twin Chinese victories excited the public and Xi's administration, breeding hopes that China might triumph in international football competitions. Although this might take at least another decade or two to become reality, China's progresses into a first-class footballing superpower have become a symbol of the country's great awakening as the world's leading nation. As two analysts nicely put it:

> Victory at soccer for China would be symbolic of their battles over the last century and a half: to modernize, to be equal, and perhaps even superior, to the world powers that once looked down on them.
> BROWN and VANDENBERG, 2018

Although the COVID-19 pandemic delayed the adoption of the revamped Club World Cup format and the United Arab Emirates was assigned to host the 2021 Club World Cup using the previous format in early 2022, China is still expected to host a tournament of 24 competing teams in the coming years (Federation Internationale de Football Association, 2020; 2021).

7 Conclusion

Compared to his predecessors, Xi's governments have devoted much attention to the country's sporting development and have shown a remarkable enthusiasm for bidding for the hosting rights of international sporting events. China's engagement, however, is never devoid of political considerations.

This chapter analyzes the different agendas underlying China's multiple bids for international sporting events under Xi's administration and reveals how the regime has leveraged the associated global processes for its political ends with increasing sophistication. Primarily, Xi's administration has capitalized on sporting events to build up governing legitimacy and reinforce intra-party and public support of Xi as the country's supreme leader to a standing matching Mao Zedong and Deng Xiaoping. The bids for the 2022 Winter games and 2019 FIBA World Cup have shown how Xi's China can boost its sense of national greatness by defeating European contestants, stoking public confidence in Xi's leadership. The 2019 Military World Games was similarly used to restore confidence in a scandal-stricken military and to project an image of China's war-fighting institutions as a modern, competent force under Xi's helm.

The three pan-Asian games (2022 Asian Games, 2020 Asian Beach Games and 2021 Asian Youth Games) showed how Xi's regime seized upon the hosting of international sporting events to build China's leading position in Asian sporting affairs and showcase the country's infrastructure readiness for mega-events. In doing so, China has tried to win the hearts and minds of athletes and officials with regard to its larger geo-economic endeavors of China. Hangzhou's bid for the Asian Games also revealed how international events had become entwined with considerations of the party-state.

China sought to host the 2020 Summer Gymnasiade as part of a powerplay to undercut the international connections and standing of Taiwan. The case showed how the Chinese state's support of a local bidding endeavor could become a blunt political instrument that could be used against recalcitrant Taipei authorities. As Xi Jinping emerged as the most powerful leader of contemporary China as he entered his second term, local officials demonstrated adherence to his mandates and instructions. This was best shown in Chengdu's successive quests for the 2021 Summer Universiade, the 2022 World Table Tennis Championships, and the 2025 World Games, which all reflected Xi's preponderance over local authorities.

Finally, the pursuits of the 2023 AFC Asian Cup and 2021 Club World Club were integral to Xi's own interest in football and his ambition to turn the country into a great footballing nation. These two cases showed how Xi's agenda could become an indelible part of China's sporting development and global sporting outreach.

These analyses affirm the view that China has been using sporting games to promote a strong national image. The country is set to quickly become a global sporting power, or at minimum a hub of international sporting events. Unlike most other great sporting nations, China's approach to international sporting outreach is distinctively state-led (or at least state-orchestrated). Even though the formal processes of bidding for sporting games originate from and are presented by potential host cities, every case this chapter has reviewed speak to the extensive level of involvement, if not intervention, from central party-state authorities (and sometimes Xi himself). This is in line with the defining characteristic of Xi's era – a marked emphasis on strong-state rule and an ambitious global quest (Mitter, 2021).

In this way, international sporting events have become an arena for competition between the great powers. An 'instrument' of governments that promises tangible political and economic yields. Our analysis echoes the view that China has tended to use international sporting events to project the perception of national greatness to both domestic and global audiences. As Brancati and Wohlforth (2021) aptly described:

> For China – a budding superpower – the Olympic Games offer the prospect of directing global attention to the country's newfound accomplishments, affording it the recognition that Chinese leaders think they deserve.

Such aspirations of achieving national greatness are best reflected in Xi remarks to the nation at the CPC centenary of July 2021: "Today, we are closer, more confident, and more capable than ever before of making the goal of national rejuvenation a reality" (Xinhua, 2021). While Xi and his administration must be aware of the enormous challenges ahead that the party-state will face, the assertiveness in presenting China as a rising nation of global importance is not limited to international sporting events but encompasses many other realms of social-cultural and economic exchange. This has been a defining characteristic of Xi's China and its engagement in the world.

In fact, Xi and his administration deeply believed that the East had been rising and the West had been falling since 2020 especially in view of the flagging economies and 'undisciplined' societies of the West following the COVID-19 outbreak (Buckley, 2021). In contrast, China appeared to have outperformed and excelled throughout the pandemic due to its authoritarian ruling under Xi. The containment approach of responding to the COVID-19, notably through maintaining 'net zero strategy,' has resulted in remarkable low infectious rate while maintaining steady economic growth (Graham-Harrison and Kuo, 2020). The Chinese authorities even leveraged the celebration of the 2022 Winter Olympics to showcase the world-leading performance of preventing the coronavirus outbreak under Xi's China (Xi, 2022). Although the Chinese public were reportedly satisfied by Xi's response to COVID, subsequent outbreaks in major cities such as Shanghai and Beijing have prompted questions about the viability of maintaining the 'net zero' approach that in effect put the cities with outbreaks under strict lockdown, preventing the localities from any social, cultural and economic activities and isolating China from the rest of the world that has been on the path of resuming to the 'new normal.'

The months-long lockdown of Shanghai has unfortunately led the postponements of the holding of the Asian Games, the Asian Beach Games, the Summer Universiade, the Gymnasiade, and the ITTF World Table Tennis Championship. China's hosting of the AFC Asian Cup, the Asian Youth Games, and the FIFA Club World Cup were also cancelled. Among them, the cancellation of the FIFA event is poised to affect Beijing's bidding of the 2030 or 2034 World Cup, according to some analysts (Duerden, 2022). Considering these development, would bidding for and hosting of the future international sporting events still be an important element attaining Xi's political ambition to the world? The answer is open-ended.

References

Aspinwall, Nick (2018) Taiwan Set to Decide on Banishing Its 'Chinese Taipei' Olympic Moniker. *The Diplomat,* 21 November, https://thediplomat.com/2018/11/taiwan-set-to-decide-on-banishing-its-chinese-taipei-olympic-moniker/, accessed 30 November 2021.

Associated Press (2017) FIFA Considering 24-team Club World Cup to Be Played in Summer. *ESPN,* 31 October, https://www.espn.com/soccer/fifa-club-world-cup/story/3251358/fifa-considering-24-team-club-world-cup-to-be-played-in-summer, accessed 30 November 2021.

Bardenhagen, Klaus (2017) China-Taiwan Tensions Show at Universiade Sports Event. *Deutsche Welle,* 20 August, https://www.dw.com/en/china-taiwan-tensions-show-at-universiade-sports-event/a-40167190, accessed 30 November 2021.

Beijing Daily (2015a) Zhuanfang Beijing Shenaowei Zhuxi Beijingshi Shizhang Wang Anshun. *Beijing Daily,* 3 June, p. 1.

Beijing Daily (2015b) Beijing Chenshu Zhanshi Zhongguo Zixin. *Beijing Daily,* 10 June, p. 4.

Beijing Youth Daily (2013) Beijing Bandongaohui 2026 Gengkaopu. *Beijing Youth Daily*, 6 November, p. B8.

Blanchard, Ben (2015) Beijing Says Sports Minister Probe Won't Affect 2022 Bid. *Reuters*, 30 June, https://www.reuters.com/article/us-olympics-china-corruption-idUSKCN0PA11320150630, accessed 30 November 2021.

Brancati, Dawn and William C. Wohlforth (2021) Why Authoritarians Love the Olympics: A Boycott of Beijing 2022 Will Do Little to Deter China. *Foreign Affairs*, 25 March, https://www.foreignaffairs.com/articles/china/2021-03-25/why-authoritarians-love-olympics, accessed 30 November 2021.

Brown, Kerry and Layne Vandenberg (2018) Football and the China Dream. *The Diplomat*, 6 July, https://thediplomat.com/2018/07/football-and-the-china-dream/, accessed 30 November 2021.

Buckley, Chris (2021) 'The East Is Rising': Xi Maps Out China's Post-COVID Ascent. *New York Times*, 3 March, https://www.nytimes.com/2021/03/03/world/asia/xi-china-congress.html, accessed 30 November 2021.

Buckley, Chris and Keith Bradsher (2018) China Moves to Let Xi Stay in Power by Abolishing Term Limit. *New York Times*, accessed 25 February, https://www.nytimes.com/2018/02/25/world/asia/china-xi-jinping.html, accessed 30 November 2021.

Butler, Nick (2016) Exclusive: Asian Youth Games set to be postponed until 2021 after Jakarta withdraw. *Inside the Games*, 24 September, https://www.insidethegames.biz/articles/1041977/exclusive-asian-youth-games-set-to-be-postponed-until-2021-after-jakarta-withdraw, accessed 30 November 2021.

Chen, Shushu (2018) Mass Sport in China. In: Jinming Zheng, Shushu Chen, Tien-Chin Tan, and Barrie Houlihan (eds.) *Sport Policy in China*. London: Routledge, pp. 150–169.

Chin, Josh and Charles Hutzler (2016) Trump's Phone Call with Taiwan President Sparks China Complaint. *Wall Street Journal*, 3 December, https://www.wsj.com/articles/trumps-phone-call-with-taiwan-president-sparks-china-complaint-1480762723, accessed 30 November 2021.

China Daily (2014) Chinese Leaders' Passion for Sports. *China Daily*, 28 March, https://www.chinadaily.com.cn/sports/2014-03/28/content_17386983.htm, accessed 30 November 2021.

China Daily (2019) Chengdu Chenggong Shenban 2022 Nian Di 56 Jie Shijie Pingpangqiu Tuanti Jinbiaosai. *China Daily*, 23 April, https://sc.chinadaily.com.cn/a/201904/23/WS5cbe6a9ea310e7f8b15785c4.html, accessed 30 November 2021.

China Global Television Network (2021) Winter Dream Meets Chinese Dream: China Delivers on Olympic Promises. *China Global Television Network*, 26 October, https://news.cgtn.com/news/2021-10-26/Winter-Dream-meets-Chinese-Dream-China-delivers-on-Olympic-promises-14FEKl6xHJS/index.html, accessed 30 November 2021.

Chu, Marcus P. (2013) The Pursuit of Regional Geopolitical Aspirations: China's Bids for the Asian Games and the Asian Winter Games since the 1980s. *The International Journal of the History of Sport*, 30(10), pp. 1048–1058.

Chu, Marcus P. (2021) *Sporting Events in China as Economic Development, National Image, and Political Ambition*. Basingstoke: Palgrave Macmillan.

Chu, Marcus P. (2022) *China, Taiwan, and International Sporting Events: Face-off in Cross Strait Relations*. Abingdon–New York: Routledge.

Duerden, John (2021) Chinese soccer plunges deeper into crisis. *Nikkei Asia*, 24 December, https://asia.nikkei.com/Business/Business-Spotlight/Chinese-soccer-plunges-deeper-into-crisis, accessed 2 January 2022.

Duerden, John (2022) Zero-COVID kicks Xi's goal of hosting China World Cup out of play. *Nikkei Asia*, 16 June, https://asia.nikkei.com/Spotlight/Sports/Zero-COVID-kicks-Xi-s-goal-of-hosting-China-World-Cup-out-of-play, accessed 15 June 2022.

Ellis, Samson and Chinmei Sung (2017) China Stealth Boycott Looms for Taiwan's Biggest Sporting Event. *Bloomberg*, 18 July, https://www.bloomberg.com/news/articles/2017-07-17/china-stealth-boycott-looms-for-taiwan-s-biggest-sporting-event, accessed 30 November 2021.

Etchells, Daniel (2015) Sri Lanka have 2017 Asian Youth Games taken away as Jakarta lined-up as replacement. *Inside the Games*, 22 May, https://www.insidethegames.biz/articles/1027477/sri-lanka-have-2017-asian-youth-games-taken-away-as-jakarta-lined-up-as-replacement, accessed 30 November 2021.

Federation Internationale de Football Association (2020) Statement from the FIFA President. *Federation Internationale de Football Association*, 18 March, https://www.fifa.com/media-releases/statement-from-the-fifa-president, accessed 30 November 2021.

Federation Internationale de Football Association (2021) FIFA Council Endorses Global Summit to Discuss the Future of Football. *Federation Internationale de Football Association*, 20 October, https://www.fifa.com/about-fifa/organisation/fifa-council/media-releases/fifa-council-endorses-global-summit-to-discuss-the-future-of-football, accessed 30 November 2021.

Graham-Harrison, Emma and Lily Kuo (2020) China's coronavirus lockdown strategy: brutal but effective, *Guardian*, 19 March, https://www.theguardian.com/world/2020/mar/19/chinas-coronavirus-lockdown-strategy-brutal-but-effective, accessed 30 November 2021.

Helin, Kurt (2015) With Help of Yao Ming, China Wins Bid to Host 2019 FIBA World Cup. *NBC Sport*, 7 August, https://nba.nbcsports.com/2015/08/07/with-help-of-yao-ming-china-wins-bid-to-host-2019-fiba-world-cup/, accessed 30 November 2021.

Houlihan, Barrie, Tien-Chin Tan, and Mick Green (2010) Policy Transfer and Learning from the West: Elite Basketball Development in the People's Republic of China. *Journal of Sport and Social Issues*, 34(1), pp. 4–28.

Huaao Xing Kong (2020) Rongju Tiyu Liliang Gongjian Saishi Mingcheng 2020 Shijie Saishi Mingcheng Fazhan Dahui Quanxin Shengji. 20 November, https://www.sports.cn/cydt/cmxx/2020/1120/367967.html, accessed 30 November 2021.

Huang, Fuhua and Fang Hong (2015) Globalization and the Governance of Chinese Sports: The Case of Professional Basketball. *The International Journal of the History of Sport,* 32(8), pp. 1030–1043.

International Basketball Federation (2014) Key Appointments Headline First Meeting of Newly-Elected Central Board, 16 September, https://www.fiba.basketball/news/pr-n56--key-appointments-headline-first-meeting-of-newly-elected-central-board, accessed 30 November 2021.

International School Sports Federation (2016) ISF to Boost Cooperation with Chinese Taipei, 25 October, https://www.isfsports.org/isf-boost-cooperation-chinese-taipei, accessed 30 November 2021.

International School Sports Federation (2017) Gymnasiade 2020 – The Bid Has Started!, 9 July, https://www.isfsports.org/gymnasiade-2020-bid-has-started, accessed 30 November 2021.

Kalathil, Shanthl (2017) Beyond the Great Firewall: How China Became a Global Information Power. *The National Endowment for Democracy,* 7 March, https://www.cima.ned.org/wp-content/uploads/2017/03/CIMA-Beyond-the-Great-Firewall_150ppi-for-web.pdf, accessed 15 June 2022.

Korean Broadcasting System (2018) FISU Proposes Seoul, Pyongyang Jointly Host 2021 Summer Universiad. *KBS World,* 14 October, http://world.kbs.co.kr/service/news_view.htm?lang=e&Seq_Code=139981, accessed 30 November 2021.

Kynge, James (2018) A Tale of Two Harbours Tells Best and Worst of China's Belt and Road. *Financial Times,* 26 September, https://www.ft.com/content/7699d13a-806a-11e8-af48-190d103e32a4, accessed 30 November 2021.

Lampert, Allison and J.R. Wu (2016) U.N. Agency Snubs Taiwan, Recognizing Beijing's One China. *Reuters,* 23 September, https://www.reuters.com/article/us-taiwan-china-idUSKCN11T08P, accessed 30 November 2021.

Liaoning Daily (2013) Liuchengshi Shenban Dongaohui Aosilu Chengwei Daremen. *Liaoning Daily,* 15 November, p. B06.

Mackay, Duncan (2019) Chengdu Set to Add 2025 World Games to 2021 Summer Universiade. *Inside the Games,* 15 March, https://www.insidethegames.biz/articles/1076813/chengdu-set-to-add-2025-world-games-to-2021-summer-universiade, accessed 30 November 2021.

Miles, Tom (2017) Shut Out of U.N. Forum, Taiwan Slams China's 'Coercion and Threats'. *Reuters,* 21 May, https://www.reuters.com/article/us-taiwan-china-idUSKCN18G0X2, accessed 30 November 2021.

Mitchell, Houston (2014) Lviv, Ukraine Withdraws Bid for 2022 Winter Olympics. *Los Angeles Times,* 30 June, http://www.latimes.com/sports/sportsnow/la-sp-sn-lviv-ukraine-2022-winter-olympics-20140630-story.html, accessed 30 November 2021.

Mitter, Rana (2021) New Characteristics for Chinese Socialism. *Foreign Affairs,* 20 December, https://www.foreignaffairs.com/articles/china/2021-12-20/new-characteristics-chinese-socialism, accessed 28 December 2021.

Moreno, Elida and Philip Wen (2017) Panama Establishes Ties with China, Ditches Taiwan in Win for Beijing. *Reuters,* 13 June, https://www.reuters.com/article/us-panama-china-idUSKBN194054, accessed 30 November 2021.

Morgan, Liam (2019a) China Confirmed as Hosts of 2023 Asian Cup at AFC Extraordinary Congress. *Inside the Games,* 4 June, https://www.insidethegames.biz/articles/1080107/china-confirmed-as-hosts-of-2023-asian-cup-at-afc-extraordinary-congress, accessed 30 November 2021.

Morgan, Liam (2019b) China Set to Host Revamped FIFA Club World Cup in 2021. *Inside the Games,* 21 October, https://www.insidethegames.biz/articles/1086199/china-set-to-host-2021-club-world-cup, accessed 30 November, 2021.

Nanjing Daily (2013) Aosilu Shenban Dongao Chengwei Daremen. *Nanjing Daily,* 15 November, p. B4.

Palmer, Dan (2018) Chengdu to Be Named as 2021 Summer Universiade Host. *Inside the Games,* 18 December, https://www.insidethegames.biz/articles/1073293/chengdu-to-be-named-as-2021-summer-universiade-host, accessed 30 November 2021.

Pavitt, Michael (2017) FISU Directly Approaching Cities as Search for 2021 Summer Universiade Host Continues. *Inside the Games,* 18 August, https://www.insidethegames.biz/articles/1054233/fisu-directly-approaching-cities-as-search-for-2021-summer-universiade-host-continues, accessed 30 November 2021.

Pavitt, Michael (2019a) Chengdu Confirmed as Host of 2025 World Games. *Inside the Games,* 9 May, https://www.insidethegames.biz/articles/1078982/chengdu-confirmed-as-host-of-2025-world-games, accessed 30 November 2021.

Pavitt, Michael (2019b) China Set to Stage 2023 Asian Cup as South Korea Focus on Women's World Cup Bid. *Inside the Games,* 17 May, https://www.insidethegames.biz/articles/1079310/china-set-to-stage-2023-asian-cup-as-south-korea-focus-on-womens-world-cup-bid, accessed 30 November 2021.

Payne, Marissa (2014) Krakow Withdraws 2022 Olympic Bid After Residents Vote 'No'. *Washington Post,* 27 May, http://www.washingtonpost.com/blogs/early-lead/wp/2014/05/27/krakow-withdraws-2022-olympic-bid-after-residents-vote-no/, accessed 30 November 2021.

People's Daily (2014) Zhongguo Aolipike Jingshen De Jianxingzhe He Hongyangzhe. 9 February, p. 2.

People's Daily (2015) Xi Jinping Huijian Guoji Aoxie Zhuxi Yaao Lishihui Zhuxi Aihamaide Qinwang. 15 January, p. 1.

Press Association (2019) Fifa Risks Row with Europe's Elite by Approving New 24-team Club World Cup. *The Guardian,* 15 March, https://www.theguardian.com/football/2019/mar/15/fifa-approves-club-world-cup-24-teams-risks-row-europe-clubs, accessed 30 November 2021.

Preuss, Holger and Christian Alfs (2011) Signaling through the 2008 Beijing Olympics – Using Mega Sport Events to Change the Perception and Image of the Host. *European Sport Management Quarterly,* 11(1), pp. 55–71.

Qi, Hang (2021) Hangzhou Chenggong Shenban Yayunhui Beihou Haiyou Zhexie Xianweirenzhi De Gushi. *Hangzhou 2022,* 6 August, https://www.hangzhou2022.cn/xwzx/jdxw/ttxw/202108/t20210806_37010.shtml, accessed 30 November 2021.

Qiushi (2021) Jianshe Tiyu Qiangguo, Xijinping Zongshuji Shizhong Gaodu Zhongshi. 25 January, http://www.qstheory.cn/zhuanqu/2021-01/25/c_1127023285.htm, accessed 30 November 2021.

Reuters (2014) Vietnam Backs Out as Host of 2019 Asian Games. *Reuters,* 17 April, https://www.reuters.com/article/us-games-asia-vietnam-idUSBREA3G18H20140417, accessed 30 November 2021.

Rowbottom, Mike (2019) History Made as Houston and Chengdu Win Right to Stage 2021 and 2022 ITTF World Championships. *Inside the Games,* 22 April, https://www.insidethegames.biz/articles/1078284/history-made-as-houston-and-chengdu-win-right-to-stage-2021-and-2022-ittf-world-championships, accessed 30 November 2021.

Rutherford, Peter (2014) Indonesia Set to Be Awarded 2018 Asian Games. *Reuters,* 17 September, https://www.reuters.com/article/uk-games-asian-2018-idUKKBN0HC19G20140917, accessed 30 November 2021.

Scott, Rick (2019) Sen. Rick Scott to FIFA Council: Reject communist China as host of Club World Cup. *US Senator Rick Scott,* 23 October, https://www.rickscott.senate.gov/sen-rick-scott-fifa-council-reject-communist-china-host-club-world-cup, accessed 30 November 2021.

Shambaugh, David (2021) *China's Leaders: from Mao to Now.* Cambridge–Medford, MA: Wiley.

Singh, Rani and Tim Winter (2019) Sports on the Silk Road. *The Diplomat,* 24 December, https://thediplomat.com/2019/12/sports-on-the-silk-road/, accessed 15 June 2022.

Sohu (2019) Haowai! Chengdu Chenggong Shenban 2022 Nian Di 56 Jie Shipingsai! *Sohu,* 22 April, https://www.sohu.com/a/309719971_330235, accessed 30 November 2021.

Sports Administration, Ministry of Education of the Republic of China (Taiwan) (2016) Jiaoyubu Cizhang Jiejian Guojixuexiaotiyuzonghui (ISF), Changtan Guojitiyu Ji Jiaoyujiaoliu. *National Sports Quarterly,* 45(4), p. 81. https://www.sa.gov.tw/wSite/public/Attachment/f1482303032230.pdf, accessed 30 November 2021.

State Council of People's Republic of China (2015) Guowuyuan Bangongting Guanyu Yinfa Zhongguo Zuqiu Gaige Fanzhan Zongti Fangan De Tongzhi, 16 March, http://www.gov.cn/zhengce/content/2015-03/16/content_9537.htm, accessed 30 November 2021.

Sullivan, Jonathan, Simon Chadwick, and Michael Gow (2019) China's Football Dream: Sport, Citizenship, Symbolic Power and Civic Spaces. *Journal of Sport and Social Issues*, 43(6), pp. 493–514.

Taipei Times (2016) Taiwan Barred from Interpol Assembly. *Taipei Times*, 6 November, https://www.taipeitimes.com/News/front/archives/2016/11/06/2003658663, accessed 30 November 2021.

Tiezzi, Shannon (2014) Xi Aims His Anti-Corruption Campaign at the PLA. *The Diplomat*, 2 July, https://thediplomat.com/2014/07/xi-aims-his-anti-corruption-campaign-at-the-pla/, accessed 30 November 2021.

Wenweipo (2017) Guofangbu: Diqijie Shijie Junren Yundonghui Jiangyu 2019 Nian 10 Yue Juxing. *Wenweipo*, 24 November, http://news.wenweipo.com/2017/11/24/IN1711240045.htm, accessed 30 November 2021.

White, Jonathan (2018) Xi Jinping Is the World's Most Powerful Soccer Coach. *Foreign Policy*, 24 June, https://foreignpolicy.com/2018/06/24/xi-jinping-is-the-worlds-most-powerful-soccer-coach/, accessed 30 November 2021.

Wilson, Stephen (2014) Stockholm Regrets Withdrawal of 2022 Games bid. *Washington Times*, 28 October, http://www.washingtontimes.com/news/2014/oct/28/stockholm-regrets-withdrawal-of-2022-games-bid/?page=all, accessed 30 November 2021.

Wu Yu-Shan (2016) Heading Towards Troubled Waters? The Impact of Taiwan's 2016 Elections on Cross-Strait Relations. *American Journal of Chinese Studies*, 23(1), pp. 59–75.

Wu, J. R. and Ben Blanchard (2016) Taiwan Loses Another Ally, Says Won't Help China Ties. *Reuters*, 21 December, https://www.reuters.com/article/us-china-taiwan-saotome-idUSKBN1492SO, accessed 21 December 2016.

Wuhan Evening News (2015) Juntihui Zaokanshang Zhongguo. *Wuhan Evening News*, 22 May, p. 3.

Xi Jinping (2017) Secure a Decisive Victory in Building a Moderately Prosperous Society in All Respects and Strive for the Great Success of Socialism with Chinese Characteristics for a New Era – Delivered at the 19th National Congress of the Communist Party Of China, 18 October, http://www.xinhuanet.com/english/download/Xi_Jinping%27s_report_at_19th_CPC_National_Congress.pdf, accessed 30 November 2021.

Xi Jinping (2022) Zai Beijing Dongaohui Canaohui Zongjie Biaozhang Dahuishang de Jianghua. *People's Daily*, 9 April, p. 2.

Xinhua (2015) Xi Jinping Huijian Guojiaoxie Zhuxi Yaaolishihui Zhuxi Aihamaide Qinwang. 22 August, http://www.xinhuanet.com//politics/2015-08/22/c_1116340559.htm, accessed 30 November 2021.

Xinhua (2017) Xi Jinping Huijian Yaaolishihui Zhuxi Aihamaide Qinwang. 27 August, http://www.xinhuanet.com/politics/2017-08/27/c_1121550547.htm, accessed 30 November 2021.

Xinhua (2018a) China's Sanya to Host 2020 Asian Beach Games. 19 August, http://www.xinhuanet.com/english/2018-08/19/c_137402045.htm, accessed 30 November 2021.

Xinhua (2018b) Xijinping Chunjie Qianxifu Sichuan Kanwang Weiwen Gezu Ganbu Qunzhong. 13 February, http://www.xinhuanet.com/politics/2018-02/13/c_1122415641.htm, accessed 30 November 2021.

Xinhua (2019a) China to Host 2021 Asian Youth Games in Shantou. 3 March, http://www.xinhuanet.com/english/2019-03/03/c_137865940.htm, accessed 30 November 2021.

Xinhua (2019b) 2021 Nian Shijubei He 2023 Nian Yazhoubei Chengban Chengshi Jiexiao. 12 December, http://m.xinhuanet.com/2019-12/28/c_1125398498.htm, accessed 30 November 2021.

Xinhua (2021) Xi Focus-Quotable Quotes: Highlights of Xi Jinping's remarks at CPC centenary ceremony. 1 July, http://www.xinhuanet.com/english/special/2021-07/01/c_1310038364.htm, accessed 30 November 2021.

Yamada, Go and Stefania Palma (2018) Is China's Belt and Road Working? A Progress Report from Eight Countries. *Nikkei Asia,* 28 March, https://asia.nikkei.com/Spotlight/Cover-Story/Is-China-s-Belt-and-Road-working-A-progress-report-from-eight-countries, accessed 30 November 2021.

Yao Yi (2014) Xijinping De Zuqiuyuan. *People.cn,* 13 June, http://cpc.people.com.cn/n/2014/0613/c164113-25145228.html, accessed 30 November 2021.

Yoon, Jean and J. R. Wu (2017) Taiwan President Says Phone Call with Trump Can Take Place Again. *Reuters,* 27 April, https://www.reuters.com/article/us-taiwan-president-idUSKBN17T0W3, accessed 30 November 2021.

Zinser, Lynn (2014) Oslo Withdraws Bid to Host 2022 Winter Games. *New York Times,* 1 October, http://www.nytimes.com/2014/10/02/sports/oslo-withdraws-bid-for-2022-olympics-citing-high-cost-of-games.html?_r=0, accessed 30 November 2021.

Index

Afghanistan   30, 53, 102, 314, 315*f*12.8, 426
Africa   52, 130, 132, 151, 152, 155, 180, 181, 184*t*7.2, 350, 413, 417, 419, 424, 432, 488
Aksai Chin   442
Al-Fahad Al-Sabah, Ahmad   482
Al-Shino, Abdulhakim   479
Alexander III   156
Almaty   477, 478
Alon, Ilan   106
Amar, Nathanel   375
Amur River   432
Anderson, Benedict   47
Anhui   173*f*7.1, 179*t*7.1, 219, 220*t*9.1, 221*f*9.1, 222*t*9.2, 223*f*9.2, 224*t*9.3, 225*f*9.3, 226*t*9.4, 227*f*9.4, 229*t*9.5, 230*f*9.5, 231*t*9.6, 232, 232*f*9.6, 233*t*9.7, 234*f*9.7, 235*t*9.8, 236, 236*f*9.8, 237, 238*t*9.9, 239*f*9.9, 240*t*9.10, 241*f*9.10, 242, 243*t*9.11, 244*f*9.11, 275, 283, 283*t*11.2, 287, 287*f*11.2, 288, 288*f*11.3, 289*f*11.4, 289*f*11.5, 290*f*11.6a, 291*f*11.6b
Aomen. *See also* Macau
Aquino, Benigno   439
Arabia   155
Aristotle   36, 40, 48
Arunachal Pradesh   442
Astana   167
Athens   38
Australia   262, 427*n*18, 427*n*19, 445, 468
Austria   315

Babones, Salvatore   109
Backer, Larry Catá   118
Badiucao   308
Bahrain   480
Balazs, Etienne   17
Baltic Sea   427
Bandurski, David   311, 312
Bangladesh   421
Barcelona   479
Barnett, Arthur Doak   168, 443
Beczkowska, Joanna   173
Belarus   426, 468
Belgium   133
Belgrade   260

Bemelmans-Videc, Marie-Louise   111
Berlin   74, 349, 351
Besley, Timothy   110
Bhutan   436, 443
Bi Gan   355, 356, 357
Biden, Joe   312, 314, 426
Bijukchhe, Narayan Man   132
Black Sea   427
Blackburn, Marsha   162
Bo Xilai   73, 90, 91, 92, 187*t*7.3
Boao   61, 423
Bocelli, Andrea   377
Bocelli, Matteo   377
Bolivia   468
Bordeaux   349
Bougon, François   16
Brancati, Dawn   490
Brands, Hal   69, 106
Brazil   130, 131, 488
Breslin, Shaun   126
Brezhnev, Leonid   8, 357
Brown, Kerry   40, 42, 50, 416, 419*n*12
Brunei   378*n*31, 436
Brussee, Vincent   121, 122
Brussels   74, 427
Brzezinski, Zbigniew   108
Burgers, Tobias   117, 119, 125
Bush, George W.   314

Cai Qi   182, 185, 188*t*7.3
Cai Xia   45, 71
Cai Xiyong   391*n*2
Callahan, William A.   126
Cambodia   18, 19, 433
Cameron, James   343
Canada   151, 444, 445
Canberra   445, 468
Cannes   349, 351
Carnoy, Martin   292
Cena, John   261
Chan, Melissa   109
Central Asia   206, 417*n*8, 419, 421, 432
Changsha   176
Chen Cheng   17
Chen Chinchih   106

Chen Duxiu 392
Chen Jianfu 73
Chen Jining 187t7.3
Chen Kaige 350
Chen Min'er 182, 185, 187t7.3
Cheng Li 22, 25, 31, 90
Chengdu 92, 176, 375, 476, 485, 486, 488, 489
Cheung, Edgar 370
Cheung, Jacky 376
Chiang Ching-kuo 17
Chiang Kai-shek 17, 436
Chongqing 6, 73, 91, 168, 175, 176, 177, 179t7.1, 180, 181, 182, 183t7.2, 184t7.2, 185, 186, 187t7.3, 188, 220t9.1, 221f9.1, 222t9.2, 223f9.2, 224t9.3, 225f9.3, 226t9.4, 227, 227f9.4, 229t9.5, 230f9.5, 231t9.6, 232, 232f9.6, 233t9.7, 234f9.7, 235t9.8, 236f9.8, 238t9.9, 239f9.9, 240t9.10, 241f9.10, 243t9.11, 244f9.11, 283, 283t11.2, 287f11.2, 288f11.3, 289f11.4, 289f11.5, 290f11.6a, 291f11.6b, 488
Chou Tzuyu 378, 378n30
Chung Jae Ho 169
Clarke, Donald 40, 42, 43, 48
Columbus, Christopher 155
Confucius 3, 4, 17, 19, 20, 26, 39, 40, 41, 42, 47, 63, 71n11, 95, 155, 258, 307, 327, 365, 377, 397, 401n20
Copenhagen 192, 195
Cracow 477, 478
Cuba 196
Cui Zi'en 354
Czechoslovakia 439

Dahl, Robert A. 110
Dalai Lama 262, 377
Dalian 187t7.3, 488
Davos 420
Deng Pufang 90
Deng Xiaoping 3, 5, 18, 19, 20, 23, 25, 26, 27, 28, 30, 31, 36, 43, 62, 67, 89, 90, 93, 94, 95, 96, 98, 101, 127n12, 154, 167, 168, 251, 252, 254, 255, 325, 338, 355, 365, 418, 418n9, 433, 435, 449, 456n1, 459, 460, 489
Diamond, Irene 114
Diamond, Larry 108, 117
Diaoyu Islands 259, 261, 441
Dickson, Bruce J. 18, 30

Dion, Celine 377
Djibouti 432
Doklam Plateau 443
Dominicana 130, 133
Donnelly, Drew 122
Dongguan 478
Dreyer, June Teufel 169
Drinhausen, Katja 118, 120, 121, 122
Duisburg 177, 184
Durham 264
Dussel, Enrique 134
Duterte, Rodrigo 440, 445

East Asia 2, 67, 262, 419, 435, 438, 439, 448, 477
East China Sea 259, 440, 441
Egypt 130, 131
Eurasia 68, 415, 417, 419, 421, 422, 423, 424, 426, 427
Europe 30, 68, 76, 96, 98, 99, 107, 128, 151, 151n1, 155, 156, 158n7, 159f6.1, 176, 180, 186, 193, 196, 206, 335, 339, 391, 413, 417, 419, 421, 423, 424, 426, 427, 427n20, 432, 468, 477, 487, 489

Fan Bingbing 349, 350
Fan Ceng 362n1
Fang Fang 264
Fedorenko, Olga 378
Fei 378n31
Flew, Terry 368, 375
Foshan 478
Foucault, Michel 37, 38, 77, 114
France 128, 155, 356, 479
Frey, Carl Benedikt 105, 106
Froumin, Isak 292
Fu Hualing 74
Fujian 24, 173f7.1, 179t7.1, 182, 185, 187t7.3, 188t7.3, 220t9.1, 221f9.1, 222t9.2, 223f9.2, 224t9.3, 225f9.3, 226t9.4, 227f9.4, 229t9.5, 230f9.5, 231t9.6, 232, 232f9.6, 233t9.7, 234f9.7, 235t9.8, 236f9.8, 238t9.9, 239f9.9, 240t9.10, 241, 241f9.10, 242, 243t9.11, 244f9.11, 283, 283t11.2, 287f11.2, 288f11.3, 289f11.4, 289f11.5, 290f11.6a, 291f11.6b, 417, 417n6, 483, 484
Fukuyama, Francis 29, 30, 110

G-Dragon 378
Gabbana, Stefano 263

INDEX 501

GAI 375
Galwan Valley 442
Gandhi, Mahatma 310
Gansu 173*f*7.1, 178*t*7.1, 219, 220*t*9.1, 221*f*9.1, 222*t*9.2, 223, 223*f*9.2, 224*t*9.3, 225*f*9.3, 226*t*9.4, 227, 227*f*9.4, 229*t*9.5, 230*f*9.5, 231*t*9.6, 232, 232*f*9.6, 233*t*9.7, 234*f*9.7, 235*t*9.8, 236*f*9.8, 238*t*9.9, 239*f*9.9, 240*t*9.10, 241*f*9.10, 242, 243*t*9.11, 244*f*9.11, 279, 280*t*11.1, 283, 283*t*11.2, 286, 287*f*11.2, 288*f*11.3, 289*f*11.4, 289*f*11.5, 290*f*11.6a, 291*f*11.6b, 400*n*19
Gao Changli 375
Gao Hua 96
Garnaut, John 64
Germany 155, 161*t*6.3, 181, 200, 479
Glasgow 196
Gomez, Selena 377
Goodman, David S.G. 62
Gow, Michael 71*n*11
Graham, Lindsey O. 162
Greater China 161*n*9, 250, 251, 376
Grünberg, Nis 118
Guan Hu 348
Guangdong 173*f*7.1, 176, 178*t*7.1, 182, 185, 187*t*7.3, 219, 220*t*9.1, 221*f*9.1, 222*t*9.2, 223*f*9.2, 224*t*9.3, 225*f*9.3, 226*t*9.4, 227, 227*f*9.4, 228, 229*t*9.5, 230*f*9.5, 231*t*9.6, 232*f*9.6, 233*t*9.7, 234*f*9.7, 235*t*9.8, 236*f*9.8, 238*t*9.9, 239*f*9.9, 240*t*9.10, 241*f*9.10, 243*t*9.11, 244*f*9.11, 271, 272, 280*t*11.1, 281, 283, 283*t*11.2, 287*f*11.2, 288*f*11.3, 289*f*11.4, 289*f*11.5, 290, 290*f*11.6a, 291*f*11.6b, 478, 482
Guangxi 173*f*7.1, 176, 178*t*7.1, 219, 220*t*9.1, 221, 221*f*9.1, 222*t*9.2, 223*f*9.2, 224*t*9.3, 225*f*9.3, 226*t*9.4, 227, 227*f*9.4, 228, 229*t*9.5, 230*f*9.5, 231*t*9.6, 232, 232*f*9.6, 233*t*9.7, 234*f*9.7, 235*t*9.8, 236*f*9.8, 237, 238*t*9.9, 239*f*9.9, 240*t*9.10, 241*f*9.10, 242, 243*t*9.11, 244*f*9.11, 279, 283, 283*t*11.2, 287*f*11.2, 288*f*11.3, 289*f*11.4, 289*f*11.5, 290*f*11.6a, 291*f*11.6b
Guangzhou 404, 478, 480, 488
Guizhou 172, 173*f*7.1, 178*t*7.1, 185, 187*t*7.3, 219, 220*t*9.1, 221, 221*f*9.1, 222*t*9.2, 223, 223*f*9.2, 224*t*9.3, 225, 225*f*9.3, 226*t*9.4, 227, 227*f*9.4, 228, 229*t*9.5, 230*f*9.5, 231*t*9.6, 232*f*9.6, 233*t*9.7, 234, 234*f*9.7, 235*t*9.8, 236, 236*f*9.8, 237, 238*t*9.9,

239*f*9.9, 240*t*9.10, 241*f*9.10, 242, 243*t*9.11, 244*f*9.11, 245, 279, 283, 283*t*11.2, 287*f*11.2, 288*f*11.3, 289*f*11.4, 289*f*11.5, 290*f*11.6a, 291*f*11.6b, 399*n*17
Gulf of Tonkin 439
Guo Baogang 3
Guo Jinlong 187*t*7.3
Guo Xiaoan 302
Gutian 361
Gwadar 426

Hague 75, 260, 378, 378*n*31
Hainan 173*f*7.1, 176, 178*t*7.1, 179*t*7.1, 220*t*9.1, 221*f*9.1, 222*t*9.2, 223*f*9.2, 224*t*9.3, 225*f*9.3, 226*t*9.4, 227*f*9.4, 229*t*9.5, 230*f*9.5, 231*t*9.6, 232*f*9.6, 233*t*9.7, 234*f*9.7, 235*t*9.8, 236*f*9.8, 238*t*9.9, 239*f*9.9, 240*t*9.10, 241*f*9.10, 242*n*2, 244*f*9.11, 279, 280*t*11.1, 282, 283, 283*t*11.2, 287*f*11.2, 288*f*11.3, 289*f*11.4, 289*f*11.5, 290*f*11.6a, 291*f*11.6b, 440, 466, 482
Han Zheng 23, 187*t*7.3
Handberg, Roger 459, 460, 469
Hangzhou 185, 188*t*7.3, 479, 481, 482, 488, 489
Hanoi 440, 481
Harari, Yuval Noah 109
Harbin 176, 274, 477
Haywood, Neil 92
He Muyang 369
He Yiting 22, 264
Hebei 172, 173*f*7.1, 176, 179*t*7.1, 180, 184*t*7.2, 219, 220*t*9.1, 221, 221*f*9.1, 222*t*9.2, 223*f*9.2, 224*t*9.3, 225, 225*f*9.3, 226*t*9.4, 227*f*9.4, 228, 229*t*9.5, 230*f*9.5, 231*t*9.6, 232, 232*f*9.6, 233*t*9.7, 234*f*9.7, 235*t*9.8, 236*f*9.8, 238*t*9.9, 239*f*9.9, 240*t*9.10, 241*f*9.10, 243*t*9.11, 244*f*9.11, 271, 272, 279, 283, 283*t*11.2, 287*f*11.2, 288*f*11.3, 289*f*11.4, 289*f*11.5, 290*f*11.6a, 291*f*11.6b
Hefei 275
Heilongjiang 173*f*7.1, 176, 179*t*7.1, 186, 220*t*9.1, 221, 221*f*9.1, 222*t*9.2, 223*f*9.2, 224*t*9.3, 225*f*9.3, 226*t*9.4, 227*f*9.4, 229*t*9.5, 230*f*9.5, 231*t*9.6, 232, 232*f*9.6, 233*t*9.7, 234*f*9.7, 235*t*9.8, 236, 236*f*9.8, 237, 238*t*9.9, 239*f*9.9, 240*t*9.10, 241*f*9.10, 242, 243*t*9.11, 244*f*9.11, 279, 283, 283*t*11.2, 287*f*11.2, 288*f*11.3, 289*f*11.4, 289*f*11.5, 290*f*11.6a, 291*f*11.6b

Henan   173f7.1, 178t7.1, 219, 220t9.1, 221f9.1, 222t9.2, 223f9.2, 224t9.3, 225f9.3, 226t9.4, 227, 227f9.4, 228, 229t9.5, 230f9.5, 231t9.6, 232, 232f9.6, 233t9.7, 234f9.7, 235t9.8, 236f9.8, 237, 238t9.9, 239f9.9, 240t9.10, 241f9.10, 243t9.11, 244f9.11, 274, 279, 280t11.1, 283, 283t11.2, 284, 287, 287f11.2, 288f11.3, 289f11.4, 289f11.5, 290, 290f11.6a, 291, 291t11.3, 291f11.6b
Hendrischke, Hans   168
Hickman, John   461
Himalayas   421, 432, 442
Hitler, Adolf   439
Ho, Denise   376
Ho, Norman   74
Ho, Wai-Chung   365, 366, 376
Hobbes, Thomas   36, 38, 48
Hollywood   343, 347
Hong Kong   2, 30, 49, 67, 161, 161n9, 161t6.3, 162, 162n10, 176, 177, 183t7.2, 184t7.2, 221f9.1, 223f9.2, 225f9.3, 227f9.4, 230f9.5, 232f9.6, 234f9.7, 236f9.8, 239f9.9, 241f9.10, 244f9.11, 250, 251, 252, 255, 261, 262, 264, 313, 316, 344t14.1, 344t14.1, 350, 352, 370, 375, 376, 379, 435, 443, 449
Hu Angang   169
Hu Jintao   19, 20, 24, 26, 48, 90, 91, 92, 93, 94, 95, 96, 256, 260, 362, 377, 397n13, 416, 433, 479
Hu Shi   390
Hu Yaobang   24
Hu, Richard   65
Hua Guofeng   26
Huan Kuming   22
Huang, Viya   257
Huang Xingguo   187t7.3
Hubei   1, 129, 173f7.1, 179t7.1, 185, 187t7.3, 220t9.1, 221, 221f9.1, 222t9.2, 223f9.2, 224t9.3, 225, 225f9.3, 226t9.4, 227f9.4, 228, 229t9.5, 230f9.5, 231t9.6, 232, 232f9.6, 233t9.7, 234f9.7, 235t9.8, 236f9.8, 238t9.9, 239f9.9, 240t9.10, 241f9.10, 243t9.11, 244f9.11, 283, 283t11.2, 287f11.2, 288f11.3, 289f11.4, 289f11.5, 290f11.6a, 291f11.6b, 480
Hunan   173f7.1, 176, 179t7.1, 219, 220t9.1, 221f9.1, 222t9.2, 223f9.2, 224t9.3, 225f9.3, 226t9.4, 227f9.4, 228, 229t9.5, 230f9.5, 231t9.6, 232, 232f9.6, 233t9.7, 234f9.7, 235t9.8, 236f9.8, 238t9.9, 239f9.9, 240t9.10, 241f9.10, 243t9.11, 244f9.11, 283, 283t11.2, 287f11.2, 288f11.3, 289f11.4, 289f11.5, 290f11.6a, 291f11.6b
Hungary   130, 132
Hutcheon, Linda   114

Ignatieff, Michael   92
India   53, 158, 159t6.2, 159f6.1, 160f6.2, 161t6.3, 195, 196, 310, 419, 421, 423, 425, 427n18, 432, 436, 442, 443, 458, 461, 468
Indian Ocean   68
Indochina   18, 421
Indonesia   262, 378n31, 413, 436, 461, 481, 481n1
Infantino, Gianni   488
Inner Mongolia   91, 173f7.1, 179t7.1, 220t9.1, 221, 221f9.1, 222t9.2, 223f9.2, 224t9.3, 225f9.3, 226t9.4, 227f9.4, 229t9.5, 230f9.5, 231t9.6, 232f9.6, 233t9.7, 234f9.7, 235t9.8, 236f9.8, 237, 238t9.9, 239f9.9, 240t9.10, 241f9.10, 243t9.11, 244f9.11, 279, 283, 283t11.2, 284, 287f11.2, 288, 288f11.3, 289f11.4, 289f11.5, 290f11.6a, 291f11.6b, 399
Introvigne, Massimo   337
Iran   162, 196, 419, 444, 468
Iraq   30, 53
Israel   458, 468
Italy   128, 130, 263, 356, 423, 427

Jakarta   421, 481, 482
Japan   66, 130, 151, 157, 159, 159f6.1, 159t6.2, 160f6.2, 161t6.3, 181, 195, 250, 253, 259, 261, 264, 348, 350, 391, 423, 427n18, 435, 436, 437, 441, 442, 458, 461, 463, 468, 486, 487
Jenkins, Patty   355
Jentleson, Bruce   109
Jia   378n31
Jia Ling   355
Jia Zhangke   351, 353, 356
Jiang Gongyan   365
Jiang Shigong   118n6
Jiang Qing   330
Jiang Zemin   19, 20, 24, 26, 30, 93, 94, 304, 333, 333n8, 362, 416, 433, 477

INDEX 503

Jiangsu 172, 173, 178*t*7.1, 187*t*7.3, 220*t*9.1, 221, 221*f*9.1, 222*t*9.2, 223*f*9.2, 224*t*9.3, 225*f*9.3, 226*t*9.4, 227, 227*f*9.4, 228, 229*t*9.5, 230*f*9.5, 231*t*9.6, 232*f*9.6, 233*t*9.7, 234*f*9.7, 235*t*9.8, 236, 236*f*9.8, 238*t*9.9, 239*f*9.9, 240*t*9.10, 241*f*9.10, 243*t*9.11, 244*f*9.11, 280*t*11.1, 281, 283, 283*t*11.2, 286, 287, 287*f*11.2, 288*f*11.3, 289*f*11.4, 289*f*11.5, 290*f*11.6a, 291*f*11.6b, 391

Jiangxi 173*f*7.1, 178*t*7.1, 219, 220*t*9.1, 221, 221*f*9.1, 222*t*9.2, 223*f*9.2, 224*t*9.3, 225, 225*f*9.3, 226*t*9.4, 227*f*9.4, 229*t*9.5, 230*f*9.5, 231*t*9.6, 232, 232*f*9.6, 233*t*9.7, 234*f*9.7, 235*t*9.8, 236*f*9.8, 237, 238*t*9.9, 239*f*9.9, 240*t*9.10, 241*f*9.10, 243*t*9.11, 244*f*9.11, 283, 283*t*11.2, 287*f*11.2, 288*f*11.3, 289*f*11.4, 289*f*11.5, 290*f*11.6a, 291*f*11.6b

Jilin 173*f*7.1, 178*t*7.1, 187*t*7.3, 220*t*9.1, 221, 221*f*9.1, 222*t*9.2, 223, 223*f*9.2, 224*t*9.3, 225, 225*f*9.3, 226*t*9.4, 227*f*9.4, 229*t*9.5, 230*f*9.5, 231*t*9.6, 232, 232*f*9.6, 233*t*9.7, 234*f*9.7, 235*t*9.8, 236*f*9.8, 238*t*9.9, 239*f*9.9, 240*t*9.10, 241*f*9.10, 242, 243*t*9.11, 244*f*9.11, 276, 279, 283, 283*t*11.2, 287*f*11.2, 288*f*11.3, 289*f*11.4, 289*f*11.5, 290*f*11.6a, 291*f*11.6b

Jinan 488
Jinjiang 483, 484

Kant, Immanuel 36
Kashmir 425
Kavanagh, Matthew M. 106
Kay, Richard S. 113
Kazakhstan 413, 417, 421, 426, 477
Kissinger, Henry 25
Kitakyushu 486
Klinger, Eduardo 133
Knight, Adam 121
Knight, John 64
Korea 66, 130, 161*t*6.3, 206, 253, 260, 261, 350, 355, 377, 378, 378*n*30, 432, 435, 436, 444, 449, 458, 461, 468, 477, 485, 487
Kovrig, Michael 444
Krasner, Stephen D. 110
Kuhn, Robert Lawrence 131
Kunming 100, 352
Kyoto 195
Kyrgyzstan 130, 132

Ladakh 442

Lady Gaga 377
Lam, Carrie 370
Lam, Dante 350
Lam, Willy Wo-Lap 68, 90
Lamond, James C. 112
Lane, Melissa 38
Laos 468
Larmore, Charles 38
Larson, Deborah W. 50
Larsson, Zara 377
Latin America 151
Latvia 315, 316*f*12.9
Lay 378*n*31
Lee, Quinby 114
Leibniz, Gottfried 155
Lele, Ajey 465, 469
Lenin, Vladimir 5, 15, 16, 17, 18, 19, 20, 22, 23, 29, 40, 42, 44, 48, 63, 64, 69, 73, 77, 95, 102, 327, 330, 331
Leung, Albert 376
Levi, Margaret 110
Li Ge. *See also* Yang Kaili
Li Hongmei 316
Li Hongzhong 185, 187*t*7.3
Li Jiaqi 257
Li Jinxi 394
Li Keqiang 23, 25, 65*n*7, 72, 425, 456
Li Peng 20, 30, 195
Li Qiang 182, 185, 187*t*7.3, 481
Li Shulei 22
Li Xianting 352
Li Zhanshu 23
Li, Chenlan Linda 169
Liang Fan 124, 302
Liang Qichao 250
Liaoning 173*f*7.1, 176, 178*t*7.1, 185, 187*t*7.3, 220*t*9.1, 221, 221*f*9.1, 222*t*9.2, 223*f*9.2, 224*t*9.3, 225*f*9.3, 226*t*9.4, 227*f*9.4, 229*t*9.5, 230*f*9.5, 231*t*9.6, 232, 232*f*9.6, 233*t*9.7, 234, 234*f*9.7, 235*t*9.8, 236*f*9.8, 237, 238*t*9.9, 239*f*9.9, 240*t*9.10, 241*f*9.10, 243*t*9.11, 244*f*9.11, 283, 283*t*11.2, 287*f*11.2, 288*f*11.3, 289*f*11.4, 289*f*11.5, 290*f*11.6a, 291*f*11.6b
Lin Biao 330
Lin Chaoxian. *See also* Lam, Dante
Lin Lucun 391
Lin, Delia 41, 47
Lin Shijie 133

Lindvall, Johannes   110, 111
Lins, Ronnie   131
Lisa   378
Lisbon   486
Lithuania   262, 424, 424n16
Liu Haifeng   270
Liu He   22
Liu Mingfu   415
Liu Qi   187t7.3
Liu Shaoqi   401n20
Liu Xiaobo   262
Liu Yazhou   415n2
Locarno   355
Logsdon, John M.   461
London   70, 74
Lovell, Julia   18
Loyalka, Prashant   292
Lu Gangzhang   391, 391n2
Lu Hao   176
Lü Ji   361
Lu Xun   364, 393, 393n7
Luo Shuze   332
Lviv   477, 478

Ma, Jack   67, 349
Ma Ying-jeou   483
Maçães, Bruno   419, 421
Macartney, George   15
Macao. *See also* Macau
Macau   173f7.1, 176, 177, 183t7.2, 184t7.2, 221f9.1, 223f9.2, 225f9.3, 227f9.4, 230f9.5, 232f9.6, 234f9.7, 236f9.8, 239f9.9, 241f9.10, 244f9.11, 250, 251, 255, 261
Machiavelli, Niccolò   36
MacInnis, Donald E.   328
MacKinnon, Rebecca   116
Madrid   479
Malaysia   130, 133, 262, 378n31, 436, 439, 461
Manila   439, 440, 441
Mann, Michael   111
Mansour, Abul-Azm   131
Mao Yexin   105, 106
Mao Zedong   3, 4, 5, 15, 16, 17, 18, 19, 20, 21, 23, 25, 26, 27, 29, 30, 36, 40, 41, 42, 47, 62, 64, 68, 72, 73, 75, 90, 92, 93, 94, 95, 96, 97, 98, 100, 101, 102, 151, 151n1, 154, 250, 251, 252, 255, 303, 325, 328, 330, 331, 338, 345, 357, 361, 362, 365, 365n3, 398n14, 414, 418, 418n9, 419n12, 421, 432, 433, 434, 459, 463, 489

Mapaila, Solly   132
Marr, Nikolai   394
Mars   77, 466, 467, 469
Marston, Cicely   106
Marx, Karl   5, 15, 16, 18, 20, 23, 29, 40, 41, 47, 48, 63, 64, 69, 77, 95, 102, 275, 327, 330, 331, 332, 333, 365, 366, 366n7, 419n12
Masaliev, Iskhak   132
Masini, Federico   131
McGregor, Richard   16
Mearsheimer, John   30
Mediterranean Sea   427
Meng Bingchun   308
Meng Wanzhou   444
Mexico   130, 134
Middle East   413
Migdal, Joel   110
Min Dahong   316
Minzner, Carl   76
Mirra, Federica   362
Mischief Reef   440, 441
Mitter, Rana   72
Moltz, James Clay   460
Mongolia   181, 183t7.2, 419, 421, 468
Montesquieu   36, 156
Moon   51, 62, 77, 460, 463, 466
Morey, Daryl   262
Moritz, Rudolf   74
Morrison, Scott   445
Moscow   1, 438
Mozur, Paul   125
Myanmar   421, 426

Nanchang   176
Nanfang   278
Nanjing   274, 352, 353, 392n4, 478
Nepal   130, 132, 421
Netherlands   161t6.3
New Delhi   425
Neyts, Johan   133
Nigeria   468
Ningxia   173f7.1, 178t7.1, 220t9.1, 221f9.1, 222t9.2, 223, 223f9.2, 224t9.3, 225f9.3, 226t9.4, 227, 227f9.4, 229t9.5, 230f9.5, 231t9.6, 232f9.6, 233t9.7, 234f9.7, 235t9.8, 236f9.8, 238t9.9, 239f9.9, 240t9.10, 241f9.10, 242n2, 244f9.11, 279, 280t11.1, 281, 283, 287f11.2, 288f11.3, 289f11.4, 289f11.5, 290f11.6a, 291f11.6b
Noriyoshi Ehara   132
North America   96, 156, 193

North Korea   432, 444, 449, 461, 468, 485
Norway   262, 477

Obama, Barack   89, 463*n*4
Okinawa Trough   441
Oliver, John   373
O'Neill, Patric Howell   125
Orwell, George   137, 337, 339
Oslo   477, 478

Pacific Ocean   6, 68, 424, 427, 448
Paektu, Mountain   377
Pakistan   421, 425, 461, 468
Palembang   481
Palmer, James   75
Panama   483
Pangong Lake   442
Paracel Islands   432, 439, 440
Paris   74, 192, 196, 206, 207, 264
Peng Shuai   444
Perry, Katy   377
Persson, Torsten   110
Peru   468
PG One   375
Philippines   75, 76, 261, 378*n*31, 436, 439, 440, 441, 445, 461, 479
Pils, Eva   70, 71, 118, 137
Plato   156
Poland   4, 151, 153, 153*t*6.1, 158*n*6, 315, 426, 477
Polit, Jakub   17
Pollpeter, Kevin   469
Pompeo, Mike   163
Portugal   419, 486
Putin, Vladimir   2, 32, 61
Pye, Lucian W.   16, 17
Pyeongchang   477

Qatar   479
Qian Xuantong   393
Qian Xuesen   458, 459, 459*n*3
Qiang Zha   272
Qianlong Emperor   15, 155
Qin Shi Huang   32, 50
Qingdao   479, 488
Qinghai   173*f*7.1, 179*t*7.1, 219, 220*t*9.1, 221, 221*f*9.1, 222*t*9.2, 223, 223*f*9.2, 224*t*9.3, 225*f*9.3, 226n.a, 226*t*9.4, 227, 227*f*9.4, 228, 229*t*9.5, 230*f*9.5, 231*t*9.6, 232, 232*f*9.6, 233*t*9.7, 234*f*9.7, 235*t*9.8, 236*f*9.8, 238*t*9.9, 239*f*9.9, 240*t*9.10, 241*f*9.10, 243*t*9.11, 286, 279, 283, 283*t*11.2, 287*f*11.2, 288*f*11.3, 289*f*11.4, 289*f*11.5, 290, 290*f*11.6a, 291*f*11.6b
Qinshi Huangdi. *See also* Qin Shi Huang
Qiong Wu   270
Qiu Sheng   357
Qu Qiubai   394, 394*n*10
Qu, Vivian   349
Quanzhou   176, 417
Quzhou   185

Rauhala, Emily   371
Rayns, Tony   352
Reagan, Ronald   39
Reinmoeller, Patrick   134
Renan, Ernest   252
Rio de Janeiro   195
Riskin, Carl   168
Risse, Thomas   110
RM   378
Robertson, Matthew   373
Robinson, David R.S.   117
Rolland, Nadège   422, 424
Romaniuk, Scott N.   119, 125
Rome   131, 424
Rotterdam   352
Rousseau, Jean-Jacques   36
Ruggie, John   446
Russia   1, 2, 15, 32, 51, 61, 74, 78, 102, 128, 156, 159, 159*f*6.1, 159*f*6.2, 160*f*6.2, 181, 183*t*7.2, 196, 206, 357, 419, 421, 424, 426, 438, 447, 448*fi*8.2, 460, 468, 478

Said, Edward   40
Sanming   185
Sanya   482
São Tomé and Príncipe   483
Sargent, Tanja Carmel   281
Scarborough Shoal   439, 440
Schmidt, Vivien A.   115
Schram, Stuart   15
Scobell, Andrew   118
Scott, James C.   112
Senkaku Islands. *See also* Diaoyu Islands
Shaanxi   173*f*7.1, 178*t*7.1, 220*t*9.1, 221*f*9.1, 222*t*9.2, 223*f*9.2, 224*t*9.3, 225*f*9.3, 226*t*9.4, 227*f*9.4, 229*t*9.5, 230*f*9.5, 231*t*9.6, 232, 232*f*9.6, 233*t*9.7, 234*f*9.7, 235*t*9.8, 236, 236*f*9.8, 238*t*9.9, 239*f*9.9, 240*t*9.10, 241*f*9.10, 243*t*9.11, 244*f*9.11, 283, 283*t*11.2, 286, 287*f*11.2, 288*f*11.3, 289*f*11.4, 289*t*11.5, 290*f*11.6a, 291*f*11.6b, 416, 417

Shambaugh, David   3, 22, 30, 327
Shandong   173*f*7.1, 178*t*7.1, 187*t*7.3, 219, 220*t*9.1, 221*f*9.1, 222*t*9.2, 223*f*9.2, 224*t*9.3, 225*f*9.3, 226*t*9.4, 227*f*9.4, 228, 229*t*9.5, 230*f*9.5, 231*t*9.6, 232, 232*f*9.6, 233*t*9.7, 234*f*9.7, 235*t*9.8, 236*f*9.8, 238*t*9.9, 239*f*9.9, 240*t*9.10, 241*f*9.10, 243*t*9.11, 244*f*9.11, 264, 276, 279, 280*t*11.1, 281n.f, 282, 283, 283*t*11.2, 285, 287*f*11.2, 288*f*11.3, 289*f*11.4, 289*t*11.5, 290, 290*t*11.6a, 291*f*11.6b
Shanghai   6, 21, 24, 65, 135, 168, 176, 177, 178*t*7.1, 180, 182, 183*t*7.2, 184*t*7.2, 185, 186, 187*t*7.3, 219, 220*t*9.1, 222*t*9.2, 224*t*9.3, 226*t*9.4, 229*t*9.5, 231*t*9.6, 232, 233*t*9.7, 234, 235*t*9.8, 237, 238*t*9.9, 240*t*9.10, 241, 242, 243*t*9.11, 274, 275, 279, 280*t*11.1, 282, 283, 283*t*11.2, 284, 286, 287, 288, 289*t*11.5, 290, 291, 291*t*11.3, 294, 348, 357, 377, 394, 404, 405, 444, 488, 491, 173*f*7.1, 221*f*9.1, 223*f*9.2, 225*f*9.3, 227*f*9.4, 230*f*9.5, 232*f*9.6, 234*f*9.7, 236*f*9.8, 239*f*9.9, 241*f*9.10, 244*f*9.11, 287*f*11.2, 288*f*11.3, 289*f*11.4, 289*f*11.5, 290*f*11.6a, 291*f*11.6b
Shantou   482
Shanxi   172, 173*f*7.1, 179*t*7.1, 220*t*9.1, 221, 221*f*9.1, 222*t*9.2, 223*f*9.2, 224*t*9.3, 225, 225*f*9.3, 226*t*9.4, 227*f*9.4, 229*t*9.5, 230*f*9.5, 231*t*9.6, 232, 232*f*9.6, 233*t*9.7, 234*f*9.7, 235*t*9.8, 236, 236*f*9.8, 238*t*9.9, 239*f*9.9, 240*t*9.10, 241*f*9.10, 242, 243*t*9.11, 244*f*9.11, 279, 280*t*11.1, 283, 283*t*11.2, 286, 287*f*11.2, 288*f*11.3, 289, 289*f*11.4, 289*t*11.5, 290*f*11.6a, 291*f*11.6b
Shaoshan   463
Shaoxing   185
Shea, Dennis C.   466
Sheng Zou   376
Shenyang   176, 479, 488
Shenzhen   65, 185, 187*t*7.3, 271, 478
Shue, Vivienne   254
Sichuan   173*f*7.1, 175, 176, 177, 178*t*7.1, 185, 186, 188*t*7.3, 219, 220*t*9.1, 221*f*9.1, 222*t*9.2, 223, 223*f*9.2, 224*t*9.3, 225, 225*f*9.3, 226*t*9.4, 227, 227*f*9.4, 228, 229*t*9.5, 230*f*9.5, 231*t*9.6, 232*f*9.6, 233*t*9.7, 234*f*9.7, 235*t*9.8, 236*f*9.8, 238*t*9.9, 239*f*9.9, 240*t*9.10, 241*f*9.10, 243*t*9.11, 249, 278, 283, 283*t*11.2, 287*f*11.2, 288*f*11.3, 289*f*11.4, 289*t*11.5, 290*f*11.6a, 291*f*11.6b, 366, 400*n*19, 476, 485, 486
Sikkim   442
Singapore   31, 177, 182, 186, 458
Song Qiang   258
Song, Victoria   378*n*31
Songzhuang   352
Soros, George   67
South Africa   130, 132
South America   487
South Asia   421
South China Sea   53, 76, 109, 260, 261, 313, 378*n*31, 432, 438, 439, 440, 445, 447, 449
South Korea   66, 130, 161*t*6.3, 206, 260, 261, 377, 378, 378*n*30, 436, 458, 461, 468, 477, 485, 487
Southeast Asia   67, 262, 419, 439
Soviet Union   15, 16, 17, 19, 22, 23, 96, 102, 151, 151*n*1, 250, 357, 426, 432, 458, 459, 460, 461, 462
Spain   128, 479, 488
Spavor, Michael   444
Spiegel, Mickey   332*n*6, 332*n*7
Spratly Islands   378*n*31, 439, 440
Sri Lanka   468, 482
Stalin, Joseph   64, 357
Stockholm   194, 477, 478
Strauss, Leo   38
Strittmatter, Kai   28
Strugatsky, Arkady and Boris   357
Sun Chunlan   187*t*7.3
Sun Yat-sen   17, 249
Sun Zhengcai   187*t*7.3
Sun Tzu   39, 449
Suzhou   176, 241, 478, 479, 488
Sweden   477
Swift, Taylor   377

Tahir, Jüme   337
Taipei   377, 436, 442, 483, 484, 489
Taiping Island   439
Taiwan   2, 17, 21, 28, 30, 67, 161*n*9, 161*t*6.3, 177, 183*t*7.2, 184*t*7.2, 250, 251, 255, 261, 262, 264, 302, 313, 316, 335, 375, 377, 378*n*30, 378*n*30, 393*n*8, 417, 432, 436, 437, 437*f*18.1, 438, 439, 441, 442, 445, 449, 476, 483, 484, 489

Taizhou   185
Taoyuan   484
Tarkovsky, Andrei   357
Tedros, Adhanom   129, 136
Teorell, Jan   110, 111
Thailand   130, 133, 262, 461
Thürmer, Gyula   132
Tiananmen Square   31, 100, 252, 376
Tianjin   6, 168, 176, 177, 178t7.1, 180, 181, 182, 183t7.2, 184t7.2, 184t7.2, 187t7.3, 219, 220t9.1, 221f9.1, 222t9.2, 223f9.2, 224t9.3, 225, 225f9.3, 226t9.4, 227f9.4, 229t9.5, 230f9.5, 231t9.6, 232, 232f9.6, 233t9.7, 234, 234f9.7, 235t9.8, 236, 236f9.8, 237, 238t9.9, 239f9.9, 240t9.10, 241f9.10, 242, 243t9.11, 244f9.11, 280t11.1, 283, 283t11.2, 287, 287f11.2, 288f11.3, 289, 289f11.4, 289f11.5, 290f11.6a, 291f11.6b, 488
Tibet   91, 173f7.1, 179t7.1, 219, 220t9.1, 221, 221f9.1, 222t9.2, 223, 223f9.2, 224n.a, 224t9.3, 225, 225f9.3, 226t9.4, 227, 227f9.4, 228, 229t9.5, 230f9.5, 231t9.6, 232, 232f9.6, 233t9.7, 234f9.7, 235t9.8, 236, 236f9.8, 237, 238t9.9, 239f9.9, 240t9.10, 241f9.10, 242, 242n2, 244f9.11, 257, 261, 263, 264, 279, 280t11.1, 283, 283t11.2, 284, 287f11.2, 288f11.3, 290, 289f11.4, 289f11.5, 290f11.6a, 291f11.6b, 327, 335, 356, 377, 399, 400m19, 435
Tilak, Jandhyala   292
Tokyo   259, 391, 427, 441, 483
Trump, Donald   53, 99, 102, 158, 161, 163, 313, 420, 449, 463n4
Tsai Ing-wen   483
Tsang, Steve   40, 41, 42, 50
Tseden, Pema   356
Tsui Hark   350
Turkey   419, 444, 479

Ukraine   1, 2, 32, 74, 78, 426, 438, 477, 478
United Arab Emirates   488
United Kingdom   15, 92, 161t6.3, 310, 416, 427n19
United States of America   10, 22, 30, 32, 36, 39, 47, 49, 51, 53, 62, 64n6, 64n6, 65, 67, 76, 78, 89, 92, 94, 99, 100, 101, 102, 109, 126, 128, 131, 151, 153, 156, 157, 158, 159, 159t6.2, 159f6.1, 160f6.2, 160, 161, 161t6.3, 162, 163, 193, 196, 250, 253, 260, 262, 306, 311, 312, 313, 314, 314f12.7, 315, 315f12.8, 316, 316f12.9, 316f12.9, 316f12.9, 317, 326, 343, 344t14.1, 344t14.1, 350, 376, 378, 415, 416n3, 418, 420, 422, 425, 426, 427n18, 427n19, 432, 436, 439, 439n1, 444, 447, 448, 448f18.2, 449, 456, 457, 458, 459, 459n3, 460, 461, 462, 463, 463n4, 465, 466, 467, 468, 469, 483, 488

Van Ryzin, Gregg G.   135
Vancouver   352
Vatican   331, 335
VaVa   375
Venezuela   196, 444, 468
Venice   351
Vietnam   161t6.3, 378n31, 432, 433, 435, 436, 439, 440, 461, 481
Vilnius   262
Voltaire   155

Wallace, Jon   171
Wang Bing   354
Wang Huning   22, 23, 65n7, 169, 170, 415n2, 416, 416n3
Wang Jisi   415
Wang Lijun   92
Wang, Maya   107, 117, 118, 124, 127, 129
Wang, Peter   107
Wang Qianyuan   263
Wang Qishan   25, 90, 97
Wang Shaoguang   169
Wang Xiji   463
Wang Xiaoshuai   356
Wang Yang   23
Wang Yi   68, 423n15, 424
Wang Yiwei   417
Washington D.C.   74, 75, 102, 426, 427, 465, 469
Wei Qiu   278
Wen Hai   354
Wen Jiabao   20, 24, 26, 91, 195
Wenzel-Teuber, Katharina   325n1
Wenzhou   185
West Asia   421
Western Pacific   448
Wilhelm II   156
Wohlforth, William C.   490

Wong, Anthony   376
Wu Jing   350
Wu Rulun   391
Wu Songjin   367
Wu Wenguang   353, 355
Wu Zhaodi   349
Wu Zhihui   392n2
Wu, Cary   135
Wuhan   1, 129, 176, 264, 274, 478, 480, 488
Wusatirakul, Tharakorn   133

Xi Zhongxun   96, 416, 416n5
Xi'an   119, 176, 276, 417, 488
Xiamen   176, 488
Xiao Tian   478
Xiao Yang   281
Xinjiang   49, 52, 91, 99, 100, 173f7.1, 178t7.1, 182, 219, 220t9.1, 221f9.1, 222t9.2, 223, 223f9.2, 224t9.3, 225, 225f9.3, 226, 227f9.4, 228, 229t9.5, 230f9.5, 231t9.6, 232, 232f9.6, 233t9.7, 234f9.7, 235t9.8, 236f9.8, 237, 238t9.9, 239f9.9, 240t9.10, 241f9.10, 243t9.11, 244f9.11, 257, 262, 264, 279, 280t11.1, 283, 283t11.2, 287f11.2, 288f11.3, 289f11.4, 289f11.5, 326, 327, 334, 337, 380, 290f11.6a, 91f11.6b, 399, 400m19, 435, 449
Xizang. *See also Tibet*
Xu Caihou   479
Xu Ke. *See also Tsui Hark*
Xue, Melanie Meng   106

Yan Dong   368n14
Yan'an   96, 361, 362
Yang Jiangang   365
Yang Kaili   370
Yang Shaoting   302
Yang, Hon-Lun   373
Yangtze River   167, 171, 175, 176, 177, 180, 183t7.2, 185, 186
Yao Dehuai   402n21
Yao Ming   479
Yasukuni shrine   259
Ye Xiaowen   332, 333
Yin Li   185, 188t7.3
Yin Liangen   368
Ying Liang   354
Ying Shuzeng   279
Yiwu   176
Yong Zhao   278
Young, Alwyn   170

Youngs, Richard   106
Yu Jianrong   91
Yu Jie   171
Yu Yang   343
Yu Zhengsheng   187t7.3
Yuan Jiajun   187t7.3
Yunnan   175, 176, 178t7.1, 219, 220t9.1, 221f9.1, 222t9.2, 223, 223f9.2, 224t9.3, 225f9.3, 226t9.4, 227, 227f9.4, 228, 229t9.5, 230f9.5, 231t9.6, 232f9.6, 233t9.7, 234f9.7, 235t9.8, 236, 236f9.8, 237, 238t9.9, 239f9.9, 240t9.10, 241f9.10, 242, 243t9.11, 244f9.11, 279, 283, 283t11.2, 287f11.2, 288f11.3, 289f11.4, 289f11.5, 290f11.6a, 291f11.6b, 352, 400m19

Zeng Jinyan   354
Zhang Binglin   250
Zhang Chunxian   334
Zhang Dejiang   187t7.3
Zhang Gaoli   187t7.3
Zhang Kejian   462
Zhang Ming   264
Zhang Qian   417n8
Zhang Qiang   287
Zhang Weiwei   22, 28
Zhang Xiaodan   70
Zhang Yimou   348, 350
Zhang Yuan   356
Zhang Zhidong   27
Zhangjiakou   477, 478
Zhao Leji   23
Zhao Lijian   136
Zhao Shuren. *See also Lu Xun*
Zhao Wei. *See also Zhao, Vicky*
Zhao, Vicky   349, 350
Zhao Ziyang   24, 433
Zhejiang   24, 91, 97, 101, 178t7.1, 182, 185, 187t7.3, 187t7.3, 188t7.3, 220t9.1, 221, 221f9.1, 222t9.2, 223f9.2, 224t9.3, 225, 225f9.3, 226t9.4, 227f9.4, 229t9.5, 230f9.5, 231t9.6, 232f9.6, 233t9.7, 234f9.7, 235t9.8, 236, 236f9.8, 237, 238t9.9, 239f9.9, 240t9.10, 241f9.10, 243t9.11, 244f9.11, 274, 275, 280t11.1, 282, 283, 283t11.2, 287f11.2, 288, 288f11.3, 289, 289f11.4, 289f11.5, 290, 290f11.6a, 291f11.6b, 481
Zheng He   155
Zheng Yongnian   31, 168

Zhengzhou   176
Zhou, Christina   68, 373
Zhou Enlai   262
Zhou Haiwen   284
Zhou Mi   378n31
Zhou Qiang   70, 70n9
Zhu Hai   369
Zhu Muzhi   257

Zhu Rikun   354
Zhu Rongji   20, 24, 26
Zhu Wenxiong   391
Zhu Xin   357
Zhuo Sinna   366
Zoellick, Robert   50
Zou Dangrong   367
Zunyi   19

www.ingramcontent.com/pod-product-compliance
Lightning Source LLC
Chambersburg PA
CBHW062112040426
42337CB00043B/3692